ACCA

PAPER F5

PERFORMANCE MANAGEMENT

BPP Learning Media is **an ACCA Approved Content Provider.** This means we work closely with ACCA to ensure this Study Text contains the information you need to pass your exam.

In this Study Text which has been reviewed by the **ACCA examination team** we:

- **Highlight** the most important elements in the syllabus and the **key skills** you will need

- **Signpost** how each chapter links to the syllabus and the Study Guide

- **Provide** lots of **exam focus points** demonstrating what is expected of you in the exam

- **Emphasise** key points in regular **fast forward** summaries

- **Test** your knowledge in **quick quizzes**

- **Examine** your understanding in our **practice question bank**

- **Reference** all the important topics in our **full index**

BPP's **Practice & Revision Kit** also supports this paper.

FOR EXAMS IN SEPTEMBER 2017, DECEMBER 2017, MARCH 2018 AND JUNE 2018

BPP
LEARNING MEDIA

First edition 2007
Tenth edition January 2017

ISBN 9781 5097 0852 9
(Previous ISBN 9781 4727 4422 7)

e-ISBN 9781 5097 0982 3

British Library Cataloguing-in-Publication Data

A catalogue record for this book
is available from the British Library

Published by

BPP Learning Media Ltd
BPP House, Aldine Place
London W12 8AA

www.bpp.com/learningmedia

Printed by

Wheatons Exeter Ltd
Hennock Road
Marsh Barton
Exeter
EX2 8RP

Your learning materials, published by BPP Learning
Media Ltd, are printed on paper obtained from
traceable sustainable sources.

We are grateful to the Association of Chartered Certified
Accountants for permission to reproduce past examination
questions. The suggested solutions in the practice answer bank
have been prepared by BPP Learning Media Ltd, unless otherwise
stated.

BPP
LEARNING MEDIA

Contents

Helping you to pass

BPP Learning Media – ACCA Approved Content Provider

As an ACCA **Approved Content Provider**, BPP Learning Media gives you the **opportunity** to use study materials reviewed by the ACCA examination team. By incorporating the examination team's comments and suggestions regarding the depth and breadth of syllabus coverage, the BPP Learning Media Study Text provides excellent, **ACCA-approved** support for your studies.

The PER alert

Before you can qualify as an ACCA member, you not only have to pass all your exams but also fulfil a three year **practical experience requirement** (PER). To help you to recognise areas of the syllabus that you might be able to apply in the workplace to achieve different performance objectives, we have introduced the **'PER alert'** feature. You will find this feature throughout the Study Text to remind you that what you are **learning to pass** your ACCA exams is **equally useful to the fulfilment of the PER requirement**.

Your achievement of the PER should now be recorded in your online *My Experience* record.

Tackling studying

Studying can be a daunting prospect, particularly when you have lots of other commitments. The **different features** of the Study Text, the **purposes** of which are explained fully on the **Chapter features** page, will help you whilst studying and improve your chances of **exam success**.

Developing exam awareness

Our Study Texts are completely **focused** on helping you pass your exam.

Our advice on **Studying F5** outlines the **content** of the paper, the **necessary skills** you are expected to be able to demonstrate and any **brought forward knowledge** you are expected to have.

Exam focus points are included within the chapters to highlight when and how specific topics were examined, or how they might be examined in the future.

Testing what you can do

Testing yourself helps you develop the skills you need to pass the exam and also confirms that you can recall what you have learnt.

We include **Questions** – lots of them – both within chapters and in the **Practice Question Bank**, as well as **Quick Quizzes** at the end of each chapter to test your knowledge of the chapter content.

Chapter features

Each chapter contains a number of helpful features to guide you through each topic.

Topic list

Topic list	Syllabus reference

What you will be studying in this chapter and the relevant section numbers, together with ACCA syllabus references.

Introduction

Puts the chapter content in the context of the syllabus as a whole.

Study Guide

Links the chapter content with ACCA guidance.

Exam Guide

Highlights how examinable the chapter content is likely to be and the ways in which it could be examined.

Knowledge brought forward from earlier studies

What you are assumed to know from previous studies/exams.

FAST FORWARD

Summarises the content of main chapter headings, allowing you to preview and review each section easily.

Examples

Demonstrate how to apply key knowledge and techniques.

Key terms

Definitions of important concepts that can often earn you easy marks in exams.

Exam focus points

When and how specific topics were examined, or how they may be examined in the future.

Formula to learn

Formulae that are not given in the exam but which have to be learnt.

PER alert

Gives you a useful indication of syllabus areas that closely relate to performance objectives in your Practical Experience Requirement (PER).

Question

Gives you essential practice of techniques covered in the chapter.

Case Study

Real world examples of theories and techniques.

Chapter Roundup

A full list of the Fast Forwards included in the chapter, providing an easy source of review.

Quick Quiz

A quick test of your knowledge of the main topics in the chapter.

Practice Question Bank

Found at the back of the Study Text with more comprehensive chapter questions. Cross referenced for easy navigation.

BPP LEARNING MEDIA

Studying F5

The F5 exam requires candidates to be able to apply management accounting techniques in business environments. The key question you need to be able to answer is 'what does it all actually mean?' Modern technology is capable of producing vast amounts of management accounting information but it has to be used to help managers make good decisions and manage effectively. The emphasis in this exam is therefore on practical elements and application to the real world. The exam does not set out to trick you: it will be fair.

1 What F5 is about

The aim of this syllabus is to develop knowledge and skills in the application of management accounting techniques. It covers a number of specialist techniques, decision-making, budgeting and standard costing, concluding with how business performance should be managed and controlled.

F5 is the middle exam in the management accounting section of the qualification structure. F2 concerns just techniques and P5 thinks strategically and considers environmental factors. F5 requires you to be able to apply techniques and think about their impact on the organisation.

2 What skills are required?

- You are expected to have a core of management accounting knowledge from your F2 studies.

- To deal with the multiple choice questions, you will need to demonstrate understanding of the subject across the entire syllabus.

- For the longer questions, you will be required to carry out calculations, with **clear workings** and a logical structure.

- You will be required to **interpret** data.

- You will be required to **explain** management accounting techniques and **discuss** whether they are appropriate for a particular organisation.

- You must be able to **apply** your skills in a practical context.

3 How to improve your chances of passing

- There is no choice in this exam; all questions have to be answered. You must therefore study the **entire syllabus**, there are no short-cuts.

- You should then practise extensively on examination-style questions. Practice will improve your ability to answer questions well, and should enable you to answer them more quickly. BPP's Practice & Revision Kit contains questions on all areas of the syllabus.

- Keep an eye out for **articles**, as the **examination team** will use **Student Accountant** to communicate with students.

- Read journals etc to pick up on ways in which real organisations apply management accounting and think about your own organisation if that is relevant.

4 Brought forward knowledge

You will need a good working knowledge of basic management accounting from ACCA F2. Chapter 1 of this Study Text revises elements of costing, and further revision material is provided in other chapters, such as those on CVP analysis and variance analysis. If you struggle with the examples and questions used to revise this knowledge, you should go back and revisit your previous work. The examination team will assume you know this material and it may form part of an exam question.

The exam paper and exam formulae

Computer-based exams

ACCA have commenced the launch of computer-based exams (CBEs) for F5–F9. They have been piloting computer-based exams in limited markets since September 2016 with the aim of rolling out into all markets internationally over a five-year period. Paper-based examinations will be run in parallel while the CBEs are phased in and BPP materials have been designed to support you, whichever exam option you choose.

Exam duration

The Skills module examinations F5–F9 contain a mix of objective and longer type questions with a duration of 3 hours for 100 marks. For paper-based exams there are an extra 15 minutes to reflect the manual effort required.

As ACCA increase their offering of F5–F9 session CBEs, they will be introducing seeded content to guarantee all exams are equivalent and fair. When the seeded content is introduced, students will be given more time to complete the exams – increasing to 3 hours and 20 minutes to take into account the inclusion of additional seeded content.

For more information on these changes and when they will be implemented, please visit the ACCA website. http://www.accaglobal.com/uk/en/student/changes-to-exams/f5-f9-session-cbe.html

Format of the exam

The exam format is the same irrespective of the mode of delivery and will comprise three exam sections:

Section	Style of question type	Description	Proportion of exam, %
A	Objective test (OT)	15 questions × 2 marks	30
B	Objective test (OT) case	3 questions × 10 marks Each question will contain 5 sub-parts each worth 2 marks	30
C	Constructed Response (Long questions)	2 questions × 20 marks	40
Total			100

Section A and B questions will be selected from the entire syllabus. The paper version of these objective test questions contain multiple choice only and the computer-based version will contain a variety. The responses to each question or sub-part in the case of OT cases are marked automatically as either correct or incorrect by computer.

The 20 mark Section C questions will mainly focus on the following syllabus areas but a minority of marks can be drawn from any other area of the syllabus:

*   Decision making techniques (syllabus area B)
*   Budgeting and control (syllabus area C)
*   Performance measurement and control (syllabus area D)

The responses to these questions are human marked.

Exam formulae

Set out below are the **formulae you will be given in the exam**. If you are not sure what the symbols mean, or how the formulae are used, you should refer to the appropriate chapter in this Study Text.

Demand curve

$P = a - bQ$

$b = \dfrac{\text{change in price}}{\text{change in quantity}}$

a = price when $Q = 0$

$MR = a - 2bQ$

Learning curve

$Y = ax^b$

Where
Y = cumulative average time per unit to produce x units
a = the time taken for the first unit of output
x = the cumulative number of units
b = the index of learning (log LR/log 2)
LR = the learning rate as a decimal

Syllabus and Study Guide

The complete F5 syllabus and study guide can be found by visiting the exam resource finder on the ACCA website: www.accaglobal.com/uk/en/student/exam-support-resources.htm.

Specialist cost and management accounting techniques

BPP
LEARNING MEDIA

Costing

Introduction

Part A of this Study Text looks at specialist cost and management accounting techniques. This chapter serves as a revision of concepts you should have covered in your previous studies.

In the following chapter we will be looking at more complex techniques, so it is important that you are familiar with the key concepts and terminology in this chapter.

Exam guide

This chapter serves as an introduction to your study of cost and management accounting techniques, as knowledge is assumed from ACCA F2 Management Accounting and is still examinable at this level. Questions in this exam will focus on interpretation rather than doing complex calculations.

1 Costing

FAST FORWARD

Costing is the process of determining the costs of products, services or activities.

Cost accounting is used to determine the cost of products, jobs or services (whatever the organisation happens to be involved in). Such costs have to be built up using a process known as **cost accumulation**.

In your earlier studies you will have learnt how to accumulate the various cost elements which make up total cost.

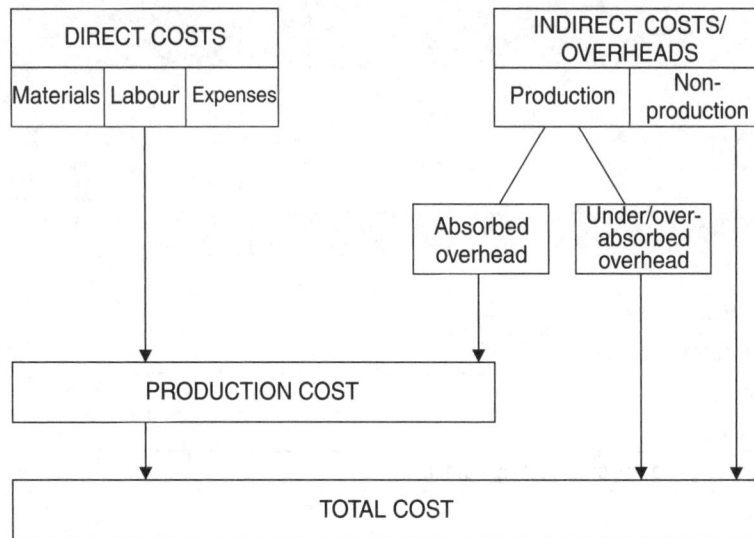

Absorption costing cost accumulation system

2 The problem of overheads

FAST FORWARD

Indirect costs, or **overheads**, are costs incurred in making a product or providing a service, but which cannot be traced directly to products or services. **Absorption costing** is a means of incorporating a fair share of these costs into the cost of each unit of product manufactured or each service provided.

If a company manufactures a product, the cost of the product will include the cost of the raw materials and components used in it and the cost of the labour effort required to make it. These are **direct costs** of the product. The company would, however, incur many other costs in making the product which are not directly attributable to a single product, but which are incurred generally in the process of manufacturing a large number of product units. These are **indirect costs** or **overheads**. Such costs include the following.

- Factory rent and rates
- Machine depreciation
- Supervision costs
- Heating and lighting

Key terms

A **direct cost** is a cost that can be traced in full to the product, service or department that is being costed.

An **indirect cost** or **overhead** is a cost that is incurred in the course of making a product, providing a service or running a department, but which cannot be traced directly and in full to the product, service or department.

In some companies, total overhead costs may be substantially greater than the total of direct production costs.

BPP
LEARNING MEDIA

It might seem unreasonable to ignore indirect costs entirely when accumulating the costs of making a product, and yet there **cannot be a completely satisfactory way of sharing out indirect costs** between the many different items of production which benefit from them.

2.1 Using absorption costing to deal with the problem of overheads

Traditionally, the view has been that a fair share of overheads should be added to the cost of units produced to obtain a full unit cost of production and sales. This fair share should **include a portion of production overhead expenditure** and possibly administration and marketing overheads too. This is the view embodied in the principles of **absorption costing**.

2.1.1 Theoretical justification for using absorption costing

In a manufacturing organisation, production overheads are incurred in making the output, so each unit of product receives some benefit from these costs. Each unit of output should therefore be charged with some of the overhead costs.

2.1.2 Practical reasons for using absorption costing

(a) **Inventory valuations**

Inventory in hand must be valued for two reasons.

(i) For the closing inventory figure in the statement of financial position
(ii) To calculate the cost of sales figure in the income statement

The valuation of inventories will affect profitability during a period because of the way in which the cost of sales is calculated.

Cost of goods sold = cost of goods produced + the value of opening inventories – the value of closing inventories

(b) **Pricing decisions**

Many companies attempt to set selling prices **by calculating the full cost of production or sales** of each product, and then adding a margin for profit. 'Full cost plus pricing' can be particularly useful for companies which do jobbing or contract work, where each job or contract is different, so that a standard unit sales price cannot be fixed. Without using absorption costing, it may be difficult to decide what the price should be to earn a satisfactory profit.

(c) **Establishing the profitability of different products**

This argument in favour of absorption costing states that, if a company sells more than one product, it will be difficult to judge **how profitable each individual product is**, unless overhead costs are shared on a fair basis and charged to the cost of sales of each product.

2.2 Using marginal costing to deal with the problem of overheads

For many planning and decision-making purposes, absorption costing is less useful as a costing method than marginal costing. In some situations, **absorption costing can actually be misleading** in the information it supplies.

Advocates of **marginal costing** take the view that only the variable costs of making and selling a product or service should be identified. **Fixed costs should be dealt with separately** and treated as a cost of the accounting period rather than shared out somehow between units produced. However, some overhead costs are variable costs, which increase as the total level of activity rises; so the marginal cost of production and sales should include an amount for variable overheads.

3 Revision of absorption costing

Absorption costing is a traditional approach to dealing with overheads, involving three stages: allocation, apportionment and absorption.

Apportionment has two stages: general overhead apportionment and service department cost apportionment.

Key term

Absorption costing is a method of product costing which aims to include in the total cost of a product (unit, job, and so on) an appropriate share of an organisation's total overhead, which is generally taken to mean an amount which reflects the amount of time and effort that has gone into producing the product.

You should have covered absorption costing in your earlier studies. We will therefore summarise the simpler points of the topic but will go into some detail on the more complex areas to refresh your memory.

Knowledge brought forward from earlier studies

Absorption costing

- Product costs are built up using absorption costing by a process of **allocation**, **apportionment** and **overhead absorption**.

- **Allocation** is the process by which whole cost items are charged directly to a cost unit or cost centre. **Direct costs** are allocated directly to cost units. **Overheads** clearly identifiable with cost centres are allocated to those cost centres but costs which cannot be identified with one particular cost centre are allocated to general overhead cost centres. The cost of a warehouse security guard would therefore be charged to the warehouse cost centre but heating and lighting costs would be charged to a general overhead cost centre.

- The **first stage of overhead apportionment** involves sharing out (or apportioning) the overheads within **general overhead cost centres** between the other cost centres using a fair basis of apportionment (such as floor area occupied by each cost centre for heating and lighting costs).

- The **second stage of overhead apportionment** is to apportion the costs of **service cost centres** (both directly allocated and apportioned costs) to production cost centres.

- After the apportionment of production overheads, all the overhead costs have been divided or shared between the production departments. The final stage in absorption costing is the **absorption** into product costs (using overhead absorption rates) of the overheads that have been allocated and apportioned to the production cost centres.

- An overhead absorption rate is calculated for each production department (or for production activity as a whole). Typically, this is an absorption rate per direct labour hour worked or an absorption rate per machine hour worked.

Question   Cost apportionment

Briefly discuss the factors which could affect the choice of the bases an organisation may use to apportion service department costs.

Answer

(a) The type of service being provided by the service department
(b) The amount of overhead expenditure involved
(c) The number of departments benefiting from the service
(d) The ability to be able to produce realistic estimates of the usage of the service by these departments
(e) The resulting costs and benefits

Question

More cost apportionment

A company is preparing its production overhead budgets and determining the apportionment of those overheads to products. Cost centre expenses and related information have been budgeted as follows.

	Total $	Machine shop A $	Machine shop B $	Assembly $	Canteen $	Maintenance $
Indirect wages	78,560	8,586	9,190	15,674	29,650	15,460
Consumable materials	16,900	6,400	8,700	1,200	600	–
Rent and rates	16,700					
Buildings insurance	2,400					
Power	8,600					
Heat and light	3,400					
Depreciation (machinery)	40,200					
Value of machinery	402,000	201,000	179,000	22,000	–	–
Power usage (%)	100	55	40	3	–	2
Direct labour (hours)	35,000	8,000	6,200	20,800	–	–
Machine usage (hours)	25,200	7,200	18,000	–	–	–
Area (sq ft)	45,000	10,000	12,000	15,000	6,000	2,000

Required

Using the direct apportionment to production departments method and bases of apportionment which you consider most appropriate from the information provided, calculate overhead totals for the three production departments.

Answer

	Total $	A $	B $	Assembly $	Canteen $	Maintenance $	Basis of apportionment
Indirect wages	78,560	8,586	9,190	15,674	29,650	15,460	Actual
Consumable materials	16,900	6,400	8,700	1,200	600	–	Actual
Rent and rates	16,700	3,711	4,453	5,567	2,227	742	Area
Insurance	2,400	533	640	800	320	107	Area
Power	8,600	4,730	3,440	258	–	172	Usage
Heat and light	3,400	756	907	1,133	453	151	Area
Depreciation	40,200	20,100	17,900	2,200	–	–	Val of mach
	166,760	44,816	45,230	26,832	33,250	16,632	
Reallocate	–	7,600	5,890	19,760	(33,250)	–	Direct labour
Reallocate	–	4,752	11,880	–	–	(16,632)	Mach usage
Totals	166,760	57,168	63,000	46,592	–	–	

Part A Specialist cost and management accounting techniques | **1: Costing**   7

4 Overhead absorption

FAST FORWARD

After apportionment, overheads are **absorbed** into products using an appropriate **absorption rate** based on budgeted costs and budgeted activity levels.

Having allocated and/or apportioned all **overheads**, the next stage in absorption costing is to **add them to, or absorb them into**, the cost of production or sales.

Overhead costs are absorbed using a predetermined rate based on budgeted figures.

4.1 Use of a predetermined absorption rate

Knowledge brought forward from earlier studies

Step 1 The overhead likely to be incurred during the coming year is estimated.

Step 2 The total hours, units or direct costs on which the overhead absorption rates are based (activity levels) are estimated.

Step 3 Absorption rate = Estimated overhead ÷ Budgeted activity level

4.2 Choosing the appropriate absorption base

Question   Absorption bases

List as many possible bases of absorption (or 'overhead recovery rates') as you can think of.

Answer

(a)   A percentage of direct materials cost
(b)   A percentage of direct labour cost
(c)   A percentage of prime cost
(d)   A percentage of factory cost (for administration overhead)
(e)   A percentage of sales or factory cost (for selling and distribution overhead)
(f)   A rate per machine hour
(g)   A rate per direct labour hour
(h)   A rate per unit

The choice of an absorption basis is a **matter of judgement and common sense**. There are no strict rules or formulae involved. However, the basis should realistically reflect the characteristics of a given production centre, avoid undue anomalies and be 'fair'. The **choice will be significant in determining the cost of individual products, but the total cost of production overheads is the budgeted overhead expenditure, no matter what basis of absorption is selected**. It is the relative share of overhead costs borne by individual products and jobs which is affected.

Question   Absorption rates

Using the information in, and the results of, the question on page 7, determine budgeted overhead absorption rates for each of the production departments using appropriate bases of absorption.

Machine shop A:	$57,168/7,200	= $7.94 per machine hour
Machine shop B:	$63,000/18,000	= $3.50 per machine hour
Assembly:	$46,592/20,800	= $2.24 per direct labour hour

4.3 Over- and under-absorption of overheads

FAST FORWARD

Over- or under-absorbed overhead occurs when overheads incurred do not equal overheads absorbed.

The rate of overhead absorption is based on estimates in the budget, of both the numerator (budgeted expenditure) and denominator (budgeted activity level), and it is quite likely that what actually occurs will differ from either one or both of these estimates. As a consequence, actual overheads incurred will probably be either greater than or less than overheads absorbed into the cost of production, and so it is almost inevitable that at the end of the accounting year there will have been an over-absorption or under-absorption of the overhead actually incurred.

- **Over-absorption** means that the **overheads charged to the cost of production or sales are greater than the overheads actually incurred**.

- **Under-absorption** means that **insufficient overheads have been included in the cost of production or sales**.

Under-absorption may also be called under-recovery of overheads; over-absorption may be called over-recovery.

Suppose that the budgeted overhead in a production department is $80,000 and the budgeted activity is 40,000 direct labour hours. The overhead recovery rate (using a direct labour hour basis) would be $2 per direct labour hour.

Suppose that actual overheads in the period are $84,000 and 45,000 direct labour hours are worked.

	$
Overhead incurred (actual)	84,000
Overhead absorbed (45,000 × $2)	90,000
Over-absorption of overhead	6,000

In this example, the cost of production has been charged with $6,000 more than was actually spent and so the recorded cost of production will be too high. The over-absorbed overhead will be an adjustment to profit at the end of the accounting period to reconcile the overheads charged to the actual overhead.

Question
Over- and under-absorption

The total production overhead expenditure of the company in the questions above was $176,533 and its actual activity was as follows.

	Machine shop A	Machine shop B	Assembly
Direct labour hours	8,200	6,500	21,900
Machine usage hours	7,300	18,700	–

Required

Using the information in and results of the previous questions, calculate the under- or over-absorption of overheads.

		$	$
Actual expenditure			176,533
Overhead absorbed			
Machine shop A	7,300 hrs × $7.94	57,962	
Machine shop B	18,700 hrs × $3.50	65,450	
Assembly	21,900 hrs × $2.24	49,056	
			172,468
Under-absorbed overhead			4,065

4.4 The reasons for under-/over-absorbed overhead

The overhead absorption rate is predetermined from budget estimates of overhead cost and activity level. Under- or over-recovery of overhead will occur in the following circumstances.

- Actual overhead costs are different from budgeted overheads.
- The actual activity level is different from the budgeted activity level.
- Actual overhead costs **and** actual activity level differ from those budgeted.

Question   Over- and under-absorption

A production department has a budgeted production overhead of $180,000 and budgeted activity of 45,000 machine hours. Overheads are absorbed on a machine hour basis.

Required

Calculate the under-/over-absorbed overhead, and note the reasons for the under-/over-absorption in the following circumstances.

(a)   Actual overheads cost $170,000 and 45,000 machine hours were worked.
(b)   Actual overheads cost $180,000 and 40,000 machine hours were worked.
(c)   Actual overheads cost $170,000 and 40,000 machine hours were worked.

Answer

The overhead recovery rate is $180,000/45,000 = $4 per machine hour.

		$
(a)	Actual overhead	170,000
	Absorbed overhead (45,000 × $4)	180,000
	Over-absorbed overhead	10,000

Reason: Actual and budgeted machine hours are the same but actual overheads cost less than expected.

		$
(b)	Actual overhead	180,000
	Absorbed overhead (40,000 × $4)	160,000
	Under-absorbed overhead	20,000

Reason: Budgeted and actual overhead costs were the same but fewer machine hours were worked than expected.

		$
(c)	Actual overhead	170,000
	Absorbed overhead (40,000 × $4)	160,000
	Under-absorbed overhead	10,000

Reason: A combination of the reasons in (a) and (b).

5 Marginal costing

FAST FORWARD

In **marginal costing**, inventories are valued at variable production cost whereas in absorption costing they are valued at their full production cost. Profit is calculated by deducting variable costs of sales from sales revenue to obtain contribution, and then deducting fixed costs to obtain a figure for profit.

Key terms

Marginal cost is the cost of one unit of a product/service which could be avoided if that unit were not produced/provided.

Contribution is the difference between sales revenue and variable (marginal) cost of sales.

Marginal costing is an alternative to absorption costing. Only variable costs (marginal costs) are charged as a cost of sales. Fixed costs are treated as period costs and are charged in full against the profit of the period in which they are incurred.

Knowledge brought forward from earlier studies

Marginal costing

- In **marginal costing**, closing **inventories are valued at marginal (variable) production cost** whereas, in **absorption costing**, inventories are **valued at their full production cost** which includes absorbed fixed production overhead.
- If the opening and closing inventory levels differ in an accounting period, the **profit reported** for the period will **differ between absorption costing and marginal costing**.
- But **in the long run, total profit for a company will be the same** whichever costing method is used, because in the long run total costs will be the same by either method of accounting. The different costing methods merely affect the reported profit for individual accounting periods.

Question

Absorption and marginal costing

A company makes and sells a single product. At the beginning of Period 1, there are no opening inventories of the product, for which the variable production cost is $4 and the sales price $6 per unit. There are no variable selling costs. Fixed costs are $2,000 per period, of which $1,500 are fixed production costs. Normal output is 1,500 units per period. In Period 1, sales were 1,200 units, production was 1,500 units. In Period 2, sales were 1,700 units, production was 1,400 units.

Required

Prepare profit statements for each period and for the two periods in total using both absorption costing and marginal costing.

Answer

It is important to notice that although production and sales volumes in each period are different, over the **full period, total production volume equals sales volume**. The total cost of sales is the same and therefore the **total profit is the same by either method** of accounting. **There are differences** in the reported profit in Period 1 and in Period 2, but these are merely **timing differences** which cancel out over a longer period of time (in this example, over the two periods).

(a) **Absorption costing.** The absorption rate for fixed production overhead is $1,500/1,500 units = $1 per unit. The fully absorbed cost per unit = $(4+1) = $5.

	Period 1		Period 2		Total	
	$	$	$	$	$	$
Sales		7,200		10,200		17,400
Production costs						
Variable	6,000		5,600		11,600	
Fixed	1,500		1,400		2,900	
	7,500		7,000		14,500	
Add opening inventory b/f (300×$5)	–		1,500		1,500	
	7,500		8,500		16,000	
Less closing inventory c/f (300×$5)	1,500		–		1,500	
Production cost of sales	6,000		8,500		14,500	
Under-absorbed overhead	–		100		100	
Total costs		6,000		8,600		14,600
Gross profit		1,200		1,600		2,800
Other costs		(500)		(500)		(1,000)
Net profit		700		1,100		1,800

(b) **Marginal costing**

The marginal cost per unit = $4.

	Period 1		Period 2		Total	
	$	$	$	$	$	$
Sales		7,200		10,200		17,400
Variable production cost	6,000		5,600		11,600	
Add opening inventory b/f (300×$4)	–		1,200		1,200	
	6,000		6,800		12,800	
Less closing inventory c/f (300×$4)	1,200		–		1,200	
Variable prod. cost of sales		4,800		6,800		11,600
Contribution		2,400		3,400		5,800
Fixed costs		2,000		2,000		4,000
Profit		400		1,400		1,800

> ✎ **Question**   **Marginal and absorption costing**

RH makes and sells one product, which has the following standard production cost.

		$
Direct labour	3 hours at $6 per hour	18
Direct materials	4 kilograms at $7 per kg	28
Variable production overhead		3
Fixed production overhead		20
Standard production cost per unit		69

Normal output is 16,000 units per annum. Variable selling, distribution and administration costs are 20% of sales value. Fixed selling, distribution and administration costs are $180,000 per annum. There are no units in finished goods inventory at 1 October 20X2. The fixed overhead expenditure is spread evenly throughout the year. The selling price per unit is $140. Production and sales budgets are as follows.

	Six months ending 31 March 20X3	Six months ending 30 September 20X3
Production	8,500	7,000
Sales	7,000	8,000

Required

Prepare profit statements for each of the six-monthly periods, using the following methods of costing.

(a) Marginal costing
(b) Absorption costing

(a) **Profit statements for the year ending 30 September 20X3**
Marginal costing basis

	Six months ending 31 March 20X3		Six months ending 30 September 20X3	
	$'000	$'000	$'000	$'000
Sales at $140 per unit		980		1,120
Opening inventory			73.5	
Std. variable prod. cost (at $49 per unit)	416.5		343.0	
	416.5		416.5	
Closing inventory (W1)	73.5		24.5	
		343		392
		637		728
Variable selling and so on costs		196		224
Contribution		441		504
Fixed costs: production (W2)	160		160	
selling and so on	90		90	
		250		250
Net profit		191		254

(b) **Profit statements for the year ending 30 September 20X3**
Absorption costing basis

	Six months ending 31 March 20X3		Six months ending 30 September 20X3	
	$'000	$'000	$'000	$'000
Sales at $140 per unit		980		1,120
Opening inventory			103.5	
Std. cost of prod. (at $69 per unit)	586.5		483.0	
	586.5		586.5	
Closing inventory (W1)	103.5		34.5	
	483.0		552.0	
(Over-)/under-absorbed overhead (W3)	(10.0)		20.0	
		473		572
Gross profit		507		548
Selling and so on costs				
Variable	196		224	
Fixed	90		90	
		286		314
Net profit		221		234

Workings

1

	Six months ending 31 March 20X3	Six months ending 30 September 20X3
	Units	Units
Opening inventory		1,500
Production	8,500	7,000
	8,500	8,500
Sales	7,000	8,000
Closing inventory	1,500	500
Marginal cost valuation (× $49)	$73,500	$24,500
Absorption cost valuation (× $69)	$103,500	$34,500

2 Budgeted fixed production o/hd = 16,000 units × $20 = $320,000 pa = $160,000 per six months

3

	Six months ending 31 March 20X3		Six months ending 30 September 20X3	
Normal output (16,000 ÷ 2)	8,000	units	8,000	units
Budgeted output	8,500	units	7,000	units
Difference	500	units	1,000	units
× std. fixed prod. o/hd per unit	× $20		× $20	
(Over-)/under-absorbed overhead	($10,000)		$20,000	

6 Absorption costing and marginal costing compared

FAST FORWARD

If opening and closing inventory levels differ, the profit reported under the two methods will be different. In the long run, total profit will be the same whichever method is used.

6.1 Reconciling the profit figures given by the two methods

The **difference in profits** reported under the two costing systems is due to the **different inventory valuation methods** used.

(a)   **If inventory levels increase** between the beginning and end of a period, **absorption costing will report the higher profit** because some of the fixed production overhead incurred during the period will be carried forward in closing inventory (which reduces cost of sales) to be set against sales revenue in the following period, instead of being written off in full against profit in the period concerned.

(b)   **If inventory levels decrease, absorption costing will report the lower profit** because, as well as the fixed overhead incurred, fixed production overhead which had been carried forward in opening inventory is released and is also included in cost of sales.

6.2 Example: Reconciling profits

The profits reported for period 1 in the question on page 12 would be reconciled as follows.

	$
Marginal costing profit	400
Adjust for fixed overhead in inventory (inventory increase of 300 units × $1 per unit)	300
Absorption costing profit	700

Exam focus point

Remember that if opening inventory values are greater than closing inventory values, marginal costing shows a bigger profit than absorption costing. If opening inventory values are lower than closing inventory values, absorption costing shows a bigger profit than marginal costing.

6.3 Marginal vs absorption costing: reporting to management

FAST FORWARD

Marginal costing is more **useful** for **decision-making** purposes, but absorption costing is needed for **financial reporting** purposes to comply with accounting standards.

We know that the reported profit in any period is likely to differ according to the costing method used, but does one method provide a more reliable guide to management about the organisation's profit position?

With marginal costing, contribution varies in direct proportion to the volume of units sold. Profits will increase as sales volume rises, by the amount of extra contribution earned. Since fixed cost expenditure does not alter, marginal costing gives an accurate picture of how a firm's cash flows and profits are affected by changes in sales volumes.

With absorption costing, in contrast, **there is no clear relationship between profit and sales volume**, and as sales volume rises the total profit will rise by the sum of the gross profit per unit plus the amount of overhead absorbed per unit. Arguably this is a confusing and unsatisfactory method of monitoring profitability.

If sales volumes are the same from period to period, marginal costing reports the same profit each period (given no change in prices or costs). In contrast, using absorption costing, profits can vary with the volume of production, even when the volume of sales is constant. **By using absorption costing there is therefore the possibility of manipulating profit, simply by changing output and inventory levels.**

6.4 Example: Manipulating profits

Gloom Co budgeted to make and sell 10,000 units of its product in 20X1. The selling price is $10 per unit and the variable cost $4 per unit. Fixed production costs were budgeted at $50,000 for the year. The company uses absorption costing and budgeted an absorption rate of $5 per unit. During 20X1, it became apparent that sales demand would only be 8,000 units. The management, concerned about the apparent effect of the low volume of sales on profits, decided to increase production for the year to 15,000 units. Actual fixed costs were still expected to be $50,000 in spite of the significant increase in production volume.

Required

Calculate the profit at an actual sales volume of 8,000 units, using the following methods.

(a)   Absorption costing
(b)   Marginal costing

Explain the difference in profits calculated.

Solution

(a)   **Absorption costing**

	$	$
Sales (8,000 × $10)		80,000
Full cost of production (15,000 × $9)	135,000	
Closing inventory (7,000 × $9)	(63,000)	
Production cost of sales	72,000	
Less: over-absorbed overhead (5,000 × $5)	(25,000)	
Cost of sales		(47,000)
Profit		33,000

(b)   **Marginal costing**

	$	$
Sales		80,000
Variable cost of production (15,000 × $4)	60,000	
Closing inventory (7,000 × $4)	(28,000)	
Variable cost of sales		32,000
Contribution		48,000
Fixed costs		50,000
Loss		(2,000)

The difference in profits of $35,000 is explained by the **difference in the increase in inventory values** (7,000 units × $5 of fixed overhead per unit). With absorption costing, the expected profit will be higher than the original budget of $10,000 (10,000 units × ($10 – 9)) simply because $35,000 of fixed overheads will be carried forward in closing inventory values. By producing to absorb overhead rather than to satisfy customers, inventory levels will, of course, increase. Unless this inventory is sold, however, there may come a point when production has to stop and the inventory has to be sold off at lower prices. Marginal costing reports a contribution of $6 per unit, or $48,000 in total for 8,000 units, which fails to cover the fixed costs of $50,000 by $2,000.

BPP
LEARNING MEDIA

Chapter Roundup

- **Costing** is the process of determining the costs of products, services or activities.

- **Indirect costs**, or **overheads**, are costs incurred in making a product or providing a service, but which cannot be traced directly to products or services. **Absorption costing** is a means of incorporating a fair share of these costs into the cost of each unit of product manufactured or each service provided.

- **Absorption costing** is a traditional approach to dealing with overheads, involving three stages: allocation, apportionment and absorption.

- **Apportionment** has two stages: general overhead apportionment and service department cost apportionment.

- After apportionment, overheads are **absorbed** into products using an appropriate **absorption rate** based on budgeted costs and budgeted activity levels.

- **Under- or over-absorbed overhead** occurs when overheads incurred do not equal overheads absorbed.

- In **marginal costing**, inventories are valued at variable production cost whereas in absorption costing they are valued at their full production cost. Profit is calculated by deducting variable costs of sales from sales revenue to obtain contribution, and then deducting fixed costs to obtain a figure for profit.

- If opening and closing inventory levels differ, the profit reported under the two methods will be different.

  In the long run, total profit will be the same whichever method is used.

- Marginal costing is more **useful** for **decision-making** purposes, but absorption costing is needed for **financial reporting** purposes to comply with accounting standards.

Quick Quiz

1   Here are some terms you should have encountered in your earlier studies. Match the term to the definition.

Terms	Definitions	
Direct cost	(a)	Specific costs of, say, an activity, which would not be incurred if the activity did not exist
Prime cost		
Overhead	(b)	Total of direct costs
Classification by function	(c)	Future cash flow which will be changed as the result of a decision
Fixed cost	(d)	Product produced by an organisation
Variable cost	(e)	Dividing costs into production, administration, selling and distribution, research and development and financing costs
Product cost		
Avoidable cost	(f)	Cost that can be traced in full to whatever is being costed
Controllable cost	(g)	Organisation's departments
Relevant cost	(h)	A cost that varies with the level of output
Cost centre	(i)	A cost that is incurred in the course of making a product but which cannot be traced directly and in full to the product
Cost unit		
	(j)	Cost that is incurred for a particular period of time and which, within certain activity levels, is unaffected by changes in the level of activity
	(k)	Cost identified with goods produced or purchased for resale and initially included in the value of inventory
	(l)	Cost which can be influenced by management decisions and actions

2   .... is the process of determining the costs of products, activities or services.

3   How is an overhead absorption rate calculated?

    A   Estimated overhead ÷ actual activity level
    B   Estimated overhead ÷ budgeted activity level
    C   Actual overhead ÷ actual activity level
    D   Actual overhead ÷ budgeted activity level

4   Over-absorption means that the overheads charged to the cost of sales are greater than the overheads actually incurred.

    ☐ True   ☐ False

5   Fill in the blanks in the statements about marginal costing and absorption costing below.

    (a)   If inventory levels .... between the beginning and end of a period, absorption costing will report the higher profit.

    (b)   If inventory levels decrease, ... costing will report the lower profit.

6   Fill in the following blanks with either 'marginal' or 'absorption'.

    (a)   Using .... costing, profits can be manipulated simply by changing output and inventory levels.

    (b)   Fixed costs are charged in full against the profit of the period in which they are incurred when .... costing is used.

    (c)   .... costing fails to recognise the importance of working to full capacity.

    (d)   .... costing could be argued to be preferable to .... costing in management accounting in order to be consistent with the requirements of accounting standards.

    (e)   .... costing should not be used when decision-making information is required.

Answers to Quick Quiz

1
Direct cost	(f)
Prime cost	(b)
Overhead	(i)
Classification by function	(e)
Fixed cost	(j)
Variable cost	(h)
Product cost	(k)
Avoidable cost	(a)
Controllable cost	(l)
Relevant cost	(c)
Cost centre	(g)
Cost unit	(d)

2   Costing

3   B

4   True

5   (a)   Increase
     (b)   Absorption

6   (a)   absorption
     (b)   marginal
     (c)   marginal
     (d)   absorption, marginal
     (e)   absorption

Now try the question below from the Practice Question Bank at the back of this Study Text

Number	Level	Marks	Approximate time
Section B Q1–5	Introductory	10	20 mins

Activity based costing

Introduction

Chapter 2 covers Part A of the syllabus, specialist cost and management accounting techniques. It has been divided into five sub-chapters to emphasise that all five techniques are equally important and equally examinable.

In this chapter we will be looking at a method of cost accumulation, **activity based costing (ABC)**, which is an alternative to traditional absorption costing. ABC attempts to overcome the problems of costing in a modern manufacturing environment, where a very large proportion of total production costs are overhead costs.

Study guide

		Intellectual level
A1	**Activity based costing**	
(a)	Identify appropriate cost drivers under ABC.	1
(b)	Calculate costs per driver and per unit using ABC.	2
(c)	Compare ABC and traditional methods of overhead absorption based on production units, labour hours or machine hours.	2

Exam guide

Questions on ABC regularly appear in the F5 exam.

1 Activity based costing   6/08, 6/10, 12/11, 12/12, 6/14, 6/15

FAST FORWARD

Activity based costing (ABC) is an alternative to traditional absorption costing as a method of costing.

ABC involves the identification of the factors **(cost drivers)** which 'cause' or 'drive' the costs of an organisation's major activities. Overheads are allocated and apportioned to activity cost centres or 'cost pools'. From these activity cost centres, the overhead costs are then absorbed into the product costs on the basis of their usage of the activity. The absorption rate for each activity is a rate per unit of the relevant cost driver.

- For activity costs that seem to relate to the volume of production, the cost driver will be volume-related (labour or machine hours).

- For activity costs that do not seem to relate to production volume, a different cost driver is identified, such as the number of production runs or number of orders received.

1.1 Reasons for the development of ABC

Traditional **absorption costing** was developed in a time when most manufacturers produced only a **narrow range of products**, so that products underwent **similar operations** and consumed **similar proportions of overheads**. In addition, **overhead costs were only a very small fraction of total production costs**: direct labour and direct material costs accounted for the largest proportion of the costs.

With the **dramatic fall** in the costs of processing information, and with the advent of **advanced manufacturing technology (AMT)**, overhead costs have become a much larger proportion of total production costs, and direct labour has become much less important. Direct labour may now account for as little as 5% of production costs. It is therefore now difficult to justify the use of direct labour hours as the basis for absorbing overheads, to produce 'realistic' product costs.

The **falling costs of information processing** have also made it possible to switch to a different and more complex system for accumulating and analysing overhead costs. ABC may now be cost effective whereas in the past its high costs could have made it difficult to justify.

Many resources are used in **non volume related support activities**, which have increased due to AMT. Non volume related support activities are activities that support production, but where the level of support activity (and so the level of cost) depends on something other than production volume – such as setting-up production runs, production scheduling and inspection. These support activities assist the efficient manufacture of a wide range of products and are **not, in general, affected by changes in production volume**. They tend to **vary in the long term according to the range and complexity** of the products manufactured, rather than the volume of output.

The wider the range and the more complex the products, the more support services are required. Consider, for example, Factory X which produces 10,000 units of one product, the Alpha, and Factory Y which produces 1,000 units each of ten slightly different versions of the Alpha. Support activity costs in Factory Y are likely to be a lot higher than in Factory X, even though the factories produce an identical number of units. For example, Factory X will need to set up only a single production run, whereas Factory Y will have to set up a production run at least ten times, for each of the ten different products. Factory Y will therefore incur more set-up costs for the same volume of production.

Traditional absorption costing systems, which assume that all products consume all support resources in proportion to production volumes, tend to **allocate**:

(a) **Too great a proportion of overheads to high volume products**, which cause relatively little diversity and hence use fewer support services; and

(b) **Too small a proportion of overheads to low volume products**, which cause greater diversity and therefore use more support services.

Activity based costing (ABC) attempts to overcome this problem.

1.2 Definition of ABC

Key term

> **Activity based costing (ABC)** is a method of costing which involves identifying the costs of the main support activities and the factors that 'drive' the costs of each activity. Support overheads are charged to products by absorbing cost on the basis of the product's usage of the factor driving the overheads.

The major ideas behind activity based costing are as follows.

(a) **Activities cause costs**. Activities include ordering, materials handling, machining, assembly, production scheduling and despatching.

(b) **Manufacturing products creates demand for the support activities**.

(c) Costs are assigned to a product **on the basis of the product's consumption of these activities**.

1.3 Outline of an ABC system

An ABC system operates as follows.

Step 1 Identify an organisation's major activities that support the manufacture of the organisation's products or the provision of its services.

Step 2 Use cost allocation and apportionment methods to charge overhead costs to each of these activities. The costs that accumulate for each activity cost centre is called a **cost pool**.

Step 3 Identify the factors which determine the size of the costs of an activity/affect the costs of an activity. These are known as **cost drivers**.

Key term

> A **cost driver** is a factor which has most influence on the cost of an activity.

Look at the following examples.

Cost pool	Possible cost driver
Ordering costs: handling customer orders	Number of orders
Materials handling costs	Number of production runs
Machine set-up costs	Number of machine set-ups
Machine operating costs	Number of machine hours
Production scheduling costs	Number of production runs
Despatching costs	Number of orders despatched

Step 4 For each cost pool/activity cost centre, calculate an absorption rate per unit of cost driver.

Step 5 Charge overhead costs to products for each activity, on the basis of their usage of the activity (the number of cost drivers they use). Overheads are charged by absorbing them into product costs at a rate per unit of cost driver.

Question
Cost driver

Which of the following definitions best describes a cost driver?

A   Any activity which causes an increase in costs
B   A collection of costs associated with a particular activity
C   A cost that varies with production levels
D   Any factor which causes a change in the cost of an activity

Answer

D   Any factor which causes a change in the cost of an activity

Exam focus point

Questions on activity based costing may require a comparison with more traditional absorption costing methods.

2 Absorption costing versus ABC
6/08, 6/10, 12/10, 12/12, 6/14

The following example illustrates the point that traditional absorption costing techniques result in a misleading and inequitable division of costs between low-volume and high-volume products, and that ABC can provide a more meaningful way of charging overhead costs to products.

2.1 Example: Activity based costing

Suppose that Cooplan manufactures four products, W, X, Y and Z. Output and cost data for the period just ended are as follows.

	Output units	Number of production runs in the period	Material cost per unit $	Direct labour hours per unit	Machine hours per unit
W	10	2	20	1	1
X	10	2	80	3	3
Y	100	5	20	1	1
Z	100	5	80	3	3
		14			

Direct labour cost per hour: **$5**

		$
Overhead costs		
Short-run variable costs		3,080
Set-up costs		10,920
Expediting and scheduling costs		9,100
Materials handling costs		7,700
		30,800

Required

Prepare unit costs for each product using:

(a)   Conventional absorption costing, and
(b)   ABC.

Assume that, in the traditional absorption costing system, overheads are absorbed at a direct labour hour rate.

Solution

(a)   Using a **conventional absorption costing approach** the absorption rate for overheads based on direct labour hours or machine hours is:

$30,800 ÷ 440 hours = $70 per direct labour.

The product costs would be as follows.

	W	X	Y	Z	Total
	$	$	$	$	$
Direct material	200	800	2,000	8,000	
Direct labour	50	150	500	1,500	
Overheads	700	2,100	7,000	21,000	
	950	3,050	9,500	30,500	44,000
Units produced	10	10	100	100	
Cost per unit	$95	$305	$95	$305	

(b)   Using **activity based costing**, it will be assumed that the number of production runs is the cost driver for set-up costs, expediting and scheduling costs and materials handling costs; and that machine hours are the cost driver for short-run variable costs. Product costs per unit are as follows.

	W	X	Y	Z	Total
	$	$	$	$	$
Direct material (no change)	200	800	2,000	8,000	
Direct labour (no change)	50	150	500	1,500	
Short-run variable overheads (W1)	70	210	700	2,100	
Set-up costs (W2)	1,560	1,560	3,900	3,900	
Expediting, scheduling costs (W3)	1,300	1,300	3,250	3,250	
Materials handling costs (W4)	1,100	1,100	2,750	2,750	
	4,280	5,120	13,100	21,500	44,000
Units produced	10	10	100	100	
Cost per unit	$428	$512	$131	$215	

Workings

1   $3,080 ÷ 440 machine hours = $7 per machine hour
2   $10,920 ÷ 14 production runs = $780 per production run
3   $9,100 ÷ 14 production runs = $650 per production run
4   $7,700 ÷ 14 production runs = $550 per production run

Summary

Product	Conventional absorption costing unit cost $	ABC unit cost $	Difference per unit $	Difference in total $
W	95	428	+333	+3,330
X	305	512	+207	+2,070
Y	95	131	+36	+3,600
Z	305	215	−90	−9,000

These figures might suggest that the traditional volume-based absorption costing system is flawed, because the low-volume products W and X are not being charged with a 'fair share' of the costs of overhead support activities.

More specifically, **traditional absorption costing may be unsatisfactory** for two main reasons.

(a) It **under-allocates overhead costs to low-volume products** (here, W and X) and **over-allocates overheads to higher-volume products** (here Z in particular).

(b) It **under-allocates overhead costs to smaller products** (here W and Y, with just one hour of work needed per unit) and **over-allocates overheads to larger products** (here X and particularly Z).

ABC addresses these problems and arguably produces a more 'realistic' or 'satisfactory' cost.

2.2 Cost drivers

ABC focuses attention on **what** factors are most influential in determining the level of support activity costs, ie the cost drivers. However, it is important to understand that activity based costs should **not be regarded as variable costs** that vary with the volume of the cost driver. Some activity costs may be variable, but many are not. Cost drivers affect or influence total costs of the activity, but not in a direct 'variable cost' relationship between activity level and cost.

(a) **Activity costs that relate to production volume**, such as power costs, should be traced to products using production **volume-related cost drivers**, such as direct labour hours or direct machine hours worked.

Overheads which do not relate to production volume but to **some other activity** should be traced to products using **transaction-based cost drivers**, such as number of production runs and number of orders received.

(b) Traditional absorption costing charges overhead costs to products in a way that ignores the costs of support activities and their cost drivers. As a consequence, it produces less satisfactory or 'reliable' product costs.

Question   Traditional costing (v) ABC

A company manufactures two products, L and M, using the same equipment and similar processes. An extract of the production data for these products in one period is shown below.

	L	M
Quantity produced (units)	5,000	7,000
Direct labour hours per unit	1	2
Machine hours per unit	3	1
Set-ups in the period	10	40
Orders handled in the period	15	60

Overhead costs	$
Relating to machine activity	220,000
Relating to production run set-ups	20,000
Relating to handling of orders	45,000
	285,000

Required

Calculate the production overheads to be absorbed by one unit of each of the products using the following costing methods.

(a)   A traditional costing approach, using a direct labour hour rate to absorb overheads
(b)   An activity based costing approach, using suitable cost drivers to trace overheads to products

Answer

(a)   **Traditional costing approach**

		Direct labour hours
Product L	= 5,000 units × 1 hour	5,000
Product M	= 7,000 units × 2 hours	14,000
		19,000

$$\therefore \text{ Overhead absorption rate } = \frac{\$285,000}{19,000}$$

$$= \$15 \text{ per hour}$$

Overhead absorbed would be as follows.

Product L	1 hour × $15 =	$15 per unit
Product M	2 hours × $15 =	$30 per unit

(b)   **ABC approach**

		Machine hours
Product L	= 5,000 units × 3 hours	15,000
Product M	= 7,000 units × 1 hour	7,000
		22,000

Using ABC the overhead costs are absorbed according to the cost drivers. The absorption rate for each cost pool is as follows.

	$			Absorption rate, ABC
Machine-hour driven costs	220,000	÷	22,000 m/c hours	= $10 per m/c hour
Set-up driven costs	20,000	÷	50 set-ups	= $400 per set-up
Order driven costs	45,000	÷	75 orders	= $600 per order

Overhead costs are therefore as follows.

		Product L $		Product M $
Machine-driven costs	(15,000 hrs × $10)	150,000	(7,000 hrs × $10)	70,000
Set-up costs	(10 × $400)	4,000	(40 × $400)	16,000
Order handling costs	(15 × $600)	9,000	(60 × $600)	36,000
		163,000		122,000
Units produced		5,000		7,000
Overhead cost per unit		$32.60		$17.43

These figures suggest that, with traditional absorption costing, Product M absorbs an 'unfair' amount of overhead costs using a direct labour hour absorption rate. If overhead costs are absorbed accordingly for each activity, based on the cost drivers for the activity, the resulting costs are more 'fair'.

ABC has both advantages and disadvantages, and tends to be more widely used by larger organisations and the service sector.

Exam focus point

There is an article on the ACCA website on the topic of activity based costing which you should read (ACCA, 2015).

As you will have discovered when you attempted the question above, there is nothing difficult about ABC. Once the necessary information has been obtained it is similar to traditional absorption costing. This simplicity is part of its appeal. Further merits of ABC are as follows.

(a) The **complexity of manufacturing has increased**, with wider product ranges, shorter product life cycles and more complex production processes. **ABC recognises this complexity with its multiple cost drivers**.

(b) In a more competitive environment, companies must be able to assess product profitability realistically. **ABC facilitates a good understanding of what drives overhead costs**.

(c) In modern manufacturing systems, overhead functions include a lot of non factory floor activities such as product design, quality control, production planning and customer services. **ABC is concerned with all overhead costs** and so it can take management accounting beyond its 'traditional' factory floor boundaries.

3.1 ABC and decision-making 12/10

Many of ABC's supporters claim that it can assist with decision-making in a number of ways.

- It provides accurate and reliable cost information.
- It establishes a long-run product cost.
- It provides cost data which may be used to evaluate different ways of delivering business.

It is particularly suited to the following types of decision.

- Pricing, where selling prices are derived by adding a profit mark-up to cost

- Promoting or discontinuing products or parts of the business, since ABC may help management to identify activity costs that may be either incurred or saved

- Developing new products or new ways to do business, because ABC focuses attention on the support activities that would be required for the new product or business procedure

Note, however, that an ABC cost is **not a variable cost**. ABC is a form of absorption costing that seeks to charge overheads to products on a more 'fair' basis than traditional absorption costing. An ABC cost is therefore **not a relevant cost** for decision-making purposes.

ABC attempts to **relate the incidence of costs to the level of activities undertaken**. A **hierarchy of activities** has been suggested (Cooper, 1990).

Classification level	Cause of cost	Types of cost	Cost driver
Unit level	Production/acquisition of a single unit of product or delivery of single unit of service	Direct materials Direct labour	Units produced
Batch level	A group of things being made, handled or processed	Purchase orders Set-ups Inspection	Batches produced

Classification level	Cause of cost	Types of cost	Cost driver
Product level	Development, production or acquisition of different items	Equipment maintenance Product development	Product lines produced
Facility sustaining level	Some costs cannot be related to a particular product line; instead, they are related to maintaining the buildings and facilities. These costs cannot be related to cost objects with any degree of accuracy and are often excluded from ABC calculations for this reason.	Building depreciation Organisational advertising	None – supports the overall production or service process

3.2 Criticisms of ABC

It has been suggested by critics that **activity based costing has some weaknesses**.

(a)   Cost apportionment may still be required at the cost pooling stage for shared items of cost, such as rent, rates and building depreciation. Apportionment can be an arbitrary way of sharing costs.

(b)   A single cost driver may not explain the cost behaviour of all items in a cost pool. An activity may have two or more cost drivers.

(c)   Unless costs are 'driven' by an activity that is measurable in quantitative terms, cost drivers cannot be used. What drives the cost of the annual external audit, for example?

(d)   There must be a reason for using a system of ABC. ABC must provide meaningful product costs or extra information that management will use. If management is not going to use ABC information for any practical purpose, a traditional absorption costing system would be simpler to operate and just as good.

(e)   The cost of implementing and maintaining an ABC system can exceed the benefits of 'improved accuracy' in product costs.

(f)   **Implementing** ABC is often problematic due to problems with understanding activities and their costs.

(g)   ABC is an absorption costing system. Absorption costing has only limited value for management accounting purposes.

Chapter Roundup

- **Activity based costing (ABC)** is an alternative to traditional absorption costing as a method of costing.

- ABC involves the identification of the factors **(cost drivers)** which 'cause' or 'drive' the costs of an organisation's major activities. Overheads are allocated and apportioned to activity cost centres or 'cost pools'. From these activity cost centres, the overhead costs are then absorbed into the product costs on the basis of their usage of the activity. The absorption rate for each activity is a rate per unit of the relevant cost driver.

- For activity costs that seem to relate to the volume of production, the cost driver will be volume related (labour or machine hours).

- For activity costs that do not seem to relate to production volume, a different cost driver is identified, such as the number of production runs or number of orders received.

- ABC has both advantages and disadvantages, and tends to be more widely used by larger organisations and the service sector.

Quick Quiz

1 Choose the correct phrases.

Traditional costing systems tend to charge **too great/too small** a proportion of overheads to high-volume products and **too great/too small** a proportion of overheads to low-volume products.

2 Fill in the blanks.

The major ideas behind ABC are as follows.

(a) Activities cause ....
(b) Producing products creates demand for the ....
(c) Costs are assigned to a product on the basis of the product's consumption of the
....

3 Match the most appropriate cost driver to each cost.

	Costs	*Cost driver*
(a)	Machine set-up costs	Number of machine hours
(b)	Machine operating costs	Number of set-ups
(c)	Materials handling and despatch	Number of orders executed

4 ABC recognises the complexity of modern manufacturing by the use of multiple cost pools. **True or false?**

5 Direct labour hours or direct machine hours are used to trace costs to products occurs with absorption costing, but not with ABC. **True or false?**

6 The cost driver for quality inspection is likely to be batch size. **True or false?**

7 ABC is not a system that is suitable for use by service organisations. **True or false?**

Answers to Quick Quiz

1   Too great
     Too small

2   (a)   Costs
     (b)   Activities
     (c)   Activities

3   (a)   Number of set-ups
     (b)   Number of machine hours
     (c)   Number of orders executed

4   True. There is a separate cost pool for each significant activity that incurs costs.

5   False. The use of volume-related cost drivers should be used for costs that do vary with production volume.

6   False. It is more likely to be the number of production runs.

7   False. It is more suitable for manufacturing but can be used to cost services in some service industries.

Now try the questions below from the Practice Question Bank at the back of this Study Text

Number	Level	Marks	Approximate time
Section A Q1	Examination	2	4 mins
Section A Q2	Examination	2	4 mins
Section A Q3	Examination	2	4 mins
Section A Q4	Examination	2	4 mins
Section A Q5	Examination	2	4 mins
Section B Q6–10	Examination	10	20 mins
Section B Q11–15	Examination	10	20 mins

Target costing

2b

Topic list	Syllabus reference
1 What is target costing?	A2 (a)
2 Implementing target costing	A2 (a)
3 Deriving a target cost	A2 (a)
4 Closing a target cost gap	A2 (c)
5 Target costing in service industries	A2 (b)

Introduction

Target costing is the second specialist cost accounting technique we will consider. It is a process which involves setting a target cost for a product by subtracting a desired profit margin from a target selling price.

In a competitive market where organisations are continually redesigning products and developing new products, target costing can be an invaluable technique for helping the organisation to make a satisfactory profit on the items that it sells.

Study guide

		Intellectual level
A2	**Target costing**	
(a)	Derive a target cost in manufacturing and service industries.	2
(b)	Explain the difficulties of using target costing in service industries.	2
(c)	Suggest how a target cost gap might be closed.	2

Exam guide

Target costing may be examined in the Section A objective test questions or it may form part of a Section B mini case study question where the calculation of a target cost may be required, followed by a multiple choice question on the theory of target costing.

1 What is target costing?

12/07

FAST FORWARD

Target costing involves setting a target cost for a product, having identified a target selling price and a required profit margin. The target cost is the target sales price minus the required profit.

In a competitive market, selling prices must be competitive. In order to sell at a competitive price and make a required amount of profit, the cost of production and sales must be kept at a level that will provide the required profit at the chosen selling price. In markets such as this, businesses can benefit from using target costing.

Target costing is concerned with designing a product and its production process so that it can be made and sold at a cost that delivers the required profit at the chosen price. It focuses on getting the expected cost of a product down to a target cost amount. Achieving a target cost will usually require some redesigning of the product and the removal of unnecessary costs. Target costing therefore encourages a business to examine its processes and costs carefully.

Functional analysis can be applied at the design stage of a new product and a target cost for each function can be set.

In many markets, new product innovation and the redesigning of existing products is a continual process. Target costing is most effective at the product design stage, and is less effective for established products that are made in established processes. At the design stage, it is easier and cheaper to make changes that reduce costs.

Here are some examples of **decisions made at the design stage** which **impact on the cost of a product**.

- The number of different components in a product, that have to be assembled in the production process
- Whether the components are standard or not: using standard components can reduce costs
- Deciding to exclude design features of the product that do not add any value for the customer
- Using cheaper materials to make the product, where this does not affect product quality
- Simplifying the production process, for example to make it easier and quicker to change over tools

Key terms

Target costing involves setting a target cost by subtracting a desired profit margin from a target selling price.

Target cost is the cost at which a product must be produced and sold in order to achieve the required amount of profit at the target selling price. When a product is first planned, its estimated cost will often be higher than its target cost. The aim of target costing is then to find ways of closing this target cost gap, and producing and selling the product at the target cost.

2 Implementing target costing Sep/Dec 15, 6/12

In an article 'Product costing/pricing strategy' (ACCA *Students Newsletter*, August 1999), a useful summary of the steps in the implementation of the target costing process was presented.

Step 1   Determine a product specification of which an adequate sales volume is estimated.

Step 2   Decide a target selling price at which the organisation will be able to sell the product successfully and achieve a desired market share.

Step 3   Estimate the required profit, based on required profit margin or return on investment.

Step 4   Calculate: Target cost = Target selling price – Target profit.

Step 5   Prepare an estimated cost for the product, based on the initial design specification and current cost levels.

Step 6   Calculate: Target cost gap = Estimated cost – Target cost.

Step 7   Make efforts to close the gap. This is more likely to be successful if efforts are made to 'design out' costs prior to production, rather than to 'control out' costs after 'live' production has started.

It is usual for estimates of target cost to be based not only on a target selling price per unit, but also on the expected volume of sales.

3 Deriving a target cost Sep/Dec 15

The target cost is calculated by starting with a market-based target selling price and subtracting a desired profit margin. The target cost is simply the target price minus the required profit.

3.1 Example: Target costing

A car manufacturer wants to calculate a target cost for a new car, the price of which will be set at $17,950. The company requires an 8% profit margin on sales.

Required

What is the target cost?

Solution

Profit required = 8% × $17,950 = $1,436
Target cost = $(17,950 – 1,436) = $16,514

The car manufacturer will then need to carefully compile an estimated cost for the new car. ABC will help to ensure that costs allocated to the new model are more accurate.

3.2 Example: Target costing and the target cost gap

Great Games, a manufacturer of computer games, is in the process of introducing a new game to the market and has undertaken market research to find out about customers' views on the value of the product and also to obtain a comparison with competitors' products. The results of this research have been used to establish a target selling price of $60. This is the price that the company thinks it will have to sell the product at to achieve the required sales volume.

Cost estimates have been prepared based on the proposed product specification.

Manufacturing cost	$
Direct material	3.21
Direct labour	24.03
Direct machinery costs	1.12
Ordering and receiving	0.23
Quality assurance	4.60

Non-manufacturing costs

Marketing	8.15
Distribution	3.25
After-sales service	1.30

The target profit margin for the game is 30% of the target selling price.

Required

Calculate the target cost of the new game and the target cost gap.

Solution

	$
Target selling price	60.00
Target profit margin (30% of selling price)	18.00
Target cost (60.00 – 18.00)	42.00
Projected cost	45.89

The projected cost exceeds the target cost by $3.89. This is the target cost gap. Great Games will therefore have to investigate ways to reduce the cost from the current estimated amount down to the target cost.

4 Closing a target cost gap   12/07

The **target cost gap** is the estimated cost less the target cost. Increasing the selling price **will not** close the cost gap. In a system of target costing, **the total target cost is split into broad cost categories**, such as development, marketing and manufacturing. **Then the manufacturing target cost per unit is split up across the different functional areas of the product. The product is designed so that each functional product area can be made within the target cost.** If a functional product area cannot be made within the target cost, so that a **cost gap** exists between the currently achievable cost and the target cost, the targets for the other areas must be reduced, or the product redesigned or scrapped. The product should be developed in an atmosphere of **continuous improvement** using **value engineering techniques** and **close collaboration with suppliers** to enhance the product (in terms of service, quality, durability and so on) and reduce costs.

Key terms

> **Value analysis** involves examining the factors which affect the cost of a product or service, so as to devise ways of achieving the intended purpose most economically at the required standards of quality and reliability.

Management can then set **benchmarks for improvement** towards the target cost, by improving production technologies and processes. Various techniques can be employed.

- Reducing the **number of components**
- Using **cheaper staff**
- Using **standard components** wherever possible
- Acquiring new, more efficient **technology**
- **Training** staff in more efficient techniques
- Cutting out **non value added activities**
- Using **different materials** (identified using **activity analysis*** etc)

*Activity analysis is an analysis of how much is being spent on particular activities.

However, as stated earlier, the most effective time to eliminate unnecessary cost and reduce the expected cost to the target cost level is during the product design and development phase, not after 'live' production has begun.

Exam focus point

> When answering a question on closing a target cost gap, you may be expected to refer to the specific circumstances of the business in the question.

5 Target costing in service industries

Target costing is difficult to use in service industries due to the **characteristics** and **information requirements** of service businesses.

5.1 Characteristics of services

> **FAST FORWARD**
>
> Unlike manufacturing companies, services are characterised by **intangibility, inseparability, variability, perishability** and no **transfer of ownership**.

Examples of service businesses include:

(a)   **Mass service** eg the banking sector, transportation (rail, air), mass entertainment
(b)   **Either/or** eg fast food, teaching, hotels and holidays, psychotherapy
(c)   **Personal service** eg pensions and financial advice, car maintenance

Key term

> 'Services are any activity or benefit that one party can offer to another that is essentially intangible and does not result in the ownership of anything. Its production may or may not be tied to a physical product.'
>
> (Kotler and Armstrong, 2010: p.248)

There are **five major characteristics** of services that distinguish services from products.

(a)   **Intangibility**. This refers to the lack of substance which is involved with service delivery. Unlike goods (physical products such as confectionery), there are no substantial material or physical aspects to a service: no taste, feel, visible presence, and so on.

(b)   **Inseparability/simultaneity**. Many services are created at the same time as they are consumed. (Think of dental treatment.) No service exists until it is actually being experienced or consumed by the person who has bought it.

(c)   **Variability/heterogeneity**. Many services face the problem of maintaining consistency in the standard of output. It may be hard to attain precise standardisation of the service offered, but customers expect it (such as with fast food). When services are delivered by humans, it is very difficult to ensure that the same service is provided in exactly the same way every time.

(d)   **Perishability**. Services are innately perishable. The services of a beautician, for example, are purchased for a period of time.

(e)   **No transfer of ownership**. Services do not result in the transfer of property. The purchase of a service only confers on the customer access to or a right to use a facility.

Services also vary widely in nature. For example, services include banking, transport, parcel delivery, energy supply, entertainment, education, hotels and holidays, car repairs and maintenance, professional services such as law and accountancy, cleaning, security services, and so on. The list is virtually endless. A feature of many services, however, is that although the labour content may be high, the material content is often quite low. With products, the material content is higher and the labour element may be lower.

5.2 Problems with target costing for services

> **FAST FORWARD**
>
> Some of the characteristics of services make it difficult to use target costing, and identify a target cost for a service having established a target selling price.

A target cost for a product is a cost for an item whose design and make-up is specified in exact detail in a product specification. A target cost is the cost for this detailed specification.

Services are much more difficult to specify exactly. This is due to some of the characteristics of a service.

(a)   Intangibility. Some of the features of a service cannot be properly specified because they are intangible. What exactly does a customer receive, for example, when they go to a cinema? When services are provided by a human, the quality of the personal service can be critically important for the customer, but this is difficult or impossible to specify.

When services do not have any material content, it is not possible to reduce costs to a target level by reducing material costs. In comparison, reducing material costs can be an effective approach to target costing for products.

(b) Variability/heterogeneity. A service can differ every time it is provided, and a standard service may not exist. For example, repairing a motor car, providing an accountancy service, or driving a delivery truck from London to Paris are never exactly the same each time. When services are variable, it is possible to calculate an estimated average cost, but this is not specific and so not ideal for target costing.

Chapter Roundup

- **Target costing** involves setting a target cost for a product, having identified a target selling price and a required profit margin. The target cost is the target sales price minus the required profit.

- Unlike manufacturing companies, services are characterised by **intangibility, inseparability, variability, perishability** and no **transfer of ownership**.

- Some of the characteristics of services make it difficult to use target costing, and identify a target cost for a service having established a target selling price.

Quick Quiz

1   Fill in the blanks using words from the list (a) to (h).

Target cost   = ... − ....

Cost gap   = ... − ....

(a)	target cost	(e)	target selling price
(b)	cost gap	(f)	estimated cost
(c)	budgeted selling price	(g)	target profit
(d)	production cost		

2   What might be effective ways of reducing the labour cost element in a product, in order to lower expected cost towards a target cost?

3   Which two of the following characteristics of services make it difficult to establish target costs for services?

(a)	Intangibility	(d)	Variability
(b)	Perishability	(e)	Simultaneity
(c)	No transfer of ownership		

4   Put the three terms below in the correct order to represent (a) the target costing process and (b) traditional costing process.

- Selling price
- Cost
- Profit

5   Indicate which of the following methods can be used to move a currently-attainable cost closer to target cost.

A   Using standard components wherever possible
B   Acquiring new, more efficient technology
C   Making staff redundant
D   Reducing the quality of the product in question

1   Target cost = (e) target selling price − (g) target profit
       Cost gap = (f) estimated cost − (a) target cost

2   Replace labour activities with automated activities: alter production methods or processes so as to improve labour efficiency

3   (a) Intangibility and (d) Variability

4   (a)   Selling price, profit, cost
       (b)   Cost, selling price, profit

5   A   Using standard components wherever possible – **can**
       B   Acquiring new, more efficient technology – **can**
       C   Making staff redundant – **can't**
       D   Reducing the quality of the product in question – **can't**

To make improvements towards the target cost, technologies and processes must be improved (**B**). The use of standard components is a way of improving the production process (**A**).

Making staff redundant will not improve technologies and processes (**C**).

Reducing the quality of the product in question does not do this either (**D**).

Now try the questions below from the Practice Question Bank

Number	Level	Marks	Approximate time
Section A Q6	Examination	2	4 mins
Section A Q7	Examination	2	4 mins
Section A Q8	Examination	2	4 mins
Section A Q9	Examination	2	4 mins
Section A Q10	Examination	2	4 mins

Life cycle costing

2c

Topic list	Syllabus reference
1 The product life cycle	A3 (a)
2 Life cycle costs	A3 (c)
3 Life cycle costing in manufacturing and service industries	A3 (b)

Introduction

Life cycle costing is the third specialist cost accounting technique we will consider. It is an approach that accumulates costs over a **product's entire life**, rather than calculating them for each accounting period through the product's life. It is used to determine the **total expected profitability** of a product over its entire life, from its design and development stage, through its market introduction, to its eventual withdrawal from the market.

It is a costing technique used primarily for planning lifetime costs and profitability. It is not a technique for recording and reporting historical costs of production and sales.

Study guide

		Intellectual level
A3	**Life cycle costing**	
(a)	Identify the costs involved at different stages of the life cycle.	2
(b)	Derive a life cycle cost in manufacturing and service industries.	2
(c)	Identify the benefits of life cycle costing.	2

Exam guide

There is an article on the ACCA website on the topic of target costing and lifecycle costing, which you should read (ACCA, 2015).

1 The product life cycle

FAST FORWARD

A **product life cycle** can be divided into five phases.

- Development
- Introduction
- Growth
- Maturity
- Decline

The 'classical' life cycle of a product has five phases or stages.

(a) **Development**. The product has a research or design and development stage. Costs are incurred but the product is not yet on the market and there are no sales revenues.

(b) **Introduction**. The product is introduced to the market. Potential customers are initially unaware of the product or service, and the organisation may have to spend heavily on advertising to bring the product or service to the attention of the market. In addition, capital expenditure costs may be incurred in order to increase the production capacity as sales demand grows.

(c) **Growth**. The product gains a bigger market as demand builds up. Sales revenues increase and the product begins to make a profit.

(d) **Maturity**. Eventually, the growth in demand for the product will slow down and it will enter a period of relative maturity, when sales have reached a peak and are fairly stable. This should be the most profitable phase of the product's life. The product may be modified or improved, as a means of sustaining its demand and making this phase of the life cycle as long as possible.

(e) **Decline**. At some stage, the market will have bought enough of the product and it will therefore reach 'saturation point'. Demand will start to fall. Eventually it will become a loss-maker and this is the time when the organisation should decide to stop selling the product or service.

The level of sales and profits earned over a life cycle can be illustrated diagrammatically as follows.

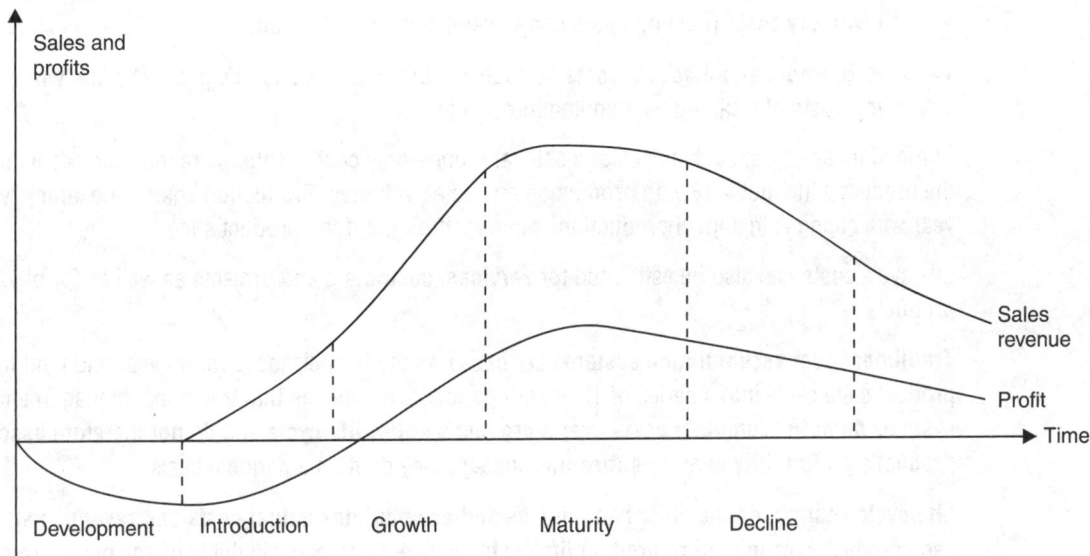

The horizontal axis measures the **duration of the life cycle**, which can last from several months to several hundred years. Children's crazes or fad products have very short lives while some products, such as binoculars (invented in the 18th century), can last a very long time.

'Generic' products have a longer life cycle than specific types of the product, which in turn have a longer life cycle than specific models of the product. For example, television continues to have a long life cycle, but global sales of black and white televisions have declined. Product models have an even shorter life: for example, Mark II may replace Mark I.

2 Life cycle costs   12/08, 12/11, 6/13, Mar/Jun 16

Life cycle costing estimates the costs and revenues attributable to a product over its entire expected life cycle.

The **life cycle costs** of a product are all the costs attributable to the product over its entire life, from product concept and design to eventual withdrawal from the market.

A product's life cycle costs are incurred **from its design stage through development to market launch, production and sales, and finally to its eventual decline and withdrawal from the market**.

The component elements of a product's cost over its life cycle could therefore include the following.

- **Research and development costs**

    - Design costs
    - Cost of making a prototype
    - Testing costs
    - Production process and equipment: development and investment

- The **cost of purchasing any technical data** required (for example purchasing the right from another organisation to use a patent)

- **Training costs** (including initial operator training and skills updating)

- **Production costs**, when the product is eventually launched in the market

- **Distribution costs** (including transportation and handling costs)

- **Marketing and advertising costs**

    - Customer service
    - Field maintenance
    - Brand promotion

- **Inventory costs** (holding spare parts, warehousing, and so on)
- **Retirement and disposal costs**, ie costs occurring at the end of a product's life, which may include the costs of cleaning up a contaminated site

Some of these costs, such as design costs, are 'once-only costs'. Others are incurred regularly throughout the product's life, but vary with production and sales volumes. Production costs for example will vary each year with changes in annual production volumes throughout the product's life.

Life cycle costs can also be estimated for **services**, customers and projects as well as for physical products.

Traditional cost accumulation systems are based on the financial accounting year and tend to dissect a product's life cycle into a series of 12-month periods. This means that traditional management accounting systems **do not accumulate costs over a product's entire life cycle** and **do not** therefore **assess a product's profitability over its entire life.** Instead they do it on a periodic basis.

Life cycle costing, on the other hand, **tracks and accumulates actual costs and revenues** attributable to each product **over the entire product life cycle.** Hence the total profitability of any given product can be determined.

Key term

> **Life cycle costing** is the accumulation of costs over a product's entire life.

2.1 Why calculate life cycle costs?

Life cycle costing has a different purpose from cost accumulation systems that measure actual costs of production and sales. Traditional costing systems are intended to measure the cost of a product in each accounting period, and the profit or loss that should be reported for the product for that period.

The **purpose of life cycle costing** is to assess the total costs of a product over its entire life, to assess the expected profitability from the product over its full life. Products that are not expected to be profitable after allowing for design and development costs, or clean-up costs, should not be considered for commercial development.

2.2 The benefits of life cycle costing   12/11

There are a number of benefits associated with life cycle costing.

(a) It helps management to assess profitability over the full life of a product, which in turn helps management to decide whether to develop the product, or to continue making the product.

(b) It can be very useful for organisations that continually develop products with a relatively short life, where it may be possible to estimate sales volumes and prices with reasonable accuracy.

(c) The life cycle concept results in earlier actions to generate more revenue or to lower costs than otherwise might be considered.

(d) Better decisions should follow from a more accurate and realistic assessment of revenues and costs, at least within a particular life cycle stage.

(e) It encourages longer-term thinking and forward planning, and may provide more useful information than traditional reports of historical costs and profits in each accounting period.

3 Life cycle costing in manufacturing and service industries

FAST FORWARD

> Both manufacturing and service organisations can use life cycle costing to estimate returns over a product/service life cycle.

With life cycle costing, all costs are traced to individual products or services over their complete life cycles. This encourages management to think of the life cycle, and ways in which this may perhaps be managed.

It has been reported that some organisations operating with an **advanced manufacturing technology** environment find that approximately 90% of a product's life cycle costs are determined by decisions made early within the cycle, at the design stage. Life cycle costing is therefore particularly useful for these organisations, to monitor spending during the early stages of a product's life cycle.

Another feature of many competitive markets is that product life cycles are getting shorter, and organisations must continually redesign existing products and develop new ones. The **planning, design and development stages of a product's cycle** are therefore **critical** to an organisation's costs and profits. Cost reduction at this stage of a product's life cycle, rather than during the production process, is one of the most important ways of reducing product cost.

Note. The techniques of life cycle costing and target costing can be combined, to plan for achieving certain levels of cost at different stages of the product's life cycle. Both are essentially forward-looking techniques of costing.

3.1 Maximising return over the product life cycle

3.1.1 Design costs out of products

Between 70% and 90% of a product's life cycle costs are determined by decisions made early in the life cycle, at the design or development stage. Careful design of the product and manufacturing and other processes will keep cost to a minimum over the life cycle.

3.1.2 Minimise the time to market

'Time to market' is the time from the conception of the product to its introduction to the market. Competitors watch each other very carefully to determine what types of product their rivals are developing. If an organisation is launching a new product it is vital to get it to the marketplace as soon as possible. This will give the product as long a period as possible without a rival in the marketplace, and should mean increased market share in the long run. Furthermore, the life span of a product may be affected by delay in its market introduction. It is not unusual for the product's overall profitability to fall by 25% if the launch is delayed by six months. This means that it is usually worthwhile incurring extra costs to keep the launch on schedule or to speed up the launch.

3.1.3 Minimise breakeven time (BET)

A short BET is very important in keeping an organisation liquid. The sooner the product is launched the quicker the research and development costs will be repaid, providing the organisation with funds to develop further products. In life cycle costing, breakeven occurs when revenue from the product has covered all the costs incurred to date, including design and development costs.

3.1.4 Maximise the length of the life span

Product life cycles are not predetermined; they can be influenced by the actions of management and competitors. For example, some products lend themselves to a number of different uses; this is especially true of materials, such as plastic, PVC, nylon and other synthetic materials. The life cycle of these materials can be extended by finding new uses for them. The life cycle of the material is then a series of individual product curves nesting on top of each other, as shown below.

By entering different national or regional markets one after another an organisation may be able to extend the growth phase of a product's life. On the other hand, in today's fast-moving world, an organisation could lose out to a competitor if it failed to establish an early presence in a particular market.

3.2 Service and project life cycles

Services have life cycles. The only difference with the life cycle of a product is that the **R&D stages** will not usually exist in the same way. The **different processes** that go into forming the complete service are important, however, and consideration should be given in advance as to how to carry them out and arrange them so as to minimise cost.

Products that take years to produce or come to fruition are usually called **projects**, and **discounted cash flow calculations** are invariably used to cost them over their life cycle in advance. The projects need to be **monitored** very carefully over their life to make sure that they **remain on schedule** and that **cost overruns** are not being incurred.

3.3 Customer life cycles

Customers also have life cycles, and an organisation will wish to **maximise the return from a customer over their life cycle**. The aim is to **extend the life cycle of a particular customer** or decrease the 'churn' rate, as the Americans say. This means **encouraging customer loyalty**. For example, some supermarkets and other retail outlets issue **loyalty cards** that offer discounts to loyal customers who return to the shop and spend a certain amount with the organisation. As existing customers tend to be more profitable than new ones they should be retained wherever possible.

Customers become more profitable over their life cycle. The profit can go on increasing for a period of between approximately 4 and 20 years. For example, if you open a bank account, take out insurance or invest in a pension, the company involved has to set up the account, run checks, and so on. The initial cost is high and the company will be keen to retain your business so that it can recoup this cost. Once customers get used to their supplier they tend to use them more frequently, and so there is a double benefit in holding on to customers.

Question   Life cycle costing

Solaris specialises in the manufacture of solar panels. It is planning to introduce a new slimline solar panel specially designed for small houses. Development of the new panel is to begin shortly and Solaris is in the process of determining the price of the panel. It expects the new product to have the following costs.

	Year 1	Year 2	Year 3	Year 4
Units manufactured and sold	2,000	15,000	20,000	5,000
	$	$	$	$
R&D costs	1,900,000	100,000	-	-
Marketing costs	100,000	75,000	50,000	10,000
Production cost per unit	500	450	400	450
Customer service costs per unit	50	40	40	40
Disposal of specialist equipment				300,000

The Marketing Director believes that customers will be prepared to pay $500 for a solar panel but the Financial Director believes this will not cover all of the costs throughout the life cycle.

Required

Calculate the cost per unit looking at the whole life cycle and comment on the suggested price.

Answer

Life cycle costs

	$'000
R&D (1,900 + 100)	2,000
Marketing (100 + 75 + 50 + 10)	235
Production (1,000 + 6,750 + 8,000 + 2,250)	18,000
Customer service (100 + 600 + 800 + 200)	1,700
Disposal	300
Total life cycle costs	22,235
Total production ('000 units)	42
Cost per unit	529.40

The total life cycle costs are $529.40 per solar panel, which is higher than the price proposed by the marketing director. Solaris will either have to charge a higher price or look at ways to reduce costs.

It may be difficult to increase the price if customers are price sensitive and not prepared to pay more. Costs could be reduced by analysing each part of the costs throughout the life cycle and actively seeking cost savings; for example, using different materials, using cheaper staff or acquiring more efficient technology.

Chapter Roundup

- A **product life cycle** can be divided into five phases.
  - Development   – Maturity
  - Introduction   – Decline
  - Growth

- Life **cycle costing** estimates the costs and revenues attributable to a product over its entire expected life cycle.

- The **life cycle costs** of a product are all the costs attributable to the product over its entire life, from product concept and design to eventual withdrawal from the market.

- Both manufacturing and service organisations can use life cycle costing, to estimate returns over a product/service life cycle.

Quick Quiz

1   **Match the following costs to the appropriate life cycle cost classification.**

Costs	Classifications
Design	Inventory costs
Energy costs	Acquisition costs
Warehousing	Maintenance costs
Transportation	Operation costs
Customer service	Product distribution costs

2   Life cycle costing is the profiling of cost over a product's production life. **True or false?**

3   Life cycle costing is particularly useful for products with a short expected life cycle. **True or false?**

4   **When are the bulk of a product's life cycle costs normally determined?**

    A   At the design/development stage
    B   When the product is introduced to the market
    C   When the product is in its growth stage
    D   On disposal

5   **Indicate which of the following items would be included in the calculation of the life cycle costs of a product.**

    A   Planning and concept design costs
    B   Preliminary and detailed design costs
    C   Testing costs
    D   Production costs
    E   Distribution and customer service costs

1 | Cost | Classification |
    |------|----------------|
    | Design | Acquisition costs |
    | Energy costs | Operation costs |
    | Warehousing | Inventory costs |
    | Transportation | Product distribution costs |
    | Customer service | Maintenance costs |

2   False. It also looks at development costs and so on which are incurred prior to production, and any dismantling costs, which are incurred once production ceases.

3   True. When the life cycle is short, estimates of life cycle costs and revenues are likely to be easier, and life cycle costs should also be easier to monitor.

4   A   At the design/development stage.

    The bulk of a product's life cycle costs will be determined at the design/development stage (being designed in at the outset during product and process design, plant installation and setting up of the distribution network).

5   The correct answers are all of them:

    A   Planning and concept design costs
    B   Preliminary and detailed design costs
    C   Testing costs
    D   Production costs
    E   Distribution and customer service costs

    Life cycle costs are incurred from design stage through to withdrawal from the market.

Now try the questions below from the Practice Question Bank

Number	Level	Marks	Approximate time
Section A Q11	Examination	2	4 mins
Section A Q12	Examination	2	4 mins
Section A Q13	Examination	2	4 mins
Section A Q14	Examination	2	4 mins
Section A Q15	Examination	2	4 mins

2d

Throughput accounting

Topic list	Syllabus reference
1 Theory of constraints	A4(a)
2 Throughput accounting	A4(a)
3 Performance measures in throughput accounting	A4(d)
4 Throughput accounting ratio	A4(b)(c)

Introduction

Throughput accounting is the fourth management accounting technique in Section A of the syllabus. It is based on the theory of constraints and is consistent with the use of just in time (JIT) production methods. The basic concept in throughput accounting is that an organisation should seek to **maximise throughput** by identifying and eliminating **bottlenecks**.

Study guide

		Intellectual level
A4	**Throughput accounting**	
(a)	Discuss and apply the theory of constraints.	2
(b)	Calculate and interpret a throughput accounting ratio (TPAR).	2
(c)	Suggest how a TPAR could be improved.	2
(d)	Apply throughput accounting to a multi-product decision-making problem.	2

Exam guide

Questions in Section B on this topic are likely to be a mixture of calculation and discussion. You may be required to use your knowledge of limiting factors from Chapter 4. You can also expect objective test questions on both the theory of constraints and throughput accounting calculations in Section A.

1 Theory of constraints   12/13

FAST FORWARD

> **Throughput accounting** supports a production management system which aims to maximise throughput, and therefore cash generation from sales. It is not concerned with 'traditional' measurements of profit, or maximisation of this profit. A **just in time (JIT) production system** is operated, with some buffer inventory kept only when there is a **bottleneck resource**.

Exam focus point

> The ACCA website contains a two-part article on **throughput accounting** and the **theory of constraints**, written by a member of the examining team (ACCA, 2015). It is recommended that you read both parts of this article.
>
> The first article summarises the story contained in a book called *The Goal* (Goldratt and Cox, 1992) that presents the theory of constraints and throughput accounting within the context of a novel. The second article talks through a practical **approach to questions on throughput accounting**.

The theory of constraints (TOC) is an **approach to production management** and optimising production performance. It was formulated by Goldratt and Cox in the US in 1986. Its key financial concept is to turn materials into sales as quickly as possible, thereby maximising the net cash generated from sales.

1.1 Throughput: sales, inventory and operational expenses

In the theory of constraints and throughput accounting, **throughput** is the money generated by a system through the sales that it makes.

Inventory is the amount of money the system has invested in purchasing things that it intends to resell within its finished products. You can think of 'inventory' in its normal sense, as stocks of materials or finished goods waiting to be used. 'Inventory' should also be considered as costs of materials purchased. **Inventory has no value** because it does not create throughput until it is used to sell products.

Throughput is the money obtained from sales minus the cost of materials that have gone into making them. In conventional cost accounting terms, the materials are the direct materials used in production. (Indirect materials are part of the fixed factory costs.)

Throughput = Sales – Material costs

Operational expenses, also known as factory expenses, are all the other costs of operations. They include both direct labour costs and overhead costs.

In throughput accounting, all operational expenses or factory expenses are assumed to be 'fixed' costs.

1.2 Bottleneck factor: the constraint

The objective should be to maximise throughput.

The theory of constraints also states that at any time there will always be a **bottleneck resource** or factor that sets a limit on the amount of throughput that is possible. This bottleneck resource could in theory be sales demand for the organisation's output, but it is more likely to be a resource that the organisation uses. This 'bottleneck resource' which prevents output and throughput from getting any higher could be:

(a) A production resource, such as time available on a type of machine, or the available amount of skilled employee time

(b) A selling resource, such as the number of sales representatives

(c) The existence of an uncompetitive selling price

(d) A need to deliver on time to particular customers

(e) A lack of product quality and reliability

(f) The lack of reliable material suppliers

In the exam, the bottleneck resource is likely to be a production factor, such as machine time or labour time. You may be familiar with the concept of 'limiting factor' in production. A bottleneck resource is a limiting factor. In the theory of constraints and throughput accounting, a bottleneck resource is also known as the **binding constraint**.

The objective of an organisation should therefore be to maximise total throughput, given the existence of a bottleneck resource.

Key terms

> **Theory of constraints (TOC)** is an approach to production management which aims to maximise sales revenue less material cost. It focuses on bottlenecks which act as constraints to the maximisation of throughput.
>
> **Throughput** is the money generated from sales minus the cost of the materials used in making the items sold.
>
> **Bottleneck resource** or **binding constraint** is an activity which has a lower capacity than preceding or subsequent activities, thereby limiting throughput.

1.3 Production scheduling and the bottleneck resource

Taking the theory of constraints a stage further, since there is one bottleneck resource, it follows that all the other resources in production and elsewhere are not bottlenecks. Since production and throughput are limited by the bottleneck resource, it follows that there will be idle capacity for all the other resources.

Idle time should be accepted. Since all operational costs are fixed, idle time is not costing any money.

Resources that are not the bottleneck resource should not be used beyond the amount required for the maximum achievable throughput, given the bottleneck resource. Using non-binding constraints beyond this amount will simply result in a build-up of inventories.

(a) In traditional cost accounting, improving efficiency and creating more inventory will increase profits. Higher inventories reduce the cost of sales and increase reported profits.

(b) In the theory of constraints, using non-bottleneck resources above the amount required for maximum throughput is wasteful. It does not increase throughput; it only increases unused inventory levels.

To avoid the build-up of work in progress, **production must be limited to the capacity of the bottleneck resource** but this capacity must be **fully utilised**.

There will be idle resources in non-bottleneck areas, but this does not matter. The focus should be on maximising throughput, given the limitation of the bottleneck.

Output through the binding constraint should never be delayed or held up otherwise sales will be lost. To avoid this happening a small **buffer inventory** should be built up immediately prior to the bottleneck constraint. This is the only inventory that the business should hold, with the exception of possibly a very small amount of finished goods inventory and raw materials, which is consistent with a just in time (JIT) approach.

Operations in the production line prior to the binding constraint should operate at the same speed as the binding constraint, otherwise excess and unwanted work in progress (other than the buffer inventory) will be built up. According to TOC, inventory costs money in terms of storage space and interest costs, and so **inventory is not desirable**.

1.4 Increasing throughput: elevating the bottleneck

The theory of constraints states that the aim should be to maximise total throughput. The only way to increase throughput is to increase the capacity of the bottleneck constraint. All the focus of management attention should be on increasing the capacity of the bottleneck resource, or 'elevating the bottleneck'.

For example, time on Machine Type X may be a bottleneck resource. The only way to increase throughput is to increase the output capacity of Machine Type X. Ways in which this might be done, without buying a new Type X machine, could include:

- Moving from working five days a week to working six or seven days a week

- Moving from working a 12-hour production day to an 18-hour or 24-hour production day

- Carrying out routine maintenance work on the machine outside normal working hours, so that it does not disrupt production

If the capacity of a bottleneck resource is elevated (increased) sufficiently it will eventually cease to be a bottleneck resource. Another resource in the system will become the new bottleneck resource.

The same approach is now used for the new bottleneck resource: maximise total throughput given the restriction of this resource, and seek to increase total throughput by increasing the capacity of the bottleneck resource.

1.5 Example: elevating the constraint

A company manufactures a single product, which is processed in turn through three machines, Machine type A, Machine type B and Machine type C. The current maximum output capacity per week on the existing machinery is as follows.

Machine type A: 1,800 units

Machine type B: 1,600 units

Machine type C: 1,500 units

The company could purchase an additional Machine type C for $8 million which would increase output capacity on Machines C by 600 units per week. It could also purchase an additional Machine type B that would cost $5 million and increase output capacity by 300 units per week.

An increase in weekly output capacity is worth (in present value terms) $50,000 per unit of additional output.

What should the company do? Should it buy either or both the additional machines?

(1)   The current bottleneck resource is Machine type C and output is restricted to 1,500 units per week. There is no point in buying an additional Machine type B unless a new Machine type C is purchased first, to elevate the bottleneck resource.

If an additional Machine type C is purchased, output capacity will increase as follows.

Machine type A: 1,800 units
Machine type B: 1,600 units
Machine type C: 2,100 units

By elevating the capacity of Machine type C, Machine type C is no longer the bottleneck resource. The new bottleneck resource is Machine type B and output is restricted to 1,600 units per week, which is 100 units per week more than the current output limit.

The benefit will be (100 units × $50,000) – $8 million = –$3,000,000 (= net loss).

(2)   If an additional Machine type C and an additional Machine type B are purchased, output capacity will increase as follows.

Machine type A: 1,800 units
Machine type B: 1,900 units
Machine type C: 2,100 units

The new bottleneck resource is Machine type A and output is restricted to 1,800 units per week, which is 300 units more than the current limit.

The benefit will be (300 units × $50,000) – $8 million – $5 million = + $2,000,000.

Conclusion. By purchasing an additional Machine type C and Machine type B, output would be increased by 300 units per week. The new bottleneck constraint would be Machine type A. The company would benefit from this by $2,000,000.

1.6 Theory of constraints: summary

Goldratt devised a **five-step approach** to summarise the key stages of **TOC**.

Step 1   **Identify** the constraint (bottleneck resource).

Step 2   Decide how to **exploit** the constraint in order to maximise throughput.

Step 3   **Subordinate** and **synchronise** everything else to the decisions made in **step 2**.

Step 4   **Elevate** the performance of the constraint.

Step 5   If the **constraint has shifted** during any of the above steps, go back to **step 1**. Do not allow inertia to cause a new constraint.

The overall aim of TOC is to **maximise throughput**. This may be called '**throughput contribution**' (sales revenue – material cost) while keeping **operational costs** (all operating costs except material costs) and **investment costs** (inventory, equipment, and so on) to a **minimum.**

1.7 Example: An illustration of the theory of constraints

Machine X can process 1,000 kg of raw material per hour, machine Y 800 kg. Of an input of 900 kg, 100 kg of processed material must wait on the bottleneck machine (machine Y) at the end of an hour of processing because machine Y does not have the capacity to produce it.

The **traditional view** is that **machines should be working, not sitting idle**. So if the desired output from the above process were 8,100 kg, **machine X would be kept in continual use** and all 8,100 kg would be processed through the machine in nine hours. There would be a **backlog** of 900 kg [8,100 – (9 hrs × 800)] of processed material in front of machine Y, however. All this material **would require handling** and storage space and **create the additional costs related to these non value added activities**. Its **processing would not increase throughput** and would not earn any money for the organisation.

2 Throughput accounting

Exam focus point

> In the December 2014 examining team's report, throughput accounting was singled out as an area of the syllabus which students continue to find challenging and it is therefore an area which needs careful consideration. The report also noted that students do not really understand what a 'bottleneck activity' is.

The concept of throughput accounting has been developed from the theory of constraints (TOC) as an alternative system of cost and management accounting in a **JIT production** environment.

Key term

> **Throughput accounting (TA)** is an approach to production management which aims to maximise sales revenue less materials cost, while also reducing inventory and operational expenses.

Throughput accounting is based on the following concepts, all derived from the TOC.

(a) **Concept 1**

In the short run, all costs in the factory (with the exception of materials costs) are **fixed costs**. These fixed costs include direct labour costs. It is useful to group all these costs and call them **Total Factory Costs (TFC)**.

(b) **Concept 2**

In a JIT environment, all inventory is a 'bad thing' and the **ideal inventory level is zero**. Products should not be made unless a customer has ordered them. When goods are made, the factory effectively operates at the rate of the slowest process, and there will be unavoidable idle capacity in other operations.

Work in progress should be **valued at material cost only** until the output is eventually sold, so that no value will be added and no profit earned until the sale takes place. Working on output just to add to work in progress or finished goods inventory creates no profit, and so should not be encouraged.

(c) **Concept 3**

Profitability is determined by the rate at which 'money comes in at the door' (that is, sales are made) and, in a JIT environment, this depends on **how quickly** goods can be produced to satisfy customer orders. Since the goal of a profit-orientated organisation is to make money, inventory must be sold for that goal to be achieved. The bottleneck resource slows the process of making money. Making money means maximising throughput.

Question

Throughput accounting

How are these concepts a direct contrast to the fundamental principles of conventional cost accounting?

Answer

Conventional cost accounting	Throughput accounting
Inventory is an asset.	Inventory is not an asset. It is a result of unsynchronised manufacturing and is a barrier to making profit.
Costs can be classified either as direct or indirect.	Such classifications are no longer useful.
Direct labour is a variable cost.	All labour costs are part of TFC, which are fixed costs.

Conventional cost accounting	Throughput accounting
Product profitability can be determined by deducting a product cost from selling price.	Profitability is determined by the rate at which money and throughput is earned.
Profit can be increased by reducing cost elements.	Profit is a function of material cost, total factory cost and throughput. Profit = throughput minus TFC.

2.1 Example: Throughput accounting in a service industry

Throughput accounting can be applied in a service industry as well as in production.

A not for profit organisation performs a medical screening service in three sequential stages.

1. Take an X-ray.
2. Interpret the result.
3. Recall patients who require further investigation / inform others that all is fine.

The 'goal unit' of this organisation will be to progress a patient through all three stages. The number of patients who complete all three stages is the organisation's throughput, and the organisation should seek to maximise its throughput. The duration of each stage and the weekly resource available is as follows.

Process	Time per patient (hours)	Total hours available per week
Take an X-ray (stage 1)	0.50	80
Interpret the result (stage 2)	0.20	40
Recall patients (stage 3)	0.40	60

The maximum number of patients (goal units) who can be dealt with in each process is as follows.

X-rays	80/0.5 = 160
Interpret results	40/0.20 = 200
Recall patients	60/0.40 = 150

The recall procedure (stage 3) is the bottleneck resource (constraint), because there are sufficient resources for the recall of only 150 patients. Throughput, and therefore the organisation's performance, cannot be improved until stage 3 can deal with more patients. There are a number of actions that the organisation could take to improve throughput.

(a) Investigate whether less time could be spent on the bottleneck activity.

(b) Ensure there is no idle time in the bottleneck resource, as this will be detrimental to overall performance.

(c) Increase the bottleneck resource available.

There is little point in improving stage 1 and stage 2 if the process grinds to a halt at stage 3. Patients are only helped when the whole process is completed and they are recalled if necessary. Increasing the bottleneck resource or the efficiency with which it is used may be relatively cheap and easy to do, as stage 3 is a relatively simple piece of administration in comparison to the first two stages that use expensive machinery and highly skilled personnel.

3 Performance measures in throughput accounting

6/09, 6/11, 12/13, 12/14

FAST FORWARD

In a throughput accounting environment, **production priority** is given to the products best able to generate throughput. Performance measures in throughput accounting are based around the concept that the aim is to maximise throughput. This is achieved by maximising the **throughput per unit of bottleneck resource**.

When an organisation makes more than one product, total throughput is maximised by **giving priority to those products that earn the largest throughput per unit of bottleneck resource**. Products should be ranked in order of priority according to their throughput per unit of bottleneck resource.

In throughput accounting, the aim is to maximise throughput. Many organisations make more than one product, and each product uses a different amount of the bottleneck resource and earns a different amount of throughput per unit.

Throughput is maximised by ranking products in order for production and sales according to the throughput that they earn per unit of bottleneck resource they consume.

The top-ranking product should be manufactured up to the limit of maximum sales demand. The second-ranking product should be made next up to the limit of maximum sales demand, then the third, and so on.

The ratio for ranking products is therefore as follows.

Throughput return per factory hour:

$$\frac{\text{Sales} - \text{direct material costs}}{\text{Usage of bottleneck resource in hours (factory hours)}}$$

3.1 Example: Maximising throughput and multiple products

WR Co manufactures three products, A, B and C. Product details are as follows.

	Product A	Product B	Product C
	$	$	$
Sales price	2.80	1.60	2.40
Materials cost	1.20	0.60	1.20
Direct labour cost	1.00	0.80	0.80
Weekly sales demand	4,000 units	4,000 units	5,000 units
Machine hours per unit	0.5 hours	0.2 hours	0.3 hours

Machine time is a bottleneck resource and maximum capacity is 4,000 machine hours per week. Operating costs including direct labour costs are $10,880 per week. Direct labour workers are not paid overtime and work a standard 38-hour week.

Required

Determine the optimum production plan for WR Co and calculate the weekly profit that would arise from the plan.

Solution

Step 1 Determine the bottleneck resource

The bottleneck resource is machine time (4,000 machine hours available each week).

Step 2 Calculate the throughput per unit for each product

	Product A	Product B	Product C
	$	$	$
Sales price	2.80	1.60	2.40
Materials cost	1.20	0.60	1.20
Throughput/unit	1.60	1.00	1.20

Step 3 Calculate throughput per unit of limiting factor (machine hours)

	Product A	Product B	Product C
Machine hours per unit	0.5 hours	0.2 hours	0.3 hours
Throughput per machine hour	$3.20*	$5.00	$4.00

* $1.60 / 0.5 hours = $3.20

Step 4 Rank products

	Product A	Product B	Product C
	3rd	1st	2nd

Step 5 Allocate resources to arrive at optimum production plan

The profit-maximising weekly output and sales volumes are as follows.

Product	Units	Bottleneck resource hours/unit	Total hours	Throughput per hour $	Total throughput $
B	4,000	0.2 hours	800	5.00	4,000
C	5,000	0.3 hours	1,500	4.00	6,000
			2,300		
A (balance)	3,400	0.5 hours	1,700	3.20	5,440
			4,000		15,440

Less: operating expenses	(10,880)
Profit per week	4,560

3.2 Throughput accounting and limiting factor analysis compared

In limiting factor analysis (covered in Chapter 4), the contribution per unit is first calculated for each product. Then a contribution per unit of scarce resource is calculated by working out how much of the scarce resource each unit requires in its production. In a throughput accounting context, a very similar calculation is performed; however, this time it is not contribution per unit of scarce resource which is calculated, but throughput return per unit of bottleneck resource. Throughput is calculated as 'selling price less direct material cost'. This is different from the calculation of 'contribution', in which both labour costs and variable overheads are also deducted from selling price.

The technical article written by the F5 examining team on the ACCA website called 'Throughput accounting and the theory of constraints – part 2', says '*It is an important distinction because the fundamental belief in throughput accounting is that all costs except direct materials costs are largely fixed – therefore to work on the basis of maximising contribution is flawed because to do so is to take into account costs that cannot be controlled in the short term anyway. One cannot help but agree with this belief really since in most businesses, it is simply not possible, for example, to hire workers on a daily basis and lay workers off if they are not busy. A workforce has to be employed within the business and available for work if there is work to do. You can not refuse to pay a worker if he is forced to sit idle by a machine for a while.*'
(ACCA, 2015).

4 Throughput accounting ratio

> The **throughput accounting ratio** (TPAR ratio) is the ratio of the throughput per unit of bottleneck resource to the factory cost per unit of bottleneck resource. This ratio should be as high as possible, and certainly more than 1.0.

The throughput accounting ratio (TPAR ratio) is a useful ratio, which you need to learn for your examination.

Throughput accounting ratio $= \dfrac{\text{Throughput per unit of bottleneck resource}}{\text{Factory cost per unit of bottleneck resource}}$

Note. Instead of 'per unit of bottleneck resource', you may come across the term 'per factory hour'. This means the same thing in this context.

The throughput per unit of bottleneck resource has been described above.

Factory cost per unit of bottleneck resource $= \dfrac{\text{Total factory costs}}{\text{Total units of bottleneck resource}}$

Note. 'Total factory costs' are also described as 'Total operating costs'. They are all the costs other than material costs, and are regarded as a fixed cost per period.

For example, suppose that a factory manufactures a single product. Each unit of product takes two hours to make on Machine X and output capacity is restricted by the available time on Machine X, which is restricted to 500 hours per week. The product has a material cost of $20 per unit and sells for $160 per unit. Total operating costs are $30,000 per week.

Throughput per Machine X hour = $(160 − 20)/2 hours = $70

Factory cost per Machine X hour = $30,000/500 hours = $60

TPAR ratio = $70/$60 = 1.17

4.1 Interpreting the TPAR ratio

Total throughput should exceed total factory costs otherwise the organisation will make a loss. This means that **the TPAR ratio should exceed 1.0**.

A TPAR ratio that is not much higher than 1.0 is barely profitable. The aim should be to achieve as high a TPAR ratio as possible.

TPAR ratios can also be used to assess the **relative earning capabilities** of different products. Products can be ranked in order of priority for manufacture and sale in order of their TPAR ratios. (Higher TPAR ratios should be given priority over lower TPAR ratios).

However, ranking products in order of priority according to their TPAR ratio will always give the same ranking as putting them in order of throughput per unit of bottleneck resource.

4.2 Example: TPAR ratios and ranking products

Corrie Company produces three products, X, Y and Z. The capacity of Corrie's plant is restricted by process Alpha. Process Alpha is expected to be operational for eight hours per day and can produce 1,200 units of X per hour, 1,500 units of Y per hour and 600 units of Z per hour.

Selling prices and material costs for each product are as follows.

Product	Selling price $ per unit	Material cost $ per unit	Throughput $ per unit
X	150	80	70
Y	130	40	90
Z	300	100	200

Operating costs are $720,000 per day.

Required

(a)   Calculate the profit per day if daily output achieved is 6,000 units of X, 4,500 units of Y and 1,200 units of Z.

(b)   Calculate the TPAR ratio for each product.

(c)   In the absence of demand restrictions for the three products, advise Corrie's management on the optimal production plan.

Solution

(a)   Profit per day = Throughput contribution – Operating costs

$$= [(\$70 \times 6,000) + (\$90 \times 4,500) + (\$200 \times 1,200)] - \$720,000$$
$$= \$345,000$$

(b)   TPAR ratio = Throughput per factory hour/Operating costs per factory hour

Operating costs per factory hour = $720,000/8 = $90,000

Product	Throughput per factory hour	Cost per factory hour	TPAR ratio
X	$70 × 1,200 = $84,000	$90,000	0.93
Y	$90 × 1,500 = $135,000	$90,000	1.50
Z	$200 × 600 = $120,000	$90,000	1.33

(c)   If it is not possible to increase the number of factory hours available, priority should be given to making and selling Product Y, since it has the highest TPAR ratio. If only Product Y is made and sold (since there is no restriction on sales demand), total output per day would be (1,500 × 8 hours) = 12,000 units of Product Y. Total throughput would be $1,080,000 (= 12,000 units × $90) per day. Total profit per day would be $1,080,000 – $720,000 = $360,000.

This is $60,000 more per day than the profit from the production mix in the answer to part (a).

The TPAR ratio of Product X is 0.93, which is less than 1.0. Product X makes less throughput per hour than its factory cost per hour.

Management should consider ways of raising the TPAR ratio above 1.0, or should give consideration to ceasing production of Product X entirely.

Question	Performance measurement in throughput accounting

Growler manufactures computer components. Health and safety regulations mean that one of its processes can only be operated eight hours a day. The hourly capacity of this process is 500 units per hour. The selling price of each component is $100 and the unit material cost is $40. The daily total of all factory costs (conversion costs) is $144,000, excluding materials. Expected production is 3,600 units per day.

Required

Calculate:

(a)   Total profit per day
(b)   Return per factory hour
(c)   Throughput accounting ratio

(a) Total profit per day = Throughput contribution – Conversion costs
= (3,600 × (100 – 40) – 144,000)
= $72,000

(b) Return per factory hour = $\dfrac{\text{Sales} - \text{direct material costs}}{\text{Usage of bottleneck resource in hours (factory hours)}}$

= $\dfrac{100 - 40}{1/500}$

= $30,000

(c) Throughput accounting ratio = $\dfrac{\text{Return per factory hour}}{\text{Total conversion cost per factory hour}}$

= $\dfrac{30,000}{144,000/8}$

= 1.67

4.3 How can a business improve a throughput accounting ratio?

In an exam question on throughput accounting, you may be asked about ways in which the TPAR ratio for a product might be increased. The ratio is increased by either:

(a) Increasing the throughput per bottleneck hour, or
(b) Reducing the operating cost per bottleneck hour.

The TPAR ratio could be increased in any of the following ways.

(a) Increase the selling price for the product. This will increase the throughput per unit, and so will increase the throughput per unit of bottleneck resource.

(b) Reducing the material cost per unit. This will increase the throughput per unit, and so will increase the throughput per unit of bottleneck resource.

(c) Reduce expenditure on operating costs/factory costs. This will reduce the operating cost per unit of bottleneck resource.

(d) Improve efficiency, and increase the number of units or product that are made in each bottleneck hour. This would increase total throughput per hour. The operating costs per hour would be unaffected, therefore the TPAR ratio would increase.

(e) Elevate the bottleneck, so that there are more hours available of the bottleneck resource. Throughput per unit of bottleneck resource would be unaffected but, since operating costs are all fixed costs and there are more bottleneck hours available, the operating cost per bottleneck hour would fall, and the TPAR ratio would increase.

However, there may be adverse consequences from some of these measures.

Measures	Consequences
• Increase sales price per unit	• Demand for the product may fall.
• Reduce material costs per unit, eg change materials and/or suppliers	• Quality may fall and bulk discounts may be lost.
• Reduce operating expenses	• Quality may fall and/or errors increase.

4.4 Throughput and limiting factor analysis

The throughput accounting approach to prioritising products for manufacture and sale is very similar to the approach of **maximising contribution per unit of scarce resource**, which you should have covered in your earlier studies.

Knowledge brought forward from earlier studies

Limiting factor analysis

- An organisation might be faced with just one limiting factor (other than maximum sales demand) but there might also be several scarce resources, with two or more of them putting an effective limit on the level of activity that can be achieved.

- Examples of limiting factors include sales demand and production constraints.

  - Labour. The limit may be either in terms of total quantity or of particular skills.
  - Materials. There may be insufficient available materials to produce enough units to satisfy sales demand.
  - Manufacturing capacity. There may not be sufficient machine capacity for the production required to meet sales demand.

- It is assumed in limiting factor analysis that management would make a product mix decision or service mix decision based on the option that would maximise profit and that profit is maximised when contribution is maximised (given no change in fixed cost expenditure incurred). In other words, marginal costing ideas are applied.

  - Contribution will be maximised by earning the biggest possible contribution per unit of limiting factor. For example, if grade A labour is the limiting factor, contribution will be maximised by earning the biggest contribution per hour of grade A labour worked.
  - The limiting factor decision therefore involves the determination of the contribution earned per unit of limiting factor by each different product.
  - If the sales demand is limited, the profit-maximising decision will be to produce the top-ranked product(s) up to the sales demand limit.

- In limiting factor decisions, we generally assume that fixed costs are the same whatever product or service mix is selected, so that the only relevant costs are variable costs.

- When there is just one limiting factor, the technique for establishing the contribution-maximising product mix or service mix is to rank the products or services in order of contribution-earning ability per unit of limiting factor.

Exam focus point

Throughput is defined as sales less material costs whereas contribution is defined as sales less **all** variable costs, including direct labour and variable overheads. Throughput assumes that all costs except direct materials are fixed in the short run.

Chapter Roundup

- **Throughput accounting** supports a production management system which aims to maximise throughput, and therefore cash generation from sales. It is not concerned with 'traditional' measurements of profit of maximisation of this profit. A **just in time (JIT) production system** is operated, with some buffer inventory kept only when there is a **bottleneck resource**.

- In a throughput accounting environment, **production priority** is given to the products best able to generate throughput. Performance measures in throughput accounting are based around the concept that the aim is to maximise throughput. This is achieved by maximising the **throughput per unit of bottleneck resource**.

- When an organisation makes more than one product, total throughput is maximised by **giving priority to those products that earn the largest throughput per unit of bottleneck resource**. Products should be ranked in order of priority according to their throughput per unit of bottleneck resource.

- The **throughput accounting ratio** (TPAR ratio) is the ratio of the throughput per unit of bottleneck resource to the factory cost per unit of bottleneck resource. This ratio should be as high as possible, and certainly more than 1.0.

Quick Quiz

1. Fill in the blanks in the statements below, using the words in the box. Some words may be used twice.

   (a) The theory of constraints is an approach to production management which aims to maximise (1).. less (2).. . It focuses on factors such as (3).. which act as (4)..

   (b) Throughput contribution = (5).. minus (6)..

   (c) TPAR ratio = (7) .... per factory hour ÷ (8) .... per factory hour

• bottlenecks	• throughput
• material costs	• constraints
• sales revenue	• factory cost

2. Fill in the right hand side of the table below, which looks at the differences between throughput accounting and traditional product costing.

Traditional product costing	Throughput accounting
Labour costs and 'traditional' variable overheads are treated as variable costs.	
Inventory is valued in the income statement and statement of financial position at total production cost.	
Variance analysis is employed to determine whether standards were achieved.	
Efficiency is based on labour and machines working to full capacity.	
Value is added when an item is produced.	

3   The following details relate to three services offered by DSF.

	V	A	L
	$ per service	$ per service	$ per service
Selling price of service	120	170	176
Direct labour	20	30	20
Variable overhead	40	56	80
Fixed overhead	20	32	40
	80	118	140
Profit	40	52	36

All three services use the same direct labour, but in different quantities.

In a period when the labour used on these services is in short supply, the most and least profitable use of the labour is:

	Most profitable	Least profitable
A	L	V
B	L	A
C	V	A
D	A	L

4   The theory of constraints is an approach to production management, which aims to maximise sales revenue less:

A   Variable overhead costs
B   All production costs
C   Material costs
D   Material and variable overhead costs

5   Throughput accounting policy is to hold zero inventories throughout all operations.

True   ☐

False   ☐

1
1 sales revenue
2 material costs
3 bottlenecks
4 constraints
5 sales revenue
6 material costs
7 throughput
8 factory cost

2

Traditional product costing	Throughput accounting
Labour costs and 'traditional' variable overheads are treated as variable costs.	They are not normally treated as variable costs.
Inventory is valued in the statement of profit or loss and statement of financial position at total production cost.	It is valued at material cost only.
Variance analysis is employed to determine whether standards were achieved.	It is used to determine why the planned product mix was not produced.
Efficiency is based on labour and machines working to full capacity.	Efficiency requires schedule adherence and meeting delivery dates.
Value is added when an item is produced.	It is added when an item is sold.

3   B

	V	A	L
	$	$	$
Selling price per service	120	170	176
Variable cost per service	60	86	100
Contribution per service	60	84	76
Labour cost per service	$20	$30	$20
Contribution per $ of labour	$3	$2.80	$3.80
Ranking	2	3	1

4   C   Material costs.

The theory of constraints focuses on factors such as bottlenecks which act as constraints to this maximisation.

5   False. A buffer inventory should be held prior to the bottleneck process.

Now try the questions below from the Practice Question Bank

Number	Level	Marks	Approximate time
Section A Q16	Examination	2	4 mins
Section A Q17	Examination	2	4 mins
Section A Q18	Examination	2	4 mins
Section A Q19	Examination	2	4 mins
Section A Q20	Examination	2	4 mins
Section B Q16–20	Examination	10	20 mins

Environmental accounting

2e

Topic list	Syllabus reference
1 Managing environmental costs	A5 (a)
2 Accounting for environmental costs	A5 (b)

Introduction

Environmental accounting is the fifth and final management accounting technique in Section A of the syllabus.

Environmental issues are becoming increasingly important in the business world. Businesses are responsible for the environmental impact of their operations and are becoming increasingly aware of problems such as carbon emissions.

The growth of environmental issues and regulations has also brought greater focus on how businesses **manage** and **account** for environmental costs.

The focus of this chapter is on methods of providing information to management on environmental costs. It does not deal with environmental reporting to shareholders and other stakeholders.

Study guide

		Intellectual level
A5	**Environmental accounting**	
(a)	Discuss the issues businesses face in the management of environmental costs.	1
(b)	Describe the different methods a business may use to account for its environmental costs.	1

Exam guide

Environmental accounting is becoming increasingly topical in the modern business environment. There is an article on the ACCA website on the topic of environmental management accounting written by a member of the examining team (ACCA, 2016). It is recommended that you read this article.

For your examination, you should try to understand the nature of environmental costs, and you should be able to describe briefly the four methods of environmental management accounting that are described in this chapter.

1 Managing environmental costs

FAST FORWARD

Environmental costs are important to businesses for a number of reasons.

- Identifying environmental costs associated with individual products and services can assist with **pricing** decisions.

- It ensures compliance with **regulatory standards**.

- There is potential for **cost savings**.

Key term

Environmental management accounting (EMA) is the generation and analysis of both financial and non-financial information in order to support internal environmental management processes.

1.1 Environmental concern and performance

Bennett and James (1998) looked at the **ways in which a company's concern for the environment can impact on its performance**.

(a) **Short-term savings** through waste minimisation and energy efficiency schemes can be substantial.

(b) Companies with poor environmental performance may face **increased cost of capital** because investors and lenders demand a higher risk premium.

(c) There are a number of **energy and environmental taxes**, such as the UK's landfill tax on waste disposal.

(d) **Pressure group campaigns** can cause damage to reputation and/or additional costs.

(e) Environmental legislation may cause the **'sunsetting'** of products and opportunities for **'sunrise' replacements**.

(f) The cost of processing input which becomes **waste** is equivalent to 5–10% of some organisations' revenue.

1.1.1 Achieving business and environmental benefits

Bennett and James went on to suggest six main **ways in which business and environmental benefits can be achieved**.

(a)   **Integrating the environment into capital expenditure decisions**. This could be done by considering environmental opposition to projects which could affect cash flows, for example.

(b)   **Understanding and managing environmental costs**. Environmental costs are often 'hidden' in overheads and environmental and energy costs are often not allocated to the relevant budgets.

(c)   **Introducing waste minimisation schemes.** Such schemes may result in the reduction or avoidance of pollution control expenditure.

(d)   **Understanding and managing life cycle costs**. For many products, the greatest environmental impact occurs upstream (such as mining raw materials) or downstream from production (such as energy to operate equipment). This has led to producers being made responsible for dealing with the disposal of products such as cars, and government and third-party measures to influence raw material choices. Organisations therefore need to identify, control and make provision for environmental life cycle costs and work with suppliers and customers to identify environmental cost reduction opportunities.

(e)   **Measuring environmental performance.** Business is under increasing pressure to measure all aspects of environmental performance, both for statutory disclosure reasons and due to demands for more environmental data from customers.

(f)   **Involving management accountants in a strategic approach to environment-related management accounting and performance evaluation.** A 'green accounting team' incorporating the key functions should analyse the strategic picture and identify opportunities for practical initiatives. It should analyse the short-, medium- and long-term impact of possible changes in the following.

   (i)   **Government policies**, such as on transport
   (ii)   **Legislation and regulation**
   (iii)   **Supply conditions**, such as fewer landfill sites
   (iv)   **Market conditions**, such as changing customer views
   (v)   **Social attitudes**, such as to factory farming
   (vi)   **Competitor strategies**

Possible action includes the following.

   (i)   Designating an **'environmental champion'** within the strategic planning or accounting function to ensure that environmental considerations are fully considered

   (ii)   Assessing whether **new data sources** are needed to collect more and better data

   (iii)   Making **comparisons** between sites/offices to highlight poor performance and generate peer pressure for action

   (iv)   Developing **checklists** for internal auditors

Such analysis and action should help organisations to better understand present and future environmental costs and benefits.

1.2 Defining environmental costs

There are many varied definitions of environmental costs. The United States Environmental Protection Agency (1995) makes a distinction between four types of cost.

(a) **Conventional costs**, such as raw materials and energy costs, have an impact on the environment.

(b) **Potentially hidden costs** are relevant costs that are captured within accounting systems but may be 'hidden' within 'general overheads'.

(c) **Contingent costs** are costs that will be incurred at a future date as a result of discharging waste into the environment, such as **clean-up** costs.

(d) **Image and relationship costs** are costs incurred to preserve the reputation of the business; for example, the costs of preparing environmental reports to ensure compliance with regulatory standards.

Environmental costs are internal or external. Internal costs are environmental costs that an organisation incurs. **External environmental costs** are costs that an organisation causes, but which are suffered by others – for example the general public. For example, unless an organisation is punished for causing environmental damage, such as pollution from toxic air emissions, society as a whole may bear the cost of the pollution and any clean-up operation.

The **internal environmental costs** for an organisation include, the costs of preventing environmental damage (such as air filters and water treatment equipment), the costs of detecting environmental damage or emissions, the costs of correcting environmental damage that is caused, and the costs of disposal of any waste.

Yet another way of looking at environmental cost is to say that an organisation incurs environmental costs when it **consumes a valuable environmental resource**, such as oil and petrol, and other forms of energy.

1.3 Identifying environmental costs

Many environmental costs are already captured within accounting systems. The difficulty lies in **pinpointing** them and **allocating** them to a specific product or service. Typical environmental costs are listed below.

*   Consumables and raw materials
*   Transport and travel
*   Waste
*   Waste and effluent disposal
*   Water consumption
*   Energy

You may be familiar with process costing. This is a method of costing for a system where output is produced in a process, and there may be some loss or wastage in the process. A principle of process costing is that, if waste or loss is expected in production, it should not be given a cost.

For example, suppose that 1,000 kilos of materials are input to a process in which 10% of input is normally lost, and the total costs of the process are $180,000. In 'traditional' process costing, the costing system would allow for normal loss and process and would not give it a cost. So if 10% loss is expected, input of 1,000 kilos will produce only 900 kilos of output, and the cost per kilo of output is therefore $200 (= $180,000/900).

The normal waste in the process is ignored for costing purposes. Waste is an environmental cost, but in this example the reported cost of loss or waste is $0.

For the purpose of environmental management accounting, this is unsatisfactory. Management should be given better information about environmental costs.

1.4 Controlling environmental costs

Once a business has **defined**, **identified** and **allocated** environmental costs, it can begin the task of trying to control them through **environmental management systems**.

1.4.1 ISO 14000

International Organization for Standardization (2015) ISO 14000 was first published in 1996 and based on earlier quality management standards. It provides a general framework on which a number of specific standards have been based (the ISO family of standards). ISO 14001 prescribes that an environmental management system must comprise:

- An **environmental policy statement**
- An assessment of environmental aspects and legal and voluntary obligations
- A management system
- Internal audits and reports to senior management
- A public declaration that ISO 14001 is being complied with

Critics of ISO 14000 claim that its emphasis on management systems rather than performance is misplaced, and that it does not include rigorous verification and disclosure requirements.

1.4.2 Management systems

Gray and Bebbington (2001) listed the functions that environmental management systems should cover.

Function	Description
Environmental review and policy development	A first review of environmental impacts of materials, issues and products and of business issues arising, as well as the development of a tailored in-house policy or measures to ensure adherence to external standards
Objectives and target development	As with all business objectives and targets, it is preferable that those set be unambiguous and achievable. Targets should be quantified within a specified time period eg reducing carbon dioxide emissions by X% within a specified time period
Life cycle assessment	This aims to identify all interactions between a product and its environment during its lifetime, including energy and material usage and environmental releases. • Raw materials used have to be traced back to the biosphere and the company recognises impact on habitat, gas balance, the energy used in the extraction and transportation and the energy used to produce the means of extraction • For intermediate stages, emissions, discharges and co-products • At the consumer purchase stage, the impact of manufacture and disposal of packaging, transport to shops and ultimately impacts of consumers using and disposing of the product
Establishment and maintenance of environmental management systems	Key features of environmental management systems (as with other management systems) including information systems, budgeting, forecasting and management accounting systems, structure of responsibilities, establishment of an environmentally friendly culture, considering impact on human resource issues such as education and performance appraisal
Regulatory compliance	Making sure that current legal requirements are being fulfilled and keeping up to date with practical implications of likely changes in legislation
Environmental impact assessment	A regular review of interactions with the environment, the degree of impact and also the impact of forthcoming major investments
Eco-label applications	Eco-labelling allows organisations to publicly identify products and services that meet the highest environmental standards. To be awarded an eco-label requires the product to be the result of a reliable quality management system

Function	Description
Waste minimisation	Whether waste can be minimised (or better still eliminated), possibility of recycling or selling waste
Pollution prevention programmes	Deciding what to target
Research, development and investment in cleaner technologies	How to bring desirable features into product development, bearing in mind product development may take several years, and opinion and legal requirements may change during that period. Desirable features may include minimum resource usage, waste, emissions, packaging and transport, recycling, disassembly and longer product life
Environmental performance and issues reporting	Consideration of the benefits and costs of reporting, how to report and what to include (policies, plans, financial data, activities undertaken, sustainability)

2 Accounting for environmental costs 12/13

The UNDSD (2003) identified a number of management accounting techniques to account for environmental costs. They include **input/output analysis, (material) flow cost accounting**, **environmental activity-based costing** and **environmental life cycle costing**.

The United Nations Division for Sustainable Development (UNDSD, 2003), as cited by ACCA (2016), identified management accounting techniques which are useful for the identification and allocation of environmental costs. They are **input/output analysis**, **flow cost accounting**, **environmental activity-based accounting** and **life cycle costing**.

You need to have a basic understanding of what these techniques are.

2.1 Input/output analysis

Input/output analysis operates on the principle that what comes in must go out. Process flow charts can help to trace inputs and outputs, particularly waste. They effectively demonstrate the details of the processes so that the relevant information can be allocated to the main activities.

Input/output analysis may involve some fairly complex modelling but, at a simple level, it measures the input to a production process or system, and the output from the system. Any difference between the amount input and the eventual output is 'residual', which is called 'waste'.

Input and output quantities are measured first, and these can then be given a cost.

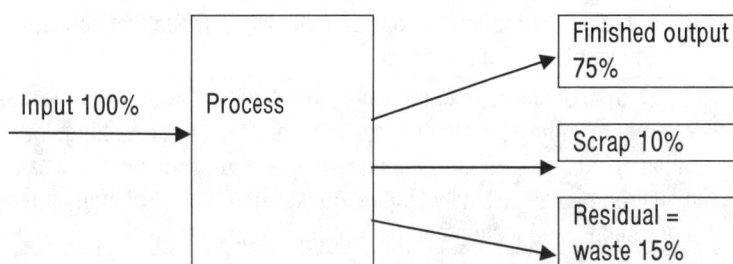

As shown in the diagram above, the input is regarded as 100% and split across the outputs which are **sold and stored goods** and **residual** (regarded as waste).

By accounting for process outputs in this way both in physical quantities and in monetary terms, businesses are forced to focus on environmental costs.

2.2 Flow cost accounting

Flow cost accounting (also known as Material Flow Cost Accounting or MFCA) is a development from input/output analysis that was originally developed in Germany in the 1990s.

With this technique, inputs and outputs are measured through each individual process of production. A distinction is made between:

(a)   Positive products: this is good output
(b)   Negative products: this is the measurement of waste

Positive products + Negative products = Total input

Positive and negative products are measured in both physical and cost terms.

Under this technique, material flows through an organisation are divided into three categories, and the cost of each category is measured separately.

- Material
- System: this is the in-house handling that is required (including labour) and its cost
- Delivery and disposal: this is the cost of transport and the cost of disposal of waste

An important focus of management attention with flow cost accounting should be to reduce the proportion of negative products in total output and increasing the proportion of positive products.

This approach is applied to each individual process within the overall production system.

2.3 Environmental activity-based costing

Activity-based costing (ABC) '... represents a method of managerial cost accounting that allocates all internal costs to the cost centres and cost drivers on the basis of the activities that caused the costs' (Bennet and James, 2000: p.89).

Environmental activity-based costing combined elements of environmental costing with an activity-based costing system. Environment costs can be divided into two categories.

(a)   Environment-related costs, such as an incinerator or a sewage treatment plant, for which costs can be directly traced

(b)   Environment-driven costs, which are normally hidden within total overheads in a conventional costing system

The main challenge with environmental activity-based costing is to:

(a)   Identify the hidden environmental costs and link them to 'environmental activities'

(b)   Charge the costs of each environmental activity to individual product costs according to the amount that each product is responsible for the environmental activity

Environmental activities and environment-driven will vary between different organisations, but they may include activities and costs relating to:

(a)   Prevention work
(b)   Detection
(c)   Corrective action
(d)   Disposal of waste

Suitable environmental activities should be identified and an activity cost centre created for it. It should be possible to trace environment-driven costs to these cost centres.

Environment costs that have been allocated and apportioned to environmental activity cost centres can then be absorbed into product costs on a suitable basis.

For example, if an environmental activity is prevention of air pollution, costs will include the costs of equipment, the cost of labour time, and so on. These costs may be absorbed into product costs using the volume of waste emissions as a cost driver. Each product will then be charged a share of the costs according to the volume of waste emitted in their manufacture.

Other environmental activities may be disposal of industrial waste, treating contaminated ground, and so on.

The general principle should be reasonably familiar to you if you understand the basics of activity-based costing (ABC).

To decide on the environmental cost drivers, the production processes involved in making a product or providing a service need to be carefully analysed. The **levels** of environmental **hazards** and **costs** need to be **established**. This may mean installing **tracking systems** to track environmental waste. Tracking waste may itself be regarded as an environmental activity, for which costs are measured.

Bennett and James stated 'the choice of an adequate allocation key (cost driver) is crucial for obtaining correct information' (2000: p.90). The four main allocations are listed below.

- Volume of emissions or waste
- Toxicity of emissions and waste treated
- Environmental impact added (volume × input per unit of volume)
- The relative costs of treating different kinds of emissions

2.4 Environmental life cycle costing

Under this method of environmental cost accounting, environmental costs for a product are considered from the **design stage** of the product right up to the **end of life costs**, such as decommissioning and removal.

As with 'normal' life cycle costing, this approach makes an assessment of expected environmental costs over the entire life of a product. These costs will include 'internal' costs that the organisation will incur. There is an argument that they should also include external environmental costs, which are costs that others in society will incur, rather than the organisation itself.

By identifying the environmental costs of a product over its entire expected life, including the costs of clean-up and disposal at the end of the product's life, management can make a decision about whether the environmental costs are acceptable, or they can consider ways of reducing the costs to a more acceptable level.

These decisions can be made before the product is actually brought into production.

Chapter Roundup

- **Environmental costs** are important to businesses for a number of reasons.
    - Identifying environmental costs associated with individual products and services can assist with **pricing** decisions.
    - It ensures compliance with **regulatory standards**.
    - There is potential for **cost savings**.
- The UNDSD (2003) identified a number of management accounting techniques to account for environmental costs. They include **input/output analysis**, **(material) flow cost accounting**, **environmental activity-based costing** and **environmental life cycle costing**.

Quick Quiz

1   What are the main elements of an environmental management system per ISO 14001?

2   Choose the appropriate words from those highlighted.

    Costs that will be incurred at a future date such as clean up costs are known as **contingent/image and relationship** costs.

    Raw materials and energy are examples of **potentially hidden/conventional** costs

3   List the three categories of material flows under a system of (material) flow cost accounting.

4   Which of the following is an example of an environmental external failure cost?

    A   Maintaining pollution equipment
    B   Decontaminating land
    C   Recycling scrap
    D   Record keeping

5   Identify four reasons why environmental costs are important to management accountants.

1
- An environmental policy
- An assessment of environmental aspects and legal and voluntary obligations
- A management system
- Internal audits and reports to senior management
- A public declaration that ISO 14001 is being complied with

2   contingent
      conventional

3
- Material
- System
- Delivery and disposal

4   B.   Decontaminating land

5   (a)   Environmental costing can help to produce more accurate product or service pricing, leading to increased profitability.

     (b)   Poor environmental behaviour can result in fines and damage to reputation.

     (c)   Recording environmental costs is important, as some may require regulatory compliance.

     (d)   Saving energy generally leads to cost savings.

Now try the questions below from the Practice Question Bank

Number	Level	Marks	Approximate time
Section A Q21	Examination	2	4 mins
Section A Q22	Examination	2	4 mins
Section A Q23	Examination	2	4 mins
Section A Q24	Examination	2	4 mins
Section A Q25	Examination	2	4 mins

Decision-making techniques

Cost volume profit (CVP) analysis

Topic list	Syllabus reference
1 A recap of basic CVP analysis	B2 (a), (b)
2 Preparing a basic breakeven chart	B2 (a)
3 Breakeven analysis in a multi-product environment	B2 (b), (e)
4 Breakeven point for multiple products	B2 (b)
5 Contribution to sales (C/S) ratio for multiple products	B2 (c)
6 Margin of safety for multiple products	B2 (b)
7 Target profits for multiple products	B2 (d)
8 Multi-product breakeven charts	B2 (e)
9 Further aspects of CVP analysis	B2 (f)

Introduction

You will have **already encountered CVP (or breakeven) analysis** in your earlier studies, so you should be reasonably familiar with the terminology or basic techniques that you will meet in this chapter. However, a brief revision of the topic is provided, before the chapter moves on to more high-level material such as multi-product CVP analysis.

Study guide

		Intellectual level
B2	**Cost volume profit analysis**	
(a)	Explain the nature of CVP analysis.	2
(b)	Calculate and interpret breakeven point and margin of safety.	2
(c)	Calculate the contribution to sales ratio, in single and multi-product situations, and demonstrate an understanding of its use.	2
(d)	Calculate target profit or revenue in single and multi-product situations, and demonstrate an understanding of its use.	2
(e)	Prepare breakeven charts and profit volume charts and interpret the information contained within each, including multi-product situations.	2
(f)	Discuss the limitations of CVP analysis for planning and decision-making.	2

Exam guide

The ACCA website contains an article on CVP analysis written by the **examining team** (ACCA, 2016). Ensure that you are familiar with this article.

1 A recap of basic CVP analysis

1.1 Knowledge brought forward from earlier studies

FAST FORWARD

Cost volume profit (CVP)/breakeven analysis is the study of the interrelationships between costs, volume and profit at various levels of activity.

1.1.1 Breakeven analysis

Key terms

- **Contribution per unit** = unit selling price – unit variable costs
- **Profit** = (sales volume × contribution per unit) – fixed costs
- **Breakeven point** = activity level at which there is neither profit nor loss

$$= \frac{\text{total fixed costs}}{\text{contribution per unit}} = \frac{\text{contribution required to breakeven}}{\text{contribution per unit}}$$

- **Contribution/sales (C/S) ratio** = profit/volume (P/V) ratio = (contribution/sales) × 100%
- **Sales revenue at breakeven point** = fixed costs ÷ C/S ratio
- **Margin of safety (in units)** = budgeted sales units – breakeven sales units
- **Margin of safety (as %)** $= \dfrac{\text{budgeted sales} - \text{breakeven sales}}{\text{budgeted sales}} \times 100\%$

- **Sales volume to achieve a target profit** $= \dfrac{\text{fixed cost} + \text{target profit}}{\text{contribution per unit}}$

1.1.2 Assumptions

(a) CVP analysis can apply to one product only, or to more than one product only if they are sold in a fixed sales mix (fixed proportions).

(b) Fixed costs per period are same in total, and unit variable costs are a constant amount at all levels of output and sales.

(c) Sales prices are constant at all levels of activity.

(d) Production volume = sales volume.

1.1.3 Example: Breakeven point and margin of safety

Question

A company makes and sells a single product. The selling price is $12 per unit. The variable cost of making and selling the product is $9 per unit and fixed costs per month are $240,000.

The company budgets to sell 90,000 units of the product a month.

Required

(a)   What is the budgeted profit per month and what is the breakeven point in sales?
(b)   What is the margin of safety?
(c)   What must sales be to achieve a monthly profit of $120,000?

Answer

(a)   Contribution per unit = $(12 – 9) = $3. The C/S ratio is 3/12 = 0.25

Budgeted profit = (90,000 × $3) – $240,000 = $30,000

Breakeven point in units of sale = $240,000/$3 per unit = 80,000 units per month

(Breakeven point in sales revenue = Fixed costs/C/S ratio = $240,000/0.25 = $960,000)

(b)   Margin of safety = (90,000 – 80,000)/90,000 = 11.1%

(c)   To achieve a profit of $120,000, total contribution must be $(240,000 + 120,000) = $360,000.

Sales must be $360,000/$3 per unit = 120,000 units (or $360,000/0.25 = $1,440,000 in sales revenue).

1.1.4 Breakeven, contribution and P/V charts   Mar/Jun 16

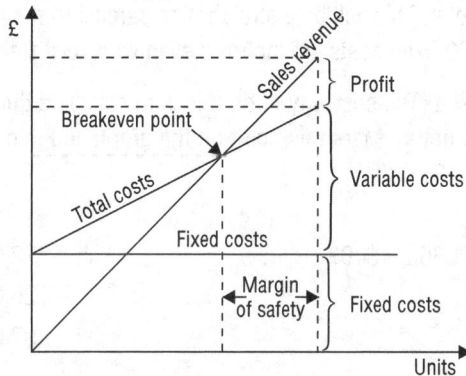

- Breakeven chart
- Contribution (contribution breakeven) chart
- Profit/volume (P/V) chart

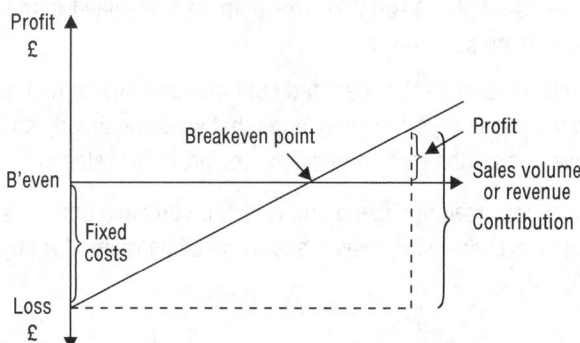

The gradient of the straight line is the contribution per unit (if the horizontal axis is measured in sales value).

2 Preparing a basic breakeven chart

In a breakeven chart, the x axis is the volume of production and sales and the y axis represents money value (revenue and cost). The chart is prepared by drawing a line to show total revenue at all levels of sales, and a total cost line to show total costs at all levels of production and sales. The **breakeven point** is where the **sales revenue** line and **total cost** line intersect.

Key term

> **Breakeven point** is the level of sales at which there is neither profit nor loss.

2.1 Example: Basic breakeven chart

A new product has the following sales and cost data.

Selling price	$60 per unit
Variable cost	$40 per unit
Fixed costs	$25,000 per month
Forecast sales	1,800 units per month

Required

Prepare a breakeven chart using the above data.

Solution

Step 1 Draw the axes and label them. Your graph should fill as much of the page as possible; this will make it clearer and easier to read.

The highest value on the vertical axis will be the monthly sales revenue.

1,800 units × $60 = $108,000

Step 2 Draw the fixed cost line and label it. This will be a straight line parallel to the horizontal axis at the $25,000 level. The $25,000 fixed costs are incurred even with zero activity.

Step 3 Draw the total cost line and label it. The best way to do this is to calculate the total costs for the maximum sales level (1,800 units). Mark this point on the graph and join it to the cost incurred at zero activity; that is, $25,000.

	$
Variable costs for 1,800 units (1,800 × $40)	72,000
Fixed costs	25,000
Total cost for 1,800 units	97,000

Step 4 Draw the revenue line and label it. Once again, start by plotting the revenue at the maximum activity level. 1,800 units × $60 = $108,000. This point can be joined to the origin, since at zero activity there will be no sales revenue.

Step 5 Mark any required information on the chart and read off solutions as required. Check that your chart is accurate by reading off the measures that we have already covered in this chapter: the breakeven point, the margin of safety, the profit for sales of 1,800 units.

Step 6 Check the accuracy of your readings using arithmetic. If you have time, it is good examination technique to check your answer and make adjustments for any errors in your chart.

The completed graph is shown below.

3 Breakeven analysis in a multi-product environment

To perform breakeven analysis for a multi-product organisation, either a **constant sales mix** must be assumed, or all products must have the **same C/S ratio**.

3.1 A major assumption

Organisations typically produce and sell a number of different products or services. This makes breakeven analysis difficult. To perform breakeven analysis in a multi-product organisation, a constant product sales mix must be assumed. In other words, we have to assume that whenever x units of product A are sold, y units of product B and z units of product C are also sold.

By assuming a constant sales mix for the products, we can calculate a weighted average contribution per unit sold. The weighting is based on the quantities or proportions of each product in the constant sales mix. This means that the unit contribution of the product that makes up the largest proportion of the mix has the greatest impact on the average contribution per mix.

As an alternative to calculating a weighted average contribution per unit of sale, we can calculate a weighted average C/S ratio.

The only situation when the mix of products does not affect the analysis is when all of the products have the same ratio of contribution to sales (C/S ratio). This is unlikely to happen in most businesses, but may occasionally occur in, say, retailing when all products are resold at the same percentage mark-up on cost.

4 Breakeven point for multiple products   12/12

The **breakeven point** for a standard sales mix of products is calculated by dividing the total fixed costs by the weighted average contribution per unit, or by the weighted average C/S ratio.

4.1 Example: Breakeven point for multiple products

PL produces and sells two products, M and N. Product M sells for $7 per unit and has a total variable cost of $2.94 per unit, while Product N sells for $15 per unit and has a total variable cost of $4.40 per unit. The marketing department has estimated that, for every five units of M sold, one unit of N will be sold. The organisation's fixed costs per period total $123,600.

Required

Calculate the breakeven point for PL.

Solution

We calculate the breakeven point as follows.

Step 1 Calculate the contribution per unit and the weighted average contribution per unit.

	M	N
	$ per unit	$ per unit
Sales price	7.00	15.00
Variable cost	2.94	4.40
Contribution	4.06	10.60

	$
Contribution from sale of 5 units of M (× $4.06)	20.30
Contribution from sale of 1 unit of N	10.60
Contribution from sale of 6 units in standard sales mix	30.90

Weighted average contribution per unit = $30.90/6 = $5.15 per unit.

Step 2 Calculate the **breakeven point in units**.

Fixed costs/Weighted average contribution per unit = $123,600/$5.15 = 24,000 units.

These are in the ratio 5:1; therefore breakeven is at the point where 20,000 units of M are sold (= 24,000 × 5/6) and 4,000 units of N are sold (= 24,000 × 1/6).

Step 3 Calculate the **breakeven point in sales revenue**.

20,000 units of M at $7 + 4,000 units of N at $15

= $140,000 + $60,000 = $200,000

It is important to note that the breakeven point is not $200,000 regardless of the sales mix of products. The breakeven point is $200,000 provided that the sales mix remains 5:1. Likewise, the breakeven point is not at a production/sales level of 24,000 units regardless of the sales mix. Rather, it is when 20,000 units of M and 4,000 units of N are sold, assuming a sales mix of 5:1.

Question	Breakeven point for multiple products

Alpha manufactures and sells three products, the Beta, the Gamma and the Delta. Relevant information is as follows.

	Beta	Gamma	Delta
	$ per unit	$ per unit	$ per unit
Selling price	135.00	165.00	220.00
Variable cost	72.80	57.90	146.20

Total fixed costs are $1,025,000.

An analysis of past trading patterns indicates that the products Beta, Gamma and Delta are sold in the ratio 3:4:5 respectively.

Required

Fill in the blanks in the sentence below.

Alpha's breakeven point in terms of revenue of the three products is ……………………….. of Beta, ……………………. of Gamma and ………............……….. of Delta, making …………..……….. in total.

The correct answer is $421,875 of Beta, $687,501 of Gamma and $1,145,833 of Delta, making $2,255,209 in total.

Step 1   Calculate weighted average **contribution per unit**.

	Beta	Gamma	Delta
	$ per unit	$ per unit	$ per unit
Selling price	135.00	165.00	220.00
Variable cost	72.80	57.90	146.20
Contribution per unit	62.20	107.10	73.80

	$
Contribution from sale of 3 units of Beta (× $62.20)	186.60
Contribution from sale of 4 units of Gamma (× $107.10)	428.40
Contribution from sale of 5 units of Delta (× $73.80)	369.00
Contribution from sale of 12 units in standard sales mix	984.00

Weighted average contribution per unit = $984/12 = $82 per unit

Step 2   Calculate the **breakeven point** in units in the standard sales mix.

= Fixed costs/Weighted average contribution per unit

= $1,025,000/$82 = 12,500 units

Step 3   Calculate the breakeven sales for each product.

Beta: 12,500 × 3/12 = 3,125 units. (Revenue × $135 = $421,875)

Gamma: 12,500 × 4/12 = 4,166.67 units (Revenue × $165 = $687,501)

Delta: 12,500 × 5/12 = 5,208.33 units (Revenue × $220 = $1,145,833)

Step 4   Calculate the **breakeven point** in terms of **revenue**.

Beta: 3,125 units × $135 = $421,875

Gamma: 4,166.67 units × $165 = $687,501

Delta: 5,208.33 units × $220 = $1,145,833

= $2,255,209 in total

5 Contribution to sales (C/S) ratio for multiple products
Sep/Dec 15

FAST FORWARD
The **breakeven point in terms of sales revenue** can be calculated by dividing the fixed costs (= required contribution) by the weighted average C/S ratio.

Formula to learn

The **breakeven point in terms of sales revenue** = fixed costs/average C/S ratio.

5.1 Calculating the ratio

An alternative way of **calculating the breakeven point** is to use the weighted **average contribution to sales (C/S) ratio** for the standard mix.

As you should already know, the C/S ratio is sometimes called the **profit/volume ratio** or **P/V ratio**.

We can calculate the breakeven point of PL (see Section 4.1) as follows.

Step 1   Calculate **revenue and contribution per mix** of 5 units of M and 1 unit of N.

	Contribution		Revenue	
	Per unit	Total	Per unit	Total
	$	$	$	$
Product M (5 units)	4.06	20.30	7	35
Product N (1 unit)	10.60	10.60	15	15
		30.90		50

Weighted average C/S ratio = $30.90/$50 = 61.8% or 0.618

Step 2   Calculate **breakeven point** (total).

= Fixed costs ÷ Weighted average C/S ratio

Fixed costs/Weighted average contribution per unit = $123,600/0.618 = $200,000 in sales revenue.

Step 3   Calculate **breakeven sales for each product**.

M = $200,000 × (35/50) = $140,000

    Sales price per unit = $7

    Therefore breakeven point in units = $140,000/$7 = 20,000 units.

N = $200,000 × (15/50) = $60,000

    Sales price per unit = $15

    Therefore breakeven point in units = $60,000/$15 = 4,000 units.

Question

C/S ratio for multiple products

Required

Calculate the breakeven sales revenue of product Beta, Gamma and Delta (see Question under 4.1 above) using the approach shown in Section 5.1.

Answer

Step 1   Calculate **revenue and contribution per mix** of 3 units of Beta, 4 units of Gamma and 5 units of Delta.

	Beta	Gamma	Delta	Total
Sales mix	3	4	5	
Revenue per unit	$135	$165	$220	
Contribution per unit	$62.20	$107.10	$73.80	
	$	$	$	$
Revenue per mix 3:4:5	405.00	660.00	1,100.00	2,165
Contribution per mix 3:4:5	186.60	428.40	369.00	984

Weighted average C/S ratio = 984/2,165 = 0.4545035

Step 2   Calculate breakeven point (total)

= Fixed costs ÷ Weighted average C/S ratio

= $1,025,000/0.4545035

= $2,255,208

Step 3 Calculate breakeven sales

Breakeven sales of Beta = 405/2,165 × $2,255,208 = $421,875

Breakeven sales of Gamma = 660/2,165 × $2,255,208 = $687,500

Breakeven sales of Delta = 1,100/2,165 × $2,255,208 = $1,145,833

Alternatively you might be provided with the individual C/S ratios of a number of products. For example. if an organisation sells two products (A and B) in the ratio 2:5 and if the C/S ratio of A is 10% whereas that of B is 50%, the average C/S ratio is calculated as follows.

$$\text{Average C/S ratio} = \frac{(2 \times 10\%) + (5 \times 50\%)}{2 + 5} = 38.6\%$$

Question
Average C/S ratio

TIM produces and sells two products, the MK and the KL. The organisation expects to sell 1 MK for every 2 KLs and have monthly sales revenue of $150,000. The MK has a C/S ratio of 20% whereas the KL has a C/S ratio of 40%. Budgeted monthly fixed costs are $30,000.

Required

What is the budgeted breakeven sales revenue?

Answer

$$\text{Average C/S ratio} = \frac{(20\% \times 1) + (40\% \times 2)}{3} = 33^1/_3\%$$

$$\text{Sales revenue at the breakeven point} = \frac{\text{fixed costs}}{\text{C/S ratio}} = \frac{\$30,000}{0.333} = \$90,000$$

The C/S ratio is a measure of how much contribution is earned from each $1 of sales of the standard mix. The C/S ratio of $33^1/_3\%$ in the question above means that, for every $1 of sales of the standard mix of products, a contribution of 33.33c is earned. To earn a total contribution of, say, $20,000, sales revenue from the standard mix must therefore be

$$\frac{\$1}{33.33c} \times \$20,000 = \$60,006$$

Question
Using the C/S ratio

Refer back to the information in the paragraph following Question: C/S ratio for multiple products. Suppose the organisation in question has fixed costs of $100,000, and wishes to earn total contribution of $200,000.

Required

What level of revenue must be achieved?

Answer

Sales revenue must be $\dfrac{\$1}{38.6c} \times \$200,000 = \$518,135$

5.2 Points to bear in mind

Any change in the proportions of products in the sales mix will change the contribution per mix and the weighted average C/S ratio. This will change the breakeven point.

(a)   If the mix shifts towards products with lower contribution margins, the breakeven point (in units) will increase and profits will fall unless there is a corresponding increase in total revenue.

(b)   A shift towards products with higher contribution margins without a corresponding decrease in revenues will cause an increase in profits and a lower breakeven point.

(c)   If sales are at the specified level but not in the specified mix, there will be either a profit or a loss depending on whether the mix shifts towards products with higher or lower contribution margins.

6 Margin of safety for multiple products   Sep/Dec 16

> The **margin of safety** for a multi-product organisation is equal to the budgeted sales in the standard mix less the breakeven sales in the standard mix. It should be expressed as a percentage of the budgeted sales.

It should not surprise you to learn that the calculation of the margin of safety for multiple products is exactly the same as for single products, but we use the standard sales mix.

6.1 Example: Margin of safety for multiple products

BA produces and sells two products. The W sells for $8 per unit and has a total variable cost of $3.80 per unit, while the R sells for $14 per unit and has a total variable cost of $4.30. For every five units of W sold, six units of R are sold. BA's expected fixed costs are $83,160 for the per period.

Budgeted sales revenue for next period is $150,040, in the standard sales mix.

Required

Calculate the margin of safety in terms of sales revenue and also as a percentage of budgeted sales revenue.

Solution

To calculate the margin of safety we must first determine the breakeven point.

Step 1   Calculate the weighted average **contribution per unit**

	W	R
	$ per unit	$ per unit
Selling price	8.00	14.00
Variable cost	3.80	4.30
Contribution	4.20	9.70

	$
Contribution from sale of 5 units of W	21.00
Contribution from sale of 6 units of R	58.20
Contribution from sale of 11 units	79.20

Weighted average contribution per unit = $72.80/11 = $7.20

Step 2   Calculate the **breakeven point** in terms of the **number of shares (total)**

= Fixed costs/Weighted average contribution per unit = $83,160/$7.20

= 11,550 units

Step 3 Calculate the **breakeven point** in terms of the **number of units of the products**

Product W: 11,550 × (5/11) = 5,250 units

Product R: 11,550 × (6/11) = 6,300 units

Step 4 Calculate the **breakeven point** in terms of **revenue**

= (5,250 × $8) + (6,300 × $14)

= $42,000 of W revenue and $88,200 of R revenue = $130,200 in total

Step 5 Calculate the **margin of safety**

= Budgeted sales − Breakeven sales

= $150,040 − $130,200 = $19,840, in the standard sales mix

As a percentage: $19,840/$150,040 = 13.2% of budgeted sales

7 Target profits for multiple products

> The sales mix required to achieve a **target profit** is the sales mix that will earn a contribution equal to the fixed costs plus the target profit.

You should already be familiar with the problem of target profits for single products in a CVP context from your earlier studies. This section expands the concept to multiple products, illustrating the calculations in several examples.

7.1 A reminder of the formula for target profits

At **breakeven point** there is no profit – that is:

Contribution = Fixed costs

Suppose an organisation wishes to achieve a certain level of profit during a period. To achieve this profit, contribution must cover fixed costs and leave the required profit.

So **Total contribution required = Fixed costs + Required profit**

Once we know the total contribution required we can calculate the sales revenue of each product needed to achieve a target profit. The method is the same as the method used to calculate the breakeven point.

Formula to learn

> The total number of units to be sold to achieve a **target profit** is calculated as (Fixed costs + Required profit)/Weighted average contribution per unit, on the assumption that products are sold in a constant sales mix.

7.2 Example: Target profits for multiple products

An organisation makes and sells three products, F, G and H. The products are sold in the proportions F:G:H = 2:1:3. The organisation's fixed costs are $80,000 per month and details of the products are as follows.

Product	Selling price $ per unit	Variable cost $ per unit
F	22	16
G	15	12
H	19	13

The organisation wishes to earn a profit of $52,000 next month. Calculate the required sales value of each product in order to achieve this target profit.

Solution

Step 1   Calculate the **weighted average contribution per unit**

	F	G	H
	$ per unit	$ per unit	$ per unit
Selling price	22	15	19
Variable cost	16	12	13
Contribution	6	3	6

	$
Contribution from 2 units of F	12
Contribution from 1 unit of G	3
Contribution from 3 units of H	18
Total contribution from sale of 6 units	33

Weighted average contribution per unit = $33/6 = $5.50

Step 2   Calculate the **required number of sales units**

= (Fixed costs + Required profit)/Weighted average contribution per unit
= ($80,000 + $52,000)/$5.50
= 24,000 units

Step 3   Calculate the required sales in terms of the number of units of the products and sales revenue of each product

Product		Units	Selling price $ per unit	Sales revenue required $
F	24,000 × 2/6	8,000	22	176,000
G	24,000 × 1/6	4,000	15	60,000
H	24,000 × 3/6	12,000	19	228,000
Total				464,000

The sales revenue of $464,000 will generate a profit of $52,000 if the products are sold in the mix 2:1:3.

Alternatively, the C/S ratio could be used to determine the required sales revenue for a profit of $52,000. The method is again similar to that demonstrated earlier when calculating the breakeven point.

7.3 Example: Using the C/S ratio to determine the required sales

We'll use the data from the example above.

Step 1   **Calculate revenue per mix of 2 units of F, 1 unit of G and 3 units of H**
= (2 × $22) + (1 × $15) + (3 × $19)
= $44 + $15 + $57
= $116

Step 2   **Calculate contribution per mix of 2 units of F, 1 unit of G and 3 units of H**
= $33 (see solution in Section 7.2)

Step 3   **Calculate weighted average C/S ratio**
= ($33/$116) × 100%
= 28.45%

Step 4   **Calculate required total revenue**
= Required contribution ÷ C/S ratio
= ($80,000 + $52,000) ÷ 0.2845
= $463,972

Step 5 **Calculate required sales from each product**: see Step 1 for proportions

Required sales of F = 44/116 × $463,972 = $175,989
Required sales of G = 15/116 × $463,972 = $59,996
Required sales of H = 57/116 × $463,972 = $227,986

Which, allowing for rounding differences, is the same answer as calculated in the first example.

8 Multi-product breakeven charts 12/12, Sep/Dec 15

FAST FORWARD

Breakeven charts for multiple products can be drawn if a constant product sales mix is assumed.

The **P/V chart** can show information about each product individually.

Exam focus point

As well as being able to carry out CVP calculations you may be asked to produce a breakeven chart in a multiple product situation. This section focuses on the procedure involved in producing multi-product breakeven charts and profit/volume (P/V) charts.

8.1 Breakeven charts

Key term

A **breakeven chart** is a chart which indicates approximate profit or loss at different levels of sales volume within a limited range.

A very serious limitation of breakeven charts is that they can show the costs, revenues, profits and margins of safety for a single product only, or at best for a single 'sales mix' of products.

Breakeven charts for multiple products can be drawn if a constant product sales mix is assumed.

For example, suppose that FA sells three products, X, Y and Z, which have variable unit costs of $3, $4 and $5 respectively. The sales price of X is $8, the price of Y is $6 and the price of Z is $6. Fixed costs per annum are $10,000.

A breakeven chart cannot be drawn, because we do not know the proportions of X, Y and Z in the sales mix.

Exam focus point

If you are not sure about this point, you should try to draw a breakeven chart with the information given. It should not be possible.

There are a number of ways in which we can overcome this problem, however.

8.1.1 Approach 1: output in $ sales and a constant product mix

Assume that budgeted sales are 2,000 units of X, 4,000 units of Y and 3,000 units of Z. A breakeven chart would make the assumption that output and sales of X, Y and Z are in the proportions 2,000: 4,000: 3,000 at all levels of activity; in other words, that the sales mix is 'fixed' in these proportions.

We begin by carrying out some calculations.

Budgeted costs		Costs		Revenue
		$		$
Variable costs of X	(2,000 × $3)	6,000	X (2,000 × $8)	16,000
Variable costs of Y	(4,000 × $4)	16,000	Y (4,000 × $6)	24,000
Variable costs of Z	(3,000 × $5)	15,000	Z (3,000 × $6)	18,000
Total variable costs		37,000	Budgeted revenue	58,000
Fixed costs		10,000		
Total budgeted costs		47,000		

The **breakeven chart** can now be drawn.

The **breakeven point** is approximately $27,500 of sales revenue. This may either be **read from the chart or computed mathematically**.

(a) The budgeted C/S ratio for all three products together is contribution/sales = $(58,000 – 37,000)/$58,000 = 36.21%.

(b) The required contribution to breakeven is $10,000, the amount of fixed costs. The breakeven point is $10,000/36.21% = $27,500 (approx) in sales revenue.

The margin of safety is approximately $(58,000 – 27,500) = $30,500.

8.1.2 Approach 2: products in sequence

The products could be plotted in a particular sequence (say X first, then Y, then Z). Using the data from Approach 1, we can calculate cumulative costs and revenues as follows.

Product	Cumulative units	Cumulative costs	Cumulative revenue
		$	$
	Nil	10,000	Nil
X (2,000 units)	2,000	16,000	16,000
Y (4,000 units)	6,000	32,000	40,000
Z (3,000 units)	9,000	47,000	58,000

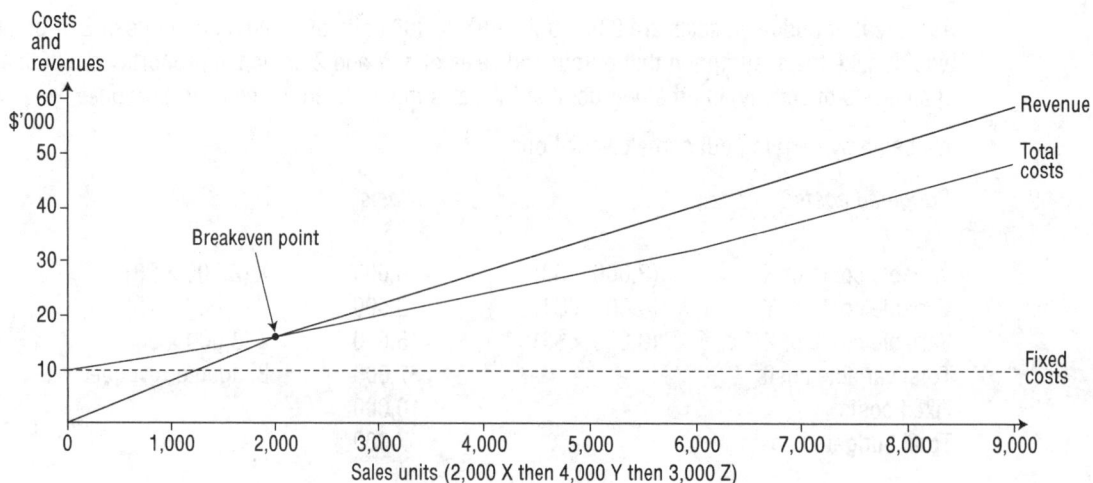

In this case the breakeven point occurs at 2,000 units of sales (2,000 units of product X). The margin of safety is roughly 4,000 units of Y and 3,000 units of Z.

8.1.3 Approach 3: output in terms of % of forecast sales and a constant product mix

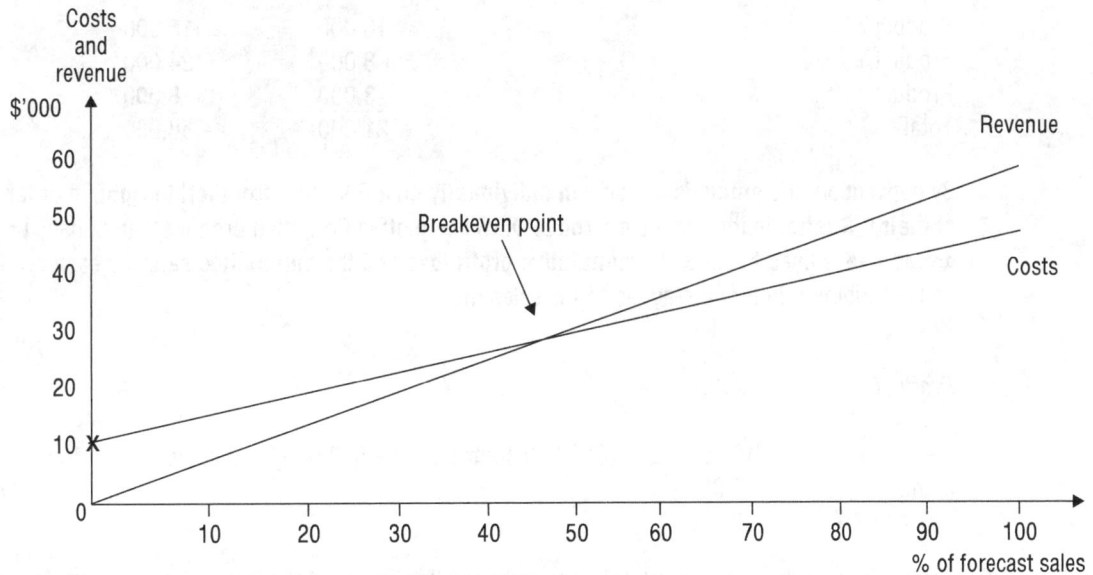

The breakeven point can be read from the graph as approximately 48% of forecast sales ($30,000 of revenue).

Alternatively, with contribution of $(58,000 – 37,000) = $21,000, 1% of forecast sales is associated with $21,000/100 = $210 contribution.

Breakeven point (%)	= fixed costs/contribution per 1%
	= $10,000/$210 = 47.62%
∴ Margin of safety	= (100 – 47.62) = 52.38%

Exam focus point

The general point of setting out these three approaches is to demonstrate that output can be viewed in several different ways.

8.2 Multi-product P/V charts

The same information could be shown on a **P/V chart**, as follows.

Multi-product P/V chart

An **addition** to the chart would **show further information about the contribution earned by each product individually**, so that their performance and profitability can be compared.

	Contribution $	Sales $	C/S ratio %
Product X	10,000	16,000	62.50
Product Y	8,000	24,000	33.33
Product Z	3,000	18,000	16.67
Total	21,000	58,000	36.21

By convention, the **products are shown individually** on a P/V chart from **left to right**, in **order of the size of their C/S ratio**. In this example, product X will be plotted first, then product Y and finally product Z. A **dotted line** is used to show the **cumulative profit/loss and the cumulative sales** as each product's sales and contribution in turn are added to the sales mix.

Product	Cumulative sales $		Cumulative profit $
X	16,000	($10,000 contribution – $10,000 fixed costs)	–
X and Y	40,000		8,000
X, Y and Z	58,000		11,000

You will see on the graph which follows that these three pairs of data are used to plot the dotted line, to indicate the contribution from each product. The **solid line** which joins the two ends of this dotted line **indicates the average profit** which will be earned from sales of the three products in this mix.

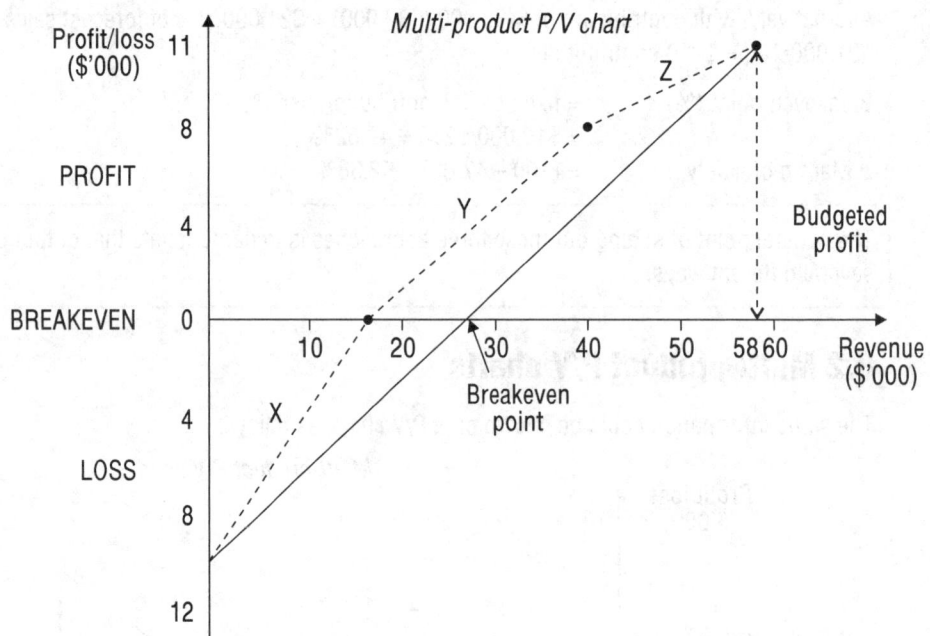

Multi-product P/V chart

The diagram **highlights** the following points.

(a)   Since X is the most profitable in terms of C/S ratio, it might be worth considering an increase in the sales of X, even if there is a consequent fall in the sales of Z.

(b)   Alternatively, the pricing structure of the products should be reviewed and a decision made as to whether the price of product Z should be raised so as to increase its C/S ratio (although an increase is likely to result in some fall in sales volume).

The **multi-product P/V chart** therefore helps to **identify** the following.

(a)   The overall company breakeven point

(b)   Which products should be expanded in output and which, if any, should be discontinued

(c) What effect changes in selling price and sales volume will have on the company's breakeven point and profit

A company sells three products, X, Y and Z. Cost and sales data for one period are as follows.

	X	Y	Z
Sales volume	2,000 units	2,000 units	5,000 units
Sales price per unit	$3	$4	$2
Variable cost per unit	$2.25	$3.50	$1.25
Total fixed costs	$3,250		

Required

Construct a multi-product P/V chart based on the above information on the axes below.

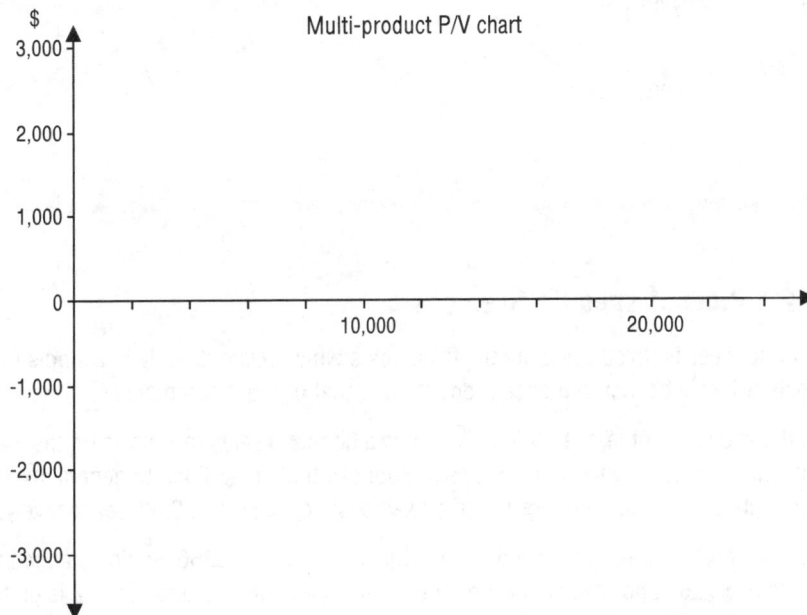

Multi-product P/V chart

Answer

	X	Y	Z	Total
				$
Contribution per unit	$0.75	$0.50	$0.75	
Budgeted contribution (total)	$1,500	$1,000	$3,750	6,250
Fixed costs				3,250
Budgeted profit				3,000

Product	Cumulative sales $		Cumulative profit $
Z	10,000	($3,750 – $3,250)	500
Z and X	16,000		2,000
Z, X and Y	24,000		3,000

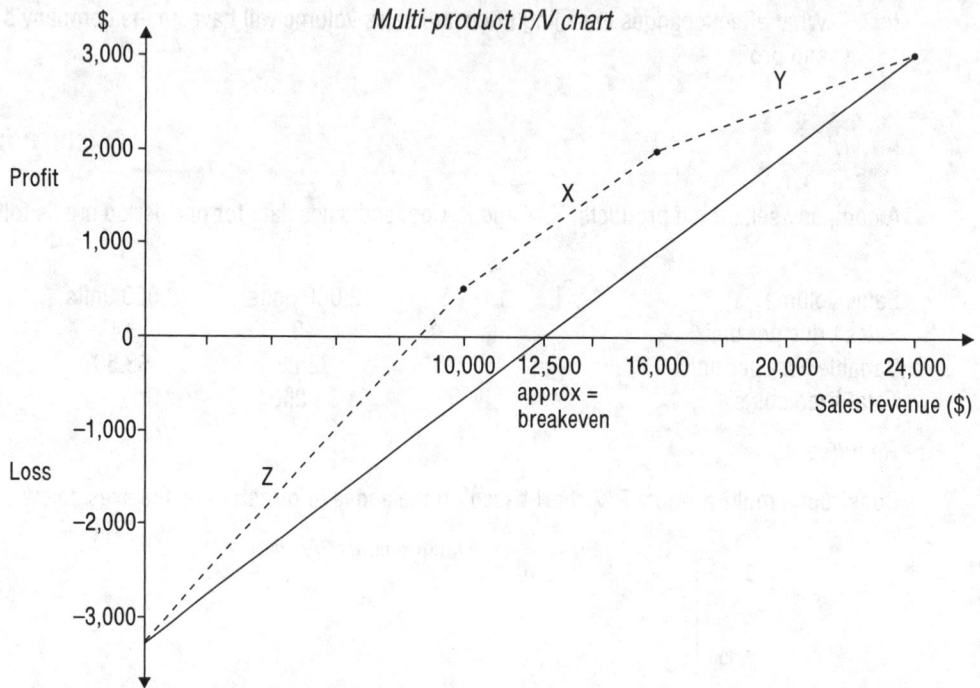

Multi-product P/V chart

8.2.1 Product-specific fixed costs

Product-specific fixed costs are the fixed costs which relate directly to a single product. Specific fixed costs will only be incurred once production of that product commences.

In the above example, the PV line assuming a constant sales mix starts on the y axis at the point where total fixed costs are incurred (–$3,250). Suppose that, in addition to general fixed costs of $3,250, products Z and X had product-specific fixed costs of $250 and $500 respectively.

Plotting product Z first, the product-specific fixed costs of $250 would be added to the total general fixed costs of $3,250 and the line for product Z would begin at –$3,500. Once Z is plotted and the MPPV line is at a profit of $250 ($3,750 – $3,500), Product X must be plotted. X has specific fixed costs of $500, therefore the MPPV line would drop vertically to show a loss of $250. X would be plotted from there to a profit of $1,250, and finally product Y with no specific fixed costs would continue as before with no drop.

The graph would appear as follows.

Profit/Loss($)

2,250
2,000

1,500
1,250
1,000

500
250
0
−250

10,000   16,000   24,000   Sales Revenue ($)

Y

X

Z

−1,000

−2,000

−3,000
−3,250
−3,500

Question

Breakeven point and sales value constraints

Sutton produces four products. Relevant data is shown below for period 2.

	Product M	Product A	Product R	Product P
C/S ratio	5%	10%	15%	20%
Maximum sales value	$200,000	$120,000	$200,000	$180,000
Minimum sales value	$50,000	$50,000	$20,000	$10,000

The fixed costs for period 2 are budgeted at $60,000.

Required

Fill in the blank in the sentence below.

The lowest breakeven sales value, subject to meeting the minimum sales value constraints, is $............

Answer

The correct answer is $390,000.

Breakeven point occurs when contribution = fixed costs.

∴ Minimum breakeven point occurs when contribution is $60,000.

Contribution achieved from minimum sales value

		$
M	5% × $50,000	2,500
A	10% × $50,000	5,000
R	15% × $20,000	3,000
P	20% × $10,000	2,000
		12,500

Product P has the highest C/S ratio and so should be produced first (as it earns more contribution per $ of revenue than the others).

Contribution from sales of P between minimum and maximum points = $170,000 × 20% = $34,000

∴ Required contribution from Product R (which has the next highest C/S ratio)

> = $(60,000 – 12,500 – 34,000)
> = $13,500

Revenue from Product R of $13,500/0.15 = $90,000 will produce $13,500 of contribution.

∴ Lowest breakeven sales

> = $130,000 (minimum sales) + $170,000 (from P) + $90,000 (from R)
> = $390,000

9 Further aspects of CVP analysis

The usefulness of CVP analysis is restricted by its **unrealistic assumptions**, such as constant sales price at all levels of activity. However, CVP has the advantage of being more **easily understood** by non-financial managers due to its graphical depiction of cost and revenue data.

Exam focus point

As well as being able to carry out CVP calculations, you may be asked to criticise the CVP approach to short-term decision-making. This means not only giving the limitations of CVP but also being aware of the advantages.

9.1 Limitations and advantages

9.1.1 Limitations

(a) It is assumed that fixed costs are the same in total and variable costs are the same per unit at all levels of output. This assumption is a great simplification.

    (i) Fixed costs will change if output falls or increases substantially (most fixed costs are step costs).

    (ii) The variable cost per unit will decrease where economies of scale are made at higher output volumes, but the variable cost per unit will also eventually rise when diseconomies of scale begin to appear at even higher volumes of output (for example the extra cost of labour in overtime working).

    The assumption is only correct within a normal range or relevant range of output. It is generally assumed that both the budgeted output and the breakeven point lie within this relevant range.

(b) It is assumed that sales prices will be constant at all levels of activity. This may not be true, especially at higher volumes of output, where the price may have to be reduced to win the extra sales.

(c) Production and sales are assumed to be the same, so that the consequences of any increase in inventory levels or of 'de-stocking' are ignored.

(d) Uncertainty in the estimates of fixed costs and unit variable costs is often ignored.

9.1.2 Advantages

(a) Graphical representation of cost and revenue data (breakeven charts) can be more easily understood by non-financial managers.

(b) A breakeven model enables profit or loss at any level of activity within the range for which the model is valid to be determined, and the C/S ratio can indicate the relative profitability of different products.

(c) Highlighting the breakeven point and the margin of safety gives managers some indication of the level of risk involved.

Chapter Roundup

- **Cost volume profit (CVP)/breakeven analysis** is the study of the interrelationships between costs, volume and profit at various levels of activity.

- In a breakeven chart, the x axis is the volume of production and sales and the y axis represents money value (revenue and cost). The chart is prepared by drawing a line to show total revenue at all levels of sales, and a total cost line to show total costs at all levels of production and sales. The **breakeven point** is where the **sales revenue** line and **total cost** line intersect.

- To perform breakeven analysis for a multi-product organisation, either a **constant sales mix** must be assumed, or all products must have the **same C/S ratio**.

- The **breakeven point** for a standard sales mix of products is calculated by dividing the total fixed costs by the weighted average contribution per unit, or by the weighted average C/S ratio.

- The **breakeven point in terms of sales revenue** can be calculated by dividing the fixed costs (= required contribution) by the weighted average C/S ratio.

- The **margin of safety** for a multi-product organisation is equal to the budgeted sales in the standard mix less the breakeven sales in the standard mix. It should be expressed as a percentage of the budgeted sales.

- The sales mix required to achieve a **target profit** is the sales mix that will earn a contribution equal to the fixed costs plus the target profit.

- **Breakeven charts** for multiple products can be drawn if a constant product sales mix is assumed.

  The **P/V chart** can show information about each product individually.

- The usefulness of CVP analysis is restricted by its **unrealistic assumptions**, such as constant sales price at all levels of activity. However, CVP has the advantage of being more **easily understood** by non-financial managers due to its graphical depiction of cost and revenue data.

Quick Quiz

1   Fill in the blanks.

   Breakeven point in units for a multi-product organisation = Total fixed costs divided by

   _____ .

   Breakeven point in sales revenue for a multi-product organisation = Total fixed costs divided by

   _____ .

2   C/S ratio = P/V ratio × 100. **True or false?**

3   Fill in the blanks.

   Margin of safety (as %) = $\left(\dfrac{\text{................. sales} - \text{................. sales}}{\text{................. sales}} \right) \times 100\%$

4   Mark the following on the breakeven chart below.

    •   Profit   •   Variable costs
    •   Sales revenue   •   Fixed costs
    •   Total costs   •   Breakeven point
    •   Margin of safety

5   Mark the following on the P/V chart below.

    •   Breakeven point   •   Contribution
    •   Fixed costs   •   Profit

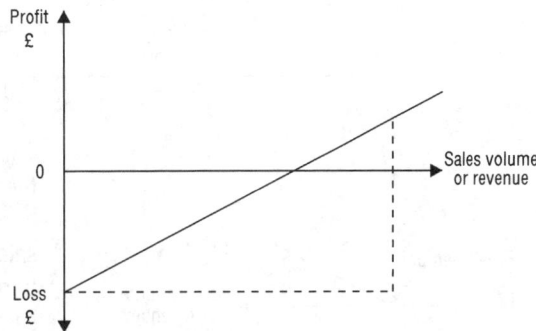

6   Which of the following is not a major assumption of breakeven analysis?

A   It can only apply to one product or a constant sales mix.
B   Fixed costs are the same in total and unit variable costs are the same at all levels of output.
C   Sales prices vary in line with levels of activity.
D   Production level is equal to sales level.

7   Choose the appropriate words from those highlighted and fill in the blanks.

When showing multiple products individually on a P/V chart, the products are shown from **left to right/right to left** in order of **increasing/decreasing** size of C/S ratio. The line joining the two ends of the dotted line (which shows ....) indicates
....

8   Choose the appropriate words from those highlighted.

The assumption in breakeven analysis that variable cost is the same per unit at all levels of output is a great simplification. The variable cost per unit will decrease where (1) **economies/diseconomies** of scale are made at higher volumes of output, but will also eventually rise where (2) **economies/diseconomies** of scale begin to appear at even (3) **higher/lower** volumes of output.

Answers to Quick Quiz

1   Weighted average contribution per unit

        Weighted average C/S ratio

2   False. The C/S ratio is another name for the P/V ratio.

3   Margin of safety (as %) = $\left(\dfrac{\text{Budgeted sales} - \text{breakeven sales}}{\text{Budgeted sales}} \right) \times 100\%$

4

5

The gradient of the straight line is the contribution per unit (if the horizontal axis is measured in sales units) or the C/S ratio (if the horizontal axis is measured in sales value).

6   C. Sales prices **are constant** at all levels of activity.

7   When showing multiple products individually on a P/V chart, the products are shown from left to right, in order of decreasing size of C/S ratio. The line joining the two ends of the dotted line (which shows the cumulative profit/loss and the cumulative sales) indicates the average profit which will be earned from sales of the products in the mix.

8   (1)   Economies
        (2)   Diseconomies
        (3)   Higher

Now try the questions below from the Practice Question Bank

Number	Level	Marks	Approximate time
Section A Q26	Examination	2	4 mins
Section A Q27	Examination	2	4 mins
Section A Q28	Examination	2	4 mins
Section A Q29	Examination	2	4 mins
Section A Q30	Examination	2	4 mins
Section C Q1	Examination	20	39 mins

Limiting factor analysis

Introduction

We have looked at **limiting factor analysis** in connection with throughput accounting in Chapter 2d and you will have encountered it in your earlier studies.

When there is more than one resource constraint, the technique of **linear programming** can be used. A multiple scarce resource problem can be solved using a **graphical method** and **simultaneous equations**.

We also look at the meaning and calculation of **shadow prices** and **slack.**

Study guide

		Intellectual level
B3	**Limiting factors**	
(a)	Identify limiting factors in a scarce resource situation and select an appropriate technique.	2
(b)	Determine the optimal production plan where an organisation is restricted by a single limiting factor, including within the context of 'make' or 'buy' decisions.	2
(c)	Formulate and solve a multiple scarce resource problem both graphically and using simultaneous equations as appropriate.	2
(d)	Explain and calculate shadow prices (dual prices) and discuss their implications on decision-making and performance management.	2
(e)	Calculate slack and explain the implications of the existence of slack for decision-making and performance management. (Excluding simplex and sensitivity to changes in objective functions)	2

Exam guide

Linear programming is a popular topic in management accounting exams and is likely to be examined as a mixture of calculations and discussion. There is an article on linear programming on the ACCA website, written by a member of the examining team (ACCA, 2015).

1 Limiting factors

FAST FORWARD

All companies have a maximum capacity for producing goods or providing services because there is a limit to the amount of resources available. There is always at least one resource that is more restrictive than others: this is known as a **limiting factor**.

Key term

A **limiting factor** is any factor that is in scarce supply and that stops the organisation from expanding its activities further, so that there is a maximum level of activity at which the organisation can operate.

Knowledge brought forward from earlier studies

- An organisation might be faced with just one limiting factor (other than maximum sales demand) but there might also be several scarce resources, with two or more of them putting an effective limit on the level of activity that can be achieved.

- Examples of limiting factors include sales demand and production constraints.

  - **Labour**. The limit may be either in terms of total quantity of labour or a limit to the availability of employees with particular skills.

  - **Materials**. There may be insufficient available materials to produce enough units to satisfy sales demand.

  - **Machine capacity**. There may not be sufficient machine capacity for the production required to meet sales demand.

- It is assumed in limiting factor analysis that management will decide to use its scarce resources in such a way as to maximise total contribution (and so profit). **In other words, marginal costing ideas are applied.**
  - If there is just one limiting factor, total contribution will be maximised by earning the biggest possible contribution per unit of limiting factor. For example, if grade A labour is the limiting factor, contribution will be maximised by earning the biggest contribution per hour of grade A labour worked.
  - The limiting factor decision therefore involves the determination of the contribution earned per unit of limiting factor by each different product.
  - If the sales demand is limited, the profit-maximising decision will be to produce the top-ranked product(s) up to the sales demand limit.
- In limiting factor decisions, we generally assume that fixed costs are the same whatever product or service mix is selected, so that the only relevant costs are variable costs.
- When there is just one limiting factor, the technique for establishing the contribution-maximising product mix or service mix is to rank the products or services in order of the contribution they earn per unit of limiting factor.
- Remember the distinction between limiting factor analysis and throughput accounting from Chapter 2d, Section 3.2. Pay attention to the question for information on which technique is expected. If the company is operating in a throughput environment, then the TA approach should be used.

Exam focus point

If a resource is the limiting factor, **contribution** will be **maximised** by earning the biggest possible contribution per unit of the limiting factor.

Where there is just one limiting factor, products should be ranked in order of priority (for production and sale) in order of the contribution they earn per unit of the limiting factor.

1.1 Example: Limiting factor decision

Sausage makes two products, the Mash and the Sauce. Unit variable costs are as follows.

	Mash	Sauce
	$	$
Direct materials	1	3
Direct labour ($3 per hour)	6	3
Variable overhead	1	1
	8	7

The sales price per unit is $14 per Mash and $11 per Sauce. During July the available direct labour is limited to 8,000 hours. Sales demand in July is expected to be as follows.

Mash	3,000 units
Sauce	5,000 units

Required

Determine the production budget that will maximise profit, assuming that fixed costs per month are $20,000 and that there is no opening inventory of finished goods or work in progress.

Solution

Step 1   Confirm that the limiting factor is something other than sales demand.

	Mash	Sauces	Total
Labour hours per unit	2 hrs	1 hr	
Sales demand	3,000 units	5,000 units	
Labour hours needed	6,000 hrs	5,000 hrs	11,000 hrs
Labour hours available			8,000 hrs
Shortfall			3,000 hrs

Labour is a limiting factor on production.

Step 2   Identify the contribution earned by each product per unit of scarce resource; that is, per labour hour worked.

	Mash $	Sauce $
Sales price	14	11
Variable cost	8	7
Unit contribution	6	4
Labour hours per unit	2 hrs	1 hr
Contribution per labour hour (= per unit of limiting factor)	$3	$4

Although the Mash earns a higher unit contribution than the Sauce, two units of Sauce can be made in the time it takes to make one unit of Mash. Because labour is in short supply it is therefore more profitable to make Sauces than Mashes.

Step 3   Determine the budgeted production and sales. Sufficient Sauces will be made to meet the full sales demand, and the remaining labour hours available will then be used to make Mashes.

(a)

Product	Demand	Hours required	Hours available	Priority for manufacture
Sauces	5,000	5,000	5,000	1st
Mashes	3,000	6,000	3,000 (bal)	2nd
		11,000	8,000	

(b)

Product	Units	Hours needed	Contribution per unit $	Total $
Sauces	5,000	5,000	4	20,000
Mashes (balance)	1,500	3,000	6	9,000
		8,000		29,000
Less fixed costs				20,000
Profit				9,000

Conclusion

(a) Unit contribution is **not** the correct way to decide priorities for production and sales.

(b) Labour hours are the scarce resource in this example, therefore **contribution per labour hour** is the correct way to decide priorities for production and sales.

(c) The Sauce earns $4 contribution per labour hour, and the Mash earns $3 contribution per labour hour. Sauces therefore make more profitable use of the scarce resource, and should be manufactured first.

(d) Sauces should be made only up to the limit of sales demand. If there is any unused labour time after this quantity of Sauces has been produced, the remaining time should be used to make the product that earns the next-highest contribution per labour hour, which in this example is the Mash.

1.2 Two potentially limiting factors

You may be asked to deal with situations where two factors are potentially the limiting factor (and there are also sales demand limitations). The approach in these situations is to find out which factor (if any) prevents the business from fulfilling maximum sales demand.

Exam focus point

> Where there is a **maximum potential sales demand** for an organisation's products, they should be ranked in order of contribution-earning ability per unit of the limiting factor. The contribution-maximising decision will be to produce the top-ranked products (or to provide the top-ranked services) up to the sales demand limit.

1.3 Example: Two potentially limiting factors

Lucky manufactures and sells three products, X, Y and Z, for which budgeted sales demand, unit selling prices and unit variable costs are as follows.

	X		Y		Z	
Budgeted sales demand	550 units		500 units		400 units	
	$	$	$	$	$	$
Unit sales price		16		18		14
Variable costs: materials	8		6		2	
labour	4		6		9	
		12		12		11
Unit contribution		4		6		3

The organisation has existing inventory of 250 units of X and 200 units of Z, which it is quite willing to use up to meet sales demand. All three products use the same direct materials and the same type of direct labour. In the next year, the available supply of materials will be restricted to $4,800 (at cost) and the available supply of labour to $6,600 (at cost).

Required

Determine what product mix and sales mix would maximise the organisation's profits in the next year.

Solution

There are **two scarce resources** that may be a limiting factor: direct materials and direct labour. However, this is not certain. Because there is a limit to sales demand, either of the following may apply.

- There is **no limiting factor at all**, except sales demand.
- There is **only one scarce resource** that prevents the full potential sales demand being achieved.

Step 1   Establish which of the resources, if any, is scarce.

	X	Y	Z
	Units	Units	Units
Budgeted sales	550	500	400
Inventory in hand	250	0	200
Minimum production to meet demand	300	500	200

	Minimum production to meet sales demand	Required materials at cost	Required labour at cost
	Units	$	$
X	300	2,400	1,200
Y	500	3,000	3,000
Z	200	400	1,800
Total required		5,800	6,000
Total available		4,800	6,600
(Shortfall)/Surplus		(1,000)	600

Materials are a limiting factor, but labour is not.

Step 2   **Rank** X, Y and Z in order of contribution earned per $1 of direct materials consumed.

	X	Y	Z
	$	$	$
Unit contribution	4	6	3
Cost of materials	8	6	2
Contribution per $1 materials	$0.50	$1.00	$1.50
Ranking	3rd	2nd	1st

Step 3   **Determine a production plan.** Z should be manufactured up to the limit where units produced plus units held in inventory will meet sales demand; then Y should be produced second and X third, until all the available materials are used up.

Ranking	Product	Sales demand less units held Units	Production quantity Units		Materials cost $
1st	Z	200	200	(× $2)	400
2nd	Y	500	500	(× $6)	3,000
3rd	X	300	175	(× $8)	1,400*
		Total available			4,800

* Balancing amount using up total available.

Step 4   **Draw up a budget.** The profit-maximising budget is as follows.

Product	Units	Material cost / unit $	Total material cost $	Contribution per $1 of material $	Total contribution $
Z opening inventory	200				
Z production	200				
	400	$2	800	$1.50	1,200
Y production	500	$6	3,000	$1.00	3,000
X opening inventory	250				
X production	175				
	425	$8	3,400	$0.50	1,700
				Total contribution	5,900

2 Limiting factor analysis – make or buy decisions and scarce resources
6/11, 6/12

FAST FORWARD

In a situation where a company is able to **subcontract work to make up a shortfall in its own in-house production capabilities**, its total costs will be minimised if those units bought from the subcontractor have the lowest extra variable cost per unit of scarce resource saved by buying. Extra variable cost is the difference between the variable cost of in-house production and the cost of buying from the subcontractor.

2.1 Combining internal and external production

An organisation might **want to do more things than it has the resources for**, and so its alternatives would be as follows.

(a) Make the best use of the available resources and ignore the opportunities to buy help from outside by subcontracting some of the work

(b) Combine internal resources with buying externally so as to produce (and sell) more and so increase profitability

Buying help from outside (subcontracting production work) is justifiable if it **adds to profits**.

A further decision is then required on how to split the work between **internal** and **external** effort. What parts of the work should be given to suppliers or subcontractors so as to maximise profitability?

In a situation where a company must **subcontract work to make up a shortfall in its own in-house capabilities**, its total costs will be minimised if those units bought have the lowest extra variable cost of buying per unit of scarce resource saved by buying. Extra variable cost is the difference between the variable cost of in-house production and the cost of buying from the subcontractor.

2.1.1 Example: Make or buy decisions with scarce resources

MM manufactures three components, S, A and T, using the same machines for each. The budget for the next year calls for the production and assembly of 4,000 of each component. The variable production cost per unit of the final product is as follows.

	Machine hours	Variable cost
		$
1 unit of S	3	20
1 unit of A	2	36
1 unit of T	4	24
Assembly		20
		100

Only 24,000 hours of machine time will be available during the year, and a subcontractor has quoted the following unit prices for supplying components: S $29; A $40; T $34.

Required

Advise MM.

Solution

The organisation's budget calls for 36,000 hours of machine time, if all the components are to be produced in-house. Only 24,000 hours are available, and so there is a shortfall of 12,000 hours of machine time, which is therefore a limiting factor. The shortage can be overcome by subcontracting the equivalent of 12,000 machine hours of output to the subcontractor.

The assembly costs are not relevant costs because they are unaffected by the decision.

The decision rule is to **minimise the extra variable costs of subcontracting per unit of scarce resource saved** (that is, per machine hour saved).

	S	A	T
	$	$	$
Variable cost of making	20	36	24
Variable cost of buying	29	40	34
Extra variable cost of buying	9	4	10
Machine hours saved by buying	3 hrs	2 hrs	4 hrs
Extra variable cost of buying per hour saved	$3	$2	$2.50

This analysis shows that it is **cheaper to buy A than to buy T** and it is **most expensive to buy S**. The **priority for making** the components in-house will be in the **reverse order**: S, then T, then A. There are enough machine hours to make all 4,000 units of S (12,000 hours) and to produce 3,000 units of T (another 12,000 hours). 12,000 hours' production of T and A must be subcontracted.

The cost-minimising and so profit-maximising make and buy schedule is as follows.

Component	Machine hours used/saved	Number of units	Unit variable cost $	Total variable cost $
Make: S	12,000	4,000	20	80,000
T	12,000	3,000	24	72,000
	24,000			152,000
Buy: T	4,000	1,000	34	34,000
A	8,000	4,000	40	160,000
	12,000			346,000

Total variable cost of components, excluding assembly costs = $346,000

Question
Make or buy and limiting factors

TW manufactures two products, the D and the E, using the same material for each. Annual demand for the D is 9,000 units, while demand for the E is 12,000 units. The variable production cost per unit of the D is $10, that of the E $15. The D requires 3.5 kg of raw material per unit, the E requires 8 kg of raw material per unit. Supply of raw material will be limited to 87,500 kg during the year.

A subcontractor has quoted prices of $17 per unit for the D and $25 per unit for the E to supply the product. How many of each product should TW manufacture in order to maximise profits?

Required

Fill in the blanks in the sentence below.

TW should manufacture .... units of D and .... units of E to maximise profits.

Answer

The correct answer is: TW should manufacture 9,000 units of D and 7,000 units of E.

	D $ per unit	E $ per unit
Variable cost of making	10	15
Variable cost of buying	17	25
Extra variable cost of buying	7	10
Raw material saved by buying	3.5 kg	8 kg
Extra variable cost of buying per kg saved	$2	$1.25
Priority for internal manufacture	1st	2nd

Production plan	Material used kg
∴ Make D (9,000 × 3.5 kg)	31,500
E (7,000 × 8 kg)	56,000
Total materials consumed (maximum available)	87,500

The remaining 5,000 units of E should be purchased from the subcontractor.

2.2 Non-financial considerations in 'make or buy' decisions

Before management can make a final decision on whether they will manufacture a product in-house, or source it from external suppliers, a number of non-financial factors should be considered. The main issues are as follows.

Control. When a product is manufactured in-house, the company has control over **quality, delivery times, reliability** and **price stability**. By outsourcing, the company becomes dependent on an external supplier, despite having no influence in the external company.

Customer perception. Customers may attach importance to producing goods or services in-house, such as providing local call centre services, and in situations where customers are making a concerted effort to support local business.

Opportunity cost. A business can prevent the under utilisation of employee skills by outsourcing low skilled tasks and reallocating staff to more specialised activities.

3 The principles of linear programming   6/08

FAST FORWARD

Linear programming is a technique for solving problems of profit maximisation or cost minimisation and resource allocation. 'Programming' has nothing to do with computers: the word is simply used to denote a series of events. If a scenario contains **two or more limiting factors**, linear programming should be used to determine the contribution-maximising or cost-minimising solution.

Linear programming is a technique that may be used to determine the contribution-maximising or cost-minimising solution to a problem when there are two (or more) limiting factors, not just one.

Ranking products in order of the contribution they earn per unit of limiting factor is not possible, because there is more than one limiting factor, and the ranking of products is likely to be different for each of the limiting factors.

Linear programming can be used to identify the contribution-maximising (or cost-minimising) solution that makes the best use of all the limiting factors.

When an organisation makes and sells just two products, a graphical method can be used to formulate the linear programming problem and then solve it.

4 The graphical method   6/08, 6/10, 6/14

FAST FORWARD

The graphical method of linear programming can be used when there are just two products (or services). The steps involved are as follows.

1   Define the problem:
    (a)   Define variables
    (b)   Establish constraints
    (c)   Construct objective function
2   Draw the constraints on a graph
3   Establish the feasible region for the optimal solution
4   Determine the optimal solution

4.1 Example: WX Co

The following example will be used throughout the chapter to illustrate the graphical method of linear programming.

WX Co manufactures two products, A and B. Both products pass through two production departments, mixing and shaping. The organisation's objective is to maximise contribution to fixed costs.

Product A is sold for $1.50 whereas product B is priced at $2.00. There is unlimited demand for product A but demand for B is limited to 13,000 units per annum. The machine hours available in each department are restricted to 2,400 per annum. Other relevant data are as follows.

Machine hours required	Mixing hrs	Shaping hrs
Product A	0.06	0.04
Product B	0.08	0.12

Variable cost per unit	$
Product A	1.30
Product B	1.70

Question   Constraints

What are the constraints in the situation facing WX Co?

Answer

These are the constraints that will prevent WX from producing and selling as much of each product as it chooses.

The constraints are machine hours in each department and sales demand for product B. There is no restriction on the availability of labour hours. Selling price cannot be a constraint.

4.2 Formulating the problem

Let's formulate the linear programming problem for WX.

Step 1   **Define the variables** ·

The variables are the items whose value we are trying to decide. In this problem, the variables are the two products that WX can make and sell; we want to decide the quantities of product A and product B that should be made in order to maximise contribution (and profit).

For the graphical method of linear programming to be possible, there can be only two variables. The variables in this problem will therefore be stated as follows.

Let x = number of units of product A produced and sold.

Let y = number of units of product B produced and sold.

Step 2   **Establish the constraints**

Constraints are anything that sets a maximum or a minimum limit on the solution. Typically, there may be a maximum limit to the sales demand for each product, or a maximum limit to the amount of a production resource available, such as the quantity of a material, labour time or machine time.

In this problem there are constraints for the maximum sales demand for product B, the maximum machine hours in the Mixing Department and the maximum machine hours in the Shaping Department.

In a linear programming problem there may also be a minimum constraint, such as a minimum quantity of a product that must be made and sold to meet a confirmed customer order.

There are also non-negativity constraints. In this example, the values of x and y cannot be negative. (You cannot produce a negative quantity of a product.)

Each constraint must now be stated as a formula or 'inequality'. An inequality is similar to an equation except that the symbol 'less than or equal to' ($\leq$) or 'greater than or equal to' ($\geq$) is used instead of the equation sign (=).

(a) Consider the Mixing Department machine hours constraint.

    (i) **Each unit of product A** requires 0.06 hours of machine time. Producing five units therefore requires 5×0.06 hours of machine time and, more generally, **producing x units will require 0.06x hours**.

    (ii) Likewise, producing **y units of product B will require 0.08y hours**.

    (iii) The total machine hours needed in the mixing department to make x units of product A and y units of product B is $0.06x + 0.08y$.

    (iv) We know that this **cannot be greater in total than 2,400 hours** and so we arrive at the following inequality.

        $0.06x + 0.08y \leq 2,400$

Question

How can the constraint facing the **Shaping Department** be written as an inequality?

Answer

The constraint facing the Shaping Department can be written as follows.

$0.04x + 0.12y \leq 2,400$

The constraint has to be a 'less than or equal to' inequality, because the amount of resource used ($0.04x + 0.12y$) has to be 'less than or equal to' the amount available of 2,400 hours.

(b) The final inequality is easier to obtain. The **number of units of product B produced and sold is y** but this has to be **less than or equal to 13,000**. Our inequality is therefore as follows.

    $y \leq 13,000$

(c) We also need to add **non-negativity constraints** ($x \geq 0$, $y \geq 0$) since negative numbers of products cannot be produced. (Linear programming is simply a mathematical tool and so there is nothing in this method which guarantees that the answer will 'make sense'. An unprofitable product may produce an answer which is negative. This is mathematically correct but nonsense in operational terms. Always remember to include the non-negativity constraints. The exam markers will not appreciate 'impossible' solutions.)

Step 3 **Construct the objective function**

The objective function is a formula that states what we are trying to achieve as a solution to the problem. The objective function is always an objective of wanting to maximise something or minimise something. Typically, the objective function will be to maximise total contribution or to minimise total cost.

In the problem we are looking at here, the objective function is to maximise total contribution. We must put this into a formula.

We know that the **contribution on each type of product** is as follows.

			$ per unit
Product A	$(1.50 – 1.30)	=	0.20
Product B	$(2.00 – 1.70)	=	0.30

The **objective of the company is to maximise contribution** and so the **objective function to be maximised** is as follows.

Maximise contribution (C): 0.2x + 0.3y

The problem has now been reduced to the following four inequalities and one equation.

Maximise contribution (C) = 0.2x + 0.3y, subject to the following constraints:

$$0.06x + 0.08y \leq 2{,}400$$

$$0.04x + 0.12y \leq 2{,}400$$

$$y \leq 13{,}000$$

$$x, y \geq 0$$

4.3 Graphing the problem

Having identified the linear programme constraints, the next step is to draw these constraints on a graph. **The constraints are all drawn as straight lines**.

Remember that a **graphical solution** is **only possible** when there are **two variables** in the problem. One variable is represented by the **x axis** of the graph and one by the **y axis**. Since non-negative values are not usually allowed, the graph shows **only zero and positive values of x and y**.

4.3.1 Rules for drawing a constraint as a straight line on a graph

There are three types of constraint that you may need to draw as lines on a graph.

(a)   A constraint 'x is less than or equal to a given amount'.

For example, $x \leq 12$

This constraint is drawn by drawing the boundary limit of this constraint. The boundary is where $x = 12$. In other words, we turn the inequality into an equation and draw a line of the equation.

To draw $x = 12$, we need to plot any two points on the graph and join them up. For example:

When $y = 0$, $x = 12$

When $y = 10$, $x = 12$

The value of x is 12 whatever the value of y.

The equation $x = 12$ is drawn as a vertical line on a graph at the point where $x = 12$.

(b)   A constraint 'y is less than or equal to a given amount'.

For example, $y \leq 15$

We turn the inequality into an equation and draw a line of the equation. Here the equation is $y = 15$.

To draw $y = 15$, we need to plot any two points on the graph and join them up. For example:

When x = 0, y = 15

When x = 10, y = 15

The value of y is 15 whatever the value of x.

The equation y = 15 is drawn as a horizontal line on a graph at the point where y = 15.

(c)   The most common type of constraint is where there is a value for both x and y; for example:

$3x + 5y \leq 45$

Once again we turn the inequality into an equation and draw a line of the equation. Here the equation is 3x + 5y = 45.

To draw this line on a graph, we need to identify two points and join them up as a straight line. The two points that are easiest to plot on the graph are:

3x + 5y = 45 when x = 0. When x = 0, y = 9, so plot x = 0, y = 9 on the graph.

3x + 5y = 45 when y = 0. When y = 0, x = 15, so plot x =15, y = 0 on the graph.

Join up these two points, and you have drawn the equation on the graph for any combination of values of x and y (where x and y are not negative values).

Let's apply these rules to the linear programming problem of WX Co.

4.3.2 Drawing the constraints in the WX Co problem

In addition to the non-negativity constraints for x and y, there are three constraints in the problem.

(a)   Mixing Department hours: **0.06x + 0.08y ≤ 2,400**

Draw a line for the equation 0.06x + 0.08y = 2,400

If x = 0, y = 30,000

If y = 0, x = 40,000

Plot these two points on the graph and join them up to shown the boundary line of the constraint.

(b)   Shaping Department hours: **0.04x + 0.12y ≤ 2,400**

Draw a line for the equation 0.04x + 0.12y = 2,400

If x = 0, y = 20,000

If y = 0, x = 60,000

Plot these two points on the graph and join them up to shown the boundary line of the constraint.

(c)   Maximum sales demand for Product B: **y ≤ 13,000**

Draw the line y = 13,000.

This is a horizontal line on the graph at the point where y = 13,000, and for all value of x.

The graph should look like this.

4.3.3 Establishing the feasible region

The feasible region in a linear programming problem is the area in the graph where the combinations of x and are all 'feasible'. In other words, any combination of the values of x and y within the feasible region comply with the constraints in the linear programming problem.

When a constraint is a 'less than or equal to' (≤) constraint, all the feasible combinations of x and y are either on the boundary line (the equation line) or below it, where values of x and y are lower.

When a constraint is a 'more than or equal to' (≤) constraint, all the feasible combinations of x and y are either on the boundary line (the equation line) or above it, where values of x and y are higher.

When the constraint is a vertical line 'x ≤ a given amount', the feasible values of x cannot exceed this amount, and so are either on the equation line or to the left of it.

The feasible region for the solution of a linear programming problem is the various combinations of x and y that comply with all the constraints in the linear programming problem.

Key term

> A **feasible region** is the area contained within all of the constraint lines shown on a graphical depiction of a linear programming problem. All feasible combinations of output are contained within or located on the boundaries of the feasible region.

In the example of WX Co, the feasible region is identified as the shaded area on the graph.

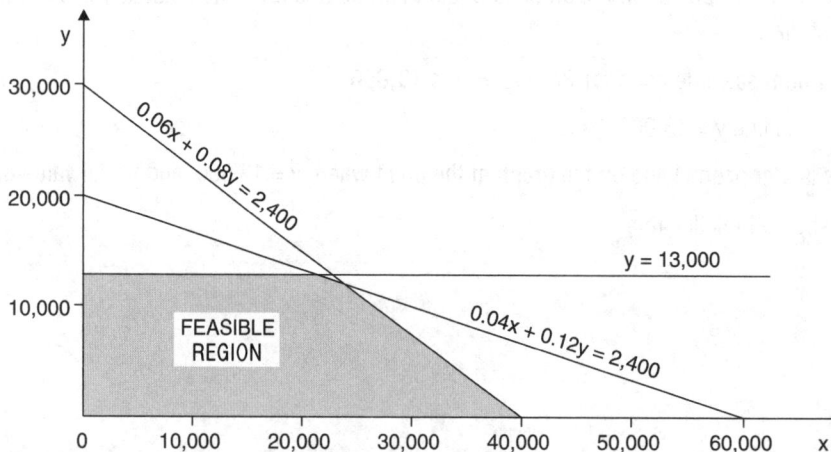

BPP
LEARNING MEDIA

Exam focus point

You may be required to draw a graph as part of an exam question. Marks will be available for labels and a title so make sure you can draw a clear graph.

4.4 Finding the optimum allocation of resources 6/08, 6/10, 12/10, 6/14

FAST FORWARD

The **optimum solution** to a linear programming problem can be found by 'sliding the iso-contribution line out'.

Having found the feasible region (which includes all the possible solutions to the problem) we need to **find which of these possible solutions is 'best'** or **optimal** in the sense that it yields the best value for the objective function – in this example, the maximum possible contribution.

Look at the feasible region of the problem faced by WX. Even in such a simple problem as this, there are a **great many possible solution points within the feasible region**. Even to write them all down would be a time-consuming process and also an unnecessary one, as we shall see.

Here is the graph of WX's problem.

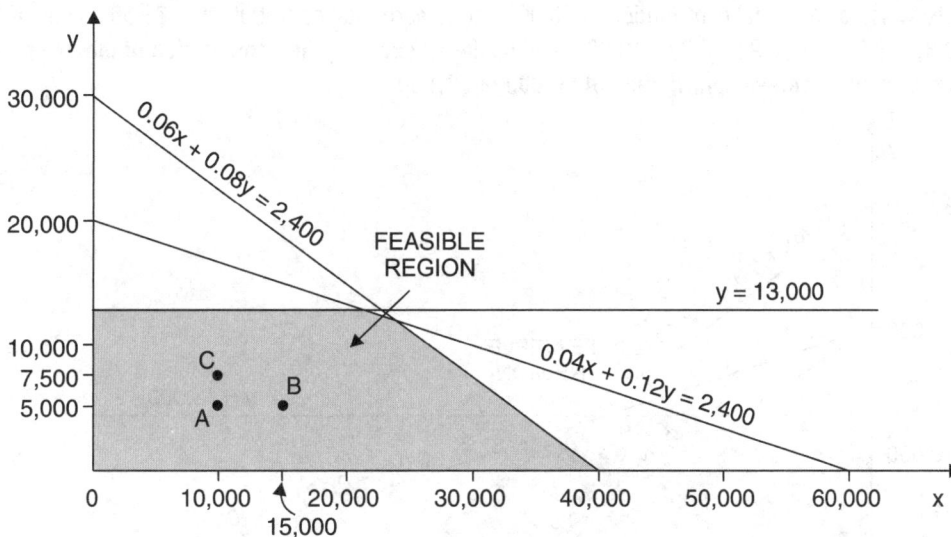

(a) Consider point A at which 10,000 units of product A and 5,000 units of product B are being manufactured. This will yield a contribution of $(10,000 \times \$0.20) + (5,000 \times \$0.30) = \$3,500$.

(b) We would clearly get more contribution at point B, where the same number of units of product B are being produced but where the number of units of product A has increased by 5,000.

(c) We would also get more contribution at point C where the number of units of product A is the same but 2,500 more units of product B are being produced.

This argument suggests that the **'best' solution** is going to be at a **point on the edge of the feasible region**, on one or more of the equation lines, rather than in the middle of it.

This still leaves us with quite a few points to look at but there is a way in which we can **narrow down still further the likely points at which the best solution will be found**. Suppose that WX wishes to earn contribution of $3,000. Given that the contribution per unit of Product A is $0.2 and the contribution per unit of Product B is $0.3, the company could sell the following combinations of the two products.

(a) 15,000 units of A, no B $(x = 15,000, y = 0)$
(b) No A, 10,000 units of B $(x = 0, y = 10,000)$.
(c) A suitable mix of the two, such as 7,500 A and 5,000 B.

The **possible combinations required to earn contribution of $3,000** could be **shown by the straight line $0.2x + 0.3y = 3,000$**.

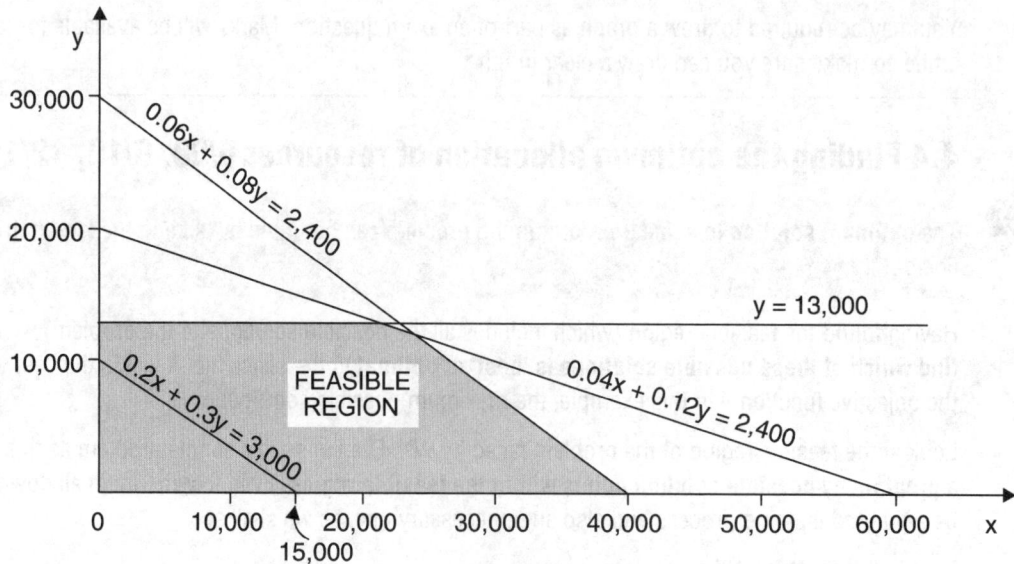

Likewise, to earn total contribution of $6,000 and to earn total contribution of $1,500, lines of 0.2x + 0.3y = 6,000 and 0.2x + 0.3y = 1,500 could be drawn **showing the combination of the two products** which would **achieve contribution of $6,000 or $1,500**.

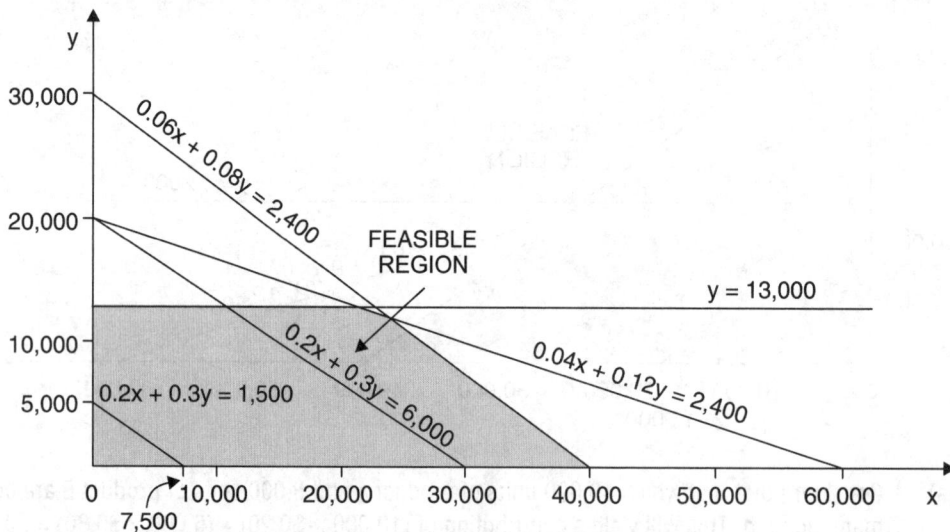

The **contribution lines are all parallel to each other**. (They are called **iso-contribution lines**, 'iso' meaning equal.) A similar line drawn for any other total contribution would also be parallel to the lines shown here. **Bigger contribution is shown by lines further from the origin** (0.2x + 0.3y = 6,000), smaller contribution by lines closer to the origin (0.2x + 0.3y = 1,500). As WX tries to increase possible contribution, we need to 'slide' any contribution line outwards from the origin, while always keeping it parallel to the other contribution lines.

As we do this there will come a point at which, if we were to move the contribution line out any further, it would cease to lie in the feasible region. Greater contribution could not be achieved, because of the constraints. In our example concerning WX this will happen, as you should test for yourself, where the contribution line just passes through the intersection of 0.06x + 0.08y = 2,400 and 0.04x + 0.12y = 2,400 (at co-ordinates (24,000, 12,000)).

The point (24,000, 12,000) will therefore give us the optimal allocation of resources (**to produce 24,000 units of A and 12,000 units of B**).

5 Using simultaneous equations

FAST FORWARD

> The optimal solution to a linear programming problem can also be found using **simultaneous equations**.

You might think that a lot of time could be saved if we started by solving the simultaneous equations in a linear programming problem and did not bother to draw the graph.

Certainly, this procedure may give the right answer, but in general, it is **not** recommended until you have shown graphically which constraints are effective in determining the optimal solution, and you have identified the feasible region. Some constraints may not affect the feasible region at all. (In particular, if a question requires 'the graphical method', you **must** draw a graph). To illustrate this point, consider the following graph.

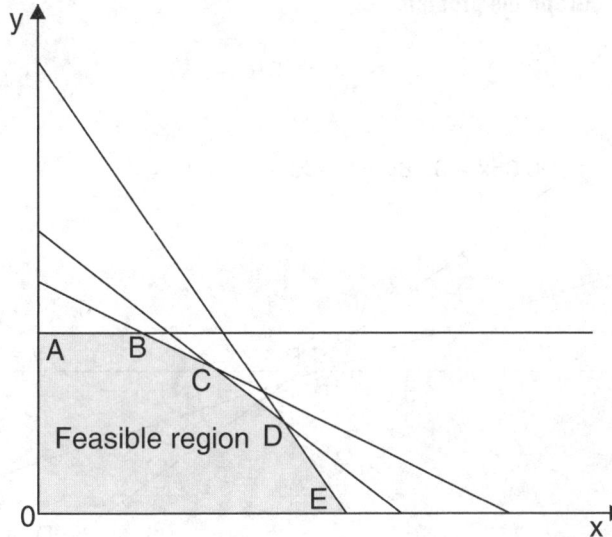

No figures have been given on the graph but the feasible region is OABCDE. When solving this problem, we would know that the optimum solution would be at one of the corners of the feasible area. We need to work out the profit at each of the corners of the feasible area and pick the one where the profit is greatest.

Once the optimum point has been determined graphically, simultaneous equations can be applied to find the exact values of x and y at this point.

Instead of a 'sliding the contribution line out' approach, **simultaneous equations** can be used to determine the optimal allocation of resources, as shown in the following example.

5.1 Example: Using simultaneous equations

The process for solving the linear programming problem for WX Co is summarised below. Let's focus on the final step to illustrate how simultaneous equations can be used to establish the contribution-maximising product mix.

Step 1

(a) **Define variables**
     x = number of units of Product A produced
     y = number of units of Product B produced

(b) **Establish the constraints**

The constraints are as follows.

$$0.06x + 0.08y \leq 2{,}400 \qquad \text{(mixing department)}$$
$$0.04x + 0.12y \leq 2{,}400 \qquad \text{(shaping department)}$$
$$y \leq 13{,}000 \qquad \text{(demand for product B)}$$
$$x, y \geq 0 \qquad \text{(non-negativity)}$$

(c) **Construct the objective function**

Product A yields a contribution of $0.20 per unit $(1.50 – 1.30).

Product B yields a contribution of $0.30 per unit $(2.00 – 1.70).

Therefore the objective is to maximise contribution (C) = 0.2x + 0.3y subject to the above constraints.

Step 2   **Graph the problem**

Step 3   **Establish feasible region**

The combinations of x and y that satisfy all three constraints are represented by the area OABCD.

Step 4   **Determine optimal solution**

Which combination will maximise contribution? Obviously, the more units of x and y, the bigger the contribution will be, and the optimal solution will be at point B, C or D. It will not be at A, since at A, y = 13,000 and x = 0, whereas at B, y = 13,000 (the same) and x is greater than zero.

Using simultaneous equations to calculate the value of x and y at each of points B, C and D, and then working out total contribution at each point from this, we can establish the contribution-maximising product mix.

Point B

(1)	y	=	13,000
(2)	0.04x + 0.12y	=	2,400
Substitute (1) into (2)	0.04x + 0.12 (13,000)	=	2,400
	0.04x + 1,560	=	2,400
	0.04x	=	840
	x	=	21,000

When x = 21,000 and y = 13,000, total contribution = $(21,000 × 0.2) + $(13,000 × 0.3) = $4,200 + $3,900 = $8,100.

Point C

(1)	$0.06x + 0.08y$	=	2,400
(2)	$0.04x + 0.12y$	=	2,400
Multiply (1) by 2			
(3)	$0.12x + 0.16y$	=	4,800
Multiply (2) by 3			
(4)	$0.12x + 0.36y$	=	7,200
Subtract (3) from (4)	$0.20y$	=	2,400
		=	12,000
Substitute in (1)	$0.06x + 0.08 (12,000)$	=	2,400
	$0.06x$	=	1,440
	x	=	24,000

When x = 24,000 and y = 12,000, total contribution = \$(24,000 × 0.2) + \$(12,000 × 0.3) = \$4,800 + \$3,600 = \$8,400.

Point D

Total contribution = $40,000 \times \$0.20 = \$8,000$.

Comparing B, C and D, we can see that contribution is maximised at C, by making 24,000 units of product A and 12,000 units of product B, to earn a contribution of \$8,400.

6 Slack and surplus 6/08, 6/14

Slack occurs when maximum availability of a resource is not used: slack is the amount of the unused resource or other constraint, where the constraint is a 'less than or equal to' constraint.

Surplus occurs when more than a minimum requirement is used: surplus is the excess over the minimum amount of constraint, where the constraint is a 'more than or equal to' constraint.

Key term

Slack occurs when maximum availability of a resource or other constraining factor is not used.

If, at the optimal solution, the amount of the resource used equals the amount of the resource available, there is **no spare capacity** of a resource and so there is **no slack**.

If, at the optimal solution, the amount of the resource used is less than the amount of the resource available, there is **spare capacity** for the resource and so there is **slack**.

For example, a machine shop makes boxes (B) and tins (T). Contribution per box is \$5 and per tin is \$7. A box requires 3 hours of machine processing time, 16 kg of raw materials and 6 labour hours. A tin requires 10 hours of machine processing time, 4 kg of raw materials and 6 labour hours. In a given month, 330 hours of machine processing time, 400 kg of raw material and 240 labour hours are available. The manufacturing technology used means that at least 12 tins must be made every month. The constraints are:

$3B + 10T \leq 330$
$16B + 4T \leq 400$
$6B + 6T \leq 240$
$\qquad T \geq 12$
$\qquad B \geq 0$

The solution is not shown in detail here, but the optimal solution is found to be to manufacture and sell 10 boxes and 30 tins.

If we substitute these values into the inequalities representing the constraints, we can determine whether the constraints are binding or whether there is slack.

| Machine time: | $(3 \times 10) + (10 \times 30) = 330$ = availability |
| | Constraint is **binding**. |

| Raw materials: | $(16 \times 10) + (4 \times 30) = 280 < 400$ |
| | There is **slack** of 120 kg of raw materials. |

| Labour: | $(6 \times 10) + (6 \times 30) = 240$ = availability |
| | Constraint is **binding**. |

If a minimum quantity of a resource must be used and, at the optimal solution, **more than that quantity is used**, there is a **surplus** on the minimum requirement. This is shown here in the production of tins where the optimal production is 30 tins but $T \geq 12$. There is therefore a **surplus** of 18 tins over the minimum production requirement.

You can see from this that slack is associated with $\leq$ constraints and surplus with $\geq$ constraints. Machine time and labour are **binding constraints** so they have been used to their full capacity. It can be argued that if more machine time and labour could be obtained, more boxes and tins could be produced and contribution increased.

6.1 Implications of slack and surplus

If the amount of slack is high, it is an indication of an inefficient use of a particular resource. If possible, the resource should be reallocated to another part of the business. Resources such as labour time may even be subcontracted to another business.

If slack is low, then management should be alert to the risk that this resource could become a binding constraint. If the resource is a particular material, management should investigate whether additional suppliers can be identified. If the resource is labour time, the human resources department should be readied for a recruitment drive should it be needed. This way, if the availability of scarce resources increases, the company is in a better position to maximise profitability.

7 Shadow prices 6/08, 6/10, 12/10

FAST FORWARD

> The **shadow price** or **dual price** of a limiting factor is the increase in value which would be created by having one additional unit of the limiting factor at its original cost.

Key term

> The **shadow price** or dual price of a constraint factor is the amount of change in the value of the objective function (for example, the increase in contribution) created by the availability of one extra unit of the limited resource at its original cost.

In terms of linear programming, the shadow price is the **extra contribution or profit that may be earned by relaxing a binding resource constraint by one unit**.

Suppose the availability of materials is a binding constraint. Suppose that if one extra kilogram becomes available then an alternative production mix becomes optimal. As a result, the contribution increases over the original production mix contribution by $2. The shadow price of a kilogram of material is therefore $2.

Note, however, that this increase in contribution of $2 per extra kilogram of material made available is calculated on the **assumption** that the **extra kilogram would cost the normal variable amount**.

Note the following points.

(a) The shadow price therefore represents the maximum **premium** above the basic rate that an organisation should be **willing to pay for one extra unit** of a resource.

(b) Since shadow prices indicate the effect of a one unit change in a constraint, they provide a measure of the **sensitivity** of the result.

(c) The **shadow price** of a constraint that is **not binding** at the optimal solution is **zero**.

(d)   Shadow prices are **only valid for a small range** before the constraint becomes non-binding or different resources become critical.

Depending on the resource in question, shadow prices enable management to make **better informed decisions** about the payment of overtime premiums, bonuses, premiums on small orders of raw materials, and so on.

7.1 Limiting factors and shadow prices

Whenever there are limiting factors, there are **opportunity costs**. These are the **benefits forgone** by using a limiting factor in one way instead of in the next most profitable way.

For example, suppose that an organisation provides two services X and Y, which earn a contribution of $24 and $18 per unit respectively. Service X requires four labour hours, and service Y two hours. Only 5,000 labour hours are available, and potential demand is for 1,000 of each of X and Y.

Labour hours are a limiting factor, and with X earning $6 per hour and Y earning $9 per hour, the profit-maximising decision would be as follows.

	Services	Hours	Contribution $
Y	1,000	2,000	18,000
X (balance)	750	3,000	18,000
		5,000	36,000

Priority is given to Y because the **opportunity cost** of providing Y instead of more of X is $6 per hour (X's contribution per labour hour), and since Y earns $9 per hour, the incremental benefit of providing Y instead of X would be $3 per hour.

If extra labour hours could be made available, more X (up to 1,000) would be provided, and an extra contribution of $6 per hour could be earned. Similarly, if fewer labour hours were available, the decision would be to provide fewer X and to keep provision of Y at 1,000, and so the loss of labour hours would cost the organisation $6 per hour in lost contribution. This $6 per hour, the **marginal contribution-earning potential of the limiting factor at the profit-maximising output level**, is referred to as the **shadow price** (or **dual price**) of the limiting factor.

Note that the shadow price only applies on the assumption that the extra unit of resource can be obtained at its **normal variable cost**. The shadow price also indicates the amount by which contribution could fall if an organisation is deprived of one unit of the scarce resource.

The shadow price of a resource is its **internal opportunity cost**. This is the marginal contribution towards fixed costs and profit that can be earned for each unit of the limiting factor that is available.

Depending on the resource in question, shadow prices enable management to make **better informed decisions** about the payment of overtime premiums, bonuses, premiums on small orders of raw materials, and so on, in order to obtain additional units of a limiting resource.

7.2 Linear programming and shadow prices

In terms of linear programming, the **shadow price** is the **extra contribution (and so profit) that may be earned by obtaining one extra unit of a binding resource constraint**.

Suppose the availability of materials is a binding constraint. If one extra kilogram becomes available so that an alternative production mix becomes optimal, with a resulting increase over the original production mix contribution of $2, the shadow price of a kilogram of material is $2.

Note, however, that this increase in contribution of $2 per extra kilogram of material made available is calculated on the **assumption** that the **extra kilogram would cost the normal variable amount**.

Note the following points.

(a)   The shadow price therefore represents the maximum **premium** above the basic rate that an organisation should be **willing to pay for one extra unit** of a resource.

(b)   Since shadow prices indicate the effect of a one unit change in a constraint, they provide a measure of the **sensitivity** of the result.

(c)   The **shadow price** of a constraint that is **not binding** at the optimal solution is **zero**. In other words, if there is slack for a constraining resource, the shadow price (dual price) of the resource is $0.

(d)   Shadow prices are **only valid for up to a limited number of additional units**, because if additional quantities of a binding constraint are obtained, another constraint will eventually become a binding constraint instead.

7.3 Example: Calculating shadow prices

This example revisits the scenario faced by WX Co which was used to demonstrate the graphical method of linear programming earlier in the chapter. The key points are recapped below.

WX manufactures two products, A and B. Both products pass through two production departments, mixing and shaping. The organisation's objective is to maximise contribution to fixed costs.

Product A is sold for $1.50 whereas product B is priced at $2.00. There is unlimited demand for product A but demand for B is limited to 13,000 units per annum. The machine hours available in each department are restricted to 2,400 per annum. Other relevant data are as follows.

Machine hours required	Mixing hrs	Shaping hrs
Product A	0.06	0.04
Product B	0.08	0.12

Variable cost per unit	$
Product A	1.30
Product B	1.70

The constraints are:

$$0.06x + 0.08y \leq 2,400$$
$$0.04x + 0.12y \leq 2,400$$
$$y \leq 13,000$$
$$x,y \geq 0$$

The objective function is:

Contribution (C) = 0.2x + 0.3y

The optimal solution is where x = 24,000 and y = 12,000, and total contribution = $(24,000 × 0.2) + $(12,000 × 0.3) = $4,800 + $3,600 = $8,400.

The availability of time in both departments are limiting factors because both are used up fully in the optimal product mix. Machine time in both departments are a limiting resource, which means that machine time in the Mixing Department and machine time in the Shaping Department both have a shadow price greater than $0.

Let us therefore calculate the effect if **one extra hour of Shaping Department machine time** was made available so that 2,401 hours were available.

The new optimal product mix would be at the intersection of the two constraint lines 0.06x + 0.08y = 2,400 and 0.04x + 0.12y = 2,401.

Solution by simultaneous equations (workings not shown) gives x = 23,980 and y = 12,015.

(You should solve the problem yourself if you are doubtful about the derivation of the solution.)

Product	Units	Contribution per unit $	Total contribution $
A	23,980	0.20	4,796.0
B	12,015	0.30	3,604.5
			8,400.5

Contribution in original problem   8,400.0

Increase in contribution from one extra hour of shaping time   0.5

The **shadow price** of an hour of machining time in the Shaping Department is therefore $0.50. It would add to total contribution if additional machine hours could be made available in the department for less than $0.50 per hour on top of the normal variable cost of the machine time.

This means that extra machine capacity could be rented, for example, provided the cost premium is less than $0.50 per hour.

This value of machine time only applies as long as shaping machine time is a limiting factor. If more and more machine hours become available, there will eventually be so much machine time that it is no longer a limiting factor.

Question

Shadow prices

What is the shadow price of one hour of machine time in the Mixing Department?

A $3   C $10.50

B $7   D $1,193

Answer

The correct answer is A.

If we assume one more hour of machine time in the Mixing Department is available, the new optimal solution is at the intersection of $0.06x + 0.08y = 2,401$ and $0.04x + 0.12y = 2,400$

Solution by simultaneous equations gives $x = 24,030$, $y = 11,990$

Product	Units	Contribution per unit $	Total contribution $
A	24,030	0.20	4,806
B	11,990	0.30	3,597
			8,403

Contribution in original problem   8,400

Reduction in contribution   3

∴ Shadow price of one hour of machine time in the mixing department is $3.

Chapter Roundup

- All companies have a maximum capacity for producing goods or providing services, because there is a limit to the amount of resources available. There is always at least one resource that is more restrictive than others: this is known as a **limiting factor**.

- In a situation where a company is able to **subcontract work to make up a shortfall in its own in-house production capabilities**, its total costs will be minimised if those units bought from the subcontractor have the lowest extra variable cost per unit of scarce resource saved by buying. Extra variable cost is the difference between the variable cost of in-house production and the cost of buying from the subcontractor.

- **Linear programming** is a technique for solving problems of profit maximisation or cost minimisation and resource allocation. 'Programming' has nothing to do with computers: the word is simply used to denote a series of events. If a scenario contains **two or more limiting factors**, linear programming should be used to determine the contribution-maximising or cost-minimising solution.

- The graphical method of linear programming can be used when there are just two products (or services). The steps involved are as follows.

   1   Define the problem:

       (a)   Define variables
       (b)   Establish constraints
       (c)   Construct objective function

   2   Draw the constraints on a graph.
   3   Establish the feasible region for the optimal solution.
   4   Determine the optimal solution.

- The **optimum solution** to a linear programming problem can be found by 'sliding the iso-contribution line out'.

- The optimal solution to a linear programming problem can also be found using **simultaneous equations**.

- **Slack** occurs when maximum availability of a resource is not used: slack is the amount of the unused resource or other constraint where the constraint is a 'less than or equal to' constraint.

- **Surplus** occurs when more than a minimum requirement is used: surplus is the excess over the minimum amount of constraint, where the constraint is a 'more than or equal to' constraint.

- The **shadow price** or **dual price** of a limiting factor is the increase in value which would be created by having one additional unit of the limiting factor at its original cost.

1   Fill in the blanks.

The shadow price of a scarce resource indicates the amount by which contribution would
.... if an organisation were deprived of one unit of the resource. The shadow
price only applies while the extra unit of resource can be obtained at its .... cost.

2   Put the following steps in the graphical approach to linear programming in the correct order.

Draw a graph of the constraints	Establish constraints
Define variables	Construct objective function
Establish the feasible region	Determine optimal product mix

3   In what circumstances does slack arise?

A   At the optimal solution, when the resource used equals the resource available

B   At the optimal solution, when a minimum quantity of a resource must be used, and more than
that quantity is used

C   At the optimal solution, when the resource used is less than the resource available

D   At the optimal solution, when a minimum quantity of resource is used

4   Choose the correct word from those highlighted.

When there is just one limiting factor, the product with the **biggest/smallest** contribution earning ability
per unit of limiting factor should be produced first.

5   Which of the following is not an example of a limiting factor?

A   Sales demand
B   Materials
C   Machine time
D   Profit

Answers to Quick Quiz

1   fall
     normal variable

2   Define variables   Draw a graph of the constraints
     Establish constraints   Establish the feasible region
     Construct objective function   Determine optimal product mix

3   C. If a resource has a maximum availability and it's not binding at the optimal solution, there will be slack.

4   Biggest

5   D.   Limiting factors are resources or demand.

Now try the questions below from the Practice Question Bank

Number	Level	Marks	Approximate time
Section A Q31	Examination	2	4 mins
Section A Q32	Examination	2	4 mins
Section A Q33	Examination	2	4 mins
Section A Q34	Examination	2	4 mins
Section A Q35	Examination	2	4 mins
Section C Q2	Examination	20	39 mins

5

Pricing decisions

Topic list	Syllabus reference
1 Pricing policy and the market	B4 (a)
2 Demand	B4 (b), (c)
3 The profit-maximising price/output level	B4 (d), (f)
4 Decisions to increase production and sales	B4 (e)
5 Price strategies	B4 (g), (h)

Introduction

All profit organisations and many non-profit organisations face the task of setting a price for their products or services.

In this chapter we will begin by looking at the **factors which influence pricing** policy. Perhaps the most important of these are the prices charged by competitors, and the **level of demand** for the organisation's products or services. In a market that is not so competitive, pricing should still be set at a level that customers will pay but which also provides a satisfactory profit.

This chapter also considers the **profit-maximising price/output level** and a range of different **pricing strategies.**

Study guide

		Intellectual level
B4	**Pricing decisions**	
(a)	Explain the factors that influence the pricing of a product or service.	2
(b)	Explain the price elasticity of demand.	1
(c)	Derive and manipulate a straight line demand equation. Derive an equation for the total cost function (including volume-based discounts).	2
(d)	Calculate the optimum selling price and quantity for an organisation, equating marginal cost and marginal revenue.	2
(e)	Evaluate a decision to increase production and sales levels, considering incremental costs, incremental revenues and other factors.	2
(f)	Determine prices and output levels for profit maximisation using the demand-based approach to pricing (both tabular and algebraic methods).	1
(g)	Explain different price strategies, including: (i) All forms of cost-plus (ii) Skimming (iii) Penetration (iv) Complementary product (v) Product line (vi) Volume discounting (vii) Discrimination (viii) Relevant cost	2
(h)	Calculate a price from a given strategy using cost plus and relevant cost.	2

Exam guide

Exam questions on pricing in Section C are likely to be a mixture of calculation and discussion and the examining team will expect a **practical application** of pricing theories.

1 Pricing policy and the market

FAST FORWARD

In the modern world there are many more **influences on price** than cost (eg competitors, product range, quality).

1.1 Influences on price   6/13

Influence	Explanation/Example
Price sensitivity	Sensitivity to price levels will vary among purchasers. Those that can pass on the cost of purchases will be the least sensitive and will therefore respond more to other elements of perceived value. For example, a business traveller will be more concerned about the level of service in looking for an hotel than price, provided that it fits the corporate budget. In contrast, a family on holiday are likely to be very price sensitive when choosing an overnight stay.
Price perception	Price perception is the way customers react to prices. For example, customers may react to a price increase by buying more. This could be because they expect further price increases to follow (they are 'stocking up').

Influence	Explanation/Example
Quality	This is an aspect of price perception. In the absence of other information, customers tend to judge quality by price. Thus a price rise may indicate improvements in quality and a price reduction may signal reduced quality.
Intermediaries	If an organisation distributes products or services to the market through independent intermediaries, such intermediaries are likely to deal with a range of suppliers and their aims concern their own profits rather than those of suppliers.
Competitors	In some industries (such as petrol retailing) pricing moves in unison; in others, price changes by one supplier may initiate a price war. Competition is discussed in more detail below.
Suppliers	If an organisation's suppliers notice a price rise for the organisation's products, they may seek a rise in the price for their supplies to the organisation.
Inflation	In periods of inflation the organisation may need to change prices to reflect increases in the prices of supplies, labour, rent, and so on.
Newness	When a new product is introduced for the first time there are no existing reference points, such as customer or competitor behaviour; pricing decisions are most difficult to make in such circumstances. It may be possible to seek alternative reference points, such as the price in another market where the new product has already been launched, or the price set by a competitor.
Incomes	If incomes are rising, price may be a less important marketing variable than product quality and convenience of access (distribution). When income levels are falling and/or unemployment levels rising, price will be more important.
Product range	Products are often interrelated, being complements to each other or substitutes for one another. The management of the pricing function is likely to focus on the profit from the whole range rather than the profit on each single product. For example, a very low price is charged for a loss leader to make consumers buy additional products in the range which carry higher profit margins (eg selling razors at very low prices while selling the blades for them at a higher profit margin).
Ethics	Ethical considerations may be a further factor, for example whether or not to exploit short-term shortages through higher prices.

1.2 Markets

The price that an organisation can charge for its products will be determined to a greater or lesser degree by the **market** in which it operates.

Here are some familiar economic terms that might feature as background for a question or that you might want to use in a written answer.

Key terms

Perfect competition: many buyers and many sellers all dealing in an identical product. Neither producer nor user has any market power and both must accept the prevailing market price.

Monopoly: one seller who dominates many buyers. The monopolist can use their market power to set a profit-maximising price.

Monopolistic competition: a large number of suppliers offer similar, but not identical, products. The similarities ensure elastic demand whereas the slight differences give some monopolistic power to the supplier.

Oligopoly: where relatively few competitive companies dominate the market. While each large firm has the ability to influence market prices, the unpredictable reaction from the other giants makes the final industry price indeterminate. Cartels are often formed.

1.3 Competition

In **established industries** dominated by a few major firms, it is generally accepted that a price initiative by one firm will be countered by a price reaction by competitors. In these circumstances, prices tend to be **fairly stable**, unless pushed upwards by inflation or strong growth in demand.

If a rival **cuts its prices** in the expectation of increasing its market share, a firm has several options.

(a)   It will **maintain its existing prices** if the expectation is that only a small market share would be lost, so that it is more profitable to keep prices at their existing level. Eventually, the rival firm may drop out of the market or be forced to raise its prices.

(b)   It may maintain its prices but respond with a **non-price counterattack**. This is a more positive response, because the firm will be securing or justifying its current prices with a product change, advertising, or better back-up services.

(c)   It may **reduce its prices**. This should protect the firm's market share so that the main beneficiary from the price reduction will be the consumer.

(d)   It may **raise its prices and respond with a non-price counterattack**. The extra revenue from the higher prices might be used to finance an advertising campaign or product design changes. A price increase would be based on a campaign to emphasise the quality difference between the firm's and the rival's products.

Question   Pricing in the modern business environment

What approach may be used to achieve a satisfactory profit when the selling price is determined by competition in the market?

Answer

The answer is **target costing**, which is explained in Chapter 2b. Price is determined by the market. Costs have to come below this price.

2 Demand

FAST FORWARD   **Economic theory** argues that the **higher the price of a good**, the **lower** will be the **quantity demanded**.

2.1 The economic analysis of demand

You will probably agree from your personal experience as a consumer that the theory of demand is essentially true: the higher the price of a good, the less will be quantity demanded. We have already seen that in practice it is by no means as straightforward as this (some goods are bought **because** they are expensive, for example, because the customer enjoys the status value of a high-priced item).

There are two extremes in the relationship between price and demand. A supplier can either **sell a certain quantity, Q, at any price** (as in graph (a)). Demand is totally unresponsive to changes in price and is said to be **completely inelastic**. Alternatively, **demand might be limitless at a certain price** P (as in graph (b)), but there would be no demand above price P and there would be little point in dropping the price below P. In such circumstances demand is said to be **completely elastic**. This situation may be faced by organisations in a highly competitive market, where they must sell at the prevailing market price. If they set their price any higher, they will not get any customers.

(a)

Price

Demand

Q

(b)

Price

P

Demand

A more **normal situation** for companies that sell a unique product or service is shown below. The **downward-sloping** demand curve shows that demand will increase as prices are lowered, or demand will fall if the selling price is raised. There is 'elasticity' in demand, because sales demand responds to changes in the selling price.

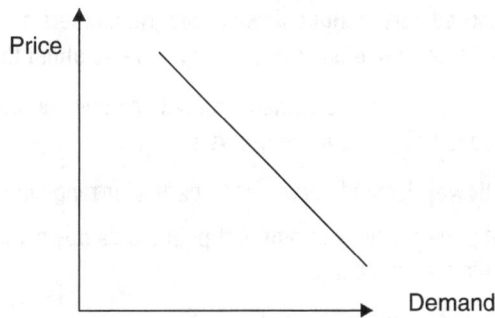

Price

Demand

2.1.1 Price elasticity of demand (η)

The **price elasticity of demand (PED)** is a measure of the extent of change in demand for a good in response to a change in its price.

Key term

Price elasticity of demand (η) is a measure of the extent of change in market demand for a good in response to a change in its price. It is measured as:

$$\frac{\text{The change in quantity demanded, as a \% of demand}}{\text{The change in price, as a \% of the price}}$$

Since the demand goes up when the price falls, and goes down when the price rises, the elasticity has a negative value. However, it is usual to ignore the minus sign.

2.1.2 Example: Price elasticity of demand

The price of a good is $1.20 per unit and annual demand is 800,000 units. Market research indicates that an increase in price of 10 cents per unit will result in a fall in annual demand of 75,000 units. What is the price elasticity of demand between prices of $1.20 and $1.30 per unit?

Solution

Annual demand at $1.20 per unit is 800,000 units.

Annual demand at $1.30 per unit is 725,000 units.

% change in demand = (75,000/800,000) × 100% = 9.375%
% change in price = (0.10/1.20) × 100% = 8.333%
Price elasticity of demand = (−9.375/8.333) = −1.125

Ignoring the minus sign, price elasticity is 1.125.

The demand for this good, at a price of $1.20 per unit, would be referred to as **elastic** because the **price elasticity of demand is greater than 1**.

2.1.3 Elastic and inelastic demand

The value of demand elasticity may be anything from zero to infinity.

Key terms

> Demand is referred to as **inelastic** if the absolute value is less than 1 and **elastic** if the absolute value is greater than 1.

Think about what this means.

(a) Where demand is **inelastic**, the **quantity demanded falls by a smaller percentage than the percentage increase in price**.

(b) Where demand is **elastic, demand falls** by a **larger percentage than the percentage rise in price**.

2.1.4 Price elasticity and the slope of the demand curve

Generally, **demand curves slope downwards**. Consumers are willing to buy more at lower prices than at higher prices. In general, **elasticity** will **vary** in value **along the length of a demand curve**.

(a) If a downward-sloping demand curve becomes **steeper** over a particular range of quantity, then demand is becoming **more inelastic**.

(b) A **shallower** demand curve over a particular range indicates **more elastic** demand.

The ranges of price elasticity at different points on a downward-sloping straight line demand curve are illustrated in the diagram below.

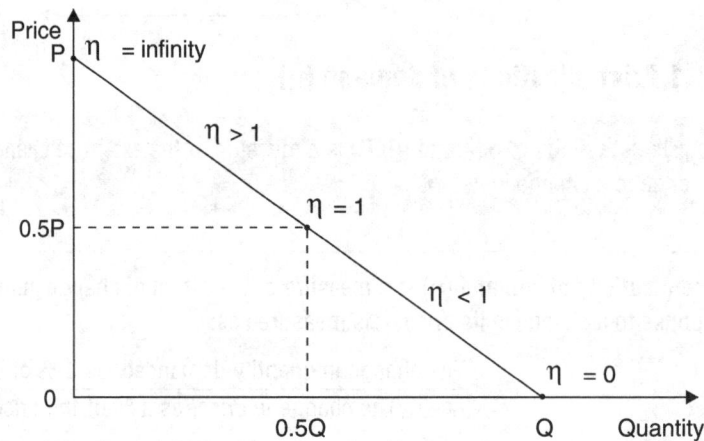

(a) At **higher prices** on a straight line demand curve (the **top** of the demand curve), **small percentage price reductions** can bring **large percentage increases in the quantity** demanded. This means that **demand is elastic** over these ranges, and **price reductions** bring **increases in total expenditure** by consumers on the commodity in question.

(b) At **lower prices** on a straight line demand curve (the **bottom** of the demand curve), **large percentage price reductions** can bring **small percentage increases in quantity**. This means that **demand is inelastic** over these price ranges, and **price increases** result in **increases in total expenditure**.

2.1.5 Special values of price elasticity

There are two special values of price elasticity of demand.

(a) **Demand is perfectly inelastic ($\eta = 0$)**. There is **no change in quantity** demanded, **regardless of the change in price**. The demand curve is **a vertical straight line** (as in graph (a) in Section 2.1).

(b)　**Perfectly elastic demand ($\eta = \infty$).** Consumers will want to **buy an infinite amount**, but **only up to a particular price** level. Any price increase above this level will reduce demand to zero. The demand curve is a **horizontal straight line** (as in graph (b) in Section 2.1).

2.1.6 Elasticity and the pricing decision

In practice, organisations will have only a rough idea of the shape of their demand curve. There will only be a limited amount of data about quantities sold at certain prices over a period of time **and**, of course, factors other than price might affect demand. Because any conclusions drawn from such data can only give an indication of likely future behaviour, management skill and expertise are also needed. Despite this limitation, an **awareness of the concept of elasticity can assist management with pricing decisions**.

(a)　(i)　In circumstances of **inelastic demand, prices should be increased** because revenues will increase and total costs will reduce (because quantities sold will reduce).

　　(ii)　In circumstances of **elastic demand**, increases in prices will bring decreases in revenue and decreases in price will bring increases in revenue. Management therefore have to **decide** whether the **increase/decrease in costs will be less than/greater than the increases/decreases in revenue**.

(b)　In situations of **very elastic demand**, overpricing can lead to a massive drop in quantity sold and hence a massive drop in profits whereas underpricing can lead to costly stock outs and, again, a significant drop in profits. **Elasticity must therefore be reduced by creating a customer preference which is unrelated to price** (through advertising and promotional activities).

(c)　In situations of **very inelastic demand**, customers are **not sensitive to price. Quality, service, product mix and location** are therefore **more important** to a firm's pricing strategy.

Question | Elasticity

Read the four statements below. Where the statement is expressed in layman's terms, rephrase it using the appropriate variant of the term **elasticity**. Where it is already phrased in terms of elasticity, translate it into layman's terms.

(a)　We doubled sales of product A by dropping the price from $1.99 to $1.75.
(b)　Price elasticity of product B is low.
(c)　Demand for product C is highly inelastic.
(d)　A large reduction in price will be necessary to stimulate further demand for product D.

Answer

Situation (a) is an example of elastic demand; (b) is a case of **inelasticity** and should be appropriately worded; (c) is the same as (b); (d) is also an example of inelasticity.

Question | Elasticity

A sales director believes that the price elasticity of demand for Product X is greater than 1, and proposes to take advantage of this by reducing the selling price for Product X. What will happen to sales revenue and profit if the price is reduced?

Answer

If price elasticity of demand is greater than 1, a reduction in the selling price will result in an increase in the sales demand, so that total sales revenue increases.

However, we do not know what will happen to total costs. Total costs will inevitably rise because more units of product will be made and sold. Without knowing more about the product's costs, we do not know by how much costs will rise.

Total profit may well increase, but there is also a possibility that profits will fall because the increase in costs will exceed the increase in revenue following the price rise.

2.2 Variables which influence demand

Here are some **variables which determine both the degree of elasticity and the volume of demand for a good in the market as a whole**.

Variable	Detail
Price of other goods	For some goods the market demand is connected to the price of other goods. Such goods are of two types.
	(a) Substitutes, so that an increase in demand for one version of a good is likely to cause a decrease in demand for others. Common examples are rival brands of the same commodity (like Coca-Cola and Pepsi), bus journeys versus car journeys, or different forms of entertainment.
	(b) Complements, so that an increase in demand for one is likely to cause an increase in demand for the other. Examples are cups and saucers, cars and components, audits and tax consultancy.
Income	A rise in income gives households more to spend and they will want to buy more goods. However, this phenomenon does not affect all goods in the same way.
	(a) Normal goods are those for which a rise in income increases the demand.
	(b) Inferior goods are those for which demand falls as income rises, such as cheap wine.
	(c) For some goods, demand rises up to a certain point and then remains unchanged, because there is a limit to what consumers can or want to consume. Examples are basic foodstuffs such as salt and bread.
Tastes or fashion	A change in tastes or fashion will alter the demand for a good, or a particular variety of a good. Changes in taste may stem from psychological, social or economic causes. There is an argument that tastes and fashions are created by the producers of products and services. There is undeniably some truth in this, but the modern focus on responding to customers' needs and wants suggests otherwise.
Expectations	If consumers have expectations that prices will rise or that shortages will occur they will attempt to stock up on the product, thereby creating excess demand in the short term.
Obsolescence	Many products and services have to be replaced periodically because of obsolescence.
	(a) In early 2017 there will be substantial demand for audits for the year ended 31 December 2016. Demand will dry up once the statutory time limit for filing audited accounts is passed. In other words, many services need to be bought repeatedly for reasons beyond the control of the consumer. A haircut is another example.
	(b) Physical goods are literally 'consumed'. Carpets become threadbare, glasses get broken, foodstuffs get eaten, children grow out of clothes.
	(c) Technological developments render some goods obsolete. Manual office equipment has been replaced by electronic equipment, because it does a better job, more quickly, quietly, efficiently and effectively.

2.3 Demand and the individual firm

We have looked at demand in the market as a whole. We also need to consider **factors that influence demand for one organisation's goods rather than another's**.

2.3.1 Product life cycle

Most products pass through the five stages of the **product life cycle**.

The product life cycle was explained in the chapter on life cycle costing. A typical product goes through several phases in its commercial life: introduction, growth, maturity and decline.

(a) During the introduction phase of the life cycle, when the market is new, price is not affected by competition. There is little or no competition, so an organisation could (in theory) charge whatever price it wanted, and hope that customers will buy at that price. A choice of pricing strategies is possible at this stage, ranging from market-skimming prices to market-penetration prices. These pricing strategies are explained in more detail later.

(b) During the growth stage, prices may start to fall as competition increases. Price reductions are possible because sales demand is increasing and, as production and sales increase, unit costs fall.

(c) In the maturity stage of the life cycle, the price may be fairly stable, but some organisations may occasionally try to win market share with price reduction offers.

(d) In the decline stage of the life cycle, prices will change again. Prices may fall as fewer customers want to buy the product. Alternatively, prices may rise because when most suppliers withdraw from the market the few remaining producers may be able to charge a higher price for a product that is now difficult to get hold of.

2.3.2 Quality

One firm's product may be perceived to be better quality than another's, and may in some cases actually be so, if it uses sturdier materials, goes faster or does whatever it is meant to do in a 'better' way. Other things being equal, the **better quality good** will be **more in demand** than other versions. Quality in a product gives the customer a sense of 'value' or benefit received, and they are prepared to pay more for extra value.

2.3.3 Marketing

You may be familiar with the 'four Ps' of the marketing mix, all of which influence demand for a firm's goods.

(a) **Price**

(b) **Product**

(c) **Place** refers to the place **where a good can be purchased**, or is likely to be purchased.

    (i) If potential buyers find that a particular version of a good is difficult to obtain, they will turn to substitutes.

    (ii) Some goods have no more than local appeal.

(d) **Promotion** refers to the various means by which firms draw attention to their products and services.

    (i) A good **brand name** is a strong and relatively permanent influence on demand.

    (ii) Demand can be stimulated by a variety of **promotional tools**, such as free gifts, money off, shop displays, direct mail and media advertising.

In recent years, emphasis has been placed, especially in marketing, on the **importance of non-profit factors** in demand. Thus the roles of product quality, promotion, personal selling and distribution and, in overall terms, brands, have grown. While it can be relatively easy for a competitor to copy a price cut, at least in the short term, it is much **more difficult to copy a successful brand image based on a unique selling proposition.** Successful branding can even imply premium pricing.

2.4 Deriving the demand equation

FAST FORWARD

You need to be able to derive the **demand equation** $P = a - bQ$.

An examination question may indicate that the demand curve for a product can be stated as a straight line equation: $P = a - bQ$.

In practice this is most unlikely to happen, but it is an aspect of pricing theory that you need to understand. You may be given sufficient information in a question to enable you to derive the demand curve.

Exam formulae

When demand is linear the equation for the demand curve is:

$P = a - bQ$

where | P | = the price
| Q | = the quantity demanded
| a | = the price at which demand would be nil
| b | = $\dfrac{\text{change in price}}{\text{change in quantity}}$

The constant a is calculated as follows.

$$a = \$(\text{current price}) + \left(\frac{\text{Current quantity at current price}}{\text{Change in quantity when price is changed by \$b}} \times \$b \right)$$

This may look rather complicated in words, but it is very easy to use once you have learned the technique.

2.4.1 Example: Deriving the demand equation

The current price of a product is \$12. At this price the company sells 60 items a month. One month the company decides to raise the price to \$15, but only 45 items are sold at this price. Determine the demand equation, which is assumed to be a straight line equation.

Solution

Step 1   **Find the price at which demand would be nil**

Assuming demand is linear, each increase of \$3 (from \$12 to \$15) in the price would result in a fall in demand of 15 units (from 60 to 45). For demand to fall to nil, the price needs to rise from its current level \$12 by as many times as there are 15 units in 60 units (60/15 = 4) ie to \$12 + (4 × \$3) = \$24.

$$a = \$(\text{current price}) + \left(\frac{\text{Current quantity at current price}}{\text{Change in quantity when price is changed by \$b}} \times \$b \right)$$

$a = \$12 + [(60/15) \times \$3)] = \$24$.

Step 2   **Calculate b**

$$b = \frac{\text{change in price}}{\text{change in quantity}} = \frac{\$15 - \$12}{60 - 45} = \frac{3}{15} = 0.2$$

The demand equation is therefore $P = 24 - 0.2Q$

Step 3   **Check your equation**

We can check this by finding Q when P is $12.

P = 24 − 0.2Q

12 = 24 − (0.2Q)
0.2Q = 24 − 12
0.2Q = 12

$Q = \dfrac{12}{0.2} = 60$

An alternative approach is to find 'b' first, then substitute the known value for 'b' into the demand function.

Step 1   **Calculate b**

$b = \dfrac{\text{change in price}}{\text{change in quantity}} = \dfrac{\$15 - \$12}{60 - 45} = \dfrac{3}{15} = 0.2$

Step 2   **Substitute the known value for 'b' into the demand function to find 'a'**

P = a − (0.2Q)

12 = a − (0.2 x 60)

12 = a − 12

a = 24

The demand equation is therefore P = 24 − 0.2Q

Step 3   **Check your equation**

We can check this by finding Q when P is $12.

12 = 24 − (0.2Q)
0.2Q = 24 − 12
0.2Q = 12

$Q = \dfrac{12}{0.2} = 60$

Question   **Deriving the demand equation**

The current price of a product is $30 and its producers sell 100 items a week at this price. One week the price is dropped by $3 as a special offer and the producers sell 150 items. Find an expression for the demand curve, assuming that this is a linear equation.

Answer

a   = $30 + (100/50 × $3)   = $36

b $= \dfrac{\$3}{150 - 100} = 0.06$

P   = 36 − 0.06Q

Check

27   = 36 − 0.06Q
0.06Q   = 36 − 27

Q $= \dfrac{9}{0.06} = 150$

2.5 The total cost function

FAST FORWARD Cost behaviour can be **modelled** using equations.

In order to decide a profit-maximising price and sales quantity, we need to consider costs as well as revenue.

Determining the optimum (profit-maximising) price and output level requires that both **cost and revenue behaviour** can be **modelled using equations**. These equations can range from simple to complex, although those you encounter in the exam will tend towards the 'simple' end of the range.

The cost function is likely to be expressed in terms of total costs = fixed costs plus variable costs.

For example, an organisation's total costs (TC) might be modelled by the equation $TC = 6,500 + 0.75Q$, where Q is the number of units sold.

Here the cost model is a simple linear equation of the form $y = a + bx$, where a ($6,500) represents the fixed costs and b ($0.75) represents the unit variable cost.

In your earlier studies, you will have covered how this equation can be derived using **linear regression analysis.** As you will remember, 'a' is the intercept of the line on the y axis and 'b' is the slope of the line.

The following graph demonstrates the total cost function.

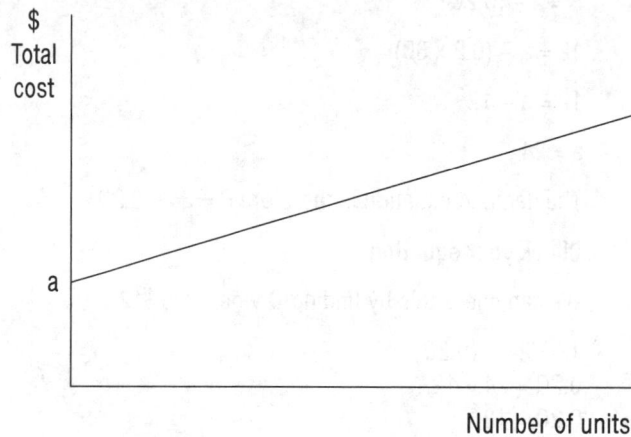

There are a number of **problems** associated with using such models.

(a) The cost model assumes fixed costs remain unchanged over all ranges of output. This is not the case for step costs. A step cost is a cost which is fixed in nature but only within certain levels of activity. An example of a step cost is the depreciation of a machine which may be fixed if production remains below 1,000 units per month. If production exceeds 1,000 units, a second machine may be required, and the cost of depreciation (on two machines) would go up a step. A sketch graph of a step cost could look like this.

Graph of step cost

(b) The cost model assumes a constant unit variable cost over all ranges of output. It therefore fails to take into account the implications of economies and diseconomies of scale. The graph below illustrates economies of scale using marginal analysis.

Marginal analysis is concerned with how a change in production (or sales volume) by one unit affects an organisation's costs and revenues. Marginal cost is the extra cost incurred when one more unit is produced.

Economies/Diseconomies of Scale

The marginal cost curve is typically U-shaped. This is because marginal costs decrease as output increases due to economies of scale. However, at some point diseconomies of scale (eg more supervision and larger workforce) appear and marginal costs begin to rise.

3 The profit-maximising price/output level   6/15

FAST FORWARD

If we assume that there is a demand curve with the equation $P = a - bQ$, and a total cost function $C = F + vQ$, we can determine the profit-maximising price for the product.

Profits are maximised where **marginal cost (MC) = marginal revenue (MR)**. The **optimal selling price** can be determined by deriving equations for MC and MR. Alternatively, the **optimum selling price** can be determined using tabulation.

Exam focus point

In the June 2015 examining team's report, it was pointed out that candidates in the exam had confused sales volume maximisation with profit maximisation. Make sure that you understand the difference between the two.

The overall objective of an organisation should be **profit maximisation**. In this section we look at how the profit-maximising price and output levels can be derived. In microeconomic theory, profits are maximised when marginal revenue = marginal cost.

If we have a demand curve $P = a - bQ$ and a total cost curve that states costs as fixed costs plus variable costs ($C = F + vQ$), we can calculate the selling price that will maximise profit. This is the price at which marginal cost equals marginal revenue (MC = MR).

3.1 Microeconomic theory and profit maximisation

In economics, **profit maximisation** is the process by which a firm determines the price and output level that returns the greatest profit. There are two common approaches to this problem.

(a) The **Total revenue (TR) – Total cost (TC)** method is based on the fact that profit equals revenue minus cost.

(b) The **Marginal revenue (MR) – Marginal cost (MC)** method is based on the fact that total profit in a perfect market reaches its maximum point where marginal revenue equals marginal cost.

To obtain the profit-maximising output quantity under the TR – TC method, we start by recognising that profit is equal to total revenue minus total cost.

From the graph above it is evident that the difference between **total costs** and **total revenue** is greatest at point Q. This is the profit-maximising output quantity.

3.2 MC = MR

Microeconomic theory suggests that as output increases, the marginal cost per unit may rise (due to the law of diminishing returns) as the quantity produced and sold increases. However, when costs are the sum of fixed costs and variable costs, the marginal MC is the variable cost per unit for each additional unit that is made and sold.

Whenever a firm is faced with a downward-sloping demand curve, the **marginal revenue per unit will decline**. By raising the sales price, total revenue may increase, but by an ever-decreasing amount.

Eventually, a level of output will be reached where the **extra cost** of making one extra unit of output is greater than the **extra revenue** obtained from its sale. It would then be unprofitable to make and sell that extra unit.

Profits will continue to be maximised only up to the output level where marginal cost has risen to be exactly equal to the marginal revenue.

Profits are maximised using marginalist theory when **marginal cost (MC) = marginal revenue (MR)**.

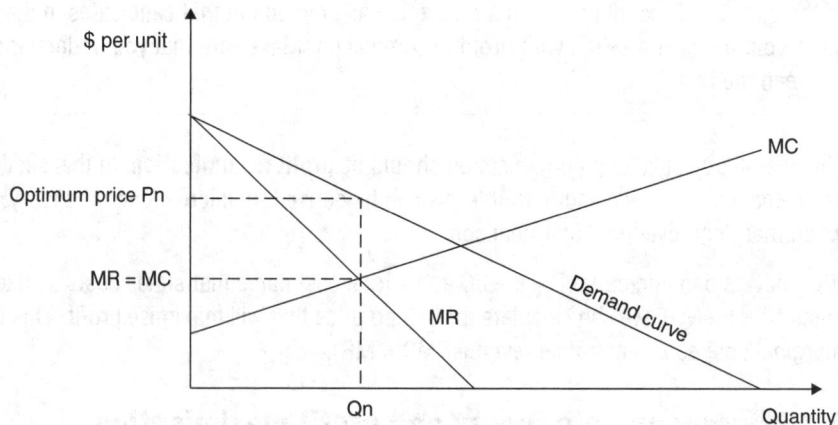

Profits are **maximised** at the point where **MC = MR**, ie at a volume of Qn units. If we add a demand curve to the graph, we can see that at an output level of Qn, the sales price per unit would be Pn.

It is important to make a clear distinction in your mind between the **sales price** and **marginal revenue**. In this example, the optimum price is Pn, but the marginal revenue is much less. This is because the 'additional' sales unit to reach output Qn has only been achieved by reducing the unit sales **price** from an amount higher than Pn for all the units to be sold, not just the marginal extra one. The increase in sales volume is therefore partly offset by a reduction in unit price; hence MR is lower than Pn.

3.3 Determining the profit-maximising selling price: using equations

The **optimal selling price** can be determined by deriving equations for MC and MR (and profits are maximised where **MC = MR**).

In your exam, you may be **provided with the equations for marginal cost and marginal revenue** or you may have to **devise them from information** in the question. Remember, **marginal cost** is the **extra cost of producing one extra unit**, **marginal revenue** is the **extra revenue from selling one extra unit**. **Marginal revenue may not be the same as** the **price** charged for all units up to that demand level, as to increase volumes the price may have to be reduced.

Section 2.4 explained how to derive an equation for the demand curve. The marginal revenue curve is derived from the demand curve.

When $P = a - bQ$

$MR = a - 2bQ$

where P = the price
       Q = the quantity demanded
       a = the price at which demand would be nil
       b = $\dfrac{\text{change in price}}{\text{change in quantity}}$

The following step-by-step approach can be applied to most questions involving algebra and pricing.

Step 1 Establish the demand function (find the values for 'a' and 'b').

Step 2 Obtain a value for MR from the demand curve. $MR = a - 2bQ$

Step 2 Establish MC (the marginal cost). This will simply be the variable cost per unit.

Step 4 To maximise profit, equate MC and MR to find Q.

Step 5 Substitute Q into the demand function and solve to find P (the optimum price).

You will need to be able to solve simple examples like those that follow.

3.3.1 Example: MC = MR

MOC makes and sells a copyrighted, executive game for two distinct markets, in which it has a monopoly. The fixed costs of production per month are $20,000 and variable costs per unit produced, and sold, are $40. (The monthly sales can be thought of as X, where $X = X_1 + X_2$, with X_1 and X_2 denoting monthly sales in their respective markets.) Detailed market research has revealed the demand functions in the markets to be as follows, with prices shown as P_1, P_2.

Market 1: $P_1 = 55 - 0.05X_1$
Market 2: $P_2 = 200 - 0.2X_2$

Note. These formulae are simply **linear equations**. They show how the price (P) can be determined for a given level of demand (X). So in market 1, at a level of demand of 100, the price (P) will be $55 - (0.05 \times 100) = 50$.

From these, the management accountant has derived that the marginal revenue functions in the two markets are as follows.

Market 1:	$MR_1 = 55 - 0.1X_1$
Market 2:	$MR_2 = 200 - 0.4X_2$

Note. In market 1, the marginal revenue if 100 units are sold is $55 - (0.1 \times 100) = 45$.

The management accountant believes there should be price discrimination; the price is currently $50 per game in either market.

Required

Analyse the information for the executive game and, given the management accountant's belief, do the following.

(a)   Calculate the price to charge in each market, and the quantity to produce (and sell) each month, to maximise profit.

(b)   Determine the revenue function for each market and the maximum monthly profit in total.

(c)   Calculate and comment on the change in total profitability and prices.

Solution

(a)   In both markets, **marginal cost = variable cost per unit** = $40

Profit is maximised when **marginal revenue = marginal cost**.

Market 1

$$55 - 0.1X_1 = 40$$
$$0.1X_1 = 15$$
$$X_1 = 15/0.1 = 150$$

and price $P_1 = 55 - (0.05 \times 150) = \$47.5$.

Hence the price in market 1 should be $47.50 per unit and 150 units should be produced.

Market 2

$$200 - 0.4X_2 = 40$$
$$0.4X_2 = 160$$
$$X_2 = 160/0.4 = 400$$

and price $P_2 = 200 - (0.2 \times 400) = \$120$.

Hence the price in market 2 should be $120 per unit and 400 units should be produced.

Total number of items to be produced per month is 550.

(b)   **Revenue = unit price × number of units sold**

Market 1

Revenue = $P_1X_1 = 55X_1 - 0.05X_1^2$

Market 2

Revenue = $P_2X_2 = 200X_2 - 0.2X_2^2$

From (a), profit is maximised when

$X_1 = 150$ and $X_2 = 400$

$P_1 = 47.5$ and $P_2 = 120$

At maximum profit:

Total revenue = $(47.5 \times 150) + (120 \times 400) = \$55,125$

Total costs = 20,000 + (40 × 550) = $42,000

Total maximum monthly profit = $13,125

(c) Currently the price is $50 in both markets.

Market 1 $50 = 55 - 0.05X_1$
$\qquad\qquad 0.05X_1 = 55 - 50 = 5$
$\qquad\qquad X_1 = 5/0.05 = 100$

Market 2 $50 = 200 - 0.2X_2$
$\qquad\qquad 0.2X_2 = 200 - 50 = 150$
$\qquad\qquad X_2 = 150/0.2 = 750$

Therefore the **total number of units** = 100 + 750 = 850.

Total revenue = $50 × 850 = $42,500.

Total cost = 20,000 + (40 × 850) = $54,000.

So the game **currently makes a loss** of $11,500.

Hence, if the prices are changed to $47.50 in market 1 and $120 in market 2, the company can expect to turn a monthly loss of $11,500 into a profit of $13,125.

You will be provided with equations representing MC and MR if they are needed. Note, however, that if a question states that the extra cost of producing one extra item is $20, say, you will be expected to realise that the MC is $20. Likewise, if you are told that **100 units are sold for $10 each**, but **101 can only be sold for $9.99**, the **MR of the 101st item is (101 × $9.99) – (100 × $10) = $8.99**.

Question
Deriving a MR equation from the demand curve

AB has used market research to determine that if a price of $250 is charged for product G, demand will be 12,000 units. It has also been established that demand will rise or fall by 5 units for every $1 fall/rise in the selling price. The marginal cost of product G is $80.

Required

If marginal revenue = a – 2bQ when the selling price (P) = a – bQ, calculate the profit-maximising selling price for product G.

Answer

$$b = \frac{\text{change in price}}{\text{change in quantity}} = \frac{\$1}{5} = 0.2$$

a = $250 + ((12,000/5) × $1) = $2,650

MR = 2,650 – (2 × 0.2)Q   = 2,650 – 0.4Q

Profits are maximised when MC = MR, ie when 80 = 2,650 – 0.4Q

$$2,650 - 80 = 2,570 \times \frac{10}{4} = 6,425$$

Profit-maximising demand   = 6,425

Now, substitute the values into the demand curve equation to find the profit-maximising selling price

P = a – bQ

P = 2,650 – (0.2 × 6,425)

∴ Profit-maximising price   = $(2,650 – 1,285)

$\qquad\qquad\qquad\qquad\qquad$ = $1,365

3.4 Determining the profit-maximising selling price: visual inspection of a tabulation of data   Mar/Jun 16

The **optimum selling price** can also be determined using tabulation.

To determine the profit-maximising selling price:

(a)   Work out the **demand curve** and hence the **price** and the **total revenue** (PQ) at various levels of demand.

(b)   Calculate **total cost** and hence **marginal cost** at each level of demand.

(c)   Finally calculate **profit** at each level of demand, thereby determining the price and level of demand at which profits are maximised.

Question   Tabulation approach to find profit-maximising price

An organisation operates in a market where there is imperfect competition, so that to sell more units of output it must reduce the sales price of all the units it sells. The following data is available for prices and costs.

Total output Units	Sales price per unit (AR) $	Average cost of output (AC) $ per unit
0	–	–
1	504	720
2	471	402
3	439	288
4	407	231
5	377	201
6	346	189
7	317	182
8	288	180
9	259	186
10	232	198

The total cost of zero output is $600.

Required

Complete the table below to determine the output level and price at which the organisation would maximise its profits, assuming that fractions of units cannot be made.

Units	Price $	Total revenue $	Marginal revenue $	Total cost $	Marginal cost $	Profit $
0						
1						
2						
3						
4						
5						
6						
7						
8						
9						
10						

The correct answer is that profit is maximised at seven units of output and a price of $317, when MR is most nearly equal to MC.

Units	Price	Total revenue	Marginal revenue	Total cost	Marginal cost	Profit
	$	$	$	$	$	$
0	0	0	0	600	–	(600)
1	504	504	504	720	120	(216)
2	471	942	438	804	84	138
3	439	1,317	375	864	60	453
4	407	1,628	311	924	60	704
5	377	1,885	257	1,005	81	880
6	346	2,076	191	1,134	129	942
7	317	2,219	143	1,274	140	945
8	288	2,304	85	1,440	166	864
9	259	2,331	27	1,674	234	657
10	232	2,320	(11)	1,980	306	340

4 Decisions to increase production and sales   12/07

FAST FORWARD

If you are required to evaluate a decision to increase production and sales levels, you will need to consider **incremental costs**, **incremental revenues** and other factors.

Key term

Incremental costs and revenues are the difference between costs and revenues for the corresponding items under each alternative being considered.   (Drury 2005: p.39)

The **incremental cost** of increasing production from 500 to 600 units per month is the additional cost of producing an extra 100 units each month. If fixed costs increase as a result of the decision, they are an incremental cost together with the increased variable costs of production.

4.1 Example: A decision to increase production

George manufactures a product which uses two types of material, A and B. Each unit of production currently sells for $10. A local trader has expressed an interest in buying 5,000 units but is only prepared to pay $9 per unit.

Current costs and revenues are as follows.

	$'000	$'000
Sales		350
Less production costs		
Material A – 1 kg per unit	25	
Material B – 1 litre per unit	50	
Labour – 1 hour per unit	75	
Variable overhead	50	
Fixed overhead	25	
Non-production costs	25	
Total cost		250
Budgeted profit		100

The following additional information has also been made available.

(a) There is minimal inventory of material available and prices for new material are expected to be 5% higher for Material A and 3% higher for Material B.

(b) George has been having problems with his workforce and is short of labour hours. He currently has the capacity to produce 36,000 units but would have to employ contract labour at $3.50 per hour to make any additional units.

(c) Included in the fixed production overhead is the salary of the production manager. He is stressed and exhausted and has threatened to leave unless he receives a pay rise of $5,000. George would not be able to fulfil any new orders without him.

Required

Evaluate whether George should accept the new order.

Solution

Workings

Current production = 350,000/10 = 35,000 units

$$\text{Current cost per unit of Material A} = \frac{\$25,000}{35,000} = \$0.71$$

$$\text{Current cost per unit of Material B} = \frac{\$50,000}{35,000} = \$1.43$$

$$\text{Current cost of labour} = \frac{\$75,000}{35,000} = \$2.14$$

	$	$
Incremental revenue (5,000 × $9)		45,000
Incremental costs		
Material A (1.05 × $0.71 × 5,000)	3,728	
Material B (1.03 × $1.43 × 5,000)	7,365	
Labour [(1,000 × $2.14) + (4,000 × $3.50)]	16,140	
Fixed overhead	5,000	
		32,233
Incremental profit		12,767

The new order would produce an additional $12,767 so is probably worthwhile but other factors may need to be considered; for example, the effect of a price cut on existing customer expectations and whether the workforce and production manager will be able to fulfil the new order with the same labour efficiency.

4.1.1 Offering volume-based discounts

Key term

> A **volume-based discount** is a discount given for buying in bulk.

An organisation may wish to consider offering a volume-based discount to customers for purchases above a certain quantity. The intention may be that, by offering the sale price discount, customers will buy more of the product.

To decide whether a volume-based discount on selling prices is financially worthwhile, the following calculation is needed.

By reducing the selling price with a volume-based discount and reducing the price from P_1 to P_2, sales volume may be expected to increase from Q_1 to Q_2. Assume that the variable cost of sale is $V per unit, and fixed costs will be unaffected by a change in sales volume.

	$
Total sales revenue at discounted price	(Q2 × P2)
Total sales revenue at non-discounted price	(Q1 × P1)
Increase in sales revenue	Difference
Increase in costs	(Q2 – Q1) × V

Change in profit = (Q2 × P2) – (Q1 × P1) – [(Q2 – Q1) × V]

For example, suppose that a company sells a product at a price of $10 per unit. The unit variable cost is $4. The sales manager believes that, by offering a customer a discount of 5% for buying at least 5,000 units a year, the customer will increase purchases from their current level of 4,000 units to a level of 5,000 units per year.

The effect on profits each year would be calculated as follows.

	$
Total sales revenue at discounted price: 5,000 × $10 × 95%	47,500
Total sales revenue at non-discounted price: 4,000 × $10	40,000
Increase in sales revenue	7,500
Increase in costs (1,000 units × $4)	4,000
Increase in annual profit from volume-based price discounting	3,500

5 Price strategies

6/10, 6/15

FAST FORWARD

The price to be charged for a product or service is often one of the most important decisions made by business organisations. There are a number of alternative pricing strategies.

5.1 Cost-plus pricing

FAST FORWARD

Full cost-plus pricing is a method of deciding the sales price by adding a percentage mark-up for profit to the full cost of the product.

In practice, cost is one of the most important influences on price. Many firms base price on simple **cost-plus rules** (costs are estimated and then a profit margin is added in order to set the price).

The 'full cost' may be a fully absorbed production cost only, or it may include some absorbed administration, selling and distribution overhead.

A business might have an idea of the percentage profit margin it would like to earn, and so might **decide on an average profit mark-up** as a general guideline for pricing decisions.

Businesses that carry out a large amount of **contract work or jobbing work**, for which individual job or contract prices must be quoted regularly, would find this a useful method to adopt. Since every job or contract is different, there are no market prices; and in the absence of a market price, adding a profit mark-up to cost provides a logical way to decide the selling price. The percentage profit **mark-up**, however, **does not have to be rigid and fixed**, but can be varied to suit different circumstances.

5.1.1 Example: Full cost-plus pricing

Markup Co has begun to produce a new product, Product X, for which the following cost estimates have been made.

	$
Direct materials	27
Direct labour: 4 hours at $5 per hour	20
Variable production overheads: machining, ½ hour at $6 per hour	3
	50

Production fixed overheads are budgeted at $300,000 per month and, because of the shortage of available machining capacity, the company will be restricted to 10,000 hours of machine time per month. The absorption rate will be a direct labour rate, however, and budgeted direct labour hours are 25,000 per month. It is estimated that the company could obtain a minimum contribution of $10 per machine hour on producing items other than product X.

The direct cost estimates are not certain as to material usage rates and direct labour productivity, and it is recognised that the estimates of direct materials and direct labour costs may be subject to an error of ± 15%. Machine time estimates are similarly subject to an error of ± 10%.

The company wishes to make a profit of 20% on full production cost from product X.

Required

Ascertain the full cost-plus based price.

Solution

Even for a relatively 'simple' cost-plus pricing estimate, some problems can arise, and certain assumptions must be made and stated. In this example, we can identify two problems.

- Should the opportunity cost of machine time be included in cost or not?
- What allowance, if any, should be made for the possible errors in cost estimates?

Different assumptions could be made.

(a) **Exclude machine time opportunity costs: ignore possible costing errors**

	$
Direct materials	27.00
Direct labour (4 hours)	20.00
Variable production overheads	3.00
Fixed production overheads	
(at $\dfrac{\$300,000}{25,000}$ = $12 per direct labour hour)	48.00
Full production cost	98.00
Profit mark-up (20%)	19.60
Selling price per unit of product X	117.60

(b) **Include machine time opportunity costs: ignore possible costing errors**

	$
Full production cost as in (a)	98.00
Opportunity cost of machine time:	
contribution forgone (½ hour × $10)	5.00
Adjusted full cost	103.00
Profit mark-up (20%)	20.60
Selling price per unit of product X	123.60

A problem with this approach is that, since the opportunity cost of machine is contribution forgone, it must include some element for profit. Adding a profit margin to a figure that already includes profit is arguably being 'greedy'. This may set the price at a high level that the customer may refuse to accept.

(c) **Exclude machine time opportunity costs but make full allowance for possible underestimates of cost**

	$	$
Direct materials	27.00	
Direct labour	20.00	
	47.00	
Possible error (15%)	7.05	
		54.05
Variable production overheads	3.00	
Possible error (10%)	0.30	
		3.30

	$	$
Fixed production overheads (4 hours × $12)	48.00	
Possible error (labour time) (15%)	7.20	
		55.20
Potential full production cost		112.55
Profit mark-up (20%)		22.51
Selling price per unit of product X		135.06

(d) **Include machine time opportunity costs and make a full allowance for possible underestimates of cost**

	$
Potential full production cost as in (c)	112.55
Opportunity cost of machine time:	
potential contribution forgone (½ hour × $10 × 110%)	5.50
Adjusted potential full cost	118.05
Profit mark-up (20%)	23.61
Selling price per unit of product X	141.66

Using different assumptions, we could arrive at any of four different unit prices in the range $117.60 to $141.66.

5.1.2 Disadvantages of full cost-plus pricing

There are several disadvantages with cost-plus pricing.

(a) It fails to recognise that, since demand may be determining price, there will be a profit-maximising combination of price and demand.

(b) There may be a need to **adjust prices to market and demand conditions**. When there is an existing market price for the product that competitors are charging, prices based on 'cost plus' may be uncompetitive.

(c) **Budgeted output volume** needs to be established. Output volume is a key factor in the overhead absorption rate and so in the calculation of full cost. If there is over- or under-absorption due to incorrect estimates of production capacity, measures of full cost will be too high or too low.

(d) A **suitable basis for overhead absorption** must be selected, where a business produces more than one product. Some products may be charged with too much overhead, so that the full cost and selling price are too high (at a price that customers may be unwilling to pay); and other products may be charged with too little overhead, so that the selling price is too low.

5.1.3 Advantages of full cost-plus pricing

Full cost-plus pricing has some advantages.

(a) It is a **quick, simple and cheap** method of pricing which can be delegated to junior managers.

(b) Since the size of the profit margin can be varied, a decision based on a price in excess of full cost should ensure that a company working at normal capacity will **cover all of its fixed costs and make a profit**.

(c) When there is no market price for the product, deciding a price by adding a profit margin to cost is a logical approach, which seeks to ensure that the organisation makes a profit.

Question   **Full cost-plus method**

A company budgets to make 20,000 units which have a variable cost of production of $4 per unit. Fixed production costs are $60,000 per annum. If the selling price is to be 40% higher than full cost, what is the selling price of the product using the full cost-plus method?

Full cost per unit = variable cost + fixed cost

Variable cost = $4 per unit

Fixed cost = $\dfrac{\$60,000}{20,000}$ = $3 per unit

Full cost per unit = $(4 + 3) = $7

$\therefore$ Selling price using full cost-plus pricing method $= \$7.00 \times \dfrac{140\%}{100}$

$$= \$9.80$$

5.2 Marginal cost-plus pricing

5.2.1 Introduction

Marginal cost-plus pricing, also called mark-up pricing, involves adding a profit margin to the marginal cost of the product.

Whereas a full cost-plus approach to pricing draws attention to net profit and the net profit margin, a variable cost-plus approach to pricing **draws attention to gross profit** and the **gross profit margin**, or **contribution**.

Profit mark up

A product has the following costs.

	$
Direct materials	5
Direct labour	3
Variable overheads	7

Fixed overheads are $10,000 per month. Budgeted sales per month are 400 units to allow the product to break even.

Required

Determine the profit mark up which needs to be added to **marginal** cost to allow the product to break even.

Breakeven point is when total contribution equals fixed costs.

At breakeven point, $10,000 = 400 (price – $15)

$\therefore$ $25 = price – $15
$\therefore$ $40 = price
$\therefore$ Profit mark up = (40 – 15) / 15 × 100% = 166%

5.2.2 Advantages of marginal cost-plus pricing

Marginal cost pricing has several advantages.

(a)   It is a **simple and easy** method to use.

(b)   The **mark-up percentage can be varied**, and so mark-up pricing can be adjusted to reflect demand conditions.

(c)   It **draws management attention to contribution**, and the effects of higher or lower sales volumes on profit. For example, if a product costs $10 per unit and a mark-up of 150% ($15) is added to reach a price of $25 per unit, management should be clearly aware that every additional $1 of sales revenue would add 60 cents to contribution and profit ($15 ÷ $25 = $0.60).

(d)   In practice, mark-up pricing is **used** in businesses **where there is a readily identifiable basic variable cost**. **Retail industries** are the most obvious example, and it is quite common for the prices of goods in shops to be fixed by adding a mark-up (20% or 33.3%, say) to the purchase cost.

5.2.3 Disadvantages of marginal cost-plus pricing

There are also disadvantages with marginal cost-plus pricing.

(a)   Although the size of the mark-up can be varied in accordance with demand conditions, it does not ensure that sufficient attention is paid to demand conditions, competitors' prices and profit maximisation.

(b)   It **ignores fixed overheads and sales volumes** in the pricing decision, but the sales price must be sufficiently high to ensure that a profit is made after covering fixed costs.

5.3 Full cost pricing versus marginal cost pricing

Perhaps the most important **criticism** of full cost pricing is that it **fails to recognise** that, since sales demand may be determined by the sales price, there will be a **profit-maximising combination** of price and demand. A full cost-based approach to pricing will be most unlikely, except by coincidence or 'luck', to arrive at the profit-maximising price. In contrast, a marginal costing approach to looking at costs and prices would be more likely to help with identifying a profit-maximising price.

5.3.1 Example: Full cost versus profit-maximising prices

Tigger has budgeted to make 50,000 units of its product, timm. The variable cost of a timm is $5 and annual fixed costs are expected to be $150,000.

The financial director of Tigger has suggested that a profit margin of 25% on full cost should be charged for every product sold.

The marketing director has challenged the wisdom of this suggestion, and has produced the following estimates of sales demand for timms.

Price per unit	Demand
$	Units
9	42,000
10	38,000
11	35,000
12	32,000
13	27,000

Required

(a)   Calculate the profit for the year if a full cost price is charged.

(b)   Calculate the profit-maximising price.

Assume in both (a) and (b) that 50,000 units of timm are produced regardless of sales volume.

Solution

(a) (i) The full cost per unit is $5 variable cost plus $3 fixed costs, ie $8 in total. A 25% mark-up on this cost gives a selling price of $10 per unit so that sales demand would be 38,000 units. (Production is given as 50,000 units.)

	$	$
Profit (absorption costing)		
Sales		380,000
Costs of production (50,000 units)		
Variable (50,000 × $5)	250,000	
Fixed (50,000 × $3)	150,000	
	400,000	
Less increase in inventory (12,000 units × 8)	(96,000)	
Cost of sales		304,000
Profit		76,000

(ii) **Profit using marginal costing** instead of absorption costing, so that fixed overhead costs are written off in the period they occur, would be as follows. (The 38,000 unit demand level is chosen for comparison.)

	$
Contribution (38,000 × $(10 − 5))	190,000
Fixed costs	150,000
Profit	40,000

Since the company cannot go on indefinitely producing an output volume in excess of sales volume, this profit figure is more indicative of the profitability of timms in the longer term.

(b) A **profit-maximising price** is one which gives the greatest net (relevant) cash flow, which in this case is the **contribution-maximising price**.

Price	Unit contribution	Demand	Total contribution
$	$	Units	$
9	4	42,000	168,000
10	5	38,000	190,000
11	6	35,000	210,000
12	7	32,000	224,000
13	8	27,000	216,000

The profit-maximising price is $12, with annual sales demand of 32,000 units.

This example shows that a **cost-based price** is **unlikely to be the profit-maximising** price, and that a **marginal costing approach**, calculating the total contribution at a variety of different selling prices, will be **more helpful** for establishing what the profit-maximising price ought to be.

5.3.2 Cost-plus pricing vs target costing

As you should remember from Chapter 2b on target costing, **target prices** are set in order to achieve a desired market share. Deduction of a desired profit margin produces the cost that has to be achieved. Design specifications and production methods are examined to establish ways in which the target cost can be met without reducing the value of the product to the customer.

Such an approach is likely to **offer greater competitive advantage** than cost-plus pricing, being far more **strategically orientated** as it **takes account of the external environment**.

However, target prices are probably more relevant to new product design and development, when the organisation identifies a selling price that will be needed if the product is to be competitive in the marketplace.

> **FAST FORWARD**
>
> Pricing strategies for new products include **market skimming** and **market penetration pricing**.

Key term

> **Price skimming** involves charging high prices when a new product is first launched on the market, in order to maximise short-term profitability. Initially there is heavy spending on advertising and sales promotion to encourage sales demand. As the product moves into the later stages of its life cycle (growth, maturity and decline), progressively lower prices are charged. The profitable 'cream' is thus skimmed off in stages until sales can only be sustained at lower prices.

Exam focus point

> In the June 2015, candidates were asked to consider a scenario and to discuss the conditions which would make market skimming a more suitable pricing strategy than their current strategy. The examining team advised that the best approach to take in this type of question was to state what each condition is and then for each one say whether the company meets the condition. Finally at the end, make a conclusion. Make sure that you can fully understand each pricing policy and that you can **apply** this knowledge to any given scenario.

The aim of market skimming is to gain **high unit profits** early in the product's life, in the hope of recovering the costs of investment quickly. High unit prices make it more likely that **competitors** will enter the market than if lower prices were to be charged.

A price skimming policy may be appropriate in the cases below.

(a) The product is **new and different**, so that customers are prepared to pay high prices so as to be one up on other people who do not own it.

(b) The strength of **demand** and the sensitivity of demand to price are **unknown**. It is better from the point of view of marketing to start by charging high prices and then reduce them if the demand for the product turns out to be price elastic than to start by charging low prices and then attempt to raise them substantially if demand appears to be insensitive to higher prices.

(c) High prices in the early stages of a product's life might generate **high initial cash flows**. A firm with liquidity problems may prefer market skimming for this reason.

(d) The firm can identify **different market segments** for the product, each prepared to pay progressively lower prices. It may therefore be possible to continue to sell at higher prices to some market segments when lower prices are charged in others. This is discussed further below.

(e) Products may have a **short life cycle**, and so need to recover their development costs and make a profit relatively quickly.

Products to which the policy has been applied include:

- Calculators
- Video recorders
- Desktop computers

5.5 Market penetration pricing   6/11

Key term

> **Penetration pricing** is a policy of low prices when a product is first launched in order to obtain strong demand for the product as soon as it is launched on the market. Low prices should encourage bigger demand.

A penetration pricing policy may be appropriate in the cases below.

(a) The firm wishes to **discourage new entrants** from entering the market.

(b) The firm wishes to **shorten the initial period** of the product's life cycle in order to enter the growth and maturity stages as quickly as possible.

(c)   There are significant **economies of scale** to be achieved from a high volume of output.

(d)   Demand is **highly elastic** and so would respond well to low prices.

Penetration prices are prices which aim to secure a substantial share in a substantial total market. A firm might therefore deliberately build **excess production capacity** and set its prices very low. As demand builds up the spare capacity will be used up gradually and unit costs will fall; the firm might even reduce prices further as unit costs fall. In this way, early losses will enable the firm to dominate the market and have the lowest costs.

5.6 Complementary product pricing

Key term

> **Complementary products** are goods that tend to be bought and used together. If an organisation makes and sells complementary products, it may wish to decide the selling prices for the products in a single pricing policy decision.

Complementary products are sold separately but are **connected** and dependent on each other for sales; for example, an electric toothbrush and replacement toothbrush heads. The electric toothbrush may be priced competitively to attract demand but the replacement heads can be relatively expensive.

On the other hand, the decision could be to set low prices for all the complementary products (or high prices for all complementary products) so that the expected sales demand for each is consistent. For example, a company selling digital book readers may also sell digital books. The prices of both may be set low in order to win sufficient sales demand for all the products. (This would be a different policy from, say, charging low prices for digital books but a high price for the reader.)

A **loss leader** is when a company sets a very low price for one product intending to make consumers buy other products in the range which carry higher profit margins. Another example is selling razors at very low prices while selling the blades for them at a higher profit margin. People will buy many of the high profit items but only one of the low profit items – yet they are 'locked in' to the former by the latter. This can also be described as **captive product pricing**.

Loss leaders are common in retailing, where stores may advertise very low prices for selected products, hoping that this will attract customers into the store where they will also buy other products that are 'normally' priced.

5.7 Product line pricing

Key term

> A **product line** is a group of products that are related to one another. A product line may be a range of branded products, and a consistent pricing policy should be applied to all the products in the range.

A **product line** is the marketing strategy of offering for sale several related products. A line can comprise related products of various sizes, types, colours, qualities or prices. Demand for and costs of the products are likely to be **interrelated.** For example, a company may manufacture a range of hygiene and skincare products, such as soaps, shower gels and bath oils, under the same brand name. With product line pricing, there will be a consistent pricing policy for all the products in the range.

There is a range of product line pricing strategies.

(a)   Set prices proportional to full or marginal cost with the same percentage profit margin for all products. This means that prices are dependent on cost and ignore demand.

(b)   Set prices reflecting the demand relationships between the products so that an overall required rate of return is achieved.

(c)   Set prices that reflect customer opinion about the quality of the products, and how they compare with similar products of competitor organisations.

5.8 Volume discounting

A **volume discount** is a reduction in price given for larger than average purchases.

The aim of a volume discount is to increase sales from large customers. The discount acts as a form of **differentiation** between types of customer (wholesale, retail, and so on).

The reduced costs of a large order will hopefully compensate for the loss of revenue from offering the discount.

5.9 Price discrimination

FAST FORWARD

With **price discrimination**, the same product or service is sold at different prices to different customers. This can be very difficult to implement in practice because it relies on the continued existence of certain market conditions for success.

In certain circumstances the **same product** can be sold at different prices to **different customers**.

Price discrimination is the practice of charging different prices for the same product to different groups of buyers when these prices are not reflective of cost differences.

There are a number of bases on which such discriminating prices can be set.

(a) **By market segment**. A ferry company running ferries from Country A to Country B would market its services at different prices in Country A and Country B, for example. Items such as cinema tickets and hairdressing services are often available at lower prices to old-age pensioners, students or juveniles.

(b) **By product version**. Many car models have 'add on' extras which enable one brand to appeal to a wider cross-section of customers. The final price need not reflect the cost price of the add on extras directly. Usually the top of the range model carries a price much in excess of the cost of provision of the extras, as a prestige appeal.

(c) **By place**. Theatre seats are usually sold according to their location so that patrons pay different prices for the same performance according to the type of seat and its location in the theatre auditorium.

(d) **By time**. This is perhaps the most popular type of price discrimination. Off-peak travel bargains, hotel prices and telephone charges are all attempts to increase sales revenue by covering variable but not necessarily average cost of provision. Railway companies are successful price discriminators, charging more to rush hour rail commuters whose demand is inelastic at certain times of the day.

Price discrimination can only be effective if a number of **conditions** hold.

(a) The market must be **segmentable** in price terms, and different sectors must show different intensities of demand. Each of the sectors must be identifiable, distinct and separate from the others, and be accessible to the firm's marketing communications.

(b) There must be little or **no** chance of a **black market** developing (this would allow those in the lower priced segment to resell to those in the higher priced segment).

(c) There must be little or **no** chance that **competitors** can and will undercut the firm's prices in the higher priced (and/or most profitable) market segments.

(d) The cost of segmenting and **administering** the arrangements should not exceed the extra revenue derived from the price discrimination strategy.

Try the following question which, although it has a few 'tricks', **looks more daunting than it is** if you keep your head and take care.

Curltown Cinemas operates a chain of 30 cinemas. Standard admission price is $7 per person, but this is subject to certain discounts. Average attendance at a cinema per month on normal price days is 5,000 people, but this is expected to be subject to seasonal variation, as follows.

Month	J	F	M	A	M	J	J	A	S	O	N	D
%	+10	−2	0	+5	−5	−5	+10	+7	−4	−4	0	+12

In December, January, July and August audiences are made up of 60% under-14s, who pay half-price admission. For the rest of the year under-14s represent only 10% of the audience. One day per month all tickets are sold at a special offer price of $1, irrespective of the age of the customer. This invariably guarantees a full house of 200 customers.

Required

(a)   What is Curltown Cinemas' total revenue from cinema admissions for a year?

(b)   If Curltown puts up prices for over-14s (other than the $1 special offer price) to $8, what will its total revenue from cinema admissions be for the year?

(c)   Should the special offer be continued?

Answer

(a)   This is simply a matter of reading the question carefully and patiently tabulating the data using a **different layout** to the one given in the question. Note that you save yourself potential error if you convert percentages into decimals as you transfer the question information into your own table. Don't forget that there are 30 cinemas.

Month	Variation	Average no	Adjusted no	Full price	Revenue @ $7.00 $	Half price	Revenue @ $3.50 $
Jan	+0.10	5,000	5,500	0.4	15,400.00	0.6	11,550.00
Feb	−0.02	5,000	4,900	0.9	30,870.00	0.1	1,715.00
Mar	+0.00	5,000	5,000	0.9	31,500.00	0.1	1,750.00
Apr	+0.05	5,000	5,250	0.9	33,075.00	0.1	1,837.50
May	−0.05	5,000	4,750	0.9	29,925.00	0.1	1,662.50
Jun	−0.05	5,000	4,750	0.9	29,925.00	0.1	1,662.50
Jul	+0.10	5,000	5,500	0.4	15,400.00	0.6	11,550.00
Aug	+0.07	5,000	5,350	0.4	14,980.00	0.6	11,235.00
Sep	−0.04	5,000	4,800	0.9	30,240.00	0.1	1,680.00
Oct	−0.04	5,000	4,800	0.9	30,240.00	0.1	1,680.00
Nov	0.00	5,000	5,000	0.9	31,500.00	0.1	1,750.00
Dec	+0.12	5,000	5,600	0.4	15,680.00	0.6	11,760.00
					308,735.00		59,832.50

	$
Total normal price ($308,735.00 + $59,832.50)	368,567.50
Special offer (12 × $1 × 200)	2,400.00
Total per cinema	370,967.50
Total per 30 cinemas	11,129,025.00

(b)   **There is no need to work out all the numbers again at the new prices.**

	$
Total as calculated above	11,129,025.00
Less: current adult normal price ($308,735 × 30)	(9,262,050.00)
Add: revised adult normal price ($308,735 × 30 × 8/7)	10,585,200.00
	12,452,175.00

(c)   If the income of $200 per cinema on the 12 special offer days is compared with an average of, say, $368,567.50/(365 – 12 days) = over $1,000, then it is clearly not worthwhile. The cinemas get average attendances of (5000 × 12)/365 = about 164 people in any case, even without special offers. (You could do **rough calculations** to estimate the overall loss of revenue per annum. Try it, making any **assumptions** you need, if you haven't done so, but not at the expense of written comments.)

However, the offer is a **loss-leader** which probably has other benefits. Customers will like it, and if the film they see is a good one they will recommend it to their friends. It may help to encourage the cinema-going habit among potential new customers. You may have thought of other relevant comments, either in favour of the policy or against it.

Exam focus point

A Section C exam question on this topic may have fewer calculations and more interpretation/analysis, so make sure you really think about the implications of price discrimination.

5.10 Relevant cost pricing

FAST FORWARD

> Special orders may require a **relevant cost** approach to the calculation of the price. A relevant cost approach is to identify a price at which the organisation will be no better off, but no worse off, if it sells the item at that price. Any price in excess of this minimum price will add to net profit.

A special order is a **one-off** revenue-earning opportunity. These may arise in the following situations.

(a)   When a business has a regular source of income but also has some **spare capacity**, allowing it to take on extra work if demanded. For example, a brewery might have a capacity of 500,000 barrels per month but only be producing and selling 300,000 barrels per month. It could therefore consider special orders to use up some of its spare capacity.

(b)   When a business has **no regular source of income** and relies exclusively on its ability to respond to demand. A building firm is a typical example, as are many types of subcontractors. In the service sector, consultants often work on this basis.

The reason for making the distinction is that in the case of (a), a firm would normally attempt to cover its longer-term running costs in its prices for its regular product. Pricing for special orders therefore does not need to consider unavoidable fixed costs, which will be incurred anyway. This is clearly not the case for a firm in (b)'s position, where special orders are the only source of income for the foreseeable future.

Exam focus point

Examination questions featuring pricing for special orders could present a scenario in which a firm has to decide whether to bid for a contract. The term 'minimum price' should be a clear indication that an incremental cost price is required.

5.10.1 Minimum pricing

The basic approach in both situations is to determine the price at which the firm would break even if it undertook the work; that is, the **minimum price** that it could afford to charge without a reduction in profit. To make a profit on the product or the order, the actual price charged should be higher than the minimum price.

A minimum price is the minimum price that would have to be charged so as to cover the following two groups of cost.

(a)   The **incremental costs** of producing and selling the item
(b)   The **opportunity costs** of the resources consumed in making and selling the item

A minimum price would leave the business no better or worse off than if it did not sell the item.

Two essential points to understand immediately about a minimum price are as follows.

(a) It is based on **relevant** costs; that is, the incremental costs plus the opportunity costs of making and selling the product or providing the service. You have covered this in your earlier studies and we will look at this aspect again in Chapter 6.

(b) It is **unlikely that a minimum price would actually be charged**, because if it were it would not provide the business with any incremental profit. However, the minimum price for an item shows the following.

    (i) An **absolute minimum** below which the price should not be set.

    (ii) The **incremental profit** that would be obtained from any price that is actually charged in excess of the minimum. For example, if the minimum price is $200 and the actual price charged is $240, the incremental profit on the sale would be $40.

If there are no **scarce resources**, and a company has **spare capacity**, the **minimum price** of a product would be an amount which equals the **incremental cost of making it**. Any price in excess of this minimum would provide an incremental contribution towards profit.

If there are scarce resources and a company makes more than one product, minimum prices would include an allowance for the **opportunity cost** of using the scarce resources to make and sell the product (instead of using the resources on the next most profitable product).

Where a firm also has to consider its **long-term costs** in the decision because it has no other way of recovering them it would have to **add a proportion of estimated unattributable costs to the price of each order**. This could be calculated on a time basis (if the job is expected to take one month, one twelfth of unavoidable costs would be included). However, this may lead to inconsistencies if, say, the unavoidable costs are borne in full by one customer in one month, but shared between several customers in another month.

Question

Relevant cost pricing

Ennerdale has been asked to quote a price for a one-off contract. The following information is available.

Materials

The contract requires 3,000 kg of material K, which is a material used regularly by the company in other production. The company has 2,000 kg of material K currently in stock which had been purchased last month for a total cost of $19,600. Since then the price per kilogram for material K has increased by 5%.

The contract also requires 200 kg of material L. There are 250 kg of material L in stock which are not required for normal production. This material originally cost a total of $3,125. If not used on this contract, the stock of material L would be sold for $11 per kg.

Labour

The contract requires 800 hours of skilled labour. Skilled labour is paid $9.50 per hour. There is a shortage of skilled labour and all the available skilled labour is fully employed in the company in the manufacture of product P. The following information relates to product P.

	$ per unit	$ per unit
Selling price		100
Less:		
Skilled labour	38	
Other variable costs	22	
		(60)
		40

Required

Prepare, on a relevant cost basis, the lowest cost estimate that could be used as the basis for a quotation.

Relevant cost – Material K

Since the material is regularly used by the company, the relevant cost of material K is the current price of the material.

Cost last month $= \dfrac{\$19{,}600}{2{,}000 \text{ kg}}$

$= \$9.80$

Revised cost (+5%) $= \$9.80 \times 1.05$

$= \$10.29$

$\therefore$ Relevant cost of Material K $= 3{,}000 \text{ kg} \times \$10.29 \text{ per kg}$

$= \$30{,}870$

Relevant cost – Material L

Since the material is not required for normal production, the relevant cost of this material is its net realisable value if it were sold.

$\therefore$ Relevant cost of Material L $= 200 \text{ kg} \times \$11 \text{ per kg}$

$= \$2{,}200$

Relevant cost – Skilled labour

Skilled labour is in short supply and therefore the relevant cost of this labour will include both the actual cost and the opportunity cost of the labour employed.

	$
Cost of skilled labour (800 hours × $9.50)	7,600
Opportunity cost of skilled labour (see working)	8,000
Relevant cost – skilled labour	15,600

Working

Skilled labour cost per unit of Product P = $38

Cost per skilled labour hour = $9.50

$\therefore$ Number of hours required per unit of Product P $= \dfrac{\$38}{\$9.50}$

$= 4 \text{ hours}$

Contribution per unit of Product P $= \$40$

$\therefore$ Contribution per skilled labour hour $= \dfrac{\$40}{4 \text{ hours}}$

$= \$10 \text{ per hour}$

$\therefore$ Opportunity cost of skilled labour $= 800 \text{ hours} \times \$10 \text{ per hour}$

$= \$8{,}000$

The total relevant costs of this contract are therefore $\$(30{,}870 + 2{,}200 + 15{,}600) = \$48{,}670$

Chapter Roundup

- In the modern world there are many more **influences on price** than cost (eg competitors, product range, quality).

- The price that an organisation can charge for its products will be determined to a greater or lesser degree by the **market** in which it operates.

- **Economic theory** argues that the **higher the price of a good**, the **lower** will be the **quantity demanded**.

- The **price elasticity of demand (PED)** is a measure of the extent of change in demand for a good in response to a change in its price.

- Most products pass through the five stages of the **product life cycle**.

- You need to be able to derive the **demand equation** $P = a - bQ$.

- Cost behaviour can be **modelled** using equations.

- If we assume that there is a demand curve with the equation $P = a - bQ$, and a total cost function $C = F + vQ$, we can determine the profit-maximising price for the product.

  Profits are maximised where **marginal cost (MC) = marginal revenue (MR)**. The **optimal selling price** can be determined by deriving equations for MC and MR. Alternatively, the **optimum selling price** can be determined using tabulation.

- If you are required to evaluate a decision to increase production and sales levels, you will need to consider **incremental costs**, **incremental revenues** and other factors.

- The price to be charged for a product or service is often one of the most important decisions made by business organisations. There are a number of alternative pricing strategies.

- **Full cost-plus pricing** is a method of deciding the sales price by adding a percentage mark-up for profit to the full cost of the product.

- **Marginal cost-plus pricing, also called mark-up pricing**, involves adding a profit margin to the marginal cost of the product.

- Pricing strategies for new products include **market skimming** and **market penetration pricing**.

- With **price discrimination**, the same product or service is sold at different prices to different customers. This can be very difficult to implement in practice because it relies on the continued existence of certain market conditions for success.

- Special orders may require a **relevant cost** approach to the calculation of the price. A relevant cost approach is to identify a price at which the organisation will be no better off, but no worse off, if it sells the item at that price. Any price in excess of this minimum price will add to net profit.

Quick Quiz

1   Fill in the blanks.

Demand is said to be elastic when a .... change in price produces a .... change in quantity demanded. PED is .... than 1.

Demand is said to be inelastic when a .... change in price produces a .... change in quantity demanded. PED is .... than 1.

2   Fill in the blanks in the formula below for the variable 'a' in the equation for a demand curve.

$$a = \$(............\,...................) + \left(\frac{..}{..} \times \$...... \right)$$

3   Cost-based approaches to pricing take more account of the external environment than target costing. **True or false?**

4   Fill in the blanks.

(a)   One of the problems with relying on a full cost-plus approach to pricing is that it fails to recognise that, since price may be determining demand, there will be a .... combination of .... and ....

(b)   An advantage of the full cost-plus approach is that, because the size of the profit margin can be varied, a decision based on a price in excess of full cost should ensure that a company working at .... capacity will cover .... and make a ....

5   Pricing based on mark-up per unit of limiting factor is particularly useful if an organisation is not working to full capacity. **True or false?**

6   Fill in the blank.

The .... price is the price at which an organisation will break even if it undertakes particular work.

7   Choose the correct word from those highlighted.

Market **skimming/penetration** pricing should be used if an organisation wishes to discourage new entrants into a market.

Answers to Quick Quiz

1   (a)   Demand is said to be elastic when a **small change** in the price produces a **large change** in the quantity demanded. PED is **greater** than 1.

    (b)   Demand is said to be **inelastic** when a small change in the price produces only a **small change in the quantity** demanded. **PED is less than 1**.

2   $$a = \text{(current price)} + \left(\frac{\text{Current quantity at current price}}{\text{Change in quantity when price is changed by \$b}} \times \$b \right)$$

3   False

4   (a)   profit-maximising combination of price and demand

    (b)   working at normal capacity will cover all of its fixed costs and make a profit

5   False. It is useful if the organisation is working at full capacity.

6   Minimum

7   Market penetration

Now try the questions below from the Practice Question Bank

Number	Level	Marks	Approximate time
Section A Q36	Examination	2	4 mins
Section A Q37	Examination	2	4 mins
Section A Q38	Examination	2	4 mins
Section A Q39	Examination	2	4 mins
Section A Q40	Examination	2	4 mins

Short-term decisions

Topic list	Syllabus reference
1 Identifying relevant costs	B1 (a), (b), (c)
2 Make or buy decisions	B5 (a), (b), (c)
3 Outsourcing	B5 (a), (b), (c)
4 Further processing decisions	B5 (d)
5 Shutdown decisions	B5 (d)

Introduction

The concept of **relevant costs** has already been revisited in this study text and their use in one-off contracts to identify a minimum price was explained in the previous chapter.

In this chapter we look in greater depth at relevant costs and at how they should be applied in **decision-making situations**.

We look at a variety of common short-run business decisions and consider how they can be dealt with using relevant costs as appropriate.

Study guide

		Intellectual level
B1	**Relevant cost analysis**	
(a)	Explain the concept of relevant costing.	2
(b)	Identify and calculate relevant costs for specific decision situations from given data.	2
(c)	Explain and apply the concept of opportunity costs.	2
B5	**Make or buy and other short-term decisions**	
(a)	Explain the issues surrounding make vs buy and outsourcing decisions.	2
(b)	Calculate and compare 'make' costs with 'buy-in' costs.	2
(c)	Compare in-house costs and outsource costs of completing tasks and consider other issues surrounding this decision.	2
(d)	Apply relevant costing principles in situations involving shutdown, one-off contracts and the further processing of joint products.	2

Exam guide

The ability to recognise relevant costs and revenues is a key skill for the F5 exam and is highly examinable. Questions will be based on practical scenarios.

1 Identifying relevant costs   12/11, 12/14, Specimen

FAST FORWARD

Relevant costs are future cash flows arising as a direct consequence of a decision.

- Relevant costs are **future costs.**
- Relevant costs are **cash flows.**
- Relevant costs are **incremental costs**, arising as a direct consequence of the decision.

1.1 When are relevant costs used?

Relevant costs are used when a decision has to be taken and the concern is whether the decision will increase profits or not, or which decision will increase profits the most. Examples of decisions where relevant costs (and benefits) are used include:

(a) Deciding whether to agree to accept a job or undertake some work at a stated price that the customer will pay

(b) Whether to sell joint products from a common process at the point where they are output from the common process, or whether they should be processed further before selling them at a higher price

(c) Whether to make products 'in house' or whether to subcontract or outsource the work to an external supplier

There are two basic types of decision where relevant costs are used.

(a) Decisions about whether to do something or whether not to do it
(b) Decisions that involve selecting between two or more different options about what to do

1.2 The approach to identifying relevant costs and benefits

To identify the relevant costs and benefits that will be affected by a decision, the approach should be to look at each item of cost or benefit in turn. (Benefits may be additional revenue or savings in costs as a result of the decision.) For each item of cost (or benefit), it is necessary to specify the relevant cost (or benefit). This is the cost (or benefit) that should be taken into account when reaching the decision.

Each item of cost or benefit should be considered in turn. In your exam, you may be required not only to identify the correct relevant cost for each item, but also to explain the logic or reasoning – in other words, explain why the cost (or benefit) that you have identified is the relevant cost.

In this section we explain the approach to identifying the relevant costs for different types of cost.

1.3 Definition of relevant costs

A relevant cost is a future cash flow arising as a direct consequence of a decision.

(a) It must be a cost that will occur in the future. Any cost that has already been incurred in the past cannot be a relevant cost.

(b) It must be a cost (or benefit) that results in cash flow. Depreciation charges and overhead absorption costs cannot be relevant costs.

(c) It must arise as a direct consequence of the decision. Any costs (or benefits) that will happen anyway, regardless of the decision, cannot be a relevant cost.

It follows from this definition that:

(a) **Sunk costs cannot be relevant costs**. Sunk costs are costs that have already been incurred.

(b) **Committed costs cannot be relevant costs**. These are costs that will be incurred in the future, but they cannot be avoided because they have already been committed by a previous decision.

In the rest of this section, we explain the approach to identifying the relevant costs for different types of cost.

1.4 Machinery user costs

A decision may involve having to use an item of machinery to do some additional work.

Once a machine has been bought its purchase cost is a **sunk** cost. **Depreciation** is not a relevant cost, because it is not a cash flow.

However, **using** machinery may involve some incremental costs. These costs may be referred to as **user costs**. They include hire charges where machinery will have to be hired or rented as a result of the decision. They also include any fall in the resale value of machinery or other assets that the organisation owns, where the fall in value will be caused by using the asset as a consequence of the decision.

1.4.1 Example: Machine user costs

Bronty Co is considering whether to undertake some contract work for a customer. The machinery required for the contract would be as follows.

(a) A special cutting machine will have to be hired for three months for the work (the length of the contract). Hire charges for this machine are $75 per month, with a minimum hire charge of $300.

(b) All other machinery required in the production for the contract has already been purchased by the organisation on hire purchase terms. The monthly hire purchase payments for this machinery are $500. This consists of $450 for capital repayment and $50 as an interest charge. The last hire purchase payment is to be made in two months' time. The cash price of this machinery was $9,000 two years ago. It is being depreciated on a straight line basis at the rate of $200 per month. However, it still has a useful life which will enable it to be operated for another 36 months.

The machinery is highly specialised and is unlikely to be required for other, more profitable jobs over the period during which the contract work would be carried out. Although there is no immediate market for selling this machine, it is expected that a customer might be found in the future. It is further estimated that the machine would lose $200 in its eventual sale value if it is used for the contract work.

What is the relevant cost of machinery for the contract?

Solution

(a) The **cutting machine** will incur an incremental cost of $300, the minimum hire charge.

(b) The historical cost of the **other machinery** is irrelevant as a past cost; depreciation is irrelevant as a non-cash cost; and future hire purchase repayments are irrelevant because they are committed costs. The only relevant cost is the loss of resale value of the machinery, estimated at $200 through use. This 'user cost' will not arise until the machinery is eventually resold and the $200 should be discounted to allow for the time value of money. However, discounting is ignored here, and will be discussed in a later chapter.

(c) **Summary of relevant costs**

	$
Incremental hire costs	300
User cost of other machinery	200
	500

1.5 Relevant cost of labour

Often the labour force will be paid irrespective of the decision made and the costs are therefore **not incremental**. Take care, however, if the labour force could be put to an **alternative use**, in which case the relevant costs are the **variable costs** of the labour and associated variable overheads **plus** the **contribution forgone** from not being able to put it to its alternative use.

For example, suppose that a special job would require 50 hours of labour time. Employees are paid $10 per hour. There is sufficient idle capacity among the workforce for 40 hours of the work. The extra ten hours would be worked in overtime, for which the additional pay is $12.50 per hour.

In this example, the relevant cost of labour is the incremental cost. Of the 50 hours required for the work, 40 hours would be paid anyway, so the cost is a committed cost that will be incurred anyway, and it is not relevant. However, there will be additional costs of $125 (10 hours at $12.50 per hour) for the overtime working, which will be an additional 'cash' cost.

Suppose that another special job will require 20 hours of skilled labour. The skilled workforce is paid $15 per hour and is working at full capacity. If the special job is undertaken, the skilled labour would be taken off other work that earns a contribution of $12 per hour, after deducting the costs of the labour and variable overheads of $1.5 per hour. In this situation the relevant cost of labour must include the variable cost of the labour plus any associated variable overhead, and the contribution that would be lost by taking the skilled workers off the other work.

	$
Labour cost of 20 hours ($\times$ $15 per hour)	300
Variable overhead costs ($\times$ $1.50 per hour)	30
Contribution forgone ($\times$ $12 per hour)	240
Total relevant cost of labour time	570

1.6 Relevant cost of materials

The relevant cost of raw materials is generally their current **replacement** cost, unless the materials have already been purchased and would not be replaced once used.

If materials have already been purchased but will not be replaced, then the relevant cost of using them is **either** (a) their current **resale** value **or** (b) the value they would obtain if they were put to an **alternative use**, if this is greater than their current resale value.

The **higher** of (a) or (b) is then the opportunity cost of the materials. If the materials have no resale value and no other possible use, then the relevant cost of using them for the opportunity under consideration would be nil.

The flowchart below shows how the relevant costs of materials can be identified, **provided that** the materials are **not in short supply**, and so have **no internal opportunity cost**.

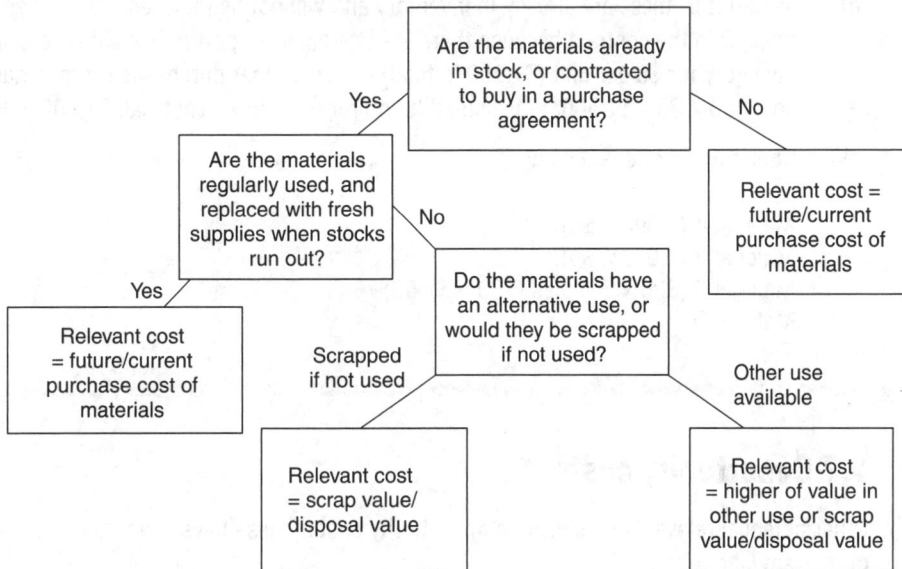

Question

Relevant cost of materials

O'Reilly Co has been approached by a customer who would like a special job to be done for them, and who is willing to pay $22,000 for it. The job would require the following materials.

Material	Total units required	Units already in inventory	Book value of units in inventory $/unit	Realisable value $/unit	Replacement cost $/unit
A	1,000	0	–	–	6
B	1,000	600	2	2.5	5
C	1,000	700	3	2.5	4
D	200	200	4	6.0	9

(a) Material B is used regularly by O'Reilly Co, and if units of B are required for this job, they would need to be replaced to meet other production demand.

(b) Materials C and D are in inventory as the result of previous overbuying, and they have a restricted use. No other use could be found for material C, but the units of material D could be used in another job as substitute for 300 units of material E, which currently costs $5 per unit (of which the company has no units in inventory at the moment).

What are the relevant costs of material, in deciding whether or not to accept the contract?

(a) **Material A**: this is not owned and would have to be bought in full at the replacement cost of $6 per unit.

(b) **Material B**: this is used regularly by the company. There is existing inventory (600 units) but if these are used on the contract under review a further 600 units would be bought to replace them. Relevant costs are therefore 1,000 units at the replacement cost of $5 per unit.

(c) **Material C**: 1,000 units are needed and 700 are already in inventory. If used for the contract, a further 300 units must be bought at $4 each. The existing inventory of 700 will not be replaced. If they are used for the contract, they could not be sold at $2.50 each. The realisable value of these 700 units is an opportunity cost of sales revenue forgone.

(d) **Material D**: these are already in inventory and will not be replaced. There is an opportunity cost of using D in the contract because there are alternative opportunities either to sell the existing inventory for $6 per unit ($1,200 in total) or avoid other purchases (of material E), which would cost $300 \times $5 = $1,500$. Since substitution for E is more beneficial, $1,500 is the opportunity cost.

(e) **Summary of relevant costs**

	$
Material A (1,000 × $6)	6,000
Material B (1,000 × $5)	5,000
Material C (300 × $4) plus (700 × $2.50)	2,950
Material D	1,500
Total	15,450

1.7 Opportunity costs

Other potential relevant costs include **opportunity costs**. These have been mentioned already in the context of relevant labour costs.

Opportunity cost is the **benefit sacrificed** by choosing one opportunity rather than the next best alternative. You will often encounter opportunity costs when there are several possible uses for a scarce resource.

For example, if a material is in short supply, it may be transferred from the production of one product to that of another product. The opportunity cost is the **contribution lost** from ceasing production of the original product.

Key term

> **Opportunity cost** is the value of a benefit sacrificed when one course of action is chosen, in preference to an alternative. The opportunity cost is represented by the forgone potential benefit from the best rejected course of action.

Question   Opportunity costs

An information technology consultancy firm has been asked to do an urgent job by a client, for which a price of $2,500 has been offered. The job would require the following.

(a) 30 hours' work from one member of staff, who is paid on an hourly basis, at a rate of $20 per hour, but who would normally be employed on work for clients where the charge-out rate is $45 per hour. No other member of staff is able to do the member of staff in question's work.

(b) The use of five hours of mainframe computer time, which the firm normally charges out to external users at a rate of $50 per hour. Mainframe computer time is currently used 24 hours a day, seven days a week.

(c) Supplies and incidental expenses of $200.

Required

Fill in the blank in the sentence below.

The relevant cost or opportunity cost of the job is $........

Answer

The correct answer is $1,800.

The relevant cost or opportunity cost of the job would be calculated as follows.

	$
Labour (30 hours × $20)	600
Opportunity cost of labour (30 hours × ($45 – $20))	750
Computer time opportunity cost (5 hours × $50)	250
Supplies and expenses	200
	1,800

2 Make or buy decisions

6/12

FAST FORWARD

> In a **make or buy decision**, the choice is between making items in-house or purchasing them from an external supplier. When there are no limiting factors restricting the in-house production capacity, the relevant costs are the differential costs between the two options.

Exam focus point

> In the exam, you may be required to apply the principles of relevant costs to a specific decision that is described in the quesiton.

There are different types of decision where relevant costs are required to evaluate the decision choices. One type of decision is the so-called 'make or buy' decision, where the choice is between making products internally, or subcontracting production to an external supplier.

Here are some examples of make or buy decisions.

(a)   Whether a company should manufacture its own components, or else buy the components from an outside supplier

(b)   Whether a construction company should do some work with its own employees, or whether it should subcontract the work to another company

(c)   Whether a service should be carried out by an internal department or whether an external organisation should be employed

The **'make'** option should give **management more direct control** over the work, but the **'buy'** option often has the benefit that the **external organisation** has a **specialist skill** and expertise in the work. Make or buy decisions should certainly **not be based exclusively on cost considerations.** Issues such as control, quality, flexibility, reliability of delivery and speed of delivery may all affect the decision to make or buy.

From the point of view of identifying relevant costs, a very important issue is whether the organisation has sufficient capacity to manufacture all the products in-house. If an organisation has the freedom of choice about whether to make internally or buy externally, it has no scarce resources that put a restriction on what it can do itself. In other words, there is no limiting factor that restricts the output capacity of in-house operations. In this situation, the **relevant costs** for the make or buy decision are the **differential costs** between the two options.

2.1 Example: Make or buy decision

Shellfish Co makes four components, W, X, Y and Z, for which costs in the forthcoming year are expected to be as follows.

	W	X	Y	Z
Production (units)	1,000	2,000	4,000	3,000
Unit marginal costs	$	$	$	$
Direct materials	4	5	2	4
Direct labour	8	9	4	6
Variable production overheads	2	3	1	2
	14	17	7	12

Directly attributable fixed costs per annum and committed fixed costs:

	$
Incurred as a direct consequence of making W	1,000
Incurred as a direct consequence of making X	5,000
Incurred as a direct consequence of making Y	6,000
Incurred as a direct consequence of making Z	8,000
Other fixed costs (committed)	30,000
	50,000

Directly attributable fixed costs are all items of cash expenditure that are incurred as a direct consequence of making the product in-house.

A subcontractor has offered to supply units of W, X, Y and Z for $12, $21, $10 and $14 respectively. Should Shellfish make or buy the components?

Solution

(a) The **relevant costs** are the differential costs between making and buying, and they consist of **differences in unit variable costs plus differences in directly attributable fixed costs**. Subcontracting will result in some **fixed cost savings.**

	W	X	Y	Z
	$	$	$	$
Unit variable cost of making	14	17	7	12
Unit variable cost of buying	12	21	10	14
	(2)	4	3	2
Annual requirements (units)	1,000	2,000	4,000	3,000
	$	$	$	$
Extra variable cost of buying (per annum)	(2,000)	8,000	12,000	6,000
Fixed costs saved by buying	(1,000)	(5,000)	(6,000)	(8,000)
Extra total cost of buying	(3,000)	3,000	6,000	(2,000)

(b) The company would save $3,000 pa by subcontracting component W (where the purchase cost would be less than the marginal cost per unit to make internally) and would save $2,000 pa by subcontracting component Z (because of the saving in fixed costs of $8,000).

(c) In this example, relevant costs are the variable costs of in-house manufacture, the variable costs of subcontracted units, and the saving in fixed costs.

(d) **Further considerations**

(i) If components W and Z are subcontracted, the company will have **spare capacity**. How should that spare capacity be profitably used? Are there hidden benefits to be obtained from subcontracting? Would the company's workforce resent the loss of work to an outside subcontractor, and might such a decision cause an industrial dispute?

(ii) Would the subcontractor be **reliable** with delivery times, and would they supply components of the same **quality** as those manufactured internally?

(iii) Does the company wish to be **flexible** and maintain better **control** over operations by making everything itself?

(iv) Are the **estimates** of fixed cost savings reliable? In the case of Product W, buying is clearly cheaper than making in-house. In the case of Product Z, the decision to buy rather than make would only be financially beneficial if it is feasible that the fixed cost savings of $8,000 will really be 'delivered' by management. All too often in practice, promised savings fail to materialise!

2.2 Make or buy decisions with a limiting factor

A manufacturing organisation may want to produce items in-house but does not have sufficient capacity to produce everything that it needs, due to a limiting factor on production, such as a shortage of machine time or labour time.

In this situation, the decision is not whether to make internally or purchase externally. The decision is about which items to make internally and which to purchase externally. The optimal decision, based on financial considerations alone, is to arrange internal production and external purchasing in a way that minimises total costs.

Make or buy decisions involving limiting factors are described in Chapter 4.

3 Outsourcing   12/07, 6/12

FAST FORWARD

> The relevant costs/revenues in decisions relating to the **operating of internal service departments or the use of external services** are the differential costs between the two options.

3.1 The trend in outsourcing

A significant trend in the 1990s was for companies and government bodies to **concentrate on their core competences** – what they are really good at (or set up to achieve) – and turn other functions over to **specialist contractors.** A company that earns its profits from, say, manufacturing bicycles, does not also need to have expertise in, say, mass catering or office cleaning. **Facilities management** companies, such as Serco and G4S, have grown in response to this.

Key term

> **Outsourcing** is the use of external suppliers for finished products, components or services. This is also known as **contract manufacturing** or **subcontracting.**

Basically, decisions about outsourcing activities or using internal staff to do the work is a form of 'make or buy' decision, and the basic principles are the same.

Reasons for the trend towards outsourcing activities include the following.

(a) Frequently the decision is made on the grounds that **specialist contractors** can offer **superior quality** and **efficiency**. If a contractor's main business is making a specific component it can invest in the specialist machinery and labour and knowledge skills needed to make that component. However, this component may be only one of many needed by the contractor's customer, and the complexity of components is now such that attempting to keep internal facilities up to the standard of specialists detracts from the main business of the customer.

(b) Contracting out manufacturing **frees capital** that can then be invested in core activities, such as market research, product definition, product planning, marketing and sales.

(c) **Contractors** have the **capacity** and **flexibility** to start production very quickly to meet sudden **variations in demand**. In-house facilities may not be able to respond as quickly, because of the need to redirect resources from elsewhere.

(d) There is not enough work to keep internal staff fully occupied, so it is cheaper to outsource the work. For example, many organisations outsource payroll administration because it is not worthwhile employing staff with knowledge of payroll work.

3.2 Internal and external services

Companies will often use specialist companies for administrative and support functions. Decisions such as the following are now common.

(a) It is often decided whether the **design and development of a new computer system** should be entrusted to in-house data processing staff or whether an external software house should be hired to do the work.

(b) It is often decided whether **maintenance and repairs** of certain items of equipment should be dealt with by in-house engineers, or whether a maintenance contract should be made with a specialist organisation.

(c) Office cleaning is often outsourced to external contractors. The management of the organisation do not want to have their time consumed by management problems relating to office cleaning, so they are happy to pay another firm to do the work and take on the operational problems.

(d) Security services are often outsourced to specialist companies. In the UK, some prison management services are outsourced by the Government to private sector contractors.

The costs **relevant** to decisions about whether or not to outsource activities are little different (if at all) to those that are taken into account in a 'conventional' make or buy situation. The relevant costs are the **differential costs** between performing the service internally or using an external provider.

Exam focus point

> The major problem in examination questions is likely to be identifying whether existing staff will be made redundant or whether they will be redeployed, and whether there are alternative uses for the other resources made available by ceasing to perform the service internally. These, it hardly needs stating, are also likely to be the major problems in practice.

3.3 Performance of outsourcers

An 'outsourcer' here means the organisation to which work is outsourced.

Once a decision has been made to outsource, it is essential that the **performance** of the outsourcer is monitored and **measured**.

Measures could include cost savings, service improvement and employee satisfaction. It is important to have **realistic goals** and expectations and to have **objective ways** to measure success.

The performance of the outsourcer, whether good or bad, can interfere with the performance assessment of an **internal function**. For example:

- Maintenance of equipment could be carried out badly by an outsourcer and this may result in increased breakdowns and reduced labour efficiency of a production team.

- If information arrives late or is incorrect, the wrong decision may be made.

3.4 Example: Outsourcing

Stunnaz is considering a proposal to use the services of a press cuttings agency. At the moment, press cuttings are collected by a junior member of the marketing department, who is also responsible for office administration (including filing), travel bookings, a small amount of proofreading and making the tea. The total annual cost of employing this person is $15,000 pa.

There is concern that the ability of this person to produce a comprehensive file of cuttings is limited by the time available. They have calculated that they need to spend about two hours of their seven and a half hour day simply reading the national and trade press, but usually only have about five hours a week for this job.

Press subscriptions currently cost $850 pa and are paid annually in advance.

The assistant makes use of a small micro-fiche device for storing cuttings. The cuttings are sent to a specialist firm once a month to be put onto fiche. Stunnaz pays $45 each month for this service. The micro-fiche reader is leased at a cost of $76 per calendar month. This lease has another 27 months to run.

The cuttings service bureau has proposed an annual contract at a cost of $1,250. Several existing users have confirmed their satisfaction with the service they receive.

Should Stunnaz outsource its press cuttings work?

Solution

Current annual costs amount to:

	$
Micro-fiche service	$45 \times 12 = 540$
Subscriptions	850
	1,390

The monthly leasing charge is a **committed cost** that must be paid whatever the decision. It is not therefore a decision-relevant cost.

Engaging the services of the press cuttings agency therefore has the **potential** to save Stunnaz $140 pa. However, this is not the final word: there are other considerations.

(a) The **'in-house' option** should give management **more direct control** over the work, but the **'outsource' option** often has the benefit that the external organisation has a **specialist skill and expertise** in the work. Decisions should certainly not be based exclusively on cost considerations.

(b) Will outsourcing create **spare capacity**? How should that spare capacity be profitably used?

(c) Are there **hidden benefits** to be obtained from subcontracting?

(d) Would the company's workforce resent the loss of work to an outside subcontractor, and might such a decision cause an **industrial dispute**?

(e) Would the subcontractor be **reliable with delivery times** and **quality**?

(f) Does the company wish to be **flexible** and **maintain better control** over operations by doing everything itself?

4 Further processing decisions   12/07, 12/13

FAST FORWARD

A further processing decision often involves joint products from a common manufacturing process. The decision is whether to sell the products at the split-off point, as soon as they emerge from the common process, or whether they should be processed further before selling them.

A joint product should be **processed further** past the split-off point if the additional sales revenue exceeds the relevant post-separation (further processing) costs.

4.1 Joint products

You should have covered joint products in your earlier studies and the following will act as a brief reminder.

Knowledge brought forward from earlier studies

- **Joint products** are two or more products which are output from the same processing operation, but which are indistinguishable from each other up to their point of separation.

- Joint products (unlike by-products from a process) have a **substantial sales value**. Often they require further processing before they are ready for sale. Joint products arise, for example, in the oil refining industry where diesel fuel, petrol, paraffin and lubricants are all produced from the same process.

- A joint product is regarded as an important saleable item, and so it should be **separately costed**. The profitability of each joint product should be assessed in the cost accounts.

- The point at which joint products become separately identifiable is known as the **split-off point** or **separation point**.

- Costs incurred prior to this point of separation are **common** or **joint costs**.

- Problems in **accounting** for joint products are basically of two different sorts.

  - How common costs should be apportioned between the joint products, in order to put a value to closing inventory and to the cost of sale (and profit) for each product. This may be necessary for financial reporting and preparing profit statements, but it has no relevance to decision making.

  - Whether it is more profitable to sell a joint product at one stage of processing, usually at the split-off point, or whether to process the product further and sell it at a later stage. This is a decision for which relevant costs and benefits should be considered.

Suppose a manufacturing company carries out process operations in which two or more joint products are made from a common process. If the joint products can be sold either in their existing condition at the 'split-off' point at the end of common processing or after further separate processing, **a decision should be taken about whether to sell each joint product at the split-off point or after further processing.**

4.2 Example: Further processing decision

The Poison Chemical Company produces two joint products, Alash and Pottum from the same process. Joint processing costs of $150,000 are incurred up to the split-off point, when 100,000 units of Alash and 50,000 units of Pottum are produced. The selling prices at the split-off point are $1.25 per unit for Alash and $2.00 per unit for Pottum.

The units of Alash could be processed further to produce 60,000 units of a new chemical, Alashplus, but at an extra fixed cost of $20,000 and variable cost of 30c per unit of input. The selling price of Alashplus would be $3.25 per unit. Should the company sell Alash or Alashplus?

Solution

The only relevant costs/incomes are those which compare the sale of Alash against the sale of Alashplus. Every other cost is irrelevant: they will be incurred regardless of what the decision is.

	Alash			Alashplus
Selling price per unit	$1.25			$3.25
	$		$	$
Total sales	125,000			195,000
Incremental post-separation processing costs	–	Fixed	20,000	
	–	Variable	30,000	50,000
Sales minus post-separation (further processing) costs	125,000			145,000

It is $20,000 more profitable to convert Alash into Alashplus.

A company manufactures four products from an input of a raw material to Process 1. Following this process, product A is processed in Process 2, product B in Process 3, product C in Process 4 and product D in Process 5.

The normal loss in Process 1 is 10% of input, and there are no expected losses in the other processes. Scrap value in Process 1 is $0.50 per litre. The costs incurred in Process 1 are apportioned to each product according to the volume of output of each product. Production overhead is absorbed as a percentage of direct wages.

Data in respect of the month of October

	Process					
	1	2	3	4	5	Total
	$'000	$'000	$'000	$'000	$'000	$'000
Direct materials at $1.25 per litre	100					100
Direct wages	48	12	8	4	16	88
Production overhead						66

	Product			
	A	B	C	D
	litres	litres	litres	litres
Output	22,000	20,000	10,000	18,000
	$	$	$	$
Selling price	4.00	3.00	2.00	5.00
Estimated sales value at end of Process 1	2.50	2.80	1.20	3.00

Required

Suggest and evaluate an alternative production strategy which would optimise profit for the month. It should not be assumed that the output of Process 1 can be changed.

Answer

During the month, the quantity of input to Process 1 was 80,000 litres. Normal loss is 10% = 8,000 litres, and so total output should have been 72,000 litres of A, B, C and D. Instead, it was only 70,000 litres. In an 'average' month, output would have been higher, and this might have some bearing on the optimal production and selling strategy.

The **central question** is whether or not the output from Process 1 should be **processed further** in Processes 2, 3, 4 and 5, or whether it should be **sold at the 'split-off' point**, at the end of Process 1. Each joint product can be looked at **individually**.

A further question is whether the **wages costs** in Process 2, 3, 4 and 5 would be avoided if the joint products were sold at the end of process 1 and not processed further. It will be assumed that all the wages costs would be **avoidable**, but none of the **production overhead** costs would be. This assumption can be challenged, and in practice would have to be investigated.

	A	B	C	D
	$	$	$	$
Selling price, per litre	4.00	3.00	2.00	5.00
Selling price at end of process 1	2.50	2.80	1.20	3.00
Incremental selling price, per litre	1.50	0.20	0.80	2.00
Litres output	22,000	20,000	10,000	18,000
	$'000	$'000	$'000	$'000
Total incremental revenue from further processing	33	4	8	36
Avoidable costs from selling at split-off point (wages saved)	12	8	4	16
Incremental benefit/(cost) of further processing	21	(4)	4	20

This analysis would seem to indicate that **products A, C and D should be further processed** in Processes 2, 4 and 5 respectively, but that **product B should be sold at the end of Process 1**, without further processing in Process 3. The saving would be at least $4,000 per month.

If **some production overhead** (which is 75% of direct wages) were also **avoidable**, this would mean that:

(a)   Selling product B at the end of Process 1 would offer further savings of up to (75% of $8,000) $6,000 in overheads, and so $10,000 in total.

(b)   The incremental benefit from further processing product C might fall by up to (75% of $4,000) $3,000 to $1,000, meaning that it is only just profitable to process C beyond the split-off point.

5 Shutdown decisions   12/09

Shutdown/discontinuance problems may sometimes be simplified into short-run relevant cost decisions. A shutdown decision is whether to close down an operation or stop making and selling a particular product or service.

5.1 The nature of shutdown decisions

Discontinuance or shutdown problems involve the following decisions.

(a)   **Whether or not to close down** a product line, department or other activity, either because it is making losses or because it is too expensive to run

(b)   If the decision is to shut down, **whether the closure should be permanent or temporary**

In practice, shutdown decisions may often involve **longer-term considerations,** and **capital expenditures and revenues**.

(a)   A shutdown should result in savings in **annual operating costs** for a number of years into the future.

(b)   Closure will probably release **unwanted non-current assets for sale**. Some assets might have a small scrap value, but other assets, in particular property, might have a substantial sale value.

(c)   **Employees** affected by the closure must be made redundant or relocated, perhaps after retraining, or else offered early retirement. There will be lump-sum payments involved which must be taken into account in the financial arithmetic. For example, suppose that the closure of a regional office would result in annual savings of $100,000, non-current assets could be sold off to earn income of $2 million, but redundancy payments would be $3 million. The shutdown decision would involve an assessment of the net capital cost of closure ($1 million) against the annual benefits ($100,000 pa).

It is possible, however, for shutdown problems to be **simplified into short-run decisions**, by making one of the following assumptions.

(a)   Non-current asset sales and redundancy costs would be negligible.

(b)   Income from non-current asset sales would match redundancy costs and so these capital items would be self-cancelling.

In such circumstances, the financial aspect of shutdown decisions would be based on **short-run relevant costs**.

5.2 Example: Adding or deleting products (or departments)

A company manufactures three products, Pawns, Rooks and Bishops. The present net annual income from these is as follows.

	Pawns $	Rooks $	Bishops $	Total $
Sales	50,000	40,000	60,000	150,000
Variable costs	30,000	25,000	35,000	90,000
Contribution	20,000	15,000	25,000	60,000
Fixed costs	17,000	18,000	20,000	55,000
Profit/loss	3,000	(3,000)	5,000	5,000

The company is concerned about its poor profit performance, and is considering whether or not to cease selling Rooks. It is felt that selling prices cannot be raised or lowered without adversely affecting net income. $5,000 of the fixed costs of Rooks are direct fixed costs which would be saved if production ceased (ie there are some attributable fixed costs). All other fixed costs, it is considered, would remain the same.

By **stopping production of Rooks**, the **consequences** would be a $10,000 fall in profits.

	$
Loss of contribution	(15,000)
Savings in fixed costs	5,000
Incremental loss	(10,000)

Suppose, however, it were possible to use the resources realised by stopping production of Rooks and **switch to producing a new item**, Crowners, which would sell for $50,000 and incur variable costs of $30,000 and extra direct fixed costs of $6,000. A new decision is now required.

	Rooks $	Crowners $
Sales	40,000	50,000
Less variable costs	25,000	30,000
	15,000	20,000
Less direct fixed costs	5,000	6,000
Contribution to shared fixed costs and profit	10,000	14,000

It would be **more profitable to shut down production of Rooks and switch** resources to making Crowners, in order to boost profits by $4,000 to $9,000.

5.3 Timing of shutdown

An organisation may also need to consider the most appropriate **timing** for a shutdown. Some costs may be avoidable in the long run but not in the short run. For example, office space may have been rented and three months' notice is required to terminate the rental agreement. This cost during the three-month notice period is therefore **unavoidable** for the three months. In the same way, supply contracts may require notice of cancellation. A month by month analysis of when notice should be given and savings made may be needed for the relevant costing and decision-making process.

5.4 Qualitative factors

With shutdown decisions, as with many other decisions involving relevant costs, the decision is not merely a matter of choosing the best financial option. **Qualitative** factors may be significant and may influence the final decision. For example:

(a)   What impact will a shutdown decision have on the morale of employees who remain?

(b)   What signal will the decision give to competitors? How will they react?

(c)   How will customers react? Will they lose confidence in the company's products?

(d)   How will suppliers be affected? If one supplier suffers disproportionately there may be a loss of goodwill and damage to future relations.

How would the above decision change if Pawns, Rooks and Bishops were manufactured in different departments, variable costs could be split down into the costs of direct materials, labour and overheads, and fixed costs could be analysed into the costs of administrative staff and equipment and premises costs?

Answer

The decision would not change at all – unless perhaps activity-based analysis of overheads was undertaken and unexpected cost patterns were revealed. The point of this exercise is to make you realise that problems that look complicated are sometimes very simple in essence even if the amount of calculations seem daunting.

Chapter Roundup

- **Relevant costs** are future cash flows arising as a direct consequence of a decision.
  - Relevant costs are **future costs.**
  - Relevant costs are **cash flows.**
  - Relevant costs are **incremental costs**, arising as a direct consequence of the decision.

- In a **make or buy decision**, the choice is between making items in-house or purchasing them from an external supplier. When there are no limiting factors restricting the in-house production capacity, the relevant costs are the differential costs between the two options.

- The relevant costs/revenues in decisions relating to the **operating of internal service departments or the use of external services** are the differential costs between the two options.

- A further processing decision often involves joint products from a common manufacturing process. The decision is whether to sell the products at the split-off point, as soon as they emerge from the common process, or whether they should be processed further before selling them.

- A joint product should be **processed further** past the split-off point if the additional sales revenue exceeds the relevant post-separation (further processing) costs.

- **Shutdown/discontinuance problems** may sometimes be simplified into short-run relevant cost decisions. A shutdown decision is whether to close down an operation or stop making and selling a particular product or service.

Quick Quiz

1   Fill in the relevant costs in the four boxes in the diagram below.

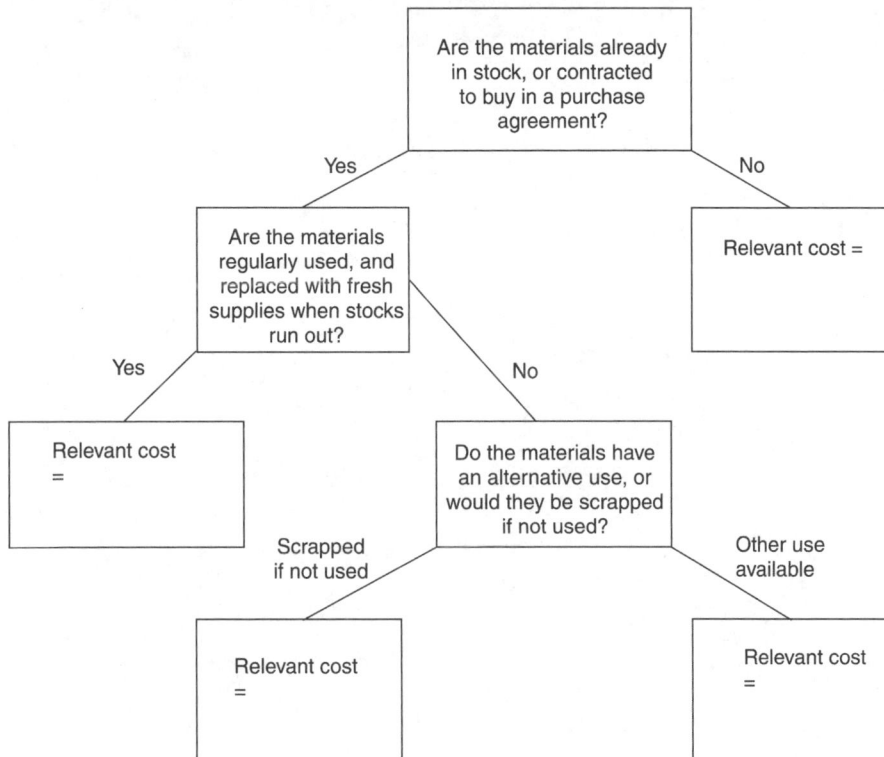

2   Choose the correct word(s) from those highlighted.

In a situation where a company must subcontract work to make up a shortfall in its own in-house capabilities, its total cost will be minimised if those units **bought out from a subcontractor/made in-house** have the **lowest/highest** extra **variable/fixed** cost of **buying out/making in-house** per unit of **scarce resource/material.**

3   In a decision about whether or not to sell a joint product at the split-off point or after further processing, joint costs are relevant. **True or false?**

4   Fill in the blanks.

Most of the decisions considered in this chapter involve calculating .... obtained from various options after identifying .... They always involve .... issues, which depend on the precise situation described.

5   What are the relevant costs in a make or buy decision?

A   The sum of the relevant costs of the two options
B   The opportunity costs associated with the decision
C   The differential costs between the two options
D   The incremental costs of the two options

1

```
                        ┌──────────────────────┐
                        │ Are the materials     │
                        │ already in stock, or  │
                        │ contracted to buy in  │
                        │ a purchase agreement? │
                        └──────────────────────┘
              Yes                            No
```

┌──────────────────────────┐   ┌──────────────────────────┐
│ Are the materials   │   │ Relevant cost =   │
│ regularly used, and   │   │ future/current   │
│ replaced with fresh   │   │ purchase cost of   │
│ supplies when stocks   │   │ materials   │
│ run out?   │   └──────────────────────────┘
└──────────────────────────┘
       Yes   No

┌──────────────────────────┐   ┌──────────────────────────┐
│ Relevant cost   │   │ Do the materials have   │
│ = future/current   │   │ an alternative use, or   │
│ purchase cost of   │   │ would they be scrapped   │
│ materials   │   │ if not used?   │
└──────────────────────────┘   └──────────────────────────┘
                  Scrapped   Other use
                  if not used   available

        ┌──────────────────────────┐   ┌──────────────────────────┐
        │ Relevant cost   │   │ Relevant cost   │
        │ = scrap value/   │   │ = higher of value in   │
        │ disposal value   │   │ other use or scrap   │
        │   │   │ value/disposal value   │
        └──────────────────────────┘   └──────────────────────────┘

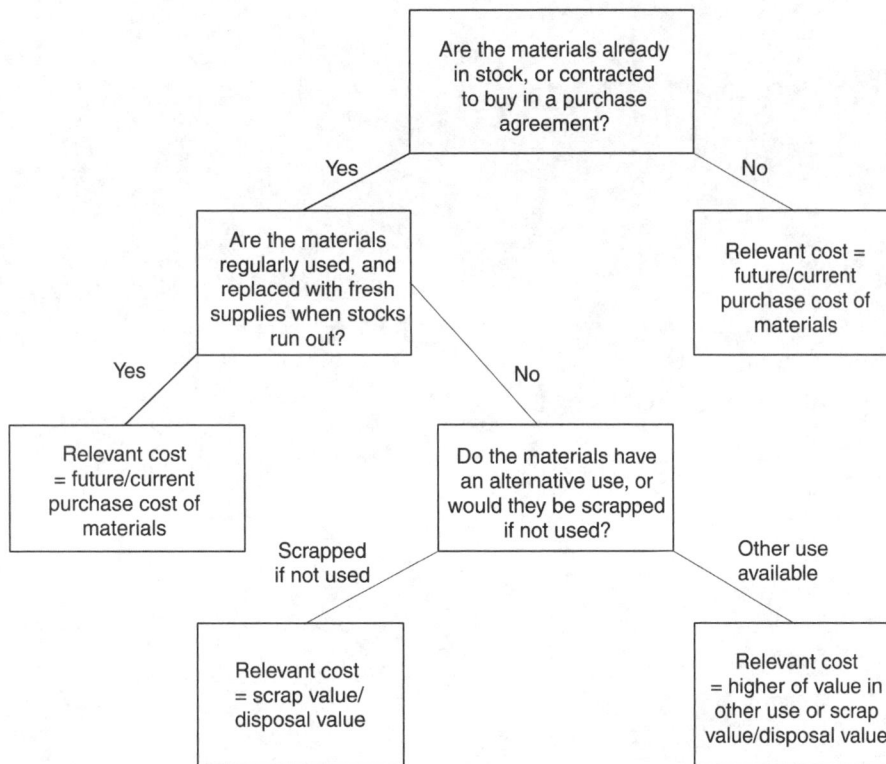

2   bought out from a subcontractor
     lowest
     variable
     buying out
     scarce resource

3   False

4   contribution

     relevant costs

     qualitative

5   C.   You need to know the difference in cost between the two options.

Now try the questions below from the Practice Question Bank

Number	Level	Marks	Approximate time
Section A Q41	Examination	2	4 mins
Section A Q42	Examination	2	4 mins
Section A Q43	Examination	2	4 mins
Section A Q44	Examination	2	4 mins
Section A Q45	Examination	2	4 mins
Section C Q3	Examination	20	39 mins

Risk and uncertainty

Topic list	Syllabus reference
1 Risk and uncertainty	B6 (a)
2 Allowing for uncertainty	B6 (a)
3 Probabilities and expected values	B6 (b), (c)
4 Other decision rules	B6 (d)
5 Decision trees	B6 (e)
6 The value of information	B6 (f)
7 Sensitivity analysis	B6 (b), (c)
8 Simulation models	B6 (b)

Introduction

Decision-making involves making decisions now about what will happen in the future. Obviously, decisions can turn out badly, or actual results can prove to be very different from the estimates on which the original decision was made. **Ideally** the decision-maker would **know with certainty** what the future consequences will be for each choice facing them. But the real world is not normally so helpful, and decisions must be made in the knowledge that their expected **consequences**, although probable perhaps, are **rarely 100% certain**.

Various **methods of bringing uncertainty and risk** into the analysis and evaluation of decisions will be described in this chapter. You may well think that some methods are more sensible or practical than others, but you should **judge** each method on its merits. You should also be prepared to apply or show an understanding of a number of different decision-making rules in your examination.

Study guide

		Intellectual level
B6	**Dealing with risk and uncertainty in decision-making**	
(a)	Suggest research techniques to reduce uncertainty, eg focus groups, market research.	2
(b)	Explain the use of simulation, expected values and sensitivity.	1
(c)	Apply expected values and sensitivity to decision-making problems.	2
(d)	Apply the techniques of maximax, maximin, and minimax regret to decision-making problems, including the production of profit tables.	2
(e)	Draw a decision tree and use it to solve a multi-stage decision problem.	1
(f)	Calculate the value of perfect and imperfect information.	2

Exam guide

Management accounting exams have increasingly expected candidates to have a good understanding of risk in decision-making. The principles of relevant costing apply to the decision-making, but in addition an element of risk or uncertainty may affect the decision. Section C questions are likely to be a mixture of calculations and explanation.

There is an article on the ACCA website written by a member of the examining team titled 'The risks of uncertainty', which you should read (ACCA, 2015).

1 Risk and uncertainty

FAST FORWARD

When there is a strong element of risk or uncertainty in a decision, the decision that is taken may be affected by the extent of the risk or uncertainty.

'Risk' and 'uncertainty' are often used to mean the same thing. However, to be more exact, 'risk' in decision-making exists when the future outcome cannot be predicted for certain, but probabilities can be estimated for each possible outcome. Uncertainty, in contrast, is when there is insufficient information to make a reliable prediction about what will happen and there are no probability estimates of different possible outcomes.

Key terms

Risk involves situations or events which may or may not occur, but whose probability of occurrence can be estimated statistically.

Uncertain events are events where the outcome cannot be estimated with a statistical probability.

In everyday usage the terms risk and uncertainty are not clearly distinguished. If you are asked to explain the difference, risk exists when probabilities of different outcomes can be estimated and uncertainty exists when there is insufficient information to assess probabilities. As a general rule, however, the terms are used interchangeably.

In the previous chapters on decision-making, the problem of risk and uncertainty has not been considered. In practice, however, risk or uncertainty can have a significant influence on decision-making. This chapter looks at different methods of assessing risk or uncertainty in order to assist decision-making.

1.1 Risk preference

People may be **risk seekers**, **risk neutral** or **risk averse**. A person's attitude to risk and uncertainty may affect the decision that is taken.

Key terms

A **risk seeker** is a decision-maker who is interested in the best outcomes, no matter how small the chance that they may occur.

A decision-maker is **risk neutral** if they are prepared to make a decision that balances risk and return. They are willing take on more risk, but only if the expected profit or return is higher. They will also accept a lower return for lower risk.

A **risk-averse** decision-maker acts on the assumption that the worst outcome might occur and will make a decision that limits or minimises the risk.

Attitudes to risk have clear implications for managers and organisations. A **risk-seeking manager** working for an **organisation** that is characteristically **risk averse** is likely to make decisions that are **not consistent with the goals of the organisation**. There may be a role for the management accountant here, who could be instructed to present decision-making information in such a way as to ensure that the manager considers **all** the possibilities, including the worst.

2 Allowing for uncertainty

FAST FORWARD

Management accounting directs its attention towards the **future** and the future is **uncertain**. For this reason a number of methods of taking **uncertainty** into consideration have evolved.

One approach to dealing with uncertainty is to obtain more information, in order to reduce the amount of uncertainty about what will happen. Reliable information reduces uncertainty.

2.1 Research techniques to reduce uncertainty

FAST FORWARD

Market research into customer habits, attitudes or intentions can be used to reduce uncertainty.

Key term

Market research is the systematic process of gathering, analysing and reporting data about markets to investigate, describe, measure, understand or explain a situation or problem facing a company or organisation.

Market research involves **tackling problems**. The assumption is that these problems can be solved, no matter how complex the issues are, if the researcher follows a line of enquiry in a **systematic** way without losing sight of the main objectives. Gathering and analysing all the facts will ultimately lead to **better decision-making**.

2.1.1 The role of market research

In the last 20 years or so market research has become a much more widespread activity. Organisations – in the private sector, the public sector and the not for profit sector – rely on research to inform and improve their **planning and decision-making**.

Market research enables organisations to understand the needs and opinions of their customers and other stakeholders. Armed with this knowledge they are able to make better quality decisions and provide better products and better services.

Thus, research influences what is provided and the way it is provided. It **reduces uncertainty and monitors performance**. A management team which possesses accurate information relating to the marketplace will be in a strong position to make the best decisions in an increasingly competitive world.

Decision-makers need data to reduce **uncertainty** and **risk** when planning for the future and to monitor business performance. Market researchers provide the data that helps them to do this.

An organisation wanting market research information will typically hire the services of a firm that specialises in market research. This firm will plan the market research exercise so as to gather information or opinions from a selected sample of individuals (or organisations). The information obtained can then be analysed **both qualitatively and statistically**.

2.1.2 Focus groups

A focus group may be used to obtain **qualitative views and opinions** from a small group of individuals. The group is asked about their opinions and attitudes towards a product or service, and members of the group are encouraged to share their views with each other as well as with the person leading the group.

Focus groups are used in marketing to obtain qualitative data about customer or consumer attitudes. They are used, for example, to obtain marketing information about attitudes to a new product or to a new advertisement for a product. They may be used in the early stages of product development, when an organisation is trying to assess the strength of consumer attitudes and to find out in detail what they think of it.

Participants in a focus group are recruited on the basis of similar demographics, lifestyles, buying attitudes or other behaviour, so that the views the group provides may be regarded as typical of the target market for the product.

Like market research, focus groups reduce uncertainty by providing information, and the information will influence decisions about designing and marketing a product.

2.1.3 Types of data collected

Data can be analysed to provide information that reduces uncertainty or enables an organisation to estimate probabilities.

The sources of data may be primary or secondary. Data may also be either qualitative or quantitative in nature.

Primary data is data that is obtained for a specific purpose and collected at first hand, typically from a sample of respondents. Market research and focus groups are sources of primary data. **Secondary data** is data that has been collected by someone else, and not for the specific purpose for which it is now being used. Secondary research is also known as **desk research**, because it can be carried out in an office by researching files or archives. Government statistics, published by the Government's statistics department or bureau, are widely used by business organisations as a source of secondary data.

Data can be either quantitative or qualitative.

(a)   **Quantitative** data is in the form of numbers and measurements. For example, quantitative data may provide a decision-maker with information about **how many** customers or competitors act in a certain way. Quantitative data can, for example, tell the researcher the numbers or percentages of consumers who are likely to buy a product and may give numerical measurements about **where**, **when** and **how** people buy goods or consumer services.

(b)   **Qualitative** data tells us **why** consumers think, buy or act the way they do. Qualitative data is used in **consumer insight** (eg understanding what makes consumers prefer one brand to another), **media awareness** (eg how much of an advertisement is noticed by the public), **new product development** studies and for many other reasons.

Qualitative research has as its specific purpose the uncovering and understanding of thought and opinion. It is carried out on relatively small samples and by using unstructured or semi-structured techniques, such as individual in-depth interviews and focus group discussions.

2.2 Worst/most likely/best outcome estimates

A fairly simple approach to assessing the uncertainty in a decision is to consider the range of possible outcomes for different decision options, and to identify:

(a)   The most likely outcome

(b)   The worst possible outcome (where 'worst possible' is an estimate of what, within reason, may happen. It is not an extreme and unlikely possibility.)

(c)   The best possible outcome (where 'best possible' is a 'within reason' estimate)

This will show the **full range of possible outcomes** from a decision, and may be used to reach a decision. For example, assessing the worst possible outcomes may help managers to reject Option A in favour of Option B because the worst possible outcome with Option A would involve an unacceptable amount of loss.

When comparing the worst possible, most likely and best possible outcomes for different decision choices, (decision options) it often helps to construct a **pay-off table**.

2.2.1 Pay-off tables   6/14

Pay-off tables **identify and record all possible outcomes (or pay-offs)** in situations where there are two or more decision options and the outcome from each decision depends on the eventual circumstances that arise ('worst possible', 'most likely' or 'best possible').

A pay-off table is a table or matrix where:

(a)   One side of the table has a different row (or column) for each decision option.
(b)   The other side of the table has a column (or row) for the eventual circumstances that may arise.

The boxes in the middle of the table record the outcome given the decision option and the circumstances that arise.

An example will help to demonstrate how a pay-off table is constructed.

2.2.2 Example: Worst/best possible outcomes

Omelette Co is trying to set the sales price for one of its products. Three prices are under consideration, and expected sales volumes and costs are as follows.

Pricing choices	Sales demand (units)	
$4	Best possible	16,000
	Most likely	14,000
	Worst possible	10,000
$4.30	Best possible	14,000
	Most likely	12,500
	Worst possible	8,000
$4.40	Best possible	12,500
	Most likely	12,000
	Worst possible	6,000

Fixed costs are $20,000 and variable costs of sales are $2 per unit.

Prepare a pay-off table for the different possible outcomes for each decision option.

Solution

Here we need to prepare a pay-off table showing **pay-offs** (contribution) **dependent on different levels of demand and different selling prices**.

In the table below, there is a column for each of the three possible pricing options, and there is a row for each of the three possible outcomes: best possible, most likely and worst possible.

The table is completed by entering the total contribution (or it could be profit, if you prefer) for each different price, given each possible outcome. The workings are not shown here.

Pay-off table

Price per unit	$4	$4.30	$4.40
Contribution per unit	$2	$2.30	$2.40
Total contribution towards fixed costs	$	$	$
Best possible	32,000	32,200	30,000
Most likely	28,000	28,750	28,800
Worst possible	20,000	18,400	14,400

So how does a pay-off table help with reaching a decision?

(a)   The highest contribution based on **most likely** sales volume would be at a price of $4.40. However, it may be argued that $4.30 would be a much better choice for price than $4.40, since the most likely profit is almost as good, the worst possible profit is not as bad, and the best possible profit is better.

(b)   However, given fixed costs of $20,000, only a price of $4 guarantees that the company would **not make a loss**, even if the worst possible outcome occurs. (The fixed costs of $20,000 would just be covered.) A risk-averse management might therefore prefer a price of $4 to either of the other two prices.

To use a pay-off table to reach a decision, we need to establish the 'rule' or 'criterion' for making the decision. There are different possible decision criteria or rules, such as the expected value (EV) rule, the maximin rule, the minimax regret rule, and so on. These are explained in the following sections.

3 Probabilities and expected values

6/11, 6/13, 6/14, Mar/Jun 16

FAST FORWARD

An expected value is a weighted average value of the different possible outcomes from a decision, where weightings are based on the probability of each possible outcome.

Expected values indicate what an outcome is likely to be in the long term, if the decision can be repeated many times over. Fortunately, many business transactions do occur over and over again.

Although the outcome of a decision may not be certain, the probabilities of different possible outcomes may possibly be estimated; for example, on the basis of historical experience of similar circumstances.

3.1 Expected values

Where probabilities are assigned to different outcomes we can measure the weighted average value of the different possible outcomes. Each possible outcome is given a weighting equal to the probability that it will occur.

The expected value (EV) decision rule is that the decision option with the highest EV of benefit or the lowest EV of cost should be selected.

3.1.1 Example: Expected values

Suppose a manager has to choose between mutually exclusive options A and B, and the probable outcomes of each option are as follows.

	Option A			Option B	
Probability		Profit	Probability		Profit
		$			$
0.8		5,000	0.1		(2,000)
0.2		6,000	0.2		5,000
			0.6		7,000
			0.1		8,000

The expected value (EV) of profit of each option would be measured as follows.

	Option A				Option B		
Prob		Profit	EV of profit	Prob		Profit	EV of profit
p		x	px	p		x	px
		$	$			$	$
0.8	×	5,000	= 4,000	0.1	×	(2,000)	= (200)
0.2	×	6,000	= 1,200	0.2	×	5,000	= 1,000
		EV =	5,200	0.6	×	7,000	= 4,200
				0.1	×	8,000	= 800
						EV	5,800

In this example, since it offers a higher EV of profit, option B would be selected in preference to A, unless further risk analysis is carried out.

3.1.2 Example: Expected values and pay-off tables

IB Newsagents stocks a weekly lifestyle magazine. The owner buys the magazines at the beginning of each week for $0.30 each and sells them at the retail price of $0.50 each.

At the end of the week unsold magazines are obsolete and have no value, so they are discarded as recycled waste. The estimated probability distribution for weekly demand is shown below.

Weekly demand in units	Probability
20	0.20
30	0.55
40	0.25
	1.00

The actual demand in each week does not affect the actual demand in the following week.

Required

If the owner is to order a fixed quantity of magazines per week, how many should that be? Since the outcomes occur every week, many times over, the EV decision rule is considered appropriate here.

Assume no seasonal variations in demand.

Solution

Start by identifying the different decision options. These are assumed here to be the different buying decisions, with three options: buy 20 per week, buy 30 per week or buy 40 per week.

The different possible outcomes are the three possibilities for actual demand: 20 units, 30 units or 40 units.

The next step is to set up a decision matrix of possible strategies (numbers bought) and possible demand.

The 'pay-off' from each combination of action and outcome is then computed.

No sale = cost of $0.30 per magazine

Sale = profit of $0.20 per magazine ($0.50 – $0.30)

Probability	Outcome (number demanded)		Decision (number bought)	
		20	30	40
		$	$	$
0.20	20	4.00	1.00*	(2.00) **
0.55	30	4.00	6.00	3.00 ***
0.25	40	4.00	6.00	8.00

* Buy 30 and sell only 20 gives a profit of (20 × $0.5) – (30 × $0.3) = $1

** Buy 40 and sell only 20 gives a loss of (20 × $0.5) – (40 × $0.3) = $(2)

*** Buy 40 and sell 30 gives a profit of (30 × $0.5) – (40 × $0.3) = $3

We can now calculate the EV of each decision option, as the weighted average value of the different possible outcomes for each option.

Decision option		EV of weekly profit
Buy 20	($4 × 0.20) + ($4 × 0.55) + ($4 × 0.25) =	$4.00
Buy 30	($1 × 0.20) + ($6 × 0.55) + ($6 × 0.25) =	$5.00
Buy 40	($(2) × 0.20) + ($3 × 0.55) + ($8 × 0.25) =	$3.25

The strategy which gives the highest expected value of pay-off is to stock 30 magazines each week.

Note. The expected value of weekly demand in this example is (20 × 0.20) + (30 × 0.55) + (40 × 0.25) = 30.5 copies, but this does not help with the calculation of the expected value of profit, because the profit is dependent on the purchase quantity as well as the sales demand quantity.)

Exam focus point

The examining team has noted that candidates often struggle to construct an accurate pay-off table. Make sure that you understand the above example which demonstrates this technique.

Question

EVs

A manager has to choose between mutually exclusive options C and D and the probable outcomes of each option are as follows.

Option C		Option D	
Probability	Cost $	Probability	Cost $
0.29	15,000	0.03	14,000
0.54	20,000	0.30	17,000
0.17	30,000	0.35	21,000
		0.32	24,000

Both options will produce an income of $30,000. Which should be chosen, on the basis of the expected value decision rule?

Answer

Option C. Do the workings yourself in the way illustrated above. Note that the probabilities are for **costs**, not profits.

3.1.3 Limitations of expected values

Making a decision between different options on the basis of expected value has some significant limitations.

(a) An expected value is a weighted average outcome that will occur in the long run if events occur many times over. It is a long-run average.

(b) The expected value of a decision may be a value that will never occur. For example, if there is a 0.7 probability of a profit of $10,000 and a 0.3 probability of a loss of $5,000, the expected value is (0.7 × $10,000) − (0.3 × $5,000) = + $5,500. The EV is a profit of $5,500, but this value cannot actually occur.

(c)   Because an EV is an average value, it ignores the extreme outcomes. For example, if there is a 0.7 probability of a profit of $10,000 and a 0.3 probability of a loss of $5,000, the expected value is a profit of $5,500. However, if the organisation cannot afford to incur a loss, making the decision on the basis of EV would be too risky.

Expected values are used to support a **risk-neutral attitude**. A risk-neutral decision-maker will ignore any variability in the range of possible outcomes and be concerned only with the expected value of outcomes.

Expected values are more valuable as a guide to decision-making where they refer to outcomes which will occur **many times over**. Examples would include the probability that so many customers per day will buy a can of baked beans, the probability that a customer services assistant will receive so many phone calls per hour, and so on.

4 Other decision rules   12/08, 6/11, 6/14

The 'play it safe' basis for decision-making is referred to as the **maximin basis**. This is short for '**maximise the minimum achievable profit**'.

A basis for making decisions by looking for the best outcome is known as the **maximax basis**, short for '**maximise the maximum achievable profit**'.

The 'opportunity loss' basis for decision-making is known as **minimax regret**.

The expected value rule is just one possible 'rule' or criterion on which to base a decision. There are other rules that a decision-maker may prefer to use. In using these alternative decision rules, it is often useful to compare the different possible outcomes of all the decision options in a **pay-off table**.

Some other ways of making a choice include the following.

(a)   **Playing safe**, and **choosing the option with the least damaging results if events were to turn out badly**

(b)   Looking for the **best outcome**, no matter how small the chance that it might occur

(c)   Looking at the opportunity loss when we choose an option but come to regret it

The 'play it safe' basis for decision-making is referred to as the **maximin basis**. This is short for '**maximise the minimum achievable profit**'. (It might also be called '**minimax**', which is short for '**minimise the maximum potential cost or loss**'). Maximin decisions are taken by **risk-averse** decision-makers.

A basis for making decisions by looking for the best outcome is known as the **maximax basis**, short for '**maximise the maximum achievable profit**'. (It can also be called the **minimin cost rule** – minimise the minimum costs or losses.) Maximax decisions are taken by **risk-seeking** decision-makers.

The 'opportunity loss' basis for decision-making is known as **minimax regret**.

4.1 Maximin decision rule

Key term

The **maximin decision rule** is that a decision-maker should select the alternative that offers the least unattractive worst outcome. This would mean choosing the alternative that **maximises** the **minimum** profits.

Suppose a businessman is trying to decide which of three **mutually exclusive** projects to undertake. Since they are mutually exclusive, only one of the projects can be selected. Each of the projects could lead to varying net profit under three possible scenarios or outcomes. (The figures in the pay-off table are figures for profit, in $'000.)

Pay-off table		Project choice		
		D	E	F
	I	100	80	60
Scenarios	II	90	120	85
	III	(20)	10	85

The maximin decision rule is to select the option that offers the best minimum profit – the best 'worst possible result' that could happen.

In this example, the worst possible is a loss of $20,000 with Project D, a profit of $10,000 with Project E and a profit of $60,000 with Project F. The best worst outcome is 60 and project F would therefore be selected (because this is a better 'worst possible' than either D or E).

4.1.1 Criticisms of the maximin rule

(a) It is **defensive** and **conservative**, being a safety-first principle of avoiding the worst outcomes without taking into account opportunities for maximising profits.

(b) It ignores the **probability** of each different outcome taking place.

4.2 Maximax decision rule

> The **maximax criterion** looks at the best possible results. Maximax means 'maximise the maximum profit'. The decision with this rule is to choose the option that could provide the maximum possible profit.

Using the example in Section 4.1 above, the maximum profit for Project D is $100,000; for Project E it is $120,000; and for Project F it is $85,000.

Project E would be chosen if the maximax rule is followed, because it offers the prospect of the biggest profit.

4.2.1 Criticisms of the maximax rule

(a) It ignores the probabilities of different outcomes.

(b) It ignores the outcomes that are less than the best possible. For some decision options, the worst possible may be more than the organisation can afford. It is a decision rule for the **risk seeker**.

Question

Maximax and maximin

A company is considering which one of three alternative courses of action, A, B and C, to take. The profit or loss from each choice depends on which one of four economic circumstances, I, II, III or IV, will apply. The possible profits and losses, in thousands of pounds, are given in the following pay-off table. Losses are shown as negative figures.

		Decision option		
		A	B	C
	I	70	60	70
Circumstance/outcome	II	–10	20	–5
	III	80	0	50
	IV	60	100	115

Required

State which option would be selected using

(a) The maximax decision rule
(b) The maximin decision rule

Answer

(a) The **best possible outcomes** are as follows.

A (circumstance III):   80
B (circumstance IV):   100
C (circumstance IV):   115

As 115 is the highest of these three figures, action C would be chosen using the maximax criterion.

(b)   The **worst possible outcomes** are as follows.

    A (circumstance II):   −10
    B (circumstance III):   0
    C (circumstance II):   −5

The best of these figures is 0 (neither a profit nor a loss), so action B would be chosen using the maximin criterion.

4.3 Minimax regret rule

> The **minimax regret rule** aims to minimise the regret from making the wrong decision. **Regret** is the opportunity lost through making the wrong decision.

The 'minimax regret' decision rule is another possible decision rule for choosing between different decision options. It is a bit more complicated than the maximin rule or the maximax rule.

With this decision rule, for each of the possible outcome situations, we compare the different values of profit (or cost) for each of the decision options.

For each outcome situation, we measure the amount of the 'regret' for each decision option.

Regret for the decision option	=	Profit from the best decision option, given the outcome circumstances or situation	−	Profit from the decision option, given the outcome circumstances or situation

For the decision option with the best outcome, given the circumstances or situation, the regret = $0. For the other decision options, the regret always has a positive value. It is the amount by which the profit is worse than if the best decision option had been taken, in view of the outcome circumstances.

The regret is calculated for all the decision options in each of the possible outcome circumstances; these are recorded in a pay-off table.

The decision rule is to select the decision option that has the lowest value of regret (= the minimum regret).

The minimax regret decision rule is that the decision option selected should be the one which **minimises the maximum potential regret** for any of the possible outcomes.

This may seem complicated, but an example should help to clarify the rule.

Using the example in Section 4.1, a table of regrets can be compiled as follows.

The pay-off table (in $'000) is as follows.

Pay-off table		Project choice		
		D	E	F
	I	100	80	60
Scenarios	II	90	120	85
	III	(20)	10	85

The regret for each decision option in each outcome situation is shown in the pay-off table below.

		Project option		
		D	E	F
	I *	0	20	40
Scenario/outcome situation	II **	30	0	35
	III ***	105	75	0
Maximum regret		105	75	40

* With outcome situation I, the best possible result is obtained from Project D, so the regret with Project D is $0. The result with Option E would be 20 worse and the result from Option F would be 40 worse. So 20 and 40 are the amounts of the regret for Options D and F respectively.

** With outcome situation II, the best possible result is obtained from Project E, so the regret with Project E is $0. The result with Option D would be 30 worse and the result from Option F would be 35 worse. So 30 and 735 are the amounts of the regret for Options D and F respectively.

*** With outcome situation III, the best possible result is obtained from Project F, so the regret with Project F is $0. The result with Option D would be 105 worse and the result from Option E would be 75 worse. So 105 and 75 are the amounts of the regret for Options D and E respectively.

The **lowest** of maximum regrets is 40 with Option F so Option F would be selected, if the minimax regret rule is used as the basis for making the decision.

4.4 Contribution tables

Questions requiring application of the decision rules often incorporate a **number of variables, each with a range of possible values**. For example, these variables might be:

- Unit price and associated level of demand
- Unit variable cost

Each variable might have, for example, three possible values.

Before being asked to use the decision rules, exam questions could ask you to **work out** the **contribution** for each of the possible outcomes, and record these in a contribution table. (Alternatively, profit figures could be required if you are given information about fixed costs.)

The **number of possible outcomes** = number of values of variable 1 × number of values of variable 2 × number of values of variable 3 etc

So, for example, if there are **two** variables, each with **three** possible values, there are **3 × 3 = 9 outcomes**.

Perhaps the easiest way to see how to draw up contribution tables is to look at an example.

4.4.1 Example: Contribution tables and the decision rules

Suppose the budgeted demand for product X will be 11,500 units if the price is $10, 8,500 units if the price is $12 and 5,000 units if the price is $14. Variable costs are estimated at either $4, $5, or $6 per unit. A decision needs to be made on the **price** to be charged.

Here is a contribution table showing the budgeted contribution for each of the nine possible outcomes.

Demand	Price	Variable cost	Unit contribution	Total contribution
	$	$	$	$'000
11,500	10	4	6	69.0
11,500	10	5	5	57.5
11,500	10	6	4	46.0
8,500	12	4	8	68.0
8,500	12	5	7	59.5
8,500	12	6	6	51.0
5,000	14	4	10	50.0
5,000	14	5	9	45.0
5,000	14	6	8	40.0

Once the table has been drawn up, the decision rules can be applied.

The decision is the selection of the selling price.

Solution

Maximin decision rule

If the maximin decision rule is used, we should select the price that provides the lowest possible total contribution, given the different possible amounts of variable cost per unit. We need to maximise the minimum contribution.

Demand/price	Minimum contribution
11,500/$10	$46,000
8,500/$12	$51,000
5,000/$14	$40,000

Set a price of $12.

Maximax decision rule

With the maximax rule, we select the option that offers the highest possible total contribution.

Demand/price	Maximum possible contribution
11,500/$10	$69,000
8,000/$12	$68,000
5,000/$14	$50,000

Set a price of $10.

Minimax regret decision rule

We need to minimise the maximum regret (lost contribution) of making the wrong decision. The regret with each decision option, given the possible amounts for variable cost per unit, are set out in the following pay-off table.

Variable cost (= outcome) $	Price (option) $10	$12	$14
4	$0	$1,000	$19,000
5	$2,000	$0	$14,500
6	$5,000	$0	$11,000
Minimax regret	$5,000	$1,000	$19,000

Using the minimax regret decision rule, a price of $12 would be charged, because this has the minimum 'worst possible value' for regret (**price of $12, maximum regret = $1,000**).

Sample working

At a variable cost of $4, the best strategy would be a price of $10. Choosing a price of $12 would mean lost contribution of $69,000 − $68,000 = $1,000, while choosing a price of $14 would mean lost contribution of $69,000 − $50,000 = $19,000.

Exam focus point

> Decision rules are a popular exam topic. The examining team has commented that candidates struggle to justify decisions with supporting calculations.

5 Decision trees

FAST FORWARD

> **Decision trees** are diagrams which illustrate the choices and possible outcomes of a decision. The possible outcomes are usually given associated probabilities of occurrence.
>
> **Rollback analysis** evaluates the EV of each decision option. You have to work from right to left and calculate EVs at each outcome point.

There has been an article in *Student Accountant* on decision trees. This is available on the ACCA website and you are strongly recommended to read it (ACCA, 2015).

A probability problem such as 'what is the probability of throwing a six with one throw of a die?' is fairly straightforward and can be solved using the basic principles of probability.

More complex probability questions, although solvable using the basic principles, require a clear logical approach to ensure that all possible choices and outcomes of a decision are taken into consideration. **Decision trees** are a useful means of analysing a probability problem.

Key term

A **decision tree** is a pictorial method of showing the different decision options in a given situation, and the possible outcomes from each decision option. Decision trees can incorporate the probabilities of both the expected outcomes and the EV of each decision option. Decision trees can also show both initial decisions and subsequent decisions, where a decision is taken in two stages, at two different times.

Exactly how does the use of a decision tree help to provide a clear and logical approach to decision-making?

- All the possible **choices** that can be made are shown as **branches** on the tree.
- All the possible **outcomes** of each choice are shown as **subsidiary branches** on the tree.

5.1 Constructing a decision tree

There are two stages in preparing a decision tree.

- Drawing the tree itself to show all the decision options or choices, and the different possible outcomes from each decision
- Putting in the numbers (the probabilities, outcome values and EVs)

Every **decision tree starts** from a **decision point** with the **decision options** that are currently being considered, and the decision that must be made 'now'.

(a) It helps to identify the **decision point**, and any subsequent decision points in the tree, with a symbol. Here, we shall use a **square shape** to indicate that a decision must be made at this point.

(b) There should be a **line**, or **branch**, for each **option** or **alternative**.

It is conventional to draw decision trees from left to right, and so a decision tree will start as follows.

In this example, the **square** is the **decision point**, and A, B, C and D represent **four alternatives** from which a choice must be made (such as buy a new machine with cash, hire a machine, continue to use existing machine, raise a loan to buy a machine).

If the outcome from any choice is certain, the branch of the decision tree for that decision option is complete.

If the outcome of a particular choice is uncertain, the various possible outcomes must be shown.

We show the various possible outcomes on a decision tree by inserting an **outcome point** on the **branch** of the tree. Each possible outcome is then shown as a **subsidiary branch**, coming out from the outcome point. The probability of each outcome occurring should be written on to the branch of the tree which represents that outcome.

To distinguish decision points from outcome points, **a circle will be used as the symbol for an outcome point**.

In the example above, there are two choices facing the decision-maker, A and B. The outcome if A is chosen is known with certainty but, if B is chosen, there are two possible outcomes: high sales (0.6 probability) or low sales (0.4 probability).

When several outcomes are possible, it may be simpler to show two or more stages of outcome points on the decision tree.

5.2 Example: Several possible outcomes

A company can choose to launch a new product, XYZ, or not. If the product is launched, expected sales and expected unit costs might be as follows.

	Sales		Unit costs
Units	Probability	£	Probability
10,000	0.8	6	0.7
15,000	0.2	8	0.3

(a) The decision tree could be drawn as follows.

(b) The layout shown above will usually be easier to use than the alternative way of drawing the tree, which is as follows.

However, both decision trees are 'correct'. You can draw whichever you prefer.

Sometimes, a **decision taken now** will lead to **other decisions to be taken in the future**. When this situation arises, the decision tree can be drawn as a **two-stage tree**, as follows.

In this decision tree, if the initial decision is to select Decision X a subsequent decision will have to be made. This subsequent decision is either a choice between A and B or else a choice between C and D will be made, depending on the outcome which occurs after choosing X.

The decision tree should be in **chronological order** from **left to right**. When there are two-stage decision trees, the first decision in time should be drawn on the left.

5.3 Example: A decision tree

Beethoven Co has a new wonder product, the vylin, of which it expects great things. At the moment the company has two courses of action open to it, to test market the product or abandon it.

If the company test markets it, the cost will be $100,000 and the market response could be positive or negative with probabilities of 0.60 and 0.40.

If the response is positive the company could either abandon the product or market it full scale.

If it markets the vylin full scale, the outcome might be low, medium or high demand, and the respective net gains (losses) would be (200), 200 or 1,000 in units of $1,000 (the result could range from a net loss of $200,000 to a gain of $1,000,000). These outcomes have probabilities of 0.20, 0.50 and 0.30 respectively.

If the result of the test marketing is negative and the company goes ahead and markets the product, estimated losses would be $600,000.

If, at any point, the company abandons the product, there would be a net gain of $50,000 from the sale of scrap. All the financial values have been discounted to the present.

Required

(a)   Draw a decision tree.
(b)   Include figures for cost, loss or profit on the appropriate branches of the tree.

Solution

The starting point for the tree is to **establish what decision has to be made now**. What are the options?

(a)   To test market
(b)   To abandon

The outcome of the 'abandon' option is known with certainty. There are two possible outcomes of the option to test market: positive response and negative response.

Depending on the outcome of the test marketing, another decision will then be made: to abandon the product or to go ahead.

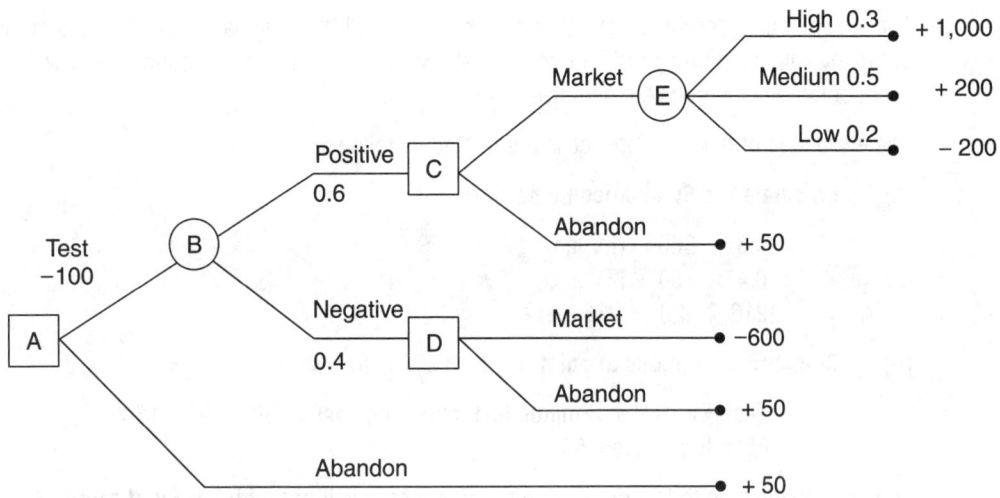

In an examination, remember to draw decision trees (and **all** diagrams) neatly, using a pen and ruler. Remember also to label decision points and branches as clearly as possible.

5.4 Evaluating the decision with a decision tree: rollback analysis

Rollback analysis evaluates the EV of each decision option. You have to **work from right to left** and calculate EVs at each outcome point.

The EV of each decision option can be evaluated, using the decision tree to help with keeping the logic on track. The basic rules are as follows.

(a)   We start on the **right-hand side** of the tree and **work back** towards the left hand side and the current decision under consideration. This is sometimes known as the **'rollback' technique** or 'rollback analysis'.

(b)   Working from **right to left**, we calculate the **EV of revenue, cost, contribution or profit** at each outcome point on the tree.

In the above example, the right-hand-most outcome point is point E, and the EV is as follows.

	Profit	Probability		
	x	p		px
	$'000			$'000
High	1,000	0.3		300
Medium	200	0.5		100
Low	(200)	0.2		(40)
			EV	360

This is the EV of the decision to market the product if the test shows positive response. It may help you to write the EV on the decision tree itself, at the appropriate outcome point (point E).

(a)   **At decision point C**, the **choice** is to select the option with the highest EV of profit (or lowest EV of cost). Here the EV of the two decision options, 'market' or 'abandon', are as follows.

(i)   Market, EV = +360 (the EV at point E)
(ii)   Abandon, value = +50

The choice would be to market the product, and so the EV at decision point C is +360.

(b)   **At decision point D**, the **choice** is again to select the option with the highest EV of profit (or lowest EV of cost). The two decision options and their associated EVs are as follows.

(i)   Market, value = −600
(ii)   Abandon, value = +50

The choice would be to abandon, and so the EV at decision point D is +50.

The second stage decisions have therefore been made. If the original decision is to test market, the company will market the product if the test shows positive customer response, and will abandon the product if the test results are negative.

The evaluation of the decision tree is completed as follows.

(a)   **Calculate the EV at outcome point B**.

$$0.6 \times 360 \quad \text{(EV at C)}$$
$$+ \quad 0.4 \times 50 \quad \text{(EV at D)}$$
$$= \quad 216 + 20 = 236.$$

(b)   **Compare the options at point A**, which are as follows.

(i)   Test: EV = EV at B minus test marketing cost = 236 − 100 = 136
(ii)   Abandon: Value = 50

The choice would be to test market the product, because it has a **higher EV of profit**.

/ **Question**   **Simple decision tree**

Consider the following diagram.

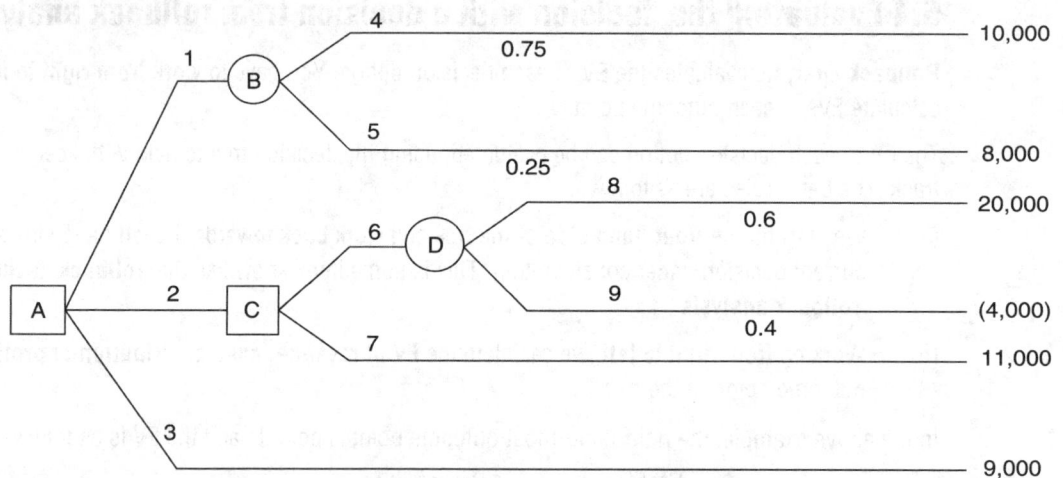

If a decision-maker wished to maximise the value of the outcome, which options should be selected?

A   Option 2 and option 7
B   Option 3
C   Option 1 and option 4
D   Option 2, option 6 and option 8

Answer

The correct answer is A.

The various outcomes must be evaluated using expected values.

EV at point B: $(0.75 \times 10,000) + (0.25 \times 8,000) = 9,500$

EV at point D: $(0.6 \times 20,000) + (0.4 \times (4,000)) = 10,400$

EV at point C: Choice between 10,400 and 11,000

EV at point A: Choice between B (9,500), C (10,400 or 11,000) and choice 3 (9,000).

If we are trying to maximise the figure, option 2 and then option 7 are chosen to give 11,000.

Evaluating decisions by using **decision trees has a number of limitations**.

(a) Decision trees are not very suitable for use with complex decisions because the decision tree becomes too big and complicated to follow.

(b) Decision trees are just a graphical way of making a decision based on the expected value rule. So the decision tree method has all the benefits and limitations of EV as a decision rule.

(c) The probabilities associated with different branches of the 'tree' are likely to be estimates, and possibly unreliable or inaccurate. (In the same way, estimates of probabilities with the EV decision rule method may be unreliable.)

6 The value of information

Perfect information is guaranteed to predict the future with 100% accuracy. **Imperfect information** is better than no information at all but could be wrong in its prediction of the future.

The **value of perfect information** is the difference between the EV of profit with perfect information and the EV of profit without perfect information.

The risk or uncertainty in a decision can be reduced by obtaining information about the likely outcome situation. Information about the likely outcome has value, because it improves the likelihood of making the best possible decision when faced with a number of different options.

The **value of information** can be calculated on the assumption that the EV decision criterion is used. The value of information is the difference between the EV of a decision if no information is available and the EV of the decision if the information is made available.

Information may be either perfect or imperfect.

Key term

> **Perfect information** is information that predicts with 100% accuracy what the outcome situation will be. Having perfect information removes all doubt and uncertainty from a decision, and enables managers to make decisions with complete confidence that they have selected the best decision option.

6.1 The value of perfect information   6/13

Step 1   If we **do not have perfect information** and we must choose between two or more decision options, we would **select** the decision option which offers the **highest EV** of profit (or lowest EV of cost). This option will not be the best decision under all circumstances. There will be some probability that what was really the best option will not have been selected, given the way actual events turn out.

Step 2   With **perfect information**, the **best decision option will always be selected**. The decision option that is selected will differ according to what the outcome situation will be. The choice will be the outcome that gives the highest profit (or lowest cost) in the circumstances that we know will occur. We can calculate an EV of profit, given the different possible outcomes and their associated probabilities. The EV of profit with perfect information should be higher than the EV of profit without the information.

Step 3   The **value of perfect information** is **the difference between the EV of profit with perfect information and the EV of profit with the information**.

BPP
LEARNING MEDIA

Part B Decision-making techniques | **7: Risk and uncertainty**   **201**

6.2 Example: The value of perfect information

The management of Ivor Ore must choose whether to go ahead with either of two **mutually exclusive** projects, A and B. The expected profits are as follows.

	Profit if there is strong demand	Profit if there is moderate demand	Profit/(loss) if there is weak demand
Option A	$4,000	$1,200	$(1,000)
Option B	$1,500	$1,000	$500
Probability of demand	0.2	0.3	0.5

Required

(a) Ascertain what the decision would be, based on expected values, if no information about demand were available.

(b) Calculate the value of perfect information about demand.

Solution

Step 1 If there is **no information** to help with the decision, the project with the higher EV of profit would be selected.

Probability	Project A		Project B	
	Profit	EV	Profit	EV
	$	$	$	$
0.2	4,000	800	1,500	300
0.3	1,200	360	1,000	300
0.5	(1,000)	(500)	500	250
		660		850

Project B would be selected and the EV of the decision is + $850.

This is clearly the better option if demand turns out to be weak. However, if demand were to turn out to be moderate or strong, project A would be more profitable. There is a 50% chance that this could happen (30% + 20%).

Step 2 **Perfect information** will indicate for certain whether demand will be weak, moderate or strong. If demand is forecast 'weak', project B would be selected. If demand is forecast as 'moderate', project A would be selected, and perfect information would improve the profit from $1,000, which would have been earned by selecting B, to $1,200.

If demand is forecast as 'strong', project A would again be selected, and perfect information would improve the profit from $1,500, which would have been earned by selecting B, to $4,000.

Forecast demand	Probability	Project chosen	Profit	EV of profit
			$	$
Weak	0.5	B	500	250
Moderate	0.3	A	1,200	360
Strong	0.2	A	4,000	800
		EV of profit with perfect information		1,410

Step 3

	$
EV of profit without perfect information (ie if project B is always chosen)	850
EV of profit with perfect information	1,410
Value of perfect information	560

Provided that the information does not cost more than $560 to collect, it would be worth having, on the assumption that the EV decision rule is applied.

WL must decide at what level to market a new product, the urk. The urk can be sold nationally, within a single sales region (where demand is likely to be relatively strong) or within a single area. The decision is complicated by uncertainty about the general strength of consumer demand for the product, and the following conditional profit table has been constructed.

		Weak	Demand Moderate	Strong
		$	$	$
Market	nationally (A)	(4,000)	2,000	10,000
	in one region (B)	0	3,500	4,000
	in one area (C)	1,000	1,500	2,000
Probability		0.3	0.5	0.2

Required

Option B should be selected, based on EVs of profit. True or false?

Answer

The correct answer is option B and so the statement is true.

Without perfect information, the option with the highest EV of profit will be chosen.

Probability	Option A (National) Profit	EV	Option B (Regional) Profit	EV	Option C (Area) Profit	EV
	$	$	$	$	$	$
0.3	(4,000)	(1,200)	0	0	1,000	300
0.5	2,000	1,000	3,500	1,750	1,500	750
0.2	10,000	2,000	4,000	800	2,000	400
		1,800		2,550		1,450

Marketing regionally (option B) has the highest EV of profit, and would be selected.

✎ Question   Perfect information

Required

Using the information in your answer to the question above (decision based on EV of profit) calculate the value of perfect information about the state of demand.

Answer

The correct answer is $1,500. It would be worth paying up to $1,500 to obtain perfect information.

If perfect information about the state of consumer demand is available, option A would be preferred if the forecast demand is strong and option C would be preferred if the forecast demand is weak.

Demand	Probability	Choice	Profit	EV of profit
			$	$
Weak	0.3	C	1,000	300
Moderate	0.5	B	3,500	1,750
Strong	0.2	A	10,000	2,000
EV of profit with perfect information				4,050
EV of profit, selecting option B				2,550
Value of perfect information				1,500

6.3 Perfect information and decision trees

When the option exists to obtain information, the decision can be shown, like any other decision, in the form of a decision tree, as follows. We will suppose, for illustration, that the cost of obtaining perfect information is $400.

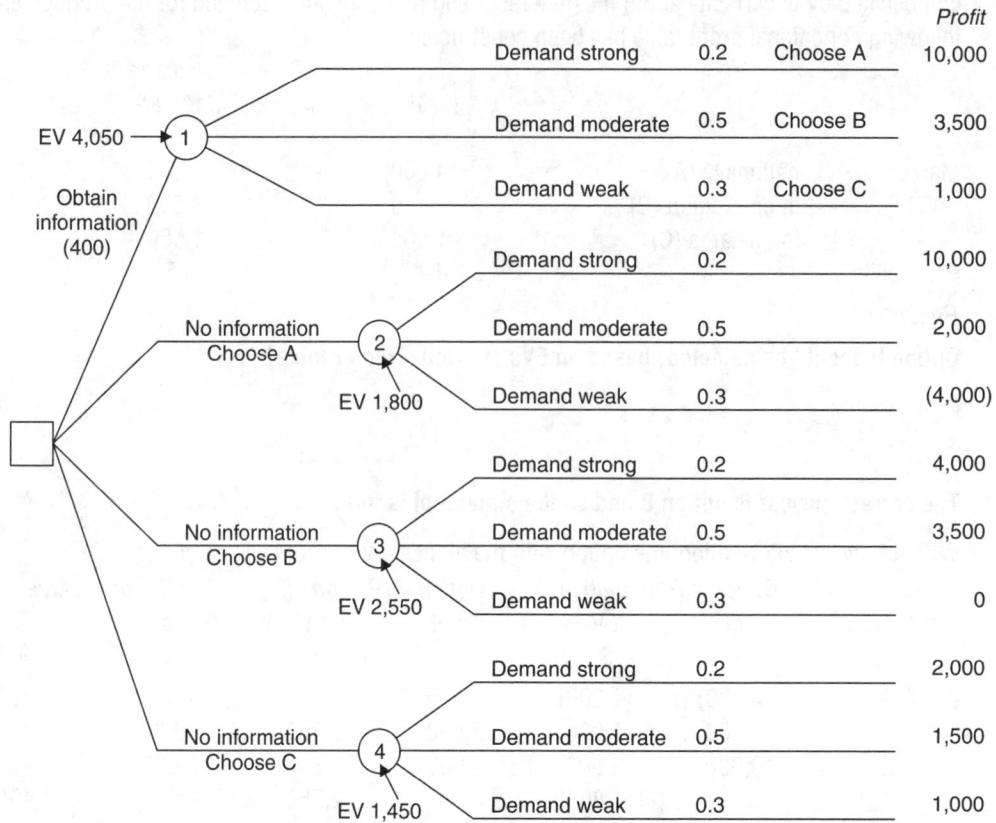

The decision would be to obtain perfect information, since the EV of profit is $4,050 – $400 = $3,650.

You should check carefully that you understand the logic of this decision tree and that you can identify how the EVs at outcome boxes 1, 2, 3 and 4 have been calculated.

6.4 The value of imperfect information

FAST FORWARD

> The **value of imperfect information** is the difference between the EV of profit with imperfect information and the EV of profit without the information.

There is one serious drawback to the 'perfect information' technique we have just looked at. In practice, **information is never perfect**. Market research findings or information from pilot tests and so on are likely to be reasonably accurate, but they can still be wrong: they provide imperfect information. It is possible, however, to arrive at an assessment of **how much it would be worth paying for such imperfect information, given that we have a rough indication of how right or wrong it is likely to be**. In other words, we can calculate the value of imperfect information provided that we have an estimate of probabilities that the information will be correct or incorrect.

Suppose that a company want to make a decision between two mutually exclusive options, Option A and Option B. The profits from each option will depend on the state of the economy in the next 12 months. Current estimates are that there is a 60% probability that the economy will be weak and a 40% probability that the economy will be strong.

The profitability with each decision option would be as follows.

	Option A	Option B
Weak economy	+ $50,000	+ $20,000
Strong economy	+ $60,000	+ $100,000

Research could be carried out into the state of the economy in the next 12 months. It has been estimated that if the true state of the economy will be weak, there is an 80% probability that the research would predict this correctly. It is also estimated that if the true state of the economy will be strong, there is an 90% probability that the research would predict this correctly.

What is the value of this imperfect information?

The value of the imperfect information is the difference between the EV of profit if no information is available and the EV of profit if the information is obtained.

(a)   *Value of decision without information*

The EV of the decision if no information is available is based on the **'prior probabilities'** of the state of the economy.

Option A: (0.6 × $50,000) + (0.4 × $60,000) $54,000

Option B: (0.6 × $20,000) + (0.4 × $100,000) $52,000

The decision would be to select Option A and the EV of profit would be $54,000.

(b)   *Value of decision with imperfect information*

If research information is obtained, the decision will be to select Option A if the research indicates a weak economy and to select Option B if the research indicates a strong economy. The different possible outcomes, and their associated probabilities, are as follows.

Actual state of economy	Research prediction	Decision	Profit	Probability		EV of profit
Weak	Weak	Option A	$50,000	(0.6 × 0.8)	0.48	24,000
Weak	Strong	Option B	$20,000	(0.6 × 0.2)	0.12	2,400
Strong	Strong	Option B	$100,000	(0.4 × 0.9)	0.36	36,000
Strong	Weak	Option A	$60,000	(0.4 × 0.1)	0.04	2,400
						64,800

The EV of profit when the decision is based on the imperfect information is $64,800. (The probabilities of the different possible outcomes with the information are called 'posterior probabilities'.)

The information is imperfect because it is not 100% certain to be correct, which means that there is a possibility that the best decision option will not be selected, in spite of obtaining the information.

The **value of the imperfect information** = EV of profit with the information minus EV of profit without the information

= $64,800 – $54,000 = **$10,800**

6.4.1 Example: The value of imperfect information

Suppose that the Small Oil Company (SOC) is trying to decide whether or not to drill on a particular site. The chief engineer has assessed the probability that there will be oil, based on past experience, as 20%, and the probability that there won't be oil as 80%.

It is possible for SOC to hire a firm of international consultants to carry out a complete survey of the site. SOC has used the firm many times before and has estimated that if there really is oil, there is a 95% chance that the report will be favourable, but if there is no oil, there is only a 10% chance that the report will indicate that there is oil.

Required

Determine whether drilling should occur.

Solution

Read the information given carefully. We are given **three** sets of probabilities.

(a) The probability that there will be oil (0.2) or there will not be oil (0.8). These outcomes are mutually exclusive.

(b) The probability that, if there is oil, the report will say there is oil (0.95) or say there is no oil (0.05).

(c) The probability that, if there is no oil, the report will say there **is** oil (0.1) or say there is no oil (0.9).

Both (b) and (c) describe conditional events, since the existence of oil or otherwise influences the chances of the survey report being correct.

SOC meanwhile faces a number of choices which we can show as a decision tree.

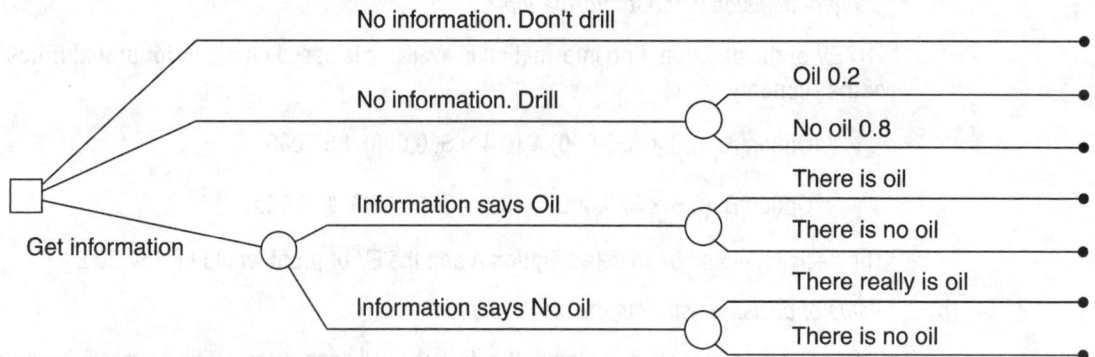

We must now calculate the probabilities of the following outcomes.

- The information will say 'oil' or 'no oil'
- The information will be right or wrong if it says 'oil'
- The information will be right or wrong if it says 'no oil'

If you check the information given in the problem, you will find that these probabilities are not given.

(a) We are told that the engineer has assessed that there is a 20% chance of oil and an 80% chance of no oil (ignoring information entirely). These are the **prior probabilities** of future possible outcomes.

(b) The **probabilities that there will be oil or no oil once the information has been obtained are posterior probabilities**.

Step 1   We can tabulate the various probabilities as percentages.

		Actual outcome					
		Oil		No oil		Total	
Survey	oil	19	(W2)	8	(W3)	27	(W4)
result:	no oil	1		72		73	
	Total	20	(W1)	80		100	

Workings

1   The engineer estimates 20% probability of oil and 80% of no oil.

2   If there is oil, ie in 20 cases out of 100, the survey will say so in 95% of these cases, ie in $20 \times 0.95 = 19$ cases. The 1 below the 19 is obtained by subtraction.

3   In the 80 per 100 cases where there is in fact no oil, the survey will wrongly say that there is oil 10% of the time; ie $80 \times 0.10 = 8$ cases. The 72 below the 8 is obtained by subtraction.

4   The horizontal totals are given by addition.

Step 2   We can now provide all the probabilities needed to complete the tree.

P (survey will say there is oil)   = 27/100   = 0.27

P (survey will say there is no oil)   = 73/100   = 0.73

If survey says oil   P (there is oil)   = 19/27 = 0.704
                            P (there is no oil)   = 8/27 = 0.296 (or 1 – 0.704)
If survey says no oil   P (there is oil)   = 1/73 = 0.014
                            P (there is no oil)   = 72/73 = 0.986 (or 1 – 0.014)

Step 3   We can now go on to complete the decision tree. Let us make the following assumptions. (In an exam question such information would have been given to you from the start.)

- The cost of drilling is $10m.
- The value of the benefits if oil is found is $70m, giving a net 'profit' of $60m.
- The cost of obtaining information from the consultants would be $3m.

An assumption is made that the decision-maker will take whichever decision the information indicates is the best. If the information says 'oil', the company will drill, and if the information says 'no oil' it will not drill.

* The information is 'no oil', so the company won't drill, regardless of whether there really is oil or not.

Step 4   We can now perform rollback analysis.

		$m
EV at point 3 =	0.704 × $60m	42.24
	0.296 × ($10m)	(2.96)
		+ 39.28

		$m
EV at point 2 =	0.27 × $39.28m	10.61
	0.73 × $0	0.00
		+ 10.61

Step 5   There are three choices.   EV

(a)   Do not obtain information and do not drill $0
(b)   Do not obtain information and drill   + $4 million
(c)   Obtain information first, decide about drilling later ($(10.61m − 3m))   + $7.61 million

The decision should be to obtain the information from a survey first.

Step 6   The value of the imperfect information is the difference between (b) and (c), $3.61 million.

7 Sensitivity analysis

> **Sensitivity analysis is a method of analysing the uncertainty in a situation or decision.** It measures the effect of changes in the estimated value of an item ('key factor') on the future outcome. It can therefore be used to assess the sensitivity of the expected outcome to variations or changes in the value of the item ('key factor').

7.1 Approaches to sensitivity analysis

Key term

> **Sensitivity analysis** is a term used to describe any technique whereby decision options are tested for their vulnerability to changes in any 'variable', such as expected sales volume, sales price per unit, material costs and labour costs.

Sensitivity analysis is a technique for analysing uncertainty about the outcome of a decision. The starting point is an estimate of what the outcome will be based on estimates for key variables, such as selling price, sales volume and unit variable cost fixed cost expenditures. Sensitivity analysis may be used because there is uncertainty about some of these estimates. Here are three useful approaches to sensitivity analysis.

(a) To estimate by **how much costs and revenues would need to differ** from their estimated values before the decision would change

(b) To estimate whether a decision would change if estimated costs were **x% higher** than estimated, or estimated revenues **y% lower** than estimated

(c) To estimate by how much costs and/or revenues would need to differ from their estimated values before the decision-maker would be **indifferent** between two options

The essence of the approach, therefore, is to carry out the calculations with one set of values for the variables and then substitute other possible values for the variables to see how this affects the overall outcome.

(a) From your studies of information technology you may recognise this as **'what if' analysis** that can be carried out using a **spreadsheet**.

(b) From your studies of **linear programming** you may remember that sensitivity analysis can be carried out to determine over which ranges the various constraints have an impact on the optimum solution.

(c) **Flexible budgeting** can also be a form of sensitivity analysis.

7.2 Example: Sensitivity analysis

Sensivite Co has estimated the following sales and profits for a new product which it may launch on to the market.

		$	$
Sales	(2,000 units)		4,000
Variable costs:	materials	2,000	
	labour	1,000	
			3,000
Contribution			1,000
Less incremental fixed costs			800
Profit			200

Required

Analyse the sensitivity of the project to changes in key variables.

Solution

(a) If incremental **fixed costs** are more than 25% above estimate (= 200/800), the project would make a loss.

(b) If **unit costs of materials** are more than 10% above estimate (200/2,000), the project would make a loss.

(c) Similarly, the project would be sensitive to an **increase in unit labour costs** of more than $200, which is 20% above estimate.

(d) Moreover, the project would become unprofitable if the selling price is more than 5% (200/4,000) below the estimate, given no change in sales volume.

(e) The **margin of safety**, given a breakeven point of 1,600 units, is (400/2,000) × 100% = 20%.

Management would then be able to judge more clearly whether the product is likely to be profitable, by making an assessment of the scale of the uncertainty in the estimates. The items to which profitability is most sensitive in this example are the selling price (5%) and material costs (10%). Sensitivity analysis can help to **concentrate management attention** on the most important factors.

8 Simulation models   12/08

FAST FORWARD

> **Simulation models** can be used to deal with decision problems when there are a large number of uncertain variables in the situation. **Random numbers** are used to assign values to the variables.

One of the chief problems encountered in decision-making is the uncertainty of the future. Where only a few factors are involved, probability analysis and expected value calculations can be used to find the most likely outcome of a decision. Often, however, in real life, there are so **many uncertain variables** that this approach does not give a true impression of possible variations in outcome.

To get an idea of what will happen in real life, one possibility is to use a **simulation model** in which the **values and the variables are selected at random**. Obviously this is a situation **ideally suited to a computer** (large volume of data, random number generation).

The term 'simulation' model is often used more specifically to refer to modelling which **makes use of random numbers**. This is the **'Monte Carlo'** method of simulation. In the business environment it can, for example, be used to examine inventory, queuing, scheduling and forecasting problems.

Random numbers are allocated to each possible value of the uncertain variable in proportion to the probabilities, so that a probability of 0.1 gets 10% of the total numbers to be assigned. These random numbers are used to assign values to the variables.

Exam focus point

> You will **not** be required to develop a simulation model in your exam. The following example is provided so that you can **understand** how simulation models are developed.

8.1 Example: Simulation and spreadsheets

A supermarket sells a product for which the daily demand varies. An analysis of daily demand over a period of about a year shows the following probability distribution.

Demand per day Units	Probability
35	0.10
36	0.20
37	0.25
38	0.30
39	0.08
40	0.07
	1.00

To develop a simulation model in which one of the variables is daily demand, we would **assign a group of numbers to each value for daily demand**. The probabilities are stated to two decimal places, and so there must be 100 random numbers in total, 00–99 (we use 00–99 rather than 1–100 so that we can use two-digit random numbers.) Random numbers are assigned in proportion to the **probabilities**, so that a probability of 0.1 gets 10% of the total numbers to be assigned; that is, 10 numbers: 0, 1, 2, 3, 4, 5, 6, 7, 8 and 9.

The assignments would therefore be as follows.

Demand per day Units	Probability	Numbers assigned
35	0.10	00-09
36	0.20	10-29
37	0.25	30-54
38	0.30	55-84
39	0.08	85-92
40	0.07	93-99

When the simulation model is run, random numbers will be generated to derive values for daily demand. For example, if the model is used to simulate demand over a ten-day period, the random numbers generated might be as follows.

19007174604721296802

The model would then **assign values** to the demand per day as follows.

Day	Random number	Demand Units
1	19	36
2	00	35
3	71	38
4	74	38
5	60	38
6	47	37
7	21	36
8	29	36
9	68	38
10	02	35

You might notice that on none of the ten days is the demand 39 or 40 units, because the random numbers generated did not include any value in the range 85–99. When a simulation model is used, there must be a long enough run to give a good representation of the system and all its potential variations.

8.2 Uses of simulation

In the example above, the supermarket would use the information to minimise inventory holding without risking running out of the product. This will reduce costs but avoid lost sales and profit.

A supermarket can also use this technique to estimate queues at checkout desks, with predicted lengths of waiting time determining the number of staff required.

Chapter Roundup

- When there is a strong element of risk or uncertainty in a decision, the decision that is taken may be affected by the extent of the risk or uncertainty.

- 'Risk' and 'uncertainty' are often used to mean the same thing. However, to be more exact, 'risk' in decision-making exists when the future outcome cannot be predicted for certain, but probabilities can be estimated for each possible outcome. Uncertainty, in contrast, is when there is insufficient information to make a reliable prediction about what will happen and there are no probability estimates of different possible outcomes.

- People may be **risk seekers**, **risk neutral** or **risk averse**. A person's attitude to risk and uncertainty may affect the decision that is taken.

- Management accounting directs its attention towards the **future** and the future is **uncertain**. For this reason a number of methods of taking **uncertainty** into consideration have evolved.

- One approach to dealing with uncertainty is to obtain more information, in order to reduce the amount of uncertainty about what will happen. Reliable information reduces uncertainty.

- **Market research** into customer habits, attitudes or intentions can be used to reduce uncertainty.

- An expected value is a weighted average value of the different possible outcomes from a decision, where weightings are based on the probability of each possible outcome.

- **Expected values** indicate what an outcome is likely to be in the long term, if the decision can be repeated many times over. Fortunately, many business transactions do occur over and over again.

- The 'play it safe' basis for decision-making is referred to as the **maximin basis**. This is short for '**maximise the minimum achievable profit**'.

- A basis for making decisions by looking for the best outcome is known as the **maximax basis**, short for '**maximise the maximum achievable profit**'.

- The 'opportunity loss' basis for decision-making is known as **minimax regret**.

- **Decision trees** are diagrams which illustrate the choices and possible outcomes of a decision. The possible outcomes are usually given associated probabilities of occurrence.

- **Rollback analysis** evaluates the EV of each decision option. You have to work from right to left and calculate EVs at each outcome point.

- **Perfect information** is guaranteed to predict the future with 100% accuracy. **Imperfect information** is better than no information at all but could be wrong in its prediction of the future.

- The **value of perfect information** is the difference between the EV of profit with perfect information and the EV of profit without perfect information.

- The **value of imperfect information** is the difference between the EV of profit with imperfect information and the EV of profit without the information.

- **Sensitivity analysis is a method of analysing the uncertainty in a situation or decision.** It measures the effect of changes in the estimated value of an item ('key factor') on the future outcome. It can therefore be used to assess the sensitivity of the expected outcome to variations or changes in the value of the item ('key factor').

- **Simulation models** can be used to deal with decision problems when there are a large number of uncertain variables in the situation. **Random numbers** are used to assign values to the variables.

Quick Quiz

1   Match the terms to the correct definitions.

Terms

(a)   Risk seeker   (c)   Risk averse
(b)   Risk neutral

Definitions

1   A decision-maker concerned with what will be the most likely outcome

2   A decision-maker interested in the best outcomes no matter how small the chance that they may occur

3   A decision-maker who acts on the assumption that the worst outcome might occur

2   Fill in the blanks.

(a)   Maximin decision rule: choosing the alternative that .... the ....
(b)   Minimax decision rule: choosing the alternative that .... the ....
(c)   Maximax decision rule: choosing the alternative that .... the............................
(d)   Minimin decision rule: choosing the alternative that .... the............................

3   How is expected value calculated?

A   Σpx   C   eΣpx
B   pΣx   D   xΣp

4   Tick the correct boxes to indicate the usefulness of expected values as a guide to decision-making in the following decisions.

	Most useful	Not as useful
(a) Whether to change the logo painted on the window of 700 retail outlets		
(b) Whether to purchase machine X or machine Y		
(c) Whether to launch product A		
(d) Deciding on the optimum daily purchases of a perishable item		

5   If the decision-maker is trying to maximise the figure, what figure would the decision-maker choose at point B in the diagram below?

A   40,000   C   13,900

B   11,800   D   22,000

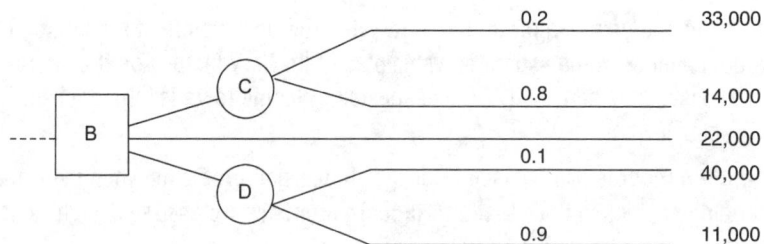

1   (a) 2; (b) 1; (c) 3

2   (a)   Maximise, minimum profits   (c)   Maximise, maximum profits
          (b)   Minimise, maximum costs/losses   (d)   Minimise, minimum costs/losses

3   A   An expected value is the sum of the different possible outcomes (x) multiplied by their associated probability of occurrence (p).

4   Expected values would be useful for decisions (a) and (d) because they are repeated several times.

5   D   Choice between $((0.2 \times 33{,}000) + (0.8 \times 14{,}000)) = 17{,}800$ at C, 22,000, and $((0.1 \times 40{,}000) + (0.9 \times 11{,}000)) = 13{,}900$ at D.

Now try the questions below from the Practice Question Bank

Number	Level	Marks	Approximate time
Section A Q46	Examination	2	4 mins
Section A Q47	Examination	2	4 mins
Section A Q48	Examination	2	4 mins
Section A Q49	Examination	2	4 mins
Section A Q50	Examination	2	4 mins
Section C Q4	Examination	20	39 mins

Budgeting and control

Budgetary systems

8

Introduction

This chapter is an introduction to Part C of the Study Text and it looks at the budgeting system and methods of preparing budgets. We look at the various stages in the **planning process**, and where the annual budget fits in to this. We also see how the budget is used in the **control process**.

We then go on to look at the **traditional approach** to budget preparation – **incremental budgeting** – as well as alternative approaches to budget preparation: **zero based budgeting**, **rolling budgets** and **activity based budgeting**.

Study guide

		Intellectual level
C1	**Budgetary systems and types of budget**	
(a)	Explain how budgetary systems fit within the performance hierarchy.	2
(b)	Select and explain appropriate budgetary systems for an organisation, including top-down, bottom-up, rolling, zero base, activity base, incremental and feed-forward control.	2
(c)	Describe the information used in budget systems and the sources of the information needed.	2
(d)	Indicate the usefulness and problems with different budget types (including fixed, flexible, zero based, activity based, incremental, rolling, top-down, bottom up, master, functional).	2
(e)	Prepare flexed budgets, rolling budgets and activity based budgets.	2
(f)	Explain the beyond budgeting model, including the benefits and problems that may be faced if it is adopted in an organisation.	
(g)	Discuss the issues surrounding setting the difficulty level for a budget.	2
(h)	Explain the benefits and difficulties of the participation of employees in the negotiation of targets.	2
(i)	Explain the difficulties of changing a budgetary system or type of budget used	2
(j)	Explain how budget systems can deal with uncertainty in the environment.	2

Exam guide

You are expected to be aware of the problems of traditional budgeting systems and why organisations may be reluctant to change to more appropriate systems. There is an article on the ACCA website titled 'Comparing budgeting techniques' written by a member of the examining team (ACCA, 2016). It is recommended that you read this article.

> One of the competencies you require to fulfil performance objective 13 is the ability to contribute to setting objectives for the planning and control of business activities. You can apply the knowledge you obtain from this chapter to help to demonstrate this competence.

1 Revision – Objectives of budgeting systems

FAST FORWARD

A budget is a **quantified plan of action** for a forthcoming accounting period.

A budget can be set from the **top down** (**imposed** budget) or from the **bottom up** (**participatory** budget).

Here are the objectives of a budgetary planning and control system.

- Ensure the achievement of the organisation's objectives
- Compel planning
- Communicate ideas and plans
- Co-ordinate activities
- Provide a framework for responsibility accounting
- Establish a system of control
- Motivate employees to improve their performance

You should be familiar with the objectives of budgetary systems from your earlier studies. The key points are summarised below.

A budgetary planning and control system is essentially a system for ensuring **communication**, **co-ordination** and **control** within an organisation. Communication, co-ordination and control are general objectives: more information is provided by an inspection of the specific objectives of a budgetary planning and control system.

Objective	Comment
Ensure the achievement of the organisation's objectives	Objectives are set for the organisation as a whole, and for individual departments and operations within the organisation. Quantified expressions of these objectives are then drawn up as targets to be achieved within the timescale of the budget plan.
Compel planning	This is probably the most important feature of a budgetary planning and control system. Planning forces management to **look ahead**, to set out **detailed plans** for achieving the targets for each department, operation and (ideally) each manager and to anticipate problems. It thus prevents management from relying on ad hoc or uncoordinated planning which may be detrimental to the performance of the organisation.
Communicate ideas and plans	A formal system is necessary to ensure that each person affected by the plans is aware of what they is **supposed to be doing**. Communication might be one-way, with managers giving **orders to subordinates**, or there might be a two-way dialogue and exchange of ideas.
Co-ordinate activities	The activities of different departments or sub-units of the organisation need to be co-ordinated to ensure **maximum integration** of effort towards common goals. This concept of coordination implies, for example, that the purchasing department should base its budget on production requirements and that the production budget should in turn be based on sales expectations. Although straightforward in concept, co-ordination is remarkably difficult to achieve, and there is often **'sub-optimality'** and conflict between departmental plans in the budget so that the efforts of each department are not fully integrated into a combined plan to achieve the company's best targets.
Provide a framework for responsibility accounting	Budgetary planning and control systems require that managers of **budget centres** are made responsible for the achievement of budget targets for the operations under their personal control.
Establish a system of control	A budget is a **yardstick** against which actual performance is measured and assessed. Control over actual performance is provided by the comparisons of actual results against the budget plan. Departures from budget can then be investigated and the reasons for the departures can be divided into **controllable** and **uncontrollable** factors.
Motivate employees to improve their performance	The interest and commitment of employees can be retained via a system of **feedback of actual results**, which lets them know how well or badly they are performing. The identification of controllable reasons for departures from budget with managers responsible provides an incentive for improving future performance.

2 The planning and control cycle

The **planning and control cycle** has seven steps.

- *Step 1.* Identify **objectives**
- *Step 2.* Identify potential **strategies**
- *Step 3.* Evaluate strategies
- *Step 4.* Choose alternative courses of action
- *Step 5.* Implement the long-term plan
- *Step 6.* Measure actual results and compare with the plan
- *Step 7.* Respond to divergences from the plan

The diagram below represents the planning and control cycle. The first five steps cover the planning process. **Planning** involves making choices between alternatives and is primarily a decision-making activity. The last two steps cover the **control** process, which involves measuring and correcting actual performance to ensure that the alternatives that are chosen and the plans for implementing them are carried out.

The planning and control cycle

Identify objectives	Step 1
Identify alternative courses of action (strategies) which might contribute towards achieving the objectives	Step 2
Evaluate each strategy	Step 3
Choose alternative courses of action	Step 4
Implement the long-term plan in the form of the annual budget	Step 5
Measure actual results and compare with the plan	Step 6
Respond to divergences from plan	Step 7

Planning process

Control process

Step 1   Identify objectives

Objectives establish the direction in which the management of the organisation wish it to be heading. They answer the question: 'Where do we want to be?'

Step 2   Identify potential strategies

Once an organisation has decided 'where it wants to be', the next step is to identify a range of possible courses of action or **strategies** that might enable the organisation to get there. The organisation must therefore carry out an **information-gathering exercise** to ensure that it has a full **understanding of where it is now**. This is known as a '**position audit**' or '**strategic analysis**' and involves looking both inwards and outwards.

(a)   The organisation must **gather information from all of its internal parts** to find out what resources it possesses: what its manufacturing capacity and capability is, what the state of its technical know-how is, how well it is able to market itself, how much cash it has in the bank, and so on.

(b)   It must also **gather information externally** so that it can assess its position in the environment. Just as it has assessed its **own strengths and weaknesses**, it must do likewise for its competitors (**threats**). Current and potential markets must be analysed to identify possible new **opportunities**. The 'state of the world' must be considered. Is it in recession or is it booming? What is likely to happen in the future?

Having carried out a strategic analysis, alternative strategies can be identified. An organisation might decide to be the lowest cost producer in the industry, perhaps by withdrawing from some markets or developing new products for sale in existing markets. This may involve internal development or a joint venture.

Step 3 Evaluate strategies

The strategies must then be evaluated **in terms of suitability, feasibility and acceptability**. Management should select those strategies that have the greatest potential for achieving the organisation's objectives.

Step 4 Choose alternative courses of action

The next step in the process is to collect the **chosen strategies** together and **co-ordinate them into a long-term financial plan.** Typically this would show the following.

- Projected cash flows
- Capital expenditure plans
- Projected long-term profits
- Financial position forecasts
- A description of the long-term objectives and strategies in words

Step 5 Implement the long-term plan

The **long-term plan** should then be **broken down into smaller parts**. It is unlikely that the different parts will fall conveniently into successive time periods. Strategy A may take two and a half years, while Strategy B may take five months, but not start until year three of the plan. It is usual, however, to break down the plan as a whole into equal time periods (usually one year). The resulting **short-term plan** is called a **budget**.

Step 6 Measure actual results and compare with plan

Actual results are recorded and analysed and information about actual results is fed back to the management concerned, often in the form of accounting reports. This reported information is **feedback** (see Section 3.2.1 below).

Step 7 Respond to divergences from plan

By comparing actual and planned results, management can then do one of three things, depending on how they see the situation.

(a) They can take control action. By identifying what has gone wrong, and then finding out why, corrective measures can be taken.

(b) They can decide to do nothing. This could be the decision when actual results are going better than planned, or when poor results were caused by something which is unlikely to happen again in the future.

(c) They can alter the plan or target if actual results are different from the plan or target, and there is nothing that management can do (or nothing, perhaps, that they want to do) to correct the situation.

Question

Planning and control cycles

Is your organisation's planning and control cycle similar to the one described here? If it differs, how does it differ? Why does it differ? Try to find out your organisation's objectives and the strategies being adopted to attain these objectives.

Answers to this question could be usefully employed in the exam.

---

3 Planning and control in the performance hierarchy

Planning and control occurs at all levels of the performance hierarchy to different degrees. The performance hierarchy refers to the system by which performance is measured and controlled at different levels of management within the organisation.

3.1 Planning

Although it implies a 'top down' approach to management, we could describe **a cascade of goals, objectives and plans** down through the layers of the organisation. The **plans** made at the **higher levels** of the performance hierarchy provide a **framework** within which the plans at the lower levels must be achieved. The **plans** at the **lower levels** are the **means** by which the plans at the higher levels are achieved.

It could therefore be argued that, without the plans allied directly to the vision and corporate objective, the operational-level and departmental plans have little meaning. **Planning** could therefore be deemed as **more significant** at the **higher levels** of the performance hierarchy than at the lower levels.

This is not to say that planning at an operational level is not important. It is just that the nature of planning differs according to the level in the management hierarchy at which it takes place.

Level	Detail
Corporate plans/strategic plans **Prepared at a strategic level by senior management**	• Focused on overall corporate performance • Environmental influence • Set overall plans and targets for units and departments • Sometimes qualitative planning (eg a programme to change the culture of the organisation)
Tactical plans **Prepared at lower management level ('management control' level), within guidelines set by senior management**	• Time horizon typically 12 months • Plans for individual departments or activities, within guidelines set by senior management • Some budgets may be prepared in non-financial terms, but all budgets are converted into money values • The overall budget is expressed in financial terms, with a budgeted income statement, budgeted end of year financial position and budgeted cash flow forecast • Provides a link between strategic plans at senior level and operational planning • Budget targets should be consistent with strategic objectives • Approved by senior management (board of directors)
Operational plans **Prepared by managers at a fairly junior level, at a practical operational level**	• Based on objectives about 'what' to achieve in operational terms • Specific (eg acceptable number of 'rings' before a phone is answered) • Operational targets likely to be quantitative • Detailed specifications of targets and standards • Based on 'how' something is achieved • Short time horizons • Operational plans should be prepared that enable budget targets to be achieved

3.2 Control

Consider how the activities of **planning** and **control** are **interrelated**.

(a) **Plans** set the targets.

(b) **Control** involves two main processes.

   (i)   **Measure** actual results against the plan.

   (ii) **Take action** to adjust actual performance to achieve the plan or to change the plan altogether.

Control is therefore **impossible without planning**.

The essence of control is the **measurement of results** and **comparing** them with the original **plan**. Any deviation from the plan indicates that **control action** is required to make the results conform more closely with the plan.

3.2.1 Feedback

Key term

> **Feedback** occurs when the results (outputs) of a system are used to control it, by adjusting the input or behaviour of the system. Feedback is information produced as output from operations; it is used to compare actual results with planned results for control purposes.

A business organisation uses feedback for control.

(a) **Negative feedback** indicates that results or activities must be brought back on course, as they are deviating from the plan.

(b) **Positive feedback** results in control action continuing the current course. You would normally assume that positive feedback means that results are going according to plan and that no corrective action is necessary: but it is best to be sure that the control system itself is not picking up the wrong information.

(c) **Feedforward control** is control based on **forecast** results: in other words, if the forecast is bad, control action is taken well in advance of actual results.

There are two types of feedback.

(a) **Single loop feedback** is control, like a thermostat, which regulates the output of a system. For example, if sales targets are not reached, control action will be taken to ensure that targets will be reached soon. The plan or target itself is not changed, even though the resources needed to achieve it might have to be reviewed.

(b) **Double loop feedback** is of a different order. It is information used to **change the plan itself**. For example, if sales targets are not reached, the company may need to change the plan.

3.2.2 Control at different levels

FAST FORWARD

> **Budgetary control** occurs at the middle management or **'management control'** levels of the performance hierarchy.

Control at the middle management or **'management control' level** of the performance hierarchy, such as standard costing and budgetary control, has the following features.

• It is exercised by measuring actual performance against planned performance in the budget or similar medium-term plans.

• Actual results are measured and reported to the managers responsible for the performance. There are formal feedback systems for reporting, and performance reports may be produced monthly, in the form of a budgetary control report or variance report.

- Reports are based mainly on feedback, ie performance information produced from within the organisation's systems. They do not make any significant use of information obtained externally, from outside the organisation.

- Comparisons of actual and budgeted performance are often expressed in financial terms.

At a more senior level of control reporting, strategic performance reports may be produced periodically (say, every three months, six months or one year). These assess performance and the organisation's strategic position in terms of the overall business plan (strategic plans). Information gathered from outside the organisation as well as information gathered internally may be used for strategic performance reports.

At an operational level, control measures are reported and monitored regularly, often on a day-to-day basis. Operational managers are expected to achieve performance standards that are set, and actual performance is compared with the standards. Many performance measures used for control purposes are non-financial in nature, such as standard times to complete a task and maximum rates of wastage or loss in process.

3.3 Other aspects of budget preparation

The following are other key points about budget preparation, included here as revision material.

Point	Detail
Long-term plan	The **starting point**; this will show **what the budget has to achieve** (the introduction of new production, the required return, and so on) and outline **how it is to be done**. It will also contain **general guidelines** on allowable price increases like wage rates. The **long-term policy** needs to be **communicated** to all managers responsible for preparing budgets so that they are aware of the context within which they are budgeting and how their area of responsibility is expected to contribute.
Limiting factor	This is the factor in the budget that **limits the scale of operations**. The limiting factor is often sales demand, but it may be production capacity when sales demand is high or when a key production resource is in short supply. Budgeting cannot proceed until the budget for the limiting factor has been prepared, since this affects all the other budgets.
Budget manual	A budget manual is a guide or instruction document to **assist functional managers** with preparing their functional budgets. It shows how figures and forecasts for the budget should be calculated, and gives other practical information. It is likely to include **proformas** showing how the information is to be presented. If budgeting is done with spreadsheets, layouts and computations may be pre-programmed, requiring only the entry of the figures. It may include a **flow diagram** showing how individual budgets are interlinked and specify deadlines by which first drafts must be prepared.
Sales budget	This contains **information on the expected volume of sales** (based on estimates or market research), the **sales mix, and selling prices**. The total revenues indicated will be used to compile the cash budget, although this information needs to be adjusted to allow for the expected timing of receipts. The volume of sales indicates the level of production required and the extent of spending on distribution and administration.
Production capacity	The level of sales anticipated is matched against opening inventory and desired closing inventory to establish the level of production. From this can be calculated the need for materials (again allowing for opening and closing inventory), labour and machine hours. In other words, production budgeting is **done in terms of physical resources initially and costed afterwards**. At this stage, too, it is likely that needs for new capital expenditure will be identified. This information will be used in preparing the capital budget.

Point	Detail
Functional budgets	Functional budgets are budgets for the different departments or functions within the organisation. **Budgets for production-related functions**, such as purchasing, engineering and inspection and testing, may be based on the budgeted volume of production. Budgets **for other areas of the organisation**, such as distribution and administration, may take the anticipated sales level as their point of reference. Vehicle costs, carriage costs, stationery and communication costs and, above all, staff costs feature in these budgets. Some budgeted, such as the budget for **research and development (R&D) spending**, may be entirely discretionary and set at a level that management consider the organisation can or should afford.
Discretionary costs	**Training and R&D** are known as 'discretionary costs' and have special features.
Consolidation and coordination	This can begin once all parts of the organisation have submitted their individual budgets. It is most **unlikely** that **all the budgets will be in line with each other** at the first attempt. Areas of **incompatibility** must be identified and the **budgets modified** in consultation with individual managers. **Spreadsheets** are invaluable at this stage, both for the consolidation itself and to allow changes to be made quickly and accurately.
Cash budget	This can only be prepared at this stage because it **needs to take account of all the plans of the organisation** and translate them into expected cash flows. Cash must be available when it is needed to enable the plans to be carried out. Overdraft facilities may need to be negotiated in advance, or some activities may need to be deferred until cash has been collected.
Master budget	The final stage, once all the necessary modifications have been made, is to prepare a **summary** of all the budgets in the form of a master budget, which generally comprises a **budgeted statement of profit or loss, a budgeted statement of financial position and a budgeted statement of cash flow.**

3.3.1 Top-down and bottom-up budgeting

'Top down' and 'bottom up' are two different approaches to budget preparation.

(a)   With **top-down budgeting**, budget targets are set at senior management level for the organisation as a whole and for each major department or activity within the organisation. The departmental budget targets are then given to the departmental managers, who are required to prepare a budget that conforms to the targets that have been imposed on them from above. Similarly, when budgets have been set at departmental level, targets are then given to managers lower down the organisation hierarchy; these managers are then required to prepare budgets that meet the targets that have been imposed on them for their area of operations.

(b)   With **bottom-up budgeting**, the budgeting process starts at a relatively low level of management. Managers are required to draft a budget for their area of operations. These are submitted to their superior, who combines the lower-level budgets into a combined budget for the department as a whole. Departmental budgets are then submitted to senior management, where they are combined into a co-ordinated budget for the organisation as a whole.

Top-down budgeting takes much less time and planning effort than bottom-up budgeting and senior management can use top-down budgets to impose their views. Bottom-up budgeting is much more time consuming, and draft budgets may have to be revised many times until they are properly co-ordinated.

However, bottom-up budgeting has two potential advantages.

(a)   It reflects the views and expectations of managers who are closer to operations and who may therefore have a better understanding of what is and what is not achievable.

(b)   Bottom-up budgeting is a form of participative budgeting process, which can have behavioural and motivational advantages. These are considered further in a later chapter.

4 Incremental budgeting

FAST FORWARD

> With the 'traditional' approach to budgeting, known as **incremental budgeting**, the budget for the next financial year is based on the actual results for the current financial year. At its simplest level, a budget based on an incremental costing approach is the actual (or budgeted) performance for the current year, adjusted for expected growth and inflation. Incremental budgeting encourages slack and wasteful spending to creep into budgets.

Key term

> **Incremental budgeting** is a method of budgeting in which next year's budget is prepared by using the current year's actual results as a starting point, and making adjustments for expected inflation, sales growth or decline and other known changes.

The main advantage of incremental budgeting is that it is a relatively straightforward way of preparing a budget.

Incremental budgeting may also be a reasonable procedure if current operations are as effective, efficient and economical as they can be. It is also appropriate for budgeting for costs, such as staff salaries, which may be estimated on the basis of current salaries plus an increment for inflation, provided that no significant changes in the workforce are anticipated and are administratively fairly easy to prepare as a result.

In general, however, it is an **inefficient form of budgeting**, as it **encourages slack** and **wasteful spending** to creep into budgets. Past inefficiencies are perpetuated because cost levels are rarely subjected to close scrutiny.

Advantages of incremental budgets	Disadvantages of incremental budgets
• Considered to be the quickest and easiest method of budgeting	• Builds in previous problems and inefficiencies
• Suitable for organisations that operate in a stable environment where historic figures are reliable and are not expected to change significantly	• Managers may spend for the sake of spending in order to use up their budget for the year and thus ensure that they get the same (or a larger) budget next year
	• Uneconomical activities may be continued. For example, a car manufacturer may continue to make parts in-house when it may be cheaper to outsource

Question
Incremental budgeting

Can incremental budgeting be used to budget for rent? What about for advertising expenditure?

Answer

Incremental budgeting is appropriate for budgeting for rent, which may be estimated on the basis of current rent plus an increment for the annual rent increase. Advertising expenditure, on the other hand, is not so easily quantifiable and is more discretionary in nature. Using incremental budgeting for advertising expenditure could allow slack and wasteful spending to creep into the budget.

4.1 Incremental budgeting in the public sector

The traditional approach to budgeting in the public sector has been incremental and this has resulted in existing patterns of public expenditure being locked in. The public spending round in the UK established an annual cycle of year on year incremental bids by departments rather than an analysis of outputs and efficiency.

5 Fixed and flexible budgets

> A **fixed budget** is a financial plan that does not change throughout the budget period, regardless of any changes from the plan in the actual volume of activity. A **flexible budget** recognises cost behaviour and changes as the actual volume of activity changes.
>
> A fixed budget is normally used for **planning purposes** and is prepared in advance of the beginning of the financial period. A flexible budget is used for **control purposes** and is normally prepared retrospectively, when the actual level of activity in a period is known.

PER alert

One of the competencies you require to fulfil performance objective 13 is to coordinate, prepare and use budgets, selecting suitable budgeting models. You can apply the knowledge you obtain from this chapter to help to demonstrate this competence.

5.1 Fixed budgets

Key term

A **fixed budget** is a budget which remains unchanged throughout the budget period, regardless of differences between the actual and the original planned volume of output or sales.

The master budget, which is prepared and approved before the beginning of the budget period, is normally a **fixed budget**. The term 'fixed' means the following.

(a) The budget is **prepared on the basis of an estimated volume of production** and an **estimated volume of sales**, but no plans are made for the event that actual volumes of production and sales may differ from budgeted volumes.

(b) When actual volumes of production and sales during a control period (month or four weeks or quarter) are achieved, the budget is **not adjusted or revised (in retrospect) to the new levels of activity**.

The major purpose of a fixed budget is for planning. It is prepared at the planning stage, when it is used to define the objectives and targets of the organisation for the budget period (financial year).

5.2 Flexible budgets

Key term

A **flexible budget** is a budget which, by recognising different cost behaviour patterns, is changed as the volume of output and sales changes. It recognises cost behaviour patterns such as changes in sales revenue and variable costs as sales volumes change, and step changes in fixed costs as activity levels rise or fall by more than a certain amount.

Flexible budgets may be used in one of two ways.

(a) **At the planning stage.** An organisation may prepare flexible budgets at the planning stage for different levels of activity. For example, suppose that a company expects to sell 10,000 units of output during the next year. A master budget (the fixed budget) would be prepared on the basis of these expected volumes. However, if the company thinks that output and sales might be as low as 8,000 units or as high as 12,000 units, it may prepare **contingency flexible budgets** at volumes of, say, 8,000, 9,000, 11,000 and 12,000 units and then assess the possible outcomes. However, preparing flexible budgets in advance adds to the time and effort required for preparing budget, and this is not common.

(b)   **Retrospectively**. At the end of each month (control period) or year, the results that should have been achieved given the actual circumstances (the flexible budget) can be compared with the actual results. As we shall see, flexible budgets are an essential factor in **budgetary control**.

Whereas fixed budgets are prepared in advance for planning purposes, flexible budgets are usually prepared retrospectively for planning purposes.

5.3 Preparing a flexible budget

Step 1   The first step in the preparation of a flexible budget is the **determination of cost behaviour patterns**, which means **deciding whether costs are fixed, variable or semi-variable**.

Step 2   The second step in the preparation of a flexible budget is to calculate the **budget cost allowance** for each cost item.

Budget cost allowance = budgeted fixed cost* + (number of units × variable cost per unit)**

* nil for variable cost
** nil for fixed cost

Semi-variable costs therefore need splitting into their fixed and variable components so that the budget cost allowance can be calculated. One method for splitting semi-variable costs is the high/low method, which we covered in Chapter 9.

5.4 Example: Preparing a flexible budget

(a)   Prepare a budget for 20X6 for the direct labour costs and overhead expenses of a production department flexed at the activity levels of 80%, 90% and 100%, using the information listed below.

(i)   The direct labour hourly rate is expected to be $3.75.

(ii)   100% activity represents 60,000 direct labour hours.

(iii)   *Variable costs*

Indirect labour	$0.75 per direct labour hour
Consumable supplies	$0.375 per direct labour hour
Canteen and other	
welfare services	6% of direct and indirect labour costs

(iv)   Semi-variable costs are expected to relate to the direct labour hours in the same manner as for the last five years.

Year	Direct labour hours	Semi-variable costs
		$
20X1	64,000	20,800
20X2	59,000	19,800
20X3	53,000	18,600
20X4	49,000	17,800
20X5	40,000 (estimate)	16,000 (estimate)

(v)   *Fixed costs*

	$
Depreciation	18,000
Maintenance	10,000
Insurance	4,000
Rates	15,000
Management salaries	25,000

(vi)   Inflation is to be ignored.

(b) Calculate the budget cost allowance (ie expected expenditure) for 20X6 assuming that 57,000 direct labour hours are worked.

Solution

(a)

	80% level 48,000 hrs $'000	90% level 54,000 hrs $'000	100% level 60,000 hrs $'000
Direct labour	180.00	202.50	225.0
Other variable costs			
Indirect labour	36.00	40.50	45.0
Consumable supplies	18.00	20.25	22.5
Canteen etc	12.96	14.58	16.2
Total variable costs ($5.145 per hour)	246.96	277.83	308.7
Semi-variable costs (W)	17.60	18.80	20.0
Fixed costs			
Depreciation	18.00	18.00	18.0
Maintenance	10.00	10.00	10.0
Insurance	4.00	4.00	4.0
Rates	15.00	15.00	15.0
Management salaries	25.00	25.00	25.0
Budgeted costs	336.56	368.63	400.7

Working

Using the high/low method:

	$
Total cost of 64,000 hours	20,800
Total cost of 40,000 hours	16,000
Variable cost of 24,000 hours	4,800
Variable cost per hour ($4,800/24,000)	$0.20

	$
Total cost of 64,000 hours	20,800
Variable cost of 64,000 hours ($\times$ $0.20)	12,800
Fixed costs	8,000

Semi-variable costs are calculated as follows.

			$
60,000 hours	(60,000 $\times$ $0.20) + $8,000	=	20,000
54,000 hours	(54,000 $\times$ $0.20) + $8,000	=	18,800
48,000 hours	(48,000 $\times$ $0.20) + $8,000	=	17,600

(b) The budget cost allowance for 57,000 direct labour hours of work would be as follows.

		$
Variable costs	(57,000 $\times$ $5.145)	293,265
Semi-variable costs	($8,000 + (57,000 $\times$ $0.20))	19,400
Fixed costs		72,000
		384,665

5.5 Factors to consider when preparing flexible budgets

The mechanics of flexible budgeting are, in theory, fairly straightforward but in practice there are a number of points to consider before figures are simply flexed.

(a) Splitting mixed costs is not always straightforward.
(b) Fixed costs may behave in a step-line fashion as activity levels increase/decrease.

(c)   Account must be taken of the assumptions on which the original fixed budget was based. Such assumptions might include the constraint posed by limiting factors, the rate of inflation, judgements about future uncertainty, the demand for the organisation's products, and so on.

(d)   By flexing a budget, a manager is effectively saying 'If I knew then what I know now, this is the budget I would have set'. It is a useful concept but can lead to some concern, as managers can become confused and frustrated if faced with continually moving targets.

We will return to flexible budgets again in Chapter 10.

6 Zero based budgeting   6/09, 12/10, 6/13, 6/15

FAST FORWARD

> The principle behind **zero based budgeting (ZBB)** is that the budget for each cost centre should be made from 'scratch' or zero. Every item of expenditure must be justified in its entirety in order to be included in the next year's budget.

Exam focus point

> In the exam, it is important to apply the knowledge from the following section, to the specifics of the scenario given. It was noted in the June 2015 exam report, that candidates did not consider the company in the question and instead just wrote down lists which had appeared in their text books. You will not be awarded marks at this level if you cannot apply the knowledge from this section to different types of scenarios.

ZBB rejects the assumption inherent in **incremental budgeting** that next year's budget should be based on the current financial year results (or the current year budget), with adjustments for incremental changes, such as growth and inflation. It is based on recognition that:

(a)   The current year's results may include wasteful spending and inefficiencies.

(b)   Budgeted activities should be reviewed and assessed to establish whether they are still required or whether they should continue at the same level of activity as in the past.

The aim of zero based budgeting is to remove unnecessary and wasteful spending from the budget. It can be particularly useful in budgeting for administrative expenses and administrative departments, where there may be a tendency to tolerate unnecessary spending.

Key term

> **Zero based budgeting** involves preparing a budget for each cost centre or activity from a zero base. Every item of expenditure has then to be justified in its entirety in order to be included in the next year's budget.

In practice, however, managers do not have to budget from zero, but can **start from their current level of expenditure and work downwards**, asking what would happen if any particular aspect of current expenditure and current operations were removed from the budget. In this way, every aspect of the budget is examined in terms of its cost and the benefits it provides and the selection of better alternatives is encouraged.

6.1 Implementing zero based budgeting

There is a three-step approach to ZBB.

- Define items or activities for which costs should be budgeted, and spending decisions should be planned: these are 'decision packages'.

- Evaluate and rank the packages in order of priority: eliminate packages whose costs exceed their value.

- Allocate resources to the decision packages according to their ranking. Where resources such as money are in short supply, they are allocated to the most valuable activities.

The implementation of ZBB involves a number of steps, but the success of ZBB depends on the application of **a questioning attitude** by all those involved in the budgeting process. Existing practices, activities and expenditures must be challenged and searching questions about their value should be asked.

- Does the activity need to be carried out?
- What would be the consequences if the activity was not carried out?
- Is the current level of provision sufficient?
- Are there alternative (and cheaper) ways of achieving the same objective?
- How much should the activity cost?
- Is the expenditure worth the benefits achieved?

The basic approach of ZBB has three steps.

Step 1   **Define decision packages**. Decision packages are activities or items in the budget about which a decision should be made. Should this activity be included in the budget or not? Decision packages are used to **rank** activities in order of priority or preference. This ranking can be used to allocate scarce resources in the budget.

Decision packages must be thoroughly documented.

There are two types of decision package.

(a)   **Mutually exclusive packages**. These are alternative methods of getting the same job done. The best option among the packages must be selected by comparing costs and benefits and the other packages are then discarded. If there are two mutually exclusive decision packages, the preferred package is selected and the other rejected for budgeting purposes.

(b)   **Incremental packages**. These divide an aspect of operations into different levels of activity. The 'base' package will contain the minimum amount of work that must be done to carry out the activity and the cost of this minimum level. The other incremental packages identify additional (incremental) work that could be done, at what cost and for what benefits.

Suppose that a cost centre manager is preparing a budget for maintenance costs. They might first consider two mutually exclusive packages.

- Package A might be to keep a maintenance team of two men per shift for two shifts each day at a cost of $60,000 per annum.

- Package B might be to obtain a maintenance service from an outside contractor at a cost of $50,000.

A **cost-benefit analysis** will be conducted because the quicker repairs obtainable from an in-house maintenance service might justify its extra cost.

If we now suppose that package A is preferred, the budget analysis must be completed by describing the incremental variations in this chosen alternative.

(a)   The 'base' package would describe the minimum requirement for the maintenance work. This might be to pay for one man per shift for two shifts each day at a cost of $30,000.

(b)   Incremental package 1 might be to pay for two men on the early shift and one man on the late shift, at a cost of $45,000. The extra cost of $15,000 would need to be justified; for example, by savings in lost production time, or by more efficient machinery.

(c)   Incremental package 2 might be the original preference, for two men on each shift at a cost of $60,000. The cost-benefit analysis would compare its advantages, if any, over incremental package 1 and so on.

Step 2   **Evaluate and rank each activity (decision package)** on the basis of its benefit to the organisation. This can be a lengthy process. Minimum work requirements (those that are essential to get a job done) will be given very high priority and so too will work which must be done to meet legal obligations. In the accounting department these would be minimum requirements to operate the payroll, purchase ledger and sales ledger systems, and to maintain and publish a set of accounts. Common problems that may occur at the ranking stage are discussed in the next section.

Step 3   **Allocate resources** in the budget according to the funds available and the evaluation and ranking of the competing packages. For example, a car manufacturer may choose to allocate significantly more funds to production processes than service and administration functions, based on the ranking of each activity in step 2.

Question
Base and incremental packages

What might the base and incremental packages for a personnel department cover?

Answer

The base package might cover the recruitment and dismissal of staff. Incremental packages might cover training, pension administration, trade union liaison, staff welfare, and so on.

6.2 The advantages and limitations of implementing ZBB

The **advantages** of zero based budgeting are as follows.

- It is possible to identify and **remove inefficient or obsolete operations**.
- It forces employees to **avoid wasteful expenditure**.
- It can **increase motivation** of staff by promoting a culture of efficiency.
- It **responds to changes** in the business environment.
- **ZBB documentation provides** an in-depth **appraisal of an organisation's operations**.
- It **challenges the status quo**.
- In summary, ZBB should result in a **more efficient allocation of resources**.

The major **disadvantage** of zero based budgeting is the enormous extra **volume of paperwork** created and the extra time required to prepare the budget. The assumptions about costs and benefits in each package must be continually updated and new packages developed as soon as new activities emerge. The following problems might also occur.

(a)   **Short-term benefits** might be **emphasised** to the detriment of long-term benefits.

(b)   It might give the impression **that all decisions have to be made in the budget**. Management must be able to meet unforeseen opportunities and threats at all times, however, and must not feel restricted from carrying out new ideas simply because they were not approved by a decision package, cost-benefit analysis and the ranking process.

(c)   It may **call for management skills** both in constructing decision packages and in the ranking process **which the organisation does not possess**. Managers may have to be trained in ZBB techniques.

(d) The organisation's **information systems may not be capable of providing suitable information**.

(e) **The ranking process can be difficult**. Managers face three common problems.

    (i) A large number of packages may have to be ranked.

    (ii) It can be difficult to rank packages which appear to be equally vital, for legal or operational reasons.

    (iii) It is difficult to rank activities which have qualitative rather than quantitative benefits – such as spending on staff welfare and working conditions.

In summary, perhaps the **most serious drawback to ZBB is that it requires a lot of management time and paperwork**. One way of obtaining the benefits of ZBB but of overcoming the drawbacks is to apply it selectively on a rolling basis throughout the organisation. This year finance, next year marketing, the year after personnel, and so on. In this way all activities will be thoroughly scrutinised over a period of time.

6.3 Using zero based budgeting

FAST FORWARD

> ZBB is particularly useful for budgeting for discretionary costs and for rationalisation purposes, in areas of operations where efficiency standards are not properly established, such as administration work.

ZBB is not particularly suitable for direct manufacturing costs, which are usually budgeted using standard costing, work study and other management planning and control techniques. It is best applied to **support expenses;** that is, expenditure incurred in departments which exist to support the essential production function. These support areas include marketing, finance, quality control, personnel, data processing, accounting, sales and distribution. In many organisations, these expenses make up a large proportion of the total expenditure. These activities are less easily quantifiable by conventional methods and are more **discretionary** in nature.

ZBB can also be successfully applied to **service industries** and **non profit making organisations**, such as local and central government departments, educational establishments and hospitals, and in any organisation where alternative levels of provision for each activity are possible and where the costs and benefits are separately identifiable.

ZBB can also be used to make **rationalisation decisions**. 'Rationalisation' is a term for cutting back on production and activity levels, and cutting costs. The need for service departments to operate above a minimum service level or the need for having a particular department at all can be questioned, and ZBB can be used to make rationalisation decisions when an organisation is forced to make spending cuts.

7 Activity based budgeting

FAST FORWARD

> At its simplest, **activity based budgeting (ABB)** is merely the use of activity based costing methods as a basis for preparing budgets.

Key term

> **Activity based budgeting** involves defining the activities that underlie the financial figures in each function and using the level of activity to decide how much resource should be allocated and how well it is being managed and to explain variances from budget.

Activity based budgeting differs from traditional budgeting in the way that budgets are prepared for overhead costs. Overhead costs are budgeted on the basis of activities, rather than on a departmental basis.

Implementing ABC (see Chapter 2a) leads to the realisation that the **business as a whole** needs to be managed with reference to **activities and the cost drivers** for those activities.

7.1 Principles of ABB

With ABB, budgeting for direct costs (direct materials, direct labour) is no different from 'traditional' budgeting. The only difference is the approach to budgeting for overhead costs.

ABB involves defining the key activities that account for overhead spending, and considering the costs of the activity. Budgeted costs will depend on the expected level of activity (volume of the cost driver). A decision is made about the planned level of activity and the resources required to sustain this activity level, and the estimated cost is included in the budget.

ABB can also be used for control purposes, comparing actual and planned costs to assess how well the activity is being **managed** and to **explain variances** from budget.

ABB is therefore based on the following **principles**.

(a) It is **activities which drive costs** and the aim is to **plan and control the causes** (drivers) of costs rather than the costs themselves, with the result that in the long term costs will be better managed and better understood.

(b) **Not all activities add value**, so activities must be examined and split up according to their ability to add value.

(c) Most departmental activities are driven by demands and decisions **beyond the immediate control** of the manager responsible for the department's budget.

(d) Traditional financial measures of performance are unable to fulfil the objective of **continuous improvement**. Additional measures which focus on drivers of costs, the quality of activities undertaken, the responsiveness to change, and so on are needed.

7.2 Example: ABB

A stores department has two main activities, receiving deliveries of raw materials from suppliers into stores and issuing raw materials to production departments. Two major cost drivers, the number of deliveries of raw materials and the number of production runs, have been identified. Although the majority of the costs of the department can be attributed to the activities, there is a small balance, termed 'department running costs', which includes general administration costs, part of the department manager's salary, and so on.

Based on activity levels expected in the next control period, the following cost driver volumes have been budgeted.

250 deliveries of raw materials
120 production runs

On the basis of budgeted departmental costs and the cost analysis, the following budget has been drawn up for the next control period.

Cost	Total $'000	Costs attributable to receiving deliveries $'000	Costs attributable to issuing materials $'000	Dept running costs $'000
Salaries – management	25	8	12	5
Salaries – store workers	27	13	12	2
Salaries – administration	15	4	5	6
Consumables	11	3	5	3
Information technology costs	14	5	8	1
Other costs	19	10	6	3
	111	43	48	20
Activity volumes		250	120	
Cost per unit of cost driver		$172	$400	$20,000

Points to note

(a) The apportionment of cost will be subjective to a certain extent. The objective of the exercise is that the resource has to be justified as supporting one or more of the activities. Costs cannot be hidden.

(b) The cost driver rates of $172 and $400 can be used to calculate product costs using ABC.

(c) Identifying activities and their costs helps to focus attention on those activities which add value and those that do not.

(d) The budget has highlighted the cost of the two activities.

7.3 Benefits of ABB

Some writers treat ABB as a complete philosophy in itself and attribute to it all the good features of strategic management accounting, zero based budgeting, total quality management, and other ideas. For example, the following claims have been made.

(a) Different **activity levels** will provide a foundation for the 'base' package and incremental packages of **ZBB**.

(b) It will ensure that the organisation's overall **strategy** and any actual or likely changes in that strategy will be taken into account, because it attempts to manage the business as the **sum of its interrelated parts**.

(c) **Critical success factors** will be identified and performance measures devised to monitor progress towards them. (A critical success factor is an activity in which a business **must** perform well if it is to succeed.)

(d) Because concentration is focused on the **whole of an activity**, not just its separate parts, there is more likelihood of **getting it right first time**. For example, what is the use of being able to **produce** goods in time for their despatch date if the budget provides insufficient resources for the distribution manager who has to **deliver** them?

Question   Activity based budget

The production department of SPI Co has four major activities, namely receiving deliveries, material handling, production runs and quality tests.

Each of these activities has an identifiable cost driver. These are provided below along with estimated volumes for the coming period.

Number of deliveries	300
Number of movements of material	400
Number of production runs	800
Number of quality tests	600

Two other activities that occur in the department are administration and supervision. While these activities are non volume related, they are necessary functions and should not be ignored in the budgeting process.

Budgeted costs for the coming period are displayed below.

	Total	Attributable to
	$'000	$'000
Management salary	50	Supervision: $45; Administration: $5
Basic wages	30	Receiving deliveries: $7; Production runs: $5; Administration: $6 Material handling: $7; Quality tests: $5
Overtime	15	Receiving deliveries: $6; Quality tests: $1; Production runs: $8
Factory overheads	12	Receiving deliveries: $3; Production runs: $2; Administration $1.5; Material handling $2; Quality tests: $1.5; Supervision: $2
Other costs	4	Receiving deliveries: $1; Supervision: $1; Administration: $2
	111	

Required

Produce an activity based budget for the coming period that shows:

(i)   Total cost for each activity
(ii) Total cost for the production department
(iii) Cost per activity unit

Answer

Activity based budget for SPI Co

	Receiving deliveries	Material handling	Production runs	Quality tests	Admin	S'vision	Total
Cost driver	No of deliveries	No of movements of material	No of production runs	No of quality tests	–	–	
Volume	300	400	800	600			
	$'000	$'000	$'000	$'000	$'000	$'000	$'000
Management salary	–	–	–	–	5	45	50
Basic wages	7	7	5	5	6	–	30
Overtime	6	–	8	1	–	–	15
Factory o'heads	3	2	2	1.5	1.5	2	12
Other	1	–	–	–	2	1	4
Total	17	9	15	7.5	14.5	48	111
Cost per activity unit	$56.67	$22.50	$18.75	$12.50			

8 Rolling budgets   12/12

FAST FORWARD

> **Rolling budgets** (also called **continuous budgets**) are budgets which are continuously updated throughout a financial year, by adding a further period (say a month or a quarter) and removing the corresponding period that has just ended.

8.1 Dynamic conditions

Actual conditions may differ from those anticipated when the budget was drawn up for a number of reasons.

(a)   **Organisational changes** may occur.

    (i)   A change in structure from a functional basis, say, to a process-based one

    (ii)   New agreements with the workforce about flexible working or safety procedures

    (iii) The reallocation of responsibilities following, say, the removal of tiers of middle management and the 'empowerment' of workers further down the line

(b)   Action may be needed to **combat an initiative by a competitor**.

(c)   **New technology** may be introduced to improve productivity, reduce labour requirements or enhance quality.

(d)   **Environmental conditions** may change: there may be a general boom or a recession, an event affecting supply or demand, or a change in government or government policy.

(e)   The level of **inflation** may be higher or lower than that anticipated.

(f)   The **level of activities** may be different from the levels planned.

Any of these changes **may make the original budget quite inappropriate**, either in terms of the numbers expected, or the way in which responsibility for achieving them is divided, or both.

There is a risk that in a period of rapid and continual change budgets cease to be useful as a plan and guide for management. To deal with this risk, budgets may be reviewed and amended regularly.

If management need to revise their plans regularly to keep them relevant and realistic, they may decide to introduce a system of **rolling budgets**.

Key term

> A **rolling budget** is a budget which is continuously updated by adding a further accounting period (a month or quarter) to the end of the budget when the corresponding period in the current budget has ended.
>
> As a result, a number of rolling budgets are prepared each year and each rolling budget covers the next 12-month period.

Rolling budgets may be used when the pace of change in the business environment is fast and continual. They represent an attempt to prepare plans which are **more realistic**, particularly with a regard to price levels, by **shortening the period between preparing budgets**.

Instead of preparing a **periodic budget** annually for the full budget period, new **budgets are prepared every 1, 2, 3 or 4 months** (so that there are 3, 4, 6, or even 12 budgets each year). **Each of these budgets would cover the next 12 months** so that the current budget is extended by an extra period as the current period ends: hence the name rolling budgets.

Suppose, for example, that a rolling budget is prepared every three months. The first three months of the budget period would be planned in great detail, and the remaining nine months in lesser detail, because of the greater uncertainty about the longer-term future. If a first continuous budget is prepared for January to March in detail and April to December in less detail, a new budget will be prepared towards the end of March, planning April to June in detail and July to March in less detail. Four rolling budgets would be prepared every 12 months on this 3 and 9 month basis, requiring, inevitably, greater administrative effort.

8.2 Example: Preparing a rolling budget

A company uses a system of rolling budgets. The sales budget is displayed below.

	Jan – Mar $	Apr – Jun $	Jul – Sep $	Oct – Dec $	Total $
Sales	78,480	86,120	91,800	97,462	353,862

Actual sales for January – March were $74,640. The adverse variance is explained by growth being lower than anticipated and the market being more competitive than predicted.

Senior management has proposed that the revised assumption for sales growth should be 2.5% per quarter.

Required

Update the budget as appropriate.

Solution

Step 1 Using the actual sales figure for January – March update the budget for the next four quarters (including a figure for January – March of the following year), incorporating a sales growth rate of 2.5%.

Apr - Jun	= $74,640 × 1.025	= $76,506
Jul – Sept	= $76,506 × 1.025	= $78,419
Oct – Dec	= $78,419 × 1.025	= $80,379
Jan – Mar	= $80,379 × 1.025	= $82,389

Step 2 **Revised budget**

	Apr – Jun $	Jul – Sep $	Oct – Dec $	Jan – Mar $	Total $
Sales	76,506	78,419	80,379	82,389	317,692

8.3 The advantages and disadvantages of rolling budgets

The **advantages** are as follows.

(a) They **reduce the element of uncertainty** in budgeting because they concentrate detailed planning and control on the near-term future, where the degree of uncertainty is much smaller.

(b) They force managers to reassess the budget regularly, and to produce budgets which are **up to date** in the light of current events and expectations.

(c) **Planning and control will be based on a recent plan** which is likely to be far **more realistic** than a fixed annual budget made many months ago.

(d) Realistic budgets are likely to have a **better motivational influence** on managers.

(e) There is **always a budget which extends for several months ahead**. For example, if rolling budgets are prepared quarterly, there will always be a budget extending over the next 9 to 12 months. This is not the case when fixed annual budgets are used.

The **disadvantages** of rolling budgets can be a deterrent to using them.

(a) They involve **more time, effort and money** in budget preparation.

(b) Frequent budgeting might have an **offputting effect on managers** who doubt the value of preparing one budget after another at regular intervals.

(c) Revisions to the budget might involve revisions to standard costs too, which in turn would involve revisions to stock valuations. This could replace a large **administrative effort** from the accounts department every time a rolling budget is prepared.

(d) The benefits of rolling budgets are limited and therefore not worth the extra cost when the rate of change in the business environment is not rapid and continual.

8.4 Continuous budgets or updated annual budgets

If the expected changes are not likely to be continuous there is a strong argument that routine updating of the budget is unnecessary. **Instead, the annual budget could be updated whenever changes become foreseeable**, so that a budget might be updated once or twice, and perhaps more often, during the course of the year. An updated annual budget, prepared in response to a significant change in circumstances, may simply be called a **revised budget**.

When a fixed budget is updated and revised, a 'rolling' 12-month budget would probably not be prepared. For example, if a budget is updated and revised in Month 8 of the year, the revised budget would relate to Months 8–12. It would not be extended to Month 7 of the following year.

9 Beyond Budgeting

Beyond Budgeting is a budgeting model which proposes that traditional budgeting should be abandoned. **Adaptive management processes** should be used rather than fixed annual budgets.

9.1 Criticisms of budgeting

There are many problems with budgets and criticisms of how they are used in organisations.

The Beyond Budgeting Round Table (BBRT), an independent research organisation, proposes that budgeting, as most organisations practise it, should be abandoned. Their website (www.bbrt.org) lists the following ten criticisms of budgeting as put forward by Hope and Fraser (2003).

(a) **Budgets are time consuming and expensive**. Even with the support of computer models it is estimated that the budgeting process uses up to 20–30% of senior executives' and financial managers' time.

(b) **Budgets provide poor value to users**. Although surveys have shown that some managers feel that budgets give them control, a large majority of financial directors wish to reform the budgetary process because they feel that finance staff spend too much time on 'lower value added activities'.

(c) **Budgets fail to focus on shareholder value**. Most budgets are set on an incremental basis as an acceptable target agreed between the manager and the manager's superior. Managers may be rewarded for achieving their short-term budgets and will not look to the longer term or take risks for fear of affecting their own short-term results.

(d) **Budgets are too rigid and prevent fast response**. Although most organisations do update and revise their budgets at regular intervals as the budget period proceeds, the process is often too slow compared with the pace at which the external environment is changing.

(e) **Budgets protect rather than reduce costs**. Once a manager has an authorised budget they can spend that amount of resource without further authorisation. A 'use it or lose it' mentality often develops so that managers will incur cost unnecessarily. This happens especially towards the end of the budget period in the expectation that managers will not be permitted to carry forward any unused resource into the budget for next period.

(f) **Budgets stifle product and strategy innovation**. The focus on achieving the budget discourages managers from taking risks in case this has adverse effects on their short-term performance. Managers do not have the freedom to respond to changing customer needs in a fast changing market because the activity they would need to undertake is not authorised in their budget.

(g) **Budgets focus on sales targets rather than customer satisfaction**. The achievement of short-term sales forecasts becomes the focus of most organisations. However, this does not necessarily result in customer satisfaction. The customer may be sold something **inappropriate to their needs**. Alternatively, if a manager has already met the sales target for a particular period, they might try to **delay sales to the next period** in order to give themselves a 'head start' towards achieving the target for the next period. Furthermore, there is an incentive towards the end of a period, if a manager feels that the sales target is not going to be achieved for the period, to **delay sales until the next period**, and thus again have a head start towards achieving the target for the next period. All these actions, focusing on sales targets rather than customer satisfaction, will have a detrimental effect on the organisation in the longer term.

(h) **Budgets are divorced from strategy**. Most organisations monitor the monthly results against the short-term budget for the month. What is needed instead is a system of monitoring the longer-term progress against the organisation's strategy.

(i) **Budgets reinforce a dependency culture**. The process of planning and budgeting within a framework devolved from senior management perpetuates a culture of dependency. Traditional budgeting systems, operated on a centralised basis, do not encourage a culture of **personal responsibility**.

(j)   **Budgets lead to unethical behaviour**. Unethical behaviour could, for example, mean building **slack** into the budget in order to create an easier target for achievement.

9.2 Beyond Budgeting concepts

Two fundamental concepts underlie the Beyond Budgeting approach.

(a)   **Use adaptive management processes for making decisions rather than tying decision-making to conformity with a rigid annual budget**. Traditional annual plans tie managers to predetermined actions which are not responsive to current situations. Managers should instead plan on a **more adaptive**, rolling basis but with the focus on cash forecasting rather than purely on cost control. Performance is monitored against world-class benchmarks, competitors and previous periods.

(b)   **Move towards devolved networks rather than centralised hierarchies**. The emphasis is on encouraging a culture of personal responsibility by delegating decision-making and performance accountability to line managers.

9.3 Implementation of Beyond Budgeting

9.3.1 Benefits

(a)   **Shift of focus.** The use of external benchmarks can lead to management focus on competitive success. Rather than comparing their performance with previous years, or on the performance of other managers within the business, the resources are used to beat competition.

(b)   **Motivation.** Rewards are team based which fosters cooperation and helps achieve corporate goals. Managers and employees are often motivated by the corporate values, rather than specific targets set in an annual budget.

(c)   **Faster response to threats and opportunities.** Operational managers are given more authority to remove the resource constraints which impede growth. The use of ratios as opposed to line by line budget authorisation encourages innovation, and can lead to an environment where managers can respond quickly to external factors.

9.3.2 Challenges

(a)   **Resistance to change.** Ultimately the success of the beyond budgeting model will depend on the needs and characteristics of the individual business. As with most alternative processes, adopting a new model will require a business to respond well to change. Managers who consistently meet their annual budget targets may resist the adoption of beyond budgeting as it threatens their position and bonuses.

The annual budget is well understood, therefore the introduction of an alternative model can cause difficulties for managers as they must now get used to an unregulated decision making environment.

(b)   **Resource constraints.** In addition, some public sector organisations may struggle to implement a beyond budgeting process due to the constraints on their resources. Public sector managers may have additional legislative constraints over certain aspects such as the movement of funds and the procurement of borrowings.

10 Information used in budget systems

FAST FORWARD

Information used in budgeting comes from a wide variety of sources.

Past data may be used as a starting point for the preparation of budgets but other information from a wide variety of sources will also be used. Each **function** of the organisation (for example, marketing, personnel and research and development) will be required to estimate revenue and expenditure for the budget period.

10.1 Sales budget information

As we have seen, for many organisations, the principal budget factor is sales volume. The sales budget is therefore often the primary budget from which the majority of the other budgets are derived. Before the sales budget can be prepared a **sales forecast** has to be made. Sales forecasting is complex and difficult and involves the use of information from a variety of sources.

- Past sales patterns
- The economic environment
- Results of market research
- Anticipated advertising
- Competition
- Changing consumer taste

- New legislation
- Distribution
- Pricing policies and discounts offered
- Legislation
- Environmental factors

10.2 Production budget information

Sources of information for the production budget will include:

(a) **Labour costs** including idle time, overtime and standard output rates per hour
(b) **Raw material costs** including allowances for losses during production
(c) **Machine hours** including expected idle time and expected output rates per machine hour

This information will come from the production department and a large part of the traditional work of **cost accounting** involves ascribing costs to the physical information produced.

11 Changing budgetary systems

An organisation wishing to **change** its budgetary practices will face a number of difficulties.

The business environment has become increasingly complex, uncertain and dynamic and organisations need to be able to adapt quickly to changing conditions. It has been argued that traditional budgets are too rigid and prevent fast response to changing conditions.

However, an organisation which decides to **change** its type of budget used, or budgetary system, will face a number of **difficulties**.

(a) **Resistance by employees.** Employees will be familiar with the current system and may have built in slack so will not easily accept new targets. New control systems that threaten to alter existing power relationships may be thwarted by those affected.

(b) **Loss of control.** Senior management may take time to adapt to the new system and understand the implications of results.

(c) **Costs of implementation.** Any new system or process requires careful implementation which will have cost implications. For example, the procedures for preparing budgets will have to be rewritten in a new budget manual. Establishing a system of zero based budgeting, for example, will require the design and documentation of a large number of decision packages.

(d) **Training.** In order to prepare and implement budgets under the new system, managers will need to be fully trained. This is time consuming and expensive.

(e) **Lack of accounting information**. The organisation may not have the **systems** in place to obtain and analyse the necessary information for preparing the new style budget. For example, an organisation needs a system of activity based costing if it is to implement activity based budgeting.

12 Budget systems and uncertainty

> **FAST FORWARD**
>
> Uncertainty can be allowed for in budgeting by means of **flexible budgeting, rolling budgets, probabilistic budgeting** and **sensitivity analysis**.

Causes of uncertainty in the budgeting process include:

(a) **Customers**. They may decide to buy less than forecast, or they may buy more.

(b) **Products/services**. In the modern business environment, organisations need to respond to customers' rapidly changing requirements.

(c) **Inflation** and movements in **interest and exchange rates**. Exchange rate fluctuations can affect the cost of imported materials, and the price that foreign customers will have to pay, which is likely to affect demand.

(d) **Materials**. The cost of raw materials may change unexpectedly.

(e) **Competitors**. They may steal some of an organisation's expected customers, or some competitors' customers may change their buying allegiance.

(f) **Employees**. They may not work as hard as was hoped, or they may work harder.

(g) **Machines**. They may break down unexpectedly.

(h) **Unrest or disaster**. There may be **political unrest** (terrorist activity), **social unrest** (public transport strikes) or minor or major **natural disasters** (storms, floods).

Rolling budgets are a way of trying to **reduce the element of uncertainty** in the plan. There are **other planning methods** which try to **analyse the uncertainty**, such as **probabilistic budgeting** (where probabilities are assigned to different conditions – see Chapter 7) and **sensitivity analysis**. These methods are suitable when the **degree of uncertainty is quantifiable** from the start of the budget period and actual results are not expected to go outside the range of these expectations.

Chapter Roundup

- A budget is a **quantified plan of action** for a forthcoming accounting period.

- A budget can be set from the **top down** (**imposed** budget) or from the **bottom up** (**participatory** budget).

- Here are the objectives of a budgetary planning and control system.

    - Ensure the achievement of the organisation's objectives
    - Compel planning
    - Communicate ideas and plans
    - Co-ordinate activities
    - Provide a framework for responsibility accounting
    - Establish a system of control
    - Motivate employees to improve their performance

- The **planning and control cycle** has seven steps

    - *Step 1.* Identify **objectives**
    - *Step 2.* Identify potential **strategies**
    - *Step 3.* Evaluate strategies
    - *Step 4.* Choose alternative courses of action
    - *Step 5.* Implement the long-term plan
    - *Step 6.* Measure actual results and compare with the plan
    - *Step 7.* Respond to divergences from the plan

- **Planning and control** occurs at all levels of the **performance hierarchy** to different degrees. The performance hierarchy refers to the system by which performance is measured and controlled at different levels of management within the organisation.

- **Budgetary control** occurs at the middle management or **'management control'** level of the performance hierarchy.

- With the 'traditional' approach to budgeting, known as **incremental budgeting**, the budget for the next financial year is based on the actual results for the current financial year. At its simplest level, a budget based on an incremental costing approach is the actual (or budgeted) performance for the current year, adjusted for expected growth and inflation. Incremental budgeting encourages slack and wasteful spending to creep into budgets.

- A **fixed budget** is a financial plan that does not change throughout the budget period, regardless of any changes from the plan in the actual volume of activity. A **flexible budget** recognises cost behaviour and changes as the actual volume of activity changes.

- A fixed budget is normally used for **planning purposes** and is prepared in advance of the beginning of the financial period. A flexible budget is used for **control purposes** and is normally prepared retrospectively, when the actual level of activity in a period is known.

- The principle behind **zero based budgeting (ZBB)** is that the budget for each cost centre should be made from 'scratch' or zero. Every item of expenditure must be justified in its entirety in order to be included in the next year's budget.

- There is a three-step approach to ZBB.

    - Define items or activities for which costs should be budgeted, and spending decisions should be planned: these are 'decision packages'.

    - Evaluate and rank the packages in order of priority: eliminate packages whose costs exceed their value.

    - Allocate resources to the decision packages according to their ranking. Where resources such as money are in short supply, they are allocated to the most valuable activities.

- ZBB is particularly useful for budgeting for discretionary costs and for rationalisation purposes in areas of operations where efficiency standards are not properly established, such as administration work.

- At its simplest, **activity based budgeting (ABB)** is merely the use of activity based costing methods as a basis for preparing budgets.

- **Rolling budgets** (also called **continuous budgets**) are budgets which are continuously updated throughout a financial year, by adding a further period (say a month or a quarter) and removing the corresponding period that has just ended.

- **Beyond Budgeting** is a budgeting model which proposes that traditional budgeting should be abandoned. **Adaptive management processes** should be used rather than fixed annual budgets.

- **Information** used in budgeting comes from a wide variety of sources.

- An organisation wishing to **change** its budgetary practices will face a number of difficulties.

- Uncertainty can be allowed for in budgeting by means of **flexible budgeting, rolling budgets, probabilistic budgeting** and **sensitivity analysis**.

1   Which of the following could not be a principal budget factor?

    (a)   Cash   (b)   Machine capacity
    (c)   Sales demand   (d)   Selling price
    (e)   Labour   (f)   Premises

2   Fill in the gaps.

A flexible budget is a budget which, by recognising ...., is designed to .... as the level of activity changes.

3   Match the descriptions to the budgeting style.

Description

(a)   Budget allowances are set without the involvement of the budget holder.
(b)   All budget holders are involved in setting their own budgets.

Budgeting style

Bottom-up budgeting
Top-down budgeting

4   Incremental budgeting is widely used and is a particularly efficient form of budgeting.

☐ True   ☐ False

5   What are the three steps of ZBB?

Step 1 ....

Step 2 ....

Step 3 ....

6   To which of the following can ZBB be usefully applied?

	Use ZBB	Do not use ZBB
Personnel		
Social services department of local government		
Direct material costs		
Sales department		
Schools		
An inefficient production department		
An efficient production department		

7   Choose the appropriate word from those highlighted.

A rolling budget is also known as a **periodic/continuous** budget.

8   If a system of a ABB is in use, how might the cost of scheduling production be flexed?

A   Number of items produced
B   Number of set-ups
C   Number of direct labour hours
D   Number of parts used in production

9   A system of zero based budgeting forces employees to remove wasteful expenditure.

☐ True   ☐ False

10   Use of zero based budgeting implies flexing budgets on the basis of differences between budgeted and actual cost-driving activities.

☐ True   ☐ False

1   (d)

2   cost behaviour patterns
        flex or change

3   (a)   Top-down budgeting
        (b)   Bottom-up budgeting

4   False. Incremental budgeting is inefficient.

5   Step 1. Define decision packages
        Step 2. Evaluate and rank activities (decision package)
        Step 3. Allocate resources

6

	Use ZBB	Do not use ZBB
Personnel	✓	
Social services department of local government	✓	
Direct material costs		✓
Sales department	✓	
Schools	✓	
An inefficient production department	✓	
An efficient production department		✓

7   It is also known as a continuous budget.

8   B   Number of set-ups

9   True

10   False. This is a common feature of **activity based** budgeting.

Now try the questions below from the Practice Question Bank

Number	Level	Marks	Approximate time
Section A Q51	Examination	2	4 mins
Section A Q52	Examination	2	4 mins
Section A Q53	Examination	2	4 mins
Section A Q54	Examination	2	4 mins
Section A Q55	Examination	2	4 mins
Section C Q5	Examination	20	39 mins

Quantitative analysis in budgeting

9

Topic list	Syllabus reference
1 Analysing fixed and variable costs: high-low method	C2 (a)
2 Learning curves	C2 (b), (c)
3 Expected values in budgeting	C2 (d)
4 Using spreadsheets in budgeting	C2 (e)

Introduction

The success of a budget is largely dependent on the degree of accuracy in estimating the revenues and costs for the budget period.

This chapter looks at the **quantitative techniques** involved in budgeting, including the **high-low method** and the concept of the **learning curve**.

We also consider how **expected values** can be used to determine the best combination of profit and risk, and the use of **spreadsheets** throughout the budgeting process.

Study guide

		Intellectual level
C2	**Quantitative analysis in budgeting**	
(a)	Analyse fixed and variable cost elements from total cost data using the high/low method.	2
(b)	Estimate the learning rate and learning effect.	2
(c)	Apply the learning curve to a budgetary problem, including calculations on steady states.	2
(d)	Discuss the reservations with the learning curve.	2
(e)	Apply expected values and explain the problems and benefits.	2
(f)	Explain the benefits and dangers inherent in using spreadsheets in budgeting.	2

Exam guide

The quantitative techniques covered in this chapter are likely to form the calculation part of a budgeting question in Section C. Techniques may also be examined regularly in short section A objective test questions, as well as featuring in Section B mini case study questions. There is an article on the ACCA website written by a member of the examining team on the topic of the learning rate and learning effect (ACCA, 2016). It is recommend that you read this article.

> ⚠️ **PER alert**
>
> One of the competencies you require to fulfil performance objective 13 of the PER is the ability to prepare and use budgets, selecting suitable budgeting models. You can apply the knowledge you obtain from this chapter of the text to help to demonstrate this competence.

1 Analysing fixed and variable costs: high-low method

> **FAST FORWARD**
>
> The **high-low method** is a quantitative technique for analysing total costs into their fixed cost and variable cost elements.

1.1 The high-low method   12/07, 12/08, 6/15

You should have encountered the high-low method in your earlier studies. It is used to separate a total cost into its fixed cost and variable cost elements. This technique is still examinable in F5. Read through the knowledge brought forward and answer the question below to jog your memory.

Exam focus point

> The examining team noted in the June 2015 report, that students had failed to recognise when the high-low method was required. This resulted in the loss of some easy marks as many students find this area of the syllabus very manageable.

Follow the steps below.

Step 1   Review records of costs in previous periods.

- Select the period with the **highest** activity level.
- Select the period with the **lowest** activity level.

Step 2   If inflation makes it difficult to compare costs, adjust by indexing up or down.

Step 3   Determine the following.

- Total costs at high activity level
- Total costs at low activity level
- Total units at high activity level
- Total units at low activity level

Step 4   The difference between total costs at the high and the low activity levels must consist entirely of variable costs, since fixed costs are the same at both activity levels. So calculate the following.

$$\frac{\text{Total cost at high activity level} - \text{total cost at low activity level}}{\text{Total units at high activity level} - \text{total units at low activity level}}$$

= Variable cost per unit (v)

Step 5   The fixed costs can be determined as follows. (Total cost at high activity level) – (total units at high activity level × variable cost per unit)

Question
High-low method

A department in a large organisation wishes to develop a method of predicting its total costs in a period. The following data have been recorded.

Month	Activity level (X) Units	Cost $
January	1,600	28,200
February	2,300	29,600
March	1,900	28,800
April	1,800	28,600
May	1,500	28,000
June	1,700	28,400

The total cost model for a period could be represented by what equation?

Answer

The highest activity level is in February and the lowest in May.

Total cost at highest activity level	= $29,600
Total cost at lowest activity level	= $28,000
Total units at highest activity level	= 2,300
Total units at lowest activity level	= 1,500

$$\text{Variable cost per unit} = \frac{29,600 - 28,000}{2,300 - 1,500} = \frac{1,600}{800} = \$2$$

Fixed costs = 29,600 – (2,300 × 2) = $25,000
Total costs = 25,000 + 2x
where x is the volume of activity in units.

1.2 The usefulness of the high-low method

The high-low method is a simple and easy to use method of estimating fixed and variable costs. However, there are a number of problems with it.

(a) The method **ignores** all cost information apart from costs at the highest and lowest volumes of activity and these may not be **representative** of costs at all levels of activity.

(b) **Inaccurate** cost estimates may be produced as a result of the assumption of a constant relationship between costs and volume of activity.

(c) Estimates are based on **historical** information and conditions may have changed.

2 Learning curves

FAST FORWARD

Learning curve theory may be useful for forecasting production time and labour costs in circumstances where a workforce makes a new product and improves its efficiency with experience and learning. However, the method has many limitations.

Whenever an individual starts a job which is **fairly repetitive** in nature and, provided that their speed of working is not dictated to them by the speed of machinery (as it would be on a production line), they are likely to become **more confident and knowledgeable** about the work as they gain experience, to become **more efficient**, and to do the work **more quickly**.

Eventually, however, when they have acquired enough experience, there will be nothing more for them to learn, and so **the learning process will stop**.

The same principle may **apply to a workforce as a whole**, when it starts to make a new product.

Key term

Learning curve theory applies to situations where the workforce as a whole improves in efficiency with experience. The **learning effect** or **learning curve effect** describes the speeding up of a job with repeated performance.

2.1 Where does learning curve theory apply?

Labour time should be expected to get shorter, with experience, in the production of items which exhibit any or all of the following features.

- Made largely **by labour effort** (rather than by a **highly mechanised** process) or where labour skill is an important factor in the production process

- Brand **new** or relatively **short lived** (the learning process does not continue indefinitely)

- **Complex** and made in **small quantities** for **special orders**

2.2 The learning rate and learning effect

Where a learning curve applies, there is a learning rate and a learning effect.

The **learning rate** is expressed as a percentage value, such as an 80% learning curve or a 70% learning curve.

The **learning effect** is that, as the workforce learns from experience how to make the new product, there is a big reduction in the time taken to make additional units.

Specifically, **every time that the cumulative output of the product doubles**, the average time to make all the units produced to date is a proportion of what it was before. This proportion is the learning rate.

So if a 90% learning curve applies, and the labour time to make the first unit is 100 hours:

(a)   The average time to make the first two units will be 90% × 100 hours = 90 hours, and the total time for the first two units will be 180 hours. Since the first unit takes 100 hours, the second unit will take 80 hours.

(b)   The average time to make the first four units will be 90% × 90 hours = 81 hours and the total time for the first four units will be 324 hours. Since the first two units take 180 hours, the third and fourth units together will take 144 hours.

This learning process continues until the learning effect comes to an end and a 'steady state' of production is achieved.

The three approaches to learning curve problems

There are two methods that can be used to deal with a learning curve scenario. Be prepared to use either or both in the exam.

*   **Method 1**. The tabular approach
*   **Method 2**. The algebraic approach

The tabular approach is quicker and easier when it can be used, but it can be used only for a limited type of problem. The algebraic approach is more likely to be examined and requires the application of a formula to calculate the cumulative average time per unit produced.

2.3 Method 1 – The tabular approach: cumulative average time and the learning rate

The **tabular approach** can only be used to calculate average times when cumulative output doubles. A table can be used to calculate:

(a)   The cumulative average time per unit
(b)   The total time to produce all the units produced so far

The rule to remember is that every time that cumulative output doubles the average production time is x% of what is was before, where x is the learning rate.

The approach is best explained with a numerical example.

2.4 Example: An 80% learning curve

For example, where an 80% learning effect occurs, the cumulative average time required per unit of output is reduced to 80% of the previous cumulative average time when output is doubled.

The first unit of output of a new product requires 100 hours. An 80% learning curve applies. The production times would be as follows.

Cumulative number of units	Cumulative avge time per unit (hours)	Cumulative total time (hours)	Incremental number of units	Incremental total time (hours)
1	100.0	100.0	–	–
2*	80.0	160.0	1	60.0
4*	64.0	256.0	2	96.0
8*	51.2	409.6	4	153.6

* Output is being **doubled** each time.

The cost of the additional time can be calculated by applying the labour hour rate to the number of labour hours (and variable overhead rate, where variable overheads vary with the number of labour hours). The learning effect does not affect material costs.

2.5 Example: The learning curve

Captain Kitts has designed a new type of sailing boat, for which the cost of the first boat to be produced has been estimated as follows.

	$
Materials	5,000
Labour (800 hrs × $5 per hr)	4,000
Overhead (150% of labour cost)	6,000
	15,000
Profit mark-up (20%)	3,000
Sales price	18,000

It is planned to sell all the yachts at full cost plus 20%. An 80% learning curve is expected to apply to the production work. The management accountant has been asked to provide cost information so that decisions can be made on what price to charge.

(a) What is the separate cost of a second yacht?

(b) What would be the cost per unit for a third and a fourth yacht, if they are ordered separately later on?

(c) If they were all ordered now, could Captain Kitts quote a single unit price for four yachts and eight yachts?

Solution

Cumulative number of units	Cumulative avge time per unit (hours)	Cumulative total time (hours)	Incremental number of units	Incremental total time (hours)	Incremental average time (hours)
1	800.0	800.0	–	–	–
2*	640.0	1,280.0 **	1	480.0	480.0
4*	512.0	2,048.0	2	768.0	384.0
8*	409.6	3,276.8	4	1,228.8	307.2

* Output is being **doubled** each time.

** 640 × 2 = 1,280, 512 × 4 = 2,048

(a) **Separate cost of a second yacht**

	$
Materials	5,000
Labour (480 hrs × $5)	2,400
Overhead (150% of labour cost)	3,600
Total cost	11,000

(b) **Cost of the third and fourth yachts**

	$
Materials cost for two yachts	10,000
Labour (768 hours × $5)	3,840
Overhead (150% of labour cost)	5,760
Total cost	19,600
Cost per yacht (÷2)	9,800

(c)   **A price for the first four yachts together and for the first eight yachts together**

		First four yachts		First eight yachts
		$		$
Materials		20,000		40,000
Labour	(2,048 hrs)	10,240	(3,276.8 hrs)	16,384
Overhead (150% of labour cost)		15,360		24,576
Total cost		45,600		80,960
Profit (20%)		9,120		16,192
Total sales price		54,720		97,152
Price per yacht	(÷4)	13,680	(÷8)	12,144

This assumes that Captain Kitts is happy to pass on the efficiency savings to the customer in the form of a lower price.

Question

Learning curve theory

Bortamord anticipates that a 90% learning curve will apply to the production of a new item. The first item will cost $2,000 in materials, and will take 500 labour hours. The cost per hour for labour and variable overhead is $5.

You are required to calculate the total cost for the first unit and for the first eight units.

Answer

Cumulative number of units	Cumulative avge time per unit (hours)	Cumulative total time (hours)	Incremental number of units	Incremental total time (hours)
1	500.0	500.0	–	–
2*	450.0	900.0	1	400.0
4*	405.0	1,620.0	2	720.0
8*	364.5	2,916.0	4	1,296.0

		Cost of first unit		Cost of first eight units
		$		$
Materials		2,000		16,000
Labour and variable o/hd (500 hrs)		2,500	(2,916 hours)	14,580
		4,500		30,580
Average cost/unit		4,500		3,822.50

2.6 Method 2 – The algebraic approach

FAST FORWARD

The formula for the learning curve is **Y = ax^b**, where b, the learning coefficient or learning index, is defined as (log of the learning rate/log of 2). The learning curve formula can be used to solve all learning curve scenarios.

Exam formula

The formula for the learning curve is **Y = ax^b**

where
- **Y** is the cumulative average time per unit to produce x units
- **x** is the cumulative number of units
- **a** is the time taken for the first unit of output
- **b** is the index of learning (logLR/log2)
- **LR** is the learning rate as a decimal

This formula is provided in the exam. It refers to time rather than labour cost. The formula can also be used to calculate the labour cost per unit. The labour **times** are calculated using the curve formula and then converted to cost.

2.6.1 Calculating the time for a specific unit

The formula approach is used to calculate the incremental time for any unit where a learning curve applies. Suppose that we want to know the time that it will take to make the third and the fifth units, where a learning curve applies.

(a) To calculate the time to make the third unit:

   (i)   Calculate the cumulative average time for the first three units and the total time for the first three units

   (ii) Calculate the cumulative average time for the first two units and the total time for the first two units

   (iii) The time for the third unit is the difference in these two totals

(b) To calculate the time to make the fifth unit:

   (i)   Calculate the cumulative average time for the first five units and the total time for the first five units

   (ii) Calculate the cumulative average time for the first four units and the total time for the first four units

   (iii) The time for the fifth unit is the difference in these two totals

This approach can be used to calculate the time required to make any unit where a learning curve applies.

2.6.2 Logarithms and the value of b

It is essential to understand how to apply the learning curve formula. You need a calculator that includes a function for calculating logarithms. Logarithms are the value of any number to the power of 10. For example, the logarithm of 3 is 0.4771213 because $10^{0.4771213} = 3$. Using a calculator, it is a simple process to obtain the log value of any number.

In the formula $Y = ax^b$, three of the items are straightforward.

- x = the cumulative number of units produced
- Y = the cumulative average time for the first x units
- a = the time to make the first unit

The only problem is calculating b.

The value of **b = log of the learning rate/log of 2**. The learning rate is expressed as a proportion, so that for an 80% learning curve, the learning rate is 0.8, and for a 90% learning curve it is 0.9, and so on.

For an 80% learning curve, b = log 0.8/log 2.

Using the button on your calculator marked 'log'

$$b = \frac{-0.0969}{0.3010} = -0.322$$

So $Y = ax^{-0.322}$

Another way of stating this is: $Y = a\,[1/x^{0.322}]$

The examining team has stated that **you should not round 'b' to less than three decimal places**. Ideally, you should keep the long number in your calculator and use that!

2.6.3 Example: Using the formula

Suppose that an 80% learning curve applies to production of a new product item ABC. To date (the end of June) 30 units of ABC have been produced. Budgeted production in July is five units. The time to make the very first unit of ABC in January was 120 hours. The labour cost is $10 per hour.

Required

(a) Calculate the time required to make the 31st unit.
(b) Calculate the budgeted total labour cost for July.

Solution

To solve this problem, we need to calculate three things.

(a) The cumulative total labour cost so far to produce 30 units of ABC

(b) The cumulative total labour cost to produce 31 units of ABC

(c) The cumulative total labour cost to produce 35 units of ABC; that is, adding on the extra 5 units for production in July

(d) The time taken to produce the 31st unit is the difference between (b) and (a). The cost of production of 5 units of ABC in July, as the difference between (c) and (a).

Time to produce the first 30 units

$Y = ax^b$

$b = \log 0.8/\log 2 = -0.09691/0.30103 = -0.3219281$

$Y = 120 \times (1/30^{0.3219281}) = 120 \times 0.3345594 = 40.147$ hours

Total time for first 30 units = 30×40.147 hours = 1,204.41 hours

Time to produce the first 31 units

$Y = 120 \times (1/31^{0.3219281}) = 120 \times 0.3310463 = 39.726$ hours

Total time for first 31 units = 31×39.726 hours = 1,231.51 hours

Time to produce the 31st unit = (1,231.51 – 1,204.41) = 27.1 hours

Time to produce the first 35 units

$Y = 120 \times (1/35^{0.3219281}) = 120 \times 0.3183619 = 38.203$ hours

Total time for first 35 units = 35×38.203 hours = 1,337.11 hours

Budgeted labour cost in July = (1,337.11 – 1,204.41) hours × $10 per hour = $1,327

Exam focus point

> This is a very examinable area of the syllabus. It was noted in the December 2014 exam report, that candidates lost easy marks when they forgot to multiply the cumulative average time by the number of units to give them the total time. This is important when calculating the incremental time for calculating an additional unit.

2.6.4 Derivation of the learning rate

The approach you should use to derive the learning rate depends on the information given in the question. If you are provided with **details about cumulative production levels of 1, 2, 4, 8 or 16 (etc) units** you can use the **first approach** shown below. If details are given about other cumulative production quantities, however, you need to use the second approach, which involves the use of logarithms.

Question

BL is planning to manufacture a new product, product A. Development tests suggest that 60% of the variable manufacturing cost of product A will be affected by a learning and experience curve. This learning effect will apply to each unit produced and continue at a constant rate of learning until cumulative production reaches 4,000 units, when learning will stop. The unit variable manufacturing cost of the first unit is estimated to be $1,200 (of which 60% will be subject to the effect of learning), while the average unit variable manufacturing cost of four units will be $405.

Required

Calculate the rate of learning that is expected to apply.

Answer

Let the rate of learning be r.

Cumulative production	Cumulative average cost
	$
1	720 (= 60% × $1,200)
2	720 × r
4	720 × r²

$$\therefore \quad \$720r^2 = \$405$$

$$r^2 = \$405/\$720 = 0.5625$$

$$r = 0.75$$

∴ The rate of learning is 75%.

2.6.5 Derivation of the learning rate using logarithms

As outlined above, the **logarithm of a number, x, is the value of x expressed in terms of '10 to the power of'**.

$10 = 10^1$	The logarithm of 10 is 1.0
$100 = 10^2$	The logarithm of 100 is 2.0
$1,000 = 10^3$	The logarithm of 1,000 is 3.0

Your **calculator** will provide you with the logarithm of any number, probably using the **button marked log 10^x**. For example, to find log of 566 using a calculator you will probably press the log button then type in 566 and the close brackets and '=', to get 2.7528, which means that $10^{2.7528} = 566$.

Logarithms are useful to us for two main reasons.

(a)   The logarithm of the product of two numbers is the sum of their logarithms: **log (c × d) = log c + log d**.

(b)   The logarithm of one number (say, f) to the power of another number (say, g) is the second number multiplied by the logarithm of the first: **log (f^g) = g log f**.

Logarithms can therefore be used to derive non-linear functions of the form **y = ax^n**.

If $y = ax^n$, the logarithm of y and the logarithm of ax^n must be the same, so **log y = log a + n log x**. **This gives us a linear function similar to y = a + nx**, the only difference being that in place of y we have to use the logarithm of y and in place of x we must use the logarithm of x.

Using simultaneous equations, we can get a value for n and a value for log a, which we can convert back into a 'normal' figure using antilogarithms (the button probably marked 10^x on your calculator).

For example, suppose the relationship between x and y can be described by the function $y = ax^n$, and suppose we know that if x = 1,000, y = 80,000 and if x = 750, y = 63,750.

Substitute these values into log y = log a + n log x.

log 80,000 = log a + n log 1,000

4.9031 = log a + 3n

∴ 4.9031 − 3n = log a   (1)

log 63,750 = log a + n log 750

4.8045 = log a + 2.8751n   (2)

Sub (1) into (2).

4.8045 = 4.9031 − 3n + 2.8751n

∴ 0.1249n = 0.0986

∴ n = 0.7894

Sub value of n into (1)

4.9031 − (3 × 0.7894) = log a

2.5349 = log a

∴ 342.69 = a

∴ Our function is **y = 342.69$x^{0.7894}$**

This technique is useful when the details given for the cumulative production levels do not take the form 1, 2, 4, 8 or 16 (etc) units.

Question   Calculation of the percentage learning effect using logs

XX is aware that there is a learning effect for the production of one of its new products, but is unsure about the degree of learning. The following data relate to this product.

Time taken to produce the first unit   28 direct labour hours

Production to date   15 units

Cumulative time taken to date   104 direct labour hours

What is the percentage learning effect?

Answer

Average time taken per unit to date = (104 ÷ 15) = 6.933 hours

Since $Y_x =$ aX^b

     6.933 = $28(15)^b$

     $15^b =$ 6.933 ÷ 28 = 0.2476

Taking logs: since 15^b = 0.2476

     b log15 =   log 0.2476

Since log15 = 1.1761 (using log 10x on your calculator)

And log 0.2476 = −0.6062

$$b = \frac{\log 0.2476}{\log 15} = \frac{-0.6062}{1.1761} = -0.515$$

$$b = \frac{\log \text{ of learning rate}}{\log 2}$$

$$-0.515 = \frac{\log \text{ of learning rate}}{0.3010}$$

Log of learning rate = −0.515 × 0.3010 = −0.155

Using the button on your calculator probably marked 10x, −0.155 converts back to a 'normal' figure of 0.70. Thus the learning rate is 70%.

2.7 Learning curves and steady state production

As long as a learning curve effect applies, the time taken to produce each additional unit is less than the time for the previous unit. This means that it is not possible to determine a standard time or standard labour cost for producing the item.

A time will be reached, however, when the learning effect no longer applies and 'steady state' production is reached for the product. When a steady state is reached, a standard time and standard labour cost for the product can be established.

The learning curve formula can be used to calculate the expected labour time and labour cost when a steady state is reached, using the same method as described above. The following example illustrates the approach.

Exam focus point

> The examining team noted in the December 2014 exam report, that even though candidates could calculate the learning rate, they didn't understand what that meant. Make sure that you understand that the lower the learning curve percentage, the quicker the staff are learning.

2.8 Example: Learning curves and standard costs

A company needs to calculate a new standard cost for one of its products. When the product was first manufactured, the standard variable cost of the first unit was as follows.

		Cost per unit
		$
Direct material	10 kg @ $4 per kg	40
Direct labour	10 hours @ $9 per hour	90
Variable overhead	10 hours @ $1 per hour	10
Total		140

During the following year, a 90% learning curve was observed in making the product. The cumulative production at the end of the third quarter was 50 units. After producing 50 units, the learning effect ended, and all subsequent units took the same time to make.

Required

What is the standard cost per unit for the fourth quarter assuming the learning curve had reached a **steady state** ie peak efficiency was reached after the 50th unit was produced?

Solution

$Y = ax^b$ where $b = \log 0.9 / \log 2$.

$b = -0.0457575/0.30103 = -0.1520031$

So $Y = ax^{-0.1520031}$

For **49 cumulative units** $Y = 10 \times (49^{-0.1520031}) = 10 \times 0.55346$ hours = 5.5346 hours.

Total time for first 49 units = 49 × 5.5346 hours = 271.2 hours.

For **50 cumulative units** $Y = 10 \times (50^{-0.1520031}) = 10 \times 0.55176$ hours = 5.5176 hours.

Total time for first 50 units = 50 × 5.5176 hours = 275.88 hours.

Time for 50th unit = (275.88 − 271.2) = 4.68 hours

This is the standard time for the product when the steady state has been reached.

Standard cost		Cost per unit
		$
Direct material	10 kg @ $4 per kg	40.00
Direct labour	4.68 hours @ $9 per hour	42.12
Variable overhead	4.68 hours @ $1 per hour	4.68
Total		86.80

In practice, the standard time may be rounded to a more convenient number, such as 4.5 hours or 5.0 hours.

2.9 The practical application of learning curve theory

What costs are affected by the learning curve?

(a)   Direct labour time and costs

(b)   Variable overhead costs, if they vary with direct labour hours worked

(c)   **Materials costs** are usually **unaffected** by learning among the workforce, although it is conceivable that materials handling might improve, and so wastage costs are reduced

(d)   **Fixed overhead expenditure** should be **unaffected** by the learning curve (although in an organisation that uses absorption costing, if fewer hours are worked in producing a unit of output, and the factory operates at full capacity, the **fixed overheads recovered or absorbed per unit** in the cost of the output **will decline** as more and more units are made)

2.10 The relevance of learning curve effects in management accounting

Learning curve theory can be used to:

(a)   Calculate the marginal (incremental) cost of making extra units of a product

(b)   **Quote selling prices for a contract**, where prices are calculated at cost plus a percentage mark-up for profit. An awareness of the learning curve can make all the difference between winning contracts and losing them, or between making profits and selling at a loss-making price

(c)   **Prepare realistic production budgets** and more **efficient production schedules**

(d)   **Prepare realistic standard costs** for cost control purposes

Considerations to bear in mind include:

(a)   **Sales projections, advertising expenditure and delivery date commitments**. Identifying a learning curve effect should allow an organisation to plan its advertising and delivery schedules to coincide with expected production schedules. Production capacity obviously affects sales capacity and sales projections.

(b) **Budgeting with standard costs**. Companies that use standard costing for much of their production output cannot apply standard times to output where a learning effect is taking place. This problem can be overcome in practice by:

    (i)   Establishing **standard times** for output, once the learning effect has worn off or become insignificant, and

    (ii)   Introducing a **'launch cost'** budget for the product for the duration of the learning period.

(c) **Budgetary control**. When learning is still taking place, it would be unreasonable to compare actual times with the standard times that ought eventually to be achieved when the learning effect wears off. **Allowances should be made** accordingly when interpreting labour efficiency variances.

(d) **Cash budgets**. Since the learning effect reduces unit variable costs as more units are produced, it should be allowed for in **cash flow projections**.

(e) **Work scheduling and overtime decisions**. To take full advantage of the learning effect, **idle production time** should be avoided and work scheduling/overtime decisions should pay regard to the expected learning effect.

(f) **Pay**. Where the workforce is paid a **productivity bonus**, the time needed to learn a new production process should be allowed for in calculating the bonus for a period.

(g) **Recruiting new labour**. When a company plans to take on new labour to help with increasing production, the learning curve assumption will have to be reviewed.

(h) **Market share**. The significance of the learning curve is that, by increasing its share of the market, a company can benefit from shop floor, managerial and technological 'learning' to achieve **economies of scale**.

2.11 Limitations of learning curve theory

Learning curve theory has some limitations.

(a) The learning curve phenomenon is **not always present**.

(b) It assumes **stable conditions** at work which will **enable learning to take place**. This is not always practicable; for example, because of **labour turnover**.

(c) It must also assume a certain degree of **motivation** among employees.

(d) Breaks between repeating production of an item must not be too long, or workers will **'forget'** and the learning process will have to begin all over again.

(e) It may be difficult to **obtain accurate data** to decide what the learning curve is.

(f) **Production techniques may change**, or product design alterations may be made, so that it takes a long time for a **'standard'** production method to emerge, to which a learning effect will apply.

(g) For purposes of planning and control, production management and workers may resist attempts to plan for reductions in the average production time, because this will put them under pressure to achieve the expected reductions. The workforce may demand some form of bonus as a reward for achieving reductions in time.

3 Expected values in budgeting

FAST FORWARD

> **Expected values** may be used in budgeting to determine the best combination of expected profit and risk.

Key term

> **Probabilistic budgeting** assigns probabilities to different conditions (most likely, worst possible, best possible) to derive an EV of budgeted profit.

A company might, for example, make the following estimates of profitability for a given budget strategy under consideration.

	Profit/(loss) $'000	Probability
Worst possible outcome	(220)	0.3
Most likely outcome	300	0.6
Best possible outcome	770	0.1

The EV of profit would be calculated as follows.

	Probability	Profit $'000	Expected value $'000
Worst possible	0.3	(220)	(66)
Most likely	0.6	300	180
Best possible	0.1	770	77
Expected value of profits			191

3.1 Example: A probabilistic budget

PIB has recently developed a new product, and is planning a marketing strategy for it. A choice must be made between selling the product at a unit price of either $15 or $17.

Estimated sales volumes are as follows.

At price of $15 per unit		At price of $17 per unit	
Sales volume	Probability	Sales volume	Probability
Units		Units	
20,000	0.1	8,000	0.1
30,000	0.6	16,000	0.3
40,000	0.3	20,000	0.3
		24,000	0.3

(a) Sales promotion costs would be $5,000 at a price of $15 and $12,000 at a price of $17.

(b) Material costs are $8 per unit.

(c) Labour and variable production overhead costs will be $5 per unit up to 30,000 units and $5.50 per unit for additional units.

(d) Fixed production costs will be $38,000.

The management of PIB wish to allow for the risk of each pricing decision before choosing $15 or $17 as the selling price.

Required

Determine which sales price would be preferred if the management selected the alternative which did the following.

(a) Minimised the worst possible outcome of profit
(b) Maximised the best possible outcome of profit

Solution

The unit contribution will be as follows.

	Price per unit	
	$15	$17
Up to 30,000 units	$2	$4
Above 30,000 units	$1.50	N/A

Sales price $15

Units of sale '000	Unit contb'n $	Total contb'n $'000	Fixed costs $'000	Profit $'000	Probability	EV of profit $'000
20	2	40	43	(3)	0.1	(0.3)
30	2	60	43	17	0.6	10.2
40	30 @ $2 10 @ $1.50	75	43	32	0.3	9.6
						19.5

Sales price $17

Units of sale '000	Unit contb'n $	Total contb'n $'000	Fixed costs $'000	Profit $'000	Probability	EV of profit $'000
8	4	32	50	(18)	0.1	(1.8)
16	4	64	50	14	0.3	4.2
20	4	80	50	30	0.3	9.0
24	4	96	50	46	0.3	13.8
						25.2

(a) The price which minimises the worst possible outcome is $15 (with a worst possible loss of $3,000).

(b) The price which maximises the best possible outcome is $17 (with a best possible profit of $46,000).

3.2 Problems and benefits of EVs in budgeting

There are problems with preparing probabilistic budgets.

(a) Preparing probabilistic budgets is more time consuming than preparing a single fixed budget.

(b) A probabilistic budget represents a weighted average of expectations, and may not reflect an outcome that is actually expected to happen.

(c) Probabilistic budgets have little practical value for the purpose of planning or control, so the cost of preparing the budgets may exceed the benefits obtained.

Probabilistic budgets may be useful in helping management to assess the risk in the budget. However, there are other ways of assessing risk, such as sensitivity analysis, especially when spreadsheets are used for preparing budgets (see below).

4 Using spreadsheets in budgeting 12/12

FAST FORWARD

Spreadsheet packages can be used to build business **models** to assist the forecasting and planning process. They are particularly useful for 'what if?' analysis.

It is quite common for managers to prepare their functional budgets using a spreadsheet. For many organisations, it is also quite common for the entire budget for the organisation as a whole to be produced on a spreadsheet.

A spreadsheet is a type of general purpose software package with **many business applications**, not just accounting ones. It **can be used to build a model**, in which data is presented in these **rows and columns**, and it is up to the model builder to determine what data or information should be presented in it, how it should be presented and how the data should be manipulated by the spreadsheet program. The most widely used spreadsheet packages are Lotus 1-2-3 and Excel.

The idea behind a spreadsheet is that the model builder should **construct a model as follows**.

(a) Identify what data goes into each row and column and by **inserting text** (for example, column headings and row identifications).

(b)   **Specify how the numerical data in the model should be derived**. Numerical data might be derived using one of the following methods.

- **Insertion into the model via keyboard input**.

- **Calculation from other data in the model** by means of a formula specified within the model itself. The model builder must insert these formulae into the spreadsheet model when it is first constructed.

- **Retrieval from data on a disk file** from another computer application program or module.

4.1 The advantages of spreadsheets

Spreadsheets have several important advantages.

(a)   A budget model can be loaded into a manager's laptop computer, so that the manager can work on the budget when they are away from the office, say, on a business trip.

(b)   The complex interrelationships of different factors in the budget can be built into the model as spreadsheet formulae. The user simply has to change values for the input variables and a new version of the budget can be prepared immediately.

(c)   Spreadsheets therefore enable managers to consider many different budget options and also carry out sensitivity analysis on the budget figures.

(d)   Spreadsheets therefore simplify and speed up a time-consuming process.

The great value of spreadsheets derives from their **simple format** of rows, columns and worksheets of data, and the ability of the data **users to have direct access themselves** to their spreadsheet model via their own PC. For example, an accountant can construct a cash flow model with a spreadsheet package on the PC on their desk: they can **create** the model, **input** the data, **manipulate** the data and **read or print the output** direct. They will also have fairly **instant access** to the model whenever it is needed, in just the time it takes to load the model into their PC. Spreadsheets therefore bring computer modelling into the everyday reach of data users.

4.2 The disadvantages of spreadsheets

Spreadsheets have significant limitations if they are not properly used.

(a)   An error in the design of the model, such as **an error in a formula**, can **affect the validity of data** throughout the spreadsheet. Such errors can be very difficult to trace.

(b)   Even if it is properly designed in the first place, it is very **easy to corrupt** a model by accidentally changing a cell or inputting data in the wrong place.

(c)   It is possible to **become overdependent on them**, so that simple one-off tasks that can be done in seconds with a pen and paper are done on a spreadsheet instead.

(d)   The possibility for experimentation with data is so great that it is possible to **lose sight of the original intention** of the spreadsheet.

(e)   Spreadsheets **cannot take account of qualitative factors** since they are invariably difficult to quantify. Decisions should not be made on the basis of quantitative information alone.

(f)   There may be security problems with risk of unauthorised access, especially if managers carry their spreadsheet around with them on a laptop.

There can be **audit trail problems**. It can be difficult to track different versions of the budget, and how the initial draft of the budget was changed over time with different assumptions and input values. There may be too many different versions of the draft budget. Some system of version control should be enforced to make sure that the current budget draft can be recognised and used by managers who are still working on it.

In summary, spreadsheets should be seen as a **tool in planning and decision-making**. The user must make the decision. It should be noted that a company may choose to integrate a software package into its own database rather than use a general purpose spreadsheet package. **Integrated software packages** such as Microsoft Works combine the most commonly used functions of many productivity software programs into one application.

4.3 'What if' analysis

Once a model has been constructed the consequences of changes in any of the variables may be tested by asking **'what if' questions, a form of sensitivity analysis**. For example, a spreadsheet may be used to develop a cash flow model, such as that shown below.

	A	B	C	D
		Month 1	*Month 2*	*Month 3*
1				
2	Sales	1,000	1,200	1,440
3	Cost of sales	(650)	(780)	(936)
4	Gross profit	350	420	504
5				
6	Receipts:			
7	Current month	600	720	864
8	Previous month		400	480
9		–	–	–
10		600	1,120	1,344
11	Payments	(650)	(780)	(936)
12		(50)	340	408
13	Balance b/f	–	(50)	290
14	Balance c/f	(50)	290	698

Typical 'what if' questions for sensitivity analysis

(a) What if the cost of sales is 68% of sales revenue, not 65%?

(b) What if payment from debtors is received 40% in the month of sale, 50% one month in arrears and 10% two months in arrears, instead of 60% in the month of sale and 40% one month in arrears?

(c) What if sales growth is only 15% per month, instead of 20% per month?

Using the spreadsheet model, the answers to such questions can be obtained simply and quickly, using the editing facility in the program. The information obtained should provide management with a **better understanding** of what the cash flow position in the future might be, and what **factors are critical** to ensuring that the cash position remains reasonable. For example, it might be found that the cost of sales must remain less than 67% of sales value to achieve a satisfactory cash position.

Chapter Roundup

- The **high-low method** is a quantitative technique for analysing total costs into their fixed cost and variable cost elements.

- **Learning curve theory** may be useful for forecasting production time and labour costs in circumstances where a workforce makes a new product and improves its efficiency with experience and learning. However, the method has many limitations.

- The formula for the learning curve is $Y = ax^b$, where b, the learning coefficient or learning index, is defined as (log of the learning rate/log of 2). The learning curve formula can be used to solve all learning curve scenarios.

- **Expected values** may be used in budgeting to determine the best combination of expected profit and risk.

- **Spreadsheet packages** can be used to build business **models** to assist the forecasting and planning process. They are particularly useful for 'what if?' analysis.

Quick Quiz

1   The costs of production runs consist of a mix of fixed and variable elements. The lowest number of production runs during the year was 120 during February, the highest number 150 during October. If the total costs of production runs in February were $80,000 and in October were $95,000, calculate the fixed and variable cost elements.

2   List five limitations of learning curve theory.

3   It takes 60 hours to make the first unit of a product and a 95% learning curve applies. How long will it take to make the second and third units?

4   *Calculate the EV of revenue using the following information.*

Sales volume	Probability	Selling price $	Probability
10,000	0.2	3.00	0.1
12,000	0.7	3.50	0.1
13,000	0.1	4.50	0.8

5   Which of the following could be considered a disadvantage of using spreadsheets in the budgeting process?

A   An error in spreadsheet design can affect the validity of the data.

B   It is possible to become overdependent on spreadsheets.

C   Data may become corrupted.

D   Spreadsheets cannot take account of qualitative factors.

1

	Number of runs	Total costs $
High	150	95,000
Low	120	80,000
Difference	30	15,000

Variable costs per run = $\dfrac{15,000}{30}$ = $500

Fixed costs = 95,000 − (500 × 150) = $20,000

2 (i) The learning curve phenomenon is **not always present**.

(ii) It assumes **stable conditions** at work which will **enable learning to take place**. This is not always practicable; for example, because of **labour turnover**.

(iii) It must also assume a certain degree of **motivation** among employees.

(iv) Breaks between repeating production of an item must not be too long, or workers will **'forget'** and the learning process will have to begin all over again.

(v) It might be difficult to **obtain accurate data** to decide what the learning curve is.

(vi) **Workers might not agree** to a gradual reduction in production times per unit.

(vii) **Production techniques might change**, or product design alterations might be made, so that it takes a long time for a **'standard'** production method to emerge, to which a learning effect will apply.

3 Average time for first 2 units = 60 × 95% = 57 hours

Total time for first two units = 57 × 2 = 114 hours

Time for 2nd unit = 114 − 60 = 54 hours.

$Y = ax^b$ and $b = \log 0.95 / \log 2 = -0.0222764/0.30103 = -0.740006$

Average time for first 3 units = $60 \times 3^{-0.740006}$ = 60 × 0.9219189 = 55.315 hours

Total time for first 3 units = 3 × 55.315 hours = 165.945 hours

Time to make 3rd unit = (165.945 − 114) = 51.945 hours = 52 hours approximately.

4 EV = ((10,000 × 0.2) + (12,000 × 0.7) + (13,000 × 0.1)) × ((3 × 0.1) + (3.5 × 0.1) + (4.5 × 0.8))
   = 11,700 × $4.25
   = $49,725

5 All of them.

<table>
<tr><td colspan="4">Now try the questions below from the Practice Question Bank</td></tr>
</table>

Number	Level	Marks	Approximate time
Section A Q56	Examination	2	4 mins
Section A Q57	Examination	2	4 mins
Section A Q58	Examination	2	4 mins
Section A Q59	Examination	2	4 mins
Section A Q60	Examination	2	4 mins
Section B Q21–25	Examination	10	20 mins

Budgeting and standard costing

10

Introduction

In this chapter we will be looking at **standard costs** and **standard costing**.

You will have studied standard costing before and have learned about the principles of standard costing and how to calculate a number of cost and sales variances. We obviously look at the topic in more depth for your studies of this syllabus.

We begin this chapter by reviewing the **main principles of standard costing** as well as looking in some detail at the **way in which standard costs are set**.

Flexible budgets are vital for both planning and control and we will look at how they are constructed and their use in the overall budgetary control process.

Study guide

		Intellectual level
C3	**Standard costing**	
(a)	Explain the use of standard costs.	2
(b)	Outline the methods used to derive standard costs and discuss the different types of cost possible.	2
(c)	Explain and illustrate the importance of flexing budgets in performance management.	2
(d)	Explain and apply the principle of controllability in the performance management system.	2

Exam guide

The contents of this chapter are likely to be examined in conjunction with variance analysis, covered in the next chapter.

1 The use of standard costs

12/08

FAST FORWARD

A **standard cost** is an estimated unit cost built up of standards for each cost element (standard resource price and standard resource usage).

Standard costing is used to value inventories, prepare cost budgets for production and provide control information (variances).

1.1 What is a standard cost?

Key term

A **standard cost** is an estimated unit cost.

The standard cost of product 12345 is set out below on a **standard cost card**.

STANDARD COST CARD				
Product: the Splodget, No 12345				
	Cost	*Requirement*	$	$
Direct materials				
A	$2.00 per kg	6 kgs	12.00	
B	$3.00 per kg	2 kgs	6.00	
C	$4.00 per litre	1 litre	4.00	
Others			2.00	
				24.00
Direct labour				
Grade I	$4.00 per hour	3 hrs	12.00	
Grade II	$5.40 per hour	5 hrs	27.00	
				39.00
Variable production overheads	$1.00 per hour	8 hrs	8.00	
Fixed production overheads	$3.00 per hour	8 hrs	24.00	
Standard full cost of production			95.00	

Notice how the standard cost is **built up from standards for each cost element**: standard quantities of materials at standard prices, standard quantities of labour time at standard rates, and so on. It is therefore determined by management's estimates of the following.

- The expected prices of materials, labour and expenses
- Efficiency levels in the use of materials and labour
- Budgeted overhead costs and budgeted volumes of activity

We will see how management arrives at these estimates later in the chapter.

But why should management want to prepare standard costs? Obviously to assist with standard costing, but what is the point of standard costing?

1.2 The uses of standard costing

Standard costing has three main **uses**.

- **To value inventories**. It is an alternative to FIFO and average cost as a method of inventory valuation.

- To **budget production costs**. When a standard per unit of product has been established, budgeting production costs becomes a fairly straightforward process.

- **To act as a control device**. This is done by establishing standards (expected costs) and comparing actual costs with the expected costs. Variances between actual and standard cost indicate aspects of operations which may be out of control.

Standard costs may also be used for the following purposes.

(a)   To **evaluate managerial performance**

(b)   To enable the principle of **'management by exception'** to be practised (a standard cost, when established, is an average expected unit cost and because it is only an average, actual results will vary to some extent above and below the average; only significant differences between actual and standard should be reported)

(c)   To provide a prediction of future costs, for use in some **decision-making** situations

(d)   To **motivate** staff and management by providing challenging targets

(e)   To provide guidance on possible ways of **improving efficiency**

Although the other uses of standard costing should not be overlooked, we will be concentrating on the control aspect and variance reporting.

1.3 Standard costing as a control technique

Key terms

> **Standard costing** involves the establishment of predetermined estimates of the costs of products or services, the collection of actual costs and the comparison of the actual costs with the predetermined estimates. The predetermined costs are known as standard costs and the difference between standard and actual cost is known as a **variance**. The process by which the total difference between standard and actual results is analysed is known as **variance analysis**.

Question

Standard costing

What are the possible advantages for the control function of an organisation of having a standard costing system?

Answer

(a)   Carefully planned standards are an aid to more accurate **budgeting**.

(b)   Standard costs provide a **yardstick** against which actual costs can be measured.

(c)   The setting of standards involves determining the **best** materials and methods which may lead to economies.

(d)   A **target of efficiency** is set for employees to reach and **cost consciousness** is stimulated.

(e)   Variances can be calculated which enable the principle of **'management by exception'** to be operated. Only the variances which exceed acceptable tolerance limits need to be investigated by management with a view to control action.

(f)   Standard costs and variance analysis can **motivate** managers to achieve better performance. However, care must be taken to distinguish between controllable and non-controllable costs in variance reporting.

1.4 Where standard costing should be used

FAST FORWARD

Standard costing is most suited to mass production and repetitive assembly work, where large quantities of a standard product are manufactured.

Although standard costing can be used in a variety of costing situations (batch and mass production, process manufacture, jobbing manufacture (where there is standardisation of parts) and service industries (if a realistic cost unit can be established)), the **greatest benefit** from its use can be gained if there is a **large amount of repetition** in the production process so that average or expected usage of resources can be determined. It is therefore most suited to **mass production** and **repetitive assembly work**. It is not well suited to production systems where items are manufactured to customer demand and specifications.

Question   Standard service costing

Can you think of a service organisation that could apply standard costing?

Answer

One example could be restaurants which deal with standard recipes for meals. If a large number of meals are produced, say, for conference delegates, mass production systems will apply. Standards may not be calculated with the same accuracy as in manufacturing environments, but the principles are still relevant. Other examples are equally valid.

Exam focus point

In an exam, you could be asked to consider whether a standard is 'meaningful'. Standards could be set for everything, but not all standards would have practical meaning or value. It is important that you can identify the industries and processes best suited to the application of standard costing.

2 Deriving standards

FAST FORWARD

The **responsibility for deriving standard costs** should be shared between **managers able to provide the necessary information** about levels of expected efficiency, prices and overhead costs.

2.1 Setting standards for materials costs

Direct materials costs per unit of raw material will be estimated by the purchasing department from their knowledge of the following.

- Purchase contracts already agreed
- Pricing discussions with regular suppliers
- The forecast movement of prices in the market
- The availability of bulk purchase discounts
- The quality of material required by the production departments

The standard cost ought to include an allowance for **bulk purchase discounts**, if these are available on all or some of the purchases, and it may have to be a weighted average price of the differing prices charged for the same product by alternative suppliers.

A decision must also be taken as to how to deal with price **inflation**. Suppose that a material costs $10 per kilogram at the moment and, during the course of the next 12 months, it is expected to go up in price by 20% to $12 per kilogram. What standard price should be selected?

(a) If the **current price** of $10 per kilogram **is used in the standard**, the reported price variance will become adverse as soon as prices go up, which could be very early in the year. If prices go up gradually rather than in one big jump, it would be difficult to select an appropriate time for revising the standard.

(b) If an **estimated mid-year price** of, say, $11 per kilogram **is used**, price variances should be favourable in the first half of the year and adverse in the second half, again assuming that prices go up gradually. Management could only really check that the price variance did not become excessively adverse (or favourable) in any month and that the price variance switched from being favourable to adverse around Month six or seven and not sooner.

Standard costing is therefore more **difficult in times of inflation but it is still worthwhile**.

- Usage and efficiency variances will still be meaningful.
- Inflation is measurable: there is no reason why its effects cannot be removed.
- Standard costs can be revised, so long as this is not done too frequently.

2.2 Setting standards for labour costs

Direct labour rates per hour will be set by reference to the payroll and to any agreements on pay rises with trade union representatives of the employees. A separate hourly rate or weekly wage will be set for each different labour grade/type of employee and an average hourly rate will be applied for each grade (even though individual rates of pay may vary according to age and experience).

Similar problems to those which arise when setting material standards in times of high inflation can be met when setting labour standards.

2.3 Setting standards for material usage and labour efficiency

To estimate the materials required to make each product (material usage) and also the labour hours required (labour efficiency), technical specifications must be prepared for each product by production experts (either in the production department or the work study department).

2.4 Setting standards for overheads

When standard costs are **fully absorbed** standard production costs (standard costs can be used in both marginal and absorption costing systems), the **absorption rate** of fixed production overheads will be **predetermined** and **based on budgeted** fixed production **overhead** and planned **production volume**.

Production volume will depend on two factors.

(a) **Production capacity** (or 'volume capacity') measured perhaps in standard hours of output (a standard hour being the amount of work achievable at standard efficiency levels in an hour), which in turn reflects direct production labour hours

(b) **Efficiency of working**, by labour or machines, allowing for rest time and contingency allowances

Suppose that a department has a workforce of ten men, each of whom works a 36-hour week to make standard units, and each unit has a standard time of two hours to make. The expected efficiency of the workforce is 125%.

(a) Budgeted capacity, in direct labour hours, would be 10 × 36 = 360 production hours per week.

(b) Budgeted efficiency is 125% so that the workforce should take only 1 hour of actual production time to produce 1.25 standard hours of output.

(c) This means in our example that budgeted output is 360 production hours × 125% = 450 standard hours of output per week. At 2 standard hours per unit, this represents production activity or volume of 225 units of output per week.

Question

ABC carries out routine office work in a sales order processing department, and all tasks in the department have been given standard times. There are 40 clerks in the department who work on average 140 hours per month each. The efficiency ratio of the department is 110%.

Required

Calculate the budgeted output in the department.

Answer

Capacity	= 40 × 140 = 5,600 hours per month
Efficiency	= 110%
Budgeted output	= 5,600 × 110% = 6,160 standard hours of work per month

2.5 Setting standards for sales price and margin

The **standard selling price** will depend on a number of factors including the following.

- Anticipated market demand
- Competing products
- Manufacturing costs
- Inflation estimates

The **standard sales margin** is the difference between the standard cost and the standard selling price.

Question

What problems do you think could occur when standards are being set?

Answer

The following problems can occur when setting standards.

(a) Deciding how to incorporate **inflation** into planned unit costs
(b) Agreeing on a **performance standard** (attainable or ideal)
(c) Deciding on the **quality** of materials to be used (a better quality of material will cost more, but perhaps reduce material wastage)
(d) Estimating materials prices where **seasonal price variations** or **bulk purchase discounts** may be significant
(e) Finding sufficient **time** to construct standards, as standard setting can be time consuming
(f) Incurring the **cost** of setting up and maintaining a system for establishing standards

2.6 Types of standard

FAST FORWARD

There are four **types of standard: ideal, attainable, current** and **basic**. These can have an impact on employee motivation.

How demanding should a standard be? Should the standard represent perfect performance or easily attainable performance? There are four types of standard.

Key terms

> An **ideal standard** is a standard which can be attained under perfect operating conditions: no wastage, no inefficiencies, no idle time, no breakdowns.
>
> An **attainable standard** is a standard which can be attained if production is carried out efficiently, machines are properly operated and/or materials are properly used. Some allowance is made for wastage and inefficiencies.
>
> A **current standard** is a standard based on current working conditions (current wastage, current inefficiencies).
>
> A **basic standard** is a long-term standard which remains unchanged over the years and is used to show trends.

The **different types of standard have a number of advantages and disadvantages.**

(a) **Ideal standards** can be seen as **long-term targets** but are not very useful for day-to-day control purposes.

(b) **Ideal standards cannot be achieved**. If such standards are used for budgeting, an allowance will have to be included to make the budget realistic and attainable.

(c) **Attainable standards** can be used for **product costing**, cost control, inventory valuation, estimating and as a basis for budgeting.

(d) **Current standards** or attainable standards provide the **best basis for budgeting**, because they represent an achievable level of productivity.

(e) Current standards **do not attempt to improve** on current levels of efficiency.

(f) **Current standards** are useful during **periods when inflation is high**. They can be set on a month by month basis.

(g) **Basic standards** are used to show **changes in efficiency or performance** over a long period of time. They are perhaps the least useful and least common type of standard in use.

2.6.1 The impact on employee behaviour of the type of standard set

The type of standard set can have an impact on the behaviour of the employees trying to achieve those standards.

Type of standard	Impact on behaviour
Ideal	Some say that they provide employees with an **incentive to be more efficient** even though it is highly unlikely that the standard will be achieved. Others argue that they are likely to have an unfavourable effect on employee motivation because the differences between standards and actual results will always be adverse. The **employees may feel that the goals are unattainable** and so **they will not work so hard**.
Attainable	Might be an **incentive to work harder** as they provide a **realistic but challenging target of efficiency**.
Current	**Will not motivate employees to do anything more than they are currently doing.**
Basic	May have an **unfavourable impact** on the motivation of employees. Over time they will discover that they are easily able to achieve the standards. They may become bored and lose interest in what they are doing if they have nothing to aim for.

3 Budgets and standards compared

Budgets and standards are very similar and interrelated, but there are important differences between them. A budget is an overall plan and a standard cost is a unit cost. Standard costs may be used for budgeting.

Budgets and standards are **similar** in the following ways.

(a) They both involve looking to the future and **forecasting** what is likely to happen given a certain set of circumstances.

(b) They are both **used for control purposes**. A budget aids control by setting financial targets or limits for a forthcoming period. Actual achievements or expenditures are then compared with the budgets and action is taken to correct any variances where necessary. A standard also achieves control by comparison of actual results against a predetermined target.

As well as being similar, **budgets and standards are interrelated**. For example, a standard unit production cost can act as the basis for a production cost budget. The unit cost is multiplied by the budgeted activity level to arrive at the budgeted expenditure on production costs.

There are, however, **important differences between budgets and standards**.

Budget	Standard cost
Gives planned total aggregate costs for a function or cost centre	Shows the unit resource usage for a single task, for example the standard labour hours for a single unit of production
Can be prepared for all functions, even where output cannot be measured	Limited to situations where repetitive actions are performed and output can be measured
Expressed in money terms	Need not be expressed in money terms. For example, a standard rate of output does not need a financial value put on it

4 Flexible budgets

Comparison of a fixed budget with the actual results for a different level of activity is of little use for control purposes. **Flexible budgets** should be used to show what cost and revenues should have been for the actual level of activity.

Key term

A **flexible budget** is a budget which, by recognising different cost behaviour patterns, changes as volume of activity (output and sales) changes.

4.1 Flexible budgets and performance management

Budgetary control involves drawing up budgets for the areas of responsibility for individual managers (production managers, purchasing managers, and so on) and regularly **comparing** actual results against expected results. The differences between actual results and expected results are reported as **variances** and these are used to provide a guideline for control action by individual managers.

Note that individual managers are held responsible for investigating differences between budgeted and actual results, and are then expected to take corrective action or amend the plan in the light of actual events.

The wrong approach to budgetary control is to compare actual results against a fixed budget. Suppose that a company manufactures a single product, Z. Budgeted results and actual results for June 20X2 are shown below.

	Budget	Actual results	Variance
Production and sales of the cloud (units)	2,000	3,000	
	$	$	$
Sales revenue (a)	20,000	30,000	10,000 (F)
Direct materials	6,000	8,500	2,500 (A)
Direct labour	4,000	4,500	500 (A)
Maintenance	1,000	1,400	400 (A)
Depreciation	2,000	2,200	200 (A)
Rent and rates	1,500	1,600	100 (A)
Other costs	3,600	5,000	1,400 (A)
Total costs (b)	18,100	23,200	5,100
Profit (a) – (b)	1,900	6,800	4,900 (F)

(a) Here the variances are **meaningless** for control purposes. Costs were higher than budget because the output volume was also higher; variable costs would be expected to increase above the costs budgeted in the fixed budget. There is no information to show whether control action is needed for any aspect of costs or revenue.

(b) For control purposes, it is necessary to know the following.

(i) Were actual costs higher than they should have been to produce and sell 3,000 Zs?
(ii) Was actual revenue satisfactory from the sale of 3,000 Zs?

The **correct approach to budgetary control** is as follows.

(a) **Identify fixed and variable costs**
(b) **Produce a flexible budget using marginal costing techniques**

Let's suppose that we have the following estimates of cost behaviour for the company.

(a) Direct materials, direct labour and maintenance costs are variable.
(b) Rent and rates and depreciation are fixed costs.
(c) Other costs consist of fixed costs of $1,600 plus a variable cost of $1 per unit made and sold.

Now that the cost behaviour patterns are known, a budget cost allowance can be calculated for each item of expenditure. This allowance is shown in a **flexible budget** as the expected expenditure on each item for the relevant level of activity. The budget cost allowances are calculated as follows.

(a) Variable cost allowances = original budgets × (3,000 units/2,000 units)

eg material cost allowance = $6,000 × $^3/_2$ = $9,000

(b) Fixed cost allowances = as original budget

(c) Semi-fixed cost allowances = original budgeted fixed costs

+ (3,000 units × variable cost per unit)

eg other cost allowances = $1,600 + (3,000 × $1) = $4,600

The budgetary control analysis should be as follows.

	Fixed budget (a)	Flexible budget (b)	Actual results (c)	Budget variance (b) – (c)
Production and sales (units)	2,000	3,000	3,000	
	$	$	$	$
Sales revenue	20,000	30,000	30,000	0
Variable costs				
Direct materials	6,000	9,000	8,500	500 (F)
Direct labour	4,000	6,000	4,500	1,500 (F)
Maintenance	1,000	1,500	1,400	100 (F)
Semi-variable costs				
Other costs	3,600	4,600	5,000	400 (A)

	Fixed budget (a)	Flexible budget (b)	Actual results (c)	Budget variance (b) – (c)
Fixed costs				
Depreciation	2,000	2,000	2,200	200 (A)
Rent and rates	1,500	1,500	1,600	100 (A)
Total costs	18,100	24,600	23,200	1,400 (F)
Profit	1,900	5,400	6,800	1,400 (F)

Note. (F) denotes a favourable variance and **(A) an adverse or unfavourable variance**.

We can **analyse** the above as follows.

(a)   In selling 3,000 units the expected profit should not have been the fixed budget profit of $1,900, but the flexible budget profit of $5,400. Instead, actual profit was $6,800 ie $1,400 more than we should have expected. One of the reasons for the improvement is that, **given output and sales** of 3,000 units, **costs were lower than expected** (and sales revenue exactly as expected).

	$
Direct materials cost variance	500 (F)
Direct labour cost variance	1,500 (F)
Maintenance cost variance	100 (F)
Other costs variance	400 (A)
Fixed cost variances	
Depreciation	200 (A)
Rent and rates	100 (A)
	1,400 (F)

(b)   Another reason for the improvement in profit above the fixed budget profit is the **sales volume** (3,000 Zs were sold instead of 2,000).

	$	$
Sales revenue increased by		10,000
Variable costs increased by:		
Direct materials	3,000	
Direct labour	2,000	
Maintenance	500	
Variable element of other costs	1,000	
Fixed costs are unchanged		6,500
Profit increased by		3,500

Profit was therefore increased by $3,500 because sales volumes increased.

(c)   A full variance analysis statement would be as follows.

	$	$
Fixed budget profit		1,900
Variances		
Sales volume	3,500 (F)	
Direct materials cost	500 (F)	
Direct labour cost	1,500 (F)	
Maintenance cost	100 (F)	
Other costs	400 (A)	
Depreciation	200 (A)	
Rent and rates	100 (A)	
		4,900 (F)
Actual profit		6,800

If management believes that any of these variances are large enough to justify it, they will investigate the reasons for them to see whether any corrective action is necessary or whether the plan needs amending in the light of actual events.

Question

The budgeted and actual results of Crunch Co for September were as follows. The company uses a marginal costing system. There were no opening or closing inventories.

Sales and production	Fixed budget 1,000 units		Actual 700 units	
	$	$	$	$
Sales		20,000		14,200
Variable cost of sales				
Direct materials	8,000		5,200	
Direct labour	4,000		3,100	
Variable overhead	2,000		1,500	
		14,000		9,800
Contribution		6,000		4,400
Fixed costs		5,000		5,400
Profit/(loss)		1,000		(1,000)

Required

Prepare a budget that will be useful for management control purposes.

Answer

We need to prepare a **flexible budget for 700 units**.

	Budget 1,000 units	per unit	Flexed budget 700 units	Actual 700 units	Variances
	$	$	$	$	$
Sales	20,000	(20)	14,000	14,200	200 (F)
Variable costs					
Direct material	8,000	(8)	5,600	5,200	400 (F)
Direct labour	4,000	(4)	2,800	3,100	300 (A)
Variable production overhead	2,000	(2)	1,400	1,500	100 (A)
	14,000	(14)	9,800	9,800	
Contribution	6,000		4,200	4,400	
Fixed costs	5,000	(N/A)	5,000	5,400	400 (A)
Profit/(loss)	1,000		(800)	(1,000)	200 (A)

By **flexing** the budget in the question above we **removed the effect on sales revenue of the difference between budgeted sales volume and actual sales volume**. However, there is still a variance of $200 (F). This means that the actual **selling price** must have been different to the budgeted selling price, resulting in a $200 (F) **selling price variance**.

4.2 The need for flexible budgets

We have seen that flexible budgets may be prepared in order to plan for variations in the level of activity above or below the level set in the fixed budget. It has been suggested, however, that since many cost items in modern industry are fixed costs, the **value** of flexible budgets in planning is dwindling.

(a) In many manufacturing industries, plant costs (depreciation, rent, and so on) are a very large proportion of total costs, and tend to be fixed costs.

(b) Wage costs also tend to be fixed, because employees are generally guaranteed a basic wage for a working week of an agreed number of hours.

(c)   With the growth of service industries, labour (wages or fixed salaries) and overheads will account for most of the costs of a business, and direct materials will be a relatively small proportion of total costs.

Flexible budgets are nevertheless necessary and, even if they are not used at the planning stage, they must be used for budgetary control variance analysis.

5 The principle of controllability

The **principle of controllability** is that managers of responsibility centres should only be held accountable for costs over which they have some influence.

5.1 Budget centres

Budgetary control is based around a system of **budget centres**. Each budget centre will have its own budget and a manager will be responsible for managing the budget centre and ensuring that the budget is met.

The selection of budget centres in an organisation is therefore a key first step in setting up a control system. What should the budget centres be? What income, expenditure and/or capital employment plans should each budget centre prepare? In addition, how will measures of performance for each budget centre be made?

A well-organised system of control should have the following features.

Feature	Explanation
A hierarchy of budget centres	If the organisation is quite large, a hierarchy is needed. Subsidiary companies, departments and work sections might be budget centres. Budgets of each section would then be consolidated into a departmental budget, departmental budgets in turn would be consolidated into the subsidiary's budget, and the budgets of each subsidiary would be **combined into a master budget** for the group as a whole.
Clearly identified responsibilities for achieving budget targets	Individual managers should be made responsible for achieving the budget targets of a particular budget centre.
Responsibilities for revenues, costs and capital employed	Budget centres should be organised so that all the revenues earned by an organisation, all the costs it incurs, and all the capital it employs are made the responsibility of someone within the organisation, at an appropriate level of authority in the management hierarchy.

Budgetary control and budget centres are therefore part of the overall system of **responsibility accounting** within an organisation.

Key term

Responsibility accounting is a system of accounting that segregates revenue and costs into areas of personal responsibility in order to monitor and assess the performance of each part of an organisation.

5.2 Controllable costs

Controllable costs are items of expenditure which can be directly influenced by a given manager within a given time span.

Care must be taken to distinguish between controllable costs and uncontrollable costs in variance reporting. The **controllability principle** is that managers of responsibility centres should only be held accountable for costs over which they have some influence. From a **motivation** point of view this is important because it can be very demoralising for managers who feel that their performance is being judged on the basis of something over which they have no influence. It is also important from a **control** point of view in that control reports should ensure that information on costs is reported to the manager who is able to take action to control them.

Responsibility accounting attempts to associate costs, revenues, assets and liabilities with the managers most capable of controlling them. As a system of accounting, it therefore distinguishes between controllable and uncontrollable costs.

Most **variable costs** within a department are thought to be **controllable in the short term** because managers can influence the efficiency with which resources are used, even if they cannot do anything to raise or lower price levels.

A cost which is not controllable by a junior manager might be controllable by a senior manager. For example, there may be high direct labour costs in a department caused by excessive overtime working. The junior manager may feel obliged to continue with the overtime to meet production schedules, but his senior may be able to reduce costs by hiring extra full-time staff, thereby reducing the requirements for overtime.

A cost which is not controllable by a manager in one department may be controllable by a manager in another department. For example, an increase in material costs may be caused by buying at higher prices than expected (controllable by the purchasing department), by excessive wastage (controllable by the production department) or by a faulty machine producing rejects (controllable by the maintenance department).

Some costs are **non-controllable**, such as increases in expenditure items due to inflation. Other costs are **controllable, but in the long term rather than the short term**. For example, production costs might be reduced by the introduction of new machinery and technology, but in the short term management must attempt to do the best they can with the resources and machinery at their disposal.

5.2.1 The controllability of fixed costs

It is often assumed that all fixed costs are non-controllable in the short run. This is not so.

(a)   **Committed fixed costs** are those costs arising from the possession of plant, equipment, buildings and an administration department to **support the long-term needs of the business**. These costs (depreciation, rent, administration salaries) are largely **non-controllable in the short term** because they have been committed by longer-term decisions affecting longer-term needs. When a company decides to cut production drastically, the long-term committed fixed costs will be reduced, but only after redundancy terms have been settled and assets sold.

(b)   **Discretionary fixed costs**, such as advertising and research and development costs, are incurred as a result of a top management decision, but could be **raised or lowered at fairly short notice** (irrespective of the actual volume of production and sales).

5.2.2 Controllability and apportioned costs

Managers should only be held accountable for costs over which they have some influence. This may seem quite straightforward in theory, but it is not always so easy in practice to distinguish controllable from uncontrollable costs. **Apportioned overhead costs provide a good example**.

Suppose that a manager of a production department in a manufacturing company is made responsible for the costs of their department. These costs include **directly attributable overhead items**, such as the costs of indirect labour employed and indirect materials consumed in the department. The department's overhead costs also include an apportionment of costs from other cost centres, such as rent and rates for the building it shares with other departments and a share of the costs of the maintenance department.

Should the production manager be held accountable for any of these apportioned costs?

(a)   Managers should not be held accountable for costs over which they have no control. In this example, apportioned rent and rates costs would not be controllable by the production department manager.

(b)   Managers should be held accountable for costs over which they have some influence. In this example, it is the responsibility of the maintenance department manager to keep maintenance costs within budget. However, their costs will be partly variable and partly fixed, and the variable cost element will depend on the volume of demand for their services. If the production department's staff treat their equipment badly we might expect higher repair costs, and the production department manager should therefore be made accountable for the repair costs that their department makes the maintenance department incur on its behalf.

(c)   Charging the production department with some of the costs of the maintenance department prevents the production department from viewing the maintenance services as 'free services'. Overuse would be discouraged and the production manager is more likely to question the activities of the maintenance department, possibly resulting in a reduction in maintenance costs or the provision of more efficient maintenance services.

5.2.3 Controllability and dual responsibility

Quite often a particular cost might be the **responsibility of two or more managers**. For example, raw materials costs might be the responsibility of the purchasing manager (prices) and the production manager (usage). A **reporting system must allocate responsibility appropriately**. The purchasing manager must be responsible for any increase in raw materials prices whereas the production manager should be responsible for any increase in raw materials usage.

Exam focus point

You can see that there are **no clear-cut rules** as to which costs are controllable and which are not. Each situation and cost must be reviewed separately and a decision taken according to the control value of the information and its behavioural impact.

Chapter Roundup

- A **standard cost** is an estimated unit cost built up of standards for each cost element (standard resource price and standard resource usage).

- **Standard costing** is used to value inventories, prepare cost budgets for production and provide control information (variances).

- Standard costing is most suited to mass production and repetitive assembly work, where large quantities of a standard product are manufactured.

- The **responsibility for deriving standard costs** should be shared between **managers able to provide the necessary information** about levels of expected efficiency, prices and overhead costs.

- There are four **types of standard: ideal, attainable, current** and **basic**. These can have an impact on employee motivation.

- Budgets and standards are very similar and interrelated, but there are important differences between them. A budget is an overall plan and a standard cost is a unit cost. Standard costs may be used for budgeting.

- Comparison of a fixed budget with the actual results for a different level of activity is of little use for control purposes. **Flexible budgets** should be used to show what cost and revenues should have been for the actual level of activity.

- The **principle of controllability** is that managers of responsibility centres should only be held accountable for costs over which they have some influence.

- **Controllable costs** are items of expenditure which can be directly influenced by a given manager within a given time span.

1   Choose the appropriate words from those highlighted.

The **greatest/least** benefit from the use of standard costing can be gained if there is a degree of repetition in the production process.

Standard costing is therefore **most/less** suited to organisations which produce to customer demand and requirements and **most/less** suited to mass production.

2   Match the type of standard with the correct definition.

Types of standard		Definitions
Ideal	(a)	Can be attained under perfect operating conditions
Attainable	(b)	Can be attained if production is carried out efficiently, machines are properly operated and/or materials are properly used
Basic		
	(c)	Based on current working conditions
Current		
	(d)	Remains unchanged over the years and is used to show trends

3   Fill in the blanks.

Standard costing is difficult in times of inflation but it is still worthwhile.

(a)   .... and .... variances will still be meaningful.

(b)   Inflation is .... : there is no reason why its effects cannot be removed.

(c)   Standard costs can be .... , as long as this is not done
      ....

4   Provide three reasons why standard costing conflicts with schemes of continuous improvement and cost reduction programmes.

5   With what kind of standards is practical capacity associated?

6   Ideal standards are long-term targets.

☐ True   ☐ False

7   Fill in the gaps.

A flexible budget is a budget which, by recognising .... , is designed to .... as the level of activity changes.

8   An extract of the costs incurred at two different activity levels is shown. Classify the costs according to their behaviour patterns and show the budget cost allowance for an activity of 1,500 units.

	1,000 units	2,000 units	Type of cost	Budget cost allowance for 1,500 units
	$	$		$
Fuel	3,000	6,000	....	....
Photocopying	9,500	11,000	....	....
Heating	2,400	2,400	....	....
Direct wages	6,000	8,000	....	....

9   Fill in the blanks.

A well-organised system of control should have the following features.

(a)   A hierarchy of ....

(b)   Clearly identified .... for achieving budget targets

(c)   Responsibilities for .... , ... and
      ....

10   Which of the following are not controllable by a production department manager?

(a)   Direct labour rate

(b)   Variable production overheads

(c)   Apportioned canteen costs

(d)   Increases in raw material costs due to inflation

(e)   Increases in overall material costs due to high levels of wastage caused by poor supervision of production workers

(f)   An increase in the level of idle time because of poorly maintained machines

(g)   Depreciation

(h)   Advertising for production workers

1   greatest
     less
     most

2   Ideal   (a)   Basic   (d)
     Attainable   (b)   Current   (c)

3   (a)   Usage and efficiency variances will still be meaningful.
     (b)   Inflation is measurable: there is no reason why its effects cannot be removed.
     (c)   Standard costs can be reviewed, as long as this is not done too frequently.

4   (a)   Efforts to improve the efficiency of operations or reduce costs will alter quantities of inputs, prices, and so on, whereas standard costing is best used in a stable, standardised, repetitive environment.
     (b)   Predetermined standards conflict with a philosophy of continual improvement.
     (c)   Standard costs often incorporate a planned level of scrap in material standards. This is at odds with the aim of 'zero defects' inherent in continuous improvement programmes.

5   Attainable standards

6   True

7   cost behaviour patterns
     flex or change

8   Variable $4,500   Fixed $2,400
     Semi-variable $10,250   Semi-variable $7,000

9   (a)   Budget centres   (c)   Revenues
     (b)   Responsibilities   Costs
                                            Capital employed

10   (a)
     (c)
     (d)
     (f)   (if there is a maintenance department)
     (g)
     (h)

Now try the questions below from the Practice Question Bank

Number	Level	Marks	Approximate time
Section A Q61	Examination	2	4 mins
Section A Q62	Examination	2	4 mins
Section A Q63	Examination	2	4 mins
Section A Q64	Examination	2	4 mins
Section A Q65	Examination	2	4 mins
Section C Q6	Examination	20	39 mins

11

Variance analysis

Topic list	Syllabus reference
1 Basic variances	Revision
2 The reasons for variances	Revision
3 Operating statements	Revision
4 Investigating variances	Revision
5 Materials mix and yield variances	C4 (a), (b), (c), (d)
6 Sales mix and quantity variances	C5 (a), (b)

Introduction

The **actual results** achieved by an organisation will usually **differ from the expected results** (the expected results being the standard costs and revenues which we looked at in the previous chapter). These differences are **variances**. You should have learned basic variances in your previous studies.

This chapter begins with revision of the **basic variances**, the reasons behind them and their presentation in **operating statements**.

It then goes on to look at more complicated variances which are more likely to be examined in F5. These are materials mix and materials yield variances, and sales mix and sales quantity variances.

Study guide

		Intellectual level
C4	**Material mix and yield variances**	
(a)	Calculate, identify the cause of, and explain mix and yield variances.	2
(b)	Explain the wider issues involved in changing material mix, eg cost, quality and performance measurement issues.	2
(c)	Identify and explain the relationship of the material price variance with the material mix and yield variances.	2
(d)	Suggest and justify alternative methods of controlling production processes.	2
C5	**Sales mix and quantity variances**	
(a)	Calculate, identify the cause of, and explain sales mix and quantity variances.	2
(b)	Identify and explain the relationship of the sales volume variances with the sales mix and quantity variances.	2

Exam guide

Basic variances, the reasons behind them and their presentation in operating statements are assumed knowledge for F5. The variance calculations set in this exam are likely to be the more complicated variances, such as materials mix and yield variances and sales mix and quantity variances. You will be required to **explain** them and **evaluate** performance.

One of the competencies you require to fulfil performance objective 13 of the PER is to use appropriate techniques to assess and to evaluate actual performance against plans. You can apply the knowledge you obtain from this section of the text to help to demonstrate this competence.

1 Basic variances

Knowledge brought forward from earlier studies

- A **variance** is the difference between an actual result and an expected result. In standard costing, cost variances are the difference between the standard costs and actual costs of units produced.
- **Variance analysis** is the process by which the **total** difference between standard and actual results is analysed.
- When actual results are better than expected results, we have a **favourable variance (F)**. If actual results are worse than expected results, we have an **adverse variance (A)**.
- The **selling price variance** measures the effect on expected profit of a selling price different to the standard selling price. It is calculated as the difference between what the sales revenue should have been for the actual quantity sold and what it was.
- The **sales volume variance** measures the increase or decrease in expected profit as a result of the sales volume being higher or lower than budgeted. It is calculated as the difference between the budgeted sales volume and the actual sales volume multiplied by the standard profit per unit.
- The material **total variance** is the difference between what the output actually cost and what it should have cost, in terms of material. It can be divided into the following two sub-variances.
- The **material price variance** is the difference between what the material did cost and what it should have cost.

- The **material usage variance** is the difference between the standard cost of the material that should have been used and the standard cost of the material that was used.
- The **labour total variance** is the difference between what the output should have cost and what it did cost, in terms of labour. It can be divided into two sub-variances.
- The **labour rate variance** is the difference between what the labour did cost and what it should have cost.
- The **labour efficiency variance** is the difference between the standard cost of the hours that should have been worked and the standard cost of the hours that were worked.
- **The variable production overhead total variance** is the difference between what the output should have cost and what it did cost, in terms of variable production overhead. It can be divided into two sub-variances.
- The **variable production overhead expenditure variance** is the difference between the amount of variable production overhead that should have been incurred in the actual hours actively worked and the actual amount of variable production overhead incurred.
- The **variable production overhead efficiency variance** is the difference between the standard cost of the hours that should have been worked for the number of units actually produced and the standard cost of the actual number of hours worked.
- **Fixed production overhead total variance** is the difference between fixed production overhead incurred and fixed production overhead absorbed. In other words, it is the under- or over-absorbed fixed production overhead.
- **Fixed production overhead expenditure variance** is the difference between the budgeted fixed production overhead expenditure and actual fixed production overhead expenditure.
- **Fixed production overhead volume variance** is the difference between actual and budgeted production/volume multiplied by the standard absorption rate per **unit**.
- **Fixed production overhead volume efficiency variance** is the difference between the number of hours that actual production should have taken and the number of hours actually taken (that is, worked) multiplied by the standard absorption rate per **hour**.
- **Fixed production overhead volume capacity variance** is the difference between budgeted hours of work and the actual hours worked, multiplied by the standard absorption rate per **hour**.

An example will be used to illustrate how these variances are calculated.

Question

Various variances

A company produces and sells one product only, the Thing, the standard cost for one unit being as follows.

	$
Direct material A – 10 kilograms at $20 per kg	200
Direct material B – 5 litres at $6 per litre	30
Direct wages – 5 hours at $6 per hour	30
Fixed production overhead	50
Total standard cost	310

The fixed overhead included in the standard cost is based on an expected monthly output of 900 units. Fixed production overhead is absorbed on the basis of direct labour hours.

During April the actual results were as follows.

Production	800 units
Material A	7,800 kg used, costing $159,900
Material B	4,300 litres used, costing $23,650
Direct wages	4,200 hours worked for $24,150
Fixed production overhead	$47,000

Required

(a) Calculate price and usage variances for each material.

(b) Calculate labour rate and efficiency variances.

(c) Calculate fixed production overhead expenditure and volume variances and then subdivide the volume variance.

Answer

(a) **Price variance – Material A**

Take the actual quantity of materials purchased/used and compare the actual prices paid for the materials with their standard price.

	$
7,800 kg should have cost (× $20)	156,000
but did cost	159,900
Price variance (actual cost exceeds standard cost)	3,900 (A)

Usage variance – Material A

Take the actual quantity of units produced and compare the actual quantity of materials used in their production with the standard quantity that should have been used. The variance is converted into a monetary value at the standard price per unit of material.

800 units should have used (× 10 kg)	8,000 kg
but did use	7,800 kg
Usage variance in kg (actual usage less than standard)	200 (F)
× standard cost per kilogram	× $20
Usage variance in $	$4,000 (F)

Price variance – Material B

	$
4,300 litres should have cost (× $6)	25,800
but did cost	23,650
Price variance	2,150 (F)

Usage variance – Material B

	$
800 units should have used (× 5 l)	4,000 l
but did use	4,300 l
Usage variance in litres	300 (A)
× standard cost per litre	× $6
Usage variance in $	$1,800 (A)

(b) **Labour rate variance**

Take the number of labour hours worked and paid for, and compare the actual amount paid with the standard rate for the hours worked.

	$
4,200 hours should have cost (× $6)	25,200
but did cost	24,150
Rate variance (actual cost less than the standard rate)	1,050 (F)

Labour efficiency variance

Take the actual quantity of units produced and compare the actual time to produce them with the standard time. The variance is converted into a monetary value at the standard rate per labour hour.

800 units should have taken (× five hrs)	4,000 hrs
but did take	4,200 hrs
Efficiency variance in hours (actual time longer than standard)	200 (A)
× standard rate per hour	× $6
Efficiency variance in $	$1,200 (A)

(c) **Fixed overhead expenditure variance**

This is the difference between budgeted and actual fixed costs.

	$
Budgeted expenditure ($50 × 900)	45,000
Actual expenditure	47,000
Expenditure variance (actual spending higher than budgeted)	2,000 (A)

Fixed overhead volume variance

This is calculated when the standard cost is a full production cost that includes absorbed fixed overhead. It is not calculated in a system of standard marginal costing; it is the difference between the budgeted and actual production volumes. It is converted into a money value at the standard production overhead cost per unit.

	Units
Budgeted production at standard rate (900 × $50)	900
Actual production at standard rate (800 × $50)	800
Volume variance in units (output less than budget)	100 (A)
Standard production overhead cost per unit	$50
Volume variance in $	$5,000 (A)

The volume variance may be analysed into an efficiency and a capacity variance. Fixed overhead efficiency variance + Capacity variance = Volume variance.

Fixed overhead volume efficiency variance

This is the same as the labour efficiency variance in hours. It is converted into a monetary value at the standard production overhead rate per hour.

	$
800 units should have taken (× five hrs)	4,000 hrs
but did take	4,200 hrs
Volume efficiency variance in hours	200 (A)
× standard absorption rate per hour	× $10
Volume efficiency variance	$2,000 (A)

Fixed overhead volume capacity variance

This is the difference between the budgeted hours of work (budgeted capacity) and the actual hours worked in production. It is converted into a monetary value at the standard production overhead rate per hour.

Budgeted hours	4,500 hrs
Actual hours	4,200 hrs
Volume capacity variance in hours	300 (A)
× standard absorption rate per hour ($50 ÷ 5)	× $10
	$3,000 (A)

Basic variance calculations are **assumed knowledge** for F5 so it is **essential** to do more practice if you struggled with this example/question.

It is assumed that you are able to calculate a sales price variance, as this variance is not included in the question above. The sales volume variance will be revised later, in the context of sales mix and quantity variances.

However, the sales price and volume variances are illustrated in the example on operating statements in Section 3.

2 The reasons for variances

6/08, 12/09, 12/10

> Knowledge brought forward from earlier studies

In an examination question you should review the information given and use your imagination and common sense to suggest possible reasons for variances.

Variance	Favourable	Adverse	Calculation	
Material price	Unforeseen discounts received Greater care in purchasing Change in material standard	Price increase Careless purchasing Change in material standard	Price Based on actual purchases What should it have cost? What did it cost?	$ X (X) X
Material usage	Material used of higher quality than standard More effective use made of material Errors in allocating material to jobs	Defective material Excessive waste Theft Stricter quality control Errors in allocating material to jobs	Usage Based on actual production What should have been used? What was used? Difference valued at standard cost per kg	Kg X (X) X $X
Labour rate	Use of workers at a lower rate of pay than standard	Wage rate increase	Rate Based on actual hours paid What should it have cost? What did it cost?	$ X (X) X
Idle time	Possible if idle time has been built into the budget	Machine breakdown Non-availability of material Illness or injury to worker	Idle time Hours worked Hours paid Difference valued at standard rate per hour	Hrs X (X) $X

Variance	Favourable	Adverse	Calculation	
Labour efficiency	Output produced more quickly than expected, because of work motivation, better quality of equipment or materials, better learning rate Errors in allocating time to jobs	Lost time in excess of standard allowed Output lower than standard set because of lack of training, substandard material, etc Errors in allocating time to jobs	Efficiency Based on actual production How long should it have taken? How long did it take? Difference valued at standard rate per hour	Hrs X (X) X $X
**Overhead expenditure	Savings in costs incurred More economical use of services	Increase in cost of services Excessive use of services Change in type of services used	Based on actual hours worked What should it have cost? What did it cost?	$ X (X) X
Overhead volume	Production or level of activity greater than budgeted	Production or level of activity less than budgeted	Budgeted units Actual units Difference valued at OAR per unit	Units X (X) X $X
Fixed overhead capacity	Production or level of activity greater than budgeted	Production or level of activity less than budgeted	Budgeted hrs worked Actual hrs worked Difference valued at OAR per hour	Hrs X (X) X X
Selling price	Unplanned price increase	Unplanned price reduction	For the quantity sold What revenue should have been generated Actual revenue	$ X (X) X
Sales volume	Additional demand	Unexpected fall in demand Production difficulties	Budgeted sales Actual sales Difference valued at standard profit per unit	Units X (X) X X

3 Operating statements

Knowledge brought forward from earlier studies

Key term

- An **operating statement** is a regular report for management which compares actual costs and revenues with budgeted figures and shows variances.

- There are several ways in which an operating statement may be presented. Perhaps the most common format is one which **reconciles budgeted profit to actual profit**. Sales variances are reported first, and the total of the budgeted profit and the two sales variances results in a figure for 'actual sales minus the standard cost of sales'. The cost variances are then reported, and an actual profit calculated.

Question

Operating statement

A company manufactures one product, and the entire product is sold as soon as it is produced. There are no opening or closing inventories and work in progress is negligible. The company operates a standard costing system and analysis of variances is made every month. The standard cost card for the product, a widget, is as follows.

STANDARD COST CARD – WIDGET

		$
Direct materials	0.5 kilos at $4 per kilo	2.00
Direct wages	2 hours at $2.00 per hour	4.00
Variable overheads	2 hours at $0.30 per hour	0.60
Fixed overhead	2 hours at $3.70 per hour	7.40
Standard cost		14.00
Standard profit		6.00
Standing selling price		20.00

Budgeted output for January was 5,100 units. Actual results for January were as follows.

Production of 4,850 units was sold for $95,600
Materials consumed in production amounted to 2,300 kilos at a total cost of $9,800
Labour hours paid for amounted to 8,500 hours at a cost of $16,800
Actual operating hours amounted to 8,000 hours
Variable overheads amounted to $2,600
Fixed overheads amounted to $42,300

Required

Calculate all variances and prepare an operating statement for January.

Answer

			$
(a)	2,300 kg of material should cost (× $4)		9,200
	but did cost		9,800
	Material price variance		600 (A)
(b)	4,850 Widgets should use (× 0.5 kg)		2,425 kg
	but did use		2,300 kg
	Material usage variance in kg		125 kg (F)
	× standard cost per kg		× $4
	Material usage variance in $		$ 500 (F)

294   **11: Variance analysis** │ Part C Budgeting and control

BPP
LEARNING MEDIA

(c)	8,500 hours of labour should cost ($\times$ $2)	17,000
	but did cost	16,800
	Labour rate variance	200 (F)

(d)	4,850 Widgets should take ($\times$ 2 hrs)	9,700 hrs
	but did take (active hours)	8,000 hrs
	Labour efficiency variance in hours	1,700 hrs (F)
	$\times$ standard cost per hour	$\times$ $2
	Labour efficiency variance in $	$3,400 (F)

| (e) | Idle time variance 500 hours (A) $\times$ $2 | $1,000 (A) |

(f)	8,000 hours incurring variable o/hd expenditure should cost ($\times$ $0.30)	2,400
	but did cost	2,600
	Variable overhead expenditure variance	200 (A)

| (g) | Variable overhead efficiency variance is the same as the labour efficiency variance: | |
| | 1,700 hours (F) $\times$ $0.30 per hour | $ 510 (F) |

(h)	Budgeted fixed overhead (5,100 units $\times$ 2 hrs $\times$ $3.70)	37,740
	Actual fixed overhead	42,300
	Fixed overhead expenditure variance	4,560 (A)

(i)	Actual production at standard rate (4,850 units $\times$ $7.40)	35,890
	Budgeted production at standard rate (5,100 units $\times$ $7.40)	37,740
	Fixed overhead volume variance	1,850 (A)

(j)	4,850 Widgets should have sold for ($\times$ $20)	97,000
	but did sell for	95,600
	Selling price variance	1,400 (A)

(k)	Budgeted sales volume	5,100 units
	Actual sales volume	4,850 units
	Sales volume variance in units	250 units (A)
	$\times$ standard profit per unit	$\times$ $6 (A)
	Sales volume variance in $	$1,500 (A)

	$	$
Budgeted profit (5,100 units $\times$ $6 profit)		30,600
Selling price variance	1,400 (A)	
Sales volume variance	1,500 (A)	
		2,900 (A)
Actual sales ($95,600) less the standard cost of sales (4,850 $\times$ $14)		27,700

OPERATING STATEMENT FOR JANUARY

	$	$
Budgeted profit		30,600
Sales variances: price	1,400 (A)	
volume	1,500 (A)	
		2,900 (A)
Actual sales minus the standard cost of sales		27,700

Cost variances

	(F) $	(A) $	
Material price		600	
Material usage	500		
Labour rate	200		
Labour efficiency	3,400		
Labour idle time		1,000	
Variable overhead expenditure		200	
Variable overhead efficiency	510		
Fixed overhead expenditure		4,560	
Fixed overhead volume		1,850	
	4,610	8,210	3,600 (A)
Actual profit for January			24,100

Check

	$	$
Sales		95,600
Materials	9,800	
Labour	16,800	
Variable overhead	2,600	
Fixed overhead	42,300	
		71,500
Actual profit		24,100

Exam focus point

Producing operating statements and reconciling actual profit to budgeted profit is **assumed knowledge** for F5 so it is **essential** to do more question practice if you struggled with this question.

3.1 Operating statements in a marginal cost environment

Knowledge brought forward from earlier studies

- There are two main differences between the variances calculated in an absorption costing system and the **variances calculated in a marginal costing system**. In a marginal costing system the only fixed overhead variance is an expenditure variance and the sales volume variance is valued at standard contribution margin, not standard profit margin.

Question   Marginal cost operating statement

Returning to the question above, now assume that the company operates a marginal costing system.

Required

Recalculate any variances necessary and produce an operating statement.

Answer

(a) There is no fixed overhead volume variance.

(b) The standard contribution per unit is $(20 − 6.60) = $13.40, therefore the sales volume variance of 250 units (A) is valued at (× $13.40) = $3,350 (A).

The other variances are unchanged, therefore an operating statement might appear as follows.

OPERATING STATEMENT FOR JANUARY

	$	$	$
Budgeted profit		30,600	
Budgeted fixed production costs		37,740	
Budgeted contribution		68,340	
Sales variances: volume		3,350 (A)	
price		1,400 (A)	
			4,750 (A)
Actual sales ($95,600) minus the standard			
variable cost of sales (4,850 × $6.60)			63,590

	(F)	(A)	
	$	$	$
Variable cost variances			
Material price		600	
Material usage	500		
Labour rate	200		
Labour efficiency	3,400		
Labour idle time		1,000	
Variable overhead expenditure		200	
Variable overhead efficiency	510		
	4,610	1,800	
			2,810 (F)
Actual contribution			66,400
Budgeted fixed production overhead		37,740	
Expenditure variance		4,560 (A)	
Actual fixed production overhead			42,300
Actual profit			24,100

Note. The profit here is the same as the profit calculated by standard absorption costing because there were no changes in inventory levels. Absorption costing and marginal costing do not always produce an identical profit figure.

4 Investigating variances

This topic should also be familiar to you from your earlier studies. The key points are recapped below.

Knowledge brought forward from earlier studies

The decision whether or not to investigate

- Before management decide whether or not to investigate the reasons for the occurrence of a particular variance, there are a number of **factors** which should be considered in assessing the **significance** of the variance.

    - **Materiality**. Because a standard cost is really only an **average** expected cost, small variations between actual and standard are bound to occur and are unlikely to be significant. Obtaining an 'explanation' of the reasons why they occurred is likely to be time consuming and irritating for the manager concerned. For such variations **further investigation is not worthwhile** since such variances are not controllable.

    - **Controllability**. Only controllable variances should be investigated. **Uncontrollable variances call for a change in plan, not an investigation into the past.**

    - **The type of standard being used**. The efficiency variance reported in any control period, whether for materials or labour, will depend on the **efficiency level set**. If, for example, an ideal standard is used, variances will always be adverse. Similarly, if basic standards are used, variances are likely to be favourable.

- **Variance trend**. Although small variations in a single period are unlikely to be significant, small variations that occur consistently may need more attention. The trend **provides an indication of whether the variance is fluctuating within acceptable control limits or becoming out of control**.

- **Interdependence between variances**. One variance might be interrelated with another, and much of it might have occurred only because the other variance occurred too. **When two variances are interdependent (interrelated) one will usually be adverse and the other favourable**. For example, an adverse selling price variance might be counterbalanced by a favourable sales volume variance.

- **Costs of investigation.** The costs of an investigation should be weighed against the benefits of correcting the cause of a variance.

Variance investigation models

- The **rule of thumb** and **statistical significance** variance investigation models and/or statistical **control charts** can be used to determine whether a variance should be investigated.

  - **The rule of thumb model**. This involves **deciding a limit**; if the size of a **variance is within the limit**, it should be considered **immaterial**. Only if it exceeds the limit is it considered materially significant, and worthy of investigation.

  - **Statistical significance model**. Historical data is used to **calculate** both a standard as **an expected average** and the **expected standard deviation** around this average when the process is under control. By assuming that variances that occur are normally distributed around this average, a **variance will be investigated if it is *more* than a distance from the expected average that the estimated normal distribution suggests is likely if the process is in control**.

  - **Statistical control charts**. By marking variances and control limits on a control chart, **investigation** is signalled not only when a particular **variance exceeds the control limit** but also when the **trend of variances shows a progressively worsening movement** in actual results (even though the variance in any single control period has not yet overstepped the control limit).

5 Materials mix and yield variances

6/10, 12/11, 12/14, Sep/Dec 15

FAST FORWARD

The **materials usage variance** can be subdivided into a materials **mix variance** and a materials **yield variance** when more than one material is used in the product.

However, calculating a mix and yield variance is only meaningful for control purposes when management is in a position to control the mix of materials used in production.

Exam focus point

There is an article on the ACCA website on material **mix** and **yield** variances written by a member of the examining team (ACCA, 2015). Ensure that you are familiar with this article.

Manufacturing processes often require that a number of different materials are combined to make a unit of finished product. When a product requires two or more raw materials in its make-up, it is often possible to **subanalyse the materials usage variance into a materials mix and a materials yield variance**.

Adding a greater proportion of one material (therefore a smaller proportion of a different material) might make the materials mix **cheaper or more expensive**. For example, the standard mix of materials for a product might consist of the following.

		$
(2/3)	2 kg of material A at $1.00 per kg	2.00
(1/3)	1 kg of material B at $0.50 per kg	0.50
		2.50

It may be possible to change the mix so that one kilogram of material A is used and two kilograms of material B. The new mix would be cheaper.

		$
(1/3)	1 kg of material A	1
(2/3)	2 kg of material B	1
		2

By changing the proportions in the mix, the **efficiency** of the combined material usage may change. In our example, in making the proportions of A and B cheaper, at 1:2, the product may now require more than three kilograms of input for its manufacture, and the new materials requirement per unit of product might be 3.6 kilograms.

		$
(1/3)	1.2 kg of material A at $1.00 per kg	1.20
(2/3)	2.4 kg of material B at $0.50 per kg	1.20
		2.40

In establishing a materials usage standard, management may therefore have to balance the **cost** of a particular mix of materials with the **efficiency** of the yield of the mix.

Once the standard has been established it may be possible for management to exercise control over the materials used in production by calculating and reviewing mix and yield variances.

Key terms

> A **mix variance** occurs when the materials are not mixed or blended in standard proportions and it is a measure of whether the actual mix is cheaper or more expensive than the standard mix.
>
> A **yield variance** arises because there is a difference between what the input should have been for the output achieved and the actual input.

5.1 When to calculate mix and yield variances

An exam question will indicate when you are required to calculate mix and yield variances. However, you should also be aware when mix and yield variances may be reported for variance analysis purposes.

(a)   **Reporting a mix and yield variance is an alternative to reporting the usage variance of each material separately**. If mix and yield variances are reported, usage variances are not reported.

(b)   A **mix variance has no practical meaning unless management is able to control the mix of materials** used in production. For example, management may be able to use a cheaper mix of materials (= favourable mix variance) by including a larger proportion of the cheapest material in the production mix.

(c)   A yield variance is a total usage variance for all the materials combined. If a mix variance is calculated, there must also be a yield variance.

It would be totally inappropriate to calculate a mix variance where the materials in the 'mix' are discrete items. A chair, for example, might consist of wood, covering material, stuffing and glue. These materials are separate components, and it would not be possible to think in terms of controlling the proportions of each material in the final product. The usage of each material must be controlled separately.

5.2 Calculating mix and yield variances

The **mix variance** is calculated as follows.

(a)   Take the **total actual quantity of materials used**.

(b)   Divide this total quantity of materials into the **standard mix** or standard proportions of the different materials used in the mix.

(c) For each item of materials, the difference between the actual quantity used and the quantity in the standard mix is a **mix variance**.

(d) Convert the mix variance for each item of material into a money value **by applying the standard price per unit** for the material.

(e) The total of the mix variance for each of the materials in the mix is the **total materials mix variance**.

The **yield variance** is calculated as follows.

(a) For the actual number of units of product manufactured, calculate the total quantity of materials that should have been used (a single total for all the materials in the mix).

(b) Compare this standard quantity of materials that should have been used with the actual total quantity of materials that was used.

(c) The difference is the yield variance in material quantities.

(d) Convert this into a monetary value by applying the weighted average cost per unit of material.

An **alternative method of calculating the yield variance** produces the same result.

(a) Take the actual total quantity of materials used and calculate how many units of output should have been produced with this quantity of materials. (This is the total quantity of materials actually used divided by the total quantity of materials in one standard unit of product.)

(b) Compare this with the actual number of units produced. The difference is the yield variance in units of finished product.

(c) Convert this into a monetary value by applying the standard material cost per unit of product.

5.3 Example: Materials usage, mix and yield variances

A company manufactures a chemical, Dynamite, using two compounds Flash and Bang. The standard materials usage and cost of one unit of Dynamite are as follows.

		$
Flash	5 kg at $2 per kg	10
Bang	10 kg at $3 per kg	30
		40

In a particular period, 80 units of Dynamite were produced from 600 kg of Flash and 750 kg of Bang.

Required

Calculate the materials usage, mix and yield variances.

Solution

(a) **Usage variance**

If we do not calculate a mix and yield variance, we would calculate a usage variance separately for each material.

	Std usage for actual output of 80 units kg	Actual usage kg	Variance kg	Standard cost per kg $	Variance $
Flash	400	600	200 (A)	2	400 (A)
Bang	800	750	50 (F)	3	150 (F)
	1,200	1,350			250 (A)

The total usage variance of $250 (A) can be analysed into a mix variance and a yield variance and these may be reported instead of the usage variance.

(b) **Mix variance**

To calculate the mix variance, it is first necessary to decide how the total quantity of materials used (600 kg + 750 kg) should have been divided between Flash and Bang. In other words, we need to **calculate the standard mix of the actual quantity of materials used**.

	Actual usage	Actual total usage in standard mix (5:10 or 1:2)	Mix variance
	kg	kg	kg
Flash	600	450	150 (A)
Bang	750	900	150 (F)
	1,350	1,350	0

The mix variance in total quantities is always 0. This must always be the case since the expected mix is based on the total quantity actually used, hence the difference between the total expected and total actual being zero.

However, the actual mix uses:

(a)   More of the cheaper material Flash (= adverse variance, because actual usage of Flash in the mix is more than the standard usage; therefore the cost for Flash is more); but

(b)   Less of the more expensive material Bang (= favourable variance, because actual usage of Bang in the mix is less than the standard usage; therefore the cost for Bang is lower).

Taking both materials together, the actual mix of materials is cheaper than the standard mix, and this will produce a favourable mix variance overall.

The mix variances in quantities are converted into a monetary value at the standard price of the materials.

	Actual usage/mix	Standard mix	Mix variance	Standard price	Mix variance
	kg	kg	kg	$ per kg	$
Flash	600	450	150 (A)	2	300 (A)
Bang	750	900	150 (F)	3	450 (F)
	1,350	1,350	0		150 (F)

The total mix variance is $150 (F).

(c) **Yield variance**

The yield variance can be calculated in total or for each individual material input.

Method 1

The weighted average cost per kilogram of materials = $40/15 kg = $2.67 per kg.

	kg
80 units of product should use in total (× 15 kg)	1,200
They did use (600 + 750)	1,350
Yield variance in kg	150 (A)
Weighted average price per kg	$2.67
Yield variance in $	$400 (A)

Method 2

	Units
1,350 kg of material should produce (÷ 15)	90
They did produce	80
Yield variance in units of output	10 (A)
Standard material cost per unit	$40
Yield variance in $	$400 (A)

The mix variance $150 (F) plus the yield variance $400 (A) add up to the usage variance $250 (A).

5.4 Interrelationship between mix and yield variance

A favourable mix variance occurs when the actual mix of materials is cheaper than the standard mix.

As a consequence of using a cheaper mix of materials, it is possible that the output/yield will be less than the standard output. In other words, a favourable mix variance may result in an adverse yield variance.

In the previous example, it is possible that by using a bigger proportion of Flash in the production mix, the actual yield of finished products (= 80 units) was less than it should have been (= 90 units).

For similar reasons, when there is an adverse mix variance because the actual mix of materials is more expensive than the standard mix, there may possibly be an interrelated favourable yield variance.

Question
Mix and yield variances

The standard materials cost of product D456 is as follows.

	$
Material X 3 kg at $2.00 per kg	6
Material Y 5 kg at $3.60 per kg	18
	24

During period 2, 2,000 kg of material X (costing $4,100) and 2,400 kg of material Y (costing $9,600) were used to produce 500 units of D456.

Required

Calculate the following variances.

(a)   Price variance
(b)   Mix variance
(c)   Yield variances – in total and for each individual material

Note. Yield variances for the individual materials are **meaningless variances**, but they have been examined once, so study the suggested solution carefully. They are calculated as the difference between:

- The standard quantity of each material for the units produced (so the standard quantities in the standard mix), and
- The actual total quantities of materials used in the standard mix.

These are converted into a monetary value at the standard price of the individual materials.

Answer

(a)

	$
2,000 kg of X should cost (× $2)	4,000
but did cost	4,100
Material X price variance	100 (A)
2,400 kg of Y should cost (× $3.60)	8,640
but did cost	9,600
Material Y price variance	960 (A)

(b)

	kg
Total quantity used (2,000 + 2,400) kg	4,400

		kg
Standard mix for actual use:	3/8 X	1,650
	5/8 Y	2,750
		4,400

	Actual quantity standard mix kg	Actual quantity actual mix kg	Mix variance kg	Standard cost per kg $	Mix variance $
X	1,650	2,000	350 (A)	2.00	700 (A)
Y	2,750	2,400	350 (F)	3.60	1,260 (F)
	4,400	4,400	–		560 (F)

(c)   Yield variance

Each unit of D456 requires

3 kg of X, costing		$6
5 kg of Y, costing		$18
8 kg		$24

4,400 kg should have yielded (÷ 8 kg)	550 units
but did yield	500 units
Yield variance in units	50 units (A)
× standard material cost per unit of output	× $24
Yield variance in $	$1,200 (A)

For individual materials

	Standard quantity standard mix kg	Actual quantity standard mix kg	Variance kg	Standard cost per kg $	Variance $
X	1,500	1,650	150 (A)	2.00	300 (A)
Y	2,500	2,750	250 (A)	3.60	900 (A)
	4,000	4,400	400 (A)		1,200 (A)

Exam focus point

With all variance calculations, it is vital that you do not simply learn formulae. You must have a thorough understanding of what your calculations are showing. This is especially true of the variances we will look at in this section and in Section 6.

5.5 Example: Losses, mix and yield

Sometimes there is expected loss in the production process.

Coope and Sorcerer Co make product T42 in a continuous process, for which standard and actual quantities in month 10 were as follows.

	Quantity kg	Standard Price per kg $	Value $	Quantity kg	Actual price per kg $	Std cost of actual usage $
Material P	40,000	2.50	100,000	34,000	2.50	85,000
Material Q	20,000	4.00	80,000	22,000	4.00	88,000
	60,000		180,000	56,000		173,000

Losses occur at an even rate during the processing operation and are expected to be 10% of materials input. So budgeted output for the month was 54,000 kg of T42 (= 60,000 kg × 90%). Actual output during the month was 51,300 kg of T42.

Required

Calculate total usage, mix and yield variances.

Solution

Usage variance

	Std usage for actual output of 51,300 kg kg	Actual usage kg	Variance kg	Standard cost per kg $	Variance $
Material P	38,000*	34,000	4,000 (F)	2.50	10,000 (F)
Material Q	19,000**	22,000	3,000 (A)	4	12,000 (A)
	57,000	56,000			2,000 (A)

* (51,300/54,000) × 40,000 = 38,000 kg

** (51,300/54,000) × 20,000 = 19,000 kg

The **total usage variance** is $2,000 (A).

Mix variance

	Actual usage/mix kg	Standard mix (2:1) kg	Mix variance kg	Standard price $ per kg	Mix variance $
Material P	34,000	37,333.33	3,333.33 (F)	2.50	8,333 (F)
Material Q	22,000	18,666.67	3,333.33 (A)	4	13,333 (A)
	56,000	56,000.00	0		5,000 (A)

The **mix variance is $5,000 (A)**.

Yield variance

The weighted average cost per kg of input materials = $180,000/60,000 = $3

	kg of material
51,300 kg of T34 should use (× 100/90)	57,000
They did use in total	56,000
Yield variance in units of T34	1,000 (F)
Standard material cost per kg of input material	$3
Yield variance in $	**$3,000 (F)**

Mix variance $5,000(A) + Yield variance $3,000 (F) = Usage variance $2,000 (A).

Exam focus point

> Question 5 of the December 2011 exam asked candidates to calculate materials usage, mix and yield (quantity) variances. The examining team noted that some candidates calculated the variances in kg but did not convert them into a monetary value using the standard costs for each ingredient.
>
> Variances need to be given a value in order to be used properly within a business. It is not sufficient to simply stop at quantity!

5.6 Issues involved in changing the mix

The materials mix variance indicates the **cost** of a change in the mix of materials and the yield variance indicates the **productivity** of the manufacturing process. A change in the mix can have wider implications. For example, rising raw material prices may cause pressure to change the mix of materials. Even if the yield is not affected by the change in the mix, the **quality** of the final product may change. This can have an adverse effect on sales if customers do not accept the change in quality. The production manager's performance may be measured by mix and yield variances but these **performance measures** may fail to indicate problems with falling quality and the impact on other areas of the business. **Quality targets** may also be needed.

5.7 Alternative methods of controlling production processes

In a modern manufacturing environment with an emphasis on quality management, using mix and yield variances for control purposes may not be possible or may be inadequate. Other control methods could be more useful.

- Rates of wastage
- Average cost of input calculations
- Percentage of deliveries on time
- Customer satisfaction ratings
- Yield percentage calculations or output to input conversion rates

We will be considering performance measures in more detail in Chapter 13.

6 Sales mix and quantity variances   6/14

FAST FORWARD

> The **sales volume variance** can be analysed further into a **sales mix variance** and a **sales quantity variance**. This may be useful for control purposes where management is in a position to control the sales mix; for example, through the allocation of spending on advertising and sales promotion.

6.1 Sales volume variance   12/14

You should be familiar with how to calculate the sales volume variance from your earlier studies. It measures the difference between the budgeted and actual sales volumes for each product, and the effect that this has had on profit. A sales volume variance in units of sale is converted into a monetary value by applying either the standard profit per unit (standard absorption costing) or the standard contribution per unit (standard marginal costing).

6.2 Sales mix and quantity variances   6/11, 6/13

If a company **sells more than one product**, it is possible to analyse the overall sales volume variance into a sales mix variance and a sales quantity variance.

Key terms

The **sales mix variance** occurs when the proportions of the various products sold are different from those in the budget.

The **sales quantity variance** shows the difference in contribution/profit because of a change in sales volume from the budgeted volume of sales.

6.3 When to calculate the mix and quantity variances

A sales mix variance and a sales quantity variance are only meaningful where management can control the proportions of the products sold.

Situations where management may be able to control the sales mix are:

(a)   Where management can control the allocation of the advertising and sales promotion budget between different products

(b)   Where the same basic product is sold in different sizes or packaging, such as large size and small size

6.4 The units method of calculation

The sales mix variance is calculated in a similar way to the materials mix variance.

(a)   Take the **total actual quantity of units sold**, for all the products combined.

(b)   Divide this total quantity of sales units into the **budgeted standard mix** or budgeted proportions of the different products in the mix.

(c) For each product, the difference between the actual quantity sold and the sales quantity in the budgeted standard mix is a **mix variance**.

(d) Convert the mix variance for each product into a monetary value by **applying the standard profit per unit** (or standard contribution per unit, where standard marginal costing is used).

(e) The total of the mix variance for each of the products in the sales mix is the **total sales mix variance**.

The **sales quantity variance** is calculated in a similar way to the materials yield variance, as follows.

(a) Calculate the weighted average standard profit per unit (or weighted average standard contribution per unit). This is calculated from the budget, as the budgeted total profit divided by the budgeted total units of sale.

(b) Calculate the difference between the actual total sales units and the budgeted total sales units. This difference is the sales quantity variance in units.

(c) Convert this variance in sales units into a monetary value by applying the weighted average standard profit (or standard contribution) per unit of sale.

The sales mix variance plus the sales quantity variance equals the total sales volume variance for all the products.

6.5 Example: Sales mix and quantity variances

Just Desserts Limited makes and sells two products, Chocolate Crunch and Strawberry Sundae. The budgeted sales and profit are as follows.

	Sales Units	Revenue $	Costs $	Profit $	Profit per unit $
Chocolate Crunch (CC)	400	8,000	6,000	2,000	5
Strawberry Sundae (SS)	300	12,000	11,100	900	3
				2,900	

Actual sales were 280 units of Chocolate Crunch and 630 units of Strawberry Sundae. The company management is able to control the relative sales of each product through the allocation of sales effort, advertising and sales promotion expenses.

Required

Calculate the sales volume variance, the sales mix variance and the sales quantity variance.

Solution

(a) **Sales volume variance**

	CC	SS
Budgeted sales	400 units	300 units
Actual sales	280 units	630 units
Sales volume variance in units	120 units (A)	330 units (F)
× standard profit per unit	× $5	× $3
Sales volume variance in $	$600 (A)	$990 (F)
Total **sales volume variance**		$390 (F)

The favourable sales volume variance indicates that profit was better than budget because on balance more units were sold than budgeted. However, the favourable variance may be due to selling a larger proportion of the more profitable product (sales mix variance) or selling more units in total (sales quantity variance).

Now we will see how to analyse this favourable volume variance into its mix and quantity elements.

(b) **Sales mix variance**

This is calculated in a similar way to the materials mix variance. Start with the total quantity of products sold and calculate what sales of each product would have been if they had been sold in the budgeted proportions.

	Actual sales mix	Standard sales mix (4:3)	Sales mix variance	Standard profit	Sales mix variance
	Units	Units	Units	$ per unit	$
CC	280	520	240 (A)	5	1,200 (A)
SS	630	390	240 (F)	3	720 (F)
	910	910	0		480 (A)

The total sales mix variance is $480 (A).

(c) **Sales quantity variance**

The standard weighted average profit per unit of sale, taken from the budget, is $2,900/700 = $29/7

	Units
Budgeted sales in total	700
Actual sales in total	910
Sales quantity variance in units	210 (F)
Standard weighted average profit per unit	$29/7
Sales quantity variance in $	**$870 (F)**

Sales mix variance $480 (A) + Sales quantity variance $870 (F) = Sales volume variance $390 (F).

The overall favourable sales volume variance was achieved by selling products in a cheaper sales mix, but achieving a higher total quantity of sales units than budgeted.

Exam focus point

Try not to confuse the sales volume profit variance with the sales quantity profit variance. The examining team has noted that candidates often learn formulae to churn out calculations, but do not appreciate what variances mean to a business. Make sure you understand why sales mix and quantity variances occur.

Chapter Roundup

- The **materials usage variance** can be subdivided into a materials **mix** variance and a materials **yield** variance when more than one material is used in the product.

- However, calculating a mix and yield variance is only meaningful for control purposes when management is in a position to control the mix of materials used in production.

- The **sales volume variance** can be analysed further into a **sales mix variance** and a **sales quantity variance**. This may be useful for control purposes where management is in a position to control the sales mix; for example, through the allocation of spending on advertising and sales promotion.

Quick Quiz

1   Fill in the blanks.

    The material price variance is the difference between ……………………………… and
    ………………………………

    The material usage variance is the difference between ……………………………… and
    ………………………………

2   If closing inventories of raw materials are valued at standard cost, the material price variance is calculated on material purchases in the period.

    True ☐   False ☐

3   Are variable production overhead variances based on hours paid or hours worked?

4   Fill in the boxes in the diagram with the names of the variances and add the appropriate definition number from the list below.

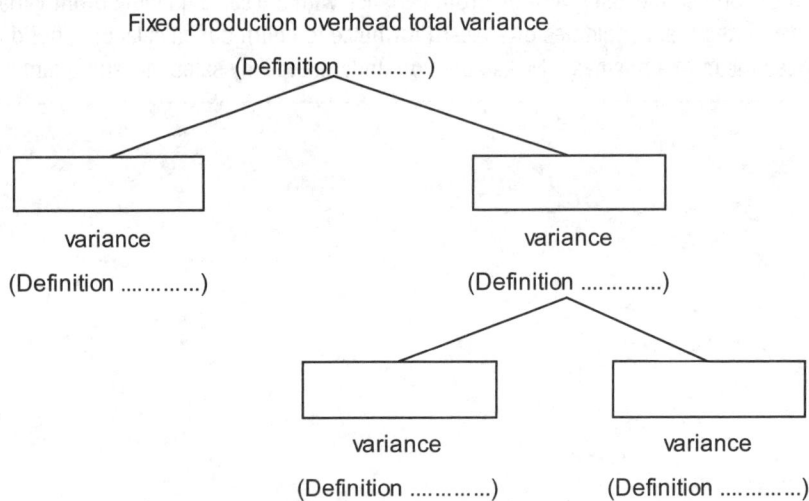

Fixed production overhead total variance

(Definition ………….)

variance

(Definition ………….)

variance

(Definition ………….)

variance

(Definition ………….)

variance

(Definition ………….)

Definitions

(1)   The difference between actual and budgeted production, multiplied by the standard absorption rate per unit

(2)   The difference between budgeted hours of work and the actual hours worked, multiplied by the standard absorption rate per hour

(3)   The under- or over-absorption of fixed production overhead

(4)   The difference between budgeted fixed production overhead expenditure and actual fixed production overhead expenditure

(5)   The difference between the number of hours that actual production should have taken, and the number of hours actually taken, multiplied by the standard absorption rate per hour

5   The sales volume variance is valued at the standard selling price per unit.

     True ☐   False ☐

6   Match the following causes of variances to the appropriate variance.

Variances		Causes	
(a)	Favourable labour efficiency	(1)	Inexperienced staff in the purchasing department
(b)	Adverse sales volume	(2)	Materials of higher quality than standard
(c)	Adverse material price	(3)	Unexpected slump in demand
(d)	Adverse selling price	(4)	Production difficulties
(e)	Adverse fixed production overhead volume	(5)	Strike
(f)	Idle time	(6)	Poor machine maintenance

7   Match the three pairs of interrelated variances.

(a)	Adverse selling price	(e)	Adverse materials price
(b)	Favourable labour rate	(f)	Favourable materials usage
(c)	Adverse materials usage	(g)	Adverse sales volume
(d)	Favourable sales volume	(h)	Idle time

8   Choose the appropriate words from those highlighted.

The materials mix variance is calculated as the difference between the **standard/actual** total quantity used in the **standard/actual** mix and the **standard/actual** quantities used in the **standard/actual** mix, valued at **standard/actual** costs.

9   Choose the appropriate words from those highlighted.

The materials yield variance is calculated on the difference between the **standard/actual** input for **standard/actual** output, and the **standard/actual** total quantity input (in the **standard/actual** mix), valued at **standard/actual** costs.

10   The total yield variance in quantity is zero.

     True ☐   False ☐

11   Choose the appropriate words from those highlighted

The sales mix variance is calculated as the difference between the **standard/actual** quantity sold in the **standard/actual** mix and the **standard/actual** quantity sold in the **standard/actual** mix, valued at **standard/actual** margin per unit.

12   Choose the appropriate words from those highlighted

The sales quantity variance is calculated as the difference between the **standard/actual** sales volume in the budgeted proportions and the budgeted sales volumes, multiplied by the **standard/actual** margin.

1   The material price variance is the difference between **what the material did cost** and what it should have cost.

The material usage variance is the difference between the standard cost of the material that should have been used and the standard cost of the material that was used.

2   True

3   Variable production overhead variances are based on hours worked.

4

Fixed production overhead total variance

(Definition 3)

Expenditure		Volume

variance   variance

(Definition 4)   (Definition 1)

Volume efficiency		Volume capacity

variance   variance

(Definition 5)   (Definition 2)

5   False. It is valued at the standard profit margin per unit.

6   (a)   (2)   (d)   (3)
    (b)   (3) or (4) or (5)   (e)   (4) or (5) or (6)
    (c)   (1)   (f)   (5) or (6)

7   (a) and (d)
    (b) and (c)
    (e) and (f)

8   The materials mix variance is calculated as the difference between the **actual** total quantity used in the **standard** mix, and the **actual** quantities used in the **actual** mix, valued at **standard** costs.

9   The materials yield variance is calculated as the difference between the **standard** input for **actual** output, and the **actual** total quantity input (in the **standard** mix), valued at **standard** costs.

10 False. It is the total mix variance in quantity which is zero.

11 The sales mix variance is calculated as the difference between the **actual** quantity sold in the **standard** mix and the **actual** quantity sold in the **actual** mix, valued at **standard** margin per unit.

12 The sales quantity variance is calculated as the difference between the **actual** sales volume in the budgeted proportions and the budgeted sales volumes, multiplied by the **standard** margin.

Now try the questions below from the Practice Question Bank

Number	Level	Marks	Approximate time
Section A Q66	Examination	2	4 mins
Section A Q67	Examination	2	4 mins
Section A Q68	Examination	2	4 mins
Section A Q69	Examination	2	4 mins
Section A Q70	Examination	2	4 mins
Section C Q7	Examination	20	39 mins

12

Planning and operational variances

Topic list	Syllabus reference
1 Revising a budget or standard cost	C6 (a), (b), (d)
2 Planning and operational variances for sales: market size and market share variances	C6 (c)
3 Planning and operational variances for materials	C6 (c)
4 Planning and operational variances for labour	C6 (c)
5 The value of planning and operational variances	C6 (b), (d)

Introduction

In this chapter we discuss the circumstances in which management may consider it appropriate to revise the budget or the standard cost.

When a budget or standard cost is revised after the budget period has begun, the reporting of variances should allow for this revision. One way of doing this is to present variances in the form of planning variances and operational variances.

We also discuss the problems of using standard costing in the modern, rapidly changing business environment.

Study guide

		Intellectual level
C6	**Planning and operational variances**	
(a)	Calculate a revised budget.	2
(b)	Identify and explain those factors that could and could not be allowed to revise an original budget.	2
(c)	Calculate, identify the cause of and explain planning and operational variances for: (i) Sales, including market size and market share (ii) Materials (iii) Labour, including the effect of the learning curve	2
(d)	Explain and discuss the manipulation issues in revising budgets.	2

Exam guide

Planning and operational variances are likely to be a frequently examined topic.

> One of the competencies you require to fulfil performance objective 13 of the PER is to monitor business activities. You can apply the knowledge you obtain from this section of the text to help to demonstrate this competence.

1 Revising a budget or standard cost

> **FAST FORWARD**
>
> Occasionally, it may be appropriate to **revise a budget or standard cost**. When this happens, variances should be reported in a way that distinguishes between variances caused by the revision to the budget and variances that are the responsibility of operational management.
>
> A planning and operational approach to variance analysis divides the total variance into those variances which have arisen because of inaccurate planning or faulty standards (**planning variances**) and those variances which have been caused by adverse or favourable operational performance, compared with a standard which has been revised in hindsight (**operational variances**).

1.1 Reasons for revising a budget or standard cost

When variances are reported in a system of budgetary control, it is usually assumed that:

(a)   The original budget or standard cost is fairly accurate or reliable.

(b)   Any differences between actual results and the budget or standard, measured as variances, are attributable to the manager who is responsible for that aspect of performance.

The manager responsible will be expected to explain the reasons for any significant variances and, where appropriate, take measures to rectify problems causing an adverse variance.

Occasionally, however, circumstances may occur that make the original budget or standard cost invalid or inappropriate.

(a)   The sales budget may have been based on expectations of the total size of the market for the organisation's product. However, due to an unexpected change in economic conditions, an unexpected technological change, a radical change in customer attitudes or unexpected new regulations affecting the marketability of a product, the market size may be much larger or much smaller than assumed when the sales budget was prepared.

(b) The standard cost of materials for a product may have been based on an assumption about what the market price for the materials should be. However, due to a major change in the market, the available market price for the materials may become much higher or much lower than originally expected when the standard cost was prepared.

(c) The standard quantity of materials for a product may be significantly altered due to an unexpected change in the product specification, requiring much more or much less of the material in the product content.

(d) The standard labour rate may become unrealistic due to an unexpected increase in pay rates for employees.

(e) The standard time to produce a unit of product may also change for unexpected reasons.

If the budget or standard cost is not revised in these circumstances, variances reported to operational managers will be unrealistic. A large part of the **variances will be due to changes that are outside the control of the operational managers**.

In these circumstances, it may be appropriate to revise the budget or revise the standard cost.

1.2 Calculating a revised budget   12/07

The syllabus requires you to be able to calculate a revised budget, which could involve revising standards for sales, materials and/or labour so that only operational variances are highlighted when actual results are compared to the revised budget.

1.2.1 Example: Revised budget

A company produces Widgets and Splodgets which are fairly standardised products. The following information relates to period 1.

The standard selling price of Widgets is $50 each and Splodgets $100 each. In Period 1, there was a special promotion on Splodgets with a 5% discount being offered. All units produced are sold and no inventory is held.

To produce a Widget they use 5 kg of X and in Period 1, their plans were based on a cost of X of $3 per kg. Due to market movements the actual price changed; if they had purchased efficiently, the cost would have been $4.50 per kg. Production of Widgets was 2,000 units.

A Splodget uses raw material Z but again the price of this can change rapidly. It was thought that Z would cost $30 per tonne but in fact they only paid $25 per tonne and if they had purchased correctly the cost would have been less, as it was freely available at only $23 per tonne. It usually takes 1.5 tonnes of Z to produce 1 Splodget and 500 Splodgets are usually produced.

Each Widget takes three hours to produce and each Splodget two hours. Labour is paid $5 per hour. At the start of Period 1, management negotiated a job security package with the workforce in exchange for a promised 5% increase in efficiency – that is, that the workers would increase output per hour by 5%.

Fixed overheads are usually $12,000 every period and variable overheads are $3 per labour hour.

Required

Produce the original budget and a revised budget allowing for controllable factors in a suitable format.

Solution

Original budget for Period 1

	$
Sales revenue ((2,000 × $50) + (500 × $100))	150,000
Material costs X (2,000 × 5kg × $3)	30,000
Material costs Z (500 × $30 × 1.5)	22,500
Labour costs ((2,000 × 3 × $5) + (500 × 2 × $5))	35,000

Variable overheads ((2,000 × 3 × $3) + (500 × 2 × $3))	21,000
Fixed overheads	12,000
Profit	29,500

Revised budget for Period 1

	$
Sales revenue ((2,000 × $50) + (500 × $100))	150,000
Material costs X (2,000 × 5kg × $4.5)	45,000
Material costs Z (500 × $23 × 1.5)	17,250
Labour costs ((2,000 × 3 × $5) + (500 × 2 × $5)) × 0.95	33,250
Variable overheads ((2,000 × 3 × $3) + (500 × 2 × $3)) × 0.95	19,950
Fixed overheads	12,000
Profit	22,550

1.2.2 When should budget revisions be allowed?

A budget revision should be allowed if something has happened which is **beyond the control** of the organisation or individual manager and which makes the original budget unsuitable for use in performance management.

Any adjustment should be **approved by senior management** who should look at the issues involved **objectively** and **independently**. **Operational issues** are the issues that a budget is attempting to control so they should **not** be subject to revision. However, it can be very **difficult to establish** what is due to operational problems (controllable) and what is due to planning (uncontrollable).

1.3 The nature of planning and operational variances

When a budget or standard cost is revised, variances are still reported as a **comparison between actual results and the original budget or standard cost**.

However, when variances are reported, a **clear distinction** should be made between:

(a)   Variances that have been caused by the revision in the budget or standard cost, for which operational managers should not be made responsible: these are called **planning variances**

(b)   Variances that are caused by differences between actual performance and the revised budget or standard, for which operational managers should be made responsible and accountable: these are called **operational variances**

Planning variances are calculated by comparing the original budget/standard cost with the revised budget/standard cost.

Operational variances are calculated in the same way as 'normal' basic variances, except that they are based on a comparison between actual results and the revised budget/standard cost.

1.4 Revising budgets: manipulation issues

When a budget or standard cost is revised, there is a potential problem. The budget or standard cost may be revised in such a way that all the reported operational variances become favourable variances, and the reason why actual results may be worse than budget is attributable entirely to planning variances, for which operational managers cannot be held responsible.

In other words, the revision to the budget or standard cost may be manipulated in such a way as to make operating results seem much better than is really the case.

To prevent manipulation, there should be strict rules about revising a budget or standard cost. In particular, the revision to the budget or standard cost should ideally be based on independent evidence (and verifiable evidence) that operational managers are not in a position to manipulate.

For example:

(a) If there is an unexpected change in the total size of the market for the company's product, there should ideally be independent evidence from an external source (such as a market research firm) about the revised expectations of the market size.

(b) If there is an unexpected change in the market price for materials, there should ideally be an official price index or price benchmark for the material item.

(c) If there is an unexpected change in the standard material usage for a product, this should ideally be evidenced by a documented change in the product specification.

Independent evidence may be difficult to obtain in many cases. When it is not available, the potential for manipulation of planning and operational variances should be recognised.

2 Planning and operational variances for sales: market size and market share variances

FAST FORWARD

> A sales budget may be revised when it is recognised that the original sales budget was based on expectations of the total market size that in retrospect are seen to be inappropriate and unrealistic.
>
> **When the sales budget is revised**, a **sales volume planning variance** may be reported. This is the difference in profit caused by the difference between the original sales budget and the revised sales budget. This planning variance is called a **market size variance**.
>
> **When the sales budget is revised**, a **sales volume operational variance** may be reported, for which operational sales managers should be held responsible. This is the difference in profit caused by the difference between actual sales volume and the sales volume in the revised sales budget. This operational variance is called a **market share variance**.

When the sales budget is revised it may be assumed that:

(a) The revision to the sales budget was due to a reassessment of the total market size for the organisation's product.

(b) However, sales management should still be expected to win the same market share (as a proportion of the total market size) as in the original budget.

On the basis of this assumption, the sales volume variance can be reported as:

(a) A **sales volume planning variance**, or **market size variance**, which is caused by the difference between the sales volume in the original budget and the sales volume in the revised budget

(b) A **sales volume operational variance**, or **market share variance**, which is caused by the difference between actual sales volume and the sales volume in the revised budget

As there has been no change in the budgeted sales price or standard cost of products, these two variances can be converted from units into a monetary value by multiplying the variance in units by the standard profit (or standard contribution) per unit.

2.1 Example: market size and market share variance

Dimsek budgeted to make and sell 400 units of its product, the Role, in the four-week period no. 8, as follows.

	$
Budgeted sales (100 units per week)	40,000
Variable costs (400 units × $60)	24,000
Contribution	16,000
Fixed costs	10,000
Profit	6,000

At the beginning of the second week, production came to a halt because inventories of raw materials ran out, and a new supply was not received until the beginning of Week 3. As a consequence, the company lost one week's production and sales. Actual results in Period 8 were as follows.

	$
Sales (320 units)	32,000
Variable costs (320 units × $60)	19,200
Contribution	12,800
Fixed costs	10,000
Actual profit	2,800

In retrospect, it is decided that the optimum budget, given the loss of production facilities in the third week, would have been to sell only 300 units in the period.

Required

Calculate appropriate planning and operational variances for sales volume.

Solution

The **sales volume planning** variance **compares the revised budget** with the **original budget**. It may be called a market size variance.

Revised sales volume, given materials shortage	300 units
Original budgeted sales volume	400 units
Sales volume planning variance in units of sales	100 units (A)
× standard contribution per unit	× $40
Sales volume planning variance in $	$4,000 (A)

Arguably, **running out of raw materials is an operational error** and so the loss of sales volume and contribution from the materials shortage is an opportunity cost that could have been avoided with better purchasing arrangements. The operational variances are variances calculated in the usual way, except that actual results are compared with the revised standard or budget. There is a sales volume variance which is an **operational variance**, as follows.

Actual sales volume	320 units
Revised sales volume	300 units
Operational sales volume variance in units	20 units (F)
(possibly due to production efficiency or marketing efficiency)	
× standard contribution per unit	× $40
Operational sales volume variance in $ contribution	$800 (F)

The operational variance for sales volume may be called a market share variance. These planning and operational variances for sales volume can be used as **control information** to reconcile budgeted and actual profit.

	$	$
Operating statement, Period 8		
Budgeted profit		6,000
Planning variance: sales volume	4,000 (A)	
Operational variance: sales volume	800 (F)	
		3,200 (A)
Actual profit in Period 8		2,800

You may have noticed that, in this example, sales volume variances were **valued at contribution forgone**. This is because it is assumed that a marginal costing system applies.

✏️ **Question**   **Sales volumes**

PG budgeted sales for 20X8 were 5,000 units. The standard contribution is $9.60 per unit. A recession in 20X8 meant that the market for PG's products declined by 5%. PG's market share also fell by 3%. Actual sales were 4,500 units.

Required

Calculate planning and operational variances for sales volume.

Answer

Planning variance

	Units
Original budgeted sales	5,000
Revised budget sales (–5%)	4,750
	250 A
@ Contribution per unit of $9.60	$2,400

Operational variance

	Units
Revised budget sales	4,750
Actual sales	4,500
	250 A
@ Contribution per unit of $9.60	$2,400

The fall in **market size** is uncontrollable by the management of PG and therefore results in a **planning** variance. The fall in **market share** is controllable and forms part of the **operational** variance.

2.2 Planning and operational variances for sales price

There may be a situation where a revision is made to the budgeted or standard selling price for a product. When this happens, a sales price planning variance and a sales price operational variance can be calculated.

The planning variance is generally outside the control of sales management, but the operational sales price variance is a sales management responsibility.

Question
Planning and operational sales variances

KSO budgeted to sell 10,000 units of a new product during 20X0. The budgeted sales price was $10 per unit, and the variable cost $3 per unit.

Actual sales in 20X0 were 12,000 units and variable costs of sales were $30,000, but sales revenue was only $5 per unit. With the benefit of hindsight, it is realised that the budgeted sales price of $10 was hopelessly optimistic, and a price of $4.50 per unit would have been much more realistic.

Required

Calculate planning and operational variances for sales price.

Answer

The only variances are selling price variances.

Planning (selling price) variance

	$ per unit
Original budgeted sales price	10.00
Revised budgeted sales price	4.50
Sales price planning variance	5.50 (A)

The planning variance is adverse because the revised sales price is lower than the sales price in the original budget. As a result, actual profit will not achieve the budgeted profit level.

The **total sales price planning variance is obtained by multiplying the planning variance per unit by the actual number of units sold** (not the budgeted number of units sold).

Sales price planning variance = $5.50 per unit (A) × 12,000 units sold

= **$66,000 (A).**

Operational (selling price) variance

The **sales price operational variance** is calculated in the same way as a 'normal' sales price variance, except that the sales price in the revised budget is used, not the original budget.

	$
12,000 units sold for (12,000 × $5)	60,000
They should have sold for (× $4.5)	54,000
Operational (selling price) variance	**6,000** (F)

3 Planning and operational variances for materials

12/13, Specimen

FAST FORWARD

Planning and operational variances can be reported for direct materials, when the standard cost is revised for the material price, material usage per unit, or both.

The same basic principles can be applied to calculating planning and operational variances for materials, when the standard material cost per unit is changed.

However:

- Operational variances are reported as a materials price and a materials usage variance. Should these variances be calculated using the original standard cost or the revised standard cost?

- The planning variance for materials is the difference between the original standard and the revised standard. But should they be converted into a total monetary value using actual material quantities or standard material quantities?

An additional problem, and one that you may be expected to deal with in your exam, is that the revised standard for materials may contain a revision to both the material price and the material quantity per unit.

The calculation of planning and operational variances for materials will be explained with two examples. The first example revises just one aspect of the standard material cost. The second example revises both the standard unit price of materials and the standard material usage per unit of product.

3.1 Example 1: Planning price and usage variances

Product X had a standard direct material cost in the budget of:

4 kg of Material M at $5 per kg = $20 per unit.

Due to disruption of supply of materials to the market, the average market price for Material M during the period was $5.50 per kg, and it was decided to revise the material standard cost to allow for this.

During the period, 6,000 units of Product X were manufactured. They required 26,300 kg of Material M, which cost $139,390.

Required

Calculate:

(a)   The material price planning variance
(b)   The material price operational variance
(c)   The material usage (operational) variance

Solution

The original standard cost was 4 kg × $5 = $20. The revised standard cost is 4 kg × $5.50 = $22.

Material price planning variance

This is the difference between the original standard price for Material M and the revised standard price.

	$ per kg
Original standard price	5.00
Revised standard price	5.50
Material price planning variance	0.50 (A)

The planning variance is adverse because the change in the standard price increases the material cost and this will result in lower profit.

The material price planning variance is converted into a total monetary amount by multiplying the planning variance per kg of material by the **actual quantity of materials used**.

Material price planning variance = 26,300 kg × $0.50 (A) = $13,150 (A).

Material price operational variance

This compares the actual price per kg of material with the revised standard price. It is calculated using the actual quantity of materials used.

	$
26,300 kg of Material M should cost (revised standard $5.50)	144,650
They did cost	139,390
Material price operational variance	5,260 (F)

Material usage operational variance

This variance is calculated by comparing the actual material usage with the standard usage in the revised standard, but it is then **converted into a monetary value by applying the original standard price for the materials, not the revised standard price**. This is an important rule.

	kg of M
6,000 units of Product X should use (× 4kg)	24,000
They did use	26,300
Material usage (operational) variance in kg of M	2,300 (A)
Original standard price per kg of Material M	$5
Material usage (operational) variance in $	$11,500 (A)

The variances may be summarised as follows.

	$	$
6,000 units of Product X at original std cost ($20)		120,000
Actual material cost		139,390
Total material cost variance		19,390 (A)
Material price planning variance	13,150 (A)	
Material price operational variance	5,260 (F)	
Material usage operational variance	11,500 (A)	
Total of variances		19,390 (A)

3.2 Example 2: Planning price and usage variances

The standard materials cost of a product is 5 kg × $7.50 per kg = $37.50. Actual production of 10,000 units used 54,400 kg at a cost of $410,000.

In retrospect it was realised that the standard materials cost should have been 5.3 kg per unit at a cost of $8 per kg. The standard cost was revised to this amount.

Required

Calculate the materials planning and operational variances in as much detail as possible.

Solution

Original standard cost: 5 kg × $7.50 per kg = $37.50 per unit of product

Revised standard cost: 5.3 kg × $8 per kg = $42.40 per unit of product

In this example, both the material price and the material usage per unit have been revised. There are planning variances for both material price and material usage.

Material price planning variance

This is the difference between the original standard price and the revised standard price.

	$ per kg
Original standard price	7.50
Revised standard price	8.00
Material price planning variance	0.50 (A)

The planning variance is adverse. The variance is converted into a total monetary amount by multiplying the planning variance per kg of material by the **actual quantity of materials used**.

Material price planning variance = 54,400 kg × $0.50 (A) = **$27,200 (A)**.

Material usage planning variance

This is the difference between the original standard usage and the revised standard usage for the quantity of units produced. **The usage planning variance is converted into a total monetary value by applying the original standard price for the material, not the revised standard price.**

	kg
10,000 units of product X should use: original standard	50,000
10,000 units of product X should use: revised standard	53,000
Material usage planning variance in kg of material	3,000 (A)
Original standard price per kg of material	$7.50
Material usage planning variance in $	$22,500 (A)

The planning variance is adverse because the revised standard is for a higher usage quantity (so higher cost and lower profit).

Material price operational variance

This is calculated using the actual quantity of materials used.

	$
54,400 kg of material should cost (revised standard $8)	435,200
They did cost	410,000
Material price operational variance	25,200 (F)

Material usage operational variance

This variance is calculated by comparing the actual material usage with the standard usage in the revised standard, and is then **converted into a monetary value by applying the original standard price for the materials**.

	kg
10,000 units of product X should use (× 5.3 kg)	53,000
They did use	54,400
Material usage (operational) variance in kg of material	1,400 (A)
Original standard price per kg of Material M	$7.50
Material usage (operational) variance in $	$10,500 (A)

The variances may be summarised as follows.

	$	$
10,000 units of product at original std cost ($37.50)		375,000
Actual material cost		410,000
Total material cost variance		35,000 (A)
Material price planning variance	27,200 (A)	
Material usage planning variance	22,500 (A)	
Material price operational variance	25,200 (F)	
Material usage operational variance	10,500 (A)	
Total of variances		35,000 (A)

4 Planning and operational variances for labour 12/12, 6/15, Mar/Jun 16

FAST FORWARD

> Planning and operational variances can be reported for direct labour, when the standard cost is revised for the labour rate per hour, the standard labour time per unit, or both.

Precisely the same argument applies to the calculation of operational variances for labour, and the examples already given should be sufficient to enable you to do the next question. If you are not sure, check the solution carefully.

Question   Planning and operational labour variances

A company makes a single product. At the beginning of the budget year, the standard labour cost was established as $8 per unit, and each unit should take 0.5 hours to make.

However, during the year, the standard labour cost was revised. A new quality control procedure was introduced to the production process, adding 20% to the expected time to complete a unit. In addition, due to severe financial difficulties facing the company, the workforce reluctantly agreed to reduce the rate of pay to $15 per hour.

In the first month after revision of the standard cost, budgeted production was 15,000 units but only 14,000 units were actually produced. These took 8,700 hours of labour time, which cost $130,500.

Required

Calculate the labour planning and operational variances in as much detail as possible.

Answer

Original standard cost = 0.5 hours × $16 per hour = $8 per unit

Revised standard = 0.6 hours × $15 per hour = $9 per unit

Planning and operational variances for labour are calculated in a similar way to planning and operational variances for materials. We need to look at planning and operational variances for labour rate and labour efficiency.

Labour rate planning variance

This is the difference between the original standard rate per hour and the revised standard rate per hour.

	$ per hour
Original standard rate	16
Revised standard rate	15
Labour rate planning variance	1 (F)

The planning variance for labour rate is favourable, because the revised hourly rate is lower than in the original standard. The variance is converted into a total monetary amount by multiplying the planning variance per hour by the **actual number of hours worked**.

Labour rate planning variance = 8,700 hours × $1 (F) = **$8,700 (F)**.

Labour efficiency planning variance

This is the difference between the original standard time per unit and the revised standard time, for the quantity of units produced. **The efficiency planning variance is converted into a total monetary value by applying the original standard rate per hour, not the revised standard rate.**

	Hours
14,000 units of product should take: original standard (× 0.5)	7,000
14,000 units of product should take: revised standard (× 0.6)	8,400
Labour efficiency planning variance in hours	1,400 (A)
Original standard rate per hour	$16
Labour efficiency planning variance in $	$22,400 (A)

The planning variance is adverse because the revised standard is for a longer time per unit (so higher cost and lower profit).

Labour rate operational variance

This is calculated using the actual number of hours worked and paid for.

	$
8,700 hours should cost (revised standard $15)	130,500
They did cost	130,500
Labour rate operational variance	0

In this example, the workforce was paid exactly the revised rate of pay per hour.

Labour efficiency operational variance

This variance is calculated by comparing the actual time to make the output units with the standard time in the revised standard. It is then **converted into a monetary value by applying the original standard rate per hour**.

	Hours
14,000 units of product should take (× 0.6 hours)	8,400
They did take	8,700
Labour efficiency (operational variance in hours)	300 (A)
Original standard rate per hour	$16
Labour efficiency (operational variance in $)	$4,800 (A)

The variances may be summarised as follows.

	$	$
14,000 units of product at original standard cost ($8)		112,000
Actual material cost		130,500
Total material cost variance		18,500 (A)
Labour rate planning variance	8,700 (F)	
Labour efficiency planning variance	22,400 (A)	
Labour rate operational variance	0	
Labour efficiency operational variance	4,800 (A)	
Total of variances		18,500 (A)

4.1 Labour planning variances and the learning curve

The learning curve was described in a previous chapter, where it was explained that when a learning curve applies to the manufacture of a new product, it is not possible to establish a standard labour cost. This is because the expected time to make each unit falls with each additional unit that is produced.

A standard labour cost can only be established when a 'steady state' is reached and production of each additional unit should take the same amount of time.

In principle, however, it would be possible to combine standard costing with the learning curve, as follows.

(a) Establish an original standard labour cost per unit, even though a learning effect will apply to production.

(b) At the end of the budget period, revise the standard time per unit. The revised standard time could be calculated using the learning curve formula and applying this to the number of units produced in the period.

(c) With the original standard cost and the revised standard cost, planning and operational variances for labour can be calculated. Because of the learning effect, the labour efficiency planning variance will always be favourable.

The examining team is very keen that candidates understand the practical problems involved with these variances and do not just concentrate on the mechanics of the calculations.

5 The value of planning and operational variances

Advantages of a system of planning and operational variances

- The analysis highlights those variances which are **controllable** (operational variances) and those which are **non-controllable** (planning variances).

- **Managers' acceptance** of the use of variances for performance measurement, and their **motivation**, is likely to increase if they know they will not be held responsible for poor planning and faulty standard setting.

- The **planning and standard-setting processes** should improve; standards should be more accurate, relevant and appropriate.

- Operational variances will provide a more realistic and **'fair' reflection of actual performance**.

Limitations of planning and operational variances, which must be overcome if they are to be applied in practice

- It is difficult to **decide in hindsight** what the **realistic standard** should have been.

- It may become **too easy to justify all the variances as being due to bad planning**, so no operational variances will be highlighted.

- Establishing realistic revised standards and analysing the total variance into planning and operational variances can be a **time-consuming** task, even if a spreadsheet package is devised.

- Even though the intention is to provide more meaningful information, **managers may be resistant** to the very idea of variances and refuse to see the virtues of the approach. Careful presentation and explanation will be required until managers are used to the concepts.

Chapter Roundup

- Occasionally, it may be appropriate to **revise a budget or standard cost**. When this happens, variances should be reported in a way that distinguishes between variances caused by the revision to the budget and variances that are the responsibility of operational management.

- A planning and operational approach to variance analysis divides the total variance into those variances which have arisen because of inaccurate planning or faulty standards (**planning variances**) and those variances which have been caused by adverse or favourable operational performance, compared with a standard which has been revised in hindsight (**operational variances**).

- A sales budget may be revised when it is recognised that the original sales budget was based on expectations of the total market size that in retrospect are seen to be inappropriate and unrealistic.

- **When the sales budget is revised**, a **sales volume planning variance** may be reported. This is the difference in profit caused by the difference between the original sales budget and the revised sales budget. This planning variance is called a **market size variance**.

- **When the sales budget is revised**, a **sales volume operational variance** may be reported, for which operational sales managers should be held responsible. This is the difference in profit caused by the difference between actual sales volume and the sales volume in the revised sales budget. This operational variance is called a **market share variance**.

- Planning and operational variances can be reported for direct materials, when the standard cost is revised for the material price, material usage per unit, or both.

- Planning and operational variances can be reported for direct labour, when the standard cost is revised for the labour rate per hour, the standard labour time per unit, or both.

Quick Quiz

1   A planning variance compares what with what?

2   If a planning efficiency variance is valued at an original standard rate, the planning rate variance is valued at the original efficiency level.

    True   ☐   False   ☐

3   A standard material cost is revised and the standard quantity of material required per unit is reduced in the revised standard, compared with the original standard. At the same time, the standard rate per unit of material is increased in the revised standard.

    (a)   The material price planning variance is _____ (favourable/adverse)

    (b)   The material usage planning variance is _____ (favourable/adverse)

4   The standard labour rate per hour in an original standard cost is $10. The standard cost is revised, and the revised labour rate per hour is $12. The labour efficiency variance in hours is 2,000 hours adverse. What is the labour efficiency operational variance in $?

    _____

5   A sales volume operational variance is sometimes called a _____ .

1   A planning variance compares an original standard with a revised standard that should or would have been used if planners had known in advance what was going to happen.

2   False. It is valued at the revised efficiency level.

3   (a)   The material price planning variance is adverse.
    (b)   The material usage planning variance is favourable.

4   2,000 hours (A) × original standard rate $10 per hour = $20,000 (A).

5   Market share variance

Now try the questions below from the Practice Question Bank

Number	Level	Marks	Approximate time
Section A Q71	Examination	2	4 mins
Section A Q72	Examination	2	4 mins
Section A Q73	Examination	2	4 mins
Section A Q74	Examination	2	4 mins
Section A Q75	Examination	2	4 mins
Section C Q8	Examination	20	39 mins
Section C Q9	Examination	20	39 mins

13

Performance analysis and behavioural aspects

Topic list	Syllabus reference
1 Using variance analysis	C7 (a), (b)
2 Behavioural implications	C7 (c)
3 Setting the difficulty level for a budget	C1 (g), C7 (d)
4 Participation in budgeting	C1 (h)
5 Variances in a JIT or TQM environment	C7 (e)
6 Standard costs in a rapidly changing environment	C7 (f)

Introduction

In this chapter we discuss the effects of standard costing and variance reporting on management and employee behaviour.

We also discuss the problems of using standard costing in the modern, rapidly changing business environment.

Study guide

		Intellectual level
C1	**Budgetary systems and types of budget**	
(a)	Explain how budgetary systems fit within the performance hierarchy.	2
(b)	Select and explain appropriate budgetary systems for an organisation, including top-down, bottom-up, rolling, zero-base, activity-base, incremental, and feed-forward control.	2
(c)	Describe the information used in budget systems and the sources of the information needed.	2
(d)	Indicate the usefulness and problems with different budget types (including fixed, flexible, zero-base, activity-base, incremental, rolling, top-down, bottom-up, master, functional.)	2
(e)	Prepare rolling budgets and activity based budgets.	2
(f)	Explain the beyond budgeting model, including the benefits and problems that may be faced if it is adopted in an organisation.	2
(g)	Discuss the issues surrounding setting the difficulty level for a budget.	2
(h)	Explain the benefits and difficulties of the participation of employees in the negotiations of targets.	2
(i)	Explain the difficulties of changing a budgetary system or type of budget used.	2
(j)	Explain how budget systems can deal with uncertainty in the environment.	2
C7	**Performance analysis**	
(a)	Analyse and evaluate past performance using the results of variance analysis.	2
(b)	Use variance analysis to assess how future performance of an organisation or business can be improved.	2
(c)	Identify the factors which influence behaviour.	2
(d)	Discuss the effect that variances have on staff motivation and action.	2
(e)	Describe the dysfunctional nature of some variances in the modern environment of JIT and TQM.	2
(f)	Discuss the behavioural problems resulting from using standard costs in rapidly changing environments.	2

Exam guide

The behavioural aspects of performance analysis and variances may form the discussion part of a Section C question, but you should also be prepared for a tricky Section A question, or Section B mini case study questions, on any of the topics in this chapter.

1 Using variance analysis

FAST FORWARD

> Variance analysis is used to analyse and evaluate past performance. It is also used for control purposes: significant variances may indicate that an aspect of performance is out of control and that measures should be taken to improve performance in the future.

1.1 Analysing past performance with variance analysis

Variance analysis compares actual performance with a budget or standard cost. Differences between actual results and the budget or standard are reported in monetary terms as variances, and variances can be used to reconcile budgeted profit and actual profit in an operating statement.The previous chapters have focused mainly on the techniques of calculating variances. For the exam, you also need to show an awareness of what variances tell us, and what control measures management should take when a variance is reported.

Basic principles of variance reporting are that:

(a) The monetary value that is given to variances should be a **reasonable indication of how much profit has been made or lost** as a result of actual performance differing from the budget or standard.

(b) The **managers responsible for variances (adverse or favourable) should be identified**, and they should be expected to account for the variance and, where appropriate, indicate what corrective or control measures they are taking.

1.1.1 Responsibility for planning variances

It was explained in the previous chapter that planning variances arise when a budget or standard cost is revised. 'Errors' in the budget or standard cost are attributable to the managers (planners) who prepared the budget or standard cost. Variances arising because the budget or standard cost was inappropriate should not be attributed to operational management.

In many cases, revisions to a budget or standard cost are due to causes outside the control of the planners. An unexpected increase in the market price for materials, for example, is beyond the control of planners. Similarly, an unexpected collapse in market demand for an industry's products, resulting in an adverse sales volume planning variance, cannot usually be 'blamed' on planners.

Even so, planning variances, where they occur, should be identified separately. Operational managers should be held responsible only for variances that may be realistically attributable to differences between actual performance and a realistic budget or standard. In other words, operational managers should be held responsible for operational variances. Unless they were also involved in the budgeting or standard-setting process, operational managers are not responsible for planning variances.

1.1.2 Responsibility for operational variances

Responsibility for operational variances should be traced to the managers who are in a position of authority and control over operations where the variances occur. Operational management responsibility for variances depends on the organisation structure and the division of authority and responsibility between management.

For example, a material price variance is the difference between actual and standard purchase costs of materials. The operational manager responsible for this variance should be the manager who makes the decisions about buying materials. This may be the head of buying in one organisation, and the production manager in a different organisation.

You should be able to identify the managers responsible for operational variances. A general guide is given in the table below.

Variance	Responsibility
Sales price variance	Sales or marketing management
Sales volume variance	Normally sales or marketing management However, if sales are less than budget due to problems with production, the production manager is responsible
Material price variance	The manager responsible for purchasing materials
Material usage variance	Normally the production manager
Labour rate variance	The manager responsible for pay rates. This may be senior management or Human Resources management. However, the production manager will be responsible for any adverse rate variances caused by working overtime and paying employees a premium rate per hour
Labour efficiency variance	Normally the production manager
Idle time variance	This depends on the cause of the idle time. It may be caused by lack of sales orders (sales management responsibility), inefficient production management (production management responsibility) or delays in deliveries of key raw material (buying manager responsibility)

1.2 Using variance analysis to improve future performance

Variance analysis is not simply a method of analysing past performance. It should provide guidance for operational management about aspects of performance that need improving. Variances should be a guide to control action and improving future performance.

It is important to understand that a reported variance is a measurement that relates to historical performance. Control action affects the future, not the past. So, for example, if an adverse labour efficiency variance of $10,000 is reported one month, and the production manager takes measures to improve efficiency:

(a)   The effect of the control measures should be to improve efficiency, but the value of the efficiency improvement in future months is unlikely to be $10,000. Control measures may result in savings of more or less than $10,000 per month, depending on how effective the measures are.

(b)   The effect of control measures should have a reasonably long-term impact, so control measures may result in savings not just in the following control period but also for a reasonably long time into the future.

1.2.1 The significance of variances

Control action to improve future performance should only be taken when a variance seems significant. Some variances are inevitable, because it is most unlikely that actual results will be exactly the same as the budget or standard.

(a)   Favourable as well as adverse variances should be investigated, with a view to taking control action if they seem significant. Control action to improve poor performance may seem an obvious requirement. However, control action to reinforce favourable performance should also be expected from management.

(b)   Variances need not be investigated if they do not seem significant. For example, variances that are less than, say, 5% of the budget or standard cost amount may be disregarded, because they fall within an acceptable tolerance limit.

(c)   Management may not use variances in a single reporting period as a guide to control action, since a variance in one month may be due to a once-only event. Instead of relying on variances reported in a single month, management may monitor cumulative variances over a period of time, and identify those that should be investigated on the basis of performance or trend over a number of months.

1.2.2 The cost of control action

Taking control measures to deal with the cause of a variance takes effort and costs money. Control measures should only be taken if it seems probable that the benefits arising from improved performance are sufficient to justify the cost of investigating the causes of the variance and taking control action.

This is a reason why insignificant variances are not investigated.

1.2.3 Improving performance

An exam question may ask about the nature of control action that an operational manager may take to deal with the cause of an adverse variance and so improve performance. The appropriate control measures will obviously depend on the circumstances and the reasons why a variance occurred, so you may need to use common sense and judgement in dealing with any question on this topic. A few ideas are set out in the following table to give you an idea of the issues that may be considered.

Variance	Possible control action
Adverse sales volume variance	Consider reducing the sales price in order to increase sales demand, although this will result in an adverse sale price variance
Adverse material price variance	Search for a supplier who is prepared to offer a lower price Consider purchasing in bulk quantities in order to obtain large-order discounts
Adverse material usage variance Adverse labour efficiency variance	Consider providing training for the workforce, with the objective of improving labour efficiency and reducing wastage of materials

2 Behavioural implications   6/10, 6/12

FAST FORWARD

Used correctly, a budgetary control and variance reporting system can **motivate** managers and employees to improve performance, but it may also produce undesirable **negative reactions**.

The purpose of a budgetary control and variance reporting system is to assist management in planning and controlling the resources of their organisation, by providing appropriate control information. The information will only be valuable, however, if it is interpreted correctly and used purposefully by managers **and** employees.

The appropriate use of control information therefore depends not only on the content of the information itself but also on the behaviour of its recipients. This is because control in business is exercised by people. Their attitude to control information will colour their views on what they should do with it and a number of behavioural problems can arise.

(a)   The **managers who set the budget** or standards are **often not the managers** who are then made **responsible for achieving budget targets**.

(b)   The **goals of the organisation as a whole**, as expressed in a budget, **may not coincide with the personal aspirations of individual managers**.

(c)   **Control is applied at different stages by different people**. A supervisor may receive weekly control reports, and act on them; their superior may receive monthly control reports, and decide to take different control action. Different managers can get in each other's way, and resent the interference from others.

2.1 Motivation

Motivation is what makes people behave in the way that they do. It comes from individual attitudes, or group attitudes. Individuals will be motivated by personal desires and interests. These may be in line with the objectives of the organisation, and some people 'live for their jobs'. Other individuals see their job as a chore, and their motivations will be unrelated to the objectives of the organisation they work for.

It is therefore vital that the goals of management and the employees harmonise with the goals of the organisation as a whole. This is known as goal congruence. Although obtaining goal congruence is essentially a behavioural problem, **it is possible to design and run a budgetary control system which will go some way towards ensuring that goal congruence is achieved**. Managers and employees must therefore be favourably disposed towards the budgetary control system so that it can operate efficiently.

The management accountant should therefore try to ensure that employees have positive attitudes towards **setting budgets, implementing budgets** (that is, putting the organisation's plans into practice) and feedback of results (**control information**).

2.2 Poor attitudes when setting budgets

Poor attitudes or hostile behaviour towards the budgetary control system can begin at the **planning stage. If managers are involved in preparing a budget** the following may happen.

(a)   Managers may **complain that they are too busy** to spend much time on budgeting.

(b)   They may **build 'slack' into their expenditure estimates**.

(c)   They may argue that **formalising a budget plan on paper is too restricting** and that managers should be allowed flexibility in the decisions they take.

(d)   They may set budgets for their budget centre and **not co-ordinate** their own plans with those of other budget centres.

(e)   They may **base future plans on past results**, instead of using the opportunity for formalised planning to look at alternative options and new ideas.

On the other hand, **managers may not be involved in the budgeting process**. Organisational goals may not be communicated to them and they might have their budget decided for them by senior management or administrative decision. It is **hard for people to be motivated to achieve targets set by someone else**.

2.2.1 Poor attitudes when putting plans into action

Poor attitudes also arise **when a budget is implemented**.

(a)   Managers may **put in only just enough effort** to achieve budget targets, without trying to beat targets.

(b)   A formal budget may **encourage rigidity and discourage flexibility**.

(c)   **Short-term planning** in a budget **can draw attention away from the longer-term consequences** of decisions.

(d)   There may be **minimal co-operation and communication** between managers.

(e)   Managers will often try to make sure that they **spend up to their full budget allowance, and do not overspend**, so that they will not be accused of having asked for too much spending allowance in the first place.

2.2.2 Poor attitudes and the use of control information

The **attitude of managers towards the accounting control information** they receive **might reduce the information's effectiveness**.

(a)   Management accounting control reports could well be seen as having a relatively **low priority** in the list of management tasks. Managers may take the view that they have more pressing jobs on hand than looking at routine control reports.

(b)   Managers may **resent control information**; they may see it as **part of a system of trying to find fault with their work**. This resentment is likely to be particularly strong when budgets or standards are imposed on managers without allowing them to participate in the budget-setting process.

(c) If budgets are seen as **pressure devices** to push managers into doing better, control reports will be resented.

(d) Managers **may not understand the information** in the control reports because they are unfamiliar with accounting terminology or principles.

(e) Managers may have a **false sense of what their objectives should be**. A production manager may consider it more important to maintain quality standards regardless of cost. They would then dismiss adverse expenditure variances as inevitable and unavoidable.

(f) **If there are flaws in the system of recording actual costs**, managers will dismiss control information as unreliable.

(g) **Control information** may be **received weeks after the end of the period** to which it relates, in which case managers may regard it as out of date and no longer useful.

(h) Managers may be **held responsible for variances outside their control**.

It is therefore obvious that management accountants and senior management should try to implement systems that are acceptable to budget holders and which produce positive effects.

2.2.3 Pay as a motivator

Many researchers agree that **pay can be an important motivator**, when there is a formal link between higher pay (or other rewards, such as promotion) and achieving budget targets. Individuals are likely to work harder to achieve budget if they know that they will be rewarded for their successful efforts. There are, however, problems with using pay as an incentive.

(a) A serious problem that can arise is that **formal reward and performance evaluation systems can encourage dysfunctional behaviour**. Many investigations have noted the tendency of managers to pad their budgets either in anticipation of cuts by superiors or to make the subsequent variances more favourable. Moreover, there are numerous examples of managers making decisions in response to performance indices, even though the decisions are contrary to the wider purposes of the organisation.

(b) The targets must be challenging but fair, otherwise individuals will become dissatisfied. **Pay can be a demotivator as well as a motivator**!

3 Setting the difficulty level for a budget

FAST FORWARD

'Aspirations' budgets can be used as **targets** to motivate higher levels of performance but a budget for **planning and decision-making** should be based on **reasonable expectations**.

The level of difficulty in a standard cost may range from very challenging to fairly undemanding: standard costs may be **ideal**, or many establish either a **target** or a **currently attainable** level of performance.

Budgets can motivate managers to achieve a high level of performance. But **how difficult** should budget targets or standard levels of efficiency be? And how might people react to targets of differing degrees of difficulty in achievement?

(a) There is likely to be a **demotivating** effect where an **ideal standard** of performance is set, because adverse efficiency variances will always be reported.

(b) A **low standard** of efficiency is also **demotivating**, because there is no sense of achievement in attaining the required standards. If the budgeted level of attainment is too 'loose', targets will be achieved easily, and there will be no impetus for employees to try harder to do better than this.

(c) A budgeted level of attainment could be the **same** as the level that has been achieved in the past. Arguably, this level will be too low. It might encourage **budgetary slack**.

Academics have argued that each individual has a **personal 'aspiration level'**. This is a level of performance, in a task with which individuals are familiar, which individuals undertake for themselves to reach.

Individual aspirations might be much higher or much lower than the organisation's aspirations, however. The solution might therefore be to have **two budgets**.

(a)   A budget for **planning and decision-making** based on **reasonable expectations**
(b)   A budget for **motivational purposes**, with more **difficult targets of performance**

These two budgets might be called an '**expectations budget**' and an '**aspirations budget**' respectively.

Similarly, the level of difficulty in a standard cost may vary.

Type of standard	
Ideal	A standard of performance that assumes the highest possible level of achievement. A desirable target, but not at all achievable at the moment. Reported variances will always be adverse. This can be demotivating for the managers responsible for performance.
Target	This is a standard cost that sets performance targets at a higher level than is currently being achieved. However, the targets are not unrealistic. Improvements in performance will be needed to turn adverse variances into favourable variances. The value of target standards depends on the strength of motivation of management to improve performance. An incentive scheme may be needed to persuade managers to 'buy in' to the target standard.
Currently attainable	This standard is based on levels of performance that are currently being achieved. They do not provide an incentive to improve performance, although they may encourage management to avoid a deterioration in performance.
Basic standard	This is an original standard that is unchanged over a long period of time. It is used to measure trends and changes in performance standards over time. It is not a useful type of standard for control purposes.

3.1 The effect of reported variances on staff action

Reported variances, if significant and adverse, should prompt managers into taking control action to improve performance. The success of a variance reporting system in achieving this objective will depend on several factors.

(a)   The manager who is considered responsible for the variance should agree and accept that the cause of the variance is their responsibility. Variances should be reported to the appropriate manager.

(b)   The manager should consider the reported variance to be 'fair'. Variances should be a realistic measure. This is a reason why it is advisable to separate planning variances from operational variances when a budget or standard needs revision. It is also a reason why variances reported using ideal standards may be demotivating.

(c)   The manager should want to do something to deal with the causes of the variance. Incentives and motivation are important factors.

(d)   Variance should be reported in a timely manner, as soon as reasonably practical. If a reported variance relates to events that occurred a long time ago, managers will be reluctant to investigate them 'now' because the variance will seem out of date.

(e)   The manager must believe that the cause of the variance is something that they are in a position to control. If a manager considers the cause of a variance to be outside their sphere of authority, or to be due to a factor that they cannot do anything to change, they will not be motivated to look for control measures.

The control culture within the organisation may also affect the response of managers to variances. If there is a 'blame culture', managers will be blamed for adverse variances and accused of poor performance. This is likely to provoke a defensive reaction, with the manager trying to justify what has gone wrong.

In contrast, if there is an 'improvement culture', variances are considered as useful indicators for control action and improving performance. Managers are not blamed for adverse variances, but encouraged to look for suitable control measures whenever significant adverse variances occur.

4 Participation in budgeting   12/11, 12/13

FAST FORWARD

A budget can be set from the **top down** (**imposed** budget) or from the **bottom up** (**participatory** budget). Many writers refer to a third style, the negotiated budget.

4.1 Participation

It has been argued that **participation** in the budgeting process **will improve motivation** and so will improve the quality of budget decisions and the efforts of individuals to achieve their budget targets (although obviously this will depend on the personality of the individual, the nature of the task (narrowly defined or flexible) and the organisational culture).

There are basically two ways in which a budget can be set: from the **top down** (imposed budget) or from the **bottom up** (participatory budget).

4.2 Imposed style of budgeting (top-down budgeting)

In this approach to budgeting, **top management prepare a budget with little or no input from operating personnel** which is then imposed on the employees who have to work to the budgeted figures.

The times when imposed budgets are effective are as follows.

- In newly formed organisations
- In very small businesses
- During periods of economic hardship
- When operational managers lack budgeting skills
- When the organisation's different units require precise co-ordination

There are, of course, advantages and disadvantages to this style of setting budgets.

Advantages

- **Strategic plans** are likely to be incorporated into planned activities.
- They **enhance** the **co-ordination** between the plans and objectives of divisions.
- They use **senior management's awareness** of total resource availability.
- They **decrease the input from inexperienced or uninformed lower-level employees**.
- They **decrease the period of time taken** to draw up the budgets.

Disadvantages

- **There may be dissatisfaction**, **defensiveness** and **low morale** among employees.
- The **feeling of team spirit** may disappear.
- The **acceptance of organisational goals** and **objectives** could be limited.
- The feeling of the budget as a **punitive device** could arise.
- **Unachievable budgets** for overseas divisions could result if consideration is not given to local operating and political environments.
- **Lower-level management initiative** may be **stifled**.

4.3 Participative style of budgeting (bottom-up budgeting)

In this approach to budgeting, **budgets are developed by lower-level managers who then submit the budgets to their superiors**. The budgets are based on the lower-level managers' perceptions of what is achievable and the associated necessary resources.

Participative budgets may be effective in the following circumstances.

- In **well-established organisations**
- In **very large businesses**
- During periods of **economic affluence**
- When operational managers have **strong budgeting skills**
- When the organisation's different units act **autonomously**

The **advantages** of participative budgets are as follows.

- They are based on **information from employees** most familiar with the department.

- **Knowledge spread** among several levels of management is pulled **together**.

- **Morale** and **motivation** is improved: employees feel more involved and that their opinions matter to senior management.

- They **increase operational managers' commitment** to organisational objectives.

- In general they are **more realistic**.

- **Co-ordination** between units is **improved**.

- **Specific resource requirements** are **included**.

- **Senior managers' overview** is mixed with operational level details.

There are, on the other hand, a number of **disadvantages** of participative budgets.

- They **consume more time**.

- When individuals are involved in negotiating their budget targets, they may want to set targets that are easily attainable rather than targets that are challenging. In other words, an ability to negotiate targets may tempt managers to introduce **budgetary slack** into their targets.

- Individuals may not properly understand the strategic and budget objectives of the organisation, and they may argue for targets that are not in the best interests of the organisation as a whole.

- **Changes implemented** by senior management may **cause dissatisfaction** if they seem to ignore the opinions of employees who have been involved in negotiating targets.

- Budgets may be **unachievable** if managers are not sufficiently experienced or knowledgeable to contribute usefully.

- They can support **'empire building'** by subordinates.

- An **earlier start** to the budgeting process will be required, compared with top-down budgeting and target setting.

4.4 Negotiated style of budgeting

At the two extremes, budgets can be dictated from above or simply emerge from below but, in practice, different levels of management often agree budgets by a process of negotiation. In the imposed budget approach, operational managers will try to negotiate the budget targets which they consider to be unreasonable or unrealistic with senior managers.

Likewise, senior management usually review and revise budgets presented to them under a participative approach through a process of negotiation with lower-level managers. **Final budgets are therefore most likely to lie between what top management would really like and what junior managers believe is feasible**. The budgeting process is hence a **bargaining process** and it is this bargaining which is of vital importance, **determining whether the budget is an effective management tool or simply a clerical device**.

5 Variances in a JIT or TQM environment

Standard costing and variance analysis may sometimes be inappropriate in a production environment based on Just in Time (JIT) methods or a Total Quality Management (TQM) approach.

The use of standard costs and variance analysis is based on certain assumptions about the way in which operations should be managed. In particular, variance analysis is based on the view that:

(a)   All resources should be used as efficiently as possible.
(b)   A standard cost is a performance target that operational managers should seek to achieve.

However, this approach to analysing performance is not always appropriate. Variances indicating adverse performance are sometimes inappropriate in a Just in Time (JIT) or Total Quality Management (TQM) environment.

5.1 Variances and a JIT environment

In a JIT manufacturing environment, production is managed on the principle that items should not be produced until they are required to meet sales orders. There should be no accumulation of inventories of work in progress and finished goods.

A JIT approach implies that if there are no sales orders, production resources should be kept idle. In addition, as explained in the earlier chapter on the theory of constraints, the volume of production should be restricted to the output capacity of the bottleneck resource, meaning that there will inevitably be idle capacity for all resources that are not the bottleneck resource.

(a)   In JIT manufacturing, idle time should therefore be expected.

(b)   In a system of standard costing, idle time is an adverse labour efficiency variance, and is undesirable.

If idle time variances are reported for a manufacturing operation that is based on JIT methods, the variances will encourage managers to use idle capacity in a productive way, by producing more and building up inventories. With increases in inventory, there will be a higher reported profit.

This is unacceptable in a JIT environment.

5.2 Variances and a TQM environment   6/12

Total Quality Management (TQM) is an approach to management that originated from different sources, and has a number of different aspects.

(a)   One aspect of TQM is the view that work should be 'right first time'. Mistakes that result in wastage and reworking of faulty output should be avoided.

(b)   Another aspect of TQM is similar to the JIT principle that items should be produced only when they are needed for the next stage in the production process, and finished goods should not be produced until they are needed for sales orders.

(c)   A third aspect of TQM is the principle of continuous improvement or 'kaizen'. This is the view that the organisation should always look for small ways of improving performance standards and that improvements should be made continually. The ideal level of performance will never be reached, because further improvements will always be possible.

Each of these principles of TQM may be inconsistent with standard costing and variance analysis. The inconsistency between standard costing and the view that production resources should be kept idle until required has already been discussed in the context of JIT.

(a)   The philosophy in TQM of 'right first time' may be inconsistent with a standard cost that includes an allowance for wastage. TQM is more consistent with environmental cost accounting (material flow cost accounting) than a costing system that allows for normal loss in the standard cost.

Part C Budgeting and control | **13: Performance analysis and behavioural aspects**   339

(b) The principle of 'kaizen' or continuous improvement is that a steady state of production will never be achieved, because further improvements will always be possible. A standard cost is based on an assumption of a desirable steady state; this view is inconsistent with the principle of continuous improvement.

5.2.1 Quality and quantity

Standard costing concentrates on **quantity** and ignores other factors contributing to effectiveness. In a **total quality environment**, however, quantity is not the main issue; quality is. Effectiveness in such an environment therefore centres on quality of output, and the cost of failing to achieve the required level of effectiveness is measured not in variances, but in terms of **internal and external failure costs**, neither of which would be identified by a traditional standard costing analysis.

Standard costing systems might measure, say, **labour efficiency** in terms of individual tasks and level of **output**. In a total quality environment, labour is more likely to be viewed as a number of **multi-task** teams who are responsible for the completion of a part of the production process. The effectiveness of such a team is more appropriately measured in terms of **reworking** required, **returns** from customers, **defects** identified in subsequent stages of production, and so on.

Traditional feedback control would seek to eliminate an adverse material price variance by requiring managers to source cheaper, possibly lower-quality supplies. This may run counter to the aim of maximising quality of output.

5.2.2 Can standard costing and TQM coexist?

Arguably, there is little point in running both a Total Quality Management programme and a standard costing system simultaneously.

(a) Predetermined standards are at odds with the philosophy of **continual improvement** inherent in a total quality management programme.

(b) Continual improvements are likely to alter methods of working, prices, quantities of inputs, and so on, whereas standard costing is most appropriate in a stable, standardised and repetitive environment.

(c) Material standard costs often incorporate a planned level of scrap. This is at odds with the TQM aim of **zero defects** and there is no motivation to 'get it right first time'.

(d) Attainable standards which make some allowance for wastage and inefficiencies are commonly set. The use of such standards conflicts with the **elimination of waste** which is such a vital ingredient in a TQM programme.

(e) Standard costing control systems make individual managers **responsible** for the variances relating to their part of the organisation's activities. A TQM programme, on the other hand, aims to make **all personnel** aware of, and responsible for, the importance of supplying the customer with a quality product.

Question

TQM and variance analysis

One of the basic tenets of total quality management is 'get it right first time'. Is variance reporting a help or a hindrance in this respect?

Answer

In theory, it should not be of any relevance at all, because variances will not occur. In practice, an organisation will not get everything right first time and variance reporting may still draw attention to areas for improvement – **if the standard and 'being right' are the same thing**.

6 Standard costs in a rapidly changing environment

The **role of standards and variances** in the rapidly changing modern business environment is open to question.

It can be argued that standard costs have limited relevance and value in the modern business world, where the environment is continually changing, and the life cycle of products can be very short.

Standard costs are appropriate for a 'steady state' production environment where the manufacturing system produces standard products, often in large quantities, using standard and repetitive production methods and processes.

In many industries today:

(a) **Products are customised** to the individual specifications of the customer. Although there may be a basic product, customers do not buy a standard product. **Standard costing is more suitable for a mass production environment**.

(b) In such countries as the UK, there are **more service industries** than manufacturing industries, and **services are often non-standard in nature** and the way they are delivered.

(c) Standard cost variances focus mainly on material cost and labour cost variances (and overhead variances may be a simple fixed cost expenditure variance). In many manufacturing companies, overhead costs are much more significant than labour costs. Variance reporting therefore fails to focus on the most important costs.

(d) Many of the variances in a standard costing system focus on the control of **short-term variable costs**. In most modern manufacturing environments, the majority of costs, including direct labour costs, tend to be fixed in the short run.

(e) In some industries, products have a very short life cycle. In these circumstances, it may not be worthwhile developing a standard cost for new products. Instead, costing techniques, such as life cycle costing and target costing, may be more appropriate for planning and control purposes.

(f) Variance reporting involves regular formal performance reports, typically every four weeks or month. Modern IT systems make it possible for operational managers to monitor performance much more frequently and 'on demand'. Variance reporting is not easily adapted to 'on demand' performance monitoring.

6.1 The role in modern business of standards and variances

However, a survey by Drury *et al* (1993) indicated the **continued widespread use of standard costing systems**. Although this survey is now somewhat out of date, the following points should be noted.

- **Planning**. Even in a TQM environment, budgets will still need to be quantified. For example, the planned level of prevention and appraisal costs needs to be determined. Standards, such as returns of a particular product should not exceed 1% of deliveries during a budget period, can be set.

- **Control**. Cost and mix changes from the plan will still be relevant in many processing situations.

- **Decision-making**. Existing standards can be used as the starting point in the construction of a cost for a new product.

- **Performance measurement**. If the product mix is relatively stable, performance measurement may be enhanced by the use of a system of planning and operational variances.

- **Product pricing**. Target costs may be compared with current standards, and the resulting 'cost gap' investigated with a view to reducing it or eliminating it using techniques such as value engineering.

- **Improvement and change**. Variance trends can be monitored over time.

- **Accounting valuations**. Although the operation of a JIT system in conjunction with backflush accounting will reduce the need for standard costs and variance analysis, standards may be used to value residual inventory and the transfers to cost of sales account.

Chapter Roundup

- Variance analysis is used to analyse and evaluate past performance. It is also used for control purposes: significant variances may indicate that an aspect of performance is out of control and that measures should be taken to improve performance in the future.

- Used correctly, a budgetary control and variance reporting system can **motivate** managers and employees to improve performance, but it may also produce undesirable **negative reactions**.

- 'Aspirations' budgets can be used as **targets** to motivate higher levels of performance but a budget for **planning and decision-making** should be based on **reasonable expectations**.

- The level of difficulty in a standard cost may range from very challenging to fairly undemanding: standard costs may be **ideal**, or many establish either a **target** or a **currently attainable** level of performance.

- A budget can be set from the **top down (imposed** budget) or from the **bottom up (participatory** budget). Many writers refer to a third style, the negotiated budget.

- Standard costing and variance analysis may sometimes be inappropriate in a production environment based on Just in Time (JIT) methods or a Total Quality Management (TQM) approach.

- The **role of standards and variances** in the rapidly changing modern business environment is open to question.

Quick Quiz

1 Complete the table below to show a possible response to each of the traditional performance measures and a consequence of that response.

Measurement	Response	Consequence of action
Purchase price variance		
Labour efficiency variance		
Cost of scrap		
Scrap factor included in standard costs		

2 What three factors are said to determine the effectiveness of participation in target setting?

   A   Nature of the task, organisation structure, personality
   B   Personality, technology, organisation structure
   C   Nature of the task, production processes, personality
   D   Personality, leadership style, aspirations

3 A budget for motivational purposes, with fairly difficult targets of performance, is an aspirations budget. **True or false?**

4 Provide five reasons why poor attitudes could arise when a budget is implemented.

5   Match the description to the correct term.

	Term		Description
(a)	Motivation	1	Exists where managers working in their own interests also act in harmony with the interests of the organisation as a whole
(b)	Goal congruence	2	Comes from individual or group attitudes
(c)	Incentive	3	Concerned with getting subordinates to run rather than walk towards desired goals

Answers to Quick Quiz

1

Measurement	Response	Consequence of action
Purchase price variance	Buy in greater bulk to reduce unit price	Excess stocks Higher holding costs Quality and reliability of delivery times ignored
Labour efficiency variance	Encourage greater output	Possibly excess stocks of the wrong products
Cost of scrap	Rework items to reduce scrap	Production flow held up by reworking
Scrap factor included in standard costs	Supervisor aims to achieve actual scrap = standard scrap	No motivation to get it right first time

2   A

3   True

4   (a)   Managers might put in only just enough effort to achieve budget targets, without trying to beat targets.

   (b)   A formal budget might encourage rigidity and discourage flexibility in operational decision-making.

   (c)   Short-term planning in a budget can draw attention away from the longer-term consequences of decisions.

   (d)   Co-operation and communication between managers might be minimal.

   (e)   Managers will often try to make sure that they spend up to their full budget allowance, and do not overspend, so that they will not be accused of having asked for too much spending allowance in the first place.

5   (a) 2; (b) 1; (c) 3

Now try the questions below from the Practice Question Bank

Number	Level	Marks	Approximate time
Section A Q76	Examination	2	4 mins
Section A Q77	Examination	2	4 mins
Section A Q78	Examination	2	4 mins
Section A Q79	Examination	2	4 mins
Section A Q80	Examination	2	4 mins

Performance measurement
and control

14

Performance management information systems

Topic list	Syllabus reference
1 Introduction to planning, control and decision-making	D1(a)
2 Management accounting information for strategic planning, control and decision-making	D1(a)
3 Management accounting information for management control	D1(a)
4 Management accounting information for operational control	D1(a)
5 Types of information systems	D1(b)
6 Open and closed systems	D1(c)

Introduction

Performance management systems, measurement and control is the final section in this Study Text.

This chapter covers issues relating to **performance management information systems** and their design.

We begin with a look at the **accounting information needs** at all levels of the organisation. Next, we consider the characteristics of a range of management information systems, including **transaction processing systems** and **executive information systems**.

The chapter concludes with a short section on **open** and **closed systems**.

Study guide

		Intellectual level
D1	**Performance management information systems**	
(a)	Identify the accounting information requirements and describe the different types of information systems used for strategic planning, management control and operational control and decision-making.	2
(b)	Define and identify the main characteristics of transaction processing systems; management information systems; executive information systems; and enterprise resource planning systems.	2
(c)	Define and discuss the merits of, and potential problems with, open and closed systems with regard to the needs of performance management.	2

Exam guide

Management accounting and information systems are an important part of the F5 syllabus because they play an integral part in producing the information that managers use for performance measurement and performance management.

Performance management information systems provide the information which enables performance measurement to take place.

You could face questions specifically on the topics in this chapter, particularly in a Section A, or you may need to use them as a framework for a wider question.

> One of the competencies you require to fulfil performance objective 12 of the PER is the ability to contribute to development and improvements of management accounting systems and internal reporting. You can apply the knowledge you obtain from this section of the text to help to demonstrate this competence.

1 Introduction to planning, control and decision-making

FAST FORWARD

> **Strategic planning** is the process of deciding on objectives for the organisation, changes in these objectives, the resources to attain these objectives, and the policies that are to govern the acquisition, use and disposition of these resources.
>
> **Management control** is the process by which managers assure that resources are obtained and used effectively and efficiently in the accomplishment of the organisation's objectives. It is sometimes called **tactics** or **tactical planning**.
>
> **Operational control** (or **operational planning**) is the process of assuring that specific tasks are carried out effectively and efficiently.

Within and at all levels of the organisation, **information** is continually flowing back and forth, being used by people to formulate **plans** and take **decisions**, and to draw attention to the need for **control** action, when the plans and decisions don't work as intended.

Key terms

> **Planning** means formulating ways of proceeding. **Decision-making** means choosing between various alternatives. These two terms are virtually inseparable: you decide to plan in the first place and the plan you make is a collection of decisions.
>
> **Strategic decisions** are long-term decisions and are characterised by their wide scope, wide impact, relative uncertainty and complexity.

> **Control** is used in the sense of monitoring something so as to keep it on course, like the 'controls' of a car, not (or not merely) in the sense of imposing restraints or exercising tyrannical power over something. We have more to say about control later in this Study Text.

1.1 Information for planning, control and decision-making

Robert **Anthony**, a leading writer on organisational control, suggested what has become a widely used hierarchy, classifying the information used at different management levels for planning, control and decision-making into three tiers: **strategic planning**, **management control** and **operational control** (Anthony, 1965).

We consider each tier in turn in Sections 2–4.

Managerial level

Top — STRATEGIC — Long-term planning decisions

Middle — TACTICAL — Medium-term planning and management control decisions

Bottom — OPERATIONAL — Operational/short-term decisions routine processing of transactions

Key terms

> **Strategic planning.** The process of deciding on objectives of the organisation, changes in these objectives, the resources used to attain these objectives, and the policies that are to govern the acquisition, use and disposition of these resources.
>
> **Management** (or **tactical**) **control.** The process by which managers assure that resources are obtained and used effectively and efficiently in the accomplishment of the organisation's objectives. It is sometimes called tactics or tactical planning.
>
> **Operational control** (or **operational planning**). The process of assuring that specific tasks are carried out effectively and efficiently.

2 Management accounting information for strategic planning, control and decision-making

FAST FORWARD

> **Management accounting information** can be used to support strategic planning, control and decision-making. Strategic management accounting differs from traditional management accounting because it has an **external** orientation and a **future** orientation.

This section identifies the accounting information requirements for strategic planning, control and decision-making.

2.1 Future uncertainty

Much strategic planning is uncertain.

(a) Strategic plans may cover a **long period** into the future, perhaps five to ten years ahead or even longer.

(b) Many strategic plans involve big changes and **new ventures**, such as capacity expansion decisions, decisions to develop into new product areas and new markets, and so on.

Inevitably, management accounting information for strategic planning will be based on incomplete data and will use **forecasts** and **estimates**.

(a) It follows that management accounting information is unlikely to give clear guidelines for management decisions and should incorporate some **risk and uncertainty analysis** (eg sensitivity analysis).

(b) For longer-term plans, **discounted cash flow techniques** ought to be used in financial evaluation.

(c) The management accountant will be involved in the following.

    (i) Project evaluation
    (ii) Managing cash and operational matters
    (iii) Reviewing the outcome of the project (post implementation review)

2.2 External and competitor orientation

Much management accounting information has been devised for internal consumption.

However, it is important to balance this with a consideration of external factors.

(a) Strategic planning and control decisions involve **environmental considerations**.

(b) A strategy is pursued in relation to **competitors**.

2.3 The challenge for management accountants

Traditional accounting systems have had a number of **perceived failings**.

(a) **Direction towards financial reporting**. It is necessary to report historical costs to shareholders, but the classifications of transactions for reporting purposes are not necessarily relevant to decision-making.

(b) **Misleading information**. This is particularly with regard to overhead absorption.

(c) **Neatness** rather than **usefulness**. Importance is placed on financial reporting templates, rather than providing solutions for management accountants.

(d) **Internal focus**. Management accounting information has been too inward looking (for example, focusing on achieving internal performance targets, like budgets). However, organisations also need to focus on customers and competition.

(e) **Inflexibility.** Traditional accounting systems have displayed an inability to cope with change, and the modern business environment.

The challenge lies in providing more relevant information for **strategic planning**, **control** and **decision-making**. Traditional management accounting systems may not always provide this.

(a) **Historical costs** are not necessarily the best guide to decision-making. One of the criticisms of management accounting is that management accounting information is biased towards the past rather than the future.

(b) **Strategic issues** are not easily detected by management accounting systems.

(c) **Financial models** of some sophistication are needed to enable management accountants to provide useful information.

2.4 What is strategic management accounting?

The aim of strategic management accounting is to provide information that is relevant to the process of strategic planning and control.

> **Strategic management accounting** is a form of management accounting in which emphasis is placed on information about factors which are external to the organisation, as well as non-financial and internally generated information.

2.4.1 External orientation

The important fact which distinguishes strategic management accounting from other management accounting activities is its **external orientation**, towards customers and competitors, suppliers and perhaps other stakeholders. For example, while a traditional management accountant would report on an organisation's own revenues, the strategic management would report on market share or trends in market size and growth.

(a) **Competitive advantage is relative**. Understanding competitors is therefore of prime importance.

For example, knowledge of competitors' costs, as well as a firm's own costs, could help inform strategic choices: a firm would be unwise to pursue a cost leadership strategy without first analysing its costs in relation to the cost structures of other firms in the industry.

(b) **Customers** determine if a firm has competitive advantage.

2.4.2 Future orientation

A criticism of traditional management accounts is that they are **backward looking**.

(a) Decision-making is a forward- and outward-looking process.
(b) Accounts are based on **costs**, whereas decision-making is concerned with **values**.

Strategic management accountants will use **relevant costs** (ie **incremental** costs and **opportunity** costs) for decision-making. We looked at this topic in Chapter 6.

2.4.3 Goal congruence

Business strategy involves the activities of many different functions, including marketing, production and human resource management. The strategic management accounting system will require **inputs from many areas of the business**.

(a) Strategic management accounting translates the consequences of different strategies into a **common accounting language for comparison**.

(b) It **relates business operations to financial performance**, and therefore helps ensure that **business activities** are **focused on shareholders' needs** for profit. In **not for profit organisations** this will not apply, as they do not focus on shareholder profitability. (We look at not for profit organisations in more detail later in this Study Text.)

It **helps to ensure goal congruence**, again by translating business activities into the common language of finance. Goal congruence is achieved when individuals or groups in an organisation take actions which are in their self-interest and also in the best interest of the organisation as a whole.

2.5 What information could strategic management accounting provide?

Bearing in mind the need for **goal congruence**, **external orientation** and **future orientation**, some **examples** of strategic management accounting are provided below.

Item	Comment
Competitors' costs	What are they? How do they compare with ours? Can we beat them? Are competitors vulnerable because of their cost structure?
Financial effect of competitor response	How might competitors respond to our strategy? How could their responses affect our sales or margins?

Item	Comment
Product profitability	A firm should want to know not just the profits or losses that are being made by each of its products but also why one product should be making good profits whereas another equally good product might be making a loss.
Customer profitability	Some customers or groups of customers are worth more than others.
Pricing decisions	Accounting information can help to analyse how profits and cash flows will vary according to price and prospective demand.
The **value of market share**	A firm ought to be aware of what it is worth to increase the market share of one of its products.
Capacity expansion	Should the firm expand its capacity and, if so, by how much? Should the firm diversify into a new area of operations, or a new market?
Brand values	How much is it worth investing in a brand which customers will choose over competitors' brands?
Shareholder wealth	Future profitability determines the value of a business.
Cash flow	A loss-making company can survive if it has adequate cash resources, but a profitable company cannot survive unless it has sufficient liquidity.
Effect of **acquisitions** and **mergers**	How will the merger affect levels of competition in the industry?
Decisions to **enter or leave a business area**	What are the barriers to entry or exit? How much investment is required to enter the market?

3 Management accounting information for management control

FAST FORWARD **Management control** is at the level below strategic planning in Anthony's decision-making hierarchy and is concerned with decisions about the efficient and effective use of resources to achieve objectives (Anthony, 1965).

Management control, which we briefly touched on in Section 1, is at the level below strategic planning in Anthony's decision-making hierarchy. While strategic planning is concerned with setting objectives and strategic targets, management control is concerned with **decisions about the efficient and effective use of an organisation's resources to achieve these objectives or targets**.

(a) **Resources** (which can be categorised as a series of 'M's): **m**oney, **m**anpower, **m**achinery, **m**ethods, **m**arkets, **m**anagement, and **m**anagement information.

(b) **Efficiency** in the use of resources means that **optimum output is achieved from the input resources used**. It relates to the combinations of men, land and capital (eg how much production work should be automated) and to the productivity of labour, or material usage.

(c) **Effectiveness** in the use of resources means that the **outputs obtained are in line with the intended objectives or targets**.

The time horizon involved in management control will be shorter than at the strategic decisions level, there will be much greater precision and the focus of information will be narrower.

Management control activities are **short-term non-strategic activities**.

3.1 Examples of management control (or tactical) planning activities

(a) Preparing budgets for the next year for sales, production, inventory levels, and so on
(b) Establishing measures of performance by which profit centres can be gauged

(c)   Developing a product for launching in the market

(d)   Planning advertising and marketing campaigns

(e)   Establishing a line of authority structure for the organisation

3.2 Examples of management control activities

(a)   Ensuring that budget targets are reached, or improved on

(b)   Ensuring that other measures of performance are satisfactory, or even better than planned

(c)   Where appropriate, changing the budget because circumstances have altered

Management control is an essentially routine affair in that it tends to be carried out in a series of **regular** planning and comparison procedures; that is, annually, monthly or weekly, so that all aspects of an organisation's activity are systematically reviewed. For example, a budget is usually prepared annually, and control reports issued every month or four weeks. Strategic planning, in contrast, might be irregular and occur when opportunities arise or are identified.

3.3 Information requirements

Features of management control information

(a)   Primarily generated **internally** (but may have a limited external component)

(b)   Embraces the **entire organisation**

(c)   **Summarised** at a relatively **low level**

(d)   **Routinely** collected and disseminated

(e)   Relevant to the **short** and **medium terms**

(f)   Often **quantitative** (labour hours, volumes of sales and production)

(g)   Collected in a **standard** manner

(h)   Commonly expressed in **money terms**

Types of information

(a)   Productivity measurements

(b)   Budgetary control or variance analysis reports

(c)   Cash flow forecasts

(d)   Manning levels

(e)   Profit results within a particular department of the organisation

(f)   Labour revenue statistics within a department

(g)   Short-term purchasing requirements

3.4 Source of information

A large proportion of this information will be generated from **within the organisation** (it has an **endogenous source**) and it will often have an accounting emphasis. Tactical information is usually prepared regularly; perhaps weekly or monthly.

3.5 Management control and strategic planning compared

The dividing line between strategic planning and management control is **not a clear one**. Many decisions include issues ranging from strategic to tactical. Nevertheless, there is a basic distinction between the two levels of decision.

(a)   The decision to launch a new brand of calorie-controlled frozen foods is a strategic plan (business strategy), but the choice of ingredients for the frozen meals involves a management control decision.

(b)   A decision that the market share for a product should be 25% is a strategic plan (competitive strategy), but the selection of a sales price of $2 per unit, supported by other marketing decisions about sales promotion and direct sales effort to achieve the required market share, would be a series of management control decisions.

Management control tends to be carried out in a series of **regular** planning and comparison procedures (annually, monthly, weekly). For example, a budget is usually prepared annually and control reports issued every month or four weeks. **Strategic planning**, in contrast, might be **irregular** and occur when opportunities arise or are identified.

4 Management accounting information for operational control

Operational control, the lowest tier in Anthony's hierarchy, is concerned with assuring that specific tasks are carried out effectively and efficiently.

The third and lowest tier in Anthony's hierarchy of decision-making consists of operational control decisions. Just as 'management control' plans are set within the guidelines of strategic plans, so too are 'operational control' plans set within the guidelines of both strategic planning and management control.

4.1 Example: Link between strategic plans and operational/management control decisions

(a) Senior management may decide that the company should increase sales by 5% per annum for at least five years – **a strategic plan**.

(b) The sales director and senior sales managers will make plans to increase sales by 5% in the next year, with some provisional planning for future years. This involves planning direct sales resources, advertising, sales promotion, and so on. Sales quotas are assigned to each sales territory – **a tactical management control decision**.

(c) The manager of a sales territory specifies the weekly sales targets for each sales representative. This is an **operational control decision**: individuals are given tasks which they are expected to achieve.

Operational control decisions are therefore much **more narrowly focused** and have a **shorter time frame** than tactical or strategic decisions.

4.2 Operational control activities

Although we have used an example of selling tasks to describe operational control, it is important to remember that this level of decision-making **occurs in all aspects of an organisation's activities**, even when the activities cannot be scheduled nor properly estimated because they are non-standard activities (such as repair work and answering customer complaints).

The scheduling of **unexpected or 'ad hoc' work** must be done at **short notice**, which is a feature of much operational decision-making. In the repairs department, for example, routine preventive maintenance can be scheduled, but breakdowns occur unexpectedly and repair work must be scheduled and controlled 'on the spot' by a repairs department supervisor.

Operational control activities can also be described as **short-term non-strategic activities**.

4.3 Information requirements

(a) **Operational information** is information which is **needed for the conduct of day to day implementation of plans**.

(b) It will include much **'transaction data'**, such as data about customer orders, purchase orders, cash receipts and payments and is likely to have an **endogenous (internal) source**.

(c) Operating information must usually be **consolidated into totals** in management reports before it can be used to prepare management control information.

(d) The amount of **detail** provided in information is likely to **vary with the purpose for which it is needed**, and operational information is likely to go into much more detail than tactical information, which in turn will be more detailed than strategic information.

(e)   Whereas tactical information for management control is often expressed in money terms, operational information, although quantitative, is more often **expressed in terms of units, hours, quantities of material, and so on.**

5 Types of information systems

You should be aware of the main characteristics of transaction processing systems, management information systems, executive information systems and enterprise resource planning systems.

5.1 Transaction processing systems

Transaction processing systems (TPS) collect, store, modify and retrieve the transactions of an organisation.

Key term

A **transaction** is an event that generates or modifies data which is eventually stored on an information system.

Transaction processing systems (TPS) collect, store, modify and retrieve the transactions of an organisation.

The four important characteristics of a TPS are as follows.

(a)   **Controlled processing**. The processing must support an organisation's operations.

(b)   **Inflexibility**. A TPS wants every transaction to be processed in the same way regardless of user or time. If it were flexible there would be too many opportunities for non-standard operations.

(c)   **Rapid response**. Fast performance is critical. Input must become output in seconds so customers don't wait.

(d)   **Reliability**. Organisations rely heavily on transaction processing systems, with failure potentially stopping business. Back-up and recovery procedures must be quick and accurate.

5.1.1 Properties of a TPS

The components of a TPS include hardware, software and people. People in a TPS can be divided into three categories – users, participants and people from the environment.

The **users** are employees of the company who own the TPS. The users will not alter data themselves, but will use the TPS to provide inputs for other information systems such as inventory control.

Participants are direct users of the system. They are the people who enter the data. Participants include data entry operators, customer service staff and people working at checkouts.

People from the environment are people who sometimes require the services of a TPS as they enter transactions and validate data, such as customers withdrawing money from an ATM.

5.1.2 Types of TPS

Batch transaction processing (BTP) collects transaction data as a group and processes it later, after a time delay, as batches of identical data.

An example of BTP is cheque clearance. A cheque is a written order asking the bank to pay an amount of money to the payee. The payee cannot withdraw the money until the cheque is cleared. This involves checking that the payer has enough money in their account to cover the cheque. It usually takes three working days – cheques are cleared in a group during a quiet period of the day.

Real time transaction processing (RTTP) is the immediate processing of data. It involves using a terminal or workstation to enter data and display results and provides instant confirmation. A large number of users can perform transactions simultaneously but access to a central online database is required.

An example of an RTTP system is a reservation system involved in setting aside a service or product for the customer to use at a future time. Such systems are commonly used for flight or train bookings and hotel reservations and require an acceptable response time, as transactions are made in the presence of customers.

5.2 Management information systems

Management information systems (MIS) convert data from mainly internal sources into information (eg summary reports, exception reports). This information enables managers to make timely and effective decisions for planning, directing and controlling the activities for which they are responsible.

Key term

Management information systems (MIS) generate information for monitoring performance (eg productivity information) and maintaining co-ordination (eg between purchasing and accounts payable).

MIS extract, process and summarise data from the TPS and provide periodic (weekly, monthly, quarterly) reports to managers.

Today MIS are becoming more flexible by providing access to information whenever needed, rather than pre-specified reports on a periodic basis. Users can often generate more customised reports by selecting subsets of data (such as listing the products with a 2% increase in sales over the past month), using different sorting options (by sales region, salesperson, highest volume of sales) and different display choices (graphical, tabular).

MIS have the following characteristics.

- Support structured decisions at operational and management control levels
- Designed to report on existing operations
- Little analytical capability
- Relatively inflexible
- An internal focus

5.3 Executive information systems

Executive information systems (EIS) draw data from the MIS and allow communication with external sources of information.

Key term

Executive information systems (EIS) provide a generalised computing and communication environment for senior managers to support strategic decisions.

Executive information systems draw data from the MIS and allow communication with **external sources** of information. EIS are designed to facilitate senior managers' access to information quickly and effectively. They have:

- Menu-driven user friendly interfaces
- Interactive graphics to help visualisation of the situation
- Communication capabilities linking the executive to external databases

An EIS summarises and tracks **strategically critical information** from the MIS and includes data from external sources, eg competitors, legislation and databases such as Reuters.

A good way to think about an EIS is to imagine the senior management team in an aircraft cockpit, with the instrument panel showing them the status of all the key business activities. EIS typically involve lots of data analysis and modelling tools, such as **what-if analysis** to help **strategic decision-making**.

A model of a typical EIS is shown below.

5.4 Enterprise resource planning systems

Executive resource planning systems (ERP systems) are modular software packages designed to integrate the key processes in an organisation so that a single system can serve the information needs of all functional areas.

Most organisations around the world have realised that, in a rapidly changing environment, it is impossible to create and maintain a custom-designed software package that will cater to all their requirements and also be completely up to date. Realising the requirement of user organisations, some of the leading software companies have designed **enterprise resource planning** software which will offer an integrated software solution to all the functions of an organisation.

ERP systems are large-scale information systems that impact an organisation's accounting information systems. These systems permeate all aspects of the organisation. A key element necessary for the ERP to provide business analysis is the data warehouse. This is a database designed for quick search, retrieval, query, and so on.

Key term

Executive resource planning systems (ERP systems) are modular software packages designed to integrate the key processes in an organisation so that a single system can serve the information needs of all functional areas.

ERP systems primarily support business operations – those activities in an organisation that support the selling process, including order processing, manufacturing, distribution, planning, customer service, human resources, finance and purchasing. ERP systems are function-rich, and typically cover all these activities – the principal benefit being that the same data can easily be shared between different departments.

This **integration** is accomplished through a database shared by all the application programs. For example, when a customer service representative takes a sales order, it is entered in the common database and it automatically updates the manufacturing backlog, the price, the credit system and the shipping schedule.

ERP systems work in **real time**, meaning that the **exact status** of everything is always available. Further, many of these systems are global. Since they can be deployed at sites around the world, they can work in **multiple languages and currencies**. When they are, you can immediately see, for example, exactly how much of a particular part is on hand at the warehouse in Japan and what its value is in yen or dollars.

5.4.1 Example: ERP

Say you are running a bicycle shop. Once you make a sale, you enter the order on the ERP system. The system then updates the inventory of bicycles in the shop, incorporates the sale into the financial ledgers, prints out an invoice, and can prompt you to purchase more bikes to replace the ones that you have sold. The ERP system can also handle repair orders and manage the spare parts inventory. It can also provide automated tools to help you forecast future sales and to plan activities over the next few weeks. There may also be data query tools present to enable sophisticated management reports and graphs to be generated. In addition, the system may handle the return of defective items from unhappy customers, the sending out of regular account statements to customers and the management of payments to suppliers.

ERP systems can assist with the scheduling and deployment of all sorts of resources, physical, monetary and human. A water company might use their ERP system to schedule a customer repair job, deploy staff to the job, verify that it got done, and subsequently bill the customer. An oil company might use it to ensure that their tankers are loaded, that a shipping itinerary is prepared and completed on schedule, and that all the equipment and people required for loading and unloading the cargo in each port are present at the right times. A bus company might use its system to manage customer bookings, record receipts and plan preventive maintenance activities for their fleet.

5.4.2 Benefits of ERP

The benefits that may be realised from a successfully implemented ERP project include:

(a)   Allowing **access** to the system to any individual with a terminal linked to the system's central server

(b)   **Decision support features**, to assist management with decision-making

(c)   In many cases, extranet **links to the major suppliers and customers**, with electronic data interchange facilities for the automated transmission of documentation, such as purchase orders and invoices

(d)   A lot of inefficiencies in the way things are done can be removed; the company can adopt so-called **'best practices'** – a cookbook of how similar activities are performed in world-class companies

(e)   A company can **restructure its processes**, so that different functions (such as accounting, shipping and manufacturing) work more closely together to get products produced

(f) An organisation can align itself to a single plan, so that all activities, all around the world, are smoothly **co-ordinated**

(g) **Standardising** Information and work practices so that the terminology used is similar, no matter where you work in the company

(h) A company could do a lot more work for a lot more customers without needing to employ so many people

6 Open and closed systems

FAST FORWARD

Systems can be **open** or **closed**.

The word **system** is impossible to define satisfactorily (the tax 'system', the respiratory 'system', the class 'system'). Basically it means **something that connects things up**.

6.1 Closed systems

Key term

> A **closed system** is isolated and shut off from the environment. Information is not received from or provided to the environment.

Closed systems are seldom, if ever, found in naturally occurring situations. A typical example of a closed system would be a chemical reaction that takes place under controlled conditions in a laboratory. Closed systems can be created to **eliminate external factors** and then used to **investigate the relationship between known variables** in an experiment.

All social systems have some interaction with the environment and so cannot be closed systems. A commercial organisation, for example, could not operate as a closed system, as it would be unable to react to the external environment and so would not be commercially or economically viable.

6.2 Open systems

Key term

> An **open system** is connected to and interacts with the environment and is influenced by it.

An open system **accepts inputs from its surroundings, processes the inputs in some manner and then produces an output**. The **input parameters** can be **foreseen** or **unpredictable**. Similarly, **outputs** can either be **predicted** or **unforeseen**. For example, consider a metal smelting works. Predictable inputs would include items like the raw materials and coal while the predictable outputs would be ash, smoke and the smelted metal. If the raw material to be smelted became contaminated in some way, it is likely that an undesirable product would be produced. These are examples of unforeseen inputs and outputs.

All social systems, including **business organisations**, are **open systems**. For example, a business is a system where management decisions are influenced by or have an influence on suppliers, customers, competitors, the Government and society as a whole. Employees are obviously influenced by what they do in their job, but as members of society at large they are also part of the external environment, just as their views and opinions expressed within the business are often a reflection of their opinions as members of society at large.

6.3 Open and closed systems and performance management

Systems are rarely either open or closed, but open to some influences and closed to others. Organisations must carefully choose the **form of management accounting system** based on the respective scenario.

The chemical laboratory could use a **closed system**. Here, performance is largely influenced by an **internally created environment** and external factors would not affect the output or result of the activity.

However, if an organisation's performance is influenced by **environmental factors**, it should operate an open system that accepts input from the external factors and examines their impact on performance output.

The advantages of an open system are:

(a) It encourages strong **communication**, which helps an organisation to operate efficiently and become effective.

(b) It adapts to the **changing environment** and there is scope for absorbing new pieces of information into the system.

(c) It highlights the **interdependencies** of different operations and processes within a business and the environment in which it operates.

(d) It helps business leaders and managers to focus on the **external factors** that shape behaviour and patterns within the organisation.

Management should consider the potential limitations of open systems.

(a) **Non-linear relationships** could exist among variables. A small change in one variable could cause a large change in another and affect the business result in a positive or negative way.

(b) It could prove **difficult to measure** the success of the system, specifically metrics relating to input, processing and output as well as the interrelationship among them.

Question — Open and closed systems

Run-Smart Co manufactures sports clothing for professional athletes. Products are designed to prevent injury and aid the post-exercise recovery process. The company regularly seeks feedback from athletes regarding the effectiveness of products and recommendations to take forward.

Required

Explain which kind of marketing system the organisation has.

Answer

Run-Smart Co operates an open system. The company interacts with its environment. It takes feedback from its customers about the effectiveness of its products and accordingly advises the product design department about customer preferences. Based on customer feedback, the company may decide to alter product design and specification.

Chapter Roundup

- **Strategic planning** is the process of deciding on objectives for the organisation, changes in these objectives, the resources to attain these objectives and the policies that are to govern the acquisition, use and disposition of these resources.

- **Management control** is the process by which managers assure that resources are obtained and used effectively and efficiently in the accomplishment of the organisation's objectives. It is sometimes called **tactics** or **tactical planning**.

- **Operational control** (or **operational planning**) is the process of assuring that specific tasks are carried out effectively and efficiently.

- **Management accounting information** can be used to support strategic planning, control and decision-making. Strategic management accounting differs from traditional management accounting because it has an **external** orientation and a **future** orientation.

- **Management control** is at the level below strategic planning in Anthony's decision-making hierarchy and is concerned with decisions about the efficient and effective use of resources to achieve objectives.

- **Operational control**, the lowest tier in Anthony's hierarchy, is concerned with assuring that specific tasks are carried out effectively and efficiently.

- **Transaction processing systems** (TPS) collect, store, modify and retrieve the transactions of an organisation.

- **Management information systems** (MIS) convert data from mainly internal sources into information (eg summary reports, exception reports). This information enables managers to make timely and effective decisions for planning, directing and controlling the activities for which they are responsible.

- **Executive information systems** (EIS) draw data from the MIS and allow communication with external sources of information.

- **Executive resource planning systems** (ERP systems) are modular software packages designed to integrate the key processes in an organisation so that a single system can serve the information needs of all functional areas.

- Systems can be **open** or **closed**.

1   Which of the following is **not** a feature of strategic management accounting?

   A   External orientation
   B   Historic focus
   C   Non-financial orientation
   D   Inputs from many areas of a business

2   What can strategic management accounting provide information or guidance about to a business?

3   Which of the following are characteristics of a transaction processing system?

   A   Reliability
   B   Controlled processing
   C   Inflexibility
   D   Rapid response

4   Match the terms to the correct definitions.

   Terms

   (a)   Transaction processing systems

   (b)   Executive information systems

   (c)   Executive resource planning systems

   Definitions

   1   Draw data from the MIS and allow communication with external sources of information

   2   Collect, store modify and retrieve the transactions of an organisation

   3   Modular software packages designed to integrate the key processes in an organisation

5   Open systems are seldom, if ever, found in naturally occurring situations. **True or false?**

6   Interaction with other systems or the outside environment is a feature of open systems. **True or false?**

1   B   Strategic management accounting is forward looking in contrast to traditional management accounting, which is a backward-looking process.

2   You could list a number of suggestions here. The Study Text gives examples but you may have others. Our list includes:

   (a)   **Competitors' costs**
   (b)   **Financial effect of competitor response**
   (c)   **Product profitability**
   (d)   **Customer profitability**
   (e)   **Pricing decisions**
   (f)   The **value of market share**
   (g)   **Capacity expansion**
   (h)   Decisions to **enter** or **leave** a **business area**
   (i)   **Brand values**
   (j)   **Shareholder wealth**
   (k)   **Cash flow**
   (l)   Effect of **acquisitions** and **mergers**
   (m)   Introduction of **new technology**

3   All of them

4   (a) 2; (b) 1; (c) 3

5   False. It is closed systems that are seldom found.

6   True

Now try the questions below from the Practice Question Bank

Number	Level	Marks	Approximate time
Section A Q81	Examination	2	4 mins
Section A Q82	Examination	2	4 mins
Section A Q83	Examination	2	4 mins
Section A Q84	Examination	2	4 mins
Section A Q85	Examination	2	4 mins

Sources of management information and management reports

15

Topic list	Syllabus reference
1 Sources of management accounting information	D2 (a)
2 Information for control purposes	D2 (b)
3 Costs of information	D2 (c),(d)
4 Costs, benefits and limitations of external information	D2 (e)
5 Controls over generating and distributing internal information	D3 (a)
6 Security and confidential information	D3 (b)

Introduction

In this chapter we look at **internal and external sources of management information** including financial accounting records, government agencies and consumer panels.

We also consider the costs, benefits and limitations of external information and the principal controls and procedures involved in generating and distributing information.

Study guide

		Intellectual level
D2	**Sources of management information**	
(a)	Identify the principal internal and external sources of management accounting information.	2
(b)	Demonstrate how these principal sources of information might be used for control purposes.	2
(c)	Identify and discuss the direct data capture and process costs of management accounting information.	2
(d)	Identify and discuss the indirect costs of producing information.	2
(e)	Discuss the limitations of using externally generated information.	2
D3	**Management reports**	
(a)	Discuss the principal controls required in generating and distributing internal information.	2
(b)	Discuss the procedures that may be necessary to ensure security of highly confidential information that is not for external consumption.	2

Exam guide

The topics covered in this chapter could form part of a scenario question in the exam or could feature as an objective test question in Section A. Ensure that you are able to **identify** and **discuss** internal and external sources of management accounting information as well as potential controls and security procedures to safeguard data.

> ⚠️ **PER alert**
>
> One of the competences you require to fulfil performance objective 12 of the PER is to monitor new developments in management accounting and consider their potential impact on performance and to management accounting systems. This data forms reports to management and is key for control and monitoring performance. In this chapter we look at information sources and procedures that may be necessary to ensure security of highly confidential information.

1 Sources of management accounting information

FAST FORWARD

> **Internal** sources of **information** include the financial accounting records and other systems closely tied to the accounting system.

Capturing data/information from inside the organisation involves the following.

(a) A **system for collecting or measuring transactions data** – eg sales, purchases, inventory and revenue – which sets out procedures for **what** data is collected, **how frequently**, **by whom** and by **what methods**, and how it is **processed** and **filed** or **communicated**

(b) **Informal communication** of information between managers and staff (eg, by word of mouth or at meetings)

(c) **Communication between managers**

1.1 Sources of monetary and non-monetary information

1.1.1 The financial accounting records

You are by now very familiar with the idea of a system of sales ledgers and purchase ledgers, general ledgers, cash books, and so on. These records provide a **history of an organisation's monetary transactions**.

Some of this information is of great value outside the accounts department – most obviously, for example, sales information for the marketing function. Other information, like cheque numbers, is of purely administrative value within the accounts department.

You will also be aware that, to maintain the integrity of its financial accounting records, an organisation of any size will have systems for and **controls over transactions**. These also give rise to valuable information.

An inventory control system is the classic example: besides actually recording the monetary value of purchases and inventory in hand for external financial reporting purposes, the system will include purchase orders, goods received notes, goods returned notes, and so on, which can be analysed to provide management information about **speed** of delivery, say, or the **quality** of supplies.

1.1.2 Other internal sources

Much information that is not strictly part of the financial accounting records nevertheless is closely tied to the accounting system.

(a) Information about personnel will be linked to the **payroll** system. Additional information may be obtained from this source if, say, a project is being costed and it is necessary to ascertain the availability and rate of pay of different levels of staff.

(b) Much information will be produced by a **production** department about machine capacity, movement of materials and work in progress, set up times, maintenance requirements, and so on.

(c) Many service businesses – notably accountants and solicitors – need to keep detailed records of the **time** spent on various activities, both to justify fees to clients and to assess the efficiency of operations.

Staff themselves are one of the primary sources of internal information. Information may be obtained either **informally** in the course of day to day business or **formally** through **meetings**, **interviews** or **questionnaires**.

Question	Sources of information

Think of at least one piece of non-monetary information that a management accountant might obtain from the following sources in order to make a decision about a new product.

(a) Marketing manager
(b) Vehicle fleet supervisor
(c) Premises manager
(d) Public relations officer
(e) Head of research

1.2 External sources of information

FAST FORWARD

External information tends to be more relevant to strategic and tactical decisions than to operational decisions. (Benchmarking is an exception.)

Capturing information from outside the organisation might be carried out formally and entrusted to particular individuals, or might be 'informal'.

1.3 Formal collection of data from outside sources

FAST FORWARD

There are many **sources** of **external information**.

(a) A company's **tax specialists** will be expected to gather information about changes in tax law and how this will affect the company.

(b) Obtaining information about any new legislation on health and safety at work, or employment regulations, must be the responsibility of a particular person – for example the company's **legal expert** or **company secretary** – who must then pass on the information to other managers affected by it.

(c) Research and development work often relies on information about other R&D work being done by another company or by government institutions. An **R&D official** might be made responsible for finding out about R&D work outside the company.

(d) **Marketing managers** need to know about the opinions and buying attitudes of potential customers. To obtain this information, they might carry out market research exercises.

Informal gathering of information from the environment **goes on all the time, consciously or unconsciously**, because the employees of an organisation learn **what is going on in the world around** them – perhaps from the media, meetings with business associates or the trade press.

Organisations hold external information, such as invoices and advertisements, **from customers and suppliers**. However, there are many occasions when an active search outside the organisation is necessary.

1.4 Specific external sources

FAST FORWARD

Secondary data, such as government statistics or data provided by online databases, is not collected by or for the user. **Primary data** – more expensive than secondary data – is more tailored to the user's exact needs. Market research is an example.

1.4.1 Directories

Examples (of business directories) include the following (although there are many others).

(a) Kompass Register (Kompass)
(b) Who owns Whom (Dun & Bradstreet)
(c) Key British Enterprises (Dun & Bradstreet)

1.4.2 Associations

There are associations in almost every field of business and leisure activity, and ACCA itself is an organisation. Associations collect and publish data for their members that can be of great interest to other users. For example, although the services of the Road Haulage Association (RHA) are geared towards transport businesses, their analysis of fuel prices rises could be useful to all motorists.

1.4.3 Government agencies

The Government is a major source of economic information and information about industry and population trends. Examples of UK Government publications are as follows. Most of these are available online and can be downloaded for free.

(a) **National Statistics**, divided into 12 separate themes such as economy, health and labour

(b) The **Digest of UK Energy Statistics** (published annually)

(c)   **Housing and Construction Statistics** (published quarterly)

(d)   **Financial Statistics** (monthly)

(e)   **Economic Trends** now published with **Labour Market Trends** in the **Economic Labour Market Review**

(f)   **Public Sector Employment Trends** (annual) gives details of employment in the public sector in the UK

(g)   **A variety of publications on the Department for Business, Innovation and Skills website** give data on industrial and commercial trends at home and overseas

(h)   **Social Trends** (annual)

Official statistics are also published by other government bodies, such as the European Union, the United Nations and local authorities.

1.4.4 Other published sources

This group includes all other publications, including some **digests** and **pocket books** and **periodicals** (often available in public libraries).

1.4.5 Syndicated services

The sources of secondary data we have looked at so far have generally been **free** because they are **in the public domain**. Inexpensiveness is an advantage that can be offset by the fact that the information is **unspecific** and needs **considerable analysis** before being useable. A middle step between adapting secondary data and commissioning primary research is the **purchase of data collected by market research companies**. The data tend to be expensive but less costly than primary research.

1.4.6 Consumer panels

A form of continuous research which result in secondary data often bought in by marketers is that generated by **consumer panels**. These constitute a representative sample of individuals and households whose buying activity in a defined area is monitored either continuously (every day, with results aggregated) or at regular intervals, **over a period of time**. There are panels set up to monitor purchases of groceries, consumer durables, cars, baby products and many others.

1.5 Information from customers

Customers can provide useful information.

(a)   Firms send out satisfaction questionnaires and market research.
(b)   Customer comments and complaints sent voluntarily can suggest improvements.

1.6 Information from suppliers

Supplier information comes in several categories.

Information	Comment
'Bid' information	A supplier pitching for a product will detail products, services and prices. This is before a deal is done.
Operational information	If a firm has placed a particular job or contract with a supplier, the supplier may provide details of the stages in the manufacturing process, eg the delivery time.
Pricing information	Component prices vary from industry to industry; some are volatile.
Technology	Technological developments in the supplier's industry can affect the type of input components, their cost and their availability.

1.7 The internet

FAST FORWARD

> The **internet** increases the richness of external data and reduces the cost of searching for it.

Key term

> The **internet** is a global network connecting millions of computers.

The internet offers efficient, fast and cost-effective **email**, and massive information **search and retrieval facilities**. There is a great deal of financial information available and users can also **access publications** and news releases issued by the Treasury and other government departments.

Businesses are also using it to **provide information (cheaply) about their own products and services** and to conduct **research** into their competitors' activities.

The internet offers a **speedy** and **impersonal** way of getting to know the basics (or even the details) of the services that a company provides.

The internet is commonly used to **access information about suppliers**.

(a)   A firm can visit a supplier's website for details of products and services.

(b)   The user can search a number of websites through a browser. Note that the internet may not contain every supplier; arguably it should not be relied on as the sole source.

(c)   A number of business to business sites have been opened. Participating members offer their services, and can offer quotes. A lot of the communication search problem is avoided.

1.8 Database information

A **management information system** or **database** should provide managers with a **useful flow** of **relevant information** which is **easy to use** and **easy to access**. Information is an important corporate resource. Managed and used effectively, it can provide considerable competitive advantage and so it is a worthwhile investment.

It is now possible to access large volumes of generally available information through databases held by public bodies and businesses.

(a)   Some companies, such as LexisNexis, charge users a subscription fee to access their electronic database. LexisNexis' clients come primarily from within the legal and accountancy profession, who use the service to access legal and public records related information.

(b)   **Public databases** are also available for inspection.

Dun & Bradstreet provides general business information. **AC Nielsen** operates online information regarding products and market share.

Developments in information technology allow businesses to have access to the databases of **external organisations**. Reuters, for example, provides an online information system about money market interest rates and foreign exchange rates to firms involved in money market and foreign exchange dealings, and to the treasury departments of a large number of companies. The growing adoption of technology at **point of sale** provides a potentially invaluable source of data to both retailer and manufacturer.

1.8.1 Online databases

Most external databases are online databases, which are very large computer files of information supplied by **database providers** and managed by '**host**' companies whose business revenue is generated through charges made to **users**. Access to such databases is open to anyone prepared to pay and who is equipped with a PC plus internet access and communication software. These days there are an increasing number of companies offering free internet access. Most databases can be accessed around the clock.

1.9 Data warehouses

A **data warehouse** contains **data from a range of internal** (for instance sales order processing system, nominal ledger) **and external sources**. One reason for including individual transaction data in a data warehouse is that the user can drill down to access transaction-level detail if necessary. Data is increasingly obtained from newer channels, such as customer care systems, outside agencies or websites.

The warehouse provides a coherent **set of information** to be **used across the organisation** for management **analysis** and **decision-making**. The reporting and query tools available within the warehouse should facilitate management reporting and analysis. This analysis can be enhanced through using **data mining** software to identify trends and patterns in the data.

2 Information for control purposes

FAST FORWARD

Much control is achieved through the **feedback** of internal information.

Control is dependent on the **receipt and processing of information**, both to plan in the first place and to compare actual results against the plan, so as to judge what control measures are needed.

Plans will be based on an **awareness of the environment** (from externally sourced information) and on the **current performance of the organisation** (based on internal information such as, for example, sales volumes and costs).

Control is achieved through **feedback** – information about actual results produced from within the organisation (that is, internal information) such as variance control reports for the purpose of helping management with control decisions.

The sources of information outlined earlier in the chapter are used to supply **management with data for control**.

For instance, **payroll records** give information on the total cost of staff and a breakdown into cost by function, role, bonuses, taxes, and so on which can show management how different cost areas are performing. As payroll is often a large cost and to some extent discretionary or variable, it is important to monitor and control.

Equally, information on **wage payments** will also be relevant to an organisation's cash flow planning. As far as possible, organisations like to keep their cash balances within certain limits. So, by knowing the amount and timing of wages and salary payments, the organisation can make any adjustments to ensure cash balances remain within the desired limits.

Information about **inventory** levels can also be instructive. For example, some lines of inventory may be slow moving, but management will need to establish why this is. Has a competitor introduced a rival product, or reduced its prices? Have there been any quality issues with the product which have damaged its reputation in the marketplace? Is the product in a long-term decline and should production of it be discontinued? In this respect, information about quantities of a product sold compared with quantities produced could also be very useful. For example, if a product is selling very well, production may need to be increased so that demand can be satisfied and any stock-outs avoided.

Customer data is vital in any business that strives to focus on customers. Thus data on buying habits, where customers shop, what they buy and who the main customers are all give feedback for control purposes.

Equally, data from customer sales accounts can provide useful information on how customer debts are aged. A report on the ageing of debt can provide management with information on how successful its receivables control policy is. Management's response will be different if half the customer debt has been outstanding for more than say, 60 days, compared with only 5% of the debt being outstanding for more than 60 days.

External data is useful for benchmarking provided the correct or appropriate benchmarks are selected.

3 Costs of information

FAST FORWARD Be aware of the **cost** of inefficient use of information.

The costs to an organisation of the collection, processing and production of internal information can be divided into three types. These are direct data capture costs, process costs, and indirect costs of producing internal information.

Cost	Examples
Direct data capture	• Use of bar coding and scanners (eg in retailing and manufacturing) • Employee time spent filling in timesheets • Secretary time spent taking minutes at a meeting
Processing	• Payroll department time spent processing and analysing personnel costs • Time for personnel to input data (eg in relation to production) on to the MIS
Inefficient use of information	• Information collected but not needed • Information stored long after it is needed • Information disseminated more widely than necessary • Collection of the same information by more than one method • Duplication of information

4 Costs, benefits and limitations of external information

FAST FORWARD There are specific **costs** not only in obtaining data but also in maintaining the infrastructure supporting data collection and distribution.

4.1 Costs

Identifying the costs of obtaining external data is not difficult. Effectively there are five types of cost.

Cost	Examples
Direct search costs	• Cost of a marketing research survey (this can be considerable) • Subscriptions to online databases • Subscriptions to magazines, services • Download fees
Indirect access costs	• Management and employee time spent finding useful information • Wasted management and employee time on unsuccessful searches for information • Spurious accuracy/redundancy • Wasted management and employee time on excessive searching • Wasted time on trying to find spurious accuracy
Management costs	• Recording, processing and dissemination of external information • Wasted time due to information overload • Wasted time on excessive processing
Infrastructure costs	• Installation and maintenance of computer networks, servers, landlines, etc to facilitate internet searching and internal electronic communication

Cost	Examples
Time theft	<ul><li>Wasted time caused by abuse of internet and email access facilities</li><li>Lost time</li><li>Cost of monitoring and disciplinary procedures</li><li>Information overload</li></ul>

As can be seen from the earlier case example, the **internet** can significantly reduce search time and cost. More information can be had for less money.

4.2 Benefits and limitations of external data

The benefits can be quantified in the following terms.

(a) The quality of **decisions** that the data has influenced

(b) **Risk/uncertainties** avoided by having the data

(c) The organisation's ability to **respond** appropriately to the environment or to **improve** its performance

One of the principal **limitations** of external data is that its **quality** cannot be guaranteed. Its **quality** will depend on the following characteristics.

(a) The **producers** of the data (they may have an axe to grind; trade associations may not include data which runs counter to the interests of its members)

(b) The **reason for the data** being collected in the first place

(c) The **collection method** (random samples with a poor response rate are particularly questionable)

(d) The **age** of the data (government statistics and information based on them are often relatively dated, though information technology has speeded up the process)

(e) **How parameters were defined** (for instance, the definition of family used by some researchers could well be very different to that used by others)

Using poor quality external data can have disastrous consequences: projects may proceed on the basis of overstated demand levels; opportunities may not be grasped because data is out of date and does not show the true state of the market.

4.2.1 Advantages arising from the use of secondary (as opposed to primary) data

(a) The data may solve the problem without the need for any primary research: **time and money is thereby saved**.

(b) **Cost savings** can be substantial because secondary data sources are a great deal **cheaper** than those for primary research.

(c) **Secondary data**, while not necessarily fulfilling all the needs of the business, can be of great use:

    (i) **Setting the parameters**, defining a hypothesis, highlighting variables; in other words, helping to focus on the central problem

    (ii) **Providing guidance**, by showing past methods of research and so on, for primary data collection

    (iii) **Helping to assimilate the primary research** with past research, highlighting trends and the like

    (iv) **Defining sampling parameters** (target populations, variables, and so on)

4.2.2 Disadvantages to the use of secondary data

(a) **Relevance**. The data may not be relevant to the research objectives in terms of the data content itself, classifications used or units of measurement.

(b) **Cost**. Although secondary data is usually cheaper than primary data, some specialist reports can cost large amounts of money. A cost-benefit analysis will determine whether such secondary data should be used or whether primary research would be more economical.

(c) **Availability**. Secondary data may not exist in the specific product or market area.

(d) **Bias**. The secondary data may be biased, depending on who originally carried it out and for what purpose. Attempts should be made to obtain the most original source of the data, to assess it for such bias.

(e) **Accuracy**. The accuracy of the data should be questioned.

The golden rule when using secondary data is **use only meaningful data**. It is obviously sensible to begin with internal sources and a firm with a good management information system should be able to provide a great deal of data. External information should be consulted in order of ease and speed of access.

5 Controls over generating and distributing internal information

FAST FORWARD **Controls** need to be in place over the generation of internal information in routine and ad-hoc reports.

5.1 Controls over generating internal information in routine reports

(a) Carry out a **cost-benefit analysis**. How **easy** is the report to prepare **compared** with the **usefulness** of the decisions that can be taken as a result of its production? The cost of preparing the report will in part be determined by **who** is preparing it. The cost can be reduced if its preparation can be **delegated** by a director to a junior member of staff.

(b) A **trial** preparation process should be carried out and a **prototype** prepared. Users should be asked to confirm that their requirements will be met.

(c) A **consistent** format and consistent definitions should be used to ensure that reporting is **accurate** and the chance of misinterpretation is minimised. Standard **house styles** will ensure that time is not wasted by managers, staff and report writers on designing alternative layouts.

(d) The **originator** of the report should be clearly identified so that users' queries can be dealt with quickly.

(e) The report should clearly set out **limits to the action** that users **can take as a result** of the information in the report. This will ensure that the organisation's system of responsibilities is maintained.

(f) The **usefulness** of the report should be **assessed** on a periodic basis to ensure that its production is necessary.

5.2 Controls over generating internal information in ad hoc reports

(a) Carry out a **cost-benefit** analysis as above.

(b) Ensure that the required information **does not already exist** in another format.

(c) Brief the report writer so that **only the relevant information** is provided.

(d) Ensure that the **originator** is clearly identified.

(e) Ensure that report writers have access to the **most up-to-date information.**

5.3 Controls over distributing internal information

FAST FORWARD A **procedures manual** sets out controls over distributing internal information.

(a) **Procedures manual** (for standard reports)

   (i) Indicates what standard reports should be issued and when (eg budgetary control report for department X on a monthly basis)

   (ii) Sets out the format of standard reports

   (iii) Makes clear who should receive particular standard reports

   (iv) Indicates whether reports should be shredded (if confidential) or just binned

   (v) Makes clear what information should be regarded as highly confidential

(b) **Other controls**

(i) **Payroll and personnel information** should be kept in a **locked** cabinet or be protected by **password** access on a computer system.

(ii) All employees should be **contractually required not to divulge confidential information**.

(iii) The internal mail system should make use of **'private and confidential' stamps**.

(iv) An appropriate **email policy** should be set up.

(1) Email is best suited to short messages rather than detailed operational problems.

(2) Email provides a relatively permanent means of communication, which may be undesirable for confidential/'off-the-record' exchanges.

(3) Staff may suffer from information overload.

(4) It is uncomfortable to read more than a full screen of information. Longer messages will either not be read properly or will be printed out (in which case they may just as well have been circulated in hard-copy form).

(v) **Physical computer security**

Internal security. Management can regulate which staff members have access to different types of data. For instance, access to HR records may be restricted to members of the HR team by keeping these records on a separate server or database. In this way, only certain terminals may access servers with sensitive or confidential data stored on them.

External security. The organisation can also protect its data from external access by using **firewalls**.

A firewall is designed **to restrict access** to a network by selectively allowing or blocking inbound traffic to parts of an organisation's system. It examines messages entering and exiting the system and blocks any that do not conform to specified criteria. In this way, firewalls can be used to protect data and databases from being accessed by unauthorised people or terminals. For example, access to key servers could be restricted to a small number of terminals only.

5.4 If information is held on a server

(a) Controls over viruses and hacking
(b) Clearly understood policy on the use of emails and corporate IT
(c) Password system to restrict access to particular files

6 Security and confidential information

Disaffected employees have potential to do deliberate damage to valuable corporate data or systems, especially if the information system is networked, because they may have access to parts of the system that they are not really authorised to use.

If the organisation is linked to an external network, **people outside** the company (hackers) may also be able to get into the company's internal network, either to steal data or to damage the system.

Various **procedures** are therefore necessary to **ensure the security of highly confidential information that is not for external consumption**.

6.1 Passwords

Passwords are a set of characters allocated to a person, terminal or facility which have to be keyed into the system before further access is permitted.

In order to access a system the user first needs to enter a string of characters. If what is entered matches a password issued to an authorised user or valid for that particular terminal, the system permits access. Otherwise the system **shuts down** and may **record the attempted unauthorised access**.

Keeping track of these attempts can alert managers to repeated efforts to break into the system; in these cases the culprits might be caught, particularly if there is an apparent pattern to their efforts.

The restriction of access to a system with passwords is effective and widely used but the widespread and growing use of PCs and networks is making physical isolation virtually impossible. The wider use of information systems requires that access to the system becomes equally widespread and easy. Requirements for system security must be balanced by the operational requirements for access: rigidly enforced isolation of the system may significantly reduce the value of the system.

6.2 Logical access systems

While **physical access control (doors, locks, and so on)** is concerned with the prevention of unauthorised persons **gaining access to the hardware**, **logical access control** is concerned with **preventing those who already have access to a terminal or a computer from gaining access to data or software**.

In a logical access system, data and software or individual computer systems will be **classified according to the sensitivity and confidentiality of data**.

(a)   Payroll data or details of the draft corporate budget for the coming year may thus be perceived as highly sensitive and made available to identified individuals only.

(b)   Other financial information may be made available to certain groups of staff only, for example members of the finance function or a certain grade of management.

(c)   Other data may be unrestricted.

A logical access system performs three operations when access is requested.

(a)   Identification of the user
(b)   Authentication of user identity
(c)   Check on user authority

6.3 Database controls

Databases present a particular problem for computer security. In theory, the database can be **accessed by large numbers of people**, and so the possibility of **alteration, unauthorised disclosure or fraud is so much greater than with application-specific files**.

It is possible to construct **complicated password systems**, and the system can be **programmed** to give a limited view of its contents to particular users or restrict the disclosure of certain types of information to particular times of day. It is possible to build a set of **privileges** into the system, allowing authorised users with a particular password to access more information.

There are problems ensuring that individuals do not circumvent the database by means of **inference**, however. If you ask enough questions, you should be able to infer from the replies the information you are really seeking.

For example, the database forbids you to ask if John is employee Category A. However, if you know there are only three employee categories, A, B, and C, and there is no prohibition on asking about categories B and C, you can work out the members of category A by process of elimination (ie neither B, nor C, therefore A).

These so-called **inference controls** exist to make this difficult by **limiting the number of queries, or by controlling the overlap between questions**.

6.4 Firewalls

Systems can have firewalls to **prevent unauthorised access into company systems**. Firewalls can be implemented in both **hardware and software**, or a combination of both. Firewalls are frequently used to **prevent unauthorised internet users from accessing private networks connected to the internet, especially intranets**. All messages entering or leaving the intranet pass through the firewall, which examines each message and blocks those that do not meet specified security criteria.

As well as preventing unauthorised access onto company systems, firewalls can also be used to help protect a company's data from corruption by viruses.

6.5 Encryption

Information transmitted from one part of an organisation to another may be intercepted. Data can be encrypted (**scrambled**) in an attempt to make it **unintelligible to eavesdroppers**.

6.6 Other safety measures

Authentication is a technique for making sure that a message has come from an authorised sender.

Dial back security operates by requiring the person wanting access to the network to dial into it and identify themselves first. The system then dials the person back on their authorised number before allowing them access.

All attempted violations of security should be automatically **logged** and the log checked regularly. In a multi-user system, the terminal attempting the violation may be automatically disconnected.

6.7 Personal data

In recent years there has been a growing popular fear that **information about individuals which is stored on computer files** and processed by computer can be **misused**.

In particular, it is felt that an individual could easily be **harmed** by the existence of computerised data about themselves which was **inaccurate** or **misleading** and which could be **transferred** to unauthorised third parties at high speed and little cost.

As a result, most countries have introduced **legislation** designed to protect the individual. In the UK, the current legislation is the Data Protection Act 1998.

6.8 Personnel security planning

Certain employees will always be placed in a position of trust; for example, senior systems analysts, the database administrator and the computer security officer. With the growth of networks, almost all employees may be in a position to do damage to a computer system. A recent report claims that 80% of hacking is done by employees.

Although most employees are honest and well intentioned, it may be relatively easy for individuals to **compromise the security** of an organisation if they wish to do so. The following types of measure are therefore necessary.

(a)   Careful recruitment
(b)   Job rotation
(c)   Supervision and observation by a superior
(d)   Review of computer usage (eg via systems logs)
(e)   Enforced vacations

The key is that **security should depend on the minimum possible number of personnel**. Although this is a weakness, it is also a strength.

6.9 Anti-virus and anti-spyware software

The growth of the internet has led to increased exposure to security risks. Two particular risks derive from exposure to **computer viruses** and to **spyware**.

Computer viruses typically arrive by email and are triggered when the user opens the email and an attachment. **The virus** is a self-replicating computer program that **infiltrates and then damages a computer system**.

Spyware is a type of program that **watches** what users do with their computer and then **sends that information** over the internet to a third party. Customers of online bank accounts have experienced particular problems with spyware when their personal financial data has been captured by keylogging software.

Software has been developed to counteract these risks. **Anti-virus software** works to achieve this by:

(a)   **Scanning files** to look for known viruses

(b)   **Identifying suspicious behaviour** from any computer program that might indicate infection

Anti-spyware software combats spyware in two ways.

(a)   Real-time protection which prevents the installation of spyware by **blocking software** and activities known to represent spyware

(b)   **Detection** and **removal** of spyware by scanning software and removing files and entries that match known spyware

Chapter Roundup

- **Internal** sources of **information** include the financial accounting records and other systems closely tied to the accounting system.

- **External information** tends to be more relevant to strategic and tactical decisions than to operational decisions. (Benchmarking is an exception.)

- There are many sources of **external information**.

- **Secondary data**, such as government statistics or data provided by online databases, is not collected by or for the user. **Primary data** – more expensive than secondary data – is more tailored to the user's exact needs. Market research is an example.

- The **internet** increases the richness of external data and reduces the cost of searching for it.

- Much control is achieved through the **feedback** of internal information.

- Be aware of the **cost** of inefficient use of information.

- There are specific **costs** to obtaining data, but also to maintaining the infrastructure supporting data collection and distribution.

- **Controls** need to be in place over the generation of internal information in routine and ad-hoc reports.

- A **procedures manual** sets out controls over distributing internal information.

- A number of procedures can be used to ensure **the security of highly confidential information that is not for external consumption**:

    - Passwords
    - Logical access systems
    - Database controls
    - Firewalls
    - Personnel security planning
    - Anti-virus and anti-spyware software

Quick Quiz

1   'Published data is always reliable.' **True or false?**

2   Provide an example for each of the following costs of obtaining external information.

Direct search costs   ……………………………………..

Indirect access costs ……………………………………..

Management costs   ……………………………………..

Infrastructure costs   ……………………………………..

Time theft   ……………………………………..

3   Organisations have many sources they can use for external data. List six of these.

4   Choose the correct words from those highlighted.

Logical/physical access control is concerned with preventing those who **do not have access/already have access** to a terminal or computer from gaining access to **hardware/data or software**.

5   Five measures to control the ability of individuals to compromise the security of an organisation were listed in the chapter. What are they?

1 ……………………………………..

2 ……………………………………..

3 ……………………………………..

4 ……………………………………..

5 ……………………………………..

6   A number of procedures can be used to make sure confidential data is kept secure. List five of these.

1   False. 'Reliability' of data for a decision is determined by its age, the sample and data definitions. By 'published' data, include the internet – a source of falsehoods as well as information.

2   See Section 4.1.

3   Directories, Trade associations, government agencies, periodicals/journals, market research data and consumer panels

4   Logical
     already have access
     data or software

5   • Careful recruitment
     • Job rotation
     • Supervision and observation by a superior
     • Review of computer usage (for example via systems logs)
     • Enforced vacations

6   Passwords, logical access systems, database controls, firewalls, encryption, personnel security planning, and anti-virus and anti-spyware software

     (We list more than five to cover all of the possibilities mentioned in the chapter)

Now try the questions below from the Practice Question Bank

Number	Level	Marks	Approximate time
Section A Q86	Examination	2	4 mins
Section A Q87	Examination	2	4 mins
Section A Q88	Examination	2	4 mins
Section A Q89	Examination	2	4 mins
Section A Q90	Examination	2	4 mins

16

Performance measurement in private sector organisations

Topic list	Syllabus reference
1 Performance measurement	D4
2 Financial performance indicators (FPIs)	D4 (a)
3 Non-financial performance indicators (NFPIs)	D4 (b), D6(e)
4 Short-termism and manipulation	D4 (d), D6 (h)
5 Improving performance	D4 (a), (b), (c), D6 (g)
6 The balanced scorecard	D4 (e)
7 Building Block model	D4 (e)
8 Target setting in qualitative areas	D4 (f), D6 (f)

Introduction

This chapter begins by introducing the term **performance measurement** and then describes various performance measures that are used by private sector organisations (other than variances).

It is important that the performance of an organisation is monitored; this is most commonly done by calculating a number of ratios.

The chapter concludes by considering alternative views of performance measurement, such as the **balanced scorecard** and **building blocks**, which offer a contrast to the more **traditional** approaches to performance measurement.

Study guide

		Intellectual level
D4	**Performance analysis in private sector organisations**	
(a)	Describe, calculate and interpret financial performance indicators (FPIs) for profitability, liquidity and risk in both manufacturing and service businesses. Suggest methods to improve these measures.	2
(b)	Describe, calculate and interpret non-financial performance indicators (NFPIs) and suggest methods to improve the performance indicated.	2
(c)	Analyse past performance and suggest ways for improving financial and non-financial performance.	2
(d)	Explain the causes and problems created by short-termism and financial manipulation of results and suggest methods to encourage a long-term view.	2
(e)	Explain and interpret the balanced scorecard, and the Building Block model proposed by Fitzgerald and Moon.	2
(f)	Discuss the difficulties of target setting in qualitative areas.	2

Exam guide

You must be able to **explain** as well as calculate performance indicators and **apply** your analysis to the organisation in the question. This topic has been a feature of all the F5 exams so far. The organisations will not necessarily be limited companies.

1 Performance measurement   6/08, 12/10

FAST FORWARD

Performance measurement aims to establish how well something or somebody is doing in relation to a plan.

Performance measures may be divided into two types.

- Financial performance indicators
- Non-financial performance indicators

Exam focus point

There is an article on the ACCA website, written by members of the examining team, which will aid your learning in this area. It is called 'Interpreting financial data' (ACCA, 2015).

Performance measurement aims to establish how well something or somebody is doing in relation to a plan. The 'thing' may be a machine, a factory, a subsidiary company or an organisation as a whole. The 'body' may be an individual employee, a manager, or a group of people.

Performance measurement is a **vital part** of the **planning and control process**.

1.1 Financial and non-financial performance measures

Measures of performance may be either financial or non-financial.

(a) Financial measures are typically measures relating to revenues, costs, profits, return on capital, asset values or cash flows. Actual performance is often measured against a financial plan, such as a budget.

(b) Non-financial measures may relate to a number of different aspects of performance, such as:

- Product or service quality
- Reliability

- Speed of performance
- Risk
- Flexibility
- Customer attitudes
- Innovation
- Capability
- Pollution

It may be asked why organisations in the private sector whose primary objective is to make profits for shareholders should be particularly concerned with non-financial aspects of performance.

The answer is quite simply that non-financial aspects of performance are often a good indicator of future financial performance. Strong financial performance is not achievable over the long term unless non-financial performance is sufficiently strong to sustain the business.

Some performance measurements combine financial and non-financial aspects of performance, especially performance that relates to the efficiency of resource utilisation or capacity utilisation. Examples are such measures as cost per patient day in the hospital service and cost per tonne-mile in the transport and distribution industry.

1.2 Performance measures

The performance measures that are used will vary between organisations. Different measures are appropriate for different businesses. Other factors that influence the design of a performance management system are:

(a) **Measurement needs resources** – people, equipment and time to collect and analyse information. The costs and benefits of providing resources to produce a performance indicator must be carefully weighed up.

(b) **Performance must be measured in relation to something**, otherwise measurement is meaningless. Overall performance should be measured against the **objectives** of the organisation and the **plans** that result from those objectives. If the organisation has no clear objectives, the first step in performance measurement is to set them. The second is to identify the factors that are critical to the success of those objectives.

(c) **Measures must be relevant**. This means finding out what the organisation does and how it does it so that measures reflect what actually occurs.

(d) **Short-** and **long-term achievement** should be measured. Short-term targets can be valuable, but exclusive use of them may direct the organisation away from opportunities that will mean success for the business in the long term.

(e) Measures should be **fair**. They should only include factors which managers can control by their decisions, and for which they can be held **responsible**. Measuring controllable costs, revenues and assets may prove controversial, however.

(f) A **variety** of measures should be used. Managers may be able to find ways to distort a single measure, but should not be able to affect a variety of measures. The balanced scorecard (Section 6) provides a method of measuring performance from a number of perspectives.

(g) **Realistic estimates** may be required for measures to be employed. These include estimates of financial items whose value is not certain, such as the cost of capital, and estimates of the impact of non-financial items.

(h) Measurement needs **responses**, and above all managers to make decisions in the best interests of the organisation. Managers will only respond to measures that they find useful. The management accountant therefore needs to adopt a modern marketing philosophy to the provision of performance measures: satisfy customer wants, not pile 'em high and sell 'em cheap.

Once suitable performance measures have been selected they must be **monitored on a regular basis** to ensure that they are providing useful information. There is little point in an organisation devoting considerable resources to measuring market share if an increase in market share is not one of the organisation's objectives.

1.3 Quantitative and qualitative performance measures

Quantitative information is information that is expressed in numbers and by measurements. Qualitative information is not numerical, and may relate to such issues as customer loyalty, employee morale and capability. Qualitative information can sometimes be converted into quantitative values through tools such as ranking scales. For example 1 = Good, 2 = Average, 3 = Poor.

(a)   An example of a **quantitative** performance measure is: 1,000 units were produced in 50 hours at a cost of $15 per unit.

(b)   An example of a **qualitative** performance measure is 'Market research indicates a very strong and positive consumer response to the new product.'

Qualitative measures are by nature **subjective** and **judgmental** but they can still be useful. They are especially valuable when they are derived from several **different sources**, as the likelihood of an unreliable judgement is reduced.

Consider the statement:

'Seven out of ten customers think our service is very reliable.'

This is a **quantitative measure** of customer satisfaction (seven out of ten), as well as a **qualitative measure** of the perceived performance of the service (very reliable).

2 Financial performance indicators (FPIs)   12/07, 12/08,12/09, 12/10, 12/12, 12/13, 6/14, Specimen

FAST FORWARD

> **Financial performance indicators** analyse return on capital, profitability, liquidity and financial risk, often in relation to a plan or budget, or in relation to performance in preceding time periods.

Financial indicators (or **monetary** measures) include:

*   Profit (both gross profit and net profit)
*   Revenue
*   Costs
*   Cash flows
*   Debt and gearing

The two most common ways of using financial measures to assess performance are:

*   Comparing actual results with the **budget** or another financial plan

*   Comparing performance in the most recent time period with performance in a **corresponding previous time period** (or analysing a **trend over time**)

Financial measures may be presented as **ratios**, such as gross profit margin (gross profit/sales), and return on capital employed (net profit/capital employed).

Monetary amounts have meaning **only in relation to something else**. Financial results should be compared against a **benchmark** such as:

*   Budgeted **sales**, **costs** and **profits**

*   **Standards** in a standard costing system

*   The **trend** over time (last year/this year, say)

*   The results of **other parts of the business**

*   The results of **other businesses**

*   **Future potential** (for example, the performance of a new business may be judged in terms of nearness to breaking even)

Knowledge of how to calculate and interpret key ratios is a weak point for many students. Make sure it is one of your strong points.

2.1 Profitability

FAST FORWARD

In private sector organisations, the most important financial performance indicators are measurements of profit.

A company ought of course to be profitable, and there are obvious checks on **profitability**.

(a)   Whether the company has made a profit or a loss on its ordinary activities
(b)   By how much this year's profit or loss is bigger or smaller than last year's profit or loss

It is probably better to consider separately the profits or losses on exceptional items if there are any. Such gains or losses should not be expected to occur again, unlike profits or losses on normal trading.

Question   Profitability

A company has the following summarised income statements for two consecutive years.

	Year 1 $	Year 2 $
Turnover	70,000	100,000
Less cost of sales	42,000	55,000
Gross profit	28,000	45,000
Less expenses	21,000	35,000
Net profit	7,000	10,000

Although the net profit margin (net profit/sales) is the same for both years at 10%, the gross profit margin is not.

$$\text{Year 1} \quad \frac{28,000}{70,000} = 40\% \qquad\qquad \text{Year 2} \quad \frac{45,000}{100,000} = 45\%$$

Is this good or bad for the business?

Answer

An increased profit margin must be good because this indicates a wider gap between selling price and cost of sales. Given that the net profit ratio has stayed the same in the second year, however, expenses must be rising. In Year 1 expenses were 30% of turnover, whereas in Year 2 they were 35% of turnover. This indicates that administration, selling and distribution expenses or interest costs require tight control.

Percentage analysis of profit between year 1 and year 2

	Year 1 %	Year 2 %
Cost of sales as a % of sales	60	55
Gross profit as a % of sales	40	45
	100	100
Expenses as a % of sales	30	35
Net profit as a % of sales	10	10
Gross profit as a % of sales	40	45

Profit on ordinary activities before taxation is generally thought to be a **better** figure to use than profit **after** taxation, because there might be unusual variations in the tax charge from year to year which would not affect the underlying profitability of the company's operations.

Another profit figure that should be calculated is **PBIT**: **profit before interest and tax**. This is the amount of profit which the company earned **before having to pay interest to the providers of loan capital**. PBIT is often the same as 'operating profit'.

PBIT = profit on ordinary activities before taxation + interest charges on long-term loan capital

PBIT is also often Gross profit – Other operating costs.

2.1.1 Sales margin (gross profit margin)

> **Sales margin** is turnover less cost of sales. It is also called gross profit.

Look at the following examples.

(a) **XYZ Printing Company**

	$'000
Turnover	89,844
Cost of sales	(60,769)
Gross profit	29,075
Distribution expenses	(1,523)
Administrative expenses	(13,300)
Goodwill amortisation	(212)
Operating profit (15.6%)	14,040

Cost of sales consists of **direct material** cost, such as paper, and **direct labour**. Distribution and administrative expenses include depreciation. **Sales margin = 32%** (29,075/89,844).

(b) **Fairway Transport, a bus company**

	$m
Turnover	1,534.3
Cost of sales	1,282.6
Gross profit	251.7
Net operating expenses	133.8
Operating profit (7.6%)	117.9

Sales margin = 16% (251.7/1,534.3). The sales margin for the bus company is much lower than for the printing company. Clearly a higher percentage of its costs are operating costs. However, is it useful or meaningful to compare the profitability of the two companies in this way?

(1) Sales margin as a measure is **not really any use in comparing companies in different industries**. Cost structures differ with the nature of business operations.

(2) **Comparisons with similar companies in the same industry** may be of interest. If an organisation has a lower sales margin than a similar business, this suggests problems in controlling costs.

(3) **Trends** in profit margin are also of interest. A falling sales margin suggests an organisation has not been able to pass on input price rises to customers.

(4) A comparison of actual profit with budgeted profit would also be of interest, but this information is not always available to the person who is analysing financial performance.

In short, the value of gross profit margin as a measure of performance depends on the **cost structure** of the industry and the **uses** to which it is put.

2.1.2 Net profit margin

For the purpose of the exam, net profit margin is either profit before interest and tax/sales or operating profit/sales, depending on the information you are given for analysis.

As with gross profit margin, net profit margin only has meaning when compared with performance in the previous period(s) or performance of similar companies in the same industry.

2.1.3 Cost/sales ratios

When there is a significant change in the net profit ratio from one year to the next, it may be useful to identify the main cause of the change. For example, if the net profit ratio falls from 8% in one year to 2% in the next year, the fall in the net profit ratio is likely to be due to a fall in the gross profit margin, or an increase in:

(a)   The ratio of sales and distribution costs to sales
(b)   The ratio of administrative costs to sales
(c)   The ratio of another cost to sales, such as R&D costs

A significant increase in the ratio of costs to sales (with a corresponding fall in profit margin) would need to be investigated.

2.1.4 Earnings per share (EPS)

EPS is a measure that relates profitability to the shareholder. It is the profit after tax (and any preference dividend) divided by the number of shares in issue.

EPS is widely used as a **measure of a company's performance**, especially in **comparing** results over a period **of several years**. A company must be able to sustain its earnings in order to pay dividends and reinvest in the business so as to achieve future growth. Investors also look for **growth in the EPS** from one year to the next.

Key term

> **Earnings per share (EPS)** is defined as the profit attributable to each equity (ordinary) share.

Question   EPS

Walter Wall Carpets made profits before tax in 20X8 of $9,320,000. Tax amounted to $2,800,000.

The company's share capital is as follows.

	$
Ordinary share (10,000,000 shares of $1)	10,000,000
8% preference shares	2,000,000
	12,000,000

Required

Calculate the EPS for 20X8.

Answer

	$
Profits before tax	9,320,000
Less tax	2,800,000
Profits after tax	6,520,000
Less preference dividend (8% of $2,000,000)	160,000
Earnings	6,360,000
Number of ordinary shares	10,000,000
EPS	63.6c

EPS on its own does not really tell us anything. It must be seen **in context**.

(a)   EPS is used for comparing the results of a company **over time**. Is its EPS growing? What is the rate of growth? Is the rate of growth increasing or decreasing?

(b)   EPS should not be used blindly to compare the earnings of one company with another. For example, if A plc has an EPS of 12c for its 10,000,000 10c shares and B plc has an EPS of 24c for its 50,000,000 25c shares, we must take account of the numbers of shares. When **earnings are** used to compare one company's shares with another, this is done using the **P/E ratio or perhaps the earnings yield**.

(c)   If EPS is to be a reliable basis for comparing results, it **must be calculated consistently**. The EPS of one company must be directly comparable with the EPS of others, and the EPS of a company in one year must be directly comparable with its published EPS figures for previous years. Changes in the share capital of a company during the course of a year cause problems of comparability.

(d)   EPS is a figure based on past data, and it is easily manipulated by changes in accounting policies and by mergers or acquisitions. **The use of the measure in calculating management bonuses makes it particularly liable to manipulation.** The attention given to EPS as a performance measure by City analysts is arguably disproportionate to its true worth. Investors should be more concerned with **future earnings**, but of course estimates of these are more difficult to reach than the readily available figure.

2.1.5 Profitability and return: the return on capital employed (ROCE)

It is impossible to assess profits or profit growth properly without relating them to the amount of funds (capital) employed in making the profits. An important profitability ratio is therefore **return on capital employed (ROCE)**, which states the profit as a **percentage of the amount of capital employed**.

Key terms

> **Return on Capital Employed** $= \dfrac{\text{PBIT}}{\text{Capital employed}}$
>
> **Capital employed** = Shareholders' funds **plus** 'payables: amounts falling due after more than one year' **plus** any long-term provisions for liabilities.
>
> = Total assets less current liabilities.

What does a company's ROCE tell us? What should we be looking for? There are three **comparisons** that can be made.

(a)   The change in ROCE from **one year to the next**

(b)   The ROCE being earned by **other companies**, if this information is available

(c)   A comparison of the ROCE with **current market borrowing rates**

   (i)   What would be the cost of extra borrowing to the company if it needed more loans, and is it earning an ROCE that suggests it could make high enough profits to make such borrowing worthwhile?

   (ii)   Is the company making an ROCE which suggests that it is making profitable use of its current borrowing?

2.1.6 Analysing profitability and return in more detail: the secondary ratios

We may analyse the ROCE to find out why it is high or low, or better or worse than last year. There are two factors that contribute towards a return on capital employed, both related to turnover.

(a)   **Profit margin**. A company might make a high or a low profit margin on its sales. For example, a company that makes a profit of 25c per $1 of sales is making a bigger return on its turnover than another company making a profit of only 10c per $1 of sales.

(b)   **Asset turnover**. Asset turnover is a measure of how well the assets of a business are being used to generate sales. For example, if two companies each have capital employed of $100,000, and company A makes sales of $400,000 a year whereas company B makes sales of only $200,000 a year, company A is making a higher turnover from the same amount of assets and this will help company A to make a higher return on capital employed than company B. Asset turnover is expressed as 'x times' so that assets generate x times their value in annual turnover. Here, company A's asset turnover is four times and company B's is two times.

Profit margin and asset turnover together explain the ROCE, and if the ROCE is the primary profitability ratio, these other two are the secondary ratios. The relationship between the three ratios is as follows.

Profit margin	×	asset turnover	=	ROCE

$$\frac{PBIT}{Sales} \quad \times \quad \frac{Sales}{Capital\,employed} \quad = \quad \frac{PBIT}{Capital\,employed}$$

It is also worth commenting on the **change in turnover** from one year to the next. Strong sales growth will usually indicate volume growth as well as turnover increases due to price rises, and volume growth is one sign of a prosperous company.

2.2 Gearing

The assets of a business must be financed somehow and, when a business is growing, the additional assets must be financed by additional capital. **Capital structure** refers to the **way in which an organisation** is **financed**, by a combination of long-term capital (ordinary shares and reserves, preference shares, loan stock, bank loans, convertible bonds, and so on) and short-term liabilities, such as a bank overdraft and trade payables.

2.2.1 Debts and financial risk

There are two main **reasons why companies should keep their debt burden under control**.

(a) When a company is heavily in debt, and seems to be becoming even more heavily so, banks and other would-be lenders are very soon likely to refuse further borrowing and the company might well find itself in trouble.

(b) When a company is earning only a modest profit before interest and tax, and has a heavy debt burden, there will be very little profit left over for shareholders after the interest charges have been paid. And so, if interest rates were to go up or the company were to borrow even more, it might soon be incurring interest charges in excess of PBIT. This might eventually lead to the liquidation of the company.

A high level of debt creates **financial risk**. Financial risk can be seen from different points of view.

(a) **The company** as a whole. If a company builds up debts that it cannot pay when they fall due, it will be forced into liquidation.

(b) **Payables**. If a company cannot pay its debts, the company will go into liquidation owing creditors money that they are unlikely to recover in full.

(c) **Ordinary shareholders**. A company will not make any distributable profits unless it is able to earn enough profit before interest and tax to pay all its interest charges, and then tax. The lower the profits or the higher the interest-bearing debts, the less there will be, if there is anything at all, for shareholders.

When a company has preference shares in its capital structure, ordinary shareholders will not get anything until the preference dividend has been paid.

2.3 Gearing ratios

FAST FORWARD

Gearing ratios measure the financial **risk** of a company's capital structure. Business risk can be measured by calculating a company's operational gearing.

Key term

Financial leverage/gearing is the use of debt finance to increase the return on equity by using borrowed funds in such a way that the return generated is greater than the cost of servicing the debt. If the return on borrowed funds is less than the cost of servicing the debt, the effect of gearing is to reduce the return on equity.

Gearing measures the **relationships between shareholders' capital plus reserves, and debt**. Debt is any loans which pay fixed interest and are secured. In this exam, overdrafts do not form part of debt in a gearing ratio.

The common gearing ratios are:

$$\text{Gearing} = \frac{\text{Debt}}{\text{Debt plus equity}} \quad \text{and} \quad \text{Gearing} = \frac{\text{Debt}}{\text{Equity}}$$

When applying the above ratios, remember **to compare like with like** (apply the same gearing ratio throughout to enable accurate comparisons to be made).

A gearing ratio of over 50% indicates **high** gearing.

There is **no absolute limit** to what a **gearing ratio** ought to be. Many companies are highly geared, but if a highly geared company is increasing its gearing it is likely to have difficulty in the future when it wants to borrow even more, unless it can also boost its shareholders' capital, either with retained profits or with a new share issue.

2.3.1 The effect of gearing on earnings

The level of gearing has a considerable effect on the earnings attributable to the ordinary shareholders. A **highly geared** company must **earn enough profit to cover its interest charges before anything is available for equity**. On the other hand, if borrowed funds are invested in projects which provide returns in excess of the cost of debt capital, then shareholders will enjoy increased returns on their equity.

Gearing, however, also **increases the probability of financial failure** occurring through a company's inability to meet interest payments in poor trading circumstances.

2.3.2 Example: Gearing

Suppose that two companies are identical in every respect except for their gearing. Both have assets of $20,000 and both make the same operating profits (profit before interest and tax: PBIT). The only difference between the two companies is that Nonlever Co is all equity financed and Lever Co is partly financed by debt capital, as follows.

	Nonlever Co	Lever Co
	$	$
Assets	20,000	20,000
10% bonds	0	(10,000)
	20,000	10,000
Ordinary shares of $1	20,000	10,000

Because Lever has $10,000 of 10% bonds it must make a profit before interest of at least $1,000 in order to pay the interest charges. Nonlever, on the other hand, does not have any minimum PBIT requirement because it has no debt capital. A company, which is lower geared, is considered less **risky** than a higher geared company because of the greater likelihood that its PBIT will be high enough to cover interest charges and make a profit for equity shareholders.

2.3.3 Operating gearing

Financial risk, as we have seen, can be measured by financial gearing. **Business risk** refers to the **risk of making only low profits**, or even losses, **due to the nature of the business** that the company is involved in. One way of measuring business risk is by calculating a company's **operating gearing** or 'operational gearing'.

Key term

> **Operating gearing or leverage** = $\dfrac{\text{Contribution}}{\text{Profit before interest and tax (PBIT)}}$

If contribution is high but PBIT is low, fixed costs will be high, and only just covered by contribution. **Business risk**, as measured by operating gearing, will be **high**. If contribution is not much bigger than

PBIT, fixed costs will be low, and fairly easily covered. Business risk, as measured by operating gearing, will be low.

2.4 Liquidity and cash flow

> A company can be profitable but at the same time get into cash flow problems. Liquidity ratios (**current** and **quick**) and **working capital turnover ratios** give some idea of a company's liquidity and ability to generate cash from its business operations.

Profitability is of course an important aspect of a company's performance, and debt or gearing is another. Neither, however, addresses directly the key issue of liquidity. A company needs liquid assets so that it can meet its debts when they fall due.

Key term

> **Liquidity** is the amount of cash a company can obtain quickly to settle its debts (and possibly to meet other unforeseen demands for cash payments too).

2.4.1 Liquid assets

Liquid funds include:

(a) Cash
(b) Short-term investments for which there is a ready market, such as investments in shares of other companies (NB **not** subsidiaries or associates)
(c) Fixed-term deposits with a bank or building society, for example six-month deposits with a bank
(d) Trade receivables
(e) Bills of exchange receivable

Some assets are more liquid than others. Inventories of goods are fairly liquid in some businesses. Inventories of finished production goods might be sold quickly, and a supermarket will hold consumer goods for resale that could well be sold for cash very soon. Raw materials and components in a manufacturing company have to be used to make a finished product before they can be sold to realise cash, and so they are less liquid than finished goods. Just how liquid they are depends on the speed of inventory turnover and the length of the production cycle.

Non-current assets are not liquid assets. A company can sell off non-current assets, but unless they are no longer needed, or are worn out and about to be replaced, they are necessary to continue the company's operations. Selling non-current assets is certainly not a solution to a company's cash needs, and so although there may be an occasional non-current asset item which is about to be sold off, probably because it is going to be replaced, it is safe to disregard non-current assets when measuring a company's liquidity.

In summary, **liquid assets are current asset items that will or could soon be converted into cash, and cash** itself. Two common definitions of liquid assets are **all current assets** or **all current assets with the exception of inventories**.

The main source of liquid assets for a trading company is sales. A company can obtain cash from sources other than sales, such as the issue of shares for cash, a new loan or the sale of non-current assets. However, a company cannot rely on these at all times and, in general, obtaining liquid funds depends on making sales and profits.

2.4.2 The current ratio

The **current ratio** is the standard test of liquidity.

Key term

> $$\text{Current ratio} = \frac{\text{Current assets}}{\text{Current liabilities}}$$

A company should have enough current assets that give a promise of 'cash to come' in order to meet its commitments to pay its current liabilities. Obviously, a ratio in **excess of 1** should be expected. In practice, a ratio comfortably in excess of 1 should be expected, but what is 'comfortable' varies between different types of business.

Companies are not able to convert all their current assets into cash very quickly. In particular, some manufacturing companies might hold large quantities of raw material inventories, which must be used in production to create finished goods. Finished goods might be warehoused for a long time, or sold on lengthy credit. In such businesses, where inventory turnover is slow, most inventories are not very liquid assets, because the cash cycle is so long. For these reasons, we calculate an additional liquidity ratio, known as the quick ratio or acid test ratio.

2.4.3 The quick ratio

Key term

$$\text{Quick ratio or acid test ratio} = \frac{\text{Current assets less inventories}}{\text{Current liabilities}}$$

This ratio should ideally be **at least 1** for companies with a **slow inventory turnover**. For companies with a **fast inventory turnover**, a quick ratio can be **less than 1** without suggesting that the company is in cash flow difficulties.

Do not forget the other side of the coin. The current ratio and the quick ratio can be bigger than they should be. A company that has large volumes of inventories and receivables might be overinvesting in working capital, and so tying up more funds in the business than it needs to. This would suggest poor management of receivables or inventories by the company.

2.4.4 The accounts receivable payment period

Key term

$$\text{Accounts receivable days or accounts receivable payment period} = \frac{\text{Trade receivables}}{\text{Credit sales turnover}} \times 365 \text{ days}$$

This is a rough measure of the average length of time it takes for a company's accounts receivable to pay what they owe.

The trade accounts receivable are not the **total** figure for accounts receivable in the statement of financial position, which includes prepayments and non-trade accounts receivable. The trade accounts receivable figure will be itemised in an analysis of the total accounts receivable, in a note to the accounts.

The estimate of accounts receivable days is only approximate.

(a) The **statement of financial position value** of accounts receivable might be **abnormally high** or low compared with the 'normal' level the company usually has. This may apply especially to smaller companies, where the size of year-end accounts receivable may largely depend on whether a few customers or even a single large customer pay just before or just after the year-end.

(b) Turnover in the income statement excludes sales tax, but the accounts receivable figure in the statement of financial position includes sales tax. We are not strictly comparing like with like.

2.4.5 The inventory turnover period

Key term

$$\text{Inventory days} = \frac{\text{Inventory}}{\text{Cost of sales}} \times 365 \text{ days}$$

This indicates the average number of days that items of inventory are held for. As with the average accounts receivable collection period, this is only an approximate figure, but one which should be reliable enough for finding changes over time.

A lengthening inventory turnover period indicates:

(a)   A **slowdown** in **trading**; or

(b)   A **build-up** in **inventory levels**, perhaps suggesting that the investment in inventories is becoming excessive.

If we add together the inventory days and the accounts receivable days, this should give us an indication of how soon inventory is convertible into cash, thereby giving a further indication of the **company's liquidity**.

2.4.6 The accounts payable payment period

$$\text{Accounts payable payment period} = \frac{\text{Average trade payables}}{\text{Credit purchases or Cost of sales}} \times 365 \text{ days}$$

The accounts payable payment period often helps to assess a company's liquidity; an increase in accounts payable days is often a sign of lack of long-term finance or poor management of current assets, resulting in the use of extended credit from suppliers, increased bank overdraft, and so on.

All the ratios calculated above will **vary by industry**; hence **comparisons** of ratios calculated with other similar companies in the same industry are important.

One of the competencies you require to fulfil performance objective 14 of the PER is to identify and use appropriate performance measurement techniques to assess aspects of performance within the organisation. You can apply the knowledge you obtain from this section of the text to help to demonstrate this competence.

Question   Liquidity and working capital ratios

Calculate liquidity and working capital ratios from the accounts of a manufacturer of products for the construction industry, and comment on the ratios.

	20X8 $m	20X7 $m
Turnover	2,065.0	1,788.7
Cost of sales	1,478.6	1,304.0
Gross profit	586.4	484.7
Current assets		
Inventories	119.0	109.0
Receivables (note 1)	400.9	347.4
Short-term investments	4.2	18.8
Cash at bank and in hand	48.2	48.0
	572.3	523.2
Payables: amounts falling due within one year		
Loans and overdrafts	49.1	35.3
Corporation taxes	62.0	46.7
Dividend	19.2	14.3
Payables (note 2)	370.7	324.0
	501.0	420.3
	$m	$m
Net current assets	71.3	102.9

Notes

1	Trade receivables	329.8	285.4
2	Trade payables	236.2	210.8

	20X8	20X7
Current ratio	572.3/501.0 = 1.14	523.2/420.3 = 1.24
Quick ratio	453.3/501.0 = 0.90	414.2/420.3 = 0.99
Receivables payment period	329.8/2,065.0 × 365 = 58 days	285.4/1,788.7 × 365 = 58 days
Inventory turnover period	119.0/1,478.6 × 365 = 29 days	109.0/1,304.0 × 365 = 31 days
Payables turnover period	236.2/1,478.6 × 365 = 58 days	210.8/1,304.0 × 365 = 59 days

As a manufacturing group serving the construction industry, the company would be expected to have a comparatively lengthy receivables turnover period, because of the relatively poor cash flow in the construction industry. It is clear that the company compensates for this by ensuring that they do not pay for raw materials and other costs before they have sold their inventories of finished goods (hence the similarity of receivables and payables turnover periods).

The company's current ratio is a little lower than average but its quick ratio is better than average and only slightly lower than the current ratio. This suggests that inventory levels are strictly controlled, which is reinforced by the low inventory turnover period. It would seem that working capital is tightly managed, to avoid the poor liquidity which could be caused by a high receivables turnover period and comparatively high payables.

3 Non-financial performance indicators (NFPIs)
12/07, 6/09, 12/10, 12/12, 12/13, Specimen

FAST FORWARD

Changes in cost structures, the competitive environment and the manufacturing environment have led to an **increased use of non-financial performance indicators** (NFPIs). Non-financial performance indicators can also be a very useful guide to future financial performance.

There has been a growing emphasis on NFPIs for a number of reasons.

(a) **Concentration on too few variables**. If performance measurement systems focus entirely on those items which can be expressed in monetary terms, managers will concentrate on only those variables and ignore other important variables that cannot be expressed in monetary terms.

(b) **Lack of information on quality**. Traditional responsibility accounting systems fail to provide information on the quality or importance of operations.

(c) **Changes in cost structures**. Modern technology requires massive investment and product life cycles have become shorter. A greater proportion of costs are sunk and a large proportion of costs are planned, engineered or designed into a product/service before production/delivery. At the time the product/service is produced/delivered, it is therefore too late to control costs.

(d) **Changes in competitive environment**. Financial measures do not convey the full picture of a company's performance, especially in a modern business environment.

(e) **Changes in manufacturing environment**. New manufacturing techniques and technologies focus on minimising throughput times, inventory levels and set-up times. However, managers can reduce the costs for which they are responsible by increasing inventory levels through maximising output. If a performance measurement system focuses principally on costs, managers may concentrate on cost reduction and ignore other important strategic manufacturing goals.

(f) **NFPIs are a better indicator of future prospects**. Financial performance indicators tend to focus on the short term. They can give a positive impression of what is happening now but problems may be looming. For example, falling quality will ultimately damage profitability.

Unlike traditional variance reports, NFPIs can be provided **quickly** for managers, per shift, daily or even hourly as required. They are likely to be easy to calculate, and easier for non-financial managers to **understand** and therefore to **use effectively**.

3.1 Which NFPIs should be measured?

The most useful NFPIs for measuring aspects of operational performance will vary between different types of business and different business circumstances. While with financial performance measures it is possible to list the most commonly used measures or ratios, this is not so easy with NFPIs.

Given an exam question in which you are asked to comment on non-financial aspects of performance of an organisation, you will need to use your judgement and try to identify the most suitable measures for the organisation in the question.

As a general guide, NFPIs may be measurements of the following aspects of performance.

(a)   **Quality** of production: wastage rates or percentage of rejects in production

(b)   **Speed** or **efficiency**, such as output per hour: average time taken per unit of activity

(c)   **Delivery**: average time between taking an order and delivery to the customer

(d)   **Reliability**: percentage of calls answered within a given target time; number of equipment failures or amount of 'down time'

(e)   **Customer satisfaction**: number of complaints

(f)   **Innovation**: number of new products developed and launched on to the market

With non-financial indicators, **anything can be measured and compared** if it is **meaningful** to do so. The measures should be **tailored** to the circumstances of the business.

3.2 NFPIs in relation to employees

NFPIs can usefully be applied to **employees** and product/service **quality**.

One of the many criticisms of traditional accounting performance measurement systems is that they **do not measure the skills, morale and training of the workforce**, which can be as **valuable to an organisation as its tangible assets**. For example, if employees have not been trained in the manufacturing practices required to achieve the objectives of the new manufacturing environment, an organisation is unlikely to be successful.

Employee attitudes and morale can be measured by **surveying** employees. Education and skills levels, promotion and training, absenteeism and labour turnover for the employees for which each manager is responsible can also be monitored.

3.3 Performance measurement in a TQM environment

Total Quality Management is a highly significant trend in modern business thinking. As **TQM embraces every activity** of a business, performance measures cannot be confined to the production process but must also cover the work of sales and distribution departments and administration departments, the efforts of external suppliers and the reaction of external customers.

In many cases the measures used will be non-financial ones. They may be divided into three types.

(a)   **Measuring the quality of incoming supplies**. Quality control should include procedures for acceptance and inspection of goods inwards and measurement of rejects.

(b)   **Monitoring work done as it proceeds**. 'In-process' controls include statistical process controls and random sampling, and measures such as the amount of scrap and reworking in relation to good production. Measurements can be made by product, by worker or work team, by machine or machine type, by department, or whatever is appropriate.

(c) **Measuring customer satisfaction**. This may be monitored in the form of letters of complaint, returned goods, penalty discounts, claims under guarantee, or requests for visits by service engineers. Some companies adopt a more proactive approach to monitoring customer satisfaction by surveying their customers on a regular basis. They use the feedback to obtain an index of customer satisfaction which is used to identify quality problems before they affect profits.

3.4 Quality of service

Service quality is measured principally by **qualitative measures**, as you might expect, although quantitative measures are used by some businesses.

(a) If it were able to obtain the information, a retailer might use the number of lost customers in a period as an indicator of service quality.

(b) Lawyers use the proportion of time spent with clients.

3.4.1 Measures of customer satisfaction

You have probably filled in **questionnaires** in fast food restaurants or on aeroplanes without realising that you were completing a customer attitude survey for input to the organisation's management information system.

Other possible measures of customer satisfaction include:

(a) Market research information on customer preferences and customer satisfaction with specific product features

(b) Number of defective units supplied to customers as a percentage of total units supplied

(c) Number of customer complaints as a percentage of total sales volume

(d) Percentage of products which fail early or excessively

(e) On-time delivery rate

(f) Average time to deal with customer queries

(g) New customer accounts opened

(h) Repeat business from existing customers

Exam focus point

> Note that many of these NFPIs can be used in not for profit and public sector organisations too.

4 Short-termism and manipulation

6/08

FAST FORWARD

> **Short-termism** is when there is a bias towards short-term rather than long-term performance. It is often due to the fact that managers' performance is measured on short-term results.

Key term

> **Short-termism** is when there is a bias towards short-term rather than long-term performance.

Organisations often have to make a trade-off between short-term and long-term objectives. Decisions which involve the **sacrifice of longer-term objectives** include the following.

(a) Postponing or abandoning capital expenditure projects, which would eventually contribute to growth and profits, in order to protect short-term cash flow and profits

(b) Cutting R&D expenditure to save operating costs, and so reducing the prospects for future product development

(c) Reducing quality control, to save operating costs (but also adversely affecting reputation and goodwill)

(d) Reducing the level of customer service, to save operating costs (but sacrificing goodwill)

(e) Cutting training costs or recruitment (so the company might be faced with skills shortages)

BPP LEARNING MEDIA

Managers may also **manipulate** results, especially if rewards are linked to performance. This can be achieved by changing the timing of capital purchases, building up inventories and speeding up or delaying payments and receipts.

4.1 Methods to encourage a long-term view

Steps that could be taken to encourage managers to take a long-term view, so that the 'ideal' decisions are taken, include the following.

(a) **Making short-term targets realistic**. If budget targets are unrealistically tough, a manager will be forced to make trade-offs between the short and long term.

(b) **Providing sufficient management information** to allow managers to see what trade-offs they are making. Managers must be kept aware of long-term aims as well as shorter-term (budget) targets.

(c) **Evaluating managers' performance** in terms of contribution to long-term as well as short-term objectives.

(d) **Link managers' rewards to share price**. This may encourage goal congruence.

(e) **Set quality-based targets** as well as financial targets. Multiple targets can be used.

5 Improving performance

One of the competencies you require to fulfil performance objective 14 of the PER is to advise on appropriate ways to maintain and improve performance. You can apply the knowledge you obtain from this section of the text to help to demonstrate this competence.

Performance is measured to assess how well or badly an organisation has performed over a given period of time. When performance is measured, the objectives should be to:

(a) Identify aspects of performance that may be a cause for concern

(b) Explain differences between actual performance and the plan or expectation, or deteriorating performance over time

(c) Consider ways of taking control measures to improve performance

In an exam question on performance measurement, it is highly likely that you will be required to do all three of these things in your answer.

5.1 Analyse performance

As explained previously, performance is analysed by comparing actual results with a target (such as a budget) or with performance in previous time periods.

The purpose of analysing performance in this way is to identify whether there are any **aspects of performance that are worse than the target or worse than the previous year, where there may be some cause for concern**.

Where performance is more or less as expected or in line with previous years, there should be no cause for concern, and no reason to investigate this aspect of performance in any detail.

5.2 Identify reasons for unexpected performance or poor performance

Having identified aspects of performance that may be a cause for some concern, the next requirement is to consider possible reasons for actual results, and why for example performance is worse this year than last year.

To identify possible reasons for disappointing performance, you may need to apply your judgement and common sense to the facts in an examination 'case study'.

The table below gives some examples of matters that you may need to consider, but these examples are illustrative and by no means exhaustive.

Aspect of performance	Possible reasons
Increase in rejection rates for faulty products	Using relatively inexperienced staff to do the work Using cheaper materials (to 'save money')
Increase in time between taking a customer order and delivering the product to the customer	Administrative delays in processing customer orders
Increase in frequency of machine breakdowns	Reduction in amount of routine maintenance work
Customer dissatisfaction with online sales service	Poor website design
Longer average time to answer customer calls in a call centre	Reduction in number of call centre staff
Declining labour productivity	Failure to train staff Increase in complexity of the work Use of inexperienced staff

5.3 Improving performance

Having identified reasons for poor performance, whether financial or non-financial, the final step is to consider and implement methods of improving performance. **Methods of improving performance should be linked to the possible reasons for the poor performance.**

The aim of corrective measures should be to tackle the problems that are the cause of the poor performance.

Illustrative control measures are shown in the table below.

Aspect of performance	Possible reasons	Possible measures to improve performance
Increase in rejection rates for faulty products	Using relatively inexperienced staff to do the work Using cheaper materials (to 'save money')	Hire more experienced staff Provide training Switch back to better-quality materials
Increase in time between taking a customer order and delivering the product to the customer	Administrative delays in processing customer orders	Set a maximum time limit for processing orders and monitor performance continually
Increase in frequency of machine breakdowns	Reduction on amount of routine maintenance work	Increase routine maintenance of machines
Customer dissatisfaction with online sales service	Poor website design	Redesign the website. Hire web design specialists if necessary
Longer average time to answer customer calls in a call centre	Reduction in number of call centre staff	Employ more staff
Declining labour productivity	Failure to train staff Increase in complexity of the work Use of inexperienced staff	Hire more experienced staff Provide training Give the most complex tasks to specialist staff

Some structured approaches to performance measurement have been developed, which combine measurements of financial and non-financial performance. Two of these are described in the next sections.

6 The balanced scorecard

> The **balanced scorecard** approach to performance measurement focuses on four different perspectives of performance, and uses both financial and non-financial indicators to set performance targets and monitor performance.

Exam focus point

> In the exam, it is important to apply the knowledge from the following section, to the specifics of the scenario given. It was noted in the December 2014 exam report, that candidates did not consider the company in the question and instead presented a generic balanced scorecard. That will not be awarded marks at this level.

Although business performance may be measured by a single financial performance indicator such as ROI, profit, or cost variances, it is often more suitable to use multiple measures of performance where each measure reflects a **different aspect of achievement**. Where multiple measures are used, several may be **non-financial**.

An important argument in favour of measuring non-financial performance is that current and future financial performance depend largely on non-financial aspects of performance.

If an organisation uses a performance measurement system for monitoring its performance, it seems appropriate that the measurement system should be formally structured, so that:

- All relevant aspects of performance are measured.

- Targets are set for all key aspects of performance.

- Actual performance is measured against targets, rather than compared with performance in previous years.

- Performance targets are consistent with each other.

Perhaps the most widely used structured approach to performance targeting and measurement is the **'balanced scorecard'**.

A balanced scorecard is a performance measurement system in which:

(a) Objectives and targets are set for **four different aspects or perspectives of performance**: a financial perspective; customer perspective; internal perspective; and innovation and learning perspective. All four perspectives are important for the long-term success of the organisation. Three of these perspectives are non-financial in nature.

(b) There should be a small number of **targets for each of the four perspectives**.

(c) The **different targets for the four perspectives should be consistent with each other**: the four perspectives are sometimes in conflict with each other and it is necessary to establish an acceptable balance between the different perspectives and targets (hence, a 'balanced' scorecard).

(e) **Actual performance is measured regularly and compared with the targets for all the perspectives**.

(f) Differences between the target and actual performance are investigated and, where appropriate, measures are taken to improve performance.

Key term

> The **balanced scorecard** approach emphasises the need to provide management with a set of information which covers all relevant areas of performance in an objective and unbiased fashion. The information provided may be both financial and non-financial and cover areas such as profitability, customer satisfaction, internal efficiency and innovation.

6.1 Perspectives

The balanced scorecard focuses on **four different perspectives**, as follows.

Perspective	Basic question	Identifying performance targets
Customer	What do existing and new customers value from us?	Gives rise to targets that matter to customers: cost, quality, delivery, inspection, handling, and so on
Internal	What processes must we excel at to achieve our financial and customer objectives?	Aims to improve internal processes and decision-making
Innovation and learning	Can we continue to improve and create future value?	Considers the business's capacity to maintain its competitive position through the acquisition of new skills and the development of new products
Financial	How do we create value for our shareholders?	Covers traditional measures such as growth, profitability and shareholder value but set through talking to the shareholder or shareholders directly

Performance targets are set once the key areas for improvement have been identified, and the balanced scorecard is the main monthly report.

The scorecard is **'balanced'**, as managers are required to think in terms of **all four** perspectives to prevent improvements being made in one area at the expense of another.

Important features of this approach are as follows.

(a)   It looks at both **internal and external** matters concerning the organisation.

(b)   It is related to the key elements of a company's **strategy**.

(c)   **Financial and non-financial** measures are linked together.

6.2 Example

An example of how a balanced scorecard might appear is offered below. Arguably, there are too many performance targets here for each of the four perspectives, but this balanced scorecard is a good illustration of issues that may be considered as critical to the organisation's success.

Balanced Scorecard

Financial Perspective	
GOALS	**MEASURES**
Survive	Cash flow
Succeed	Monthly sales growth and operating income by division
Prosper	Increase market share and ROI

Customer Perspective	
GOALS	**MEASURES**
New products	Percentage of sales from new products
Responsive supply	On-time delivery(defined by customer
Preferred supplier	Share of key accounts' purchases
	Ranking by key accounts
Customer partnership	Number of co-operative engineering efforts

Internal Business Perspective	
GOALS	**MEASURES**
Technology capability	Manufacturing configuration vs competition
Manufacturing excellence	Cycle time
	Unit cost
	Yield
Design productivity	Silicon efficiency
	Engineering efficiency
New project introduction	Actual introduction schedule vs plan

Innovation and Learning Perspective	
GOALS	**MEASURES**
Technology leadership	Time to develop next generation of products
Manufacturing learning	Process time to maturity
Product focus	Percentage of products that equal 80% sales
Time to market	New product introduction vs competition

6.3 Example: Balanced scorecard and not for profit organisations

Balanced scorecards are used most in private sector organisations, where reward systems may be based on success in achieving targets in each of the four perspectives. It is also possible, however, to use a balanced scorecard in not for profit organisations.

Not for profit organisations such as charities are likely to have significantly different goals in comparison to profitable businesses. The following are goals that may be relevant to a charity.

Financial perspective

- Increase income from charitable donations
- Improve margins

Internal business perspective

- Reduce overheads
- Claim back tax on gift aid

Customer perspective

- Continued donor support
- Donor involvement in initiatives

Innovation and learning perspective

- More projects supported
- More fundraisers
- More money pledged

Required

Suggest some performance measures for each of the goals outlined above.

Solution

The balanced scorecard for the charity may appear as follows.

Financial perspective	
GOALS	**MEASURES (KPI)**
Income from charitable donations	Donations received
Improved margins	Lower costs and/or increased income from all sources

Customer perspective	
GOALS	**MEASURES (KPI)**
Continued donor support	Pledges given and direct debits set up
Donor involvement in initiatives	Fundraising and charity dinners

Internal business perspective	
GOALS	**MEASURES (KPI)**
Reduce overheads	Lower overheads measured by monitoring and accounts
Claim back tax on gift aid	Improved reclaim times for gift aided donation

Innovation and learning perspective	
GOALS	**MEASURES (KPI)**
More projects supported	Number of projects given support
More fundraisers	Number of fundraisers recruited
More money pledged	Amount of donations promised

Note. KPI = Key Performance Indicator

Question

Spotlight Productions has in the past produced just one fairly successful product. Recently, however, a new version of this product has been launched. Development work continues to add a related product to the product list. Given below are some details of the activities during the month of November.

Units produced	– existing product	25,000
	– new product	5,000
Cost of units produced	– existing product	$375,000
	– new product	$70,000
Sales revenue	– existing product	$550,000
	– new product	$125,000
Hours worked	– existing product	5,000
	– new product	1,250
Development costs		$47,000

Required

(a) Suggest and calculate performance indicators that could be calculated for each of the four perspectives on the balanced scorecard.

(b) Suggest how this information would be interpreted.

Answer

(a) **Customer**

- Percentage of sales represented by new products $= \dfrac{\$125,000}{\$550,000 + \$125,000} \times 100$

$= 18.5\%$

Internal

- Productivity   – existing product $= \dfrac{25{,}000 \text{ units}}{5{,}000 \text{ units}}$

                                    $= 5 \text{ units per hour}$

                – new product $= \dfrac{5{,}000 \text{ units}}{1{,}250 \text{ units}}$

                                    $= 4 \text{ units per hour}$

- Unit cost   – existing product $= \dfrac{\$375{,}000}{25{,}000 \text{ units}}$

                                    $= \$15 \text{ per unit}$

                – new product $= \dfrac{\$70{,}000}{5{,}000 \text{ units}}$

                                    $= \$14 \text{ per unit}$

Financial

- Gross profit   – existing product $= \dfrac{\$550{,}000 - 375{,}000}{\$550{,}000}$

                                    $= 32\%$

                – new product $= \dfrac{\$125{,}000 - 70{,}000}{\$125{,}000}$

                                    $= 44\%$

Innovation and learning

- Development costs as % of sales $= \dfrac{\$47{,}000}{\$675{,}000}$

                                    $= 7\%$

(b)   Using a range of performance indicators will allow Spotlight Productions to look at the success of the new product in wider terms than just its profitability. For example, productivity is lower for the new product than the existing product, so managers may wish to examine the processes involved in order to make improvements. Sales of the new product look very promising but some additional measure of customer satisfaction could provide a better view of long-term prospects.

7 Building Block model

FAST FORWARD

> Fitzgerald and Moon's **building blocks** for **dimensions**, **standards** and **rewards** attempt to overcome the problems associated with performance measurement of service businesses.

Performance measurement in service businesses has sometimes been perceived as more difficult than in manufacturing businesses.

Fitzgerald and Moon (1996) suggested that a performance management system in a service organisation can be analysed as a combination of three building blocks.

- Dimensions of performance
- Standards
- Rewards

Dimensions of performance	
Profit	
Competitiveness	
Quality	
Resource utilisation	
Flexibility	
Innovation	

Standards	**Rewards**
Ownership	Clarity
Achievability	Motivation
Equity	Controllability

7.1 Dimensions of performance

Dimensions of performance are the aspects of performance that are measured. Fitzgerald and Moon suggested that there are six aspects to performance measurement that link performance to corporate strategy. These are shown in the diagram above.

Some performance measures that might be used for each of these dimensions are as follows.

Dimension of performance	Possible measure of performance
Financial performance	Profitability Profit growth Gross profit margin, net profit margin
Competitiveness	Growth in sales Retention rate for customers Success rate in converting enquiries into sales
Service quality	Number of complaints Customer satisfaction, as revealed by customer opinion surveys
Flexibility	Mix of different types of work done by employees Speed in responding to customer requests
Resource utilisation	Efficiency/productivity measures Capacity utilisation rates
Innovation	Number of new services offered within the previous year or two years

Fitzgerald and Moon also suggested that the dimensions of performance should distinguish between the 'results' of actions taken in the past and 'determinants' of future performance.

(a)   Financial performance and measures of competitiveness are performance measures that have resulted from measures taken in the past.

(b)   Quality, flexibility, resource utilisation and innovation are all aspects of performance that will determine the success (or otherwise) of the organisation in the future.

7.2 Standards

The second part of Fitzgerald and Moon's framework for performance measurement concerns setting the standards or targets of performance, once the measures for the dimensions of performance have been selected.

There are three aspects to setting standards of performance.

- Individuals need to feel that they 'own' the standards and targets for which they will be made responsible.

- Individuals also need to feel that the targets or standards are realistic and achievable.

- The standards and targets should be seen as 'fair' and equitable for all the managers in the organisation.

7.3 Rewards

The third aspect of Fitzgerald and Moon's performance measurement framework is rewards. This refers to the structure of the rewards system, and how individuals will be rewarded for the successful achievement of performance targets.

There are three aspects to consider in a reward system.

- The system of setting targets and rewarding individuals for achieving the targets should be clear. Clarity will improve the motivation to achieve the targets.

- Achievement of performance targets should be suitably rewarded.

- Individuals should be made responsible only for aspects of performance that they are in a position to control.

> One of the competencies you require to fulfil performance objective 14 of the PER is to use review and reward systems to monitor and assess performance. You can apply the knowledge you obtain from this section of the text to help to demonstrate this competence.

Question — Competitiveness and resource utilisation

A service business has collected some figures relating to its year just ended.

		Budget	Actual
Customer enquiries:	New customers	6,000	9,000
	Existing customers	4,000	3,000
Business won:	New customers	2,000	4,000
	Existing customers	1,500	1,500
Types of service performed:	Service A	875	780
	Service B	1,575	1,850
	Service C	1,050	2,870
Employees:	Service A	5	4
	Service B	10	10
	Service C	5	8

Required

Calculate figures that illustrate competitiveness and resource utilisation.

Answer

Competitiveness can only be measured from these figures by looking at how successful the organisation is at converting enquiries into firm orders.

Percentage of enquiries converted into firm orders

	Budget	Actual
New customers (W1)	33%	44%
Existing customers (W1)	37.5%	50%

Resource utilisation can be measured by looking at average services performed per employee.

	Budget	Actual	Rise
Service A (W2)	175	195	+11.4%
Service B (W2)	157.5	185	+17.5%
Service C (W2)	210	358.75	+70.8%

Workings

1   For example 2,000/6,000 = 33%
2   For example 875/5 = 175

What comments would you make about these results? How well is the business doing?

Exam focus point

> Be prepared to think up performance measures for different areas of an organisation's business. Remember to make the measures relevant to the organisation in question. There is little point in suggesting such measures as waiting times in queues to assess the quality of the service provided by an educational establishment.

Question

Performance indicators

Suggest two separate performance indicators that could be used to assess each of the following areas of a fast food chain's operations.

(a)   Food preparation department
(b)   Marketing department

Answer

Here are some suggestions.

(a)   Material usage per product   (b)   Market share
       Wastage levels   Sales revenue per employee
       Incidences of food poisoning   Growth in sales revenue

---

8 Target setting in qualitative areas

The balanced scorecard and Fitzgerald and Moon's Building Block model are based on the assumption that performance targets can be set and measured for non-financial aspects of performance. This presumes that all key non-financial aspects of performance can be measured and quantified.

In practice, this is not necessarily the case. Some critical non-financial aspects of performance may be difficult to quantify, or to quantify in a reliable way. There are several problems with qualitative non-financial performance targets.

(a)   There is often a problem with selecting a suitable measure of performance. For example, an important objective for an organisation may be winning and retaining customer loyalty. But how is a reliable target for customer loyalty decided?

     (i)   Opinion research by a market research firm and setting a 'target score for loyalty'?

     (ii)   The percentage of customers who make a repeat order within x months?

     Similarly, a performance objective may be to deliver a high standard of service to a customer, but how is service quality defined? Having defined service quality, how is it measured?

(b)   By its very nature, qualitative data is not quantified. At best, qualitative measures are converted into quantitative measures using a subjective scoring system. When performance is not quantified, it is difficult to target and monitor.

(c)   Data collection and management information systems. An organisation may have a well-established system for measuring quantitative data, especially in the areas of accounting and sales statistics. It is much less likely to have a reliable and comprehensive system for collecting data about qualitative aspects of performance.

Chapter Roundup

- **Performance measurement** aims to establish how well something or somebody is doing in relation to a plan.

- Performance measures may be divided into two types.
  - Financial performance indicators
  - Non-financial performance indicators

- **Financial performance indicators** analyse return on capital, profitability, liquidity and financial risk, often in relation to a plan or budget, or in relation to performance in preceding time periods.

- In private sector organisations, the most important financial performance indicators are measurements of profit.

- **Gearing ratios** measure the financial **risk** of a company's capital structure. Business risk can be measured by calculating a company's operational gearing.

- A company can be profitable but at the same time get into cash flow problems. Liquidity ratios (**current** and **quick**) and **working capital turnover ratios** give some idea of a company's liquidity and ability to generate cash from its business operations.

- Changes in cost structures, the competitive environment and the manufacturing environment have led to an **increased use of non-financial performance indicators** (NFPIs). Non-financial performance indicators can also be a very useful guide to future financial performance.

- NFPIs can usefully be applied to **employees** and product/service **quality**.

- **Short-termism** is when there is a bias towards short-term rather than long-term performance. It is often due to the fact that managers' performance is measured on short-term results.

- The **balanced scorecard** approach to performance measurement focuses on four different perspectives of performance, and uses both financial and non-financial indicators to set performance targets and monitor performance.

- Fitzgerald and Moon's **building blocks** for **dimensions, standards** and **rewards** attempt to overcome the problems associated with performance measurement of service businesses.

1   Give five examples of a financial performance measure.

- ....
- ....
- ....
- ....
- ....

2   How do quantitative and qualitative performance measures differ?

3   Choose the correct words from those highlighted.

In general, a current ratio **in excess of 1/less than 1/approximately zero** should be expected.

4   **Service quality** is measured principally by quantitative measures.

True   ☐   False   ☐

5   Fill in the blanks.

NFPIs are less likely to be .... than traditional profit-related measures and they should therefore offer a means of counteracting ....

6   What are the three most important features of the balanced scorecard approach?

7   Fill in the blanks.

The five characteristics of a service business are .... , ..., ..., ... and ....

8   Fitzgerald and Moon's standards for performance measurement systems are ownership, achievability and controllability. **True or false?**

9   Fill in the gaps.

Fitzgerald and Moon's dimensions of performance can be divided into results (............................... and ....) and determinants (..............................., ..., ... and ....) .

1
- Profit
- Revenue
- Costs
- Share price
- Cash flow

2 Quantitative measures are expressed in numbers whereas qualitative measures are not.

3 in excess of 1

4 False. Service quality is measured principally by **qualitative** measures.

5 manipulated
   short-termism

6
- It looks at both internal and external matters concerning the organisation.
- It is related to the key elements of a company's strategy.
- Financial and non-financial measures are linked together.

7 Heterogeneity/variability   Simultaneity/inseparability
   Perishability   No transfer of ownership
   Intangibility

8 False. They are ownership, achievability and equity.

9 *Results*

   Financial performance
   Competitive performance

   Determinants

   Quality   Innovation
   Flexibility   Resource utilisation

> Now try the questions below from the Practice Question Bank

Number	Level	Marks	Approximate time
Section A Q91	Examination	2	4 mins
Section A Q92	Examination	2	4 mins
Section A Q93	Examination	2	4 mins
Section A Q94	Examination	2	4 mins
Section A Q95	Examination	2	4 mins

17

Divisional performance and transfer pricing

Topic list	Syllabus reference
1 Divisionalisation	D5
2 Return on investment (ROI)	D5 (c)
3 Residual income (RI)	D5 (c), (d)
4 Transfer pricing	D5 (a), (b)

Introduction

This chapter looks at **divisional performance** and **transfer pricing** which is a system of charging other divisions of your organisation when you provide them with your division's goods or services.

In a **divisionalised organisation** structure of any kind, if one division does work that is used by another division, transfer pricing may be required. Do not be misled by the term 'price': there is not necessarily any suggestion of **profit** as there usually is with an external selling price. But as we shall see, transfer pricing is particularly appropriate where divisions are designated as **profit centres**.

Study guide

		Intellectual level
D5	**Divisional performance and transfer pricing**	
(a)	Explain and illustrate the basis for setting a transfer price using variable cost, full cost and the principles behind allowing for intermediate markets.	2
(b)	Explain how transfer prices can distort the performance assessment of divisions and decisions made.	2
(c)	Explain the meaning of, and calculate, Return on Investment (ROI) and Residual Income (RI), and discuss their shortcomings.	2
(d)	Compare divisional performance and recognise the problems of doing so.	2

Exam guide

You may be required to calculate transfer prices in this exam. You must be able to explain how and why they are used and the problems they can create. There are two articles on the ACCA website on transfer pricing which you should read (ACCA, 2015 and ACCA, 2016). You should also read 'Decentralisation and the need for performance measurement' (ACCA, 2016).

1 Divisionalisation

FAST FORWARD

Divisionalisation is a term for the division of an organisation into divisions. Each divisional manager is responsible for the performance of the division. A division may be a cost centre (responsible for its costs only), a profit centre (responsible for revenues and profits) or an investment centre or Strategic Business Unit (responsible for costs, revenues and assets).

There are a number of advantages and disadvantages to **divisionalisation**.

In general, a large organisation can be **structured in one of two ways: functionally** (all activities of a similar type within a company, such as production, sales and research, are under the control of the appropriate departmental head) or **divisionally** (split into divisions in accordance with the products or services made or provided).

Divisional managers are therefore responsible for all operations (production, sales, and so on) relating to their product, the functional structure being applied to each division. It is possible, of course, that only part of a company is divisionalised and activities such as administration are structured centrally on a functional basis with the responsibility of providing services to **all** divisions.

1.1 Decentralisation

In general, a **divisional structure will lead to decentralisation** of the decision-making process and divisional managers may have the freedom to set selling prices, choose suppliers, make product mix and output decisions, and so on. Decentralisation is, however, a matter of degree, depending on how much freedom divisional managers are given.

1.2 Advantages of divisionalisation

(a) Divisionalisation can **improve** the **quality of decisions** made because divisional managers (those taking the decisions) know local conditions and are able to make more informed judgements. Moreover, with the personal incentive to improve the division's performance, they ought to take decisions in the division's best interests.

(b)   **Decisions should be taken more quickly** because information does not have to pass along the chain of command to and from top management. Decisions can be made on the spot by those who are familiar with the product lines and production processes and who are able to react to changes in local conditions quickly and efficiently.

(c)   The authority to act to improve performance should **motivate divisional managers**.

(d)   Divisional organisation **frees top management** from detailed involvement in day-to-day operations and allows them to devote more time to strategic planning.

(e)   Divisions provide **valuable training grounds for future members of top management** by giving them experience of managerial skills in a less complex environment than that faced by top management.

(f)   In a large business organisation, the **central head office will not have the management resources or skills to direct operations closely enough itself**. Some authority must be delegated to local operational managers.

1.3 Disadvantages of divisionalisation

(a)   A danger with divisional accounting is that the business organisation will divide into a number of self-interested segments, each acting at times against the wishes and interests of other segments. Decisions might be taken by a divisional manager in the best interests of their own part of the business, but against the best interest of other divisions and possibly against the interests of the organisation as a whole.

A task of **head office** is therefore to try to **prevent dysfunctional decision-making** by individual divisional managers. To do this, head office must reserve some power and authority for itself so that divisional managers cannot be allowed to make entirely independent decisions. A **balance** ought to be kept **between decentralisation** of authority to provide incentives and motivation, **and retaining centralised authority** to ensure that the organisation's divisions are all working towards the same target, the benefit of the organisation as a whole (in other words, **retaining goal congruence** among the organisation's separate divisions).

(b)   It is claimed that the **costs of activities that are common** to all divisions, such as running the accounting department, **may be greater** for a divisionalised structure than for a centralised structure.

(c)   **Top management**, by delegating decision-making to divisional managers, may **lose control** since they are not aware of what is going on in the organisation as a whole. (With a good system of performance evaluation and appropriate control information, however, top management should be able to control operations just as effectively.)

1.4 Responsibility accounting

Responsibility accounting is the term used to describe decentralisation of authority, with the performance of the decentralised units measured in terms of accounting results.

With a system of responsibility accounting there are five types of **responsibility centre: cost centre; revenue centre; profit centre; contribution centre; and investment centre**.

The creation of divisions allows for the operation of a system of **responsibility accounting**. There are a number of types of responsibility accounting unit, or responsibility centre that can be used within a system of responsibility accounting.

In the weakest form of decentralisation a system of **cost centres** might be used. As decentralisation becomes stronger the responsibility accounting framework will be based around **profit centres**. In its strongest form **investment centres** are used.

Type of responsibility centre	Manager has control over ...	Principal performance measures
Cost centre	Controllable costs	Variance analysis Efficiency measures
Revenue centre	Revenues only	Revenues
Profit centre	Controllable costs Sales prices (including transfer prices)	Profit
Contribution centre	As for profit centre except that expenditure is reported on a marginal cost basis	Contribution
Investment centre	Controllable costs Sales prices (including transfer prices) Output volumes Investment in non-current assets and working capital	Return on investment Residual income Other financial ratios

2 Return on investment (ROI) 12/08, 6/11, 6/12, Sep/Dec 15

FAST FORWARD

The performance of an investment centre is usually monitored using either or both **return on investment (ROI)** and **residual income (RI)**.

ROI is generally regarded as the **key performance measure**. The main reason for its **widespread use** is that it **ties in directly with the accounting process**, and is identifiable from the statement of profit or loss and statement of financial position. However, it does have limitations, as we will see later in this chapter.

Key term

Return on investment (ROI) shows how much profit has been made in relation to the amount of capital invested and is calculated as (profit/capital employed) × 100%.

For example, suppose that a company has two investment centres, A and B, which show results for the year as follows.

	A $	B $
Profit	60,000	30,000
Capital employed	400,000	120,000
ROI	15%	25%

Investment centre A has made double the profits of investment centre B and in terms of profits alone has therefore been more 'successful'. However, B has achieved its profits with a much lower capital investment and so has earned a much higher ROI. This suggests that B has been a more successful investment than A.

2.1 Measuring ROI

FAST FORWARD

There is no generally agreed method of calculating ROI, and it can have **behavioural implications** and lead to dysfunctional decision-making when used as a guide to investment decisions. It focuses attention on short-run performance whereas investment decisions should be evaluated over their full life.

ROI can be measured in different ways.

2.1.1 Profit after depreciation as a % of net assets employed

This is probably the **most common method**, but it does present a problem. If an investment centre maintains the same annual profit, and keeps the same assets without a policy of regular replacement of non-current assets, its ROI will increase year by year as the assets get older. This **can give a false impression of improving performance over time**.

For example, the results of investment centre X, with a policy of straight-line depreciation of assets over a five-year period, might be as follows.

Year	Non-current assets at cost $'000	Depreciation in the year $'000	NBV (mid year) $'000	Working capital $'000	Capital employed $'000	Profit $'000	ROI
0	100			10	110		
1	100	20	90	10	100	10	10.0%
2	100	20	70	10	80	10	12.5%
3	100	20	50	10	60	10	16.7%
4	100	20	30	10	40	10	25.0%
5	100	20	10	10	20	10	50.0%

This table of figures is intended to show that an investment centre can **improve its ROI** year by year simply **by allowing its non-current assets to depreciate**, and there could be a **disincentive** to investment centre managers to **reinvest in new or replacement assets**, because the centre's ROI would probably fall.

This example has used a mid-year NBV but a year end or start of year NBV can also be used.

Question — ROI calculation (1)

A new company has non-current assets of $460,000 which will be depreciated to nil on a straight line basis over 10 years. Net current assets will consistently be $75,000, and annual profit will consistently be $30,000. ROI is measured as return on net assets.

Required

Calculate the company's ROI in Years 2 and 6.

Answer

Year 2 – 6.8%
Year 6 – 11.6%

A further disadvantage of measuring ROI as profit divided by net assets is that, for similar reasons, it is not **easy to compare** fairly the **performance of investment centres**.

For example, suppose that we have two investment centres.

	Investment centre P		Investment centre Q	
	$	$	$	$
Working capital		20,000		20,000
Non-current assets at cost	230,000		230,000	
Accumulated depreciation	170,000		10,000	
Net book value		60,000		220,000
Capital employed		80,000		240,000
Profit		$24,000		$24,000
ROI		30%		10%

Investment centres P and Q have the same amount of working capital, the same value of non-current assets at cost and the same profit. However, P's non-current assets have been depreciated by a much bigger amount (presumably P's non-current assets are much older than Q's) and so P's ROI is three times the size of Q's ROI. The conclusion might therefore be that P has performed much better than Q. This comparison, however, would not be 'fair', because the difference in performance might be entirely attributable to the age of their non-current assets.

The arguments for using net book values for calculating ROI

(a)   It is the **'normally accepted'** method of calculating ROI.

(b)   Organisations are continually buying new non-current assets to replace old ones that wear out and so, on the whole, the **total net book value** of all non-current assets together **will remain fairly constant** (assuming nil inflation and nil growth).

2.1.2 Profit after depreciation as a % of gross assets employed

Instead of measuring ROI as return on net assets, we could measure it as return on gross assets ie before depreciation. This would **remove the problem of ROI increasing over time as non-current assets get older**.

If a company acquired a non-current asset costing $40,000, which it intends to depreciate by $10,000 pa for four years, and if the asset earns a profit of $8,000 pa after depreciation, ROI might be calculated on net book values or gross values, as follows.

Year	Profit $	NBV (mid-year value) $	ROI based on NBV	Gross value $	ROI based on gross value
1	8,000	35,000	22.9%	40,000	20%
2	8,000	25,000	32.0%	40,000	20%
3	8,000	15,000	53.3%	40,000	20%
4	8,000	5,000	160.0%	40,000	20%

The ROI based on **net book value** shows an **increasing trend over time**, simply because the asset's value is falling as it is depreciated. The ROI based on gross book value suggests that the asset has **performed consistently** in each of the four years, which is probably a more valid conclusion.

Question
ROI calculation (2)

Repeat **Question: ROI calculation (1)**, measuring ROI as return on gross assets.

Answer

Year 2 – 5.6%
Year 6 – 5.6%

However, using gross book values to measure ROI has its **disadvantages**. Most important of these is that measuring ROI as return on gross assets ignores the age factor, and **does not distinguish between old and new assets**.

(a)   **Older non-current assets** usually **cost more to repair and maintain**, to keep them running. An investment centre with old assets may therefore have its profitability reduced by repair costs, and its ROI might fall over time as its assets get older and repair costs get bigger.

(b)   **Inflation** and **technological change alter the cost of non-current assets**. If one investment centre has non-current assets bought ten years ago with a gross cost of $1 million, and another investment centre in the same area of business operations has non-current assets bought very recently for $1 million, the quantity and technological character of the non-current assets of the two investment centres are likely to be very different.

2.1.3 Constituent elements of the investment base

Although we have looked at how the investment base should be valued, we need to consider its appropriate constituent elements.

(a)   If a **manager's performance is being evaluated**, only those **assets** which can be **traced directly to the division** and are **controllable by the manager should be included**. Head office assets or investment centre assets controlled by head office should not be included. So, for example, only those cash balances actually maintained within an investment centre itself should be included.

(b)   If it is the performance of the investment centre that is being appraised, **a proportion of the investment in head office assets would need to be included** because an investment centre could not operate without the support of head office assets and administrative backup.

2.1.4 Profits

We have looked at how to define the asset base used in the calculations but what about profit? If the **performance of the investment centre manager is being assessed** it should seem reasonable to **base profit on the revenues and costs controllable by the manager** and exclude service and head office costs except those costs specifically attributable to the investment centre. If it is the **performance of the investment centre that is being assessed, however, the inclusion of general service and head office costs would seem reasonable**.

Exam focus point

> The profit figure for ROI should always be the amount before any interest is charged.

2.1.5 Massaging the ROI

If a manager's large bonus depends on ROI being met, the manager may feel pressure to massage the measure. The **asset base** of the ratio can be **altered** by increasing/decreasing payables and receivables (by speeding up or delaying payments and receipts).

2.2 ROI and new investments

If investment centre performance is judged by ROI, we should expect that the managers of investment centres will probably decide to undertake new capital investments **only if these new investments are likely to increase the ROI of their centre**.

Suppose that an investment centre, A, currently makes a return of 40% on capital employed. The manager of centre A would probably only want to undertake new investments that promise to yield a return of 40% or more, otherwise the investment centre's overall ROI would fall.

For example, if investment centre A currently has assets of $1,000,000 and expects to earn a profit of $400,000, how would the centre's manager view a new capital investment which would cost $250,000 and yield a profit of $75,000 pa?

	Without the new investment	With the new investment
Profit	$400,000	$475,000
Capital employed	$1,000,000	$1,250,000
ROI	40%	38%

The **new investment** would **reduce the investment centre's ROI** from 40% to 38%, and so the investment centre manager would probably decide **not to undertake** the new investment.

If the group of companies of which investment centre A is a part has a target ROI of, say, 25%, the new investment would presumably be seen as **beneficial for the group as a whole**. But even though it promises to yield a return of 75,000/250,000 = 30%, which is above the group's target ROI, it would still make investment centre A's results look worse. The manager of investment centre A would, in these circumstances, be motivated to do not what is best for the organisation as a whole, but what is **best for his division**.

ROI should not be used to guide investment decisions but there is a difficult **motivational** problem. If management performance is measured in terms of ROI, any decisions which benefit the company in the long term but which reduce the ROI in the immediate short term would reflect badly on the manager's reported performance. In other words, good investment decisions would make a manager's performance seem **worse** than if the wrong investment decision were taken instead.

3 Residual income (RI)

FAST FORWARD

> RI can sometimes give results that avoid the **behavioural** problem of **dysfunctionality**. Its weakness is that it does not facilitate comparisons between investment centres nor does it relate the size of a centre's income to the size of the investment.

An alternative way of measuring the performance of an investment centre, instead of using ROI, is residual income (RI). **Residual income** is a **measure of the centre's profits after deducting a notional or imputed interest cost**.

(a)   The centre's profit is **after deducting depreciation** on capital equipment.

(b)   The imputed cost of capital might be the organisation's cost of borrowing or its weighted average cost of capital.

Key term

> **Residual income** is a measure of the centre's profits after deducting a notional or imputed interest cost.

Question

RI

A division with capital employed of $400,000 currently earns an ROI of 22%. It can make an additional investment of $50,000 for a five year life with nil residual value. The average net profit from this investment would be $12,000 after depreciation. The division's cost of capital is 14%.

What are the residual incomes before and after the investment?

Answer

	Before investment $	After investment $
Divisional profit ($400,000 × 22%)	88,000	100,000
Imputed interest		
(400,000 × 0.14)	56,000	
(450,000 × 0.14)		63,000
Residual income	32,000	37,000

3.1 The advantages and weaknesses of RI compared with ROI

The advantages of using RI

(a)   Residual income will **increase** when investments earning above the cost of capital are undertaken and investments earning below the cost of capital are eliminated.

(b)   Residual income is **more flexible** since a different cost of capital can be applied to investments with **different risk** characteristics.

The **weakness** of RI is that it **does not facilitate comparisons** between investment centres nor **does it relate the size of a centre's income to the size of the investment**.

3.2 RI versus ROI: marginally profitable investments

Residual income will increase if a new investment is undertaken which earns a profit in excess of the imputed interest charge on the value of the asset acquired. Residual income will go up even if the investment only just exceeds the imputed interest charge, and this means that 'marginally profitable' investments are likely to be undertaken by the investment centre manager.

In contrast, when a manager is judged by ROI, a marginally profitable investment would be less likely to be undertaken because it would reduce the average ROI earned by the centre as a whole.

3.2.1 Example: ROI versus residual income

Suppose that Department H has the following profit, assets employed and an imputed interest charge of 12% on operating assets.

	$	$
Operating profit	30,000	
Operating assets		100,000
Imputed interest (12%)	12,000	
Return on investment		30%
Residual income	18,000	

Suppose now that an additional investment of $10,000 is proposed, which will increase operating income in Department H by $1,400. The effect of the investment would be:

	$	$
Total operating income	31,400	
Total operating assets		110,000
Imputed interest (12%)	13,200	
Return on investment		28.5%
Residual income	18,200	

If the Department H manager is made responsible for the department's performance, they would **resist the new investment if they were to be judged on ROI**, but would **welcome the investment if they were judged according to RI**, since there would be a marginal increase of $200 in residual income from the investment, but a fall of 1.5% in ROI.

The marginal investment offers a return of 14% ($1,400 on an investment of $10,000) which is above the 'cut-off rate' of 12%. Since the original return on investment was 30%, the marginal investment will reduce the overall divisional performance. Indeed, any marginal investment offering an accounting rate of return of less than 30% in the year would reduce the overall performance.

Exam focus point

Examination questions on residual income may focus on the sort of behavioural aspects of investment centre measurement that we have discussed above; for example, why it is considered necessary to use residual income to measure performance rather than ROI, and why residual income might influence an investment centre manager's investment decisions differently.

4 Transfer pricing   6/10, 12/11, 12/13, 6/14, 6/15, Mar/Jun 16

FAST FORWARD

Transfer prices are a way of promoting **divisional autonomy**, ideally without prejudicing the **measurement of divisional performance** or discouraging **overall corporate profit maximisation**.

Transfer prices should be set at a level which ensures that profits for the organisation as a whole are maximised.

The examining team noted in the June 2015 exam report that transfer pricing questions are answered poorly on a consistent basis. A guide to answering this type of question was given as, 'logically consider the minimum transfer price, the maximum transfer price, then discuss what a reasonable transfer price would therefore be'.

Transfer pricing is used when divisions of an organisation need to charge other divisions of the same organisation for goods and services they provide to them. For example, subsidiary A might make a component that is used as part of a product made by subsidiary B of the same company, but that can also be sold to the external market, including makers of rival products to subsidiary B's product. There will therefore be two sources of revenue for A.

(a)   External sales revenue from sales made to other organisations

(b)   Internal sales revenue from sales made to other responsibility centres within the same organisation, valued at the transfer price

A **transfer price** is the price at which goods or services are transferred from one department to another, or from one member of a group to another.

4.1 Problems with transfer pricing

4.1.1 Maintaining the right level of divisional autonomy

Transfer prices are particularly appropriate for **profit centres** because if one profit centre does work for another the size of the transfer price will affect the costs of one profit centre and the revenues of another.

However, as we have seen, a danger with profit centre accounting is that the business organisation will **divide into a number of self-interested segments**, each acting at times against the wishes and interests of other segments. Decisions might be taken by a profit centre manager in the best interests of their own part of the business, but against the best interests of other profit centres and possibly the organisation as a whole.

4.1.2 Ensuring divisional performance is measured fairly

Profit centre managers tend to put their own profit performance above everything else. Since profit centre performance is measured according to the profit they earn, no profit centre will want to do work for another and incur costs without being paid for it. Consequently, profit centre managers are likely to dispute the size of transfer prices with each other, or disagree about whether one profit centre should do work for another or not. Transfer prices **affect behaviour and decisions** by profit centre managers.

4.1.3 Ensuring corporate profits are maximised

When there are disagreements about how much work should be transferred between divisions, and how many sales the division should make to the external market, there is presumably a **profit-maximising level of output and sales for the organisation as a whole**. However, unless each profit centre also maximises its own profit at this same level of output, there will be interdivisional disagreements about output levels and the profit-maximising output will not be achieved.

4.1.4 The ideal solution

Ideally a transfer price should be set at a level that overcomes these problems.

(a)   The transfer price should provide an 'artificial' selling price that enables the **transferring division to earn a return for its efforts**, and the **receiving division to incur a cost for benefits received**.

(b)   The transfer price should be set at a level that enables **profit centre performance** to be **measured 'commercially'**. This means that the transfer price should be a fair commercial price.

(c)   The transfer price, if possible, should encourage profit centre managers to agree on the amount of goods and services to be transferred, which will also be at a level that is consistent with the aims of the organisation as a whole, such as **maximising company profits**.

In practice it is difficult to achieve all three aims.

Question

The transfer pricing system operated by a divisional company has the potential to make a significant contribution towards the achievement of corporate financial objectives.

Required

Explain the potential benefits of operating a transfer pricing system within a divisionalised company.

Answer

Potential benefits of operating a transfer pricing system within a divisionalised company include the following.

(a)   It can lead to **goal congruence** by motivating divisional managers to make decisions, which improve divisional profit and improve profit of the organisation as a whole.

(b)   It can prevent **dysfunctional decision-making** so that decisions taken by a divisional manager are in the best interests of their own part of the business, other divisions and the organisation as a whole.

(c)   Transfer prices can be set at a level that enables divisional performance to be measured 'commercially'. A transfer pricing system should therefore report a level of divisional profit that is a **reasonable measure of the managerial performance** of the division.

(d)   It should ensure that **divisional autonomy** is not undermined. A well-run transfer pricing system helps to ensure that a balance is kept between divisional autonomy to provide incentives and motivation, and centralised authority to ensure that the divisions are all working towards the same target; the benefit of the organisation as a whole.

4.2 General rules

FAST FORWARD

The **limits within which transfer prices should fall** are as follows.

*   **The minimum**. The sum of the supplying division's marginal cost and opportunity cost of the item transferred.
*   **The maximum**. The lowest market price at which the receiving division could purchase the goods or services externally, less any internal cost savings in packaging and delivery.

The **minimum** results from the fact that the **supplying division will not agree to transfer if the transfer price is less than the marginal cost + opportunity cost of the item transferred** (because if it were, the division would incur a loss).

The **maximum** results from the fact that the **receiving division will buy the item at the cheapest price possible**.

4.2.1 Example: general rules

Division X produces product L at a marginal cost per unit of $100. If a unit is transferred internally to division Y, $25 contribution is forgone on an external sale. The item can be purchased externally for $150.

*   **The minimum**. Division X will not agree to a transfer price of less than $(100 + 25) = $125 per unit.
*   **The maximum**. Division Y will not agree to a transfer price in excess of $150.

The difference between the two results ($25) represents the savings from producing internally as opposed to buying externally.

4.2.2 Opportunity cost

The **opportunity cost** included in determining the lower limit will be one of the following.

(a)   The maximum contribution forgone by the supplying division **in transferring internally rather than selling goods externally**.

(b)   The contribution forgone by **not using the same facilities** in the producing division **for their next best alternative use**.

If there is **no external market** for the item being transferred, and **no alternative uses for** the division's facilities, the **transfer price = standard variable cost of production**.

If there is an **external market** for the item being transferred and **no alternative, more profitable use** for the facilities in that division, the **transfer price = the market price**.

4.2.3 Example: The transfer price at full and spare capacity

The factors that influence the transfer price charged when divisions are operating at **full capacity** and **spare capacity** are best illustrated using an example.

Until recently, Strike Co focused exclusively on making soles for work boots and football boots. It sold these rubber soles to boot manufacturers. Last year the company decided to take advantage of its strong reputation by expanding into the business of making football boots. As a consequence of this expansion, the company is now structured as two independent divisions, the Boot Division and the Sole Division.

The Sole Division continues to make rubber soles for both football boots and work boots and sells these soles to other boot manufacturers. The Boot division manufactures leather uppers for football boots and attaches these uppers to rubber soles. During its first year the Boot Division purchased its rubber soles from outside suppliers so as not to disrupt the operations of the Sole Division.

Strike management now wants the Sole Division to provide at least some of the soles used by the Boot Division. The table below shows the contribution margin for each division when the Boot Division purchases from an outside supplier.

Boot Division		*Sole Division*	
	$		$
Selling price of football boot	100	Selling price of sole	28
Variable cost of making boot (not including sole)	45	Variable cost per sole	21
Cost of sole purchased from outside suppliers	25		
Contribution margin per unit	30	Contribution margin per unit	7

The information above indicates that the total contribution margin per unit is $37 ($30 + $7).

Required

What would be a fair transfer price if the Sole Division sold 10,000 soles to the Boot Division?

Solution

The answer depends on how busy the Sole Division is – that is, whether it has **spare capacity**.

No spare capacity

As indicated above, the Sole Division charges $28 and derives a contribution margin of $7 per sole. The Sole Division has **no spare capacity** and produces and sells 80,000 units (soles) to outside customers. Therefore, the Sole Division must receive from the Boot Division a payment that will at least cover its variable cost per sole **plus** its lost contribution margin per sole (the **opportunity cost**). If the Sole Division cannot cover that amount (the **minimum** transfer price), it should not sell soles to the Boot Division. The minimum transfer price that would be acceptable to the Sole Division is $28, as shown below.

$21 (variable cost) + $7 (opportunity cost) = $28

Spare capacity

The minimum transfer price is different if a division has spare capacity. Assume the Sole Division produces 80,000 soles but can only sell 70,000 to the open market. As a result, it has available capacity of 10,000 units. In this situation, the Sole Division does not lose its contribution margin of $7 per unit, and therefore the minimum price it would now accept is $21 as shown below.

$21 (variable cost) + $0 (opportunity cost) = $21

In this case the Boot Division and the Sole Division should **negotiate** a transfer price within the range of $21 and $25 (cost from outside supplier).

4.3 The use of market price as a basis for transfer prices

If an **external market price exists** for transferred goods, profit centre managers will be aware of the price they could obtain or the price they would have to pay for their goods on the external market, and they would inevitably **compare** this price **with the transfer price**.

4.3.1 Example: Transferring goods at market value

A company has two profit centres, A and B. A sells half its output on the open market and transfers the other half to B. Costs and external revenues in an accounting period are as follows.

	A $	B $	Total $
External sales	8,000	24,000	32,000
Costs of production	12,000	10,000	22,000
Company profit			10,000

Required

What are the consequences of setting a transfer price at market value?

Solution

If the transfer price is at market price, A would be happy to sell the output to B for $8,000, which is what A would get by selling it externally instead of transferring it.

	A $	A $	B $	B $	Total $
Market sales		8,000		24,000	32,000
Transfer sales		8,000		–	
		16,000		24,000	
Transfer costs		–	8,000		
Own costs	12,000		10,000		22,000
		12,000	18,000		
Profit		4,000		6,000	10,000

The **transfer sales of A are self-cancelling with the transfer cost of B**, so that the total profits are unaffected by the transfer items. The transfer price simply spreads the total profit between A and B.

Consequences

(a)   A earns the same profit on transfers as on external sales. B must pay a commercial price for transferred goods, and both divisions will have their profit measured in a fair way.

(b)   A will be indifferent about selling externally or transferring goods to B because the profit is the same on both types of transaction. B can therefore ask for and obtain as many units as it wants from A.

A **market-based** transfer price therefore seems to be the **ideal** transfer price.

4.4 The merits of market value transfer prices

4.4.1 Divisional autonomy

In a decentralised company, divisional managers should have the **autonomy** to make output, selling and buying **decisions which appear to be in the best interests of the division's performance.** (If every division optimises its performance, the company as a whole must inevitably achieve optimal results.) Thus a **transferor division should be given the freedom to sell output on the open market**, rather than to transfer it within the company.

'Arm's length' transfer prices, which give profit centre managers the freedom to negotiate prices with other profit centres as though they were independent companies, will tend to result in a market-based transfer price.

4.4.2 Corporate profit maximisation

In most cases where the transfer price is at market price, **internal transfers** should be **expected**, because the **buying division** is likely to **benefit** from a better quality of service, greater flexibility and dependability of supply. **Both divisions** may **benefit** from cheaper costs of administration, selling and transport. Using a market price as the transfer price would therefore **result in decisions which would be in the best interests of the company or group as a whole**.

4.4.3 Divisional performance measurement

Where a **market price exists**, but the **transfer price is a different amount** (say, at standard cost plus), divisional managers will **argue** about the volume of internal transfers.

For example, if division X is expected to sell output to division Y at a transfer price of $8 per unit when the open market price is $10, its manager will decide to sell all output on the open market. The manager of division Y would resent the loss of their cheap supply from X, and would be reluctant to buy on the open market. A wasteful situation would arise where X sells on the open market at $10, where Y buys at $10, so that administration, selling and distribution costs would have been saved if X had sold directly to Y at $10, the market price.

4.5 The disadvantages of market value transfer prices

Market value as a transfer price does have certain **disadvantages**.

(a)   The **market price may be a temporary one**, induced by adverse economic conditions or dumping, or it might depend on the volume of output supplied to the external market by the profit centre.

(b)   A transfer price at market value might, under some circumstances, **act as a disincentive to use up any spare capacity** in the divisions. A price based on incremental cost, in contrast, might provide an incentive to use up the spare resources in order to provide a marginal contribution to profit.

(c)   Many products **do not have an equivalent market price** so that the price of a similar, but not identical, product might have to be chosen. In such circumstances, the option to sell or buy on the open market does not really exist.

(d)   There might be an **imperfect external market** for the transferred item so that, if the transferring division tried to sell more externally, it would have to reduce its selling price.

4.6 Cost-based approaches to transfer pricing

FAST FORWARD

Problems arise with the use of **cost-based** transfer prices because one party or the other is liable to perceive them as unfair.

Cost-based approaches to transfer pricing are often used in practice, because in practice the following conditions are common.

(a) There is **no external market** for the product that is being transferred.

(b) Alternatively, although there is an external market, it is an **imperfect** one because the market price is affected by such factors as the amount that the company setting the transfer price supplies to it, or because there is only a limited external demand.

In either case there will not be a suitable market price on which to base the transfer price.

4.6.1 Transfer prices based on full cost

Under this approach, the **full cost** (including fixed overheads absorbed) incurred by the supplying division in making the 'intermediate' product is charged to the receiving division. The obvious drawback to this is that the division supplying the product **makes no profit** on its work so is not motivated to supply internally. In addition, there are a number of alternative ways in which fixed costs can be accounted for. If a **full cost-plus** approach is used, a **profit margin** is also included in this transfer price. The supplying division will therefore gain some profit at the expense of the buying division.

4.6.2 Example: Transfer prices based on full cost

Suppose a company has two profit centres, A and B. A can only sell half its maximum output of 800 units externally because of limited demand. It transfers the other half of its output to B which also faces limited demand. Costs and revenues in an accounting period are as follows.

	A $	B $	Total $
External sales	8,000	24,000	32,000
Costs of production in the division	13,000	10,000	23,000
Profit			9,000

Division A's costs included fixed production overheads of $4,800 and fixed selling and administration costs of $1,000.

There are no opening or closing inventories. It does not matter, for this illustration, whether marginal costing or absorption costing is used. For the moment, we shall ignore the question of whether the current output levels are profit maximising and congruent with the goals of the company as a whole.

If the transfer price is at full cost, A in our example would have 'sales' to B of $6,000 (($13,000 – 1,000) × 50%). Selling and administration costs are not included, as these are not incurred on the internal transfers. This would be a cost to B, as follows.

	A $	A $	B $	B $	Company as a whole $
Open market sales		8,000		24,000	32,000
Transfer sales		6,000		–	
Total sales, inc transfers		14,000		24,000	
Transfer costs			6,000		
Own costs	13,000		10,000		23,000
Total costs, inc transfers		13,000		16,000	
Profit		1,000		8,000	9,000

The **transfer sales of A are self-cancelling with the transfer costs of B** so that total profits are **unaffected by the transfer items**. The transfer price simply spreads the total profit of $9,000 between A and B.

The obvious **drawback** to the transfer price at cost is that **A makes no profit** on its work, and the manager of division A would much prefer to sell output on the open market to earn a profit, rather than transfer to B, regardless of whether or not transfers to B would be in the best interests of the company as a whole. Division A needs a profit on its transfers in order to be motivated to supply B; therefore transfer pricing at cost is inconsistent with the use of a profit centre accounting system.

An **intermediate product** is one that is used as a component of another product; for example, car headlights or food additives.

4.6.3 Transfer price at variable cost

A variable cost approach entails charging the variable cost (which we assume to be the same as the marginal cost) that has been incurred by the supplying division to the receiving division.

The problem is that with a transfer price at marginal cost the **supplying division does not cover its fixed costs**.

4.7 Identifying the optimal transfer price

Here are some guiding rules for identifying the optimal transfer price.

(a)   The **ideal transfer price** should **reflect the opportunity cost** of sale to the supply division and the opportunity cost to the buying division. Unfortunately, full information about opportunity costs may not be easily obtainable in practice.

(b)   Where a **perfect external market price exists and unit variable costs and unit selling prices are constant**, the **opportunity cost** of transfer will be **external market price** or **external market price less savings in selling costs**.

(c)   In the **absence of a perfect external market price for the transferred item**, but where **unit variable costs are constant**, and the **sales price per unit of the end product is constant**, the **ideal transfer price** should reflect the opportunity cost of the resources consumed by the supply division to make and supply the item and so should be at **standard variable cost + opportunity cost of making the transfer**.

(d)   When **unit variable costs and/or unit selling prices are not constant**, there will be a **profit-maximising level of output** and the **ideal transfer price** will only be found by sensible **negotiation** and careful **analysis**.

   (i)   Establish the output and sales quantities that will optimise the profits of the company or group as a whole.

   (ii)   Establish the transfer price at which both profit centres would maximise their profits at this company-optimising output level.

   There may be a range of prices within which both profit centres can agree on the output level that would maximise their individual profits and the profits of the company as a whole. Any price within the range would then be 'ideal'.

4.8 Transfer pricing calculations

4.8.1 Sub-optimal decisions

Note that, as the level of transfer price increases, its effect on a division within the organisation could lead to sub-optimalisation problems for the organisation as a whole.

4.8.2 Example: Sub-optimal decisions

For example, suppose division B could buy the product from an outside supplier for $10 instead of paying $15 ($6,000/(800/2)) to division A. This transfer price would therefore force division B to buy the product externally at $10 per unit, although it could be manufactured internally for a variable cost of $(13,000 – 4,800 – 1,000)/800 = $9 per unit.

Although division B (the buying division) would save ($15 − $10) = $5 per unit by buying externally, the organisation as a whole would lose $400, as follows.

	Per unit
	$
Marginal cost of production	9
External purchase cost	10
Loss if buy in	1

The overall loss on transfer/purchase of 400 units is therefore 400 × $1 = $400.

This loss of $1 per unit assumes that any other use for the released capacity would produce a benefit of less than $400. If the 400 units could also be sold externally for $20 per unit, the optimal decision for the organisation as a whole would be to buy in the units for division B at $10 per unit.

	Per unit
	$
Market price	20
Marginal cost	9
Contribution	11
Loss if buy-in	(1)
Incremental profit	10

The overall incremental profit would therefore be 400 × $10 = $4,000.

4.8.3 Example: Prices based on full cost plus

If the transfers are at cost plus a margin of, say, 10%, A's sales to B would be $6,600 (($13,000 − 1,000) × 50% × 1.10).

	A		B	Total
	$	$	$	$
Open market sales		8,000	24,000	32,000
Transfer sales		6,600	–	
		14,600	24,000	
Transfer costs			6,600	
Own costs	13,000		10,000	23,000
		13,000	16,600	
Profit		1,600	7,400	9,000

Compared to a transfer price at cost, **A gains some profit** at the expense of B. However, A makes a bigger profit on external sales in this case because the profit mark-up of 10% is less than the profit mark-up on open market sales. The choice of 10% as a profit mark-up was arbitrary and unrelated to external market conditions.

The transfer price **fails on all three criteria** (divisional autonomy, performance measurement and corporate profit measurement) for judgement.

(a) Arguably, the transfer price does not give A fair revenue or charge B a reasonable cost, and so their profit **performance is distorted**. It would certainly be unfair, for example, to compare A's profit with B's profit.

(b) Given this unfairness, it is likely that the **autonomy** of each of the divisional managers is **under threat**. If they cannot agree on what is a fair split of the external profit, a decision will have to be imposed from above.

(c) It would seem to give A an incentive to sell more goods externally and transfer less to B. This may or **may not be in the best interests of the company as a whole**.

In fact, we can demonstrate that the method is **flawed from the point of view of corporate profit maximisation**. Division A's total production costs of $12,000 include an element of fixed costs. Half of division A's total production costs are transferred to division B. However, from the point of view of division B, the cost is entirely variable.

The cost per unit to A is $15 ($12,000 ÷ 800) and this includes a fixed element of $6 ($4,800 ÷ 800), while division B's own costs are $25 ($10,000 ÷ 400) per unit, including a fixed element of $10 (say). The **total variable cost is really** $9 + $15 = **$24**, but from division **B's point of view** the **variable cost** is $15 + $(25 – 10) = **$30**. This means that division B will be unwilling to sell the final product for less than $30, whereas any price above $24 would make a contribution to overall costs. Thus, if external prices for the final product fall, B might be tempted to cease production.

4.8.4 Example: Transfer prices based on variable or marginal cost

A variable or marginal cost approach entails charging the variable cost (which we assume to be the same as the marginal cost) that has been incurred by the supplying division to the receiving division. As above, we shall suppose that A's cost per unit is $15, of which $6 is fixed and $9 variable.

	A		B		Company as a whole	
	$	$	$	$	$	$
Market sales		8,000		24,000		32,000
Transfer sales		3,600		–		
		11,600		24,000		
Transfer costs	–		3,600			
Own variable costs	7,200		6,000		13,200	
Own fixed costs	5,800		4,000		9,800	
Total costs and transfers		13,000		13,600		23,000
(Loss)/Profit		(1,400)		10,400		9,000

4.8.5 Divisional autonomy, divisional performance measurement and corporate profit maximisation

(a) This result is **deeply unsatisfactory for the manager of division A** who could make an additional $4,400 ($(8,000 – 3,600)) profit if no goods were transferred to division B, but all were sold externally.

(b) Given that the manager of division A would prefer to transfer externally, **head office** are likely to have to **insist** that internal transfers are made.

(c) For the company overall, external transfers only would cause a large fall in profit, because division B could make no sales at all.

Point to note. Suppose no more than the current $8,000 could be earned from external sales and the production capacity used for production for internal transfer would remain idle if not used. Division A would be indifferent to the transfers at marginal cost, as they do not represent any benefit to the division.

If more than the $8,000 of revenue could be earned externally (ie division A could sell more externally than at present), division A would have a strong disincentive to supply B at marginal cost.

Chapter Roundup

- Divisionalisation is a term for the division of an organisation into divisions. Each divisional manager is responsible for the performance of the division. A division may be a cost centre (responsible for its costs only), a profit centre (responsible for revenues and profits) or an investment centre or Strategic Business Unit (responsible for costs, revenues and assets).

- There are a number of advantages and disadvantages to **divisionalisation**.

- **Responsibility accounting** is the term used to describe decentralisation of authority, with the performance of the decentralised units measured in terms of accounting results.

  With a system of responsibility accounting there are five types of **responsibility centre: cost centre; revenue centre; profit centre; contribution centre; and investment centre**.

- The performance of an investment centre is usually monitored using either or both **return on investment (ROI)** and **residual income (RI)**.

- There is no generally agreed method of calculating ROI and it can have **behavioural implications** and lead to dysfunctional decision-making when used as a guide to investment decisions. It focuses attention on short-run performance whereas investment decisions should be evaluated over their full life.

- RI can sometimes give results that avoid the **behavioural** problem of **dysfunctionality**. Its weakness is that it does not facilitate comparisons between investment centres nor does it relate the size of a centre's income to the size of the investment.

- Transfer prices are a way of promoting **divisional autonomy**, ideally without prejudicing the **measurement of divisional performance** or discouraging **overall corporate profit maximisation**.

- Transfer prices should be set at a level which ensures that profits for the organisation as a whole are maximised.

- The **limits within which transfer prices should fall** are as follows.

  - **The minimum**. The sum of the supplying division's marginal cost and opportunity cost of the item transferred.

  - **The maximum**. The lowest market price at which the receiving division could purchase the goods or services externally, less any internal cost savings in packaging and delivery.

- Problems arise with the use of **cost-based** transfer prices because one party or the other is liable to perceive them as unfair.

1   Choose the correct words from those highlighted.

ROI based on profits as a % of net assets employed will (a) **increase/decrease** as an asset gets older and its book value (b) **increases/reduces**. This could therefore create an (c) **incentive/disincentive** to investment centre managers to reinvest in new or replacement assets.

2   An investment centre with capital employed of $570,000 is budgeted to earn a profit of $119,700 next year. A proposed fixed asset investment of $50,000, not included in the budget at present, will earn a profit next year of $8,500 after depreciation. The company's cost of capital is 15%. What is the budgeted ROI and residual income for next year, both with and without the investment?

	ROI	*Residual income*
Without investment	………………..	………………..
With investment	………………..	………………..

3   'The use of residual income in performance measurement will avoid dysfunctional decision-making because it will always lead to the correct decision concerning capital investments.' **True or false?**

4   To prevent dysfunctional transfer price decision-making, profit centres must be allowed to make autonomous decisions. **True or false?**

5   Which of the following is not a disadvantage of using market value as a transfer price?

   A   The market price might be a temporary one.
   B   Use of market price might act as a disincentive to use up spare capacity.
   C   Many products do not have an equivalent market price.
   D   The external market might be perfect.

6   Fill in the blanks.

Ideally, a transfer price should be set that enables the individual divisions to maximise their profits at a level of output that maximises ……………………………………………… .

The transfer price which achieves this is unlikely to be a ………………………………….. transfer price or a ………………………….. transfer price.

If optimum decisions are to be taken, transfer prices should reflect ……………………………………… .

Answers to Quick Quiz

1   (a)   increase
    (b)   reduces
    (c)   disincentive

2
	ROI	Residual income
Without investment	21.0%	$34,200
With investment	20.7%	$35,200

3   False

4   False. They cannot be allowed to make entirely autonomous decisions.

5   D

6   profit for the company as a whole; market-based; cost-based; opportunity costs

Now try the questions below from the Practice Question Bank

Number	Level	Marks	Approximate time
Section A Q96	Examination	2	4 mins
Section A Q97	Examination	2	4 mins
Section A Q98	Examination	2	4 mins
Section A Q99	Examination	2	4 mins
Section A Q100	Examination	2	4 mins
Section C Q10	Examination	20	39 mins

18

Further aspects of performance management

Topic list	Syllabus reference
1 Not for profit organisations	D6 (a), (c)
2 Performance measurement in not for profit organisations	D6 (b)
3 Value for money	D6 (d)
4 Non-financial performance indicators (NFPIs)	D6 (e)
5 Target setting in qualitative areas	D6 (f)
6 Short-termism and manipulation	D6 (h)
7 External considerations	D7 (a), (b), (c)
8 Behaviour aspects of performance management	D7 (d)

Introduction

This final chapter on performance measurement looks at performance analysis in not for profit organisations and the public sector. The problems of having **non-quantifiable** and **multiple** objectives are discussed.

We then go on to consider how **external considerations** are allowed for in performance measurement and finally identify and explain the **behaviour aspects** of performance management.

Study guide

		Intellectual level
D6	**Performance analysis in not for profit organisations and the public sector**	
(a)	Comment on the problems of having non-quantifiable objectives in performance management.	2
(b)	Comment on the problems of having multiple objectives in this sector.	2
(c)	Explain how performance could be measured in this sector.	2
(d)	Outline Value for Money (VFM) as a public sector objective.	1
(e)	Describe, calculate and interpret non-financial performance indicators (NFPIs) and suggest methods to improve the performance indicated.	2
(f)	Discuss the difficulties of target setting in qualitative areas.	2
(g)	Analyse past performance and suggest ways for improving financial and non-financial performance.	2
(h)	Explain the causes and problems created by short-termism and financial manipulation of results and suggest methods to encourage a long term view.	2
D7	**External considerations and behavioural aspects**	
(a)	Explain the need to allow for external considerations in performance management, including stakeholders, market conditions and allowance for competitors.	2
(b)	Suggest ways in which external considerations could be allowed for in performance management.	2
(c)	Interpret performance in the light of external considerations.	2
(d)	Identify and explain the behaviour aspects of performance management.	2

Exam guide

Scenarios in your exam may relate to not for profit organisations and the public sector and you need to understand their particular needs and issues. Always **apply** your answers to the specific organisation. There is a two part article on the ACCA website on the topic of not for profit organisations, written by a member of the examining team (ACCA, 2015). It is recommended that you read both of these articles.

1 Not for profit organisations

FAST FORWARD

One possible definition of a **not for profit seeking organisation** is that its first objective is to be involved in non loss making operations to cover its costs, profits only being made as a means to an end.

Although most people would 'know one if they saw it', there is a surprising problem in clearly defining what counts as a not for profit organisation.

It has been suggested that not for profit organisations can be defined by recognising that their first objective is to be involved in **non loss making operations** in order to cover their costs and that profits are only made as a means to an end (such as providing a service, or accomplishing some socially or morally worthy objective).

1.1 Objectives and not for profit organisations

Not for profit organisations have **multiple objectives** which are **difficult to define**.

A major problem with many not for profit organisations, particularly government bodies, is that it is extremely **difficult to define their objectives** at all. In addition, they tend to have **multiple objectives**, so that even if they could all be clearly identified it is impossible to say which is the overriding objective.

Question
Objectives

What objectives might the following not for profit organisations have?

(a)   An army
(b)   A local council
(c)   A charity
(d)   A political party
(e)   A college

Answer

Here are some suggestions.

(a)   To defend a country
(b)   To provide services for local people (such as the elderly)
(c)   To help others/protect the environment
(d)   To gain power/enact legislation
(e)   To provide education

More general objectives for not for profit organisations include:

- Surplus maximisation (equivalent to profit maximisation)
- Revenue maximisation (as for a commercial business)
- Usage maximisation (as in leisure centre swimming pool usage)
- Usage targeting (matching the capacity available)
- Full/partial cost recovery (minimising subsidy)
- Budget maximisation (maximising what is offered)
- Producer satisfaction maximisation (satisfying the wants of staff and volunteers)
- Client satisfaction maximisation (the police generating the support of the public)

It is difficult to judge whether **non-quantifiable objectives** have been met. For example, assessing whether a charity has improved the situation of those benefiting from its activities is difficult to research. Statistics related to product mix, financial resources, size of budgets, number of employees, number of volunteers, number of customers serviced and number and location of facilities are all useful for this task.

The primary objectives of commercial manufacturing and service organisations are likely to be fairly similar and centre on satisfying shareholders.

Exam focus point

In an exam, if faced with a question on the public sector, remember that you are likely to have had extensive contact with a variety of public sector organisations and have seen something of how they work. Your greatest contact is likely to have been with the public education system, but you will probably have had contact with some local government authorities which provide a wide variety of services, from street cleaning, to leisure facilities, to fire services. You may also have had contact with the health service.

Think now about your experiences and use them in the exam.

2 Performance measurement in not for profit organisations

FAST FORWARD There are a range of problems in measuring performance of not for profit organisations.

Commercial organisations generally have market competition and the profit motive to guide the process of managing resources economically, efficiently and effectively. However, not for profit organisations cannot by definition be **judged by profitability** and do **not** generally have to be **successful against competition**, so other methods of assessing performance have to be used.

As we have already said, a major problem with many not for profit organisations, particularly government bodies, is that it is extremely **difficult to define their objectives** at all, let alone find one which can serve a yardstick function in the way that profit does for commercial bodies.

Question — Objectives for non profit seeking organisations

One of the objectives of a local government body could be 'to provide adequate street lighting throughout the area'.

(a) How could the 'adequacy' of street lighting be measured?

(b) Assume that other objectives are to improve road safety in the area and to reduce crime. How much does 'adequate' street lighting contribute to each of these aims?

(c) What is an excessive amount of money to pay for adequately lit streets, improved road safety and reduced crime? How much is too little?

Answer

Mull over these questions and discuss them in class or with colleagues if possible. It is possible to suggest answers, perhaps even in quantitative terms, but the point is that there are no **easy** answers, and no right or wrong answers.

You might consider (partly depending on your political point of view) that it is therefore not necessary to measure performance in not for profit organisations. However, few would argue that such bodies should be given **whatever amount of money** they say they need to pursue their aims, with no **check** on whether it is spent well or badly.

(a) Without information about what is being achieved (outputs) and what it is costing (inputs) it is impossible to make **efficient resource allocations**. These allocation decisions rely on a range of performance measures which, if unavailable, may lead managers to allocate resources based on subjective judgement, personal whim or in response to political pressure.

(b) Without performance measures, managers will not know the **extent to which operations are contributing to effectiveness and efficiency**; when diagnostic interventions are necessary; how the performance of their organisation **compares** with similar units elsewhere; and how their performance has **changed** over time.

(c) **Government** may require performance information to decide how much to spend in the public sector and where within the sector it should be allocated. In particular, they will be interested to know the results that may be achieved as a consequence of a particular level of funding, or to decide whether or not a service could be delivered more effectively and efficiently in the private sector. Likewise, **people who provide funds for** other kinds of not for profit organisations are entitled to know whether their money is being put to good use.

2.1 How can performance be measured?

FAST FORWARD

Performance is judged in terms of inputs and outputs, hence the **value for money criteria** of **economy, efficiency** and **effectiveness**.

Performance is usually judged in terms of **inputs and outputs** and this ties in with the 'value for money' criteria that are often used to assess not for profit organisations (covered in Section 3).

- **Economy** (spending money frugally)
- **Efficiency** (getting out as much as possible for what goes in)
- **Effectiveness** (getting done, by means of the above, what was supposed to be done)

More formal definitions are as follows.

Key terms

Effectiveness is the relationship between an organisation's outputs and its objectives.

Efficiency is the relationship between inputs and outputs.

Economy is attaining the appropriate quantity and quality of inputs at the lowest cost.

We will look at these concepts in more depth in Section 3.

2.2 Problems with performance measurement of not for profit organisations

(a) **Multiple objectives**

As we have said, they tend to have multiple objectives, so that even if they can all be clearly identified it is impossible to say which is the overriding objective.

(b) **Measuring outputs**

Outputs can seldom be measured in a way that is generally agreed to be meaningful. (For example, are good exam results alone an adequate measure of the quality of teaching?) Data collection can be problematic. For example, unreported crimes are not included in data used to measure the performance of a police force.

(c) **Lack of profit measure**

If an organisation is not expected to make a profit, or if it has no sales, indicators such as ROI and RI are meaningless.

(d) **Nature of service provided**

Many not for profit organisations provide services for which it is difficult to define a cost unit. For example, what is the cost unit for a local fire service? This problem does exist for commercial service providers but problems of performance measurement are made simple because profit can be used.

(e) **Financial constraints**

Although every organisation operates under financial constraints, these are more pronounced in not for profit organisations. For instance, a commercial organisation's borrowing power is effectively limited by managerial prudence and the willingness of lenders to lend, but a local authority's ability to raise finance (whether by borrowing or via local taxes) is subject to strict control by central government.

(f) **Political, social and legal considerations**

(i) Unlike commercial organisations, public sector organisations are subject to strong political influences. Local authorities, for example, have to carry out central government's policies as well as their own (possibly conflicting) policies.

(ii) The public may have higher expectations of public sector organisations than commercial organisations. A decision to close a local hospital in an effort to save costs, for example, is likely to be less acceptable to the public than the closure of a factory for the same reason.

(iii) The performance indicators of public sector organisations are subject to far more onerous legal requirements than those of private sector organisations.

(iv) While profit-seeking organisations are unlikely in the long term to continue services making a negative contribution, not for profit organisations may be required to offer a range of services, even if some are uneconomical.

2.3 Solutions

2.3.1 Inputs

Performance can be judged in terms of inputs. This is very common in everyday life. If somebody tells you that their suit cost $750, you would generally conclude that it was an extremely well designed and good quality suit, even if you did not think so when you first saw it. The drawback is that you might also conclude that the person wearing the suit had been cheated or was a fool, or you may happen to be of the opinion that no piece of clothing is worth $750. So it is with the inputs and outputs of not for profit organisations.

2.3.2 Judgement

A second possibility is to accept that performance measurement must to some extent be subjective. Judgements can be made by **experts** in that particular not for profit activity or by the **persons who fund the activity**.

2.3.3 Comparisons

We have said that most not for profit organisations do not face competition but this does not mean that all are unique. Bodies like local governments, health services, and so on can judge their performance **against each other** and **against the historical results of their predecessors**. And, since they are not competing with each other, there is less of a problem with confidentiality and so **benchmarking** is easier.

In practice, **benchmarking** usually encompasses:

- Regularly comparing aspects of performance (functions or processes) with best practitioners
- Identifying gaps in performance
- Seeking fresh approaches to bring about improvements in performance
- Following through with implementing improvements
- Following up by monitoring progress and reviewing the benefits

2.3.4 Quantitative measures

Unit cost measurements like 'cost per patient day' or 'cost of borrowing one library book' can fairly easily be established to allow organisations to assess whether they are doing better or worse than their counterparts.

Efficiency measurement of inputs and outputs is illustrated in three different situations, as follows.

(a) **Where input is fixed**

$$\frac{\text{Actual output}}{\text{Maximum output obtainable for a given input}}$$ 25/30 miles per gallon = 83.3% efficiency

(b) **Where output is fixed**

$$\frac{\text{Minimum input needed for a given output}}{\text{Actual input}}$$

55/60 hours to erect scaffolding = 91.7% efficiency

(c) **Where input and output are both variable**

Actual output ÷ actual input
compared with
standard output ÷ standard input

$9,030/7,000 meals = $1.29 per meal

$9,600/7,500 meals = $1.28 per meal
Efficiency = 99.2%

As a further illustration, suppose that at a cost of $40,000 and 4,000 hours (inputs) in an average year two policemen travel 8,000 miles and are instrumental in 200 arrests (outputs). A large number of possibly meaningful measures can be derived from these few figures, as the table below shows.

	$40,000	*4,000 hours*	*8,000 miles*	*200 arrests*
Cost $40,000		$40,000/4,000 = $10 per hour	$40,000/8,000 = $5 per mile	$40,000/200 = $200 per arrest
Time 4,000 hours	4,000/$40,000 = 6 minutes patrolling per $1 spent		4,000/8,000 = ½ hour to patrol 1 mile	4,000/200 = 20 hours per arrest
Miles 8,000	8,000/$40,000 = 0.2 of a mile per $1	8,000/4,000 = 2 miles patrolled per hour		8,000/200 = 40 miles per arrest
Arrests 200	200/$40,000 = 1 arrest per $200	200/4,000 = 1 arrest every 20 hours	200/8,000 = 1 arrest every 40 miles	

These measures **do not necessarily identify cause and effect** (do teachers or equipment produce better exam results?) **or personal responsibility and accountability**. Actual performance needs to be compared as follows.

(a) With standards, if there are any
(b) With similar external activities
(c) With similar internal activities
(d) With targets
(e) With indices
(f) Over time, as trends

Not for profit organisations are forced to use a **wide range** of indicators and can be considered early users of a **balanced scorecard** approach (covered in Chapter 16).

3 Value for money

Sep/Dec 15

Public sector organisations are now under considerable pressure to prove that they operate economically, efficiently and effectively, and are encouraged from many sources to draw up action plans to achieve **value for money** as part of the continuing process of good management.

Although much has been written about value for money (VFM), there is no great mystique about the concept. The term is common in everyday speech and so is the idea.

Value for money means providing a service in a way which is economical, efficient and effective.

To drive the point home, think of a bottle of washing up liquid for cleaning dishes. We'll call it Angeldishes. The advertising says Angeldishes is good 'value for money' because it washes twice as many plates as any other washing up liquid. Bottle for bottle it may be more expensive, but plate for plate it is cheaper. Not only this, but Angeldishes gets plates 'squeaky' clean. To summarise, Angeldishes gives us VFM because it exhibits the following characteristics.

- **Economy** (more clean plates per $ spent)
- **Efficiency** (more clean plates per squirt)
- **Effectiveness** (plates as clean as they should be)

The assessment of economy, efficiency and effectiveness should be a part of the normal management process of any organisation, public or private.

(a) Management should carry out **performance reviews** as a regular feature of their control responsibilities.

(b) Independent assessments of management performance can be carried out by 'outsiders', perhaps an internal audit department, as **value for money audits (VFM audits)**.

Value for money is important **whatever level of expenditure** is being considered. Negatively it may be seen as an approach to spreading costs in public expenditure fairly across services but positively it is necessary to ensure that the desired impact is achieved with the minimum use of resources.

3.1 Economy

Economy is concerned with the cost of inputs, and it is achieved by **obtaining those inputs at the lowest acceptable cost**. Economy **does not mean straightforward cost cutting,** because resources that are of a suitable **quality** to provide the service to the desired standard must be acquired. Cost cutting should not sacrifice quality to the extent that service standards fall to an unacceptable level. Economising by buying poor quality materials, labour or equipment is a 'false economy'.

3.2 Efficiency

Efficiency means the following.

(a) **Maximising output for a given input**; for example, maximising the number of transactions handled per employee or per $1 spent.

(b) **Achieving the minimum input for a given output**. For example, a government department may be required to pay unemployment benefit to millions of people. Efficiency will be achieved by making these payments with the minimum labour and computer time.

3.3 Effectiveness

Effectiveness means ensuring that the **outputs** of a service or programme have the **desired impacts**; in other words, finding out whether they **succeed in achieving objectives** and, if so, to what extent.

3.4 Studying and measuring the three Es

Economy, efficiency and effectiveness can be studied and measured with reference to the following.

(a) **Inputs**

    (i)   Money

    (ii)   Resources – the labour, materials, time, and so on consumed, and their cost

    For example, a VFM audit into state secondary education would look at the efficiency and economy of the use of resources for education (the use of schoolteachers, school buildings, equipment, cash) and whether the resources are being used for their purpose: what is the pupil/teacher ratio and are trained teachers being fully used to teach the subjects they have been trained for?

(b) **Outputs**; in other words, the **results of an activity**, measurable as the services actually produced, and the quality of the services.

    In the case of a VFM audit of secondary education, outputs would be measured as the number of pupils taught and the number of subjects taught per pupil; how many examination papers are taken and what is the pass rate; what proportion of students go on to further education at a university or college.

(c)   Impacts, which are the effects that the outputs of an activity or programme have in terms of achieving policy objectives.

Policy objectives might be to provide a minimum level of education for all children up to the age of 16, and to make education relevant for the children's future jobs and careers. This might be measured by the ratio of jobs vacant to unemployed school leavers. A VFM audit could assess to what extent this objective is being achieved.

As another example from education, suppose that there is a programme to build a new school in an area. The **inputs** would be the **costs of building** the school, and the resources used up; the **outputs** would be the **school building** itself; and the **impacts** would be the **effect that the new school has on education in the area** it serves.

4 Non-financial performance indicators (NFPIs)

In Chapter 16 Section 3, we covered the reasons for a growing emphasis on NFPIs and how aspects such as quality and customer satisfaction can be measured. These aspects can be applied to the public sector also. As with profit-seeking businesses, not for profit organisations can measure quality, efficiency, delivery, reliability, customer satisfaction and innovation. VFM and the 3Es include performance measures which are non-financial.

5 Target setting in qualitative areas

In Chapter 16 Section 8 we discussed the difficulties of measuring non-financial aspects of performance. The same problems arise for not for profit and public sector organisations. Problems include selecting a suitable measure for performance, having data which by its very nature is not quantified and a lack of system for collecting data about qualitative areas.

6 Short-termism and manipulation

In Chapter 16 Section 4 we discussed how organisations often make a trade off between short term and long term objectives. This applies to not for profit and public sector organisations too.

7 External considerations

Performance management needs to allow for **external considerations**, including stakeholders, market conditions and allowance for competitiors.

7.1 Stakeholders

Key term

> **Stakeholders** are groups of people or individuals who have a legitimate interest in the activities of an organisation. They include customers, employees, the community, shareholders, suppliers and lenders.

There are three broad types of stakeholder in an organisation.

- **Internal** stakeholders (employees, management)
- **Connected** stakeholders (shareholders, customers, suppliers, financiers)
- **External** stakeholders (the community, government, pressure groups)

The stakeholder approach suggests that **corporate objectives** are, or should be, **shaped** and **influenced** by **those** who have **sufficient involvement or interest** in the organisation's operational activities.

7.1.1 Internal stakeholders: employees and management

Because employees and management are so **intimately connected** with the company, their objectives are likely to have a **strong influence** on how it is run. They are interested in the following issues.

(a) The **organisation's continuation and growth**. Management and employees have a special interest in the organisation's continued existence.

(b) Managers and employees have **individual interests** and goals which can be harnessed to the goals of the organisation.

- Jobs/careers
- Money
- Benefits
- Satisfaction
- Promotion

For managers and employees, an organisation's social obligations will include the provision of safe working conditions and anti-discrimination policies.

7.1.2 Connected stakeholders

Increasing shareholder value should assume a **core role** in the strategic management of a business. If management performance is measured and rewarded by reference to changes in **shareholder value** then shareholders will be happy because managers are likely to **encourage long-term share price growth**.

Connected stakeholder	Interests to defend	
Shareholders (corporate strategy)	• Increase in shareholder wealth, measured by profitability, P/E ratios, market capitalisation, dividends and yield • Risk	
Bankers (cash flows)	• Security of loan	• Adherence to loan agreements
Suppliers (purchase strategy)	• Profitable sales • Payment for goods	• Long-term relationship
Customers (product market strategy)	• Goods as promised	• Future benefits

Even though **shareholders** are deemed to be interested in return on investment and/or capital appreciation, many want to **invest** in **ethically sound** organisations.

7.1.3 External stakeholders

External stakeholder groups – the Government, local authorities, pressure groups, the community at large, professional bodies – are likely to have quite diverse objectives.

External stakeholder	Interests to defend		
Government	• Jobs	• Training	• Tax
Interest/pressure groups/charities/'civil society'	• Pollution	• Rights	• Other

It is external stakeholders in particular who **induce social and ethical obligations**.

7.1.4 Performance measures

Organisations may need to develop performance measures to ensure that the needs of stakeholders are met.

Stakeholder	Measure
Employees	Morale index
Shareholders	Share price, dividend yield
Government	Percentage of products conforming to environmental regulations
Customers	Warranty cost, percentage of repeat customers

There is a strong link here to the balanced scorecard approach and the need to have a range of non-financial performance indicators as well as financial performance indicators.

7.2 Economic environment

Economic growth

- Has the economy grown or is there a recession?
- How has demand for goods/services been affected?

Local economic trends

- Are local businesses rationalising or expanding?
- Are office/factory rents increasing/falling?
- In what direction are house prices moving?
- Are labour rates on the increase?

Inflation

(a) Is a high rate making it difficult to plan, owing to the uncertainty of future financial returns? Inflation and expectations of it help to explain short-termism.

(b) Is the rate depressing consumer demand?

(c) Is the rate encouraging investment in domestic industries?

(d) Is a high rate leading employees to demand higher money wages to compensate for a fall in the value of their wages?

Interest rates

- How do these affect consumer confidence and liquidity, and therefore demand?
- Is the cost of borrowing increasing, thereby reducing profitability?

Exchange rates

- What impact do these have on the cost of overseas imports?
- Are prices that can be charged to overseas customers affected?

Government fiscal policy

(a) Are consumers increasing/decreasing the amount they spend due to tax and government spending decisions?

(b) How is the Government's corporation tax policy affecting the organisation?

(c) Is sales tax (VAT) affecting demand?

Government spending

Is the organisation a supplier to the Government (such as a construction firm) and therefore affected by the level of spending?

7.3 Competition

We considered the effects of competitors' behaviour in Chapter 5 when we looked at **pricing strategies**. Performance management must consider information on competitors' prices and cost structures and identify which features of an organisation's products add most value. Management accounting information has to be produced speedily and be up to date so that managers can react quickly and effectively to **changing market conditions**.

8 Behaviour aspects of performance management

FAST FORWARD

It is generally considered to be unreasonable to assess managers' performance in relation to matters that are beyond their control. Therefore **management performance measures** should **only include those items that are directly controllable by the manager** in question.

If people **know** that their performance is being **measured** then this will **affect the standard** of their performance, particularly if they know that they will be **rewarded** for achieving a certain level of performance.

Ideally, performance **measures** that **reward behaviour** which **maximises the corporate good** will be devised. In practice, however, it is not quite so simple.

(a)   There is a danger that managers and staff will **concentrate** only on what they know is **being measured**. This is not a problem if every important issue has a measure attached to it, but such a system is difficult to devise and implement in practice.

(b)   **Individuals** have their own goals, but good performance that satisfies their own sense of what is important will not necessarily work towards the **corporate good**. Each individual may face a **conflict** between taking action to ensure organisational goals and action to ensure personal goals.

Point (b) is the problem of **goal congruence**.

8.1 Example: Performance measurement and behaviour

(a)   As we saw in Chapter 17, a divisional manager whose performance is assessed on the basis of their division's ROI might reject a proposal that produces an ROI greater than the group's target return if it reduces their division's overall return.

(b)   Traditional feedback control would seek to eliminate an adverse material price variance by requiring managers to source cheaper, possibly lower quality, suppliers. This may run counter to an organisational objective to implement a system of TQM with the aim of reducing quality costs.

8.2 Measuring managerial performance

It is difficult to devise performance measures that relate specifically to a manager to judge their performance as a manager. It is possible to calculate statistics to assess the manager as an employee, like any other employee (days absent, professional qualifications obtained, personability, and so on), but this is not the point. As soon as the issue of **ability as a manager** arises it is necessary to **consider them in relation to their area of responsibility**. If we want to know how good a manager is at marketing, the only information there is to go on is the marketing performance of their division (which may or may not be traceable to their own efforts).

8.3 The controllability principle

As we have seen, the **controllability principle** is that managers of responsibility centres should only be held accountable for costs over which they have some influence. From a motivation point of view this is important because it can be very demoralising for managers who feel that their performance is being judged on the basis of something over which they have no influence. It is also important from a control point of view, in that control reports should ensure that information on costs is reported to the manager who is able to take action to control them.

8.4 Reward schemes and performance measurement

In many organisations, senior management try to motivate managers and employees by offering organisational rewards (more pay and promotion) for the achievement of certain levels of performance. The conventional theory of reward structures is that, if the organisation establishes procedures for formal measurement of performance, and **rewards individuals for good performance**, individuals will be more likely to direct their efforts towards achieving the organisation's goals.

8.4.1 Problems associated with reward schemes

(a)   A serious problem that can arise is that performance-related pay and performance-evaluation systems can **encourage dysfunctional behaviour**. Many investigations have noted the tendency of managers to pad their budgets either in anticipation of cuts by superiors or to make subsequent variances more favourable.

(b)   Perhaps of even more concern are the numerous examples of managers making **decisions that are contrary to the wider purposes of the organisation**.

(c)   Schemes designed to **ensure long-term achievements** (that is, to combat short-termism) **may not motivate** since efforts and reward are too distant in time from each other (or managers may not think they will be around that long!).

(d)   It is questionable whether any performance measures or set of measures can provide a **comprehensive assessment of what a single person achieves** for an organisation. There will always be the old chestnut of lack of goal congruence, employees being committed to what is measured, rather than the objectives of the organisation.

(e)   **Self-interested performance** may be encouraged at the **expense of teamwork**.

(f)   High levels of output (whether this is number of calls answered or production of product X) may be achieved at the expense of **quality**.

(g)   In order to make bonuses more accessible, **standards and targets may have to be lowered**, with knock-on effects on quality.

(h)   They **undervalue intrinsic rewards** (which reflect the satisfaction that an individual experiences from doing a job and the opportunity for growth that the job provides) given that they promote extrinsic rewards (bonuses and so on).

Chapter Roundup

- One possible definition of a **not for profit seeking organisation** is that its first objective is to be involved in non-loss operations to cover its costs, profits only being made as a means to an end.

- Not for profit organisations have **multiple objectives** which are **difficult to define**.

- There are a range of problems in measuring the performance of not for profit organisations.

- Performance is judged in terms of inputs and outputs, hence the **value for money criteria** of **economy, efficiency** and **effectiveness**.

- Public sector organisations are now under considerable pressure to prove that they operate economically, efficiently and effectively, and are encouraged from many sources to draw up action plans to achieve **value for money** as part of the continuing process of good management.

- Performance management needs to allow for **external considerations** including stakeholders, market conditions and allowance for competitiors.

- It is generally considered to be unreasonable to assess managers' performance in relation to matters that are beyond their control. Therefore, **management performance measures** should **only include those items that are directly controllable by the manager** in question.

Quick Quiz

1   What general objectives of non profit seeking organisations are being described in each of the following?

    (a)   Maximising what is offered
    (b)   Satisfying the wants of staff and volunteers
    (c)   Equivalent to profit maximisation
    (d)   Matching capacity available

2   The public service funding system operates on the basis that performance against non-financial objectives leads to a reduction in the level of funding. **True or false?**

3   Match the definition to the term.

Terms		Definition	
(a)	Economy	(1)	Ensuring outputs succeed in achieving objectives
(b)	Efficiency	(2)	Getting out as much as possible for what goes in
(c)	Effectiveness	(3)	Spending money frugally

4   Economy means cost cutting. **True or false?**

5   Six problems of measuring performance in non profit seeking organisations were described in this chapter. Which two are missing from the list below?

    (a)   Multiple objectives   (c)   Lack of profit measure
    (b)   Measuring output   (d)   Nature of service provided

Answers to Quick Quiz

1.   (a)   Budget maximisation
      (b)   Producer satisfaction maximisation
      (c)   Surplus maximisation
      (d)   Usage targeting

2.   False

3.   (a) (3); (b) (2); (c) (1)

4.   False

5.   Financial constraints
   Political/social/legal considerations

Now try the questions below from the Practice Question Bank

Number	Level	Marks	Approximate time
Section A Q101	Examination	2	4 mins
Section A Q102	Examination	2	4 mins
Section A Q103	Examination	2	4 mins
Section A Q104	Examination	2	4 mins
Section A Q105	Examination	2	4 mins
Section C Q11	Examination	20	39 mins

Practice question and answer bank

Section A questions

1   Are the following statements about Activity Based Costing (ABC) true or false?

		True	False
(1)	In a system of ABC, there is no under- or over-absorption of overheads.	☐	☐
(2)	In a system of ABC, a larger proportion of overheads is attributed to low volume products than in a traditional absorption costing system.	☐	☐

2   The following statements have been made about activity-based costing.

(1)   Unlike traditional absorption costing, ABC identifies variable overhead costs for allocation to product costs.

(2)   ABC can be used as an information source for budget planning based on activity rather than incremental budgeting.

Which of the above statements is/are true?

A   1 only
B   2 only
C   Neither 1 nor 2
D   Both 1 and 2

3   **Which THREE of the following statements about activity-based costing are correct?**

(1)   Implementation of ABC is unlikely to be cost-effective when variable production costs are a low proportion of total production costs.

(2)   In a system of ABC, for costs that vary with production levels, the most suitable cost driver is likely to be direct labour hours or machine hours.

(3)   Activity based costs are not the same as relevant costs for the purpose of short-run decision making.

(4)   Activity based costing is a form of absorption costing.

A   1, 2 and 3
B   2, 3 and 4
C   1, 3 and 4
D   1, 2 and 4

4   Ohno Co uses activity based costing and produces three products called EM, TM and GM.

Ohno Co expects to incur the following indirect production costs next year.

Cost pools	$	Cost driver
Machine set up costs	328,800	Number of batches (ie set ups)
Material ordering costs	266,000	Number of purchase orders

The following information also applies.

Product	EM	TM	GM
Budgeted production (units)	40,000	32,000	44,000
Batch size (units)	400	500	400
Number of purchase orders per batch	3	2	4

What is the cost per machine set-up?

$ ☐

5   Ohyes Co uses activity based costing and produces three products called ET, TT and GT.

Ohyes Co expects to incur the following indirect production costs next year.

Cost pools	$	Cost driver
Machine set up costs	328,800	Number of batches
Material ordering costs	266,000	Number of purchase orders

The following information also applies.

Product	ET	TT	GT
Budgeted production (units)	40,000	32,000	44,000
Number of batches	40	20	55
Number of purchase orders per batch	3	2	4

What is the cost per purchase order?

$ [   ]

6   **Are the following statements about target costing true or false?**

	True	False

(1)   When applying target costing to a product in the design stage of
      development, the production specification may be changed in order to
      achieve the target cost.   ☐   ☐

(2)   Target costing must take into consideration all the expected lifetime
      costs of the product.   ☐   ☐

7   A company has developed a new product and has estimated the costs as follows.

- Direct materials: 50kg required at a cost of $2.50 per kg

- Direct labour: 25% chance that each unit will take 1.5 hours, 30% chance that each unit will
  take 2 hours and 45% chance that each unit will take 2.5 hours

- Labour is paid at a rate of $15 per hour.

- Variable overheads will be incurred at a rate of $8 per labour hour

- The company believes it will be able to sell the product at $200 per unit and it requires a
  profit margin of 25%.

What is the value of the cost gap for this product?

$ [   ]

8   S Company is a manufacturer of multiple products and uses target costing. It has been noted that
    Product P currently has a target cost gap and the company wishes to close this gap.

Which of the following may be used to close the target cost gap for product P?

A   Use overtime to complete work ahead of schedule
B   Substitute current raw materials with cheaper versions
C   Raise the selling price of P
D   Negotiate cheaper rent for S Company's premises

9   **Use the words below to complete the following paragraphs**. (Each word can be used more than once)

- reduce
- set
- value
- target
- design
- accept
- start
- standard
- expected
- end
- increase

A company manufactures and sells a range of products. It is not dominant in the market in which it operates so has to [   ] the market price for each of its products. [   ] costing can be used to ensure that a new product is viable. Its aim is to [   ] costs incurred due to the product's [   ] and occurs at the [   ] of the lifecycle. If the [   ] cost is greater than the target cost, major changes are introduced to [   ] costs.

10   A furniture manufacturer wants to calculate a target cost for a new table. The table will be priced at $600. The company requires a 7% profit margin on sales.

What is the target cost of the table?

$ [   ]

11   Which of the following is **NOT** a way of maximising return over a product life cycle?

A   Design costs out of the product
B   Minimise the time to market
C   Maximise the break even time
D   Maximise the length of the life span

12   The following statements have been made about life cycle costing.

(1)   Life cycle costing is needed in order to plan for the maximum length of commercial life for new products.

(2)   Life cycle costing is particularly suited to businesses that manufacture products with long life cycles and who have significant research and development costs.

Which of the above statements is/are true?

A   1 only
B   2 only
C   Neither 1 nor 2
D   Both 1 and 2

13 **This question appeared in the June 2015 exam.**

The following statements have been made about life cycle costing:

(1) It focuses on the short-term by identifying costs at the beginning of a product's life cycle

(2) It identifies all costs which arise in relation to the product each year and then calculates the product's profitability on an annual basis

(3) It accumulates a product's costs over its whole life time and works out the overall profitability of a product

(4) It allocates costs to each stage of a product's life cycle and writes them off at the end of each stage

Which of the above statements is/are correct?

A   1 and 3 only
B   3 only
C   1 and 4 only
D   2 only

14 The following statements have been made about life cycle costing:

(1) Clean up costs should be included when assessing the profitability of a product
(2) It is useful for organisations that develop products with a relatively short life

Which of the above statements is/are correct?

A   1 only
B   2 only
C   Neither 1 nor 2
D   Both 1 and 2

15 Moonface is developing a new piece of technology with the following expected costs.

	Year 1	Year 2	Year 3	Year 4
No of units made and sold	3,000	16,000	20,000	4,000
	$'000	$'000	$'000	$'000
R&D costs	4,750	250		
Marketing costs	250	188	125	25
Production costs	2,400	14,400	15,000	3,400
Disposal costs				750

What is the life cycle cost per unit?

$ _____

16 **This question appeared in the June 2015 exam.**

The following statements have been made in relation to the concepts outlined in throughput accounting:

(1) Inventory levels should be kept to a minimum
(2) All machines within a factory should be 100% efficient, with no idle time

Which of the above statements is/are correct?

A   1 only
B   2 only
C   Both 1 and 2
D   Neither 1 nor 2

17   **This question appeared in the June 2015 exam.**

X Co uses a throughput accounting system. Details of product A, per unit, are as follows:

Selling price	$320
Material costs	$80
Conversion costs	$60
Time on bottleneck resource	6 minutes

What is the return per hour for product A?

A $40
B $2,400
C $30
D $1,800

18   The following production budget is for a company that makes two products, A and B. The company's budgeted output and sales are restricted by a maximum number of 3,500 direct labour hours available in the budget period.

	Product A	Product B
Output and sales	2,000 units	10,000 units
Direct labour hours per unit	0.5	0.25
	$ per unit	$ per unit
Budgeted direct material cost per unit	8.00	5.00
Budgeted direct labour cost per unit	8.00	4.00
Budgeted production overhead cost per unit	19.50	8.00
Budgeted sale price per unit	40.00	25.00

If the company were to use a throughput accounting system, what would be the throughput accounting ratio (TPAR) for Product B (to 2 dp)?

☐

19   CD plc produces a single product, the BC, which passes through three different processes, Alpha, Beta and Gamma. The throughput per hour of the three processes is 25, 30 and 32 units of BC respectively. The organisation operates for ten hours a day, 5 days a week for 50 weeks of the year. The BC can be sold for $420 per unit and it has a material cost of $170 per unit. It is anticipated that annual conversion costs will be $1,800,000.

What is the throughput accounting ratio per day? (to 2 decimal places)

☐

20   The following data relate to a manufacturing company. At the beginning of August there was no inventory. During August 2,000 units of product X were produced, but only 1,750 units were sold. The financial data for product X August were as follows:

	$
Materials	40,000
Labour	12,600
Variable production overheads	9,400
Fixed production overheads	22,500
Variable selling costs	6,000
Fixed selling costs	19,300
Total costs for X for August	109,800

The value of inventory of X at 31 August using a throughput accounting approach is:

A $5,000
B $6,175
C $6,575
D $13,725

21   What is the cost of waste called in flow cost accounting?

    A   System costs
    B   Environment-related costs
    C   Delivery and disposal costs
    D   The cost of negative products

22   **Which of the following environmental costs should NOT be included in an environmental cost budget?**

    A   Cost of cleaning up contaminated sites
    B   Costs of using pollution-prevention methods and technology
    C   Cost of fines for environmental contamination
    D   Cost of recycling waste

23   **Which of the following environmental costs is an external environmental cost?**

    A   Licence fees
    B   Payments of fines and charges
    C   Costs of monitoring emissions
    D   Traffic congestion

24   **This question appeared in the June 2015 exam.**

When activity based costing is used for environmental accounting, which statement is correct for environment-related costs and environment-driven costs?

    A   Environment-related costs can be attributed to joint cost centres and environment-driven costs cannot be

    B   Environment-driven costs can be attributed to joint cost centres and environment-related costs cannot be

    C   Both environment-related costs and environment-driven costs can be attributed to joint cost centres

    D   Neither environment-related costs nor environment-driven costs can be attributed to joint cost centres

25   The following statements have been made about cost classifications.

    (1)   Repairs under warranty are an external failure cost
    (2)   Lower selling price for sub quality goods is an internal failure cost

Which of the above statements is/are correct?

    A   1 only
    B   2 only
    C   Both 1 and 2
    D   Neither 1 nor 2

26   A company makes and sells two products, X and Y. The following budget has been prepared.

	Product X	Product Y
Budgeted units of production and sale	8,000	10,000
	$	$
Sales price per unit	18.00	21.60
Variable cost per unit	7.75	10.00
Fixed cost per unit	6.00	6.00

What is the breakeven point in sales revenue, to the nearest $100?

$ [   ]

27   A product has the following costs.

	$
Direct materials	15
Direct labour	9
Variable overheads	16

Fixed overheads are $9,000 per month. Budgeted sales per month are 450 units to allow the product to break even.

Fill in the blank in the sentence below.

The mark-up which needs to be added to marginal cost to allow the product to break even at the budgeted units is

☐ %.

28   HG plc manufactures four products. The unit cost, selling price and bottleneck resource details per unit are as follows.

	Product W	Product X	Product Y	Product Z
	$	$	$	$
Selling price	56	67	89	96
Material	22	31	38	46
Labour	15	20	18	24
Variable overhead	12	15	18	15
Fixed overhead	4	2	8	7

Assuming that labour is a unit variable cost, if budgeted unit sales are in the ratio W : 2, X : 3, Y : 3, Z : 4 and monthly fixed costs are budgeted to be $15,000, the number of units of W that would be sold per month at the budgeted breakeven point is nearest to:

A   106 units
B   142 units
C   212 units
D   283 units

29   Co X makes two products Y and Z, which it sells in the ratio 4:2. (This ratio is based on the sales revenue.) The sales prices and variables costs of Y and Z are as follows:

	Sales price	Variable costs
Y	$61	$42
Z	$95	$63

Fixed costs for the business are $200,000.

What is the breakeven revenue for the business (to the nearest whole number)?

A $322,000
B $612,000
C $620,000
D $857,000

30 **This question appeared in the June 2015 exam.**

The following information is available for a manufacturing company which produces multiple products:

(1) The product mix ratio
(2) Contribution to sales ratio for each product
(3) General fixed costs
(4) Method of reapportioning general fixed costs

Which of the above are required in order to calculate the breakeven sales revenue for the company?

A   All of the above
B   1, 2 and 3 only
C   1, 3 and 4 only
D   2 and 3 only

31 The following draft annual budget has been prepared for the machining room of a production centre. The machining room makes four components which are then transferred to an assembly and fitting department.

	Component			
	W	X	Y	Z
Variable cost per unit	$20	$15	$8	$15
Fixed cost per unit	$25	$20	$16	$30
Hours per unit	3 hours	2 hours	1 hour	1.5 hours
Cost of buying from external supplier	$60	$46	$24	$48
Budgeted production (units)	4,000	3,000	6,000	2,000

The machining room has a maximum capacity of 24,000 hours per year, but any quantity of any of the components can be purchased from an external supplier if required. It is essential that the budgeted quantities of all four components be delivered to the assembly and fitting department. This means that some of the budgeted requirement for components will have to be purchased externally.

In order to optimise the financial return, which component should be purchased externally?

A   Component W
B   Component X
C   Component Y
D   Component Z

32 A company makes two products, X and Y, with the same machines and the same direct labour workforce. The following information is available for the next budget period.

	Labour hours per unit	Machine hours per unit
Product X	0.6 hours	0.3 hours
Product Y	0.5 hours	0.2 hours

During the period there will be a maximum of 20,000 machine hours and 48,000 direct labour hours available, and these resources could be limiting factors on output and sales. If linear programming is used to determine the optimum production quantities of Product X and Product Y, which one of the following would be a constraint in the linear programming model?

A $0.3x + 0.2y \leq 48,000$
B $0.5x + 0.2y \leq 20,000$
C $0.6x + 0.3y \leq 20,000$
D $0.6x + 0.5y \leq 48,000$

33 **This question appeared in the June 2015 exam.**

A company manufactures three products using different amounts of the same grade of labour, which is in short supply. The following budgeted data relates to the products:

Per unit:	P1	P2	P3
	$	$	$
Selling price	120	140	95
Materials ($2 per kg)	(40)	(32)	(22)
Labour ($10 per hour)	(10)	(20)	(11)
Variable overheads	(20)	(28)	(24)
Fixed overheads	(6)	(9)	(12)
Profit per unit	44	51	26

What order should the products be manufactured in to ensure that profit is maximised?

	P1	P2	P3
A	2nd	1st	3rd
B	2nd	3rd	1st
C	1st	3rd	2nd
D	1st	2nd	3rd

34 ABC Co makes three products, budget information is provided below.

	A	B	C
	$	$	$
Selling price	50	68	94
Material A	20	30	40
Material B	5	8	10
Labour	10	5	15
Demand (units)	1,000	2,000	3,000

Material A is in short supply and ABC Co only have 10,000 kgs available. Material A costs $10 per kg.

What is the optimum production plan for ABC Co?

A   1000 As, 0 Bs and 2,975 Cs
B   0 As, 2,000 Bs and 3,000 Cs
C   1,000 As, 2,000 Bs and 500 Cs
D   1,000 As, 2,000 Bs and 3,000 Cs

35 KP makes 2 products, the K and the P.

	K	P
	$	$
Selling price	160	98
Mat C	20	0
Mat D	20	20
Labour	60	40
Fixed costs per unit	15	10

Labour is in short supply and KP have only 21,000 hours available per month. Labour is paid $20 per hour.

What is the maximum contribution they can earn in the month?

$ ☐

36 A company currently sells a product for $40 and at this price, demand is 16,000 units per month. It has been estimated that for every $3 increase or reduction in the price, monthly demand will fall or increase by 2,000 units.

What is the formula for the demand curve for this product?

A   48 – 0.0001875Q
B   64 – 0.0015Q
C   64 – 0.003Q
D   64 – 0.015Q

37 Which of the following pricing policies is the most appropriate for a new product for which the price elasticity of demand is expected to be inelastic?

A   Marginal cost plus
B   Market skimming
C   Penetration pricing
D   Price discrimination

38 A company currently sells a product for $60 and at this price, demand is 20,000 units per month. It has been estimated that for every $2 increase or reduction in the price, monthly demand will fall or increase by 1,000 units.

What is the formula for the demand curve for this product?

☐ - ☐ Q

39 A product has the following costs.

	$
Direct materials	8
Direct labour	10
Variable overheads	4

Fixed overheads are $15,000 per month. Budgeted sales per month as 500 units

What is the profit mark up (the nearest whole percentage) which needs to be added to marginal cost to establish a selling price that will allow the product to breakeven?

☐ %

40 When is a market penetration pricing policy appropriate?

A   If a product is new and different
B   If demand is highly elastic
C   If demand is inelastic
D   If there is no possibility of economies of scale

41 A company uses its direct labour workforce to make a product for which the sales price and unit cost are as follows.

	$
Selling price	80
Direct materials	10
Direct labour (2 hours)	20
Variable overheads (2 hours)	4
Fixed overheads (2 hours)	30

The workforce is operating at full capacity and it is not possible to obtain any additional labour hours in the near future. A customer has asked the company to perform a special job that would require 20 hours of direct labour time.

What would be the relevant cost of diverting labour from its existing work to perform the special job for the customer?

$ ☐

42 A company wants to decide whether to make its materials in-house or whether to sub-contract production to an external supplier. In the past it has made four materials in-house, but demand in the next year will exceed in-house production capacity of 8,000 units. All four materials are made on the same machines and require the same machine time per unit: machine time is the limiting production factor. The following information is available.

Material	W	X	Y	Z
Units required	4,000	2,000	3,000	4,000
Variable cost of in-house manufacture	$8 per unit	$12 per unit	$9 per unit	$10 per unit
Directly attributable fixed cost expenditure	$5,500	$8,000	$6,000	$7,000
Cost of external purchase	$9 per unit	$18 per unit	$12 per unit	$12 per unit

If a decision is made solely on the basis of short-term cost considerations, what materials should the company purchase externally?

A   4,000 units of W and 1,000 units of Z
B   4,000 units of W and 4,000 units of Z
C   3,000 units of Y and 2,000 units of Z
D   1,000 units of Y and 4,000 units of Z

43 Jetson Co produces three products:

	George	*Elroy*	*Jane*
Sales price	$60	$75	$85
Material cost	$15	$30	$22
Labour cost @ $6 per hour	$33	$27	$48
Demand	10,000 units	8,000 units	9,000 units

Labour is restricted to 120,000 hours. In order to meet demand, Jetson is considering using a subcontractor to produce the products that cannot be produced in-house due to the restriction on labour hours. The subcontractor has prepared the following quote:

George = $55
Elroy = $66
Jane = $82

Calculate the number of units of George that will be manufactured in-house.

A   0
B   2,181
C   7,819
D   10,000

44 Your company regularly uses material X and currently has in inventory 500 kg for which it paid $1,500 two weeks ago. If this were to be sold as raw material, it could be sold today for $2.00 per kg. You are aware that the material can be bought on the open market for $3.25 per kg, but it must be purchased in quantities of 1,000 kg.

What is the relevant cost of 600 kg needed to be used in a job for a customer?

A $1,325
B $1,825
C $1,950
D $3,250

45 A company is launching a new product. In order to manufacture this new product, two types of labour are required. The new product required 5 hours of skilled labour and 5 hours of semi skilled.

A skilled employee is available and is currently paid $10 per hour. A replacement would, however, have to be obtained at a rate of $9 per hour for the work that would otherwise be done by the skilled employee. The current rate for semi skilled workers is $5 per hour and an additional employee would be appointed for this work.

What is the relevant cost of labour to be used in making one unit of the new product?

A $45
B $50
C $70
D $75

46 The following pay-off table shows the monthly contribution that would be earned from each of four mutually exclusive options (options A-D) given three different outcome situations. It is not possible to predict or estimate the probability of each outcome scenario.

If the choice of option is made on the basis of the minimax regret criterion, which option will be selected?

Outcome situation	Option A	Option B	Option C	Option D
Outcome 1	32,000	40,000	25,000	22,000
Outcome 2	50,000	40,000	80,000	60,000
Outcome 3	75,000	38,000	50,000	52,000

47 **Match the type of investor to the attitude to risk:**

Risk averse   (i)   Minimax regret   (ii)   Relevant costing
                 (iii) Perfect information   (iv)   Maximin
                 (v)   Maximax   (iv)   Expected values

Risk seeker   (i)   Minimax regret   (ii)   Relevant costing
                 (iii) Perfect information   (iv)   Maximin
                 (v)   Maximax   (iv)   Expected values

Risk neutral   (i)   Minimax regret   (ii)   Relevant costing
                 (iii) Perfect information   (iv)   Maximin
                 (v)   Maximax   (iv)   Expected values

48 A company can choose from four mutually exclusive investment projects. The return on the project will depend on market conditions.

The table below details the returns for each possible outcome:

	A	B	C	D
Poor	$400,000	$700,000	$450,000	$360,000
Average	$470,000	$550,000	$500,000	$400,000
Good	$600,000	$300,000	$800,000	$550,000

If the company applies the maximin rule it will invest in:

A Project A
B Project B
C Project C
D Project D

49   A supplier will supply company A in batches of 100 units, but daily demand is unpredictable. Company A has prepared a payoff table to reflect the expected profits if different quantities are purchased and in differing market demand conditions.

Market conditions	Probability	Purchase 100	Purchase 200	Purchase 300	Purchase 400
Weak	15%	50	(100)	(200)	(250)
Average	25%	120	120	250	100
Strong	50%	90	200	300	400
Exceptional	10%	80	300	400	500

If the maximin criteria is applied, how many units would be purchased from the supplier?

A   100
B   200
C   300
D   400

50   A supplier will supply company B in batches of 100 units, but daily demand is unpredictable. Company B has prepared a payoff table to reflect the expected profits if different quantities are purchased and in differing market demand conditions.

Market conditions	Probability	Purchase 100	Purchase 200	Purchase 300	Purchase 400
Weak	15%	50	(100)	(200)	(250)
Average	25%	120	120	250	100
Strong	50%	90	200	300	400
Exceptional	10%	80	300	400	500

If the maximax criteria is applied, how many units would be purchased from the supplier?

A   100
B   200
C   300
D   400

51   The following statements have been made about budgeting.

(1)   An incremental budget is a budget which is designed to change as the volume of output changes.

(2)   Zero-based budgeting is used to compare the incremental cost and related benefits of activities.

Which of the above statements is/are true?

A   1 only
B   2 only
C   Neither 1 nor 2
D   Both 1 and 2

52   Which of the following is a characteristic of feedback?

A   It is used mainly for planning purposes
B   It is secondary data
C   It comes from internal sources within the organisation
D   It consists entirely of financial information

53   **A budget that is continuously updated by adding a further accounting period (a month or a quarter) when the earlier accounting period has expired is known as a:**

A   Zero base budget
B   Rolling budget
C   Periodic budget
D   Flexible budget

54   The following statements have been made about zero base budgeting.

(1)   The zero base budgeting process seeks to identify long-term benefits and improvements, even if they are sometimes made at the expense of short-term profitability.

(2)   A barrier to the use of zero base budgeting is the possibility that management may not have the skills to apply it.

Which of the above statements is/are true?

A   1 only
B   2 only
C   Neither 1 nor 2
D   Both 1 and 2

55   **A control system that reacts to historical changes in the business environment, usually to maintain a desired state of operations, is known as:**

A   Feedback control
B   Feedforward control
C   A rolling budget
D   Top-down control

56   A company incurs the following costs at various activity levels:

Total cost	Activity level
$	units
250,000	5,000
312,500	7,500
400,000	10,000

Using the high-low method what is the variable cost per unit?

A $25
B $30
C $35
D $40

57   The total cost of production for two levels of activity is as follows:

	Level 1	Level 2
Production (units)	3,000	5,000
Total cost ($)	6,750	9,250

The variable production cost per unit and the total fixed production cost both remain constant in the range of activity shown.

What is the level of fixed costs?

A $2,000
B $2,500
C $3,000
D $3,500

58 The first unit of an entirely new product took 160 labour hours to make and the labour cost was $3,200. Four units have now been produced and it is thought that a 75% learning curve applies to the work.

What will be the expected labour cost of the fifth unit to be produced?

A $1,004
B $1,231
C $1,641
D $1,800

59 Which of the following is generally regarded as a benefit of using spreadsheets for budgeting?

A   Audit trail
B   Complexity of modelling
C   Greater participation in budgeting process
D   Use of sensitivity analysis

60 **This question appeared in the June 2015 exam.**

A company predicted that the learning rate for production of a new product would be 80%. The actual learning rate was 75%. The following possible reasons were stated for this:

(1) The number of new employees recruited was lower than expected

(2) Unexpected problems were encountered with production

(3) Unexpected changes to Health and Safety laws meant that the company had to increase the number of breaks during production for employees.

Which of the above reasons could have caused the difference between the expected rate of learning and the actual rate of learning?

A   All of the above
B   2 and 3 only
C   1 only
D   None of the above

61 In which of the following production environments is the use of standard costs most appropriate?

A   For mass produced products
B   In a JIT production environment
C   In a target costing environment
D   In a TQM production environment

62 **Which of the following statements about standard costing is NOT correct?**

A   Standard costing is less applicable in a modern manufacturing environment where a large proportion of total costs are overhead costs that are fixed in the short term

B   Managers expect to access up to date performance information on-line, and standard costing systems do not easily provide this

C   Management may prefer alternative methods of performance reporting instead of standard costing

D   Managers no longer rely on formal budgetary control reports to monitor performance

63 **Which type of standard cost is most useful for monitoring trends in performance over time?**

A   Attainable standard
B   Basic standard
C   Current standard
D   Ideal standard

64 **Which of the following describes a 'basic standard' within the context of budgeting?**

   A   A standard which is kept unchanged over a period of time

   B   A standard which is based on current price levels

   C   A standard set at an ideal level, which makes no allowance for normal losses, waste and machine downtime

   D   A standard which assumes an efficient level of operation, but which includes allowances for factors such as normal loss, waste and machine downtime

65 **Which of the following statements about standard costing is NOT true?**

   A   Standard costing is useful where products are customised to a customer's specifications.
   B   Standard costing provides useful information to assist management in controlling costs
   C   Standard costing makes it easier to value inventory
   D   Standard costing can be used to predict future costs and set budgets

66 Spendthrift Co purchased 6,850 kg of material at a total cost of $32,195. The material price variance was $1,370 adverse.

   The standard price per kg was $ ☐ (to the nearest cent)

67 A standard unit of product contains two materials, P and Q. The standard direct materials cost is:

		$
Material P	0.1 kg at $8 per kg	0.8
Material Q	0.3 kg at $4 per kg	1.2
Total direct material cost		2.0

Management can control the mix of the materials and so, in standard costing variance reports, direct materials variances are reported as mix and yield variances.

In the period just ended, 45,000 units of finished products were made. They used 6,900 kg of Material P, which cost $7 per kg, and 12,600 kg of Material Q, which cost $5 per kg.

What was the adverse direct materials yield variance?

   $ ☐

68 In the budget period just ended, a very large adverse direct materials usage variance has been reported. Control action should be taken. Which one of the following actions might help to improve materials usage rates?

   A   Alter the mix of materials to a cheaper mix
   B   Reduce the sale price of the company's products
   C   Switch to a cheaper materials supplier
   D   Give production staff some training

69 The following data have been extracted from the budget working papers of WR Co:

Activity (machine hours)	Overhead cost
	$
10,000	13,468
12,000	14,162
16,000	15,549
18,000	16,242

In November 20X3, the actual activity was 13,780 machine hours and the actual overhead cost incurred was $14,521. Give your answer to the nearest $10.

Calculate the total overhead expenditure variance for November 20X3.

$ [   ] Favourable/Adverse (select the correct option)

70 **Which of the following would NOT explain a favourable direct materials usage variance?**

A   Using a higher quality of materials than that specified in the standard.
B   A reduction in materials wastage rates.
C   An increase in suppliers' quality control checks.
D   Achieving a lower output volume than budgeted.

71 A company sells a single product. Budgeted and actual sales data for the period just ended are as follows.

	Sales	Sales price per unit	Cost per unit
Budget	20,000 units	$50	$40
Actual results	17,000 units	$48	$42

The budget was based on an expectation that the company would maintain its 20% share of the market. It was subsequently recognised that the actual market size, due to unforeseen changes in customer buying behaviour, was only 90,000 units. It was therefore decided to report sales volume variances as a market share variance and a market size variance.

What was the market share variance, and should this be controllable by operational sales managers?

A $6,000 (A): controllable by operational managers
B $10,000 (A): controllable by operational managers
C $18,000 (A): not controllable by operational managers
D $20,000 (A): not controllable by operational managers

72 SG Co budgeted to make and sell 900 units of product M during September. The standard selling price per unit of M is $27. At the beginning of September, a new competitor entered the market and SG Co was forced to reduce the selling price in order to maintain sales volumes. By the end of September, 900 units had been sold for a total of $18,000. In retrospect it is decided that a realistic standard selling price for September, given the unexpected extra competition, was $18 per unit.

Calculate the sales price planning variance.

$ [   ] Adverse / Favourable (select the correct option)

73   **This question appeared in the June 2015 exam.**

Caf Co budgeted to sell 10,000 units of a new product in the period at a budgeted selling price of $5 per unit. Actual sales volumes in the period were as budgeted but the actual sales price achieved was only $4 per unit. This was because a competitor launched a similar product at the same time. Caf Co had been aware that this was going to happen when it prepared its budget and, had it known this, it would have revised its expected selling price to $3.80 per unit, which was the price of the competitor's product.

What is the sales price planning variance?

A $12,000 A
B $12,000 F
C $2,000 F
D $2,000 A

74   **This question appeared in the June 2015 exam.**

The following budgeted data for a particular period was available for a company selling two products:

	Sales price per unit	Variable cost per unit	Sales volume in units
Product A	$20	$8	15,840
Product B	$24	$11	10,560

The actual results for the period were as follows:

	Sales price per unit	Variable cost per unit	Sales volume in units
Product A	$22	$8	14,200
Product B	$26	$11	12,500

What is the sales quantity contribution variance?

A $3,720 F
B $3,720 A
C $4,320 F
D $4,320 A

75   **Which of the following variances should a production manager be held responsible for?**

A   Material price planning variance
B   Material price operational variance
C   Material usage planning variance
D   Material usage operational variance

76   **In which of the following circumstances are participative budgets likely to be effective?**

(1)   In very large organisations
(2)   During periods of economic affluence
(3)   When an organisation's different units act autonomously
(4)   In newly-formed organisations

A   4 only
B   1 and 2
C   1, 2 and 3
D   1, 2, 3 and 4

77   Participation by staff in the budgeting process is often seen as an aid to the creation of a realistic budget and to the motivation of staff. There are, however, limitations to the effectiveness of such participation.

Which of the following illustrates one of these limitations?

A   Participation allows staff to buy into the budget
B   Staff suggestions may be ignored leading to de-motivation
C   Staff suggestions may be based on local knowledge
D   Budgetary slack can be built in by senior manager as well as staff

78   Which of the following statements about budgeting and motivation are true?

(1)   A target is more motivating than no target at all
(2)   The problem with a target is setting an appropriate degree of difficulty
(3)   Employees who are challenged tend to withdraw their commitment

A   All of them
B   2 and 3 only
C   1 and 2 only
D   3 only

79   Which of the following best describes a top-down budget?

A   A budget which has been set by scaling down individual expenditure items until the total budgeted expenditure can be met from available resources

B   A budget which is set by delegating authority from top management, allowing budget holders to participate in setting their own budgets

C   A budget which is set without permitting the ultimate budget holder to participate in the budgeting process

D   A budget which is set within the framework of strategic plans determined by top management

80   In which of the following circumstances are participative budgets effective?

(1)   In decentralised organisations
(2)   During periods of economic affluence
(3)   When an organisation's different units act autonomously

A   All of them
B   2 and 3 only
C   1 and 2 only
D   3 only

81   The following statements have been made about management information.

(1)   Budgetary control information comes mainly from sources outside the organisation.
(2)   An EIS provides an integrated database system for the management of operations.

Which of the above statements is/are true?

A   1 only
B   2 only
C   Neither 1 nor 2
D   Both 1 and 2

82 **This question appeared in the June 2015 exam.**

The following statements have been made about transaction processing systems and executive information systems:

(1) A transaction processing system collects and records the transactions of an organisation

(2) An executive information system is a way of integrating the data from all operations within the organisation into a single system

Which of the above statements is/are true?

A   1 only
B   2 only
C   Both 1 and 2
D   Neither 1 nor 2

83 **Which of the following correctly describes a management information system?**

A   A system which measures and corrects the performance of activities of subordinates in order to make sure that the objectives of an organisation are being met and the plans devised to attain them are being carried out

B   A system by which managers ensure that information is obtained and used effectively and efficiently in the accomplishment of the organisation's objectives

C   A system which involves selecting appropriate information so that management can prepare a long-term plan to attain the objectives of the organisation

D   A collective term for the hardware and software used to drive a database system with the outputs, both to screen and print, being designed to provide easily assimilated information for management

84 **Which of the following combinations describe the purposes of management information?**

A   Planning, negotiating and decision making
B   Control, decision making and publication
C   Decision making, negotiating and implementing
D   Planning, control and decision making

85 **Which of the following statements is/are true?**

(1) Enterprise Resource Planning (ERP) systems use complex computer systems, usually comprehensive databases, to provide plans for every aspect of the business.

(2) Enterprise Resource Planning (ERP) systems are accounting oriented information systems which aid in identifying and planning the enterprise wide resources needed to resource, make, account for and deliver customer orders.

A   1 only
B   2 only
C   Both 1 and 2
D   Neither 1 nor 2

86 **This question appeared in the June 2015 exam.**

Which of the following is an external source of information?

A   Value of sales, analysed for each customer
B   Value of purchases, analysed for each supplier
C   Prices of similar products, analysed for each competitor company
D   Hours worked, analysed for each employee

87   **Which of the following is NOT an internal source of management information?**

A   Personnel records
B   Production department records
C   Financial statements of competitors
D   Detailed time records

88   Data used by the management that has been obtained from an official government source is an example of:

A   External primary data
B   External secondary data
C   Internal primary data
D   Internal secondary data

89   The following statements have been made about data and information.

(1)   In-depth analysis of data on a database in order to identify undiscovered trends or patterns in the data is known as data mining.

(2)   Large public databases are a major source of feedback for many commercial organisations.

Which of the above statements is/are true?

A   1 only
B   2 only
C   Neither 1 nor 2
D   Both 1 and 2

90   Which one of the following is often used to protect an intranet from unauthorised access by an external hacker?

A   Anti-virus software
B   Data encryption
C   Firewall
D   Passwords

91   The following statements have been made about a balanced scorecard (BSC) performance reporting system.

(1)   There must be just one key performance indicator (KPI) for each of the four perspectives of performance.

(2)   A performance target to reduce the amount of wastage in production would relate to the innovation and learning perspective of the BSC.

Which of the above statements is/are true?

A   1 only
B   2 only
C   Neither 1 nor 2
D   Both 1 and 2

92   Which of the following elements in the Building Block model of performance management (Fitzgerald and Moon) relates to setting standards of performance?

A   Achievability
B   Competitiveness
C   Controllability
D   Motivation

93   EJET is an airline company that operates domestically and internationally using a fleet of 20 aircraft. Passengers book flights using the internet or by telephone and pay for their flights at the time of booking using a debit or credit card.

EJET currently measures its performance using financial ratios. The new Managing Director has suggested that non-financial measures are equally important as financial measures and provide further insights into company performance.

Indicate the statements shown below that are valid:

A   Non-financial measures are less likely to be manipulated than traditional financial ratios.

B   Non-financial measures may discourage dysfunctional behaviour by airline staff.

C   Financial ratios do not need to be linked with non-financial measures.

D   Non-financial measures are a better indicator of future prospects than financial ratios which focus on the short term.

E   Internal efficiency can be measured by the number of flight take-offs that are on time.

F   Non-financial performance measures do not need to be developed and refined over time as they always remain relevant.

G   Customer satisfaction can be measured in terms of the number of failed attempts to make a booking due to website crashes.

94   A government department is responsible for monitoring the performance of schools providing education for pupils aged between 11 and 18.

There is a separate government department that sets final examinations that help determine entry to university and support pupils' job applications.

The head teachers at individual schools are responsible for teaching and submitting selected pupils for these examinations.

Which of the following statements is valid in the context of this scenario?

A   Poor performance in terms of financial indicators should be ignored if a school is performing well in non-financial terms.

B   Non-financial performance indicators cannot be manipulated by school head teachers.

C   It is generally valid to compare the pass rates of different schools in the final examinations.

D   Non-financial indicators are generally more important than financial indicators in the public sector

95   **This question appeared in the June 2015 exam.**

The following ratios have been calculated for a company:

Gross profit margin   42%
Operating profit margin   28%
Gearing (debt/equity)   40%
Asset turnover   65%

What is the return on capital employed for the company?

A   27.3%
B   18.2%
C   11.2%
D   16.8%

96   The following information relates to an investment centre, which is a separate product division in a large company.

	$
Net current assets	60,000
Non-current assets	240,000
Profit before depreciation	50,000
Depreciation	10,000

The company's cost of capital is 10%. What is the most appropriate measure of the centre's Return on Investment (ROI)?

A   3.3%
B   13.3%
C   16.7%
D   20.8%

97   There are two profit centres, A and B. Profit centre A transfers a product to profit centre B, but could also sell the product in an external market at a price of $30. The marginal cost of making the product in profit centre A is $8 per unit and the full cost is $14 per unit. There would be a variable cost of $1 per unit for sales and distribution to customers in the external market, but no such costs for internal transfers.

To avoid disputes between the profit centre managers, what should be the transfer price for the product?

$ [   ]

98   SWAL has two divisions, SW and AL, which operate as profit centres and have full autonomy in making, buying and selling decisions.

SW manufactures SW+ at a cost of $12 per unit. The market price of SW+ is $16 per unit.

AL uses SW+ in manufacturing its own product. The transfer price of SW+ when transferred from Division SW to Division AL is set at full production cost plus 20%.

Which one of the following independent circumstances represents dysfunctional behaviour arising from SWAL's transfer pricing policy?

A   SW refuses to sell SW+ to AL as there is unlimited demand for SW+ in the external market.

B   AL refuses to order from SW as it can buy SW+ from the open market at lower than current transfer price. As a result, SW sells all its units on the open market.

C   SW refuses to transfer below market price so AL is forced to buy from the external market.

D   SW agrees to sell to AL but has to cancel the sale in order to fulfil an urgent customer order who is willing to pay a higher price for immediate delivery.

99   **This question appeared in the June 2015 exam.**

A division is considering investing in capital equipment costing $2.7m. The useful economic life of the equipment is expected to be 50 years, with no resale value at the end of the period. The forecast return on the initial investment is 15% per annum before depreciation. The division's cost of capital is 7%?

What is the expected annual residual income of the initial investment?

A $0
B   ($270,000)
C $162,000
D $216,000

100 **This question appeared in the June 2015 exam.**

At the start of the year, a division has non-current assets of $4 million and makes no additions or disposals during the year. Depreciation is charged at a rate of 10% per annum on all non-current assets held at the end of the year. Working capital is $0.5 million at the start of the year although this is expected to increase by 20% by the end of the year. The budgeted profit of the division after depreciation is $1.2 million.

What is the expected ROI of the division for the year, based on average capital employed?

A   27.59%
B   26.37%
C   18.39%
D   31.58%

101 For a not for profit organisation with multiple objectives, which aspect of performance is the most difficult to assess?

A   Financial
B   Economy
C   Efficiency
D   Effectiveness

102 A government body uses measures based on the 3Es to measure value for money generated by a publicly funded hospital. It considers the most important performance measure to be 'cost per successfully treated patient'

Which of the 3Es best describes the above measure?

A   Externality
B   Economy
C   Efficiency
D   Effectiveness

103 Which TWO of the following are most likely to be performance measures for a not for profit organisation?

(1)   Efficient resource allocation.
(2)   Return on investment (ROI) and residual income (RI)
(3)   Minimising the cost of resources used.
(4)   Success measured against competition

A   1 and 2
B   2 and 3
C   3 and 4
D   1 and 3

104 Which of the following is an example of an internal stakeholder?

A   Shareholders
B   Employees
C   Suppliers
D   Financiers

105 Insert the correct words into the performance measures.

Stakeholder	Measure		
Employees	morale		
Shareholders	dividend		
Government			of products conforming to environmental regulations
Customers			of repeat customers

Options

percentage

yield

index

Section B questions

Solo   20 mins

Solo makes and sells a single product. The following data relate to Periods 1 to 3.

	$
Variable cost per unit	30
Selling price per unit	55
Fixed costs per period	6,000

Normal activity is 500 units and there were no opening inventories at the start of Period 1. The marginal costing operating statement for Periods 1 to 3 is shown below.

Marginal costing operating statement

	Period 1		Period 2		Period 3	
	$	$	$	$	$	$
Sales		27,500		22,000		30,250
Variable production costs	15,000		15,000		13,500	
Add: Opening inventory	–		–		3,000	
Less: Closing inventory	–		(3,000)		–	
Variable production cost of sales		15,000		12,000		16,500
Contribution		12,500		10,000		13,750
Fixed costs		6,000		6,000		6,000
Profit for period		6,500		4,000		7,750

Required

1   Production and sales for Period 1 were as follows:

	Period 1 units
Sales	500
Production	500

Calculate the profit for period 1 based on absorption costing principles.

$ _____   **(2 marks)**

2   Production and sales for Period 2 was as follows:

	Period 2 Units
Sales	400
Production	500

There was no opening inventory in Period 2. Calculate the profit for Period 2 based on absorption costing principles.

$ _____   **(2 marks)**

3   Production and sales for Period 3 was as follows:

	Period 3 Units
Sales	550
Production	450

The opening inventory in Period 3 was 100 units. Calculate the profit for Period 3 based on absorption costing principles.

$ _____   **(2 marks)**

4   Calculate the figure for over/(under) absorption of production overheads for Period 3

$ _____ **over/under**   **(2 marks)**

5   When Solo compares their profits reported under absorption costing and marginal costing during a period when the level of inventory increased:

☐   Absorption costing profits will be higher and closing inventory valuations lower than those under marginal costing.

☐   Absorption costing profits will be higher and closing inventory valuations higher than those under marginal costing.

☐   Marginal costing profits will be higher and closing inventory valuations lower than those under absorption costing.

☐   Marginal costing profits will be higher and closing inventory valuations higher than those under absorption costing.   **(2 marks)**

(Total = 10 marks)

Southcott

Southcott Co is a firm of financial consultants which offers short revision courses on taxation and auditing for professional examinations. The firm has budgeted annual overheads totalling $152,625. Until recently the firm has applied overheads on a volume basis, based on the number of course days offered. The firm has no variable costs and the only direct costs are the consultants' own time which they divide equally between their two courses.

The following information relates to the past year and is expected to remain the same for the coming year.

Course	No of courses sold	Duration of course	No of enquiries per course	No of brochures printed per course
Auditing	50	2 days	175	300
Taxation	30	3 days	70	200

All courses run with a maximum number of students (30), as it is deemed that beyond this number the learning experience is severely diminished, and the same centre is hired for all courses at a standard daily rate. The firm has the human resources to run only one course at any one time.

Required

6   Calculate the overhead cost per course for auditing using traditional volume based absorption costing to the nearest dollar.

$ [   ]   **(2 marks)**

The firm is considering the possibility of adopting an activity based costing (ABC) system and has identified the overhead costs as shown below.

Details of overheads

	$
Centre hire	62,500
Enquiries administration	27,125
Brochures	63,000
Total	152,625

7   Calculate the overhead cost of centre hire which would be allocated to an auditing course under activity based costing to the nearest dollar.

$ [   ]   **(2 marks)**

8   Calculate the overhead cost of brochure printing which would be allocated to a taxation course under activity based costing to the nearest dollar.

$ [   ]   **(2 marks)**

9   Calculate the overhead cost of enquiries administration which would be allocated to a taxation course under activity based costing.

$ [   ]   **(2 marks)**

10   A member of Southcott Co's finance team has said that activity based costing (ABC) provides more accurate product costs than a traditional absorption costing system. He gave a number of statements supporting this claim.

Which of the following statements does **NOT** support his claim?

- [ ] ABC uses cost drivers to allocate overhead costs to products by cost pool
- [ ] ABC identifies value added and non-value added activities
- [ ] ABC assigns overheads to each major activity
- [ ] ABC uses both volume based and non-volume based cost drivers

(2 marks)

(Total = 10 marks)

Abkaber

Abkaber assembles three types of motorcycle at the same factory: the 50cc Sunshine; the 250cc Roadster and the 1000cc Fireball. It sells the motorcycles throughout the world. In response to market pressures Abkaber has invested heavily in new manufacturing technology in recent years and, as a result, has significantly reduced the size of its workforce.

Historically, the company has allocated all overhead costs using total direct labour hours, but is now considering introducing Activity Based Costing (ABC). Abkaber's accountant has produced the following analysis.

	Annual output (units)	Annual direct labour Hours	Selling price ($ per unit)	Raw material cost ($ per unit)
Sunshine	2,000	200,000	4,000	400
Roadster	1,600	220,000	6,000	600
Fireball	400	80,000	8,000	900

The three cost drivers that generate overheads are:

Deliveries to retailers	–	the number of deliveries of motorcycles to retail showrooms
Set-ups	–	the number of times the assembly line process is re-set to accommodate a production run of a different type of motorcycle
Purchase orders	–	the number of purchase orders.

The annual cost driver volumes relating to each activity and for each type of motorcycle are as follows:

	Number of deliveries to retailers	Number of set-ups	Number of purchase orders
Sunshine	100	35	400
Roadster	80	40	300
Fireball	70	25	100

The annual overhead costs relating to these activities are as follows:

	$
Deliveries to retailers	2,400,000
Set-up costs	6,000,000
Purchase orders	3,600,000

All direct labour is paid at $5 per hour. The company holds no inventories.

Required

11 Calculate the total costs of producing the budgeted amount of Sunshine motorcycles based on the existing method of attributing overheads.

$ [   ]

(2 marks)

12 Calculate the total costs of producing the budgeted amount of Roadster motorcycles based on the existing method of attributing overheads.

$ [   ]

(2 marks)

13 Calculate the amount of overhead in respect of set up costs, which would be attributed to the production of the budgeted amount of Roadster motorcycles, under ABC costing principles.

$ [   ]

(2 marks)

14 Calculate the amount of overhead in respect of purchase orders, which would be attributed to the budgeted amount of Fireball motorcycles, using ABC costing principles.

$ [   ]

(2 marks)

15 Which of the following could be used to describe activity based budgeting (ABB)?

Select all that apply.

☐ A method of budgeting based on an activity framework and utilising cost driver data in the budget setting and variance feedback processes

☐ The use of costs determined using ABC as a basis for preparing budgets

☐ The definition of the activities that underlie the financial figures in each function and the use of the level of activity to decide how much resource should be allocated, how well it is being managed and to explain variances from budget **(2 marks)**

(Total = 10 marks)

Bottlenecks   20 mins

F Co makes and sells two products, A and B, each of which passes through the same automated production operations. The following estimated information is available for period 1.

Product unit data

	A	B
Direct material cost ($)	2	40
Variable production overhead cost ($)	28	4

Original estimates of production/sales of products A and B are 120,000 units and 45,000 units respectively. The selling prices per unit for A and B are $60 and $70 respectively.

Maximum demand for each product is 20% above the estimated sales levels.

Total fixed production overhead cost is $1,470,000. This is absorbed by products A and B at an average rate per hour based on the estimated production levels.

One of the production operations has a maximum capacity of 3,075 hours which has been identified as a bottleneck, limiting the overall estimated production/sales of products A and B. The bottleneck hours required per product unit for products A and B are 0.02 and 0.015 respectively.

Required

16 Using limiting factor analysis, calculate the contribution per bottleneck hour of Product B to the nearest dollar.

$ [   ]   **(2 marks)**

17 If F Co chooses to prioritise Product B, calculate the value (in $) of the maximum net profit.

$ [   ]   **(2 marks)**

18 Using throughput analysis, calculate the return per bottleneck hour of Product A.

$ [   ]   **(2 marks)**

19 If F Co choose to prioritise the manufacture of Product A, calculate the value (in $) of the maximum net profit using throughput analysis.

$ [   ]   **(2 marks)**

20 The throughput return per hour of Product B is $2,000. Calculate the throughput accounting ratio for Product B (to 2 dp).

[   ]   **(2 marks)**

(Total = 10 marks)

Bench Co

20 mins

Bench Co has developed two new products, Product A and Product B. The first batch of 15 units of Product A will take 350 labour hours to produce. There will be an 80% learning curve that will continue until 390 units have been produced. Batches after this level will each take the same amount of time as the 26th batch. The batch size will always be 15 units.

For Product B, the company has estimated that a 75% learning curve will apply. The time to produce the first unit was 1,600 hours.

Note. The learning index for an 80% learning curve is –0.3219. The learning index for a 75% learning curve is –0.415

Ignore the time value of money.

21 Calculate the cumulative average time per batch for the first 26 batches of Product A (give your answer to two d.p).

    ☐ hours   **(2 marks)**

22 The total time for the first 16 batches of Product A was 2,500 hours. What was the actual learning rate (closest to the nearest %)?

    ☐ %   **(2 marks)**

23 What is the expected time to produce the 9th unit of Product B (give your answer to the nearest hour)?

    ☐ hours   **(2 marks)**

24 Which **THREE** of the following conditions are necessary for learning curve theory to apply?

    ☐ A relatively new product.
    ☐ A manual, rather than mechanised production process.
    ☐ A relatively complex production process.
    ☐ Production in batches of equal size.
    ☐ Constant labour wage rates.   **(2 marks)**

25 Which of the following statements is **FALSE** in relation to learning curve theory?

    ☐ The learning curve theory states that the average time per unit produced is assumed to decease by a constant percentage every time total output doubles

    ☐ When a certain level of units have been produced the learning process comes to an end and any extra units produced tend to take the same amount of time

    ☐ The formula for the learning curve is $Y = aX^b$ where Y is the cumulative average time per unit to produce X units, X is the cumulative number of units, a is the time taken for the first unit of output, and b is the index of learning.   **(2 marks)**

                                                              (Total = 10 marks)

Section C questions

1 BD Company   39 mins

For some time the BD company has sold its entire output of canned goods to supermarket chains which sell them as 'own label' products. One advantage of this arrangement is that BD incurs no marketing costs, but there is continued pressure from the chains on prices, and margins are tight.

As a consequence, BD is considering selling some of its output under the BD brand. Margins will be better but there will be substantial marketing costs.

The following information is available.

	Current year's results – 20X2 (adjusted to 20X3 cost levels)	Forecast for 20X3 (assuming all 'own label' sales)
Sales (millions of cans)	18	19
	$ million	$ million
Sales	5.94	6.27
Manufacturing costs	4.30	4.45
Administration costs	1.20	1.20
Profit	0.44	0.62

For 20X3 the unit contribution on BD brand sales is expected to be $33\frac{1}{3}\%$ greater than 'own label' sales, but variable marketing costs of 2c per can and fixed marketing costs of $400,000 will be incurred.

Required

(a) Prepare a contribution breakeven chart for 20X3 assuming that all sales will be 'own label'.

(7 marks)

(b) Prepare a contribution breakeven chart for 20X3 assuming that 50% of sales are 'own label' and 50% are of the BD brand.   **(7 marks)**

Note. The breakeven points and margins of safety must be shown clearly on the charts.

(c) Comment on the positions shown by the charts and your calculations and discuss what other factors management should consider before making a decision.   **(6 marks)**

   Ignore inflation.   **(Total = 20 marks)**

2 RAB Consulting   39 mins

RAB Consulting specialises in two types of consultancy project.

- Each type A project requires 20 hours of work from qualified researchers and 8 hours of work from junior researchers.

- Each type B project requires 12 hours of work from qualified researchers and 15 hours of work from junior researchers.

Researchers are paid on an hourly basis at the following rates.

Qualified researchers	$30/hour
Junior researchers	$14/hour

Other data relating to the projects:

Project type

	A	B
	$	$
Revenue per project	1,700	1,500
Direct project expenses	408	310
Administration*	280	270

* Administration costs are attributed to projects using a rate per project hour. Total administration costs are $28,000 per four-week period.

During the four-week period ending on 30 June 20X0, owing to holidays and other staffing difficulties the number of working hours available are:

Qualified researchers	1,344
Junior researchers	1,120

An agreement has already been made for 20 type A projects with XYZ group. RAB Consulting must start and complete these projects in the four-week period ending 30 June 20X0.

A maximum of 60 type B projects may be undertaken during the four-week period ending 30 June 20X0.

RAB Consulting is preparing its detailed budget for the four-week period ending 30 June 20X0 and needs to identify the most profitable use of the resources it has available.

Required

(a) Calculate the contribution from each type of project. **(2 marks)**

(b) Determine the optimal production plan for the four-week period ending 30 June 20X0, assuming that RAB is seeking to maximise the profit earned. You should use a linear programming graph, identify the feasible region and the optimal point and accurately calculate the maximum profit that could be earned using whichever equations you need. **(12 marks)**

(c) Explain the meaning of a shadow price and calculate the shadow price of qualified researcher time. **(6 marks)**

(Total = 20 marks)

3 AB

39 mins

AB produces a consumable compound X, used in the preliminary stage of a technical process that it installs in customers' factories worldwide. An overseas competitor, CD, offering an alternative process which uses the same preliminary stage, has developed a new compound, Y, for that stage which is both cheaper in its ingredients and more effective than X.

At present, CD is offering Y only in its own national market, but it is expected that it will not be long before it extends its sales overseas. Both X and Y are also sold separately to users of the technical process as a replacement for the original compound that eventually loses its strength. This replacement demand amounts to 60% of total demand for X and would do so for Y. CD is selling Y at the same price as X ($64.08 per kg).

AB discovers that it would take 20 weeks to set up a production facility to manufacture Y at an incremental capital cost of $3,500 and the comparative manufacturing costs of X and Y would be:

	X	Y
	$ per kg	$ per kg
Direct materials	17.33	4.01
Direct labour	7.36	2.85
	24.69	6.86

AB normally absorbs departmental overhead at 200% of direct labour: 30% of this departmental overhead is variable directly with direct labour cost. Selling and administration overhead is absorbed at one half of departmental overhead.

The current sales of X average 74 kg per week and this level (whether of X or of Y if it were produced) is not expected to change over the next year. Because the direct materials for X are highly specialised, AB has always had to keep large inventories in order to obtain supplies. At present, these amount to $44,800 at cost. Its inventory of finished X is $51,900 at full cost. Unfortunately, neither X nor its raw materials have any resale value whatsoever: in fact, it would cost $0.30 per kg to dispose of them.

Over the next three months AB is not normally busy and, in order to avoid laying off staff, has an arrangement with the trade union whereby it pays its factory operators at 65% of their normal rate of pay for the period while they do non-production work. AB assesses that it could process all its relevant direct materials into X in that period, if necessary.

There are two main options open to AB.

(i)   To continue to sell X until all its inventories of X (both of direct materials and of finished inventory) are exhausted, and then start sales of Y immediately afterwards.

(ii)   To start sales of Y as soon as possible and then to dispose of any remaining inventories of X and/or its raw materials.

Required

(a)   Recommend, with supporting calculations, which of the two main courses of action suggested is the more advantageous from a purely cost and financial point of view.   **(10 marks)**

(b)   Identify three major non-financial factors that AB would need to consider in making its eventual decision as to what to do.   **(6 marks)**

(c)   Suggest one other course of action that AB might follow, explaining what you consider to be its merits and demerits when compared with your answer at (a) above.   **(4 marks)**

(Total = 20 marks)

4 Stow Health Centre   39 mins

Stow Health Centre specialises in the provision of sports/exercise and medical/dietary advice for clients. The service is provided on a residential basis and clients stay for whatever number of days suits their needs.

Budgeted estimates for the year ending 30 June 20X1 are as follows.

(i)   The maximum capacity of the centre is 50 clients per day for 350 days in the year.

(ii)   Clients will be invoiced at a fee per day. The budgeted occupancy level will vary with the client fee level per day and is estimated at different percentages of maximum capacity as follows.

Client fee per day	Occupancy level	Occupancy as percentage of maximum capacity
$180	High	90%
$200	Most likely	75%
$220	Low	60%

(iii)   Variable costs are also estimated at one of three levels per client day. The high, most likely and low levels per client day are $95, $85 and $70 respectively.

The range of cost levels reflects only the possible effect of the purchase prices of goods and services.

Required

(a)   Prepare a summary which shows the budgeted contribution earned by Stow Health Centre for the year ended 30 June 20X1 for each of nine possible outcomes.   **(6 marks)**

(b)   State the client fee strategy for the year to 30 June 20X1 which will result from the use of each of the following decision rules.

        (i)   Maximax
        (ii)   Maximin
        (iii)   Minimax regret

Your answer should explain the basis of operation of each rule. Use the information from your answer to (a) as relevant and show any additional working calculations as necessary. **(10 marks)**

(c)   The probabilities of variable cost levels occurring at the high, most likely and low levels provided in the question are estimated as 0.1, 0.6 and 0.3 respectively.

Using the information available, determine the client fee strategy which will be chosen where maximisation of expected value of contribution is used as the decision basis. **(4 marks)**

(Total = 20 marks)

5 NYE Co   39 mins

NYE Co manufactures three standard products which it sells to several large wholesale chains. Production is highly automated and occurs in large batches. Goods are shipped to customers in slightly smaller batches. Details of a typical month's output are as follows.

	Product X	Product Y	Product Z
Units of output	50,000	100,000	225,000
Production machine hours (PMH) per unit of output	0.3 PMH	0.2 PMH	
Production batch size (units)	1,250	2,000	3,750
Shipment batch size (units)	1,000	1,000	2,500

Two types of indirect labour are employed – 4 quality control inspectors (at a cost of $4,000 each per month) and 9 administrators (at a monthly cost of $3,500 each). Each employee works a standard 180 hours per month.

The role of the quality control staff is to inspect a sample from each batch of output produced. The standard inspection time is 4 hours per batch. The administrators perform two tasks – shipment processing work (which takes 3 hours per batch shipped) and monitoring of production (at a rate of 1 hour of administrator time for every 600 units of output).

In addition to the production machinery (which has a capacity of 100,000 production machine hours [PMH] per month) there are two additional types of specialised machinery which perform automated production setup and automated shipment loading procedures. Details of these two machines are provided below.

	Production setup machinery	Shipment loading machinery
Monthly capacity	800 hours	520 hours
Usage rates	5 hours per batch produced	2 hours per batch shipped

Required

(a)   Use activity based budgeting to assess whether the resources currently owned or employed by the company are sufficient to meet typical monthly output. Comment on any significant surplus/shortfall in resource. **(14 marks)**

(b)   Briefly outline THREE advantages that may be claimed for the use of activity based budgeting rather than a traditional incremental budgeting system. **(6 marks)**

(Total = 20 marks)

6 McDreamy   39 mins

McDreamy is in an industry sector which is recovering from the recent recession. The directors of the company hope next year to be operating at 85% of capacity, although currently the company is operating at only 65% of capacity. 65% of capacity represents output of 10,000 units of the single product which is produced and sold. One hundred direct workers are employed on production for 200,000 hours in the current year.

The flexed budgets for the current year are as follows.

Capacity level	55%	65%	75%
	$	$	$
Direct materials	846,200	1,000,000	1,153,800
Direct wages	1,480,850	1,750,000	2,019,150
Production overhead	596,170	650,000	703,830
Selling and distribution overhead	192,310	200,000	207,690
Administration overhead	120,000	120,000	120,000
Total costs	3,235,530	3,720,000	4,204,470

Profit in any year is budgeted to be $16\frac{2}{3}\%$ of sales.

The following percentage increases in costs are expected for next year.

	Increase %
Direct materials	6.0
Direct wages	3.0
Variable production overhead	7.0
Variable selling and distribution overhead	7.0
Fixed production overhead	10.0
Fixed selling and distribution overhead	7.5
Administration overhead	10.0

Required

(a) Prepare for next year a flexible budget statement on the assumption that the company operates at 85% of capacity; your statement should show both contribution and profit. **(12 marks)**

(b) State **three** problems which may arise from the change in capacity level. **(3 marks)**

(c) Explain what is meant by the principle of controllability. **(5 marks)**

(Total = 20 marks)

Helping hand. Profit may be expressed either as a percentage of cost of sales (**mark-up**) or as a percentage of sales (**margin**).

- If profit is x% of sales (**margin**), then profit is also $\left(\dfrac{x}{100-x} \times 100\%\right)$ of cost of sales (**mark-up**)

- If profit is 16.67% of sales (**margin**), then profit is also 20% $\left(\dfrac{16.67}{100-16.67} \times 100\%\right)$ of cost of sales (**mark-up**)

---

7 Chem Co

Chem Co manufacture a single product, product W, and have provided you with the following information which relates to the period which has just ended.

Standard cost per unit of product W

Materials:

Material	Kilos	Price per kilo $	Total $
F	15	4	60
G	12	3	36
H	8	6	48
	35		144

Labour:

	Hours	Rate per hour $	
Department P	4	10	40
Department Q	2	6	12
			196

Budgeted sales for the period are 4,500 units at $260 per unit. There were no budgeted opening or closing inventories of product W.

The actual materials used were as follows.

Materials:

Material	Kilos	Price per kilo $	Total $
F	59,800	4.25	254,150
G	53,500	2.80	149,800
H	33,300	6.40	213,120

Labour:

	Hours	Rate per hour $	Total $
Department P	20,500	10.60	217,300
Department Q	9,225	5.60	51,660

4,100 units of product W were produced and sold for $1,115,800.

Required

(a) Calculate the following material variances.

    (1)   Price   (3)   Mix

    (2)   Usage   (4)   Yield   **(8 marks)**

(b) Calculate the following labour variances for each of the production departments.

    (1)   Cost   (3)   Rate

    (2)   Efficiency   **(4 marks)**

(c) Calculate the sales variances.   **(3 marks)**

(d) Comment on your findings to help explain what has happened to the yield variance.   **(5 marks)**

                                                (Total = 20 marks)

8 Truffle Co

Truffle Co makes high quality, hand-made chocolate truffles which it sells to a local retailer. All chocolates are made in batches of 16, to fit the standard boxes supplied by the retailer. The standard cost of labour for each batch is $6.00 and the standard labour time for each batch is half an hour. In November, Truffle Co had budgeted production of 24,000 batches; actual production was only 20,500 batches. 12,000 labour hours were used to complete the work and there was no idle time. All workers were paid for their actual hours worked. The actual total labour cost for November was $136,800. The production manager at Truffle Co has no input into the budgeting process.

At the end of October, the managing director decided to hold a meeting and offer staff the choice of either accepting a 5% pay cut or facing a certain number of redundancies. All staff subsequently agreed to accept the 5% pay cut with immediate effect.

At the same time, the retailer requested that the truffles be made slightly softer. This change was implemented immediately and made the chocolates more difficult to shape. When recipe changes such as these are made, it takes time before the workers become used to working with the new ingredient mix, making the process 20% slower for at least the first month of the new operation.

The standard costing system is only updated once a year in June and no changes are ever made to the system outside of this.

Required

(a) Calculate the total labour rate and total labour efficiency variances for November, based on the standard cost provided above. **(4 marks)**

(b) Analyse the total labour rate and total labour efficiency variances into component parts for planning and operational variances in as much detail as the information allows. **(8 marks)**

(c) Assess the performance of the production manager for the month of November. **(8 marks)**

(Total = 20 marks)

9 Linsil (FMC, 6/04, amended)

39 mins

Linsil has produced the following operating statement reconciling budgeted and actual gross profit for the last three months, based on actual sales of 122,000 units of its single product:

Operating statement	$	$	$
Budgeted gross profit			800,000
Budgeted fixed production overhead			352,000
Budgeted contribution			1,152,000
Sales volume contribution variance		19,200	
Sales price variance		(61,000)	
			(41,800)
Actual sales less standard variable cost of sales			1,110,200

Planning variances	Favourable	Adverse	
Material	18,099		
Labour		286,358	
			(268,259)
Operational variances			
Material		16,635	
Labour	117,998		
			101,363
Actual contribution			943,304
Budgeted fixed production overhead		(352,000)	
Fixed production overhead expenditure variance		27,000	
Actual fixed production overhead			(325,000)
Actual gross profit			618,304

The standard direct costs and selling price applied during the three-month period and the actual direct costs and selling price for the period were as follows:

	Standard	Actual
Selling price ($/unit)	31.50	31.00
Direct material usage (kg/unit)	3.00	2.80
Direct material price ($/kg)	2.30	2.46
Direct labour efficiency (hrs/unit)	1.25	1.30
Direct labour rate ($/hr)	12.00	12.60

After the end of the three-month period and prior to the preparation of the above operating statement, it was decided to revise the standard costs retrospectively to take account of the following.

1   A 3% increase in the direct material price per kilogram;

2   A labour rate increase of 4%;

3   The standard for labour efficiency had anticipated buying a new machine leading to a 10% decrease in labour hours; instead of buying a new machine, existing machines had been improved, giving an expected 5% saving in material usage.

Required

(a)   Calculate the revised standard costs.   **(4 marks)**

(b)   Using the information provided demonstrate how the planning and operational variances in the operating statement have been calculated.   **(8 marks)**

(c)   Explain the significance of separating variances into planning and operational elements and the problems which could arise.   **(8 marks)**

(Total = 20 marks)

10 Divisional performance measures   39 mins

(a)   Compare and contrast the use of residual income and return on investment in divisional performance measurement, stating the advantages and disadvantages of each.   **(7 marks)**

(b)   Division Y of Chardonnay currently has capital employed of $100,000 and earns an annual profit after depreciation of $18,000. The divisional manager is considering an investment of $10,000 in an asset which will have a ten-year life with no residual value and will earn a constant annual profit after depreciation of $1,600. The cost of capital is 15%.

Calculate the following and comment on the results.

(i)   The return on divisional investment before and after the new investment
(ii)   The divisional residual income before and after the new investment   **(8 marks)**

(c)   Explain the potential benefits of operating a transfer pricing system within a divisionalised company.   **(5 marks)**

(Total = 20 marks)

11 Non profit seeking organisations   39 mins

(a)   The absence of the profit measure in non profit seeking organisations causes problems for the measurement of their efficiency and effectiveness.

Required

(i)   Explain why the absence of the profit measure should be a cause of the problems referred to.   **(8 marks)**

(ii)   Explain how these problems extend to activities within business entities which have a profit motive. Support your answer with examples.   **(4 marks)**

(b)   A public health clinic is the subject of a scheme to measure its efficiency and effectiveness. Among a number of factors, the 'quality of care provided' has been included as an aspect of the clinic's service to be measured. Three features of 'quality of care provided' have been listed.

(1)   Clinic's adherence to appointment times
(2)   Patients' ability to contact the clinic and make appointments without difficulty
(3)   The provision of a comprehensive patient health monitoring programme

Required

(i)   Suggest a set of quantitative measures which can be used to identify the effective level of achievement of each of the features listed.   **(6 marks)**

(ii)   Indicate how these measures could be combined into a single 'quality of care' measure.
                                                                                                      (2 marks)

                                                                                        (Total = 20 marks)

Section A solutions

1   Statement 1 is false and statement 2 is true. ABC is a system of absorption costing and if overheads are charged on the basis of a budgeted rate there will be under- or over-absorption.

   In a system of ABC, a larger proportion of overheads is charged to low volume products. In traditional absorption costing overheads are allocated in proportion to production volumes. This tends to allocate too small a proportion of overheads to low volume products.

2   B   The correct answer is: 2 only.

   ABC is a method of absorption costing that uses cost drivers to calculate absorption rates per unit of overhead activity. It then apportions overhead costs to products. It is not a technique for identifying variable overhead costs.

   ABC can be used as a basis for preparing budgets. This approach to budgeting is called activity based budgeting (ABB).

3   B   The correct answers are:

   2   In a system of ABC, for costs that vary with production levels, the most suitable cost driver is likely to be direct labour hours or machine hours.

   3   Activity based costs are not the same as relevant costs for the purpose of short-run decision making.

   4   Activity based costing is a form of absorption costing.

   Implementation of ABC is likely to be cost-effective when variable production costs are a low proportion of total production costs and overhead costs, traditionally assumed to be fixed costs, are a large proportion of total production costs.

   At a unit level, the cost driver for production-related overheads is likely to be direct labour hours or machine hours.

   It is a mistake to associate activity-based costs with the variable costs of an activity. Some of the costs may be variable in the short run, but others are not. So ABC costs should not be treated as relevant costs for the purpose of short-term decision making. It is more appropriate to think of ABC as a form of absorption costing, where overheads are allocated to activities and products on a more meaningful basis than with traditional absorption costing.

4   $1,200

   Cost per machine set-up = Machine set up costs / total number of batches

   $$\text{Total number of batches} = \frac{40,000\,\text{units}}{400\,\text{units}} + \frac{32,000\,\text{units}}{500\,\text{units}} + \frac{44,000\,\text{units}}{400\,\text{units}} = 274\,\text{batches}$$

   $$\text{Cost per machine set-up} = \frac{\$328,800}{274} = \$1,200$$

5   $700

   Cost per machine set-up = Material ordering costs / total number of purchase orders

   Total number of purchase orders = (40 × 3) + (20 × 2) + (55 × 4) = 380

   $$\text{Cost per purchase order} = \frac{\$266,000}{380} = \$700$$

6   Statement 1 is true and statement 2 is false. The product specification may be changed; for example, by using more standard components or changing the materials content of the product. However, changes should not reduce the value of the product to the customer, because this will affect the price the customer will be prepared to pay. Target costing may be combined with life cycle costing, but this is not necessary.

7   The correct answer is: $23.30

Direct materials	=	$50 \times \$2.50$	= $125
Labour time	=	$(0.25 \times 1.5) + (0.3 \times 2) + (0.45 \times 2.5)$	= 2.1 hours
Labour cost	=	$2.1 \times \$15$	= $31.50
Variable overhead	=	$2.1 \times \$8$	= $16.80
Total expected cost	=	$173.30	
Target cost	=	$200 - (200 \times 0.25)$	= $150
Cost gap	=	$173.3 - 150$	= $23.30

8   B   The correct answer is: Substitute current raw materials with cheaper versions.

Reducing the target cost gap should focus on ways of reducing the direct or variable costs of the product. This can be achieved by using a substitute cheaper raw material, but without affecting product quality. Reducing fixed overhead costs is not a way of reducing the gap. Using overtime is likely to increase costs and the target cost gap. Raising the selling price does not affect the cost gap directly, although it may lead to a reassessment of the target cost.

9   A company manufactures and sells a range of products. It is not dominant in the market in which it operates so has to **accept** the market price for each of its products. **Target** costing can be used to ensure that a new product is viable. Its aim is to **reduce** costs incurred due to the product's **design** and occurs at the **start** of the lifecycle. If the **expected** cost is greater than the target cost, major changes are introduced to **reduce** costs.

10   $558

Profit required = 7% × $600 = $42

Target cost = $600 − $42 = $558

11   C   Return will be increased if the breakeven time is shortened, not maximised.

12   C   The correct answer is: Neither 1 nor 2.

Life cycle costing does not have as an objective the maximisation of the commercial life of new products. Costs are estimated on the basis of the expected life of a product.

Life cycle costing is particularly suited to businesses that manufacture products with short life cycles and who have significant research and development costs.

13   B   All the statements are false except for statement 3.

14   D   Both statements are correct.

Life cycle costing is the accumulation of costs of a product's entire life cycle. Products that are not expected to be profitable after allowing for clean up costs should not be considered.

Life cycle costing can be very useful for organisations that continually develop products with a relatively short life, where it may be possible to estimate sales volumes and prices with reasonable accuracy.

15    $966

	$'000
R&D costs (4,750 + 250)	5,000
Marketing (250 + 188 + 125 + 25)	588
Production (2,400 + 14,400 + 15,000 + 3,400)	35,200
Disposal	750
Total life cycle costs	41,538
Total production ('000 units)	43
Cost per unit	966

16   A   The first statement is correct as throughput accounting discourages production for inventory purposes and is often used in a just in time environment.

The second statement is incorrect as in throughput accounting it is the bottleneck resource which should be 100% efficient which actually may mean unused capacity elsewhere.

17   B   ($320 - $80)/(6/60) = $2,400

18   1.60

Total factory costs: [2,000 units × $(8 + 19.50)] + [10,000 × $(4 + 8)] = $175,000
Factory cost per unit of bottleneck resource = $175,000/3,500 hours = $50
Product B throughput per unit = $25 − $5 = $20
Product B throughput per unit of bottleneck resource = $20/0.25 = $80
TPAR = $80/$50 = 1.60

19   Process Alpha is the bottleneck as it can only process 25 units of BC per hour. There are 10 working hours per day $\therefore$ 250 units per day.

Throughput return per day is $(420 − 170) × 250 = $62,500.

Conversion costs per day is $\dfrac{\$1,800,000}{(5 \times 50)} = \$7,200.$

Throughput accounting ratio = $\dfrac{\$62,500}{\$7,200} = 8.68$

20   A   The correct answer is: $5,000.

The total cost of producing 2,000 units using a throughput approach is:

	$
Materials	40,000

The cost per unit is $20 ($40,000 ÷ 2,000).

For the remaining inventory of 250 units the cost would be 250 × $20 = $5,000

21   D   In flow cost accounting, a distinction is made between positive and negative products, but a cost is attributed to each. Cost consists of materials, system costs and delivery and disposal costs.

22   C   The correct answer is: Cost of fines for environmental contamination.

A company may incur costs for contamination of the environment, but this cost should not be included within budgeted (and so 'acceptable') environmental costs.

23   D   The correct answer is: Traffic congestion.

This is an external environmental impact and the cost is picked up by the rest of society. The other costs are internal costs.

24   A   This is the correct option as environment-driven costs are allocated to general overheads, not joint cost centres.

25 C   Both statements are true. Repairs after the products have left the factory are an external failure cost. Having to reduce the price before the products leave the factory are an internal failure cost.

26 $196,400

	Product X	Product Y	Total
	$	$	$
Sales revenue	144,000	216,000	360,000
Variable costs	62,000	100,000	162,000
Contribution			198,000
Fixed costs	48,000	60,000	108,000

Contribution/Sales ratio = 198,000/360,000 = 0.55
Breakeven point = $108,000/0.55 = $196,364

27 The correct answer is: 50%.

Breakeven point is when total contribution equals fixed costs.

At breakeven point, $9,000 = 450 (selling price – $40)

$\therefore$ $20 = price – $40

$\therefore$ price = $60

$\therefore$ Mark-up = $((60 - 40) /40) \times 100\% = 50\%$

28 D   The correct answer is: 283 units.

Contribution per mix

= $(2 \times \$7) + (3 \times \$1) + (3 \times \$15) + (4 \times \$11) = \$106$

$\therefore$ Breakeven point in number of mixes = $15,000/$106 = 141.5

$\therefore$ Number of W sold at breakeven point = $2 \times 141.5 = 283$ units

If you chose 142 you took the breakeven number of mixes but did not multiply by 2 to get the number of units of W as there are 2 units of W in each mix.

If you chose 106 units then this is the contribution per mix. You did not go on then to calculate the BE point or number of units of W.

If you chose 212 you simply multiplied the contribution per mix by 2 and missed out the intermediate stage of calculating the breakeven point.

29 C   Breakeven sales revenue = fixed costs/weighted average c/s ratio
Contribution Y: 61–42 = 19
Contribution Z: 95–63 = 32
Total contribution for mix = $(19 \times 4) + (32 \times 2) = 140$
Total sales = $(61 \times 4) + (95 \times 2) = 434$
C/S ratio = 140/434 = 0.3226

Breakeven revenue = $200,000/0.3226 = $619,963 or $620,000 rounded up

30 B   The method of apportioning general overheads is not required to calculate the breakeven sales revenue.

31 A

	Component			
	W	X	Y	Z
Additional cost of external purchase	$40	$31	$16	$33
Hours saved	3	2	1	1.5
Extra cost per hour saved	$13.3	$15.5	$16	$22
Ranking for external purchase	1st	2nd	3rd	4th

32   D   The two maximum constraints would be $0.6x + 0.5y \leq 48{,}000$ and $0.3x + 0.2y \leq 20{,}000$

33   C

	1	2	1.1
Labour hours per unit	P1	P2	P3
	$	$	$
Profit per unit	44	51	26
Add back fixed costs	6	9	12
Contribution per unit	50	60	38
Contribution per labour hour	50	30	34.55
Ranking	1st	3rd	2nd

34   C

	A	B	C
	$	$	$
Selling price	50	68	94
Material A	(20)	(30)	(40)
Material B	(5)	(8)	(10)
Labour	(10)	(5)	(15)
Contribution per unit	15	25	29
Kgs of Mat A per unit	2	3	4
Contribution per kg A	7.5	8.33	7.25
Rank	2	1	3

Optimal production plan:

		kgs
Available		10,000
Make max number of Bs	(2,000 × 3)	(6,000)
Make max number of As	(1,000 × 2)	(2,000)
		2,000
Use rest to make Cs @ 4kg	2,000/4 = 500	(2,000)

35   The correct answer is: $420,000

	K	P
	$	$
Selling price	160	98
Mat C	20	0
Mat D	20	20
Labour	60	40
Contribution	60	38
Labour hours	3	2
Contribution per hour	20	19
Rank	1	2

Optimal production plan:

We are not told that there is a maximum demand for either product, therefore assume the 21,000 hours are used to manufacture Ks @$20 per hour = $420,000

36   B   Price at which demand is $0 = \$40 + (16{,}000/2{,}000) \times \$3 = \$64$

When $P = a - bQ$, $b = 3/2{,}000 = 0.0015$

37   B   If demand is expected to be inelastic with regard to price, low prices are not going to affect market demand significantly, so market skimming will almost certainly result in profit maximisation. Price discrimination will not offer any benefit when demand is price inelastic.

38 $100 - 0.002Q$

Price at which demand is $0 = \$60 + (20{,}000/1{,}000) \times \$2 = \$100$

When $P = a - bQ$, $b = 2/1{,}000 = 0.002$

39   136%

Breakeven point is when total contribution equals fixed costs.
At breakeven point, $15,000 = 500 (price - $22)
So $30 = price – $22
So $52 = price
So profit mark up = ($52 – $22) / $22 ×100% = 136%

40   B   If demand is highly elastic.

If demand is highly elastic it responds well to low prices.

If a product is new and different, market skimming would be more appropriate. Customers would be prepared to pay high prices so as to be one up on other people who do not own the product.

Market penetration pricing is appropriate if there are significant economies of scale to be achieved from a high volume of output, so that quick penetration into the market is desirable in order to gain unit cost reductions.

41    $700

	$ per hour
Labour cost	10
Variable overhead cost	2
Lost contribution (80 – 34)/2	23
Relevant cost per hour	35

Total relevant cost = 20 hours × $35 = $700

42   B   The correct answer is: 4,000 units of W and 4,000 units of Z.

	W	X	Y	Z
	$	$	$	£
Extra cost per unit of external purchase	1	6	3	2
Total extra cost of external purchase	4,000	12,000	9,000	8,000
Fixed costs saved by not making in-house	(5,500)	(8,000)	(6,000)	(7,000)
Difference	(1,500)	4,000	3,000	1,000

It would save $1,000 in cash to buy Material W externally. If full production can be achieved for the other materials, only W would be purchased externally. However, there is insufficient capacity to produce all three materials in-house.

If in-house production of Material Z is reduced to 3,000 units, the additional cost of external purchase would be only $6,000, so that $1,000 would be saved by purchasing all of Z externally.

The easiest way of understanding this is to look at the total costs associated with Product Z depending on which course of action is chosen:

- Buy them all in ($12 × 4,000 units) = $48,000

- Buy in 1,000 ($12 × 1,000) = $12,000 and make the remaining 3,000 ($10 × 3,000) + 7,000 specific fixed costs = $49,000

Therefore it is best to buy in all 4,000 units despite having the capacity to make 3,000.

43 B The correct answer is: 2,181 units.

Labour is a limiting factor. Therefore, to determine the order of production the saving per limiting factor of manufacturing in-house for each product must be calculated:

	George	Elroy	Jane
	$	$	$
Subcontractor	55	66	82
Variable costs	48	57	70
Saving	7	9	12
Labour hours	5.5	4.5	8.0
Saving/hour	1.27	2.00	1.50

Elroy has the greatest saving of manufacturing in-house per labour hour so should be prioritised to be manufactured in-house, followed by Jane, then George.

8,000 units of Elroy = 36,000 hrs (84,000 hours remaining)

9,000 units of Jane = 72,000 hrs (12,000 hours remaining)

12,000 hrs / 5.5 hrs per George = 2,181 units of George can be produced in-house.

44 C The correct answer is: $1,950.

The material is in regular use so the relevant cost is 500 kg in inventory at the replacement cost of $3.25. The other 100 will need to be purchased at a cost of $3.25.

The total is therefore $600 \times 3.25 = \$1,950$.

If you selected $1,325 you valued the inventory at their resale value. The items are in regular use so they would not be resold.

$1,825 values the items at their original purchase price but this is a sunk cost.

$3,250 is the cost of the full 1,000 kg that must be purchased. However, as the material is regularly used it can be kept in inventory till needed.

45 C The correct answer is: $70.

The rate of $10 per hour is not relevant because it would be paid anyway. The relevant hourly rate is the incremental cost of $9 per hour.

Skilled labour 5 hour × $9 = 45

Semi skilled 5 hours × $5 = 25

Total = $70

If you chose $45 you missed out the semi skilled labour.

If you chose $50 you costed all of the hours at the $10 per hour which is the rate for the skilled employee, but not the relevant one in this scenario.

If you chose $75 you then added the 5 hours at $5 to this $50. In other words all hours were costed using normal hourly rates.

46 D Regret table

Outcome situation	Option A	Option B	Option C	Option D
	$	$	$	$
Outcome 1	8,000	0	15,000	18,000
Outcome 2	30,000	40,000	0	20,000
Outcome 3	0	37,000	25,000	23,000
Max regret	30,000	40,000	25,000	23,000

The lowest maximum regret is $23,000.

47 The correct answers are:

Attitude to risk	Decision making method adopted
Risk averse	Maximin
Risk seeker	Maximax
Risk neutral	Expected values

Maximax decisions are taken by risk-seeking decision makers, also known as optimists, as they aim to maximise the maximum return available.

Maximin decision are taken by risk-averse decision-makers, also known as pessimists, as they aim to maximise the minimum return available.

A decision maker who bases these decisions on expected values is concerned with the most likely outcome and therefore ignores the variability of the returns. This is known as a risk-neutral approach to decision making.

48 C The correct answer is: Project C.

Maximin = maximise the minimum achievable return. The minimum achievable returns for each project are:

Project A	Project B	Project C	Project D
$400,000	$300,000	$450,000	$360,000

The maximum return from these is $450,000, project C.

49 The correct answer is: 100

Market conditions	Probability	Purchase 100	Purchase 200	Purchase 300	Purchase 400
Weak	15%	50	(100)	(200)	(250)
Average	25%	120	120	250	100
Strong	50%	90	200	300	400
Exceptional	10%	80	300	400	500
Minimum return		50	(100)	(200)	(250)

Therefore choose to purchase 100 as this has the lowest, minimum return.

50 D The correct answer is: 400

Market conditions	Probability	Purchase 100	Purchase 200	Purchase 300	Purchase 400
Weak	15%	50	(100)	(200)	(250)
Average	25%	120	120	250	100
Strong	50%	90	200	300	400
Exceptional	10%	80	300	400	500
Maximum return		120	300	400	500

Therefore choose to purchase 400 as this has the highest possible return.

51 B The definition in statement 1 is a definition of a flexible budget. Incremental decision packages in ZBB are used to measure the incremental cost of an activity or incremental activity, and to assess the benefits that this will provide. Incremental decision packages can be ranked according to the net benefit they will provide.

52 C Feedback is used mainly for control reporting purposes. It is primary data. It comes from internal sources within the organisation. It may consist of both financial and non-financial information.

53 B The correct answer is: Rolling budget.

Sometimes this is known as a continuous budget as the budget period is continually being extended.

54 B The answer is: 2 only.

Only the second statement is correct. The zero base budgeting process seeks to identify short-term benefits and improvements, and there is a risk that these may be implemented at the expense of longer-term objectives. ZBB calls for management skills that managers often lack.

55 A The correct answer is: Feedback control.

An example of feedforward control is using the information from a forecast, rather than a historical result, to decide on appropriate control measures. Feedback is where past actual figures have been compared to a plan and this has necessitated making corrective action going forward. A rolling budget is a budget model that is regularly updated to take account of a changing environment. Top down is a form of control where the budget is imposed upon the lower levels of the organisation from those above.

56 B

	Activity level Units	Cost $
Highest	10,000	400,000
Lowest	5,000	250,000
	5,000	150,000

$$\text{Variable cost per unit} = \frac{\$150,000}{5,000\,\text{units}} = \$30$$

57 C

	Production Units	Total cost $
Level 2	5,000	9,250
Level 1	3,000	6,750
	2,000	2,500

$$\text{Variable cost per unit} = \frac{\$2,500}{2,000\,\text{units}}$$

$$= \$1.25 \text{ per unit}$$

Fixed overhead = $9,250 − ($1.25 × 5,000) = $3,000

58 A $Y = ax^b$
Time taken for the first unit of output (a) = 160
Learning index (b) = log 0.75/log 2 = −0.1249387/0.30103 = −0.4150374

Time to produce the first 4 units
Cumulative average time for first 4 units = 160 × 4$^{-0.4150374}$ = 160 × 0.5625 = 90 hours
Total time for first 4 units = 4 × 90 hours = 360 hours

Time to produce the first 5 units
Cumulative average time for first 5 units = 160 × 5$^{-0.4150374}$ = 160 × 0.5127449 = 82.03918 hours
Total time for first 5 units = 5 × 82.03918 hours = 410.196 hours

Time to produce the 5th unit = (410.196 − 360) = 50.2 hours
Cost per hour = $3,200/160= $20 per hour
Cost for 5th unit = 50.2 hours × $20 = $1,003.92

59	D	There is a poor or non-existent audit trail with spreadsheets. Spreadsheets and participation in budgeting are unrelated. Models can be complex, but there is a greater risk of errors in formulae in the model. The use of spreadsheets does, however, greatly assist risk and uncertainty analysis.
60	C	The learning rate was actually better than expected and only 1 could cause it to improve.
61	A	Standard costing is most appropriate when the products manufactured are identical. This occurs in a mass production environment.
62	D	The correct answer is: Managers no longer rely on formal budgetary control reports to monitor performance.

62 D (cont.) Formal arrangements for monitoring performance are very widely used. Budgetary control reporting (if not standard costing variance reports) is an effective way of providing control information and performance information.

63	B	The correct answer is: Basic standard

A basic standard is left unchanged, so that changes in variances over time indicate a trend in prices and efficiency over time.

64	A	A basic standard is a long-term standard which remains unchanged over the years and is used to show trends. The descriptions given in B, C, and D describe a current standard, an ideal standard, and an attainable standard respectively.
65	A	Standard costing is useful where products are non standard or are customised to a customer's specifications.

Standard costs work well when homogenous items are being produced, because the company can have an expected usage of inputs for each product, which can be used to value each item of inventory. This simplifies the bookkeeping as well as having the benefit of being useful as a future cost prediction tool. Variance analysis can be used to understand if the standard costs were achieved during a control period.

66 The correct answer is: $4.50

Standard cost of material purchased – Actual cost of material purchased = Price variance

Standard cost $= \$32,195 - \$1,370$
$= \$30,825$

Standard price per kg $= \dfrac{\$30,825}{6,850}$
$= \$4.50$

67 $7,500

	Units
19,500 kg should yield ($\div 0.4$)	48,750
but did yield	45,000
Yield variance in units	3,750 (A)
$\times$ Standard material cost per unit of output	$2
Yield variance in $	$7,500 (A)

68	D	Adverse materials usage may be caused partly by inefficiencies or errors by production staff. Training may improve their ability to do the work and improve materials usage rates.

69   The correct answer is: $260 Favourable.

The overhead cost given, includes both fixed and variable costs. Fixed and variable budgeted overhead costs can be separated using the high/low method.

	Hours	$
High	18,000	16,242
Low	10,000	13,468
	8,000	2,774

The variable cost per machine hour can be estimated as $\dfrac{\$2,774}{8,000}$ = $0.34675

The fixed cost is $10,000, being the difference between variable overheads of 10,000 × 0.34675 and total cost of $13,468.

The total overhead variance for November is: Fixed overhead + Variable overhead for quality achieved - Total actual overhead cost incurred.

Budgeted cost ($10,000 + 13,780 × $0.34675)

Total actual overhead cost incurred

$	
14,778	
14,521	
257	(F)

70   D   The correct answer is: Achieving a lower output volume than budgeted.

The direct materials usage variance compares the standard material usage for the actual production with the actual material used. This means that the budgeted output volume is not relevant because it is not included in the calculation of the variance.

Using higher quality materials and increasing quality control checks are both likely to lead to a reduction in wastage rates which will lead to lower usage and a favourable materials usage variance.

71   B   In retrospect the market size was 90,000 units and if the company maintained a 20% market share it would have sold 18,000 units.

Market share variance:

	Units
Expected sales to maintain market share	18,000
Actual sales	17,000
Market share variance in sales units	1,000 (A)
Standard profit per unit	$10
Market share variance in $ profit	$10,000 (A)

72   The correct answer is: 8,100 Adverse.

Original standard selling price per unit	$27
Revised standard selling price per unit	$18
Planning variance per unit	$9 (A)
× sales volume in units	× 900
Sales price planning variance	$8,100 (A)

73   A   Planning variance = ($3.80 - $5) × 10,000 = $12,000 A

74 A

	Actual sales units in std mix	Standard sales units in std mix	Difference in units	Standard contribution	Variance
Product A	16,020	15,840	180 F	$12	$2,160 F
Product B	10,680	10,560	120 F	$13	$1,560 F
					$3,720 F

75 D   Material usage operational variance. Material usage variances are in the production manager's control. Material price variances are usually the responsibility of the purchasing manager.

Operational variances can be controlled by a line manager. In this instance the production manager can control efficiencies within the production process, influencing the operational variance. Planning variances are attributable to the manager responsible for approving the original standard, usually a more senior director

76 C   The correct answers are:

- In very large organisations
- During periods of economic affluence
- When an organisation's different units act autonomously.

Imposed budgets are likely to be most effective in newly-formed organisations. But participative budgets are likely to be effective in all other organisations.

77 B   Staff suggestions may be ignored leading to de-motivation. Psuedo-participation occurs when managers pretend to involve staff but actually ignore their input. This may lead to a less realistic budget and will certainly be de-motivating if the staff involved find out what is going on.

78 C   It is generally agreed that the existence of some form of target or expected outcome is a greater motivation than no target at all. Therefore (1) is true. The establishment of a target, however, raises the question of the degree of difficulty or challenge of the target. Therefore (2) is true. If the performance standard is set too high or too low sub-optimal performance could be the result.
The degree of budget difficulty is not easy to establish. It is influenced by the nature of the task, the organisational culture and personality factors. Some people respond positively to a difficult target. Others, if challenged, tend to withdraw their commitment. So (3) is not true.

79 C   A budget which is set without permitting the ultimate budget holder to participate in the budgeting process.

80 A   Participative budgeting should be used in all three circumstances.

81 C   Budgetary control information comes mainly from sources inside the organisation.

An Enterprise Resource Planning (ERP) system provides an integrated database system for the management of operations.

82 A   Statement 2 describes an enterprise resource planning system, not an executive information system.

83 D   This is the correct definition of a management information system.

84 D   Planning, control and decision making.

85 C   They are both true.

86 C   All of the others are internal sources of information.

87 C   The financial statements of competitors are an external source of management information.

88	B	Data from a government source is external data since it comes from a source outside the organisation. It is secondary data because it was not produced for the specific purpose for which management are using it.
89	A	Feedback is information captured within an organisation by measuring output from the system. Information from an external source cannot be feedback.
90	C	Passwords are used to prevent access to files and programs within a system, rather than preventing access to the system at all.
91	C	There can be (and usually are) several key performance indicators for each of the four perspectives of performance. A performance target to reduce the amount of wastage in production would relate to the internal perspective of the BSC.
92	A	There are three aspects to setting standards in the Building Block model: ownership, achievability and equity (fairness).

93   The correct answers are:

A   Non-financial measures are less likely to be manipulated than traditional financial ratios

B   Non-financial measures may discourage dysfunctional behavior by airline staff.

D   Non-financial measures are a better indicator of future prospects than financial ratios which focus on the short term.

E   Internal efficiency can be measured by the number of flight take-offs that are on time.

G   Customer satisfaction can be measured in terms of the number of failed attempts to make a booking due to website crashes.

Financial ratios do not need to be linked with non-financial measures is incorrect. The linkage via performance models such as the Balanced Scorecard will help to improve performance as financial ratios do not give the full picture.

As businesses develop, non-financial performance measures do need to be developed and refined over time so they can remain relevant.

94   D   The correct answer is:

  • Non-financial indicators are generally more important than financial indicators in the public sector.

The public sector is funded by government therefore financial indicators involving profit will be of little use in measuring performance.

95   B   ROCE can be calculated by multiplying the operating profit margin and the asset turnover.

28% × 65% = 18.2%

96   B   ($40,000/$300,000) × 100% = 13.3%

97   $29

The transfer price should be the opportunity cost for profit centre B of not being able to sell the product in the external market. This is the external market price minus the variable selling and distribution cost: $30 – $1 = $29.

98   C   The correct answer is: SW refuses to transfer below market price so AL is forced to buy from the external market.

This action will result in dysfunctional behaviour as both divisions' actions are not in the interest of the company. Head Office intervention should resolve the problem in the short term.

Distractors:

SW refuses to sell SW+ to AL as there is unlimited demand for SW+ in the external market.

Since there is full autonomy, SW will want to satisfy external demand to maximise its profits and that of the group.

AL refuses to order from SW as it can buy SW+ from the open market at lower than current transfer price. As a result, SW sells all its units in open market.

No dysfunctional behaviour as both divisions' actions will maximise group profits.

SW agrees to sell to AL but has to cancel the sale in order to fulfill an urgent customer order, willing to pay a higher price for immediate delivery.

Since both divisions have autonomy in making buying and selling decisions, this short term action will not result in dysfunctional behaviour.

99 C Divisional profit before depreciation = $2.7m × 15% = $405,000 per year.
Less depreciation = $2.7m × 1/50 = $54,000 per year
Divisional profit after depreciation = $351,000
Imputed interest = $2.7m × 7% = $189,000
Residual income = $162,000

100 A Opening capital employed = $4m + $0.5m = $4.5m
Closing capital employed = ($4m × 0.9) + ($0.5m × 1.2) = $3.6m + $0.6 = $4.2m
Average capital employed = $4.35m
Profit after depreciation = $1.2m
Therefore ROI = $1.2m/$4.35m = 27.59%

101 D When an organisation has multiple objectives, especially when these are not ranked in order of importance, it is difficult to assess performance. Some objectives may be met, but performance with regard to other objectives may be very poor and disappointing.

102 C Efficiency

103 D Efficient resource allocation and minimising the cost of resources used.

Not for profit organisations do not usually measure themselves against competition. However, sometimes they use benchmarking against similar departments or organisations. Not for profit organisations don't use ROI or RI.

104 B Employees. The others are all connected stakeholders.

105

Stakeholder	Measure		
Employees	morale	index	
Shareholders	dividend	yield	
Government		Percentage	of products conforming to environmental regulations
Customers		Percentage	of repeat customers

Section B solutions

Solo

> **Top tips**. Remember that when inventory levels **increase**, absorption costing reports the **higher** profit figure because some of the fixed production overhead will be carried forward in closing inventory (which reduces the cost of sales and therefore increases the profit).

1   $6,500

As opening and closing inventory levels are the same (zero), absorption costing and marginal costing will report the same profits.

Absorption costing operating statement

	Period 1	
	$	$
Sales		27,500
Production costs		
Variable	15,000	
Fixed	6,000	
	21,000	
Add: Opening inventory b/fwd	–	
Less: Closing inventory c/fwd	–	
Production cost of sales	21,000	
Under-absorbed overhead	–	
Total production costs		21,000
Profit for period		6,500

The absorption rate for fixed costs is $\dfrac{\$6,000}{500\,\text{units}} = \$12$ per unit

500 units produced = 500 × $12 per unit = $6,000 fixed costs

2   $5,200

In period 2, closing inventory is 100 units higher than opening inventory. This means that absorption costing will report higher profits than marginal costing. The difference in profits is 100 units × OAR = 100 units × $12 = $1,200. So absorption profit = marginal profit + $1,200 = $4,000 + $1,200 = $5,200.

Absorption costing operating statement

	Period 2	
	$	$
Sales		22,000
Production costs		
Variable	15,000	
Fixed	6,000	
	21,000	
Add: Opening inventory b/fwd	–	
Less: Closing inventory c/fwd	*(4,200)	
Production cost of sales	16,800	
Under-absorbed overhead	–	
Total production costs		16,800
Profit for period		5,200

The absorption rate for fixed costs is $\dfrac{\$6,000}{500\,\text{units}} = \$12$ per unit

Inventory is valued at $30 + $12 = $42 per unit
* 100 units at $42 per unit = $4,200

3    $6,550

Opening inventory is period 3 = 100 units. Closing inventory units = opening inventory units + production units – sales units. Closing inventory = 100 + 450 – 550 = 0. So inventory has decreased during the period and therefore marginal costing will report a higher profit than absorption costing. Absorption costing profit = $7,750 – (100 × $12) = $6,550.

Absorption costing operating statement

	Period 3	
	$	$
Sales		30,250
Production costs		
Variable	13,500	
Fixed	5,400	
	18,900	
Add: Opening inventory b/fwd	*4,200	
Less: Closing inventory c/fwd	–	
Production cost of sales	23,100	
Under-absorbed overhead	600	
Total production costs		23,700
Profit for period		6,550

The absorption rate for fixed costs is $\dfrac{\$6,000}{500\,\text{units}}$ = $12 per unit

Inventory is valued at $30 + $12 = $42 per unit
* 100 units at $42 per unit = $4,200

4    $600 under absorbed

Fixed costs per period per budget = $6,000

Fixed costs absorbed = $12 × 450 = $5,400

Under absorbed overhead = $6,000 – $5,400 = $600

5   The correct answer is:

- Absorption costing profits will be higher and closing inventory valuations higher than those under marginal costing.

Closing inventory valuation under absorption costing will always be higher than under marginal costing because of the absorption of fixed overheads into closing inventory values.

The profit under absorption costing will be greater because the fixed overhead being carried forward in closing inventory is greater than the fixed overhead being written off in opening inventory.

Southcott

Top tips. The original absorption basis was course days and so you simply needed to calculate the number of course days (number of courses × duration of course) for each course and total the results. Dividing total overheads by this figure gives an overhead cost per course day. Overheads are included in the cost of a course on the basis of the course duration.

The ABC **principles** applied to a service organisation are the **same** as those you would apply when dealing with a manufacturing organisation.

Step 1   Determine the cost driver for each category of overhead.
Step 2   Calculate a cost per cost driver (cost/number of cost drivers)

Step 3   Include overhead in the cost of a course on the basis of the number of cost drivers generated by a course.

6    $1,607

	Auditing	Taxation	Total
No of courses sold	50	30	
Duration of course (days)	2	3	
No of course days	100	90	190

Overhead cost per course day = $\dfrac{\$152,625}{190}$ = $803.29

Overhead cost per course

Auditing $803.29 × 2 days = $1,606.58

7    $658

Overhead cost of centre hire per auditing course using activity based costing

Centre hire cost per course day = $\dfrac{\$62,500}{190}$ = $328.95

Number of days per auditing course = 2

Centre hire cost per auditing course = 2 × $328.95 = $657.90

8    $600

Brochure cost per brochure printed = $\dfrac{\$63,000}{(50 \times 300) + (30 \times 200)}$ = $3 per brochure

Number of brochures printed per taxation course = 200

Cost of brochure printing allocated to a taxation course = 200 × $3 = $600

9    $175

Enquiries administration cost per enquiry = $\dfrac{\$27,125}{(50 \times 175) + (30 \times 70)}$ = $2.50

Number of enquiries per taxation course = 70

Cost of enquiries allocated to a taxation course = 70 × $2.50 = $175

10   The correct answer is:

- ABC identifies value added and non-value added activities.

The results of ABC must be interpreted by management before they can be used to identify which activities add value and which do not.

The other statements explain why ABC gives more accurate information than traditional absorption costing.

Abkaber

11    $ 6,600,000

Existing method

	Sunshine
	$
Direct labour (W1)	1,000,000
Materials (W2)	800,000
Overheads (at $24) (W3)	4,800,000
Total costs	6,600,000

Workings

1   **Labour cost**

    Sunshine   200,000 hrs × $5 per hour = $1,000,000

2   **Material cost**

    Sunshine   2,000 × 400 = $800,000

3   **Overhead per labour hour**

	$
Total overhead cost =	12,000,000
Total labour hours =	500,000 hrs
Overhead per labour hour =	$\dfrac{\$12,000,000}{500,000} = \$24$

12   **$7,340,000**

Existing method

	Roadster
	$
Direct labour ($5 per hr) (W1)	1,100,000
Materials (W2)	960,000
Overheads (at $24) (W3)	5,280,000
Total costs	7,340,000

Workings

1   **Labour cost**

    Roadster   220,000 hrs × $5 per hour = $1,100,000

2   **Material cost**

    Roadster   1,600 × 600 = $960,000

3   **Overhead per labour hour**

	$
Total overhead cost =	12,000,000
Total labour hours =	500,000 hrs
Overhead per labour hour =	$\dfrac{\$12,000,000}{500,000} = \$24$

13   **$2,400,000**

Overheads

$$\frac{\text{Overhead cost of set-ups}}{\text{Total number of set-ups}} = \frac{\$6,000,000}{100} = \$60,000$$

Set-up cost overheads

    Roadster $60,000 × 40 = $2,400,000

14   **$450,000**

Overheads

$$\frac{\text{Overhead cost of purchase orders}}{\text{Total number of purchase orders}} = \frac{3,600,000}{800} = \$4,500$$

Purchase order overheads

    Fireball $4,500 × 100 = $450,000

15   The correct answer is: All of the statements can be used to describe ABB.

    ABB can be applied on a number of levels and hence various definitions are appropriate.

Bottlenecks

16 $1,733

We are told that one of the production operations is the bottleneck, limiting production/sales.

	B
	$
Direct material cost	40
Variable production overhead cost	4
	44
Selling price	70
Contribution per unit	26
Bottleneck hours per unit	0.015
Contribution per bottleneck hour	$1,733
	1

17 $3,331,500

Determine profit-maximising product mix

Product	Demand			Hours required	Hours available		Units of production
B	45,000 × 1.2 =	54,000	(× 0.015)	810	810	(÷ 0.015)	54,000
A	120,000 × 1.2 =	144,000	(× 0.02)	2,880	2,265	(÷ 0.02)	113,250
				3,690	3,075		

Maximum profit calculation

Product	Units	Contribution per unit	Total contribution
			$
A	113,250	× $30	3,397,500
B	54,000	× $26	1,404,000
			4,801,500
Less: fixed production overhead			1,470,000
Maximum net profit			3,331,500

18 $2,900

Throughput return per production hour of the bottleneck resource = (selling price – material cost)/hours on the bottleneck resource

Rank products on the basis of throughput return per bottleneck hour

	A
	$
Selling price	60
Material cost	2
Throughput return	58
Bottleneck hours per unit	0.02
Return per bottleneck hour	$2,900

19 $3,732,000

Determine profit-maximising product mix

Product	Demand	Hours required	Hours available		Units of production
A	144,000	2,880	2,880	(÷ 0.02)	144,000
B	54,000	810	195 (bal)	(÷ 0.015)	13,000
		3,690	3,075		

Maximum profit calculation

Product	Units	Throughput return per unit	Total return $
A	144,000	× $58	8,352,000
B	13,000	× $30	390,000
Total throughput return			8,742,000
Less: overhead costs			
shown as variable in limiting factor analysis ((120,000 × $28) + (45,000 × $4))			(3,540,000)
fixed			(1,470,000)
Maximum net profit			3,732,000

20   1.23

TA ratio = throughput return per hour/conversion cost per hour

Conversion cost per hour = overhead costs/bottleneck hours
  = $(3,540,000 + 1,470,000)/3,075
  = $1,629.27

∴ TA ratio for B = $2,000/ $1,629.27 = 1.2275 = 1.23 (to 2 dp)

Bench Co

21   122.63 hours

Cumulative average time per batch for the first 54 batches

$Y = ax^b$

Where Y = the cumulative average time per unit to produce x units

x = the cumulative number of units

a = the time taken for the first unit of output

b = the index of learning (logLR/log2)

The cumulative average time per batch, with a learning curve of 80% is therefore

$Y = aX^{-0.3219}$

where a = the time for the first batch (350 hours) and X is the number of the batch. For the 26th batch, X = 26.

$Y = 350 \times 26^{-0.3219}$

  = 350 × 0.35036 = 122.63

The cumulative average time per batch for the first 26 batches is 122.63 hours.

22   82%

Batches	Total time	Average time/unit
1	350	350
2		350 × r
4		350 × r2
8		350 × r3
16	2,500	350 × r4

$2,500 = 16 \times 350\ r^4$

$2,500/(16 \times 350) = r^4$

$r = 0.82$ or 82%

23   385 hours

Cumulative average time for the first 8 units = $1,600 \times 75\% \times 75\% \times 75\% = 675$ hours

Cumulative average time for the first 9 units = ax^b where $a = 1,600$, $x = 9$, and $b = -0.415$

Cumulative average time for the first 9 units = $1,600 \times 9^{-0.415}$

$= 1,600 \times 0.401748 = 642.7968$

		hours
Total time for first 9 units	(9×642.7968)	5,785
Total time for first 8 units	(8×675)	5,400
		385

24   The correct answers are:

- A relatively new product.
- A manual, rather than mechanised production process.
- A relatively complex production process.

If a product is relatively new it means that workers are still learning.

If a process is manual (as opposed to one that is mechanised), learning can reduce the time taken.

If the production process is relatively complex there are processes and techniques to learn.

Production can be in batches of any size – equal sizes just make the calculations easier.

Changing labour rates do not affect the application of learning curve theory.

25   The FALSE statement is:

- The learning curve theory states that the average time per unit produced is assumed to decease by a constant percentage every time total output doubles

The important word 'cumulative' is missing and the sentence should read:

The learning curve theory states that the cumulative average time per unit produced is assumed to decrease by a constant percentage every time total output doubles.

Cumulative average time means the average time per unit for all units produced so far, back to and including the first unit made.

Section C solutions

1 BD Company

Top tips. The F5 exam could include a full question on the topic so ensure you make a good attempt at this one.

To draw up a **contribution breakeven chart** you need to **know** three things.

- Selling price per can
- Variable cost per can
- Fixed costs

These can all be calculated from information in the question with varying degrees of difficulty/ease.

As CVP analysis is based on **marginal costing principles**, and given that information in the question is provided for two time periods, you have a rather large hint that you need to split the manufacturing costs into fixed and variable components using the **high-low method**. It is safe to assume that the **administration** costs are **fixed**, as they are the **same** in both time periods. Selling price per unit is a straightforward calculation.

You then have enough information to draw up the chart. You can always calculate breakeven point and margin of safety and compare them with your chart to ensure that you have marked them on the chart correctly. (Did you actually see the note in the requirements asking you to show them on the chart?)

Part (b) involves **multi-product** CVP analysis. The data for the chart is not difficult to derive, but the calculation of breakeven point must be based on contribution per mix, **the standard mix being one own label, one BD brand**.

An exam question may ask for some written analysis, and this question is no exception. The points you need to make are not particularly technical, but are simply grounded in common sense. If option 2 shows the higher profit, **lower breakeven point** (so that **not so many sales are required to cover costs**) and **a higher margin of safety** (which means that the **difference between expected sales and breakeven sales is likely to be higher**), it should be the better option. There are, of course, **other factors** that might affect that decision.

Assumption. Manufacturing costs for the BD brand will be the same as for own label brands.

Initial workings

Manufacturing costs

We need to analyse the cost behaviour patterns by separating the manufacturing costs into their fixed and variable elements, using the high-low method.

	Sales Millions	Costs $ million
20X3	19	4.45
20X2	18	4.30
	1	0.15

Variable manufacturing cost per can = $0.15

Fixed manufacturing cost = $4.45 million − (19 million × $0.15)
= $1.6 million

Selling prices

Selling price per can in 20X3	= 6.27/19	= $0.33
∴ Unit contribution per can	= $0.33 − $0.15	= $0.18
∴ Contribution per can of BD brand	= $0.18 × 133 1/3%	= $0.24
Variable cost per can of BD brand	= $0.15 + $0.02	= $0.17
∴ Selling price per can of BD brand	= $0.17 + $0.24	= $0.41

(a) **Data for chart**

	$ million	$ million
Variable costs (19 million × $0.15)		2.85
Fixed costs: manufacturing	1.60	
administration	1.20	
		2.80
Total costs		5.65

$$\text{Breakeven point} = \frac{\text{fixed costs}}{\text{contribution}} = \frac{\$2.8m}{\$0.18}$$

$$= 15.55 \text{ million cans}$$

$$= \$5.13 \text{ million sales}$$

Margin of safety = 19m − 15.55m = 3.45 million cans = $1.14 million sales

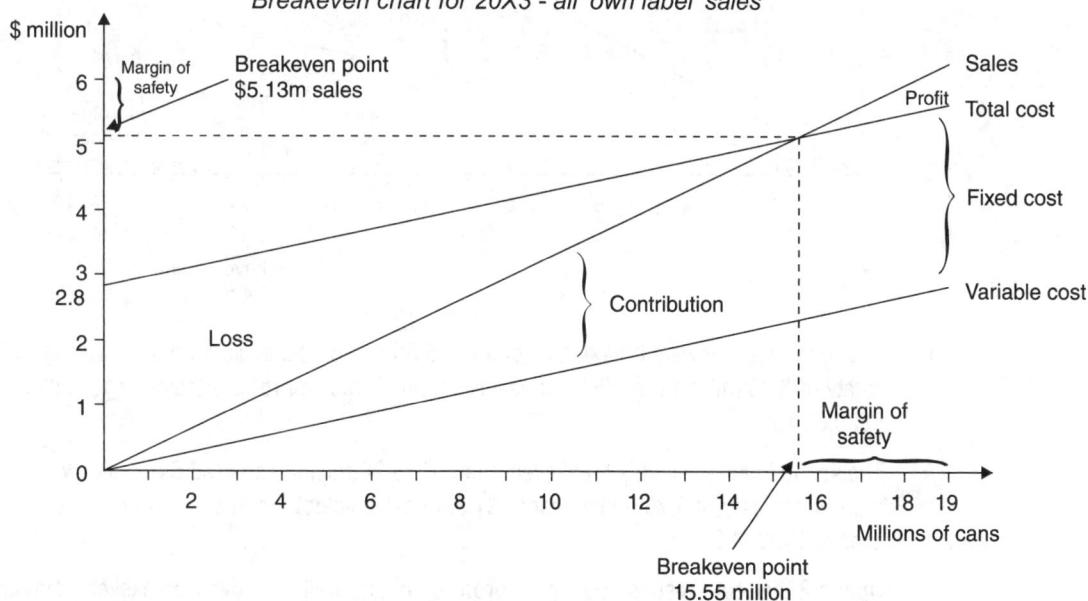

Breakeven chart for 20X3 - all 'own label' sales

(b) **Data for chart**

		$ million	$ million
Variable costs:	own label (9.5m × $0.15)		1.425
	BD brand (9.5m × $0.17)		1.615
			3.040
Fixed costs:	manufacturing	1.600	
	administration	1.200	
	marketing	0.400	
			3.200
Total costs:			6.240
Sales value:	own label (9.5m × $0.33)		3.135
	BD brand (9.5m × $0.41)		3.895
			7.030

Our standard mix is 1 own label, 1 BD brand.

$$\text{Breakeven point} = \frac{\text{fixed costs}}{\text{contribution per mix}} = \frac{\$3.2m}{\$(0.18+0.24)} = \frac{\$3.2m}{\$0.42}$$

$$= 7.62 \text{ million mixes} = 15.24 \text{ million cans}$$

$$= 7.62 \times (\$(0.33 + 0.41)) \text{ million sales} = \$5.64 \text{ million sales}$$

Margin of safety $= 19m - 15.24$ million $= 3.76$ million cans $= 1.88$ million mixes

$$= 1.88 \times (\$(0.33 + 0.41)) \text{ million sales}$$

$$= \$1.39 \text{ million sales}$$

Profit = $7.03 million – $6.24 million = $790,000

Breakeven chart for 20x3 – 50% 'own label', 50% BD brand

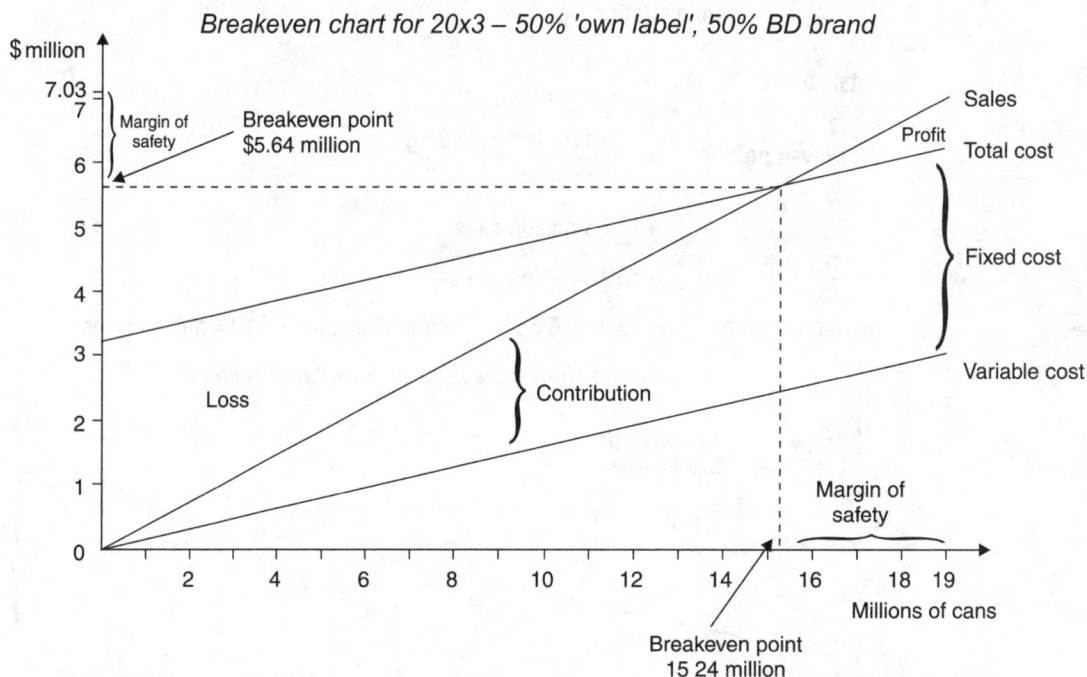

(c)   The **first chart** shows a breakeven point of 15.55 million cans ($5.13m sales value) and a margin of safety of 3.45 million cans ($1.14m sales value). Forecast profit for sales of 19 million cans is $620,000.

The **second chart** shows a breakeven point of 15.24 million cans ($5.64m sales value) and a margin of safety of 3.76 million cans ($1.39m sales value). Forecast profit for sales of 19 million cans is $790,000.

Option 2 therefore results in a higher profit figure, as well as a lower breakeven point and increased margin of safety. On this basis it is the better of the two options.

Other factors which management should consider before making a decision

(i)   The supermarket chains may put the same pressure on margins and prices of the BD brand as they do on the own label brands.

(ii)   Customers may realise that the BD brand is the same product as the own label brand and may not be willing to pay the premium price.

(iii)   If the mix of sales can be changed in favour of the BD brand then profits will improve still further.

BPP
LEARNING MEDIA

2 RAB Consulting

> **Top tips**. This is a straightforward linear programming question. The best way to approach graphical linear programming questions is to work through the **six steps** we recommend in the text.
>
> - Define variables
> - Establish objective function
> - Establish constraints
> - Graph the problem
> - Define feasible region
> - Determine optimal solution
>
> Notice the approach we have taken to choosing our sample **iso-contribution line**. This is something that students often find difficult, so choose easy **numbers (related to the coefficients of the variables)**, making sure that the line then falls within the feasible region.

(a)

		Type A $ per project		Type B $ per project
Revenue		1,700		1,500
Variable costs				
Labour				
– qualified researchers	(20 hrs × $30)	600	(12 hrs × $30)	360
– junior researchers	(8 hrs × $14)	112	(15 hrs × $14)	210
Direct project expenses		408		310
		1,120		880
Contribution		580		620

(b) ## Step 1   **Define variables**

Let a = number of type A projects
Let b = number of type B projects

Step 2   **Establish objective function**

Maximise contribution (C) = 580a + 620b, subject to the constraints below.

Step 3   **Establish constraints**

Qualified researchers time: $20a + 12b \leq 1,344$
Junior researchers time: $8a + 15b \leq 1,120$
Agreement for type A: $a \geq 20$
Maximum for type B: $b \leq 60$
Non-negativity: $b \geq 0$

Step 4   **Graphing the problem**

Constraints

Qualified researcher time: if a = 0, b = 112
                  if b = 0, a = 67.2

Junior researcher time: if a = 0, b = 74.67
                  if b = 0, a = 140

Agreement for type A: graph the line a = 20

Maximum for type B: graph the line b = 60

Step 5   **Define feasible region**

Iso-contribution line

580a + 620b = 35,960 (where 35,960 = 58 × 62 × 10) goes through the points (62, 0) and (0, 58)

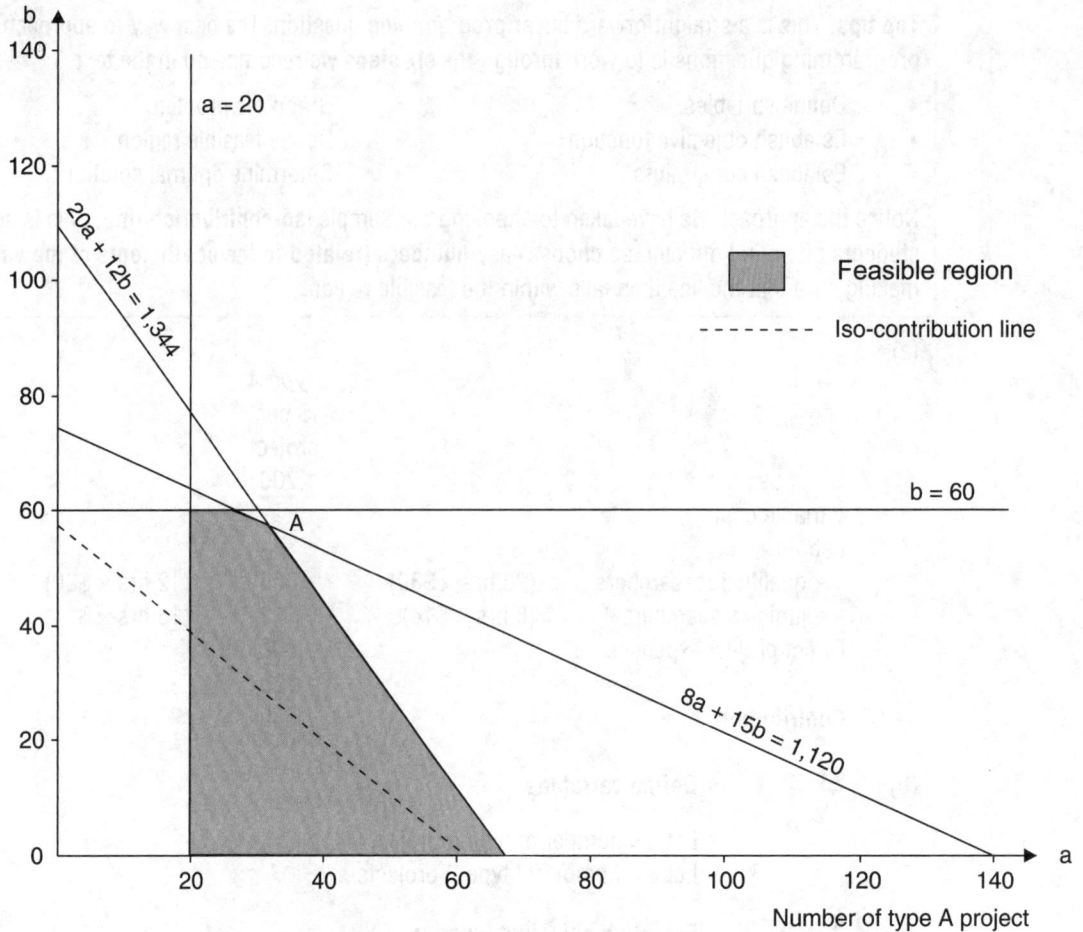

Graph to show profit-maximising mix of projects

Moving the iso-contribution line away from the origin, we see that it leaves the feasible area at the intersection of the two time constraints (point A).

Step 6 Determine optimal solution

Find the co-ordinates of A

$20a + 12b$	$= 1{,}344$	(1)	
$8a + 15b$	$= 1{,}120$	(2)	
$20a + 37.5b$	$= 2{,}800$	(3)	(2) × 2.5
$25.5b$	$= 1{,}456$		(3) − (1)
b	$= 57.10$		
$20a + 685.20$	$= 1{,}344$		substitute into (1)
a	$= 32.94$		

The profit-maximising mix of projects is 32.94 of type A and 57.10 of type B.

Profit for profit-maximising mix

		$
Contribution from type A:	32.94 × $580	19,105
Contribution from type B:	57.10 × $620	35,402
Total contribution		54,507
Less: fixed costs		(28,000)
		26,507

(c) **Shadow price**

The shadow price is the **extra contribution** or profit that may be earned if one more unit of a **binding resource** or **limiting factor** becomes available.

It can be used to inform managers of the **maximum price** that should be paid for more of a scarce resource over and above the basic rate. The shadow price of a constraint that is not binding at the optimal solution is zero.

Calculation of shadow prices

At the optimal solution, A = 32.94 and B = 57.10
Contribution = $54,507

Qualified researchers

$(32.94 \times 20) + (57.10 \times 12) = 1,344 =$ availability

The constraint is **binding**. If one more hour of labour was available, the new optimal product mix would be at the intersection of the lines:

$$20a + 12b = 1,345 \ (1)$$
$$8a + 15b = 1,120 \ (2)$$

$(2) \times 2.5$

$$20a + 37.5b = 2,800 \ (3)$$

$(3) - (1)$

$$25.5b = 1,455$$
$$b = 57.06$$

Substitute into (1)

$$20a + 684.72 = 1,345$$
$$a = 33.01$$

Contribution $= (580 \times 33.01) + (620 \times 57.06) = \$54,523$

The **shadow price** of one hour of qualified researcher's time is the extra contribution generated which is $16.

3 AB

Top tips. This question has four ingredients of a good and testing problem on decision-making.

- It tests your ability to grasp the **nature of a decision problem**, and think about the assumptions you may have to make. It is assumed that inventory in hand of finished X, valued at $51,900 at full cost, is valued at the full cost of production and not at the full cost of sale.

- It tests your knowledge of **relevant costs**. For example, the $3,500 capital cost of Y will be incurred whatever course of action is taken, although with the alternative recommendation we have made the spending could be deferred by 33 weeks. Selling and administration overhead has been assumed to be a fixed cost and so is irrelevant to the decision.

- It includes a consideration of **non-financial factors**. We looked at the workforce, customers' interests and competition – you may have focused on different areas.

- Part (c) of the question introduced the very practical issue **of searching for alternative opportunities**. For example, the alternative course of action we have suggested seems the most obvious one, but you might think otherwise, and a sensible alternative would be equally acceptable as a solution.

(a) **Full cost of production per kg of X**

	$
Direct materials	17.33
Direct labour	7.36
Production overhead (200% of labour)	14.72
	39.41

The quantity of inventory in hand is therefore $51,900/$39.41 = 1,317 kg

At a weekly sales volume of 74 kg, this represents 1,317/74 = about 18 weeks of sales

It will take 20 weeks to set up the production facility for Y, and so inventory in hand of finished X can be sold before any Y can be produced. This **finished inventory** is therefore **irrelevant** to the decision under review; it will be sold whatever decision is taken.

The problem therefore centres on the inventory in hand of direct materials. Assuming that there is no loss or wastage in manufacture and so 1 kg of direct material is needed to produce 1 kg of X then inventory in hand is $44,800/$17.33 = 2,585 kg.

This would be converted into 2,585 kg of X, which would represent sales volume for 2,585/74 = 35 weeks.

If AB sells its existing inventories of finished X (in 18 weeks) there are **two options**.

(i)   To produce enough X from raw materials for 2 more weeks, until production of Y can start, and then dispose of all other quantities of direct material – ie 33 weeks' supply.

(ii) To produce enough X from raw materials to use up the existing inventory of raw materials, and so delay the introduction of Y by 33 weeks.

The relevant costs of these two options

(i)   **Direct materials**. The relevant cost of existing inventories of raw materials is $(0.30). In other words the 'cost' is a benefit. By using the direct materials to make more X, the company would save $0.30 per kg used.

(ii) **Direct labour**. It is assumed that, if labour is switched to production work from non-production work in the next three months, they must be paid at the full rate of pay, and not at 65% of normal rate. The **incremental** cost of labour would be 35% of the normal rate (35% of $7.36 = $2.58 per kg produced).

Relevant cost of production of X

	$
Direct materials	(0.30)
Direct labour	2.58
Variable overhead (30% of full overhead cost of $14.72)	4.42
Cost per kg of X	6.70

Relevant cost per kg of Y

	$
Direct materials	4.01
Direct labour	2.85
Variable overhead (30% of 200% of $2.85)	1.71
	8.57

(**Note**. Y cannot be made for 20 weeks, and so the company cannot make use of spare labour capacity to produce any units of Y.)

It is cheaper to use up the direct material inventories and make X ($6.70 per kg) than to introduce Y as soon as possible, because there would be a saving of ($8.57 − $6.70) = $1.87 per kg made.

AB must sell X for at least 20 weeks until Y could be produced anyway, but the introduction of Y could be delayed by a further 33 weeks until all inventories of direct material for X are used up. The saving in total would be about $1.87 per kg × 74 kg per week × 33 weeks = $4,567.

(b) **Non-financial factors that must be considered in reaching the decision**

(i) **The workforce**. If the recommended course of action is undertaken, the workforce will produce enough units of X in the next 13 weeks to satisfy sales demand over the next year (with 18 weeks' supply of existing finished goods inventories and a further 35 weeks' supply obtainable from direct materials inventories). When production of Y begins, the direct labour content of production will fall to $2.85 per kg – less than 40% of the current effort per kg produced – but sales demand will not rise. The changeover will therefore mean a big drop in labour requirements in production. Redundancies seem inevitable, and might be costly. By switching to producing Y as soon as possible, the redundancies might be less immediate, and could be justified more easily to employees and their union representatives than a decision to produce enough X in the next three months to eliminate further production needs for about nine months.

(ii) **Customers' interests**. Product Y is a superior and 'more effective' compound than X. It would be in customers' interests to provide them with this improved product as soon as possible, instead of delaying its introduction until existing inventories of direct materials for X have been used up.

(iii) **Competition**. CD is expected to start selling Y overseas, and quite possibly in direct competition with AB. CD has the advantage of having developed Y itself, and appears to use it in the preliminary stage of an alternative technical process. The competitive threat to AB is twofold:

(1) CD might take away some of the replacement demand for Y from AB so that AB's sales of X or Y would fall.

(2) CD might compete with AB to install its total technical process into customers' factories, and so the competition would be wider than the market for compound Y.

(c) **Alternative course of action**

(i) Produce enough units of X in the next 13 weeks to use up existing inventories of direct materials.

(ii) Start sales of Y as soon as possible, and offer customers the choice between X and Y. Since X is an inferior compound, it would have to be sold at a lower price than Y.

Merits of this course of action

(i) The workforce would be usefully employed for the next 13 weeks and then production of Y would begin at once. Although redundancies would still seem inevitable, the company would be creating as much work as it could for its employees.

(ii) AB's customers would be made aware of the superiority of Y over X in terms of price, and of AB's commitment to the new compound. AB's marketing approach would be both 'honest' and would also give customers an attractive choice of buying the superior Y or, for a time, an inferior X but at a lower price. This might well enhance AB's marketing success.

Demerits of this course of action

(i) It is unlikely to be a profit-maximising option, because selling X at a discount price would reduce profitability.

(ii) Customers who get a discount on X might demand similar discounts on Y.

(iii) Some customers might query the technical differences between X and Y, and question why AB has been selling X at such a high price in the past – this might lead to some customer relations difficulties.

(iv) AB must decide when to reduce the price of X, given that Y cannot be made for 20 weeks. The timing of the price reduction might create some difficulties with customers who buy X just before the price is reduced.

4 Stow Health Centre

Top tips. Did you get confused in part (a)? The occupancy level will vary with the client fee per day, while the variable cost per client day is independent. In other words, at each of the **three different levels of client fee** per day, there are **three possible levels of variable cost** per client and so $3 \times 3 =$ **9 possible levels of contribution per client day**.

The most tricky aspect of part (b) was dealing with the **minimax regret decision rule**. This rule involves choosing the strategy which will **minimise the maximum regret** (ie drop in contribution) from choosing one option instead of the best option. This requires you to draw up an **opportunity loss table**. This will show the **drop in contribution** at **each level of variable cost** from **choosing a level of client fee which is not the best option**. For example, at a variable cost of $95 per day, the best strategy would be a client fee of $200 per day. The opportunity loss from using a fee of $180 would be the difference between the contributions at the two fee levels.

For part (c) you simply need to **calculate an EV of variable cost per day**. You are then faced with a situation of one level of client fee per day and one level of variable cost per day at each level of 'demand'.

(a) We need to calculate budgeted contribution and so the summary will need to show the various income (fee) and variable cost levels.

	Client fee per day		
Variable cost per day	$180	$200	$220
$	$	$	$
95	1,338,750	1,378,125	1,312,500
85	1,496,250	1,509,375	1,417,500
70	1,732,500	1,706,250	1,575,000

Workings

Number of client days:
Maximum capacity = $50 \times 350 = 17,500$
High occupancy level = $90\% \times 17,500 = 15,750$
Most likely occupancy level = $75\% \times 17,500 = 13,125$
Low occupancy level = $60\% \times 17,500 = 10,500$

Number of client days × contribution per client day (fee − variable cost) = contribution

(b) (i) The **maximax** decision rule involves choosing the outcome with the **best possible result**, in this instance choosing the outcome which **maximises contribution**. The decision-maker would therefore choose a **client fee of $180 per day**, which could result in a contribution of $1,732,500.

(ii) The **maximin** decision rule involves choosing the outcome that offers the **least unattractive worst outcome**, in this instance choosing the outcome which **maximises the minimum contribution**. The decision-maker would therefore choose a **client fee of $200 per day**, which has a lowest possible contribution of $1,378,125. This is better than the worst possible outcomes from client fees per day of $180 and $220, which would provide contributions of $1,338,750 and $1,312,500 respectively.

(iii) The **minimax regret** decision rule involves choosing the **outcome that minimises the maximum regret** from making the wrong decision, in this instance choosing the outcome which minimises the opportunity lost from making the wrong decision.

We can use the calculations performed in (a) to draw up an **opportunity loss table**.

Client fee per day	Variable cost per day $95	$85	$70	Maximum regret
$	$	$	$	$
180	39,375 (W1)	13,125 (W4)	0 (W7)	39,375
200	0 (W2)	0 (W5)	26,250 (W8)	26,250
220	65,625 (W3)	91,875 (W6)	157,500 (W9)	157,500

The minimax regret decision strategy would be to **choose a client fee of $200** to minimise the maximum regret at $26,250.

Workings

1   At a variable cost of $95 per day, the best strategy would be a client fee of $200 per day. The opportunity loss from using a fee of $180 would be $(1,378,125 – 1,338,750) = $39,375.

2   The opportunity loss in this case is $(1,378,125 – 1,378,125) = $0.

3   The opportunity loss in this case is $(1,378,125 – 1,312,500) = $65,625.

4   At a variable cost of $85 per day, the best strategy would be a client fee of $200 per day. The opportunity loss from using a fee of $180 would be $(1,509,375 – 1,496,250) = $13,125.

5   The opportunity loss in this case is $(1,509,375 – 1,509,375) = 0.

6   The opportunity loss in this case is $(1,509,375 – 1,417,500) = $91,875.

7   At a variable cost of $70 per day, the best strategy would be a client fee of $180 per day. The opportunity loss from using a fee of $180 would be $(1,732,500 – 1,732,500) = $0.

8   The opportunity loss in this case is $(1,732,500 – 1,706,250) = $26,250.

9   The opportunity loss in this case is $(1,732,500 – 1,575,000) = $157,500.

(c)   **Expected value of variable costs** = $(0.1 \times \$95) + (0.6 \times \$85) + (0.3 \times \$70) = \$81.50$.

We can now calculate an expected value of budgeted contribution at each client fee per day level.

	Client fee per day		
Variable cost	$180	$200	$220
$81.50	1,551,375	1,553,312.50	1,454,250

If **maximisation of EV of contribution is used as the decision basis**, a **client fee of $200 per day** will be selected, with an EV of contribution of $1,555,312.50 (although this is *very* close to the EV of contribution which results from a client fee of $180).

5 NYE Co

Text reference. Activity based budgeting is covered in Chapter 8.

Top tips. This is a relatively straightforward question designed to give you practice at applying the principles of ABB. Show all your workings to part (a) to maximise your score.

Part (b) is a straightforward discussion of ABB versus traditional budgeting systems. Even if you struggled with the calculations in part (a), you should be able to pick up a number of marks here.

		Marks
(a)	Number of PMH	1
	Number of batches produced	1
	Number of batches shipped	1
	Indirect labour hours	2
	Machinery hours	2
	Indirect labour staff numbers	3
	Machine capacity	2
	Comment re shortfall of production machine capacity	1
	Comment re surplus of administrators	1
		14
(b)	Up to 1 mark per well explained point	6
		20

(a) ## Step 1   Calculate amount of activities required for typical monthly output

	Product X	Product Y	Product Z	Total
Number of PMH	15,000 PMH	20,000 PMH	90,000 PMH	125,000 PMH
	$(50,000 \times 0.3)$	$(100,000 \times 0.2)$	$(225,000 \times 0.4)$	
Number of batches produced	40	50	60	150
	$(50,000 / 1,250)$	$(100,000 / 2,000)$	$(225,000 / 3,750)$	
Number of batches shipped	50	100	90	240
	$(50,000 / 1,000)$	$(100,000 / 1,000)$	$(225,000 / 2,500)$	

Step 2   Calculate the resource required to perform the amount of activities identified in step 1

Indirect labour

Quality control	= 150 batches produced × 4 inspection hours = **600 inspection hours**
Administration	= 240 batches × 3 administration hours = 720 administration hours
	+ 375,000 units of output / 600 = 625 administration hours
	= **1,345 administration hours**

Machinery

Production machinery	= 125,000 PMH (calculated in Step 1)
Setup machinery	= 150 batches produced × 5 hours = 750 hours
Shipment loading machinery	= 240 batches shipped × 2 hours = 480 hours

Step 3   Assess whether resources currently owned or employed by the company are sufficient to meet the requirements identified in steps 1 and 2

Indirect labour – staff numbers

	Quality control inspectors	Administrators
Number employed at present	4 inspectors	9 administrators
Number required	3.33 inspectors	7.47 administrators
	(600 hours / 180 hours each)	(1,345 hours / 180 hours each)
Surplus/(shortfall)	**0.67 inspectors**	**1.53 administrators**

Machine capacity

	Production machinery	Setup machinery	Shipment loading machinery
Capacity of existing equipment	100,000 PMH	800 hours	520 hours
Capacity required	125,000 PMH	750 hours	480 hours
Surplus/(shortfall)	(25,000 PMH)	50 hours	40 hours

From the above it is clear that the company has too little production machine capacity. Unless this bottleneck is removed the budgeted levels of output of some or all of the three products will not be achieved.

It is also evident that the company has a surplus of administrators. The company currently employs 9 administrators, which is 1.5 more than it needs. Since the cost of employing an administrator is $3,500 per month, the cost of this spare capacity is $5,250 per month. The company should consider how this idle time cost can be avoided. Redundancy may be one option, but only after NYE Co has considered the full long-term consequences (including redundancy payments).

(b)   Advantages claimed for the use of activity based budgeting include the following:

Resource allocation is **linked** to a **strategic plan** for the future, prepared after considering alternative strategies. **Traditional budgets** tend to **focus on resources and inputs** rather than on objectives and alternatives.

New **high priority activities** are **encouraged**, rather than focusing on the existing planning model. Activity based budgeting **focuses** on **activities**. This allows the identification of the cost of each activity. It also allows the **ranking of activities** where financial constraints limit the range of activities that may be achieved.

There is **more focus** on **efficiency** and **effectiveness** and the alternative methods by which they may be achieved. Activity based budgeting assists in the operation of a **total quality philosophy**.

It avoids arbitrary cuts in specific budget areas in order to meet the overall financial targets. Non-value added activities may be identified as those which should be eliminated.

It tends to **increase management commitment** to the **budget process**. This should be achieved since the activity analysis enables management to focus on the objectives of each activity. Identification of primary and secondary activities and non-value added activities should also help in motivating management in activity planning and control.

6 McDreamy

Top tips. Make sure you read the question carefully especially on the calculation of capacity levels. Note that at 65% capacity 10,000 units are produced.

Part (b) requires you to apply your knowledge and part (c) is a straightforward regurgitation of text book knowledge.

(a) **Flexible budget statement for next year operating at 85% capacity**

	Workings		
Output	1	13,077 units	
		$	$
Sales revenue	9		5,911,484
Variable costs			
Direct materials	2	1,386,162	
Direct wages	3	2,357,129	
Variable production overhead	4	489,734	
Variable selling and distribution overhead	5	69,962	
			4,302,987
Contribution			1,608,497
Fixed costs			
Production overhead	6	330,000	
Selling and distribution overhead	7	161,250	
Administration overhead	8	132,000	
			623,250
Profit			985,247

Workings

1   65% of capacity = 10,000 units
∴100% of capacity = 10,000 ÷ 0.65 = 15,385 units
∴ 85% of capacity = (10,000 ÷ 0.65) × 0.85 = 13,077 units
∴ 75% of capacity = 11,538
∴ 55% of capacity = 8,462

2   Current direct material cost per unit   = $1,000,000 ÷ 10,000
= $100 per unit

∴ Flexible budget allowance for next year   = $100 × 1.06 × 13,077
= $1,386,162

3   Current direct wages cost per unit   = $1,750,000 ÷ 10,000
= $175 per unit

∴ Flexible budget allowance for next year   = $175 × 1.03 × 13,077
= $2,357,129

4   Production overhead increases by $53,830 for an increase in activity of (10,000 – 8,462) units

∴ Variable production overhead per unit = $35
∴ Variable overhead allowance for 85% capacity   = 13,077 × $35   = $457,695
Plus 7% increase $32,039
Total allowance $489,734

5   Selling overhead increases by $7,690 for an increase in activity of (10,000 – 8,462) units.

∴ Variable cost per unit = $5
∴ Variable overhead allowance for 85% capacity   = 13,077 × $5   = $65,385
Plus 7% increase $4,577
Total allowance $69,962

6

	$
Total production overhead at 65% activity	650,000
Less variable overhead (10,000 × $35 (W4))	350,000
Fixed overhead this year	300,000
Plus 10% increase	30,000
Total allowance	330,000

	$
Total selling overhead at 65% activity	200,000
Less variable overhead (10,000 × $5 (W5))	50,000
Fixed overhead this year	150,000
Plus 7.5% increase	11,250
Total allowance	161,250

8   Administration overhead = $120,000 × 1.1 = $132,000

9   The cost and selling price structure is as follows.

	%
Sales price	100.00
Profit	16.67
Cost	83.33

$$\therefore \text{Profit as a percentage of cost} = \frac{16.67}{83.33} \times 100\% = 20\% \text{ of cost}$$

	$
Total cost ($4,302,987 + $623,250)	4,926,237
Profit at 20% of cost	985,247
∴ Sales value	5,911,484

(b)   Three **problems** which may **arise from the change in capacity level** are as follows.

(i)   There is likely to be a requirement for **additional cash for working capital**, for example inventory levels and debtors will probably increase. This additional cash may not be available.

(ii)   It will probably be necessary to **recruit more direct labour**. The activities involved in advertising, interviewing and training may lead to increased costs.

(iii)   It may be necessary to **reduce the selling price** to sell the increased volume. This could have an **adverse effect on profits**.

(c)   **The principle of controllability** is that managers of responsibility centres should only be held accountable for costs over which they have some influence.

Budgetary control is based around a system of **budget centres**. Each budget centre will have its own budget and a manager will be responsible for managing the budget centre and ensuring that the budget is met.

Budgetary control and budget centres are therefore part of the overall system of **responsibility accounting** within an organisation.

Controllable costs are items of expenditure which can be directly influenced by a given manager within a given time span.

Care must be taken to distinguish between controllable costs and uncontrollable costs in variance reporting. The **controllability principle** is that managers of responsibility centres should only be held accountable for costs over which they have some influence. From a **motivation** point of view this is important because it can be very demoralising for managers who feel that their performance is being judged on the basis of something over which they have no influence. It is also important from a **control** point of view in that control reports should ensure that information on costs is reported to the manager who is able to take action to control them.

Responsibility accounting attempts to associate costs, revenues, assets and liabilities with the managers most capable of controlling them. As a system of accounting, it therefore distinguishes between controllable and uncontrollable costs.

Most **variable costs** within a department are thought to be **controllable in the short term** because managers can influence the efficiency with which resources are used, even if they cannot do anything to raise or lower price levels.

A cost which is not controllable by a junior manager might be controllable by a senior manager. For example, there may be high direct labour costs in a department caused by excessive overtime working. The junior manager may feel obliged to continue with the overtime to meet production schedules, but his senior may be able to reduce costs by hiring extra full-time staff, thereby reducing the requirements for overtime.

A cost which is not controllable by a manager in one department may be controllable by a manager in another department. For example, an increase in material costs may be caused by buying at higher prices than expected (controllable by the purchasing department) or by excessive wastage (controllable by the production department) or by a faulty machine producing rejects (controllable by the maintenance department).

Some costs are **non-controllable,** such as increases in expenditure items due to inflation. Other costs are **controllable, but in the long term rather than the short term**. For example, production costs might be reduced by the introduction of new machinery and technology, but in the short term, management must attempt to do the best they can with the resources and machinery at their disposal.

7 Chem Co

> **Top tips**. There are quite a lot of calculations in this question. While it's easy to say that you should split your time so that you spend enough time on the written elements, written element (d) is dependent on your answer to the earlier calculations.
>
> Work through (d) carefully, and make sure you understand the link between the different variances.

(a) (1) **Price variances**

		$	$
Material F			
59,800 kg should have cost ($\times$ \$4)		239,200	
but did cost		254,150	
			14,950 (A)
Material G			
53,500 kg should have cost ($\times$ \$3)		160,500	
but did cost		149,800	
			10,700 (F)
Material H			
33,300 kg should have cost ($\times$ \$6)		199,800	
but did cost		213,120	
			13,320 (A)
Total material price variance			17,570 (A)

(2) **Usage variances**

	kg	$
Material F		
4,100 units should have used ($\times$ 15 kg)	61,500	
but did use	59,800	
Usage variance in kg (actual usage less than standard)	1,700 (F)	
$\times$ standard cost per kg		4
Usage variance in $		6,800 (F)
Material G		
4,100 units should have used ($\times$ 12 kg)	49,200	
but did use	53,500	
Usage variance in kg (actual usage exceeds standard)	4,300 (A)	
$\times$ standard cost per kg		3
Usage variance in $		12,900 (A)

		kg	$
Material H			
4,100 units should have used (× 8 kg)		32,800	
but did use		33,320	
Usage variance in kg (actual usage exceeds standard)		500 (A)	
× standard cost per kg			6
Usage variance in $			3,000 (A)
Total material price variance			9,100 (A)

(3) **Mix variances**

Total kg used = 146,600 kg

Standard mix for actual use

			kg
F	$^{15}/_{35}$ × 146,600 =		62,829
G	$^{12}/_{35}$ × 146,600 =		50,263
H	$^{8}/_{35}$ × 146,600 =		33,508
			146,600

	Actual quantity standard mix	Actual quantity actual mix	Variance	Standard cost per kg	Variance
	kg	kg	kg	$	$
F	62,829	59,800	3,029 (F)	4	12,116 (F)
G	50,263	53,500	3,237 (A)	3	9,711 (A)
H	33,508	33,300	208 (F)	6	1,248 (F)
	146,600	146,600	–		3,653 (F)

Total mix variance = $3,653 (F)

(4) **Yield variance**

The yield variance can be calculated in total or for each material input.

In total

146,600 kg input should yield (÷35)	4188.57 units
146,600 kg input did yield	4100 units
	88.57 (A)
@ $144 per unit	$12,754 (A)

	Standard quantity standard mix	Actual quantity standard mix	Variance	Standard cost per kg	Variance
	kg	kg	kg	$	$
F	61,500	62,829	1,329 (A)	4	5,316 (A)
G	49,200	50,263	1,063 (A)	3	3,189 (A)
H	32,800	33,508	708 (A)	6	4,248 (A)
	143,500	146,600	3,100 (A)		12,753 (A)

(b) (1)

		Dept P		Dept Q	Total
		$		$	$
4,100 units should have cost	(× $40)	164,000	(× $12)	49,200	213,200
but did cost		217,300		51,660	268,960
Labour cost variance		53,300 (A)		2,460 (A)	55,760 (A)

(2)

		Dept P		Dept Q	Total
4,100 units should have taken	(× 4)	16,400 hrs	(× 2)	8,200 hrs	
but did take		20,500 hrs		9,225 hrs	
		4,100 hrs (A)		1,025 hrs (A)	
× standard rate per hour		× $10		× $6	
Labour efficiency variance		41,000 (A)		$6,150 (A)	$47,150 (A)

(3)

		Dept P $		Dept Q $	Total $
20,500 hrs/9,225 hrs should have cost	(× $10)	205,000	(× $6)	55,350	260,350
but did cost		217,300		51,660	268,960
Labour rate variance		12,300 (A)		3,690 (F)	8,610 (A)

(c)

	$
4,100 units should have sold for (× $260)	1,066,000
but did sell for	1,115,800
Selling price variance	49,800 (F)
Budgeted sales for period	4,500 units
Actual sales volume	4,100 units
Volume variance in units	400 units (A)
× standard profit per unit ($(260 – 144))	× $116
Sales volume profit variance	$46,400 (A)

(d) **Adverse yield variance**

An analysis of the materials mix variance (see (a)(3)) shows that 3,029 kg of F and 208 kg of H (the more expensive materials) were replaced by 3,237 kg of G (the cheapest material). This **substitution of cheaper material** could have led to the adverse yield variance. It is **also** possible that the yield variance was because the material G that was used was of a **lower than standard quality** since it was purchased at a price below its standard price.

Adverse efficiency variance

The adverse labour efficiency variance may have been due to Material G taking longer to process than normal because it was of a poor quality. Alternatively, the fact that in Department Q the **actual rate was less than the standard rate could mean that less skilled labour was used** than provided for in the standard, and that this then **lowered productivity** with the result that the **yield was lower than expected**.

8 Truffle Co

Text reference. Basic variances are covered in Chapter 11. Planning and operational variances are covered in Chapter 12.

Top tips. You should find part (a) relatively straightforward. Labour rate and efficiency variances are assumed knowledge from Paper F2.

Part (b) contains some of the trickier variances stated on the F5 syllabus. As a check, the sum of all variances in part (b) should equal the sum of the labour rate variance and the labour efficiency variance calculated in part (a). Ensure you leave enough time to assess the performance of the production manager, based on your calculations (part (c)).

Easy marks. There are easy marks available in part (a) for calculating the labour rate and efficiency variances.

		Marks
(a)	Rate and efficiency variances:	
	Rate variance	2
	Efficiency variance	2
		4
(b)	Planning and operational variances:	
	Labour rate planning variance	2
	Labour rate operational variance	2
	Labour efficiency planning variance	2
	Labour efficiency operational variance	2
		8
(c)	Discussion:	
	Only operational variances controllable	1
	No labour rate operating variance	1
	Planning variance down to company, not manager	2
	Labour efficiency total variance looks bad	2
	Manager has performed well as regards efficiency	2
	Standard for labour time was to blame	2
	Conclusion	2
		max 8
		20

(a) **Labour variances**

Standard cost per labour hour = $6.00 / 0.5 = $12.00

Labour rate variance

	$
12,000 hours of work should have cost (× $12 per hr)	144,000
but did cost	136,800
Labour rate variance	7,200 (F)

Labour efficiency variance

20,500 batches should have taken (× 0.5 hrs)	10,250 hrs
but did take	12,000 hrs
Efficiency variance in hours	1,750 hrs (A)
× standard rate per hour	× $12
Efficiency variance	$21,000 (A)

(b) **Planning and operational variances**

Labour rate planning variance

	$
Standard rate	12.00
Revised rate ($12 × 0.95)	11.40
Variance	0.60 (F)
× actual hours paid (12,000)	× 12,000
Labour rate planning variance	$7,200 (F)

Labour rate operational variance	$
Revised cost of actual hours (12,000 × $12 × 95%)	136,800
Actual cost of actual hours	136,800
Labour rate operational variance	$nil

Labour efficiency planning variance |
---|---
Standard hours for actual production (20,500 × 0.5 hrs per batch) | 10,250 hrs
Revised hours for actual production (20,500 batches × 0.5 hrs per batch × 1.2) | 12,300 hrs
Variance | 2,050 hrs (A)
× standard rate per hour | × $12
Labour efficiency planning variance | $24,600 (A)

Labour efficiency operational variance |
---|---
20,500 batches should have taken (20,500 × 0.5 × 1.2) | 12,300 hrs
but did take | 12,000 hrs
Variance | 300 hrs (F)
× standard rate per hour | × $12
Labour efficiency operational variance | $3,600 (F)

Alternative solution

The following solution, calculating the **labour efficiency operational variance** using the **revised standard rate per hour**, and the **labour rate planning variance** based on **revised hours for actual production** also scored full marks.

Note that whilst this approach does not reconcile to the labour rate and efficiency variances calculated in part (a), it does **reconcile to the total labour variance ($13,800 adverse).**

Labour rate planning variance	$
Standard rate	12.00
Revised rate ($12 × 0.95)	11.40
Variance	0.60 (F)
× revised hours for actual production (12,300)	× 12,300
Labour rate planning variance	$7,380 (F)

Labour rate operational variance	$
Revised cost of actual hours (12,000 × $12 × 95%)	136,800
Actual cost of actual hours	136,800
Labour rate operational variance	$nil

Labour efficiency planning variance |
---|---
Standard hours for actual production (20,500 × 0.5 hrs per batch) | 10,250 hrs
Revised hours for actual production (20,500 batches × 0.5 hrs per batch × 1.2) | 12,300 hrs
Variance | 2,050 hrs (A)
× standard rate per hour | × $12
Labour efficiency planning variance | $24,600 (A)

Labour efficiency operational variance |
---|---
20,500 batches should have taken (20,500 × 0.5 × 1.2) | 12,300 hrs
but did take | 12,000 hrs
Variance | 300 hrs (F)
× revised standard rate per hour | × $11.40
Labour efficiency operational variance | $3,420 (F)

(c) **Performance of the production manager for the month of November**

The total labour rate variance calculated in part (a) suggests that the production manager has managed to secure **labour at a lower rate** than budgeted (favourable variance of $7,200). However, the total labour efficiency variance (adverse variance of $21,000) would appear to indicate that he or she has been extremely poor at controlling his or her **staff's efficiency**.

These variances should be split into **planning and operational variances** to give a truer indication of performance. Planning variances arise due to **inaccurate** planning and/or faulty standards (factors that are outside the control of production manager). Therefore, the production manager should only be assessed on operational variances.

Labour rate

The labour rate operational variance was $nil. This means that the workforce were paid the **agreed reduced rate** of $11.40 per hour. It is unlikely that the production manager paid anyone for overtime, as this would have increased the hourly rate.

The production manager cannot take credit for the favourable total labour rate variance. The labour rate planning variance of $7,200 indicates that the reduced labour rate was beyond the production manager's control and was **secured by the company**.

Labour efficiency

The total labour efficiency variance is $21,000 adverse.

The planning variance is **$24,600 adverse**. This is because the standard labour time per batch was not updated in November to reflect the fact that it would take **longer to produce the truffles** as a result of the retailer requesting the truffles to be made slightly softer. The production manager cannot be held responsible for this variance.

In contrast, the operational variance is **$3,600 favourable**. When the truffle recipe changed in November, it was expected that the production process would take 20% longer for the first month as the workers became used to working with the **new ingredient mix**. The workers actually took less than the 20% extra time predicted, yielding a **favourable operational variance**. The production manager can take credit for this variance.

In summary, the production manager **performed well** in the month of November.

9 Linsil

Text references. Variance analysis is covered in Chapter 11 and planning and operational variances in Chapter 12.

Top tips. Ensure that you can explain and discuss variances as you can expect an exam question to involve written elements as well as calculations. Remember, a planning variance is the difference between the original standard cost and the revised standard cost, multiplied by the actual units produced. An operational variance is the difference between the revised standard cost of the actual units produced and the actual cost.

(a)
Revised standard costs

Direct material price	2.30×1.03	2.369	$/kg
Direct material usage	$3.00 \times 95\%$	2.85	kg/unit
Direct labour rate	12.00×1.04	12.48	$/hr
Direct labour hours	$1.25 \times 100/90$	1.39	hrs/unit

(b)

Material	$
Actual material costs (for 122,000 units)	
(122,000 × 2.80 kg × $2.46)	840,336
Revised standard cost (for 122,000 units)	
(122,000 × 2.85 kg × $2.369)	823,701
Total operational variance	16,635 (A)
Revised standard cost	823,701
Original standard	
(122,000 × 3.00 kg × £2.30)	841,800
Total planning variance	18,099 (F)

Labour	$
Actual labour costs	
(122,000 × 1.30 hrs × $12.60)	1,998,360
Revised standard cost	
(122,000 × 1.39 hrs × $12.48)	2,116,358
Total operational variance	117,998 (F)
Revised standard cost	2,116,358
Original standard cost	
(122,000 × 1.25 hrs × $12.00)	1,830,000
Total planning variance	286,358 (A)

(c)   The planning and operational variance approach attempts to divide a total variance into a group of variances which have arisen because of inaccurate planning or faulty standards (**planning variances**) and a group of variances which have been caused by adverse or favourable operational performance (**operational variances**).

A **planning variance** compares an original standard with a revised standard that should or would have been used if planners had known in advance what was going to happen. Planning variances are **uncontrollable** (see below) by operational managers, but can be avoided through better planning.

An **operational variance** compares an actual result with the revised standard. Operational variances are **controllable** by managers.

Planning and operational variances are based on the principle that variances ought to be reported by taking as the main starting point a standard which can be seen, in hindsight, to be the **optimum** that should have been achievable. For example, in the example given in the question, the standard direct labour rate should have been $12.48 rather than $12.00.

Exponents of this approach argue that the monetary value of variances ought to be a **realistic reflection** of what the causes of the variances have cost the organisation. In other words they should show the cash (and profit) gained or lost as a consequence of operating results being different to what should have been achieved. Variances can be valued in this way by comparing actual results with a realistic standard or budget.

Planning variances arise because the original standard and revised (more realistic) standards are different, and these have nothing to do with operational performance. In most cases, it is unlikely that anything could be done about planning variances: they are not controllable by operational managers but by senior management.

Problems

The reasons behind **why planning variances arise** may need to be investigated. It needs to be understood how certain pieces of information get missed or otherwise omitted from the standard setting process.

It can also be too easy to justify **all** the variances are being due to bad planning, so no operational variances will be highlighted.

It is difficult to **decide in hindsight** what the realistic standard should have been, and establishing retrospective standards is time consuming.

10 Divisional performance measures

> **Top tips**. Parts (a) and (b) require you to demonstrate knowledge you should have picked up directly from the text. No application skills are required at all in this instance.
>
> That being said, it is vital that you do not learn the advantages and disadvantages of ROI and RI in a parrot fashion as they underlie the very core of the chapter. You **must understand how and why ROI affects managerial behaviour**, for example. You are just as likely to get a written question on this area as a calculation-based one.
>
> The calculations required in (b) should not have caused you any problems.
>
> Part (c) is **basic book knowledge** and so you should have been able to score quite a few of the marks available.

(a)   The **residual income (RI)** for a division is calculated by deducting from the divisional profit an imputed interest charge, based on the investment in the division.

The **return on investment (ROI)** is the divisional profit expressed as a percentage of the investment in the division.

Both methods use the **same basic figure for profit and investment**, but **residual income** produces an **absolute** measure whereas the **return on investment** is expressed as a **percentage**.

Both methods suffer from **disadvantages** in measuring the profit and the investment in a division which include the following.

(i)   Assets must be valued consistently at historical cost or at replacement cost. Neither valuation basis is ideal.

(ii)   Divisions might use different bases to value inventory and to calculate depreciation.

(iii) Any charges made for the use of head office services or allocations of head office assets to divisions are likely to be arbitrary.

In addition, **return on investment** suffers from the following **disadvantages**.

(i)   Rigid adherence to the need to maintain ROI in the short term can discourage managers from investing in new assets, since average divisional ROI tends to fall in the early stages of a new investment. Residual income can overcome this problem by highlighting projects which return more than the cost of capital.

(ii)   It can be difficult to compare the percentage ROI results of divisions if their activities are very different: residual income can overcome this problem through the use of different interest rates for different divisions.

(b)   (i)   **Return on divisional investment (ROI)**

	Before investment	After investment
Divisional profit	$18,000	$19,600
Divisional investment	$100,000	$110,000
Divisional ROI	18.0%	17.8%

The ROI will fall in the short term if the new investment is undertaken. This is a problem which often arises with ROI, as noted in part (a) of this solution.

(ii)   **Divisional residual income**

	Before investment	After investment
	$	$
Divisional profit	18,000	19,600
Less imputed interest: $100,000 \times 15\%$	15,000	
$110,000 \times 15\%$		16,500
Residual income	3,000	3,100

The residual income will increase if the new investment is undertaken. The use of residual income has highlighted the fact that the new project returns more than the cost of capital (16% compared with 15%).

(c)   **Potential benefits of operating a transfer pricing system within a divisionalised company**

      (i)   It can lead to **goal congruence** by motivating divisional managers to make decisions, which improve divisional profit and improve profit of the organisation as a whole.

      (ii)   It can prevent **dysfunctional decision making** so that decisions taken by a divisional manager are in the best interests of his own part of the business, other divisions and the organisation as a whole.

      (iii) Transfer prices can be set at a level that enables divisional performance to be measured 'commercially'. A transfer pricing system should therefore report a level of divisional profit that is a **reasonable measure of the managerial performance** of the division.

      (iv) It should ensure that **divisional autonomy** is not undermined. A well-run transfer pricing system helps to ensure that a balance is kept between divisional autonomy to provide incentives and motivation, and centralised authority to ensure that the divisions are all working towards the same target, the benefit of the organisation as a whole.

11 Non profit seeking organisations

> **Top tips**. Like many examination questions, part (a) can be answered by taking a **logical, structured approach** that is offered to you by the wording of the question itself. You can take (1) **efficiency** and (2) **effectiveness** in turn (this solution opts to deal with effectiveness first) and explain for each why the absence of a profit measure causes problems. This suggests that you need to explain why the **presence of a profit measure** helps with the assessment of efficiency and effectiveness.
>
> Take note of the **examples about objectives** we have provided in part (a) – they may prove **useful in your exam** as this requirement is perhaps one of the more likely to appear on the subject of non profit seeking organisations.
>
> Note the need to provide **examples** in part (a)(ii) – this means at least one! As well as the given similarity between profit-seeking and non-profit seeking organisations, don't forget that the **distinctions between the two types of organisation are becoming blurred.**
>
> For part (b), remember that indicators need to be **compared against a yardstick** to be of any use for performance measurement purposes. The fact that 8% of appointments were cancelled is useless information. When considered in conjunction with a target of 5%, it becomes useful!

(a)   (i)   **Effectiveness** refers to the use of resources so as to achieve desired ends or objectives or outputs.

            In a profit-making organisation, objectives can be expressed financially in terms of a target profit or return. The organisation, or profit centres within the organisation, can be judged to have operated effectively if they have achieved a target profit within a given period.

            In non-profit seeking organisations, effectiveness cannot be measured in this way. The organisation's objectives cannot be expressed in financial terms at all, and non-financial objectives need to be established. The effectiveness of performance could be measured in terms of whether targeted non-financial objectives have been achieved, but there are several **problems** involved in trying to do this.

            (1)   The organisation might have several **different objectives** which are difficult to reconcile with each other. Achieving one objective might only be possible at the expense of failing to achieve another. For example, schools have the objective of providing education. They teach a certain curriculum, but by opting to educate students in some subjects, there is no time available to provide education in other subjects.

            (2)   A non-profit seeking organisation will invariably be **restricted in what it can achieve by the availability of funds**. The health service, for example, has the objective of providing health care, but since funds are restricted there is a limit to the amount of

care that can be provided, and there will be competition for funds between different parts of the service.

(3) The objectives of non-profit seeking organisations are also difficult to establish because the **quality** of the service provided will be a significant feature of their service. For example, a local authority has, amongst its various different objectives, the objective of providing a rubbish collection service. The effectiveness of this service can only be judged by establishing what standard or quality of service is required.

(4) With differing objectives, none of them directly comparable, and none that can be expressed in profit terms, **human judgement** is likely to be involved in deciding whether an organisation has been effective or not. This is most clearly seen in government organisations where political views cloud opinion about the government's performance.

Efficiency refers to the rate at which resources are consumed to achieve desired ends. Efficiency measurements compare the output produced by the organisation with the resources employed or used up to achieve the output. They are used to control the consumption of resources, so that the maximum output is achieved by a given amount of input resources, or a certain volume of output is produced within the minimum resources being used up.

In profit-making organisations, the efficiency of the organisation as a whole can be measured in terms of return on capital employed. Individual profit centres or operating units within the organisation can also have efficiency measured by relating the quantity of output produced, which has a **market value** and therefore a quantifiable financial value, to the resources (and their costs) required to make the output.

In non-profit seeking organisations, output does not usually have a market value, and it is therefore more difficult to measure efficiency. This difficulty is compounded by the fact that since these organisations often have **several different objectives**, it is difficult to compare the efficiency of one operation with the efficiency of another. For example, with the police force, it might be difficult to compare the efficiency of a serious crimes squad with the efficiency of the traffic police, because each has its own 'outputs' that are not easily comparable in terms of 'value achieved'.

In spite of the difficulties of measuring effectiveness and efficiency, control over the performance of non-profit seeking organisations can only be satisfactorily achieved by assessments of **'value for money'** (economy, efficiency and effectiveness).

(ii) The same problems extend to **support activities** within profit-motivated organisations, where these activities are not directly involved in the creation of output and sales. Examples include research and development, the personnel function, the accountancy function and so on.

(1) Some of the outputs of these functions **cannot be measured in market values**.

(2) The **objectives** of the functions are **not easily expressed** in quantifiable terms.

Examples

(1) Within the personnel department, outputs from activities such as training and some aspects of recruitment can be given market price values by estimating what the same services would cost if provided by an external organisation. Other activities, however, do not have any such market valuation. Welfare is an example. Its objective is to provide support for employees in their personal affairs, but since this objective cannot easily be expressed as quantifiable targets, and does not have a market price valuation, the effectiveness and efficiency of work done by welfare staff cannot be measured easily.

(2) Within the accountancy department, outputs from management accountants are management information. This does not have an easily-measured market value, and information's value depends more on quality than quantity. The contribution of

management accounting to profitability is difficult to judge, and so the efficiency and effectiveness of the function are difficult to measure.

(b)   (i)   To measure effectiveness, we need to establish objectives or targets for performance. Since these cannot be expressed financially, **non-financial targets** must be used. The effective level of achievement could be measured by comparing actual performance against target.

(1)   **Adherence to appointment times**

- Percentage of appointments kept on time
- Percentage of appointments no more than 10 minutes late
- Percentage of appointments kept within 30 minutes of schedule
- Percentage of cancelled appointments
- Average delay in appointments

A **problem** with these measures is that there is an implied assumption that all patients will be at the clinic by their appointed time. In practice, this will not always be the case.

(2)   **Patients' ability to contact the clinic and make appointments**

- Percentage of patients who can make an appointment at their first preferred time, or at the first date offered to them

- Average time from making an appointment to the appointment date

- Number of complaints about failure to contact the clinic, as a percentage of total patients seen

- If the telephone answering system provides for queuing of calls, the average waiting for answer times for callers and the percentage of abandoned calls

(3)   **Comprehensive monitoring programme**

Measures might be based on the definition of each element or step within a monitoring programme for a patient. It would then be possible to measure the following.

- Percentage of patients receiving every stage of the programme (and percentage receiving every stage but one, every stage but two, and so on)

- If each stage has a scheduled date for completion, the average delay for patients in the completion of each stage

(ii)   A **single quality of care** measure would call for subjective judgements about the following.

(1)   The key **objective**/objectives for each of the three features of service
(2)   The relative **weighting** that should be given to each

The objectives would have to be measured on comparable terms and, since monetary values are inappropriate, an index based on percentage or a points-scoring system of measurement might be used. A target index or points score for achievement could then be set, and actual results compared against the target.

Bibliography

Bibliography

ACCA (1999) Product costing/pricing strategy. *Students Newsletter*

ACCA (2015) *F5 examiner's report – June 2015* [Online]. Available from: http://www.accaglobal.com/zm/en/student/exam-support-resources/fundamentals-exams-study-resources/f5/examiners-reports.html [Accessed 29 November 2016].

ACCA (2015) *Activity based costing* [Online]. Available from: http://www.accaglobal.com/uk/en/student/exam-support-resources/fundamentals-exams-study-resources/f5/technical-articles.html [Accessed 29 November 2016].

ACCA (2016) *Comparing budgeting techniques* [Online]. Available from: http://www.accaglobal.com/uk/en/student/exam-support-resources/fundamentals-exams-study-resources/f5/technical-articles.html [Accessed 29 November 2016].

ACCA (2016) *Cost-volume-profit analysis* [Online]. Available from: http://www.accaglobal.com/uk/en/student/exam-support-resources/fundamentals-exams-study-resources/f5/technical-articles.html [Accessed 29 November 2016].

ACCA (2016) *Decentralisation and the need for performance measurement* [Online]. Available from: http://www.accaglobal.com/uk/en/student/exam-support-resources/fundamentals-exams-study-resources/f5/technical-articles.html [Accessed 29 November 2016].

ACCA (2015) *Decision Trees* [Online]. Available from: http://www.accaglobal.com/uk/en/student/exam-support-resources/fundamentals-exams-study-resources/f5/technical-articles.html [Accessed 29 November 2016].

ACCA (2016) *Environmental management accounting* [Online]. Available from: http://www.accaglobal.com/uk/en/student/exam-support-resources/fundamentals-exams-study-resources/f5/technical-articles.html [Accessed 29 November 2016].

ACCA (2015) *Interpreting financial data* [Online]. Available from: http://www.accaglobal.com/uk/en/student/exam-support-resources/fundamentals-exams-study-resources/f5/technical-articles.html [Accessed 29 November 2016].

ACCA (2016) *The learning rate and learning effect* [Online]. Available from: http://www.accaglobal.com/uk/en/student/exam-support-resources/fundamentals-exams-study-resources/f5/technical-articles.html [Accessed 29 November 2016].

ACCA (2015) *Linear programming* [Online]. Available from: http://www.accaglobal.com/uk/en/student/exam-support-resources/fundamentals-exams-study-resources/f5/technical-articles.html [Accessed 29 November 2016].

ACCA (2015) *Materials mix and yield variances* [Online]. Available from: http://www.accaglobal.com/uk/en/student/exam-support-resources/fundamentals-exams-study-resources/f5/technical-articles.html [Accessed 29 November 2016].

ACCA (2015) *Not for profit organisations – part 1* [Online]. Available from: http://www.accaglobal.com/uk/en/student/exam-support-resources/fundamentals-exams-study-resources/f5/technical-articles.html [Accessed 29 November 2016].

ACCA (2015) *Not for profit organisations – part 2* [Online]. Available from: http://www.accaglobal.com/uk/en/student/exam-support-resources/fundamentals-exams-study-resources/f5/technical-articles.html [Accessed 29 November 2016].

ACCA (2015) *The risks of uncertainty* [Online]. Available from: http://www.accaglobal.com/uk/en/student/exam-support-resources/fundamentals-exams-study-resources/f5/technical-articles.html [Accessed 29 November 2016].

ACCA (2015) *Target costing and lifecycle costing* [Online]. Available from: http://www.accaglobal.com/uk/en/student/exam-support-resources/fundamentals-exams-study-resources/f5/technical-articles.html [Accessed 29 November 2016].

ACCA (2015) *Throughput accounting and the theory of constraints – part 2* [Online]. Available from: http://www.accaglobal.com/uk/en/student/exam-support-resources/fundamentals-exams-study-resources/f5/technical-articles.html [Accessed 29 November 2016].

ACCA (2015) *Throughput accounting and the theory of constraints – part 2* [Online]. Available from: http://www.accaglobal.com/uk/en/student/exam-support-resources/fundamentals-exams-study-resources/f5/technical-articles.html [Accessed 29 November 2016].

ACCA (2015) *Transfer pricing* [Online]. Available from: http://www.accaglobal.com/uk/en/student/exam-support-resources/fundamentals-exams-study-resources/f5/technical-articles.html [Accessed 29 November 2016].

ACCA (2016) *Transfer pricing* [Online]. Available from: http://www.accaglobal.com/uk/en/student/exam-support-resources/fundamentals-exams-study-resources/f5/technical-articles.html [Accessed 29 November 2016].

Anthony, R. N. (1965) *Planning and control systems: A framework for analysis*, 1st edition. Boston, Division of Research, Harvard Business School.

Bennett, P. and James, P. (2000) *The green bottom line: environmental accounting for management : current practice and future trends*, 2nd edition. Sheffield, Greenleaf Publishing Limited.

Cooper, R. (1990a) Cost classifications in unit-based and activity-based manufacturing cost systems, Journal of Cost Management, Fall, 4-14

Drury, C. (2005) *Management and cost accounting*, 6th edition. London, Thomson Learning.

Drury, C., Braund, S., Osborne, P. and Tayles, M. (1993) A survey of management accounting practices in UK manufacturing companies, ACCA Research Paper, Chartered Association of Certified Accountants

Fitzgerald, L. and Moon, P. (1996) *Performance measurement in service industries: Making it work.* 1st edition. Chartered Institute of Management Accountants.

Goldratt, E.M. and Cox, J. (1992) *The Goal.* 2nd edition. London, Gower Publishing Ltd.

Gray, R.H. and Bebbington, J. (2001) *Accounting for the environment,* 2nd edition. London, SAGE publications Ltd.

Hope, J. and Fraser, R. (2003) *Beyond Budgeting*, 1st edition. Harvard Business School Publishing Corporation.

International Organization for Standardization (2015) *ISO 14000 – Environmental management* [Online}. Available from: http://www.iso.org/iso/iso14000 [Accessed 29 November 2016].

Kotler, P. and Armstrong, G. (2010) *Principles of Marketing.* 13th edition. London, Pearson Education Ltd

United Nations Division of Sustainable Development

United States Environmental Protection Agency (1995) *An introduction to environmental accounting as a business management tool* [Online]. Available from: https://archive.epa.gov/p2/archive/web/pdf/busmgt.pdf [Accessed 29 November 2016].

BPP
LEARNING MEDIA

Index

Review Form – Paper F5 Performance Management (01/17)

Please help us to ensure that the ACCA learning materials we produce remain as accurate and user-friendly as possible. We cannot promise to answer every submission we receive, but we do promise that it will be read and taken into account when we update this Study Text.

Name: _____   Address: _____

_____

_____

How have you used this Text?
(Tick one box only)

☐ Home study (book only)

☐ On a course: college _____

☐ With 'correspondence' package

☐ Other _____

Why did you decide to purchase this Text? *(Tick one box only)*

☐ Have used BPP Study Texts in the past

☐ Recommendation by friend/colleague

☐ Recommendation by a lecturer at college

☐ Saw information of BPP website

☐ Saw advertising

☐ Other _____

During the past six months do you recall seeing/receiving any of the following?
(Tick as many boxes as are relevant)

☐ Our advertisement in ACCA *Student Accountant*

☐ Our advertisement in *PQ*

☐ Our brochure with a letter through the post

☐ Our website www.bpp.com

Which (if any) aspects of our advertising do you find useful?
(Tick as many boxes as are relevant)

☐ Prices and publication dates of new editions

☐ Information on Study Text content

☐ Facility to order books off-the-page

☐ None of the above

Which BPP products have you used?

Study Text	☑	*Home Study Package*	☐
Kit	☐	*i-Pass*	☐
Passcards	☐		

Your ratings, comments and suggestions would be appreciated on the following areas.

	Very useful	Useful	Not useful
Introductory section	☐	☐	☐
Chapter introductions	☐	☐	☐
Key terms	☐	☐	☐
Quality of explanations	☐	☐	☐
Case studies and other examples	☐	☐	☐
Exam focus points	☐	☐	☐
Questions and answers in each chapter	☐	☐	☐
Fast forwards and chapter roundups	☐	☐	☐
Quick quizzes	☐	☐	☐
Question Bank	☐	☐	☐
Answer Bank	☐	☐	☐
Index	☐	☐	☐

Overall opinion of this Study Text   Excellent ☐   Good ☐   Adequate ☐   Poor ☐

Do you intend to continue using BPP products?   Yes ☐   No ☐

On the reverse of this page is space for you to write your comments about our Study Text. We welcome your feedback.

The author of this edition can be emailed at: accaqueries@bpp.com

Please return this form to: Head of ACCA & FIA programmes, BPP Learning Media Ltd, FREEPOST, London, W12 8AA

TELL US WHAT YOU THINK

Please note any further comments and suggestions/errors below. For example, was the text accurate, readable, concise, user-friendly and comprehensive?